W9-COO-863

Effective Instructional Strategies

FOR EXCEPTIONAL CHILDREN

Edited by
Edward L. Meyen
University of Kansas
Glenn A. Vergason
Georgia State University
Richard J. Whelan
University of Kansas Medical Center

No Longer Property of
Phillips Memorial Library

LOVE PUBLISHING COMPANY
Denver, Colorado 80222

Phillips Memorial
Library
Providence College

LC
396.5
E3X

All rights reserved. No part of this publication may be reproduced,
stored in a retrieval system or transmitted, in any form or by any means,
electronic, mechanical, recording or otherwise,
without the prior written permission of the publisher.

Copyright © 1988 Love Publishing Company
Printed in the U.S.A.
ISBN 0-89108-201-8
Library of Congress Catalog Card Number 87-83464

Contents

One

Instructional Organization

Edward L. Meyen

Although exceptional children and youth today may possess the same attributes and needs of their counterparts of decades past, instructional settings in which they find themselves have changed. No longer are they necessarily the focus of intense instruction in homogeneous groups or the sole responsibility of a particular teacher. Today they frequently find themselves in very heterogeneous groups, and the responsibility for their instruction is shared by a number of teaching personnel. If there has been a constant in the history of special education instruction, it has been a state of change in the delivery of instruction or in the instructional settings where specialized instruction is intended to occur. No other population of students has presented educators as much difficulty in determining where they should be taught, in addition to how.

Throughout the history of special education, a lineage of efficacy studies has contrasted the performances of students in special education with their counterparts in regular classes. The results have been consistently equivocal—sometimes favoring regular class placement and other times showing no significant differences. This has contributed to considerable indecision over time as to the most effective and appropriate instructional setting. Today most students with special needs spend considerable time in regular instructional settings, and momentum is building to further dissipate the presumed differences between regular and special education instruction through what is being referred to as the regular education initiative (Will, 1985). If history repeats itself, another shift in instructional settings will occur.

In searching for more effective teaching strategies, the tendency in special education has been to focus on restructuring the instructional setting rather than emphasizing interventions applicable to varied settings. Special schools, special classes, resource rooms, itinerant teachers, consulting teachers, crisis teachers, resource teachers, mainstreaming, and now the regular education initiative all impact on the instructional setting. They do not alter the attributes of students or necessarily influence teaching interventions. To a large extent they represent attempts to restructure the conditions under which teaching occurs based on the belief system of professionals, not research.

Each delivery system has met with varying success, and collectively each is periodically called into question. As questions evolve, shifts in the delivery of instruction eventually follow. And as these shifts occur, exceptional children and youth find themselves in still another configuration that becomes the instructional setting in which teaching and learning occur. Presumably each shift is toward a more effective instructional setting. In the quest for effective teaching strategies, special educators appear to operate on the assumption that the instructional setting—rather than learner attributes or how they interact with teaching styles—is the critical variable.

The arguments by Will (1985), Wang, Reynolds, and Walberg (1985, 1986), and Lilly (1986) favoring full integration in regular education are reasonable views. Certainly evidence is lacking to support any particular instructional setting for special needs students—making views on regular school initiatives as valid as any. And clearly many needs of students with mildly handicapping conditions are undifferentiated from those of students in migrant programs, bilingual students, and others who have difficulties in academic achievement but who do not qualify for special education services.

Consolidating special education and the other "special help" initiatives into a comprehensive program for all students who have special needs and moving away from the categorical dimensions of special education may be necessary in the evolution of quality instruction for all students. On the other hand, it could become just another shift motivated by social, economic, or philosophical, rather than educational, concerns. This continuum in the development of special education pedagogy brings into question the issue of what is the best route to achieve effective instruction for special needs students—a focus on instructional intervention or on instructional settings.

This section of the book is concerned with instructional organization for exceptional students and does not discuss delivery systems or philosophical considerations underlying special education—hence, these introductory comments on shifts in delivery systems and the momentum that is building for still another shift in how the instructional needs of exceptional children and youth are met (i.e., the regular school initiative). The rationale for this discussion is to remind readers that instructional variables and learner behaviors cannot be separated from the conditions under which instruction occurs. No generation of exceptional students has had the advantage of completing its education without being enmeshed in a major shift in how the public schools organize themselves to teach exceptional children and youth. To precisely measure the effects of these shifts or to sort out the cumulative consequences of these shifts and the concomitant changes in instruction on learners may not be possible, but to ignore them precludes a valid analysis of the soundness of underlying decisions.

As special education prepares for another "rethinking" of how exceptional students should be educated, or as the lack of evidence on the success of contemporary practices builds, regular education, in addressing the instructional needs of nonhandicapped students, is focusing on initiatives identified as "effective schools," "school effectiveness," and "effective teaching." The emphasis in this movement is on successful practices with particular attention to learner-teacher interactions. These initiatives also are being addressed to some degree in special education, but the more dominant concern for effective instructional strategies appears to be occurring in regular education. Many districts are organizing their professional development programs around topics and experiences related to the research literature on effective schools. Building-level teams are being organized and resource allocations are frequently based on the extent to which programs are applying the principles of effective teaching. The primary difference between the regular school initiative for special education and the effective schools movement is the latter's focus on known instructional practices in the school effectiveness movement rather than on philosophical issues or the logic of similarities in learner attributes.

Admittedly, instructional settings have considerable influence on the effectiveness of instruction. The instruction of special needs students, however, requires powerful interventions that transcend the conditions of the setting. As long as major shifts continue to occur, approaches to meeting the educational needs of exceptional students and the process of achieving effective instruction will be slow and inconsistent. There obviously has been a concern for researching interventions for the teaching of exceptional students. Unfortunately, these research efforts tend to be overshadowed by the issue of "where." The concerns for "where" have tended to have a significant contribution on the search for more effective instructional strategies in special education. The purpose of this book is to provide a resource on strategies that have proved to be effective in teaching exceptional children and youth. Consequently, the emphasis is on *what* rather than where instruction ought to occur for exceptional children and youth.

When the emphasis is on the learner-teacher interaction in instructional settings, the perspective becomes one of relating learner attributes to known effective teaching strategies. Because effectiveness in the education of exceptional children and youth tends to be viewed in the more general context of philosophical, social, and organizational concerns, it is important to examine two levels of perspectives: (a) policy trends related to effective instruction and (b) effective instructional practices. At the more general organizational level, special education does not appear to have influenced the reform movement in public education or personnel preparation for roles in regular education. Over 30 reports on reform needs in education have been released by commissions, professional associations, educational agencies, and task forces. In examining these reports it is apparent that the needs of exceptional children and youth have not been seriously considered. For example, almost no reference is made to special education or the needs of exceptional children and youth (or personnel preparation for special education) in reports such as *A Nation at Risk* by the National Commission on Excellence in Education (1984), *Tomorrow's Teachers*, a report of the Holmes Group (1986), *A Nation Prepared: Teachers for the 21st Century*, by the Carnegie Forum on Education and the Economy (1986), and *Leaders for America's Schools*, recently released by the National Commission on Excellence in Educational Administration (1987).

If the emerging regular school initiative for the education of special needs students is to be successful, it must be viewed by those responsible for proposing changes in the organization of schools, the preparation of teachers, the K–12 curriculum, and the assessment of pupil performance. Unless this occurs, special education will continue to be faced with convincing regular educators at the operational level that proposed changes are not necessary only for special education students but are beneficial to all students. A similar situation exists in the literature evolving on successful-practices-in-the-school reports such as *The Superintendent's Can-Do Guide to School Improvement*, (Dianda, 1984), published by the Council for Educational Development and Research, and *What Works: Research About Teaching and Learning*, by the U.S. Department of Education (1986). Again, we find almost no attention given to the needs of or intervention applications to exceptional children and youth.

If special education is to operationalize a closer, more integrated relationship with regular education through effective instruction, interests in the groups concerned with reform and effective schools must be merged. Inherent in this process must be an examination of practices and strategies found to be successful with nonhandicapped students to ascertain their generalization to exceptional children and youth. If the regular education initiative is sound in its underlying assumption that the needs of mildly handicapped students are more effectively met through integration in regular education, there is an implied assumption that instructional practices found to be successful with nonhandicapped students are also likely to be applicable to special needs students. This calls for some form of interface between the school-teaching effectiveness literature in regular education and special education.

In the global context of instructional organization, the regular education initiative (Will, 1985) should have some parallel effort in regular education. Otherwise it becomes incumbent upon special educators to again initiate the change and to strive for some way to create the necessary readiness on the part of regular educators to ensure that the new shift (in *where* exceptional children and youth are educated) is meaningful. Certainly more attention is being given to educational policy and effective instruction in regular education than during any decade in recent history. Not only is public education the target of reform, but so is the preparation of teachers. And one would assume that if regular education were to share the views of those promulgating shifts in the education of exceptional children and were concerned about how schools are organized to deliver effective instruction to exceptional children and youth, this population of students would receive attention in the educational reform literature.

In an attempt to broaden the reader's perspective of instructional organization, two types of articles have been selected for this section of the book. The perspective reflected in the Berliner manuscript is the application of research to teaching. Although the research literature reviewed by Berliner is not specific to the education of children and youth with disabilities, it does represent a research base applicable to teaching exceptional children, particularly in regular class settings. More important, it represents a summary of the research knowledge base on teaching with which all teachers should be familiar. Too often, under the guise that exceptional learners differ significantly from nonhandicapped peers in their responsiveness to teaching strategies, special educators tend to focus only on the special education research base. But much can be learned from the broader research base on teaching. Berliner's discussion on research related to pre-instructional factors (content decisions, time allocation decisions, pacing decisions, grouping decisions, and decisions about activities structure) is particularly applicable.

The other articles are specific to teaching exceptional children and youth. They relate to linking strategies with an emphasis on instructional organization. *Instructional organization*, as used in this book, refers to what teachers need to know—i.e., the knowledge base on teaching, as well as the knowledge base on the relationship of learner attributes to instructional intervention and environments conducive to teaching and learning. It includes organizational decisions made largely by administrators in response to national and state trends, as well as classroom management, decisions on instructional resources, assessment, placement decisions, and teaching strategies.

Preparation for instructional organization begins long before the teacher encounters the students in the instructional setting. Effective teaching requires an approach to instructional organization that builds on decisions that result in students being grouped for instruction according to predetermined attributes. Given appropriate decisions prior to placement in the instructional setting, the teacher's responsibilities shift to instructional interventions and management strategies that result in optimum learning. For exceptional children and youth, the process of instructional organization at the teaching level is complicated by the wide array of learner attributes and the variability in how the student's attributes interact with instructional strategies. Teachers of exceptional children must possess an understanding of the knowledge base on effective teaching as validated with nonhandicapped students, as well as principles most effective with exceptional students.

As the reader will note, this section of the book is not totally independent of the other two sections (teaching presentation and assessment). The knowledge based on effective strategies does not lend itself to a division of dichotomous information. The general emphasis in each section does vary, however, with teaching effectiveness being the common theme.

REFERENCES

Carnegie Forum on Education and the Economy. (1986) *A nation prepared: Teachers for the 21st century.* New York: Carnegie Corp.

Dianda, M. R. (1984). *The superintendent's can-do guide to school improvement.* Washington, DC: Council for Educational Development and Research.

The Holmes Group (1986, April) *Tomorrow's Teachers.* East Lansing, MI: Author.

Lilly, M. S. (1986, March). The relationship between general and special education: A new face on an old issue. *Counterpoint, 6*(1), 10.

National Commission on Excellence in Education. (1984, March). *A nation at risk.* Cambridge, MA: U.S.A. Research.

National Commission on Excellence in Educational Administration. (1987). *Leaders for America's schools.* Tempe, AZ: University Council for Educational Administration.

U.S. Department of Education. (1986). *What works: Research about teaching and learning.* Washington, DC: Government Printing Office.

Wang, M. C., Reynolds, M. C., & Walberg, H. J. (1985, December). *Rethinking special education.* Position paper prepared for discussion at a Wingspread conference in Racine, WI.

Wang, M. C., Reynolds, M. C., & Walberg, H. J. (1986, July). *Reflections on research and practices in special education: A case of disjointedness*. Position paper prepared for discussion at Wingspread Conference on the Education of Children with Special Needs, Racine, WI.

Will, M. C. (1985, December). Educating children with learning problems: A shared responsibility. Remarks before the Wingspread Conference on the Education of Children with Special Needs, Racine, WI.

Special education has a long history of building its own research base on teaching. Although this approach has resulted in the development of effective instructional interventions, much of the research on teaching in general education, while applicable to teaching children with disabilities, has been somewhat ignored. Berliner provides a detailed review of research on effective teaching. His discussion of research related to pre-instructional factors and during-instruction factors is particularly applicable to special education.

In contrast to many critics of education, Berliner presents an optimistic perspective on the research base related to teaching. The key factor, however, is the extent to which research results are translated into teaching strategies and incorporated into teacher training curricula. Inclusion of Berliner's article broadens the emphasis on instruction from special education settings to the school setting in general. Given that most students with disabilities spend considerable time in regular class, special educators should be familiar with the full spectrum of research on effective teaching.

The Half-Full Glass: A Review Of Research on Teaching

David C. Berliner

There is a well-known adage about what is seen when the liquid in a glass is at the midpoint. A pessimist describes the glass as half empty, while an optimist describes the glass as half full. Both statements are absolutely accurate. Nevertheless, the choice of the terms used by optimists and pessimists to describe what they see can lead to vastly different beliefs and actions. I am a minority in a profession where too many observers see the findings of research on teaching as, at most, constituting a half-empty glass.

The pessimism we suffer from in our profession is, perhaps, understandable. Until 1963 and the publication of the *Handbook of Research on Teaching* (Gage, 1963), there really was no field of research on teaching. Only a small number of scientists could be identified as having a primary interest in research on teaching. Coincidental with the publication of the *Handbook* came massive federal involvement in educational research and development. Centers at Stanford, the University of Texas, and the University of Wisconsin, among others, were funded to study teaching and instruction. The mid 1960s also saw federal monies used to start educational laboratories such as the Far West Laboratory for Educational Research and Development and Research for Better Schools. The laboratories were given the mission of improving the practice of schooling and of teacher education. The result of federally supported and independent research efforts over the last 20 years has been an enormous increase in our knowledge about sensible, effective, and efficient teaching practices. The glass is, I believe, at least half full. So why are so few drinking? Three reasons immediately come to mind.

First, the past has seen research on teaching being oversold to educators. At the turn of the century the eminent educational psychologist E. L. Thorndike promised a revolution in education. He believed that empirical science and statistical inference would allow us to determine optimum ways to teach. Thorndike's promise of a scientific revolution based on psychological inquiry was misguided for a number of reasons, among which was his failure to adequately recognize the political and sociological forces that affect the schools and teacher education programs. A second reason is an outgrowth of the Great Depression. In society at large there grew a general mistrust of science and technology and a lack of faith in scientific inquiry in education as a means of improvement. Finally, as noted above, the field of research on teaching took its modern form only about 20 years ago. Reliable and replicable research has accumulated rapidly, but only recently. There has been only a short time in which to change deeply held beliefs about the utility of research on teaching.

Thus, because of promises unkept, societal and unique professional conditions resulting in a pervasive mistrust of research (and researchers) in education, and the recency of the development of the field of inquiry called research on teaching, we find the professional educator slow to respond to the remarkably bountiful yield of knowledge acquired over the last two decades. There exists in education a belief that the glass is half empty. In contrast, I believe the glass has at least reached the half-full point.

What is it we now know about teaching that is so useful? Let me start by recognizing that teaching is a highly cognitive activity that requires an extraordinary level of competence for making decisions in complex and dynamic environments. Perhaps every teacher has always said this was the case. But with recent research we have learned something about how such complex decision making takes place, and what factors must be considered in the decision process. This review of research is framed as a review of factors that can be controlled or influenced by teachers and that are known to affect student behavior, attitudes, and achievement. Two purposes are served by organizing the review in this way. The complexity of the decisions teachers must deal with is made explicit and we see also that there are well-documented ways for teachers to make sensible choices about how they should go about teaching. Both are important points to make in any program of preservice or inservice education of teachers.

PREINSTRUCTIONAL FACTORS

Content decisions, time allocation decisions, pacing decisions, grouping decisions and decisions about activity structures are among the many preinstructional issues to be decided upon by teachers. Each such decision is known to affect the attitudes, behaviors, and achievement of students. Thus, they must be carefully considered by teachers.

Content Decisions

Until recently it has always been assumed that the district curriculum directors, superintendents, school boards, and state departments of education determined the content that is taught. This is only partly true. The final arbiter of what it is that gets taught is the classroom teacher. The teacher makes the final content choices. In a study of how such content decisions are made (Fisher and others, 1978), one elementary school teacher was observed for over 90 days. During that period of time she taught nothing about fractions, despite the fact that the topic was mandated by the State for instruction at that grade. When the teacher was asked why she did not teach any fractions, she said, "I don't like fractions!" That is a very human response, illustrating the power that teachers have in deciding the content of the curriculum.

We have recently learned from the Michigan State research team (Schwille and others, 1981) that the perceived *effort* required to teach a subject matter area, the perceived *difficulty* of the subject matter area for students, and the teachers' *personal feelings of enjoyment* while teaching a subject matter area influence the teachers' choice of content. One striking example in their data illustrates this point. An elementary school teacher who enjoyed teaching science taught 28 times more science than one who said she did not enjoy teaching science. And from Carew and Lightfoot's (1979) intensive study of four classes we see how the content concerns of a teacher can come to dominate all aspects of classroom life. One of their teachers, Ms. Allen, made reading the central part of classroom life. Eighty-five percent of all interactions with her first grade students were in academic contexts and 75 percent of those were in reading contexts. For the students in her class all feelings of personal competence and self-concept as a learner derived from evaluations of their competence as readers. In that class the teacher's decisions about the importance of reading as the preeminent content area dominated all other aspects of classroom life.

The empirical data relating content coverage or content emphasis to achievement is clear (see the review by Berliner and Rosenshine, 1977). Walker and Schaffarzick (1974) wrote an insightful article on this issue a number of years ago. Even the summary of the International Evaluation of Achievement (Husen, 1967) noted that content emphasis was among the determining factors accounting for difference in achievement between countries. And, more recently, the empirical work of Cooley and Leinhardt (1980) resulted in their comment that the opportunity to learn a given content area was perhaps the most potent variable in accounting for student achievement in that area. With the evidence about the powerful effects of the content variable so clear, it is interesting to note the casualness with which such content decisions get made. As Buchmann and Schmidt (1981) of the Institute for Research on Teaching say:

> During the school day, elementary school teachers can be a law unto themselves, favoring certain subjects at their discretion. What is taught matters, hence arbitrariness in content decisions is clearly inappropriate. If personal feelings about teaching subject matters are not bounded by an impersonal conception of professional duties, children will suffer the consequences. Responsibility in content decision-making requires that teachers examine their own conduct, its main springs and potential effects on what is taught. (pp. 17–18)

Time Allocation Decisions

Related to the issues involved in content decisions are those decisions about time allocations for subject matter areas. The elementary teacher, as opposed to the junior or senior high school teacher, allocates that most precious of scarce resources—time. The Beginning Teacher Evaluation Study (Fisher and others, 1978; Denham and Lieberman, 1980) is one of the many sources for empirical evidence relating allocated time to achievement. What is important to bring to everyone's attention is the incredible variation in the time allocations that are made by different teachers. While observing fifth grade teachers, it was noticed that one teacher could find only 68 minutes a day for instruction in reading and language arts, while another teacher was able to find 137 minutes a day. At second grade, one teacher allocated 47 minutes a day for reading and language arts, another teacher managed to find 118 minutes a day, or 2½ times more time per day to teach reading and language arts. In mathematics the same variability was shown. One second grade teacher allocated 16 minutes a day to instruction in mathematics, another teacher constrained by the same length of the school day somehow found 51 minutes a day to allocate to mathematics. From such data it is not difficult to infer why this is a management issue of great consequence.

Another time management issue has to do with the ways in which time *within* a curriculum area is scheduled. This decision is of equal importance for those teaching at elementary levels and for those who teach at higher levels where departmentalization often occurs and allocations of time to subject matter areas are fixed. One fifth grade teacher, observed for half the school year, allocated 5,646 minutes to comprehension-type activities such as drawing inferences, identifying main ideas in prose, and paraphrasing what was read (Berliner, 1979). These skills are considered critical for language arts, science, social studies, and any other curriculum areas heavily dependent on prose instruction. This figure stands starkly in contrast with the data from another fifth grade teacher who allocated only 917 minutes to comprehension activities. Such marked variability in time in particular content areas lends, inevitably, to differences in achievement.

Pacing Decisions

Related to choice of content, and time allocations between and within content area is the issue of pace of instruction. The evidence for the power of the pacing variable keeps mounting. The more a teacher covers, the more students seem to learn. This is hardly shocking news. But again, it is the variability across classes that is most impressive. One teacher adjusts the pace in the workplace and covers half the text in a semester, another finishes it all. One teacher has 20 practice problems covered in a lesson, another manages to cover only 10. One teacher has students who develop a sight vocabulary of 100 words before Christmas, another teacher's students learn only 50. A remarkable finding reported by Shavelson (1983) concerns the teachers' differential treatment of ability groups over what would be expected if they were in uniform ability groups. Once teachers formed ability groups, they tended to pace the groups differently. That in itself sounds sensible. But the high groups were paced as much as 15 times faster than the low groups, increasing dramatically the difference in what the high and low groups will be exposed to in the school curriculum. The choice of pace, like the choice of content and the decisions about the time to be spent learning particular content areas, determines student achievement. For example, Barr (1980), who has completed a number of studies of pacing, found that 80 percent of the variance in measures of basal reading achievement could be accounted for by the pace of instruction.

Grouping Decisions

Teachers, like any other sensible managers, try to form work groups. Grouping is a very rational response to what Dreeben (1978) pointed out as one of the most salient characteristics of classrooms—their collective nature. But the decisions about the size and composition of the group for various subject matter areas is very complex. We have yet to uncover why many teachers will choose to have no work groups in mathematics instruction, three homogeneous ability groups in reading instruction, and three or four heterogeneously formed discussion groups for social studies. We do know, however, that the size and composition of the work groups affect achievement. For example, Webb (1980) shows how the middle ability child suffers a loss in achievement while the low ability child shows some gains in achievement when they are in mixed ability groups, over what would be expected if they were in uniform ability groups. We have also learned that irrelevant criteria can be used as the basis for group assignment, and that such assignments can be of long duration. Rist (1973) poignantly described how one teacher formed three work groups on the eighth day of kindergarten. It appeared that she used as the basis of assignment those well known correlates of academic ability—clothing, cleanliness, and body odor. The assignments made at the beginning of kindergarten, to what was obviously the group expected to be lowest in achievement, were, in general, still in force three years later when second grade groups were observed. The evidence suggests that the assignment of students to work groups is occasionally like a life-long sentence and always results in students in different groups learning different things while in school.

Decisions About Activity Structures

Activity or task structures, such as reading circle or seatwork or recitation, Doyle (1977) noted, each have *functions* and *operations* (rules or norms) associated with them. The activity structures that are characteristically used by a teacher determines teacher behavior, as well as student behavior, attitudes, and achievement. For example, Bossert (1978) noted that:

> Teachers who relied on recitation were less able to establish close social ties with their students than were teachers who primarily utilized small groups and individualized projects. Recitation places teachers at the center of control. It forces them to rely on equitable, impersonal sanctions (usually short verbal desists) and on the authority of office rather than on more personalized influence mechanisms. By contrast, small groups and individualized instruction increases opportunities for teachers to covertly "bend" classroom rules to handle individual problems and facilitates teacher involvement in, rather than simply teacher direction of, the activity. (p. 46)

The difference in rapport between teachers and students is clearly noticeable in the recitation oriented versus the individualized instruction oriented classrooms. Different activity structures in these different classrooms give rise to differences in the behavior and the attitudes of the participants in the activity. Again, as Bossert (1978) noted:

> It was not that the teachers who used recitation were less concerned or less empathic, but rather that recitation precludes the individualization and involvement allowed by other activities. (pp. 46–47)

Teachers, who must choose between recitation, lecture, discussion, reading circle, computer-mediated instruction, television, seatwork, and so on, must also learn that each activity structure limits or enhances certain factors that affect instruction (see Berliner and others, 1983). Each structure shows characteristic variations in duration, number of students, opportunity for responding and whether such responding is public or private, opportunities for feedback to students and whether such feedback is public or private, and so on. Teachers do not, usually, know how to make these kinds of cost/benefit decisions when choosing activity structures. They must now learn to do so, since the more we learn in psychology about the operations of behavior settings, ecological settings or contexts, the more we learn how powerful they are in determining the behavior of the participants in that setting.

Summary of Preinstructional Factors

A set of complex decisions must be made, primarily, before instruction takes place. Teachers need to be acutely aware of the power they have when making certain decisions to facilitate or retard achievement, to affect the attitudes of students, and to control student classroom behavior. Among the powerful variables that impact on students are those involved in content decisions, time allocation decisions, pacing decisions, grouping decisions, and decisions about activity structures for instruction. The complexity of the task and the number of powerful variables teachers can control also show up during the teaching performance itself. To that topic we turn next.

DURING-INSTRUCTION FACTORS

When teachers are working with students scores of factors affect whether or not learning will occur. Among these are few that seem to be powerful and replicable. These include engaged time, time management, success rate, academic learning time, monitoring, structuring, and questioning. These are discussed briefly, in turn.

Engaged Time

As with allocated time, the fact that engaged time or time on task is associated with achievement is not news. The fact that engaged time is so variable across classes is what is now well documented. There are classes where engagement rates are regularly under 50 percent, and those where engagement rates are regularly about 90 percent (Fisher and others, 1978). One hour of allocated mathematics instruction, then, can result in either 30 minutes or 54 minutes of actual delivered instruction to students. In a single week, differences of such a magnitude can yield a difference of about two hours in the amount of mathematics that is actually engaged in by students. It is no wonder that in reading, mathematics, or science, at any grade level, large variations in engaged time by students is a strong predictor of achievement. Rossmiller (1982) recently found consistent and strong relations between time on task and achievement in reading and mathematics as he studied students over a three-year period. The results are shown in Figure 1. The importance of time on task for lower ability children is shown clearly here. The effect is less powerful for students of high ability, but time on task is still a consistent predictor of achievement. Teachers need to be aware of engaged time rates—for individual students and for the class as a whole—in order to ensure that a sufficient amount of time allocated to instruction in a content area is used by students in productive ways.

Time Management

Time must be controlled after it is allocated or it is lost. And it is easy to lose time in the dynamic world of the classroom. For example, transition times (the start up time and time needed to put things away) can mount rapidly. This results in large losses of the time allocated to a content area. In the study of one class (Fisher and others, 1978) where the school day was around 300 minutes, transition times was coded at 76 minutes. The teacher had a listening center, a math facts table, a career education table, a silent reading table, a science center, a cooking station, and more. Students in this class moved in and out of these stations at a rapid rate throughout the day, according to a complex schedule. While trying to be very creative, this teacher actually was losing one fourth of the instructional time each day to commuting.

When given feedback about their behavior, very rapid changes can take place in the ways teachers go about their jobs. Simple management hints can make a big difference. For example, we asked one teacher to write the language arts assignments of her different reading groups on the board at the start of recess, so that the first student into the classroom after recess can start work and the teacher does not have to wait until the last student wanders in to give oral instructions. Savings of six minutes a day in this class occurred with that simple advice. This is not trivial. That adds about 180 student learning minutes a day. It provides a half-hour more of instruction a week, and, potentially, it adds 18 hours of instructional time per year.

One district that recently tried to audit how time is spent had phenomenal success. They estimated that they added the equivalent of 10–16 days of instructional time per school year. Such time was worth 2–3 million dollars if it had to be purchased. Managing time is serious business in industry and education. In education, however, we probably have not realized how easy it is to lose time through poor management, and do not generally observe teachers long enough and regularly enough to provide them with feedback about this important variable.

Monitoring Success Rate

The Beginning Teacher Evaluation Study provided more evidence in a convincing body of knowledge about the relationship between high success rates and achievement. For younger students and for the academically least able, almost errorless performance during learning tasks results in higher test performance and greater student satisfaction (Marliave and Filby, in press). Rosenshine (1983) has reviewed the data from a number of studies and concluded that during the initial phases of learning, during recitation or small group work, success rate in reading should be at about the 70–80 percent level. When students are reviewing or practicing, as in seatwork, engaging in drill activities, or working on homework, student responses should be rapid, smooth, and almost always correct. Brophy's (1983) recent comments on this issue are relevant:

FIGURE 1* *The Amount of Variance in Reading and Mathematics Achievement Accounted for by Time on Task for Students of Different Ability Levels Over Three Years*

Variance Accounted for by Time on Task Variables

Grade and Academic Year	*Lowest 25% in Ability*		*Middle 50% in Ability*		*Highest 25% in Ability*	
	Reading	*Math*	*Reading*	*Math*	*Reading*	*Math*
3rd grade 1979–1980	.55	.30	.08	.11	.14	.06
4th grade 1980–1981	.27	.18	.06	.12	.04	.04
5th grade 1981–1982	.73	.12	.16	.19	.16	.16

**Adapted from Rossmiller (1982).*

> . . . bear in mind that we are talking about independent seatwork and homework assignments that students must be able to progress through on their own. These assignments demand application of hierarchically organized knowledge and skills that must be not merely learned but mastered to the point of overlearning if they are going to be retained and applied to still more complex material. Confusion about what to do or lack of even a single important concept or skill will frustrate students' progress, and lead to both management and instructional problems for teachers. Yet, this happens frequently. Observational studies suggest that, to the extent that students are given inappropriate tasks, the tasks are much more likely to be too difficult than too easy.

Data from some of the classes of the Beginning Teacher Evaluation Study (Fisher and others, 1978) support Brophy's assertion. Students were coded in some classes as making almost 100 percent errors in their workbooks or during their group work, as much as 14 percent of the time that they were observed. That is, students in some classes were observed to experience total failure in their learning activities for many consecutive minutes of the school day. As might be expected, the percent of time students spent in activities in which they had high error rates was correlated negatively with achievement.

Success rate, then, appears to be another powerful variable with known effects on achievement. Like other such classroom variables, it needs to be monitored, evaluated, and often modified.

Academic Learning Time

A relatively new variable, created after extensive observation and testing of students was completed, is academic learning time (ALT). Virtually all the variables discussed earlier can be related to ALT, which is defined as time engaged with materials or activities related to the outcome measure being used (often an achievement test), during which a student experiences a high success rate. We may visually represent ALT as in Figure 2. The ALT variable is likely to become one of the most useful concepts for judging whether student learning is taking place at a particular point in time in some particular curricular areas. It is appropriate to think of ALT as a proxy variable for student learning: ALT is a variable that can be observed and measured in the classroom, and it has known relations with student learning.

The practical importance of academic learning time in relation to achievement is illustrated by an example from an analysis of reading instruction in second grade (Fisher and others, 1978). Consider an imaginary second-grade student, Sam, whose reading score in October was average among the sample of students under study. That is, Sam was at the 50th percentile. If Sam experiences an average amount of ALT (573 minutes total, or 23 minutes per day in reading), he can be expected to show average reading achievement in December. In other words, Sam will once again be at the 50th percentile. He would have learned quite a bit between October and December, but would not have changed his relative standing in the total sample.

Now let us follow another student, Claire, who also began as an average student. Suppose Claire experienced only 4 minutes per day of ALT (100 minutes total) for the

FIGURE 2 Defining Academic Learning Time (ALT)

Interpretation: The time allocated for instruction is shown visually in (a). During some of this time, students are engaged, as shown in (b). Some of the time students are engaged is time related to the outcome measures that are used to assess instruction. This is shown visually in (c). The time allocated, whether engaged or not, and whether related to the outcome measures or not, can by yielding low, medium, or high success rates for students (d). That portion of allocated time that is time engaged in activities related to the outcome measures and which provides students with a high success rate is defined as Academic Learning Time, as shown in (e).

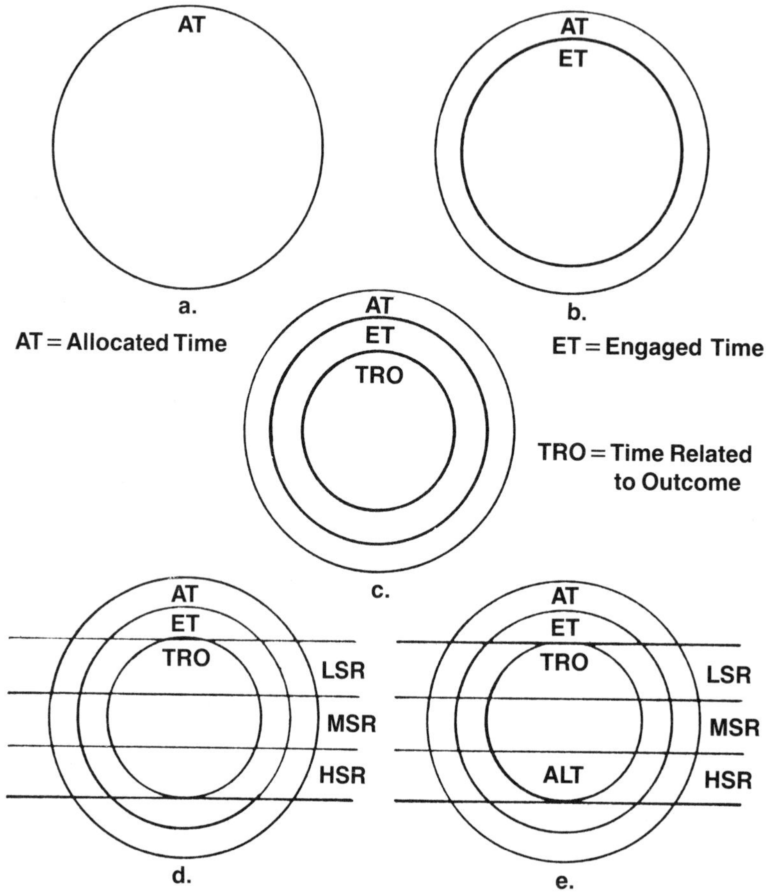

LSR = Low Success Rate
MSR = Medium Success Rate
HSR = High Success Rate

ALT = Academic Learning Time

time period between October and December. Clair would be expected to show almost no change in raw score and would decline considerably in relative terms. In percentile terms, Claire would go from the 50th percentile in October to about the 39th percentile in December in terms of relative standing in the sample. If this same average student had experienced very large amounts of ALT, say 52 minutes per day between October and December, then she could be expected to show considerable improvement in reading achievement relative to the other students in the study. Claire would then have started at the 50th percentile in October, and she would be predicted to have moved to the 66th percentile in relative standing by December.

Thus, the student who accrues a large amount of ALT appears to benefit substantially. At least, these are the predictions that researchers have for groups of students who experience these differential amounts of ALT. And these predictions are derived from data collected on hundreds of elementary-school students.

In the example given it may appear that this range of 4 to 52 minutes per day in ALT is unrealistically large. However, these were times that actually occurred in the classes studied by Fisher and others (1978, 1980). Furthermore, it is easy to imagine how either four or 52 minutes per day of ALT might come about for a particular student. If 50 minutes of reading instruction per day is allocated to a student who pays attention about one-third of the time, and only one-fourth of the student's reading time is a high level of success, the student will experience only about four minutes of ALT—engaged reading time at a high success level. Similarly, if 100 minutes per day is allocated to reading for a student who pays attention 85 percent of the time and is at a high level of success for almost two-thirds of that time, that student will experience about 52 minutes a day of ALT.

Teachers must learn to keep ALT in mind as they instruct, because large differences in the amount of ALT built up by different students generally result in wide variation in student achievement. Teachers should know the outcome measures that are used for instruction, assign activities related to those outcome measures, see to it that enough time is allocated for students, find ways to keep students engaged, and see to it that the younger or less bright students in particular spend large percentages of time in high-success experiences. Under such conditions students will accumulate a good deal of ALT. Students and classes that accumulate high levels of ALT are those that are likely to achieve more than students or classes with lower accumulations of ALT.

Monitoring

A good deal of classroom work in today's schools is done by students on their own. Students may spend large segments of the elementary-school day in seat work, working individually on a contract in reading, doing the ditto sheets related to a science lesson, or finishing the workbook pages on a topic in mathematics. In three different studies of schooling, examining hundreds of classrooms for students age 8–11, researchers found that students worked privately about 50 percent of the time (Angus, Evans, and Parkin, 1975; Good and Beckerman, 1978; McDonald, 1976). Very little substantive interaction between a student and his or her teachers, classroom aides, or peers, occurs in the schools.

When students are left to work privately and are not monitored by the teacher or classroom aide, they often spend less time engaged in the activities for which they are responsible. In classes where a good deal of work is done by students on their own, the engagement rate in academic subjects usually declines if teachers do not keep their monitoring behavior at a high level. It appears that the classroom in which the teacher moves rapidly about, monitoring students and raising the number of substantive interactions with students, is the class where students do well. A substantive interaction between a teacher and student takes place when the teacher checks to see if the student is doing things correctly, asks questions, gives the student academic feedback, and so on. The greater the number of substantive interactions that take place, the more likely it is that students will achieve academically (Fisher and others, 1978, 1980).

Structuring

During an ethnographic study of more and less effective teachers (Tikunoff, Berliner, and Rist, 1975), the importance of structuring was made manifest. While analyzing protocols of reading and mathematics lessons, sometimes the teacher's intent could not be inferred. That is, the readers did not have a clue about why the lesson was occurring, where it fit in the scheme of things, or what students needed to focus on for success at the task. Almost invariably, the teachers that were judged to be unclear about communicating their goals and giving directions were less effective in promoting academic achievement. Through additional data collection (Fisher and others, 1980), it was concluded that students:

> pay attention more when the teacher spends time discussing the goals or structures of the lesson and/or giving directions about what students are to do. (p. 26)

Further, it was noted that both success rate and attention were improved when teachers spent more time structuring the lesson and giving directions.

Structuring is especially important in classes where seatwork is used frequently. In those classes children work alone a good deal of the time. Therefore, it is not surprising that children who do not have a clear handle on what they are to do easily find ways to do nothing. Jerome Bruner (1981) has reached a similar conclusion. In visits to schools he saw many children unable to figure out what was expected of them. He felt that some simple attention to this basic management function would easily improve achievement in classrooms.

Structuring affects attention and success rate: It is sometimes not done at all, sometimes it is done only minimally, and sometimes it is overdone. The case of too much structuring was reported by Hassenpflug (1981) of Wisconsin. Her field notes documented how the directions given for many of the worksheet assignments in third grade actually lasted longer than the amount of time needed by most of the children to finish the assignment! In any case, what is worth noting is that structuring is the responsibility of the teacher, it affects performance, and it can be taught.

Questioning

From the time of Socrates to the present, educators have used questioning as an instructional technique. We have learned from research that elementary-school teachers ask many questions—150 per hour when teaching science or social studies (Gall, 1970), and that high-school teachers also ask many hundreds of questions per day. We have confirmed a suspicion long held by observers of schools—that the cognitive level of the questions that teachers ask is very low. A question's cognitive level is that level of thought believed to be required for a student to consider and answer a question. Bloom's taxonomy is one way of categorizing questions (Bloom and others, 1956). Using that categorization system to classify questions asked by teachers in the classroom, we find that most teachers ask lower-order knowledge-level questions (such as, "When did Columbus discover America?"). Teachers less often ask higher-order questions that require application, synthesis of knowledge, evaluation, or analysis of information (for example, "Why did Columbus want to reach the East?"). Trachtenberg (1974) analyzed over 61,000 questions in the workbooks, tests, and teachers' manuals accompanying nine world history textbooks. Over 95 percent of those questions were lower-order. These data are not very appealing philosophically, since most of us value the higher-order, more thought-provoking questions. Nevertheless, the lower-order question has been found to serve some positive functions. It promotes participation, establishes a factual data base from which more relevant higher-order discussions can arise, and provides high-success experiences for students. Moreover, in the case of students of lower socioeconomic standing, high levels of lower-order questions seem to correlate positively with achievement (Brophy and Everston, 1976).

Although it is not customary for teachers to ask many higher-level cognitive questions, when they do, another problem arises. They may receive and accept answers that do not match the level of cognitive thought required by the question. An analysis of questions and answers in hundreds of teacher-student interchanges showed that the odds are only about 50–50 that an analysis, synthesis or application-level question will be responded to with an answer reflecting analysis, synthesis, or application (Mills and others, 1980). Thus, teachers would appear to need experience in more than phrasing questions—they need to learn to classify answers as well.

Perhaps the most important point about questions is that higher-order questions do facilitate learning. In a review of the effects of higher-order questions, Redfield and Rousseau (1981) found that teachers who ask more higher-order questions have students who achieve considerably more. The overall effect is such that a typical student exposed to a lesson without higher-order questions may be expected to perform at the 50th percentile on a test related to that lesson. In contrast, if that same student had been exposed to a lesson where many intelligent higher-order questions were asked, the student would be performing at about the 75th percentile on the same test!

Finally, research informs us that we should consider carefully Rowe's (1974) finding that students' answers to questions are of much better quality if teachers wait longer than they usually do between asking a question and requesting a response. This increased wait-time results in increased appropriateness of the response, increased confidence in responding, an increase in the variety of responses, and an increase in the cognitive level of responses. This is not a bad return for a simple adjustment in teaching style—going from the typical one second to the recommended three or more seconds of wait-time. Clearly, there is much to master in this oldest of pedogogical forms—the question. Training is probably not now as extensive in this area as it ought to be.

Summary of During-Instruction Factors

In this section of the review we have noted a number of factors under a teacher's control that can affect student attitude, achievement, and classroom behavior. Mentioned briefly were engaged time, time management, success rate, academic learning time, monitoring, structuring, and questioning. Programs of professional education for teachers should see to it that teachers become familiar with these factors. But teacher educators should *not* make the mistake of presenting each of these factors as single variables that alone will determine achievement. Instructional behavior is multifaceted and it is, no doubt, the interaction of dozens of significant variables like these that affect achievement. If a person makes a change from being a smoker to being a non-smoker, or from being a sedentary person to being on an active schedule, or goes from being on a diet where beef is used a lot to a diet where grain is used a lot, we hope for some improvement in general health and longevity. But any one such change is not expected to make a really big difference. If all the changes in lifestyle noted above were made, marked positive effects on health and longevity are much more likely to occur. The interactive teaching variables are like that. Independently, they may have some slight positive effects, but it will be hard to detect them. When used in combination and when they become a teacher's normal and customary pattern of interactive teaching, these variables are much more likely to affect achievement in noticeable ways.

CLIMATE FACTORS

For want of a better term, we shall use the term *climate* to describe characteristics of classroom environments that appear to lead to achievement. Four such factors seem particularly important—the communication of academic expectations for achievement; development of a safe, orderly and academically focused environment for work; quick, fair and sensible management of deviancy; and the development of cooperative environments for learning.

Communicating Academic Expectations for Achievement

The voluminous literature on expectancy effects in education has been reviewed by Brophy and Good (1974) and more recently by Cooper (1979) and by Good (in press). The expectation literature is consistently (though not unanimously) interpreted to show that there are powerful effects on performance when teachers communicate their goals for performance to those they are teaching. If teachers set high but attainable goals for academic performance, academic achievement usually increases. If teachers set goals for performance that are low, academic achievement usually decreases.

The evidence on the differential treatment accorded to high and low ability students is believed to provide clues to the mechanism by which expectancies about performance are communicated. Good (in press) summarized this literature as follows: In comparison to students for whom teachers hold high expectations about performance, the students perceived to be low performers are most often seated farther away from the teacher; treated as groups, not individuals; smiled at less; made eye contact with less; called on less to answer questions; are given less time to answer those questions; have their answers followed up less frequently; are praised more often for marginal and inadequate answers; are praised less frequently for successful public responses; interrupted in their work more often; and so forth. This kind of treatment differential between students for whom teachers hold high and low expectations appears to influence their performance in predictable ways.

The communication of expectations does not just create a classroom climate. The expectations of teachers and administrators can permeate a school, creating a school climate. The work of Rutter and others (1979), as well as Brookover and Lezotte (1977), Edmonds (1979), Vanezky and Winfield (1979), makes this point. Rutter and others (1979) found marked differences in the outcomes of secondary schools attributable to school level variables such as expectations. Their data revealed that "Children had better academic success in schools . . . where the teachers expressed expectations that a high proportion of the children would do well in national examinations" (p. 188). Furthermore, the beneficial effects of high expectations are felt in areas other than academic achievement. Again, from Rutter and others (1979):

> The findings showed that schools which expected children to care for their own resources had better behavior, better attendance, and less delinquency. In a similar way, giving children posts or tasks of responsibility was associated with better pupil behavior. The message of confidence that the pupils can be trusted to act with maturity and responsibility is likely to encourage pupils to fulfill those expectations. (p. 188)

Thus, the process by which expectations about academic performance are communicated must be learned by teachers if they are to create a positive educational environment for students.

Developing a Safe, Orderly and Academically Focused Environment for Work

The evidence on effective classrooms and effective schools is amazingly congruent. There is always an indication of higher achievement in classes or schools where there is present an orderly, safe environment, a business-like manner among the teachers, and a schoolwide system that reflects thoughtfulness in promulgating academic programs, focuses on achievement, holds students accountable for achievement, and rewards achievement. Where such evidence of order and focus are missing, achievement is lower. Case studies of unusually effective classes in the Beginning Teacher Evaluation Study (Fisher and others, 1978) showed this rather clearly. And Rutter and his colleagues (1979) found similar variables related to achievement when they looked between schools, rather than between classes. Purkey and Smith (1983, p. 445), after reviewing the effective schools literature, comment:

> The seriousness and purpose with which the school approaches its task is communicated by the order and discipline it maintains in its building. . . . evidence exists indicating that clear, reasonable rules, fairly and consistently enforced, not only can reduce behavior problems that interfere with learning but also can promote feelings of pride and responsibility in the school community. (p. 41)

Those who train teachers must remember that these findings about order and academic focus do constitute a real and present danger. Literal interpretations of these findings can lead to overcontrol and to such a strict academic focus that it denies the arts or produces debilitating levels of anxiety among students. But a lack of order and a lack of an academic focus have been empirically determined to lead to low levels of achievement and may, therefore, constitute an equally serious threat to the nation.

The power of these variables is clear. The ability to balance these forces is the problem that teachers face. The complexity of teachers is once again highlighted, as teachers must decide how to demonstrate that such things as playfulness and order are not incompatible, and that societal and individual needs must *both* be kept in perspective.

Sensible Management of Deviancy

Jacob Kounin, in an enormously influential work (1970), has given us a set of concepts that help us understand the process of maintaining a workplace free from deviance and in which students attend to their assignments. He gave us *withitness*, describing how effective managers nip behavioral problems in the bud; *overlappingness*, describing how effective classroom managers handle more than one thing at a time; he also described the need for *signals* for academic work; the effects of *momentum* and *smoothness* in lessons on student behavior, and the positive effects on attention of *group alerting, accountability* and *variety* in teaching. These variables have, for the most part, been verified or appropriately qualified in the work of Brophy and Evertson (1976) and Anderson, Evertson, and Brophy (1979), among others. Borg and Ascione (1982) have taken these concepts and developed training materials for teachers. Borg's work provides clear evidence of changed teacher and student behavior as a function of this kind of training. The students in classes where teachers had been taught management skills were markedly more on task and showed less deviant behavior. At the University of Texas, Evertson and Emmer and their colleagues (Evertson and others, 1981; and Emmer and others, 1981) have developed sensible management training programs for elementary and for junior high school teachers.

Field tests of these eminently sensible suggestions from research and practice that are designed to help keep management problems to a minimum show that they do work.

This technology for creating learning environments that are relatively free from behavior problems has been developed, primarily over the last decade. (See, for example, Borg and Ascione, 1982; Duke, 1979, 1982). We have only to figure out how to provide the time so that teachers can learn the technology that can be used for controlling the management climate in their classes. Proper control of this climate variable can result in increased achievement through a reduction of time lost due to management problems and by helping to foster a safe and orderly environment in which it is possible for students to learn the school curriculum that was selected for them.

Developing Cooperative Learning Environments

In the last few years, just as we have done in the area of behavior management in classrooms, we have developed technology to help teachers enhance the interpersonal relationships between members of different social classes, races, sexes, or different ability groups. The key element in these approaches to developing cooperative environments is the requirement that every member of a group participate in activities that can be successfully completed only through interdependent and cooperative behavior. In Teams-Games-Tournaments (Slavin, 1980) heterogeneous groups are formed to compete for prizes obtainable through academic achievement. A clever point system is used so that low ability and high ability students can each contribute the same number of points to the team. Over 2,000 schools have tried Teams-Games-Tournaments with some success. The use of this technology usually improves cooperative behavior among students and often improves academic achievement as well.

A different approach is used by Aronson and his colleagues. They required that each member of the group have some of the information needed to solve a problem, thus ensuring that everyone in a group is responsible for success. The techniques used by Johnson and Johnson (1975) and by Sharon (1980) in Israel accomplish similar goals. Technology now exists to create productive and cognitive classroom learning environments. Alas, such technology is not finding its way quickly into programs of teacher education.

Summary of Climate Factors

In this section four climate variables that affect achievement were noted. It was reported that when a teacher communicates high academic expectations, and such expectations become a part of the classroom and school ethos, achievement is positively affected; when teachers create classrooms that are safe, orderly, and academically focused, achievement is increased; when the technology now available to teach sensible management of behavior problems is used, the opportunity for learning increases; and when the technology now available to create cooperative learning environments is used, positive results ensue. Teaching takes place in a context. It can never be decontextualized. The context, that environment for learning that must be developed in order for classrooms or schools to be judged successful, appears to require a press for both prosocial and academically oriented behavior.

POST-INSTRUCTIONAL FACTORS

After an instructional sequence is over, some measure of student learning is usually devised. We have learned, recently, at least two interesting facts about testing that contribute to effective teaching. And we have some new concerns about two other post-instructional factors that have been discussed for years—grades and feedback to students.

Tests

There has been a growing concern that what occurs in classrooms is not represented on some of the standardized tests that are often used to assess student learning and teachers' and school districts' competency. This concern has taken many forms, from concern about whether students have had the "opportunity to learn" what is on the tests used to measure achievement, to content analysis of curriculum and achievement tests to see what degree of overlap or congruence between tests and the curriculum actually does exist. The latter kind of concern gave rise to research that examined each topic in three widely used mathematics textbooks and each test item in five widely used standardized tests (Freeman and others, 1980). In the *best* case, 71 percent of the topics that were on each test were also covered in the text. Thus, in the best case about 30 percent of what was tested had never been covered in school by students. In the *worst* case, 47 percent of the topics that were tested were never covered by the text. That is, the test that is used in some districts to evaluate student learning, teacher competency, and district effectiveness has more than half its items derived from topics never covered by students in that district! The lessons from recent research is clear—if teachers, schools, and districts are ever to look effective, they must learn to use tests that accurately reflect what they teach. The congruence between what is taught and what is tested must be high.

A second issue in testing, especially with the advent of the microcomputer, is that test items can be used to diagnose "buggy" algorithms (Brown and Burton, 1978). J. S. Brown, in particular, has challenged the assumption that a wrong answer shows lack of knowledge. Instead, he has demonstrated convincingly how people may possess the wrong knowledge for a particular task. For example, when a student solves a problem such as 143 minus 28 and answers 125, and then solves 256 minus 179 and answers 123, we see evidence of algorythmic or logical functioning in subtraction. The student subtracts the smaller number from the larger number each time, regardless of which number is on top. The student's solutions show evidence of learning and consistency. They also show, however, that the student has learned faulty or "buggy" algorithms. Hundreds of examples now are being developed to show how teachers can learn what a student knows but is incorrect. Scoring test items wrong is wasteful—items can supply hypotheses about the buggy algorithms in use by students, a first step toward correcting a student's errors.

Grades

The overuse and the coercive power of grades had, in the 1960s, been condemned by many educational reformers. It was thought that learning was lessened when external grading policies were applied. That appears not to be true. In fact, the evidence is persuasive that grades do motivate students to learn more in a given subject area (Gage and Berliner, 1984). The judicious use of grades that are tied to objective performance, as in mastery and some other instructional programs, appears to be related to increased achievement and positive student attitudes.

Feedback

Substantial use of corrective feedback in the academic areas, contingent praise for correct or proper behavior, and the use of students' ideas as a way of letting students know that their contributions are valued, all show positive relations to achievement and attitude (Gage and Berliner, 1984). Such feedback to students is not often found at high rates in classes, despite its logical and empirically determined effectiveness. Criticism, as a form of feedback, if emotionally neutral has been found to be accepted by students, but it has long been recognized that sarcasm and personal attacks are negatively related to achievement and should not be used as feedback for inappropriate behavior. Ignoring inappropriate behavior and other techniques are recommended by behavior modification advocates who have had great success in changing student behavior (see Sulzer-Azaroff and Mayer, 1977).

Summary of Post-Instructional Factors

Briefly mentioned were some teaching practices that typically occur after an instructional episode is completed, and which relate to achievement. It was noted that tests should be used to assess student knowledge, teacher competency, and district effectiveness *only* if the tests and curriculum match. Evidence suggests that our schools are a good deal more effective than is generally recognized, because we seriously underestimate what is learned by students when schools rely on tests that do not measure what is taught. We have also learned that tests need not be designed to be summative, as they so often are. A formative test, designed to systematically diagnose a student's faulty knowledge can be created. Teachers can then more precisely prescribe the kinds of remediation necessary for students with particular needs. Grades and feedback were also mentioned as affecting achievement. Perhaps much of this section can be summarized by the word "accountability." In study after study we learn that when students learn that they are accountable for their academic work because someone gives them feedback in the form of grades, rewards, or criticism for their homework, classwork, or test performance, there is evidence of increased achievement.

RESEARCH AND THE PRACTICE OF CLASSROOM TEACHING

A good deal of the research cited has been derived from correlational studies or studies of single variables as investigators searched for some effect on student attitude, behavior, or achievement. Teaching—real, live, honest-to-goodness classroom teaching—is extremely complex and extremely dynamic. A very legitimate concern, then, is whether the factors mentioned are found to hold up *in situ*. The evidence, while scanty, is reassuring. For example, the Missouri Math project of Good and Grouws (1979) used training procedures based on the available research (and old-fashioned common sense). Elementary school teachers were trained to

- check the previous day's work and reteach where necessary (this factor is related to the comments on grading and feedback, noted earlier).
- present new content or skills, proceeding rapidly, but in small steps, while giving detailed instructions and explanations (this factor is related to the comments about pacing, success rate, and structuring, noted earlier).
- have students practice the material, while providing feedback and corrections (this factor is related to the comments on questioning, feedback, and monitoring, noted earlier).
- have students do independent practice (this factor is related to the comments about allocated time, engaged time, success rate and feedback, noted earlier).
- provide weekly and monthly reviews (this factor is related to the comments about grades and feedback).

The training program helped teachers to develop a safe and orderly environment for learning. In addition, the teachers developed a climate characterized by an academic orientation. The program was unambiguously successful. Teachers trained by Good and Grouws had students who achieved considerably more than did the students of teachers who did not use the procedures recommended in the training program. Thus, it appears that the dozen or more factors drawn upon by Good and Grouws as they developed training materials proved, in combination, to be effective in regular classroom use. Moreover, the variables that teachers were trained to attend to showed a fascinating pattern when the actual implementation of those variables in classes was studied.

The experimental group of teachers learned to use 15 teaching practices. A comparison of the classroom behavior of the trained and untrained teachers showed that in classroom use, the trained teachers used eight teaching practices at rates different from the untrained teachers (that is, training changed their teaching behavior) and that seven teaching practices were not implemented at rates different than those used by untrained teachers. The interesting pattern shown in the data was that *each* of the eight recommended teaching practices that were implemented by the trained teachers showed a significant relationship with student achievement, and that *none* of the seven recommended teaching practices that were not implemented showed a significant relationship with achievement (Gage and Giaconia, 1981).

The same pattern of relations was shown to hold in the study by Anderson, Evertson, and Brophy (1979). In that experimental study the research on teaching was culled to provide over two dozen recommendations for the teaching of reading in first grade. Teachers who were trained to use the whole set of recommended teaching practices had students who achieved more than did the students of teachers who were not trained. Again, we find evidence that the variables derived from research on teaching can be used to train teachers and in turn, to increase student achievement. Moreover, as in the Good and Grouws study, those teaching practices actually implemented in the trained teachers classes were usually related to student achievement, and those teaching practices that did not actually become a salient part of the teacher's regular classroom behavior usually showed no relationship to achievement. The data from both studies are shown in Figures 3 and 4.

FIGURE 3 The Relationship between the Implementation of Recommended Teaching Practices and Achievement in the Study by Good and Grouws (1979) *

		Significance of the Relationship between Teaching Practice and Achievement		
		Significant	**Not Significant**	
Recommended Teaching Practices Actually Implemented in the Classroom	**Yes**	8	0	8
	No	0	7	7
		8	7	15

Source: Gage and Giaconia (1981).

FIGURE 4 The Relationship between the Implementation of Recommended Teaching Practices and Achievement in the Study by Anderson, Evertson, and Brophy (1979) *

		Significance of the Relationship between Teaching Practice and Achievement		
		Significant	**Not Significant**	
Recommended Teaching Practices Actually Implemented in the Classroom	**Yes**	12	2	14
	No	8	9	17
		20	11	31

Source: Gage and Giaconia (1981).

The implications of these two studies, analyzed in this way, must be made clear: when the research on teaching is used to develop training procedures for teachers, teachers can learn the recommended teaching practices, and if they implement the teaching practices that they have learned they can effect in a positive way student classroom behavior and achievement. That is why, in my opinion, there is cause to be optimistic. The glass is half full.

Other studies that have used research on teaching as guides to improve teaching practice have also been successful. The research team at Stanford did inservice training of elementary teachers and was able to show a positive effect on student achievement (Crawford and others, 1978). In a study with low income Hawaiian children, remarkable increases in reading achievement were noted when a program was instituted using time-on-task, success rate, structuring, monitoring, questioning, and so on. The program worked when it was placed within the Hawaiian cultural context that was familiar to the children (Tharp, 1982). Many of the research variables mentioned above were shown to affect achievement in a study by Stallings, Needles, and Stayrook (1979), and many of these same variables were found to distinguish between effective and less effective secondary school teachers (Evertson, Anderson, and Brophy, 1979). There is good reason to believe that a list of factors such as those presented in this essay, or by Hunter in this volume, or by Rosenshine (1983), or by Good (in press), does represent a reliable knowledge base for the inservice and preservice education of teachers. What will it take to convince the teacher education community to use such knowledge?

Gage (1983) has addressed this problem and his logic will be followed here. When a relationship occurs between a teaching practice and an educational outcome we value, we have "an implication." Implications range along a continuum of strength that may be labeled as going from a *shred* (a glimmer of an insight) to a *suggestion*, to a *recommendation*, to an *imperative*, and on to a *categorical imperative*, where the failure to use certain knowledge would be morally reprehensible. In medicine, extremely small increases in health or longevity due to diet or the use of the new beta-blocker anti-heart-attack drugs become the basis for recommendations and imperatives. Beta-blockers have only a small (though significant) effect on death rate. Yet, a physician who will not order beta blockers for someone recovering from a heart attack could well be sued for malpractice.

There are many variables recently uncovered in educational research that show as strong or stronger a relationship with student achievement and student behavior as variables in medical practice show to longevity and general health. But in medicine such relationships become imperatives, while in education they are treated as shreds—the merest glimmer of an implication. Our research is much less at fault than are our attitudes toward research. Perhaps this essay and this volume will help to change people's opinions about whether in research on teaching the glass is half full or half empty.

REFERENCES

Anderson, L. M.; Evertson, C. M.; and Brophy, J. E. "An Experimental Study of Effective Teaching in First Grade Reading Groups." *The Elementary School Journal* 79 (1979): 193–223.

Angus, M. J.; Evans, K. W.; and Parkin, B. *An Observational Study of Selected Pupil and Teacher Behavior in Open Plan and Conventional Design Classrooms*. Australian Open Area Project, Technical Report No. 4. Perth, Australia: Educational Department of Western Australia, 1975.

Barr, R. C. "School, Class, Group, and Pace Effects on Learning." Paper presented at the meeting of the American Educational Research Association, April 1980, Boston, Mass.

Berliner, D. C. "Tempus Educare." In *Research on Teaching*. Edited by P. L. Peterson and M. J. Walberg. Berkeley, Calif.: McCutchan, 1979.

Berliner, D. C. "Developing Conceptions of Classroom Environments: Some Light on the T in Classroom Studies of ATI." *Educational Psychologist* 18 (1983): 1–13.

Berliner, D. C., and Rosenshine, B. V. "The Acquisition of Knowledge in the Classroom." In *Schooling and the Acquisition of Knowledge*. Edited by R. C. Anderson, R. J. Spiro, and W. E. Montague. Hillsdale, N.J.: Erlbaum, 1977.

Bloom, B. S.; Engelhart, M. B.; Furst, E. J.; Hill, W. M., and Krathwohl, D. R. *Taxonomy of Educational Objectives: The Classification of Educational Goals. Handbook I: Cognitive Domain*. New York: Longman Green, 1956.

Borg, W. R., and Ascione, F. R. "Classroom Management in Elementary Mainstreaming Classrooms." *Journal of Educational Psychology* 74 (1982): 85–95.

Bossert, S. T., "Activity Structures and Student Outcomes." Paper presented at the National Institute of Education's Conference on School Organization and Effects, San Diego, Calif., January 1978.

Brookover, W. B., and Lezotte, L. *Changes in School Characteristics Coincident with Changes in Student Achievement*. East Lansing, Mich.: College of Urban Development, Michigan State University, 1977.

Brophy, J. "Classroom Organization and Management." *The Elementary School Journal* 83 (1983): 265–286.

Brophy, J., and Evertson, C. *Learning from Teaching: A Developmental Perspective*. Boston, Mass.: Allyn and Bacon, 1976.

Brophy, J. E., and Evertson, C. M. *Process-Product Correlations In the Texas Teacher Effectiveness Study*. Final Report No. 74–4. Austin: Research and Development Center for Teacher Education, University of Texas, 1979.

Brophy, J. E., and Good, T. L. *Teacher-Student Relationships: Causes and Consequences*. New York: Holt, Reinhardt and Winston, 1974.

Brown, J. S., and Burton, R. R. "Diagnostic Models for Procedural Bugs in Basic Mathematical Skills," *Cognitive Science* 1 (1978): 155–192.

Bruner, J. "On Instructability." Paper presented at the meeting of the American Psychological Association, Los Angeles, Calif., August 1981.

Buchmann, M., and Schmidt, W. H. *The School Day and Teachers' Content Commitments*. IRT Research Series #83. East Lansing: Institute for Research on Teaching, Michigan State University, 1981.

Carew, J., and Lightfoot, S. L. *Beyond Bias*. Cambridge, Mass.: Harvard University Press, 1979.

Cooley, W. W., and Leinhardt, G. "The Instructional Dimensions Study." *Educational Evaluation and Policy Analysis* 2, 1 (1980): 7–25.

Cooper, H. "Pygmalion Grows Up: A Model for Teacher Expectation, Communication and Performance Influence." *Review of Educational Research* 79 (1979): 389–410.

Crawford, J.; Gage, N. L.; Corno, L; Stayrook, W.; Mittman, A.; Schunk, D.; Stallings, J.; Baskin, E.; Harvey, P.; Austin, D.; Cronin, D.; and Newman, R. *An Experiment on Teacher Effectiveness and Parent-Assisted Instruction in the Third Grade* (3 Vols.). Stanford, Calif.: Center for Educational Research at Stanford, 1978.

Denham, C., and Lieberman, A., eds. *Time to Learn*. Washington, D.C.: U.S. Department of Education, National Institute of Education, 1980.

Doyle, W. "Paradigms for Research on Teacher Effectiveness." In *Review of Research in Education* (Vol. 5). Edited by L. S. Shulman. Itasca, Ill.: Peacock Publishers, 1977.

Dreeben, R. "The Collective Character of Instruction." Paper presented at the meeting of the American Educational Research Association, Toronto, Canada, March 1978.

Duke, D., ed. *Classroom Management*. Seventy-eighth yearbook of the National Society for the Study of Education. Part II. Chicago: University of Chicago Press, 1979.

Duke, D. L., ed. *Helping Teachers Manage Classrooms*. Alexandria, Va.: Association for Supervision and Curriculum Development, 1982.

Edmonds, R. "Some Schools Work and More Can." *Social Policy* 9 (March/April 1979): 28–32.

Emmer, E. T.; Evertson, C. M.; Clements, B. S.; Sanford, J. P.; and Worsham, M. E. *Organizing and Managing the Junior High School Classroom*. Austin: Research and Development Center for Teacher Education, University of Texas, 1981.

Evertson, C. M.; Anderson, L. M.; and Brophy, J. E. *The Texas Junior High School Study: Final Report of Process-Product Relationships* (R & D Report #4061). Austin: Research and Development Center for Teacher Education, University of Texas, 1978.
Evertson, C. M.; Emmer, E. T.; Clements, B. S.; Sanford, J. P.; Worsham, M. E.; and Williams, E. L. *Organizing and Managing the Elementary School Room*. Austin: Research and Development Center for Teacher Education, University of Texas, 1981.
Fisher, C. W.; Berliner, D. C.; Filby, N. N. Marliave, R. S.; Cahen, L. S.; and Dishaw, M. M. "Teaching Behaviors, Academic Learning Time and Student Achievement: An Overview." In *Time to learn*. Edited by C. Denham and A. Lieberman. Washington, D.C.: U.S. Department of Education, National Institute of Education, 1980.
Fisher, C. W.; Filby, N. N.; Marliave,R. S.; Cahen, L. S.; Dishaw, M. M.; Moore, J. E.; and Berliner, D. C. *Teaching Behaviors, Academic Learning Time and Student Achievement*. Final Report of Phase III-B, Beginning Teacher Evaluation Study. Technical Report V-1. San Francisco, Calif.: Far West Laboratory for Educational Research and Development, 1978.
Freeman, D.; Kuhs, T.; Porter, A.; Knappen, L.; Floden, R.; Schmidt, W.; and Schwille, J. *The Fourth Grade Mathematics Curriculum as Inferred from Textbooks and Tests*. East Lansing: Michigan State University, Institute for Research on Teaching, Report #82, 1980.
Gage, N. L., ed. *Handbook of Research on Teaching*. Chicago, Ill.: Rand McNally, 1963.
Gage, N. L. "When Does Research on Teaching Yield Implications for Practice?" *Elementary School Journal* 83 (1983): 492–496.
Gage, N. L., and Berliner, D. C. *Educational Psychology*, 3rd ed. Boston, Mass.: Houghton-Mifflin, 1984.
Gage, N. L., and Giaconia, R. "Teaching Practices and Student Achievement: Causal Connections." *New York University Education Quarterly* 113, 3 (1981): 2–9.
Gall, M. D. "The Use of Questioning in Teaching." *Review of Educational Research* 40 (1970): 707–721.
Good, T. L. "Classroom research: Past and future." In *Handbook of Teaching and Policy*. Edited by L. S. Shulman and G. A. Sykes. New York: Longman, in press.
Good, T. L., and Beckerman, T. M. "Time on Task: A Naturalistic Study in Sixth Grade Classrooms." *Elementary School Journal* 78 (1978): 193–201.
Good, T. L., and Grouws, D. "The Missouri Mathematics Effectiveness Project: An Experimental Study in Fourth-Grade Classrooms." *Journal of Educational Psychology* 71 (1979): 355–362.
Hassenpflug, A. M. *The Use and Understanding of School Time by Third Graders: An Ethnographic Case Study*. Technical Report No. 574. Madison: Research and Development Center for Individualized Schooling, University of Wisconsin, 1981.
Husen, T. *International Study of Achievement in Mathematics: Comparison of Twelve Countries* (Vols. 1 and 2). New York: John Wiley, 1967.
Johnson, D., and Johnson R. *Learning Together and Alone*. Englewood Cliffs, N.J.: Prentice-Hall, 1975.
Kounin, J. *Discipline and Group Management in Classrooms*. New York: Holt, Reinhart, and Winston, 1970.
McDonald, F. J. *Research on Teaching and Its Implications for Policy Making: Report on Phase II of the Beginning Teacher Evaluation Study*. Princeton, N.J.: Educational Testing Service, 1976.
Marliave, R., and Filby, J. N. "Success Rates: A Measure of Task Appropriateness." In *Perspectives on Instructional Time*, Edited by C. W. Fisher and D. C. Berliner. New York: Longman, in press.
Mills, S. R., Rice, C. T.; Berliner, D. C.; and Rousseau, E. W. "The Correspondence Between Teacher Questions and Student Answers in Classroom Discourse." *Journal of Experimental Education* 48 (1980): 194–209.
Purkey, S. C., and Smith, M. C. "Effective Schools: A Review." *The Elementary School Journal* 93 (1983): 428–452.
Redfield, D. L., and Rousseau, E. W. "A Meta-Analysis of Experimental Research on Teacher Questioning Behavior." *Review of Educational Research* 51 (1981): 237–245.
Rist, R. C. *The Urban School: A Factory for Failure*. Cambridge: Massachusetts Institute of Technology Press, 1973.
Rosenshine, B. V. "Teaching Functions in Instructional Programs." *The Elementary School Journal* 83 (1983): 335–352.
Rossmiller, R. A. "Managing School Resources to Improve Student Achievement." Paper presented at the State Superintendent Conference for District Administrators, Madison, Wisc., September 1982.
Rowe, M. B. "Wait Time and Rewards as Instructional Variables: Their Influence on Language, Logic and Fate Control. Part One, Wait Time." *Journal of Research in Science Teaching* 11 (1974): 81–94.

Rutter, M.; Maughan, B.; Mortimore, P.; and Ousten, J. *Fifteen Thousand Hours*. Cambridge, Mass.: Harvard University Press, 1979.

Schwille, J.; Porter, A.; Belli, A.; Floden, R.; Freeman, D.; Knappen, L.; Kuhs, T.; and Schmidt, W. J. *Teachers as Policy Brokers in the Content of Elementary School Mathematics*. (National Institute of Education Contract No. P–80–0127). East Lansing: Institute for Research on Teaching, Michigan State University, 1981.

Sharon, S. "Cooperative Learning in Small Groups: Recent Methods and Effects on Achievement Attitudes and Ethnic Relations." *Review of Educational Research* 50 (1980): 241–271.

Shavelson, R. J. "Review of Research on Teachers' Pedagogical Judgments, Plans, and Decisions." *Elementary School Journal* 83 (1983): 392–414.

Slavin, R. "Cooperative learning." *Review of Educational Research* 50 (1980): 315–342.

Stallings, J.; Needles, M.; and Stayrook, N. *How to Change the Process of Teaching Basic Reading Skills in Secondary Schools*. Menlo Park, Calif.: SRI International, 1979.

Sulzer-Azaroff, B., and Mayer, R. G. *Applying Behavior Analysis Procedures with Children and Youth*. New York: Holt, Reinhart, and Winston, 1977.

Tharp, R. G. "The Effective Instruction of Comprehension: Results and Description of the Kamehameha Early Education Program." *Reading Research Quarterly* 17 (1982): 503–527.

Tikunoff, W. J.; Berliner, D. C.; and Rist, R. C. *An Ethnographic Study of the Forty Classrooms of the Beginning Teacher Evaluation Study Known Sample*. Technical Report 75–105. San Francisco, Calif.: Far West Laboratory for Educational Research and Development, 1975.

Trachtenberg, D. "Student Tasks in Text Material: What Cognitive Skills Do They Tap?" *Peabody Journal of Education* 52 (1974): 54–57.

Vanezky, R. L., and Winfield, L. F. *Schools That Succeed Beyond Expectations in Teaching Reading*. Final Report, National Institute of Education, Grant No. NIE-G-78–0027. Newark, Del.: College of Education, University of Delaware, 1979.

Walker, D. F., and Schaffarzick, J. "Comparing Curricula." *Review of Educational Research* 44 (1974): 83–111.

Webb, N. M. "A Process-Outcome Analysis of Learning in Group and Individual Settings." *Educational Psychologist* 15 (1980): 69–83.

David C. Berliner is Professor, Department of Educational Psychology, University of Arizona, Tucson.

From *Using What We Know About Teaching* (1984 Yearbook), edited by P. L. Hosford, pp. 51–77 (Alexandria, VA: Association for Superivision and Curriculum Development). Used by permission.

The ecology of the classroom is an important factor in classroom management. Even though students are responsible for their own behavior, the influence of peers, teachers, and the environment in general exerts considerable influence on students' behavior. Any examination of student behavior must take into consideration the context in which the behavior is occurring. The authors direct the reader's attention to teacher behavior as a contributor to student misbehavior. This is an excellent reference for both beginning and experienced teachers. The selection is research-based and is presented from a classroom perspective.

Classroom Management: Teacher-Child-Peer Relationships

James M. Kauffman, Patricia L. Pullen, and Eileen Akers

Most teachers spend little or none of their teaching time in concentrating solely on an individual student, whether for academic instruction or behavior management. The reality of the classroom demands that teachers instruct and manage students in groups. Moreover, research indicates that the most effective instruction typically occurs in small groups, with the teacher requiring both group and individual responses (Stevens & Rosenshine, 1981; Wallace & Kauffman, 1986). Although special education is concerned with individuals, the notion of individualization often has been misunderstood and misapplied to special education (Lloyd, 1984; Strain, Odom & McConnell, 1984). In short, both instruction and behavior management in the classroom almost always involve a teacher, an exceptional child, and the child's peers. When a classroom management problem arises, all three—teacher, child, and peers—are very much in it together.

The "togetherness" involved in problem behavior was first emphasized by special educators who described classrooms as microcommunities or social ecologies (e.g., Graubard, Rosenberg, & Miller, 1971; Hobbs, 1966; Rhodes, 1967, 1970). Research based on the ecological principles of mutual influence and interdependency has clearly established the fact that every person in the classroom—adult or child—influences the behavior of every other individual in that environment (Kauffman, 1985).

Thus, classroom management strategies must take into account not only the teacher's influence on children but children's influence on the teacher and on each other as well.

Relationships among teachers, children, and peers suggest looking for mutual influences in the causes of misbehavior; they suggest also an array of strategies, including direct management by the teacher, self-control techniques, and peer-directed interventions. We will briefly examine potential contributions to misbehavior on the part of teachers and children; then we will describe possible interventions.

POTENTIAL CONTRIBUTIONS TO MISBEHAVIOR

When children misbehave, adults may be a part of the problem. Through their expectations, demands, and reactions to children's behavior, adults influence the course of interactions for better or for worse. Adults thus bear much responsibility for how children behave. Teachers, as are parents, are called upon to shape children's behavior through their conscious manipulation of the child's physical and social environment. Teachers' tasks include selecting curriculum, giving directions, setting expectations, controlling consequences, and otherwise structuring the environment to obtain and support desirable conduct.

Nevertheless, children share responsibility for their misbehavior. They are not merely passive recipients of adults' manipulations. Children are active partners in determining how they are treated by their parents, teachers, and peers. Their physical, cognitive, and behavioral characteristics play a significant role in determining how others will approach them, what others will expect of them, and how others will respond to them. Their developmental tasks include learning how to encourage others to approach them and how to be rewarding to others—in short, how to join appropriate "communities of reinforcement," how to become enmeshed in mutually gratifying and appropriate social exchanges (Strain, Odom & McConnell, 1984).

When misbehavior occurs, teachers too often assign an unrealistic burden of responsibility to themselves or to children. Teachers must, certainly, assume primary responsibility for analysis of and intervention in troublesome behavior. To blame the child, to see the problem as hopeless or the child as simply unmanageable, is all too easy. In this era of emphasis on the accountability of teachers, however, the following should be remembered: *Inadequate teaching is not the only possible cause of a child's academic or social problems*. We should examine, therefore, the major contributions that both teachers and children can make to problems of classroom management.

Teachers' Contributions

The child development literature and research in classrooms indicate, as Kauffman (1985) has noted, a variety of ways in which teachers may contribute to children's misbehavior. Both the research literature and our classroom experience suggest that the following teacher characteristics will negatively influence classroom discipline and learning:

- inconsistency in management techniques
- reinforcement of the wrong behavior
- formation of inappropriate expectations for children
- nonfunctional or irrelevant instruction
- insensitivity to children's legitimate individuality
- demonstration or encouragement of undesirable models
- irritability and overreliance on punishment
- unwillingness to try new strategies or to seek suggestions from other professionals.

Teachers certainly do not *purposely* encourage children to misbehave, but they sometimes have blind spots in their classroom management practices that set the stage for behavior problems. Figure 1 is a checklist for teachers; it is intended to encourage introspection and self-monitoring that may indicate how the classroom environment might be altered to reduce the probability that problems will arise or continue.

Children's Contributions

The work of Swift and Spivack (1969, 1973) and others has indicated differences between the behavior of poor achievers and the behavior of high achievers in elementary and secondary schools. The behavioral characteristics of low achievers not only inhibit or preclude academic success, but they produce stress in the teacher and peers as well. Following are some of the most common characteristics known to contribute to academic and behavior management problems:

- overdependency on the teacher
- difficulty concentrating and paying attention
- becoming upset under pressure to achieve
- sloppiness and impulsivity in responding
- teasing, annoying, or interfering with other children
- negativism about work, self, teacher, or peers
- poor personal hygiene
- extreme social withdrawal or refusal to respond
- self-stimulation or self-injury
- physical or verbal aggression toward teacher or peers.

Teachers should not be surprised that these characteristics call forth negative affect and behavior from a child's peers or from themselves. These and similar characteristics suggest targets for behavioral intervention. Figure 2 includes items that a teacher might use as a checklist in considering the selection of behaviors for intervention.

INTERVENTIONS

When behavior management problems arise in the classroom, one should consider first the possible contributions that the teacher, the child, and peers are making

FIGURE 1 Possible Contributions to Misbehavior: A Checklist of Teacher Behavior

☐ *Am I consistent in responding to children's behavior?* If your response to children's conduct—good or bad—is unpredictable, children will have difficulty learning how they are to behave. Your students should know what the consequences of appropriate behavior and misbehavior will be. Give clear directions; hold firm to your expectations; and be consistent in following through with rewards and punishment.

☐ *Am I rewarding the right behavior?* Children who present difficult management problems often are ignored when they are behaving appropriately. Often, about the only time they receive attention is when they are criticized or reprimanded for misbehavior. Sometimes teachers make the mistake of praising them (for something else) or making physical contact with them (in attempts to offer loving correction) when they misbehave. Make sure that children are receiving your attention primarily when they are behaving appropriately. You must make certain that desirable conduct receives a hefty amount of recognition and that misbehavior does not.

☐ *Are my expectations and demands appropriate for children's abilities?* When expectations are too high, children feel too much pressure and experience too much failure. When expectations are too low, children become bored and may feel resentful. Make certain that your expectations fit each child's ability level so that the child is challenged while his or her progress is obvious.

☐ *Am I tolerant enough of children's individuality?* Children have as much right as adults to express their individuality. Many children rebel against teachers who demand strict uniformity and regimentation or are unwilling to encourage appropriate individuality. Make certain that your rules and expectations allow sufficient room for harmless preferences and idiosyncracies.

☐ *Am I providing instruction that is useful to children?* People do not learn quickly or happily when they see no point in what they are doing. First, you must make sure that you have chosen the most important things to teach. When children do not see the importance of what you are teaching, you must point out to them the value of what they are learning. If they still do not understand, you must find a way to make the material interesting or worth their while—perhaps by offering meaningful rewards of privileges for learning.

☐ *Are children seeing desirable models?* Children are great imitators of their teachers and their high-status peers. Make certain that if children are imitating you, they are behaving appropriately. Monitor your own behavior, and change it if necessary. Call attention to the desirable conduct of children's peers. Point out the kind of behavior you want to see.

☐ *Am I generally irritable and overreliant on punishment as a control technique?* Teachers set a tone in their classrooms by their general attitudes toward persons and events. A teacher who is easily upset, frequently short-tempered, quick to punish minor misbehavior, and hesitant in expressing approval is virtually certain to foster irritability and defiance in students. General irritability and a focus on punishment suggest depression; and a teacher's depression may contribute to children's depressive behavior.

☐ *Am I willing to try a different tack on the problem or to seek the help of colleagues or consultants?* A teacher who resists the suggestions of others, who insists on "going it alone," or who discards any different approach as useless or doomed to failure is not likely to be successful for long. Teaching today presents complex behavior management problems for which even the most competent teacher needs consultation. An attitude of openness and a willingness to look outside oneself are essential to success.

---

to the difficulty. Even if the teacher's self-assessment or the assessment of a colleague or consultant leads to the conclusion that the teacher's behavior is exemplary for highly competent professionals, intervention must begin with a change in teacher behavior. A different strategy must be tried. We offer several suggestions for the selection of interventions.

Perhaps the most useful suggestion we can make is that the simplest, most direct approaches to solving the problem should be tried *first*. If simple instructions, reminders, or models of appropriate behavior will suffice, more complicated interventions are a waste of time and effort. Typically, a teacher must try more than one intervention before hitting on one that does, in fact, provide a solution.

Second, ideas and advice from others should be sought. Often, another educator (fellow teacher, principal, supervisor, school psychologist, consultant, or student teacher, for example) may offer a workable or adaptable suggestion. Printed materials, including professional books and journals, might be the source of ideas that a teacher may find practical. Although individual teachers often do come up with solutions to their own problems, a fresh perspective on the problem sometimes is needed. Teachers must remember that people—including competent teachers, good parents,

FIGURE 2
Possible Contributions to Misbehavior: A Checklist of Child Behavior

☐ *Is the child overdependent on you?* Children who cannot work independently are a constant source of interruption of the teacher's work and their peers' concentration. Their frequent demands for help, or their refusal to work without the teacher's constant oversight, are wearing on the teacher and may trigger rivalry from peers.

☐ *Does the child have difficulty concentrating and paying attention?* Learning requires focused attention. A child's lack of attention to task requires additional teacher effort, provides an inappropriate model for peers, raises the probability of disruptive behavior, and lowers the probability of academic success.

☐ *Does the child become easily upset under pressure to achieve?* The world contains many sources of pressure for productive activity and achievement. Therefore, a classroom without any pressure whatsoever for achievement is an unrealistic and debilitating environment. Children's resistance to expectations for performance is a source of frustration for the teacher and for peers who are striving to achieve.

☐ *Is the child's work sloppy? Are responses impulsive?* Reflective, careful work is needed in the workplace, and it should be expected in the classroom. Teachers are justified in requiring reasonably neat, thoughtful responses. Teaching is difficult and progress is slow when the child has not learned good work habits and impulse control.

☐ *Does the child tease, annoy, or interfere with the work of other students?* Annoyance or hassle by neighbors or coworkers is a common and sometimes serious source of stress for adults and children. A child who interferes with the lives of others becomes a source of bad feelings and a sinkhole for the energies of teachers and peers.

☐ *Is the child negative toward schoolwork, self, teacher, or peers?* Fault-finding, whining, and criticism—whether directed toward others or oneself—induce negative responses in others. These characteristics often are indicative of depression, and they tend to make others feel depressed.

☐ *Does the child have poor personal hygiene or habits of self-care?* People, young or old, who are dirty or smelly are less likely to be approached socially or to be befriended by others than are those who maintain good hygiene and self-care. Teachers will have difficulty being positive toward children whose odor or appearance is offensive.

☐ *Is the child unusually withdrawn or reticent?* A withdrawn or reticent child is easily overlooked by teachers and peers. A child with those characteristics is unlikely to be drawn into positive, reciprocal social exchanges without special intervention.

☐ *Does the child engage in self-stimulation or self-injury?* Excessive or socially inappropriate self-stimulation is incompatible with learning and social acceptance. Self-stimulation and self-injury usually are off-putting to others and inhibit normal psychological and physical development.

☐ *Is the child aggressive toward teachers or peers?* Aggression in the form of verbal threats, intimidation, extortion, or physical attack heightens anxiety and stress in all parties involved. An aggressive child can be expected to induce hostility and counter-aggression in others.

and well adjusted children—have occasional difficulty with close interpersonal relationships simply because they cannot step back and view them as an outsider.

Third, teacher-child-peer interrelationships must be considered. Sometimes, focusing intervention on the individual child is sufficient; typically, it is not. Teachers should consider the possibility of employing group contingencies involving two or more children. Many classroom problems involve the entire group's misbehavior. Frequently, an exceptional child in a regular class of low-achieving, disruptive students compounds the management problem, and the regular teacher's skill in handling the situation may be a critical variable in determining the success of a mainstreaming effort for that student.

General strategies for behavior management have been widely published (e.g., Kerr & Nelson, 1983; Morris, 1985; Smith, 1984; Wallace & Kauffman, 1986), and behavior management principles now are typically taught in special education teacher training programs. For this reason, we will not outline the most basic management strategies or behavior principles a teacher should know. Rather, we will present some basic considerations required in managing problems involving children and their peers, along with several case reports illustrating successful intervention strategies.

Group Disruption: When to Focus on an Individual

When one child disrupts the group, the most appropriate intervention is not necessarily a group contingency. The best strategy may be to focus on containing the disruptive student's instigation of misbehavior, perhaps by employing a technique that gets the child actively involved in self-control. In deciding whether to approach the problem with a group-oriented contingency or a plan focused on the individual, the extent to which peers are reinforcing the disruptive child's behavior or launching their own counter-aggression must be assessed.

If disruption almost always begins with the target child and peers offer relatively little reinforcement for the target child's disruptive behavior, the most efficient plan may be to intervene with the target child alone. The following case illustrates a special education teacher's management of an individual child who was disrupting the class.[1]

LaRouche, a 13-year-old from a low-income family, was enrolled in my seventh-grade class for the mildly mentally retarded. A highly distractible child, he often sought attention through inappropriate behavior such as mumbling snide remarks, and he was in continual motion—a real treat to teach! His parents usually cooperated in attending parent-teacher conferences. Unfortunately, however, they tended to respond to LaRouche's school problems with physical punishment. Therefore, I have tried to manage his behavior in school without involving the parents.

In my classroom LaRouche was on a behavior contract. One provision of his contract was that he would lose 3 points for any specified infraction of classroom rules of which he was aware. This provision applied not only to my

[1] *This case was described by Gena C. Johnson, a special education teacher in Orange County, Virginia.*

special education class but to his exploratory classes (where he was mainstreamed) as well.

A specific problem with which I had to deal recently was that LaRouche, when seated close to his friends, had a tendency to provoke a particular female student (B. T.) by mumbling verbal abuse regarding her history of head lice. Whenever LaRouche mumbled "tinder bugs," a verbal battle began, the rest of the class "grasped the moment" (to put it mildly), and LaRouche and his friends were off-task for several minutes.

My first move in trying to resolve this problem was to ask B. T. to ignore LaRouche's remarks. I also seated LaRouche in the front of the class near the position I assume most frequently when I am teaching. This seemed the simplest, most obvious tactic. Unfortunately, it was not effective in dealing with the problem. My records showed that LaRouche and company averaged about 12 to 14 "tinder bugs" incidents per day before I changed the seating arrangement; we were still having about 8 to 10 per day.

The second intervention was to continue to encourage B. T. to ignore LaRouche's remarks but to arrange an explicit contingency in his contract, as follows: I tapped him on the shoulder each time he made a remark directed to B. T.—a signal that he had lost 3 points. At first this seemed to be working, but within a week LaRouche was up to his old tricks again, 8 to 10 times per day.

My third try was to seat LaRouche in the back of the room, away from the group, to continue taking points off his daily contract for inappropriate remarks, and to position his seat facing the chalkboard, where I wrote his daily schedule. Every 10 minutes LaRouche was allowed to write his initials on the board if he had remained on-task and not made any inappropriate remarks. His schedule included 8 half-hour periods, meaning that he could write his initials up to 24 times each day. I explained to him that he could exchange the initials for tangible rewards, such as pencils, ink pens, notebook paper, erasers, or other items. The minimum number of initials required for earning a reward on any given day was 21, allowing for a few slips. With this arrangement, LaRouche's "tinder bugs" incidents dropped to 2 or fewer per day.

LaRouche was thrilled with the tangible rewards he earned. In addition, just getting to write his initials on the board was a reinforcer for him.

The case of LaRouche illustrates the management of disruptive behavior that involved peers by concentrating on the individual child who was the source of disruption. It also illustrates a teacher's discovery that reinforcement of desirable conduct (Deitz & Repp, 1983) was more effective than response cost punishment (Walker, 1983). Moreover, the case shows that simple, low-cost interventions can be highly effective in resolving seemingly intractible problems.

Group Disruption: The Use of Group-Oriented Contingencies

When misbehavior is widespread in a group and pinpointing a single instigator of disruption is difficult, a group-oriented contingency may be the intervention of choice. Group-oriented contingencies make use of peer pressure—a phenomenon all teachers recognize but that many do not use to best advantage in the classroom. Ideally, a teacher should strive to prevent negative peer pressure (e.g., students getting peers' attention for clowning) and use positive peer pressure to encourage achievement and appropriate behavior. A variety of group-oriented procedures have been devised, only a few of which will be briefly described here (see Greenwood & Hops, 1981, for further discussion).

Independent or Standardized Group Contingencies

Standardized contingencies are those that apply to individual students regardless of the performance of the group. A contingency of this type is group-oriented only in that it applies to each member of the group equally. An advantage of an independent contingency is that no child is penalized for the behavior of anyone else; each child receives the reward or punishment he or she alone has earned, and each child has access to rewards or suffers punishment under exactly the same terms. A distinct disadvantage, however, is that peer pressure is unlikely to be harnessed because one child's behavior in no way influences the consequences for another.

Dependent Group Contingencies

Dependent group contingencies are those under which consequences for a group of students depend on the performance of one member of the group (or, perhaps, a small subgroup). This type of arrangement makes peer pressure much more likely than under an independent contingency. An example of a dependent group contingency is the "hero procedure" used by Patterson (1965). Patterson and his colleagues made "heros" of hyperactive, disruptive students by allowing them to earn rewards for paying attention and behaving appropriately—rewards that were shared with the entire class.

A well executed dependent group contingency can have a distinct advantage: Problem students' peers tend to "root for" them and do what they can to encourage improvement because they have something to gain by doing so. A disadvantage is that it can easily be mismanaged, resulting in possible threats, criticism, or harassment from peers when the target student or subgroup does not perform adequately.

Interdependent Group Contingencies

Interdependent group contingencies are those in which the same requirements apply to all members of the group but consequences depend on the combined or total performance of the group. Group members must work together to earn a reward in which they all share equally. An example of an interdependent group contingency is the "good behavior game" (Barrish, Saunders, & Wolf, 1969), which has been used in a variety of forms by several research groups (Greenwood & Hops, 1981). The essential features of the game are as follows: (1) The teacher states certain rules that apply to all members of the class, (2) all members of the class can earn points for the class (or their "team," a subgroup of the class) by behaving according to the rules, and (3) the class (or team) earns rewards, depending on the number of points earned. In some cases the class or team has earned rewards for accumulating fewer than a certain number of points, which were given for specific misbehaviors; in other cases, the class or team has been rewarded for accumulating greater than a certain number of points for appropriate conduct.

An interdependent contingency, when it is used skillfully, has the advantage of appropriate peer pressure and competition. A possible disadvantage is negative peer reaction when success of the group is spoiled by too high expectations or by persistent misbehavior of a single individual or small group.

Teachers who use group-oriented contingencies can guard against negative peer pressure in several ways: (1) being sure that the performance standard for reward is not too high—beginning with a criterion that can be reached easily and gradually increasing the requirement for reward; (2) emphasizing reward for appropriate behavior rather than punishment for misbehavior; (3) encouraging everyone to participate in the group-oriented contingency but not requiring participation; (4) keeping the competition fair by making certain the teams are about equal in ability to perform; and (5) allowing for students who do not work well in a group competition and eliminating saboteurs from the contingency.

Skillful use of group-oriented contingencies can play a major role in preventing referral of students for special education and in successfully mainstreaming identified exceptional children. If a regular classroom teacher finds more effective means of controlling disruptive behavior, it is less likely that a given student in that class will be referred, and it is more likely that a mainstreamed student will be successful in that class. The following case illustrates a regular classroom teacher's use of an interdependent group-oriented approach.[2]

As a first-year math teacher instructing seventh and eighth graders, I soon became aware of the fact that effective behavior management is a key element in successful instruction. For the most part, my classes fairly quickly came under stimulus control. One of my eight classes, however, did not, and I had to take special steps to remedy the situation.

The class consisted of 24 students, one of whom was labeled learning disabled. This was a mixed group in terms of achievement—12 students on grade level and 11 above. The class met during the last period of the school day, when students are often tired and cranky. During the day these students had only one 30-minute break (for lunch) and approximately 25 minutes of physical activity during gym. The classroom was small for the number of students and desks, and temperature control was poor (the room was often unbearably hot and stuffy). In addition, the school was constructed with relatively "open" classrooms, such that passersby were a constant source of disruption.

The less desirable behaviors of these students included physical aggression, out-of-seat, talking out, off-task, and rudeness to each other, as well as to me. Two factors were of primary importance in selecting a behavior management system for this class. First, as a public school teacher, I carried a heavy class load, so it was important to find a system that not only would be effective but also would demand a minimum amount of time for implementation. In this respect a group-oriented contingency was appealing, in that it

[2] *This case was described by John Jeanes, a regular education teacher in Orange County, Virginia.*

would require less time and record keeping than a token economy or similar system. Second, taking into account the dynamics, an interdependent contingency was most attractive, since the majority of students in the class supported and encouraged disruptive behavior.

As targets for intervention, I chose two high-incidence behaviors that are incompatible with academic learning: *talking-out* and *out-of-seat*. I defined talking out as any vocalization, verbal or nonverbal, made without the student having raised his or her hand and receiving my verbal recognition. I defined out-of-seat as a student's buttocks losing contact with the chair or movement of the chair from its position in front of the desk. For purposes of assessment and intervention, however, I considered these behaviors together as disruptions. My aide and I recorded disruptions daily so that we could report the level of the problem to the class and assess any change resulting from our intervention. We kept separate records of disruptions during direct instructional time and seatwork.

Our 5 days of baseline showed that disruptive behavior was occurring about 6.5 times per minute—about 260 incidents per class period! I explained my concern to the students, and during a discussion of the problem we agreed on a plan for trying to get it under control. The immediate criterion we agreed upon was that disruptions should be reduced to no more than 50 per class period. The long-term goal was to reduce disruptions to no more than 7 per period. We agreed that if the class could meet the criterion for a given day, the students would all share a positive reinforcer—5 minutes of free time at the end of the period, during which they could do as they pleased as long as they were orderly and kept their voices down to a reasonable level.

The students immediately showed enthusiasm for the plan, and it was immediately successful. The criteria we set were 50 the first day, 20 the second, then 15, 12, 10, 8, and 7. The class occasionally did not meet the criterion. Once the criterion had been exceeded on a given day, the students thought they had nothing to gain by behaving appropriately, and their behavior reverted back to baseline levels. To deal with this difficulty, I incorporated an additional reinforcer: a "free day" with a group-selected video contingent upon a cumulative average target behavior being met within criterion over a specified period of time. This feature kept the group from losing control because students had "blown it" for the day (that is, they still had something to work for).

All in all, I would have to say that the group-oriented contingency I used was an unqualified success. Not only did disruptive behavior decline dramatically, but academic performance improved as well. A few minutes of free time at the end of each class period and an occasional "free day" seems a small price to pay for the instructional time and improved behavior that were gained.

We now examine a somewhat more complex case in which teachers, a target child, and the child's regular class peers found it necessary to work out a solution to a problem involving their interrelationships. The following case illustrates use of an interdependent group contingency and a self-control strategy.[3]

James, a 9-year-old, came to my first-grade class in November. He previously had been enrolled in two other schools in the area and had been re-

[3] *This case was managed by author Akers with the assistance of author Pullen.*

tained in first grade. He was visually impaired and wore very thick glasses. His glasses corrected his vision adequately for mobility, but he held his face very close to his reading material and had acquired the habit of reading over his glasses. He felt more secure being placed close to the board or at the front of the group in any presentation in the auditorium.

In addition to his visual impairment, James suffered from an asthmatic condition that was aggravated by some weather conditions. His mother reported that he could not attend school in Wisconsin, where they had lived previously, because of the severe winter cold. Consequently, he had received homebound instruction there.

James was smaller than most of the other children, and his physical unattractiveness was a problem. His long, dirty hair, thick, smudged glasses, dirty clothing, and unpleasant odor made him the target of other children's teasing. Even though they teased him, James truly seemed to want to be friends with other children. He discovered that he could attract his peers' attention not only by his appearance but by his silly and gross antics, such as falling out of his chair, crawling on the floor, making loud animal-like noises, eating like a dog, and picking his nose. Other children responded to his behavior by laughing or by commenting on how disgusting he was, or both. He loved other children's attention, positive or negative.

Part of the problem in managing James' behavior was created by the composition of the class: 16 boys and 7 girls. Six of the boys had been retained, were physically larger than James, had been together in the same class for 2 years, and enjoyed having a victim or scapegoat.

Academically, James was more advanced than the reading group in which he was placed initially. He therefore went to another teacher for reading and stayed with me for math, spelling, language, health, and home room. He went to other teachers for science, social studies, art, music, and physical education. James could make exceptional contributions to class discussions, but he disliked the routine type of work required in handwriting and math.

James had a short attention span and was easily distracted. When he tired of doing his assignments, he drew pictures, distracted others, or engaged in other forms of inappropriate behavior, as described previously. He was unable to function in any large-group setting, and he had difficulty adjusting to special teachers (e.g., music, art, physical education), from whom I received many complaints about his misbehavior.

I tried several positive behavior modification techniques with James—all with limited success. For example, I used "Happy Grams" (positive smiling-face notes home) daily (something I use in an ongoing system with the entire group). I also tried class meetings in which we discussed James's behavior, parent conferences, daily notes home, and frequent compliments for appropriate behavior. A long conference with his mother—who was not fastidious herself and who did not see James's cleanliness and appearance as her responsibility—finally did result in some improvement in his appearance and hygiene. This resulted in somewhat better treatment from his peers. Significant behavior problems persisted, however, and I was ready to try anything new.

Pat and I discussed a combination of self-monitoring and an interdependent group contingency. We devised a means of monitoring the behavior of the entire class and a self-monitoring procedure for James. I made a large chart on the chalkboard, divided into two sections. I put a smiling face on one side of the chart whenever everyone ignored one of James's inappropriate behaviors. If a classmate responded in any way to the behavior, I put an X on the other side of the chart. Initially, I also praised the individual or the entire group when making the smiling face, commenting on the specific desirable peer behavior (e.g., "I'm proud of Chris because he kept right on working on his math sheet" when James tried to distract him). When I made an X on the chart, I almost never called attention to the guilty party. The class knew who was responsible.

Quite soon I saw peer pressure operating to get smiling faces and to keep the class from getting Xs. Clearly, James was getting less reinforcement from his peers, and the class was looking forward to receiving a reward. I had promised the class that if, at the end of the week, the smiling faces outnumbered the Xs, everyone would be able to participate in a special treat—a sing-along with Ms. Pullen, who would bring her guitar and teach them new songs.

James's self-monitoring involved his keeping smiling faces and Xs in a folder. He made his own smiling faces for behaving appropriately, and his own Xs for misbehavior. He took pride in maintaining his folder and was extremely trustworthy in recording. In the beginning, I gave him a nod for inappropriate behavior and praised him for desirable behavior, signaling him what to record.

Eventually James began to make his own judgments about the acceptability of his behavior, and his smiling faces increased while his Xs decreased. In addition, his attention span increased and the quality of his academic work improved. I also received more good reports from his special teachers, who were quite receptive to the idea of self-monitoring. Through it all, James seemed to acquire a much improved self-image and to obtain a sense of accomplishment.

SUMMARY

Both teachers and pupils can contribute to problems of behavior management. Teachers and children exert reciprocal influence. Management is not simply a matter of teachers managing children. Teachers' introspection may indicate ways in which their own behavior might foster the misbehavior of their students. Although certain pupil characteristics may produce stress for the teacher and classroom peers and contribute to undesirable teacher and peer conduct, the teacher generally is responsible for initiating intervention to improve children's behavior.

Intervention should be as simple and direct as possible. Ideas and suggestions of other professionals should be sought when difficulties are encountered, and teacher-child-peer relationships should be carefully considered in selecting interventions. When a group disruption is primarily the result of one child's misconduct, the most appropriate intervention may focus on that individual. When all or many members of the group are disruptive, group-oriented contingencies are typically the intervention of choice. A target child whose misbehavior involves many members of the class often may be managed by a combination of self-control and interdependent group contingency strategies. Group management skills are particularly important in maintaining exceptional children in regular classes, where teacher-child-peer relationships are critical to successful mainstreaming.

REFERENCES

Barrish, H. H., Saunders, M., & Wolf, M. M. (1969). Good behavior game: Effects of individual contingencies for group consequences on disruptive behavior in a classroom. *Journal of Applied Behavior Analysis, 2*, 119–124.

Deitz, D. E. D., & Repp, A. C. (1983). Reducing behavior through reinforcement. *Exceptional Education Quarterly, 3*(4), 34–46.
Graubard, P. S., Rosenberg, H., & Miller, M. (1971). Ecological approaches to social deviancy. In B. L. Hopkins & E. Ramp (Eds.), *A new direction for education: Behavior analysis 1971*. Lawrence: Kansas University Department of Human Development.
Greenwood, C R., & Hops, H. (1981). Group-oriented contingencies and peer behavior change. In P. S. Strain (Ed.), *The utilization of classroom peers as behavior change agents*. New York: Plenum.
Hobbs, N. (1966). Helping the disturbed child: Psychological and ecological strategies. *American Psychologist, 21,* 1105–1115.
Kauffman, J. M. (1985). *Characteristics of children's behavior disorders* (3rd ed.). Columbus, OH: Charles E. Merrill.
Kerr, M. M., & Nelson, C. M. (1983). *Strategies for managing behavior problems in the classroom*. Columbus, OH: Charles E. Merrill.
Lloyd, J. W. (1984). How shall we individualize instruction—or should we? *Remedial & Special Education, 5*(1), 7–15.
Morris, R. J. (1985). *Behavior modification with exceptional children*. Glenview, IL: Scott, Foresman.
Patterson, G. R. (1965). An application of conditioning techniques to the control of a hyperactive child. In L. P. Ullmann & L. Krasner (Eds.), *Case studies in behavior modification*. New York: Holt, Rinehart, & Winston.
Rhodes, W. C. (1967). The disturbing child: A problem of ecological management. *Exceptional Children, 33*, 449–455.
Rhodes, W. C. (1970). A community participation analysis of emotional disturbance. *Exceptional Children, 37,* 309–314.
Smith, D. D. (1984). *Effective discipline*. Austin, TX: Pro-Ed.
Stevens, R., & Rosenshine, B. (1981). Advances in research on teaching. *Exceptional Education Quarterly, 2*(1), 1–9.
Strain, P. S., Odom, S. L., & McConnell, S. (1984). Promoting social reciprocity of exceptional children: Identification, target behavior selection, and intervention. *Remedial & Special Education, 5*(1), 21–28.
Swift, M. S., & Spivack, G. (1969). Clarifying the relationship between academic success and overt classroom behavior. *Exceptional Children, 36,* 99-104.
Swift, M. S., & Spivack, G. (1973). Academic success and classroom behavior in secondary schools. *Exceptional Children, 39*, 392–399.
Walker, H. M. (1983). Applications of response cost in school settings: Outcomes, issues and recommendations. *Exceptional Education Quarterly, 3*(4), 47–55.
Wallace, G., & Kauffman, J. M. (1986). *Teaching students with learning and behavior problems* (3rd ed.). Columbus, OH: Charles E. Merrill.

James Kauffman is Professor of Education, Department of Curriculum, Instruction, and Special Education, Curry School of Education, University of Virginia, Charlottesville. Patricia Pullen is a clinical instructor in the Curry School and a special education teacher at Jackson Via Elementary School, Charlottesville. Eileen Akers is a clinical instructor in the Curry School, president of the Charlottesville Education Association, and a first grade teacher at Jackson Via Elementary School.

Cognitive and behavioral technologies have been combined to enhance the learning of mildly handicapped students. Gerber reviews the learning problems and discusses how this new technology may offer real help to the mildly handicapped. The concept of *cognitive engagement* is explained, including the fact that self-regulation is an integral part of such practices. Studies relating to cognitive-behavioral training are reviewed, showing the effectiveness of these procedures in improving handicapped students' attention to task and subsequent improvement in achievement.

Cognitive-Behavioral Training In the Curriculum: Time, Slow Learners, and Basic Skills

Michael M. Gerber

Whatever disagreement exists concerning identification of various subtypes of mildly handicapped (MH) learners, a consensus probably exists that these students learn at a slower rate than do their normally achieving peers. The idea of "slower rate" implies managerial as well as cognitive-behavioral concerns. In part, slower rate of acquisition is a function of discrepancies between time allocated by teachers for learning and time during which MH students are cognitively engaged with the content of learning tasks (i.e., academic learning time). MH students may be more predisposed to exhibit "off-task," or inappropriate task orientation, behaviors than their normally achieving peers. These students quite literally "waste" time, presenting teachers with difficult management problems.

If task orientation behaviors were the only problems, however, academic gains for these students should be obtainable simply by increasing the percentage of allocated time that they appear to be actively engaged in learning. In fact, this line of reasoning has led to many intervention strategies that have sought to increase the probability of "on-task" behaviors through use of adult managed (e.g., see Kauffman & Hallahan, 1979) or student managed (e.g., see Hallahan & Sapona, 1983) procedures.

Another line of thought—one for which practical implications are less well researched in special education—holds that even under conditions of optimal attentional behavior *during* tasks, MH students are always "slower" learners because they have difficulty allocating attention efficiently to information *within* tasks. (For general discussion of evidence favoring an attentional deficit hypothesis, see Hallahan & Reeve, 1980; for contrary evidence and arguments, see a recent paper by Samuels & Miller, 1985). If this hypothesis is true, MH students, under available conditions of instruction, will require *absolutely* more learning time than faster learning peers *if they are to develop similar levels of mastery and automaticity.* Therefore, slower rates of acquisition present instructional design, as well as general managerial, problems.

Further, if observable amounts of task engagement are only a general consequence of variable degrees of cognitive efficiency, the reason that measures of time on-task correlate only moderately and inconsistently with achievement measures, and why some students invariably "need differing amounts of time to achieve the same learning goals" (Karweit & Slavin, 1981, p. 171), becomes clearer. Unfortunately, special education has no well developed theories that relate macro teaching and management variables (such as allocated learning time, instructional grouping, and instructional design) to within-student, cognitive or micro variables (such as coding, strategy generation, and structure of knowledge). By discussing how cognitive-behaviorial training methods might facilitate acquisition of basic skills in MH students, this article is intended as a step in this direction.

THE GENERAL EDUCATION DILEMMA

Recent work by Gettinger and her colleagues has renewed interest in and brought fresh perspective to the role of time in classroom learning. A study by Gettinger (1984a) supports the hypothesis that the ratio of time spent in learning (TSL) to time needed to learn (TTL) for normally achieving students is a reliable predictor of achievement, whether measured by criterion task accuracy, retention, tested achievement, or teacher ratings of performance. Moreover, Gettinger and White (1979) showed that the TSL:TTL ratio was a more adequate predictor of task-specific learning than IQ for elementary students of normal intelligence. When TSL was student determined, Gettinger and Lyon (1983) found that about two-thirds of the variability in discrepancies between TTL and TSL in a sample of boys exhibiting classroom behavior problems could be accounted for mostly by prior achievement and a combination of variables related to attention, including level of interest, locus of control, and self-concept.

These findings suggest a spiral of transacting events in which insufficient time to learn on earlier occasions increases the need for learning time in the present. Inadequate acquisition of basic skills and critical knowledge, as a function of insufficient learning time, results in a cognitive-behavioral status that requires progressively more time to learn hierarchically more difficult material on future occasions.

If classroom learning time is viewed as a scarce and relatively fixed resource, interventions based on differences in time needed to learn require strategies directed not only toward learners but also toward time constraints inherent to classroom teaching. Ideally, interventions must acknowledge and address in an integrated fashion the overt behavior—covert cognition dualism associated with "slow" rates of learning (Gerber, 1983). That is, MH learners exhibit overt learning behaviors that, though sometimes discernibly different, similarly restrict them to less than best use of available learning time.

Moreover, salient learning characteristics of MH students, however variable for defined subgroups, also appear to be related to some level of cognitive inefficiency. Therefore, even if intervention strategies successfully induce all of the *behavioral* concomitants associated with "attention to task," the typical amounts of time allocated for classroom learning still will be insufficient to assure rates of acquisition for some MH students that are equivalent to acquisition rates of their normally achieving peers.

From a purely pragmatic perspective, without trying to disentangle characteristics thought to be diagnostic of discrete handicapping conditions, MH students can be expected to (a) take longer to reach the same achievement criteria as set for their classmates, and (b) require more instructional effort or more powerful instructional techniques, or both. These expectations have important implications for various approaches to mainstreaming, but especially for what is being called the "general education initiative"—a set of recent policy proposals aimed at increasing the role of regular classrooms and teachers in the education of many or most students now classified as mildly handicapped (Will, 1986). From a policy, or macroanalytic, perspective, these implications should be considered with reference to two "laws of motion" operating in all classrooms.

1. *The Law of Time-Achievement Exchange*

Teachers in typical classrooms can control time or achievement, but not both. If they fix the amount of time that they will teach toward some particular instructional objective, achievement as a function of individual differences will vary. On the other hand, if teachers attempt to fix achievement, time needed as a function of individual differences likewise must vary.

2. *The Law of Distributed Outcomes*

Teachers can try to maximize the mean level of achievement for the class as a whole, or they can attempt to minimize variability of learning outcomes. If instructional resources (and technology) are assumed to be relatively fixed, however, they cannot do both. This means in practice that instructional effort will result either in smaller differences between slower and faster students at the end of a specified instructional period or in greater differences (i.e., greater mean outcomes) driven by achievement of faster students.

These "laws" continually force teachers to decide whether to continue investment of instructional time and effort in MH students who have not yet obtained mastery of some objective, or to reallocate their time to begin instruction toward mastery of new objectives by more modal students. As long as individual students differ from one another in instructionally meaningful ways, these laws will generally hold, regardless of how students are classified or instructionally grouped. Obviously, these laws constantly tend to operate to the disadvantage of MH students being taught in mainstream settings.

Although some empirical evidence (Brown & Saks, 1984) suggests that teachers tend to choose variance-reducing teaching procedures (presumably by directing instructional effort toward lower achieving students), studies of teacher decision making tend to support the view that teachers, as a cognitive convenience, prefer to direct instruction to the large middle group of students in their classes (e.g., see Shavelson & Stern, 1981).

Being able to transfer instructional responsibility for their most difficult students to a subsystem such as special education helps teachers accomplish both these objectives (Gerber & Semmel, 1985). By removing these most difficult, time consuming students, teachers instantly achieve smaller class achievement variances and increase the number of students falling into an instructionally tractable modal range. Therefore, attempts to maintain effort-demanding, slower-learning students in regular classrooms without either increases in critical teaching resources or implementation of new, more powerful instructional technologies will yield inevitably disappointing results. A relentlessly growing gap between achievement and age can be expected to develop, coupled with an ever decreasing amount of public school time remaining. The consequences are high rates of referral to special education and a burgeoning number of students classified (Gerber, 1984a); and high rates of drop-out or "push-out" (Zigmond & Thornton, 1985) of MH students invariably result.

THE NEED FOR NEW APPROACHES

What appears to be needed is a new approach to curriculum that encourages instructional efficiency in how teachers allocate and use available time, but also cognitive efficiency for learners depicted as "slow" relative to a modal group of peers. This approach requires both a theoretical and practical integration of variables arising from cognitive-behavioral research as well as from classroom instructional research.

Implications of Cognitive-Behavioral Research for Classroom Instruction

Several recent reviews have attempted to integrate cognitive-behavioral intervention research and draw suitable implications for practice (Corno & Mandinach, 1983; Doyle, 1983; Frederiksen, 1984). In trying to understand "cognitive engagement," for example, Corno and Mandinach (1983) viewed students as:

> . . . actively engaged in a variety and range of cognitive interpretations—of their environments and themselves—which, in turn, influence the amount and kind of effort they will expend on classroom tasks. (p. 89)

"Cognitive engagement," therefore, represents processing of task-specific information but also, and simultaneously, some degree of cognitive self-regulation. This self-regulatory component minimally includes deliberate planning and monitoring during performance of academic tasks. The actual degree of self-regulated learning, however, also reflects the degree to which "some of the processes are overtaken by classroom teachers, other students, or features of written instruction (p. 89)."

It follows that, while academic "tasks" are the natural and basic units of classroom learning (Doyle, 1983), teachers are able to adjust the cognitive demands implicit to different types of school tasks for learners differing in maturity and ability by varying the directness of instruction. Presumably, slow or immature learners are assisted cognitively when instruction is "direct." Doyle (1983) asserted that learning "procedural" or "routine" tasks (e.g., computation, decoding) is particularly facilitated by direct instruction in specific solution algorithms (p. 177). He described procedural tasks—what teachers might recognize as "basic skills"—as those that can be performed "without understanding by simply knowing how to follow a series of computational steps," while what he called "understanding tasks" requires "knowledge about why the computational steps work (p. 165)."

Cognitive Elements within Direct Instruction

The power and conceptual simplicity of methods collectively known as "direct instruction" procedures have achieved a rough consensus among researchers about teacher behavior variables that are critical for effective instruction of students with mild handicaps (Good, 1983; Rosenshine, 1983; Stevens & Rosenshine, 1981). Generally speaking, techniques derived from these pragmatic, intervention-oriented perspectives emphasize active effort by the teacher to elicit as many correctable or reinforceable responses from students as possible within instructional time constraints. Moreover, these techniques typically require careful attention to the amount and type of environmental structuring necessary to assure controlled and consistent student achievement, especially for simple, delimited, academic responses. Some of the features of this structuring include.

- Grouping by immediate instructional needs.
- Careful sequencing (programming) of academic skills to be taught.
- Modeling.
- Rapid pacing to achieve high-density response opportunities.
- Use of response signals to control attention and pace.
- Use of choral as well as independent responding.
- Immediate corrective feedback, including adequate, contingent reinforcement.
- Ample, monitored practice.

The literature contains ample demonstration and review of the power, utility, and broad applicability of these techniques for all aspects of curriculum and across a range of learner characteristics (e.g., Becker, 1977; Becker & Carnine, 1981; Carnine, 1983; Engelmann, 1969; Lloyd, 1975; Lloyd, Cullinan, Heins, & Epstein, 1980). Therefore, they will not be discussed further here. It is necessary to point out, however, that successful demonstration of these and related active, or "hot," teaching techniques, particularly with students presumed to have mild handicaps, generally has not been derived from theoretical models of learning specific to exceptional children. Cognitive processes are subsumed for teaching under one of three categories of knowledge: (a) basic concepts ("forms"), (b) relationships ("joining forms"), and (c) cognitive "routines" (Carnine, 1983, p. 23). Although Becker (1977) and Carnine (1983) have argued that there are cognitive as well as behavioral reasons for the observed effectiveness of direct instruction procedures, application in practice has been largely atheoretical and relegated by some to the status of an engineering problem.

Specifically, teachers are advised to control events that have empirically demonstrated relationships to desirable child outcomes. No insight into individual differences among learners is considered necessary. Instead, there is a conscious pragmatism in selecting techniques that are so economical and potent that reliable—though perhaps not optimal—gains are achieved independent of individual differences. Consequently, it has become common to treat these techniques as instances of "good" or "effective" teaching, without analysis of how, as educational treatments, they may uniquely interact with specific learning characteristics (i.e., aptitudes) of students prone to be identified as mildly handicapped. Some students, however, require little more than a verbal hint, while others require the full panoply of highly structured techniques to acquire the same knowledge or display the same level of skilled behavior.

More strictly behavioral versions of direct instruction regard basic academic skills as presenting problems of instructional, not learner, strategy. Researchers working in this tradition attempt to specify "procedures needed to teach general cases and to cumulatively build knowledge within sets of related concepts (Becker, 1977, p. 531)." This approach avoids becoming tediously additive because it:

> . . . seeks to identify the smallest set of rote memory items and set of rules for combining these items that will provide skills for attacking problems of a given type while also developing the basis for attacking related problems. (Lloyd et al., 1980, p. 11)

Invention and Problem Solving

Learners, even handicapped learners, are never really cognitively passive during tasks requiring even simple algorithms. Rather, young and cognitively immature learners can be observed engaging in a form of problem solving as well as simple retrieval of task-specific knowledge. For example, work on young children's early spelling by Read (1975), Henderson and Beers (1980), and Bissex (1980) demonstrates that normally achieving students progress through a series of predictable stages actively struggling to induce the rule system that governs spelling. Gerber (1984b), Cook (1981), and Bookman (1984), for example, have shown that similar, though lagged, developments can be observed in students described as dyslexic or learning disabled.

These studies showed that students, whether novice or handicapped, naturally attempt to induce or "invent" rule systems to simplify and economize cognitive effort while learning how to spell. Error making during these natural problem solving attempts tends to be systematic rather than random, representing incomplete knowledge or inefficient algorithms rather than absence of knowledge and rote memorization.

Unfortunately, despite their being naturally inventive in problem solving academic tasks, teachers cannot depend upon the ability of slow learners to induce basic algorithms that are optimal, durable, or flexible unless additional instruction is provided in "higher level executive control processes and knowledge structures for representing tasks and selecting solution strategies (Doyle, 1983, p. 178)." This caution implies a need for teaching general as well as task-specific problem solving procedures, where how to coordinate and effectively use task-imposed, teacher-arranged, and learner-generated "structure" is the general "problem" to be solved.

Following Simon (1973), Frederiksen (1984) noted that "novices" seeking to acquire expertise in a field of knowledge are confronted by two classes of problems—well-structured and ill-structured problems. Well-structured problems generally are those for which a necessary and sufficient set of explicit algorithms can be stated, taught, or induced. Ill-structured problems, on the other hand, do not provide such unambiguous or even stable instructional targets. To solve the latter problems, learners or teachers must contrive some structure where there appears to be none. Short of some sudden, inexplicable insight, novices must repeatedly practice manipulation of elements or procedures associated with these problems until a relative automaticity in performing some component operations develops, thereby freeing attentional resources for manipulation of less tractable components.

Analogously, response demands associated with tasks meant to train "basic skills" pose "problems" that are ill-structured from the perspective of immature or slow learners. In early stages of acquisition, demands for elemental responses involving, for example, recall and manipulation of sound-symbol or number-numeral associations similarly require repeated practice until some response components are sufficiently automatized to allow attention to other components, or to problems of application such as composition in writing, word problems in arithmetic, or comprehension in reading. How teachers design and manage tasks to teach skills underlying these applications can increase or decrease the "structure," and hence, the cognitive burden for learners.

Nevertheless, a "brute force" approach to teaching these skills has been most common. This approach typically involves repetitive practice to induce rote memorization. For normally achieving, or modal, learners, naturally inclined to be self-organizing and self-regulating, this approach is economical because these students tend to spontaneously and rapidly generate facilitating problem solving approaches, and having mastered "basic" knowledge, they soon are able to attack tasks requiring its deliberate (i.e., skilled) application, such as writing sentences, reading passages, and higher level computation.

Limitations of "Brute Force" Approaches For Mildly Handicapped Students

For MH students, unlike most learners, "brute force" learning does not come easily. First, they often fail to spontaneously generate sufficiently powerful or reliable memorization strategies. Second, they often require more time than their normally achieving peers to practice to increase both accuracy and speed of performance to desirable levels. Third, and perhaps most important, they often do not know why they are memorizing the information, in what context it is meaningful, or how to internalize the "structure" provided implicitly by teachers as part of task design and instructional presentation.

Failure to develop proficiency in fundamental skills is one of the factors that works to the cumulative disadvantage of MH students, in terms of specific content mastery as well as in terms of their perceived teachability by classroom teachers. At the microanalytic level, failure to become proficient in basic academic skills contributes to generalized and cumulative deficiencies in both knowledge and ability to cognitively manage higher order academic tasks. At the macroanalytic level, the classroom presence of students who are unable to use basic academic skills accurately and rapidly contributes to teachers' perceptions that some students are absolutely unresponsive to conventional methods of instruction offered in regular class environments. Perceptions like these ultimately decrease teachers' willingness to invest much additional instructional effort in "slower" students and concomitantly increase the probability that these students will be referred for "special" education as "handicapped."

What is the solution? Probably, training of generic problem solving ability must begin *in parallel* with teaching of basic skills, not only to facilitate acquisition of these skills, but also to establish patterns of conscious attention to the generic aspects of "executive work" common to all problem solving situations. To accomplish the latter goal, basic skills learning has been described as an early and prototypical type of problem solving for which a growing body of cognitive-behavioral training (CBT) literature may have great relevance.

ELEMENTS OF COGNITIVE BEHAVIORAL TRAINING

Despite conceptual fuzziness and confusion over ill-defined samples of mildly handicapped learners, the past decade has seen a promising shift to more instructionally oriented special education research. Some of this research in particular appears to combine elements of cognitive theory and behavioral technology into what might be labeled generically as *cognitive-behavioral training (CBT) intervention models*. When focused on applied academic tasks and classroom performance rather than laboratory analogues, this growing body of work has intuitive appeal for many practitioners. The formal requirements for conducting instructional research (e.g., see Belmont & Butterfield, 1977; Cohen & deBettencourt, 1983) have encouraged researchers to provide extensive and explicit descriptions of instructional methods and techniques. Unlike much special education research literature, these descriptions present teachers with an unusually accessible and potentially rich source of practical information about how to systematically integrate cognitive-behavioral and content goals.

Furthermore, if use of CBT methods results in greater capacity for self-management of learning, as its proponents claim, the perceived "teachability" of MH students by classroom teachers should increase, which in turn should increase the willingness of teachers to invest instructional effort in MH students regardless of classroom setting. The past years have seen CBT-related methods applied increasingly and with generally encouraging results to both differentiated and nondifferentiated groups of students whose shared, common characteristic is that of poor and cumulatively worsening responsiveness to conventional methods of instruction.

Therefore, special education research on various approaches to and targets for use of CBT methods with mildly handicapped students has burgeoned. Reviews of experimental findings and speculations about their implications for special education have appeared in unusually rapid succession (e.g., see Abikoff, 1979; Harris, 1982; Rooney & Hallahan, 1985; Sheinker, Sheinker, & Stevens, 1984). Although CBT has not been viewed as a method for enhancing acquisition of basic skills, it not only might prove useful for facilitating acquisition of basic skills but also might provide a model for conceptualizing a truly "special" education curriculum that would address rate as well as content of learning problems for those described as mildly handicapped.

Although few studies have attempted to use CBT methods directly to facilitate acquisition of basic skills, several studies would appear to provide fertile ground for elaboration and experimentation because they have (a) attempted a cognitive-behavioral intervention directly, (b) used some form of explicit, direct instructional method that provides cognitive "structure," or (c) conducted analyses of cognitive components reflected in task performance (e.g., reading: Bos, 1982; Carnine, 1983; Samuels, 1979; Frederiksen, Warren, & Roseberry, 1985; Palincsar & Brown, 1984; Pflaum & Pascarella, 1980; handwriting: Graham, 1983; Kosiewicz, Hallahan, Lloyd & Graves, 1982; Robin, Armel, & O'Leary, 1975; spelling: Bissex, 1980; Bookman, 1984; Farnham-Diggory & Nelson, 1984; Frith, 1980; Gerber, 1984b, 1984c, 1985, in press; Graham & Freeman, 1985; Lovitt, 1975; Nulman & Gerber, 1984; composition: Ballard & Glynn, 1975; Harris & Graham, 1985; arithmetic: Baroody, 1984; Carpenter, Moser & Romberg, 1982; Cullinan, Lloyd, & Epstein, 1981; Grimm, Bijou, & Parsons, 1973; Lloyd, 1980; Lloyd, Saltzman, & Kauffman, 1981; Lovitt & Curtiss, 1968; Russell & Ginsburg, 1984).

Some non-trivial theoretical and empirical issues remain to be resolved while research proceeds in this direction. Most researchers have viewed CBT as a means for facilitating organization of previous knowledge or behaviors into a more efficacious problem solving routine (e.g., see Brown, Campione, & Day, 1981; Palincsar & Brown, 1984). Because higher order academic tasks, such as reading comprehension, are typically targeted, extensive pretraining has been necessary before CBT can be effectively applied. But an unwarranted tendency has been to dismiss CBT techniques with younger students because of assumptions about their cognitive immaturity and lack of basic knowledge. This remains, in the author's judgment, an empirical question. Moreover, MH students, unlike their normally achieving younger peers, have accrued considerable (though perhaps inadequate) declarative and procedural knowledge about academic tasks.

Regardless of whether CBT procedures will prove successful with younger students, more intensive and systematic research on CBT training of basic skills with MH students seems desirable. Specifically, opinions held by some researchers that CBT is effective chiefly as a means for enhancing on-task behavior during independent practice or other drill activities require further exploration. Some have speculated, for example, that CBT:

> . . . works best when children are working on tasks for which they already have the skills. We are skeptical about how successful the procedure would be for children when they are in the acquisition stages of learning. (Hallahan & Sapona, 1983, p. 619)

The approach associated with this latter opinion has been well documented by Hallahan and his colleagues at the University of Virginia Learning Disabilities Research Institute since 1979 (Hallahan et al., 1983). LD students selected on the basis of their observed distractibility, and trained to self-monitor and record their attention, subsequently showed marked and reliable improvements over baseline in attention to task. Moreover, they showed consistent gains in academic "productivity" (number of observable, correct or appropriate responses per minute), leading to the logical inference that observed changes in "attention" were associated with desirable cognitive activity and not merely its behavioral concomitants.

Nevertheless, the inference that self-monitoring training of this type might have to be restricted to overt attention difficulties during practice of known responses presents some conceptual and practical disappointments. First, were it true, it certainly reduces the breadth of application of the technique, however easy to implement, for helping students acquire new skills. It might be argued that increasing cognitive engagement during drill makes use of that time more efficient, thereby "freeing" time for direct instruction of new skills. Presumably, though, during instruction of new material, students would be as difficult to teach, relative to their normally achieving peers, as ever.

Positive changes in overall efficacy of instruction would seem not to be strongly influenced by use of the CBT methods in this case, if at all. Self-regulation of the kind and quality expected from normally achieving students would be only partially achieved; successful learning would still depend more on externally provided structuring, as opposed to internally controlled processing, of information. A dependency on external structure, in turn, is part of what makes teaching slow learners effortful. Hallahan and his colleagues recognized this problem and have suggested that "a more curriculum-oriented view is warranted (Rooney & Hallahan, 1985, p. 49)."

For example, Gerber and Niemann (in preparation) recently have applied CBT methods similar to those used in Virginia's attention self-monitoring studies in a multiple baseline design to train a distractable LD student to monitor the quality of his performance, rather than his on-task behavior, on three tasks: reading comprehension, listening comprehension, and expository writing. The self-monitoring question used in previous work ("Was I paying attention?") was replaced with questions for each task that specifically directed "attention" to the criterion performance expected after each task ("Will I be able to answer the questions at the end?" "Am I checking capitals, punctuation, and spelling?") In addition, to test Hallahan and Sapona's speculation that CBT would not be useful at acquisition stages of learning, the student was provided difficult materials judged to be at his instructional level—not practice material.

Results indicated improvement above levels achieved at baseline or during reinforcement on measures of reading comprehension and writing accuracy *in addition to* increases in on-task behavior. Relative failure of listening comprehension to show meaningful improvement was interpreted to mean that the verbal self-monitoring induced by training was itself distracting during a listening activity. The findings from the other two tasks, however, were interpreted as indications that CBT could enhance performance on difficult material in which responses were still uncertain and problematic. Moreover, increased on-task behavior was obtainable without the necessity of directly training self-monitoring of on-task behavior. That is to say, when CBT was used to induce attention to the problem solving nature of difficult material, the behavioral concomitants of "on-task behavior" logically followed.

From a macroanalytic perspective, though these findings give reason to hope for application of CBT methods beyond independent practice, the question of learning rate remains. Are MH students to be taught individual skills in a more or less linear fashion in hopes that greater generalized competence will emerge from a sufficiently large repertoire? Stated differently, can a qualitative shift in learner competence be expected to occur as a function of incremental changes in the number of discrete skills acquired? Or, similar to Zeno's paradox, is there an infinity of definable skills, or subskills within skills, to be learned, making it practically hopeless to tailor some new version of CBT for each item in the curriculum?

There appears to be no escaping the need for a decision on how to apportion time between directly teaching what students must learn and teaching them more general means for approaching some class of academic tasks more effectively. Some researchers, such as Ann Brown (e.g., see Brown et al., 1981, p. 14) remain optimistic that CBT can contribute to both specialized and generalized ability. Nonetheless, as suggested by experiences of Hallahan and his colleagues in Virginia (e.g., Rooney & Hallahan, 1985), one time, highly focal interventions, however successful, will have to be rethought in terms of ongoing curriculum.

CBT Effects on Knowledge Search and Structure

Whether approached from a cognitive or a behavioral perspective, CBT improves organization of task response. By providing a self-managed problem solving routine, the information load (or "problem space") associated with even basic skills tasks is reduced to more manageable proportions. If mildly handicapped students can be taught to approach learning tasks in a more structured, organized fashion, it is reasonable to expect that they also will be more efficient. This is because "structure," as Hall (1980) has noted, implies organization.

Structure also implies a transactional relationship between operations devoted to searching a knowledge base for relevant information and the structure of that knowledge base. For example, how quickly and efficiently one can reduce uncertainty by using what is known may determine to some degree both the reliability and future accessibility of newly appended knowledge. Conversely, the degree of organization with which knowledge has accumulated in the past may severely constrain the possible speed and efficiency of search procedures when confronting learning problems in the present.

To the extent that trained "strategies" impose structure by controlling information organization and sequencing, as well as timing and rate of response demand, to define "strategies" as overt behaviors or as internalized, cognitive processes is a matter of pedagogical indifference. Again from the teacher's standpoint, when understood in this sense, teaching clearly can be optimal or suboptimal for different learners. For mildly handicapped students particularly, effective teaching, like direct instruction, provides highly constraining structure that serves as an environmental proxy for absent or ineffective "strategies."

Although CBT might be viewed as useful only "as needed" whenever task performance roadblocks are confronted, however, to impact rate and quality of acquisition over time, CBT should be a formal part of the everyday curriculum. This, in fact, has been suggested (Borkowski & Cavanaugh, 1979; Borkowski & Konarski, 1981). The puzzle, from both a theoretical and applied point of view, has been whether there is, or could be, a simultaneous means of approaching specific *and* general learner competence that respects both individual and content differences but also can be implemented with reasonable economy of time and effort in real classrooms.

This type of approach will not likely take the form of single, elaborate intervention late in the elementary school career of most mildly handicapped students. More logically, the approach would have to be systematically associated with the curriculum that intends to impart basic academic knowledge and skills—parallel in a sense to the way in which teachers attempt to subtly embed instruction in school-appropriate, task orientation behaviors (e.g., following directions, being alert to learning cues, beginning and ending tasks on time, proper use of tools/materials) in most primary grade lessons.

What would be novel in using CBT throughout the early curriculum, however, would be making the "hidden" portion of the curriculum that deals with problem solving and task management more overt and more potent for slower learners. Normally achieving students, or those who will be considered normally achieving in later grades, internalize useful and generalized task handling routines after relatively short exposures to teacher-imposed or task-imposed structure. From the teacher's perspective, their dependable ability to divide attention between information within the task and information about the task makes them easier to teach.

Behaviors indicative of developing self-regulation in early learning are subtle, however, as is their relationship to success and speed of acquisition. Because faster learning students appear to be so responsive to instruction, the critical role of mediating student behaviors often is overlooked or appreciated as an undifferentiated part of what causes these students to seem so "teachable." Unless their relevance in the teacher-learner system is recognized, teachers will not formally adopt CBT-type methods for directly developing or exploiting these behaviors more fully in slower learning students.

Consider, for example, normally achieving 6-year-olds who enter first grade and encounter what Doyle (1983) has referred to as "academic work" for the first time. Behaviors that they have only observed and imitated before, such as writing letters, decoding written words, and adding quantities, now are explored with interest, enthusiasm, and concentration. But now they also are required to complete a series of "tasks" that, independent of any innate attractiveness, require intentional remembering, purposeful comprehension, deliberate and facile retrieval and use of both declarative and procedural knowledge, and practice of selected responses until some standard of mastery is achieved. Even casual observation of these students strikingly reveals behavioral signs of emerging metacognitive capacity in parallel with their processing of task-specific information.

To illustrate, in addition to performing the components of any required response, one "average" first grader recently was observed to comment to herself (and to any available adult audience) on things she noticed about her own performance on a variety of ordinary paper-and-pencil letter tasks requiring simple decoding, letter writing, and simple addition. These comments sometimes were limited to labeling the behavior in relation to salient features in the stimulus field but also included comments that clearly represent early efforts to construct a self-regulatory transaction between task-specific information and meta-awareness of "self-engaged-in-task." Her comment and motor responses flowed with continuity, intention, and rhythmicity. This is not to say that she never was observed to be "off-task." Most of the self-talk, however, was clearly task-related. Her comments never appeared to punctuate a series of pencil responses so much as glue them together, serving a variety of functions such as:

- Schematizing—recognition of analogies between some aspect of the task and previous experience or knowledge; e.g. (reading), "This word has /E/ sound in it just like . . ."
- Self-Monitoring—statements or behavior interpretable as indication of planfulness, error consciousness, and attempts to control impulse; e.g. (writing), "Oops. I made a mistake." . . ." I'm being very careful, aren't I?"
- Strategizing—discovery or invention of algorithms or rules for reducing response uncertainty; e.g. (adding), "First you say this number, then you hold up that many fingers, then you . . ."
- Recruitment—bids for reinforcement, correction, or help; e.g. (spelling), "Is this right?" . . ." I got it right, didn't I?" . . ." How do you spell . . . ?"

In addition to whatever intrinsic learning benefit is derived from these behaviors, these students clearly will be attractive and rewarding to teach. The benefit-cost ratio relating pupil performance to teacher effort is likely to be high, compared to the payoff expected by teachers exerting equivalent effort for the kind of students typically considered mildly handicapped. In short, these normally achieving students don't require as much external structure or management; their demonstrated capacity for simultaneous, or at least rapidly shifting, processing at different levels of task engagement represents an emerging orderliness and self-regulation during academic work that prepares for and also must facilitate future as well as present learning.

When "basic skills" are still difficult puzzles rather than automatized responses, success in inventing or discovering increasingly efficient algorithms is similarly assisted by the ability to overview one's problem solving behavior without losing place or tempo. For example, without direct prompting or instruction, normal preschoolers given a simple addition task (counting blocks for each addend, then combining sets and recounting) were observed by Groen and Resnick (1977) to discover a more efficient algorithm (i.e., naming, then counting from largest addend) simply as a result of continued practice. As naming and physical counting out of blocks to match addends became more rapid, a portion of the process was transformed from being overt to covert, making problem solution more likely, faster, and certainly less cumbersome.

As a general rule, if responses become not only more accurate, but also faster (e.g., see Ackerman & Dykman, 1982; Chi & Gallagher, 1982; Sternberg, 1981; Sternberg & Wagner, 1982), a task-oriented excess capacity is generated that can be used to operate not on the response but rather on the procedure used to generate that response. Increasing automaticity of invented or discovered algorithms, whether "correct" or not, permits and encourages a kind of metacognitive housekeeping that aims to reduce mental effort by replacing or transforming components of old response generation procedures with more efficient ones.

CBT and Effective Teaching

Though a multi-element training technology suitable for general curricular use has not yet been developed, notable advances have been made. Egeland (1974), for example, was able to train impulsive children general "search-and-scan" rules that led to improved performance on several laboratory tasks, but also appeared to improve performance on a test of reading comprehension 5 months after training.

Kendall and Wilcox (1980) have created a more elaborate training program that has resulted in practical (not merely statistically significant) improvements for a group of impulsive children. Their training program was unique because it combined, but differentiated, concrete (task-specific) and conceptual (generalized) training targets and procedures. Children were trained in a range of actual behavior and academic problem situations. Six training components used in both types of training consisted of modeling and practice in using verbal self-instructions but were made problem- or task-specific during concrete training, while they were presented more abstractly for application to problems in general during conceptual training. These components are:

1. Problem definition.
2. Problem approach.
3. Focusing attention.
4. Problem solution.
5. Self-reinforcement.
6. Coping with errors.

Some evidence has been developing also that supports not only the separability of cognitive and metacognitive processes (Slife, Weiss, & Bell, 1985) but also the possibility of training strategic use of both during tasks requiring deliberate memorization (Ghatala, Levin, Pressley, & Lodico, 1985). Recent studies by Ghatala and her colleagues have shown that even primary grade students can and will abandon ineffective strategies more rapidly and use appropriate strategies more effectively during deliberate memory tasks as a result of being trained to monitor and evaluate utility of task strategies.

In these studies, when students were prompted to use a detrimental strategy, its use probably resulted in an increase in response uncertainty; that is, the specific task demands became more, not less, problematic. Because high uncertainty results in more, not less, cognitive effort, detrimental procedures tended to be more spontaneously replaced by more natural (and inevitably more adequate) mnemonic strategies. On the other hand, when students had been prompted to use a strategy that was more efficient than one they might naturally generate, response uncertainty was reduced reliably and rapidly, relatively little mental effort was required, and a functional capacity "excess" was created with which the prompted strategy could be integrated with whatever mnemonic skills repertoire already existed.

Whereas these examples suggest that normally achieving, younger students benefit with relatively little external pacing and control, mildly handicapped students in upper elementary grades most often have been perceived as being incapable of functioning successfully without substantial teacher direction and environmental constraint. These perceptions typically lead to attempts to "overpower" slow learners with environmental management in the earliest stages of basic skills acquisition, rather than to "empower" them by systematic training in task self-management. When they are older, and their failure on more complex learning tasks is more dramatic, more heroic interventions are attempted, including CBT. These latter attempts possibly come too late to assist learners in developing an appropriately generic task management repertoire. Rather than bind metacognitive knowledge to the organization and structure of student ability to search, retrieve, and apply declarative and procedural knowledge about "basic" academic tasks, CBT then can be used only in very focal applications that serve to enhance specific (i.e., task) competence, but not generalized learning ability.

Time and Technology

Theoretical and empirical studies of CBT have contributed to new conceptual and methodological approaches to research and instructional design for children thought to be mildly handicapped. Moreover, this work, as a body, has tended to bring a strong theoretical basis to more behaviorally derived techniques for decreasing impulsivity and increasing self-control. In their development to date, CBT methods have captured and uniquely organized what appear to be critical features of the most powerful instructional techniques.

In Walberg's (1984) summarization of data on a variety of general teaching approaches across student types and subject matter, his analyses show that manipulations of reinforcement contingencies—an intervention providing minimal structure by linking some pattern of antecedent and consequent events to responses—produced an average effect size of 1.20. Individualized tutoring, on the other hand, produced an average effect size of 2.00.

Because individualized tutoring may not be feasible, Bloom (1984) compared Walberg's data to data from "mastery learning" studies in which teachers provided each student with sufficient time and corrective feedback over trials to assure performance at some targeted level. Although conventional approaches to instruction result in estimated effect sizes of about .50, or .76 when enhanced by methods to assure "cognitive entry prerequisites," mastery learning alone resulted in an effect size of 1.00, and an effect size of 1.60 when enhanced by "cognitive entry prerequisites" (i.e., preskills and previous knowledge).

These data are particularly interesting in light of Palincsar and Brown's (1984) conclusion from a long series of studies that to be successful, cognitive training must "force" students to be cognitively active (engaged) during learning tasks, provide corrective feedback on appropriate use of trained tactics or strategies, and provide "instruction in why, when, and where such activities should be applied" (p. 122). Similarly, Bloom (1984) argued that as effort is made to assure that students possess ideas or skills necessary for learning new material:

> . . . they become more positive about their ability to learn the subject, and they put in more active learning time than do control students. (p. 7)

From a direct instruction perspective, Carnine (1983) reported on two studies with similar implications for cumulative effects from structuring thinking during teaching. In the first, systematic preskills training of simple multiplication was compared with a no-preskills training condition in which each error was corrected and retaught as it occurred. Over 30% more teaching time was required to reach criterion levels of performance without preskills training. Moreover, students trained in preskills transferred their knowledge more readily to a new set of items. In a second study of the effects of overt versus covert procedures for learning to read lists of phonetically simple words, the group that received instruction in component skills, including a "sounding out" operation, reached criterion 16 minutes faster than a group that received only "look-say" practice. On a transfer task, the component skills group averaged over three times as many correct responses.

These general investigations of teaching technology and its relationship to rate of learning support the general thesis that "good" instruction provides or elicits the amount of structure most likely to maximally reduce response uncertainty. Moreover, the amount of structure that must be provided by teaching methods appears to relate inversely to the cognitive maturity of prospective learners. Various well established techniques—overtly controlling incentives and attention to informative environmental cues (e.g., reinforcement), intensively guiding and monitoring attention to task and responding (e.g., tutoring), presenting "sufficient" response and feedback opportunities (e.g., direct instruction, mastery learning), assuring that necessary preskills are usable and available (e.g., some forms of direct instruction, mastery learning, cognitive training), and direct teaching of demonstrably useful overt behaviors related to task-specific performance (e.g., phonics instruction)—find common ground in their ability to make correct responding on a target task more probable by reducing response uncertainty or organizing information more efficiently for students than they are able to accomplish spontaneously on their own.

If these techniques can be applied systematically as part of a curriculum focused on enhancing cognitive-behavioral self-regulation during learning, the seemingly unresolvable problems of time and learning rate posed by slower learning, mildly handicapped students, whether in restrictive or less restrictive environments, may be addressed with new optimism.

REFERENCES

Abikoff, H. (1979). Cognitive training interventions in children: A review of a new approach. *Journal of Learning Disabilities, 12*, 65–77.

Ackerman, P. T., & Dykman, R. A. (1982), Automatic and effortful information-processing deficits in children with learning and attention disorders. *Topics in Learning & Learning Disabilities, 2*(2), 12–22.

Ballard, K. D., & Glynn, T. (1975). Behavioral self-management in story writing with elementary school age children. *Journal of Applied Behavior Analysis 8*, 387–398.

Baroody, A. J. (1984). The case of Felicia: A young child's strategies for reducing memory during mental addition. *Cognition & Instruction, 1*(1), 109–116.

Becker, W. C. (1977). Teaching reading and language to the disadvantaged—what we have learned from field research. *Harvard Educational Review, 47* 518–543.

Becker, W. C. & Carnine, D. W. (1981). Direct instruction: A behavior theory model for comprehensive educational intervention with the disadvantaged. In S. W. Bijou & R. Ruis (Eds.), *Behavior modification: Contributions to education*. Hillsdale, NJ: Lawrence Erlbaum.

Belmont, J. M., & Butterfield, E. C. (1977). The instructional approach to developmental cognitive research. In R. Kail & J. Hagen (Eds.), *Perspectives on the development of memory and cognition* (pp. 437–481). Hillsdale, NJ: Lawrence Erlbaum.

Bissex, G. L. (1980). *GYNS AT WRK*. Cambridge, MA: Harvard University Press.

Bloom, B. S. (1984). The 2 sigma problem: The search for methods of group instruction as effective as one-to-one tutoring. *Educational Researcher, 13*(6), 4–16.

Bookman, M. (1984). Spelling as a cognitive-developmental linguistic process: Implications for testing and teaching. *Academic Therapy*.

Borkowski, J. G., & Cavanaugh, J. C. (1979). Maintenance and generalization of skills and strategies by the retarded. In N. R. Ellis (Ed.), *Handbook of mental deficiency: Psychological theory and research* (2nd ed.) (pp. 569–617). Hillsdale, NJ: Lawrence Earlbaum.

Borkowski, J. G., & Konarski, E. A. (1981). Educational implications of efforts to train intelligence. *Journal of Special Education, 15*(2), 289–305.

Bos, C. S. (1982). Getting past decoding: Assisted and repeated readings as remedial methods for learning disabled students. *Topics in Learning & Learning Disabilities, 1*(4), 51–57.

Brown, A. L., Campione, J. C., & Day, J. D. (1981). Learning to learn: On training students to learn from texts. *Educational Researcher, 10*(2), 14–21.

Brown, B. W., & Saks, D. H. (1983, April). *An economic approach to measuring teachers' preferences in allocating time to students*. Paper presented at the annual meeting of the American Educational Research Association, Montreal, Canada.

Carnine, D. (1983). Direct instruction: In search of instructional solutions for educational problems. In *Interdisciplinary voices in learning disabilities and remedial education* (pp. 1–66). Austin, TX: Pro-Ed.

Carpenter, T., Moser, J., & Romberg, T. (Eds.) (1982). *Addition and subtraction: A cognitive perspective*. Hillsdale, NJ: Lawrence Erlbaum.

Chi, M. T. H., & Gallagher, J. D. (1982). Speed of processing: A developmental source of limitation. *Topics in Learning & Learning Disabilities, 2*(2), 23–32.
Cohen, S., & deBettencourt, L. (1983). Teaching children to be independent learners: A step-by-step strategy. *Focus on Exceptional Children, 16*(3), 1–12.
Cook, L. (1981). Misspelling analysis in dyslexia: Observation of developmental strategy shifts. *Bulletin of the Orton Society, 31,* 123–134.
Corno, L., & Mandinach, E. B. (1983). The role of cognitive engagement in classroom learning and motivation. *Educational Psychologist, 18*(2), 88–108.
Cullinan, D., Lloyd J., & Epstein, M. H. (1981). Strategy training: A structured approach to arithmetic instruction. *Exceptional Education Quarterly, 2*(1), 41–49.
Doyle, W. (1983). Academic work. *Review of Educational Research, 53*(2), 159–199.
Egeland, B. Training impulsive children in the use of more efficient scanning techniques. *Child Development, 45,* 165–171.
Engelmann, S. (1969). *Preventing failure in the primary grades.* Chicago: SRA.
Farnham-Diggory, S., & Nelson, B. (1984). Cognitive analyses of basic school tasks. *Applied Developmental Psychology, 1,* 21–74.
Frederiksen, J. R., Warren, B. M., & Roseberry, A. S. (1985). A componential approach to training reading skills: Part 1. Perceptual units training. *Cognition & Instruction, 2*(2), 91–130.
Frederiksen, N. (1984). Implications of cognitive theory for instruction in problem solving. *Review of Educational Research, 54*(3), 363–407.
Frith, U. (1980). *Cognitive processes in spelling.* London: Academic Press.
Gerber, M. M. (1983). Learning disabilities and cognitive strategies: A case for training or constraining problem solving? *Journal of Learning Disabilities, 16*(5), 255–260.
Gerber, M. M. (1984a). The Department of Education's Sixth Annual Report to Congress on P. L. 94–142: Is congress getting the full story? *Exceptional Children, 51*(3), 209–224.
Gerber, M. M. (1984b). Investigations of orthographic problem-solving ability in learning disabled and normally achieving students. *Learning Disability Quarterly, 7,* 157–164.
Gerber, M. M. (1984c). Techniques to teach generalizable spelling skills. *Academic Therapy, 20*(1), 49–58.
Gerber, M. M. (1985). Spelling as concept-driven problem solving. In B. Hutson (Ed.), *Advances in reading/language research* (Vol. 3) (pp. 39–75). Greenwich, CT: JAI Press.
Gerber, M. M. (in press). Generalization of spelling strategies by LD students as a result of contingent imitation/modeling and mastery criteria. *Journal of Learning Disabilities.*
Gerber, M. M., & Niemann, C. (in preparation). *Self-monitoring and acquisition of new academic skills.*
Gerber, M. M., & Semmel, M. I. (1985). The microeconomics of referral and reintegration: A paradigm for evaluation of special education. *Studies in Educational Evaluation, 11,* 13–29.
Gettinger, M. (1984a). Achievement as a function of time spent in learning and time needed for learning. *American Educational Research Journal, 21*(3), 617–628.
Gettinger, M. (1984b). Applying learning principles to remedial spelling instruction. *Academic Therapy, 20*(1), 41–48.
Gettinger, M. & Lyon, M. A. (1983). Predictors of the discrepancy between time needed and time spent in learning among boys exhibiting behavior problems. *Journal of Educational Psychology, 75*(4), 491–499.
Gettinger, M., & White, M. A. (1979). Which is the stronger correlate of school learning? Time to learn or measured intelligence? *Journal of Educational Psychology, 71,* 405–412.
Ghatala, E., Levin, J. R., Pressley, M., & Lodico, M. G. (1985). Training cognitive strategy monitoring in children. *American Educational Research Journal, 22*(2), 199–215.
Good, T. L. (1983). Classroom research: A decade of progress. *Educational Psychologist, 18*(3), 127–144.
Graham, S. (1983). The effect of self-instructional procedures on LD students' handwriting performance. *Learning Disability Quarterly, 6*(2), 231–234.
Graham, S., & Freeman, S. (1985). Strategy training and teacher vs. student-controlled study conditions: Effects of learning disabled students' spelling performance. *Learning Disability Quarterly, 8*(4), 267–274.
Grimm, J. A., Bijou, S. W., & Parsons, J. A. (1973). A problem solving model for teaching remedial arithmetic to handicapped young children. *Journal of Abnormal Child Psychology, 1,* 26–39.
Groen, G., & Resnick, L. B. (1977). Can preschool children invent addition algorithms? *Journal of Educational Psychology, 69,* 645–652.

Hall, R. J. (1980). Cognitive behavior modification and information-processing skills of exceptional children. *Exceptional Education Quarterly, 1*(1), 9–15.

Hallahan, D. P., Hall, R. J., Ianna, S. O., Kneedler, R. D., Lloyd, J. W., Loper, A. B., & Reeve, R. E. (1983). Summary of research findings at the University of Virginia Learning Disabilities Research Institute. *Exceptional Education Quarterly, 4*(1), 95–114.

Hallahan, D. P., & Reeve, R. (1980). Selective attention and distractibility. In B. Keogh (Ed.), *Advances in special education* (Vol. 1) (pp. 141–181). Greenwich, CT: JAI Press.

Hallahan, D. P., & Sapona, R. (1983). Self-monitoring of attention with learning-disabled children: Past research and current issues. *Journal of Learning Disabilities, 16*(10), 616–620.

Harris, K. R. (1982). Cognitive-behavior modification: Application with exceptional students. *Focus on Exceptional Children, 15*(2), 1–16.

Harris, K. R., & Graham, S. (1985). Improving learning disabled students' composition skills: Self-control strategy training. *Learning Disability Quarterly, 8*, 27–36.

Henderson, E. H., & Beers, J. W. (Eds.). (1980). *Developmental and cognitive aspects of learning to spell—a reflection of word knowledge*. Newark, DE: International Reading Association.

Karweit, N., & Slavin, R. E. (1981). Measurement and modeling choices in studies of time and learning. *American Educational Research Journal, 18*(2), 157–171.

Kauffman, J. M., & Hallahan, D. P. (1979). Learning disability and hyperactivity. In B. B. Lahey & A. E. Kazdin (Eds.), *Advances in child clinical psychology* (Vol. 2) (pp. 71–105). New York: Plenum.

Kendall, P. C., & Wilcox, L. E. (1980). Cognitive-behavioral treatment for impulsivity: Concrete versus conceptual training in non-self-controlled problem children. *Journal of Consulting & Clinical Psychology, 48*, 80–91.

Kosiewicz, M. M., Hallahan, D. P., Lloyd, J. W., & Graves, A. W. (1982). Effects of self-instruction and self-correction procedures on handwriting performance. *Learning Disability Quarterly, 5*, 71–78.

Lloyd, J. (1975). The pedagogical orientation: An argument for improving instruction. *Journal of Learning Disabilities, 8*(2), 74–78.

Lloyd, J. (1980). Academic instruction and cognitive behavior modification: The need for attack strategy training. *Exceptional Education Quarterly, 1*(1), 53–63.

Lloyd, J., Cullinan, D., Heins, E. D., & Epstein, M. H. (1980). Direct instruction: Effects on oral and written language comprehension. *Learning Disability Quarterly, 3*(4), 70–76.

Lloyd, J. W., Saltzman, N. J., & Kauffman, J. M. (1981). Predictable generalization in academic learning as a result of preskills and strategy training. *Learning Disability Quarterly, 4*, 203–216.

Lovitt, T. (1975). Specific research recommendations and suggestions for practitioners. *Journal of Learning Disabilities, 8*, 504–517.

Lovitt, T. C., & Curtiss, K. A. (1968). Effects of manipulating an antecedent event on mathematics response rate. *Journal of Applied Behavioral Analysis, 1*, 329–333.

Nulman, J. H., & Gerber, M. M. (1984). Improving spelling performance by imitating a child's errors. *Journal of Learning Disabilities, 17*, 328–333.

Palincsar, A. S., & Brown, A. L. (1984). Reciprocal teaching of comprehension-fostering and comprehension-monitoring activities. *Cognition & Instruction, 1*(2), 117–175.

Pflaum, S. W., & Pascarella, E. T. (1980). Interactive effects of prior reading achievement and training in context on the reading of learning disabled children. *Reading Research Quarterly, 16*, 138–158.

Read, C. (1975). *Children's categorization of speech sounds in English*. Urbana, IL: National Council of Teachers of English.

Robin, A. L., Armel S., & O'Leary, K. D. (1975). The effects of self-instruction on writing deficiencies. *Behavior Therapy, 6*, 178–187.

Rooney, K. J., & Hallahan, D. P. (1985). Future directions for cognitive behavior modification research: The quest for cognitive change. *Remedial & Special Education, 6*(2), 46–51.

Rosenshine, B. (1983). Teaching functions in instructional programs. *Elementary School Journal, 83*, 335–351.

Russell, R. L., & Ginsburg, H. P. (1984). Cognitive analysis of children's mathematics difficulties. *Cognition & Instruction, 1*(2), 217–244.

Samuels, S. J., (1979). The method of repeated readings. *Reading Teacher, 32*, 403–408.

Samuels, S. J., & Miller, N. L. (1985). Failure to find attention differences between learning disabled and normal children on classroom and laboratory tasks. *Exceptional Children, 51*(5), 358–375.

Shavelson, R. J., & Stern, P. (1981). Research on teachers' pedagogical thoughts, judgments, decisions, and behavior. *Review of Educational Research, 51,* 444–498.
Sheinker, A., Sheinker, J. M., & Stevens, L. J. (1984). Cognitive strategies for teaching the mildly handicapped. *Focus on Exceptional Children, 17*(1), 1–15.
Simon, H. A. (1973). The structure of ill-structured problems. *Artificial Intelligence, 4,* 181–201.
Slife, B. D., Weiss, J., & Bell, T. (1985). Separability of metacognition and cognition: Problem solving in learning disabled and regular students. *Journal of Educational Psychology, 77*(4), 437–445.
Sternberg, R. J. (1981). Cognitive-behavioral approaches to the training of intelligence in the retarded. *Journal of Special Education, 15*(2), 165–183.
Sternberg, R. J., & Wagner, R. K. (1982). Automatization failure in learning disabilities. *Topics in Learning & Learning Disabilities, 2*(2), 1–11.
Stevens, R., & Rosenshine, B. (1981). Advances in research on teaching. *Exceptional Education Quarterly, 2*(1), 1–9.
Walberg, H. J. (1984). Improving the productivity of America's schools. *Educational Leadership, 41*(8), 19–27.
Will, M. C. (1986). Educating children with learning problems: A shared responsibility. *Exceptional Children, 52*(5), 411–415.
Zigmond, N., & Thornton, H. B. (April, 1985). *Follow-up postsecondary-age LD graduates and dropouts.* Paper presented at the annual meeting of the American Educational Research Association, Chicago.

Michael Gerber is an Associate Professor of Special Education, University of California, Santa Barbara.

Direct instruction is a teaching process based on a theory of instruction developed by Siegfried Engelmann and Douglas Carnine. It has been expanded and developed by individuals primarily at the University of Oregon and Ohio State University. Direct instruction involves precise, step-by-step instructional procedures. The present article examines the use of this technique to teach reading comprehension. As such, it is highly effective. The technique also has been used to teach most other academic subjects.

Direct Instruction in Reading Comprehension

Russell Gersten and Douglas Carnine

We can be precise.
—Charles Olson (from "The King Fishers," cited by Creeley 1966, p. 171.)

The recent report by the National Commission on Reading (Anderson et al. 1985) concluded:

> *Direct instruction* needs to be distinguished from questioning, discussion, and guided practice. Direct instruction in comprehension means explaining the steps in a thought process that give birth to comprehension. It may mean that the teacher models a strategy by thinking aloud about how he or she is going about understanding a passage. The instruction includes information on why and when to use the strategy. Instruction of this type is the surest means of developing the strategic processing that was identified earlier as characteristic of skilled readers. (p. 72)

Fifteen years of research have gone into developing and evaluating direct instruction in reading comprehension at the University of Oregon. This research was based on the proposition that precise principles of instructional design can be developed for instruction even in an area as complex as reading comprehension, and that these procedures can (and should) be empirically investigated. The general model that guided the research (Englemann and Carnine 1982) was originally developed as part of Project Follow Through, a U.S. Office of Education research and training project aimed at improving the academic achievement of low-income students in 20 communities—from Arkansas to New York City.

In Follow Through, we faced a perennial problem, recently articulated by Duffy: "How can teachers, despite the complexities of classroom context, provide instruction beyond the routine level?" (1983, p. 135). In order to work effectively with teachers, Follow Through consultants were forced to make decisions about the structure and nature of reading texts, the nature and sequence of comprehension strategies to be taught in these texts, and the specific procedures used to teach these skills. We focused on what many would consider mundane decisions: the best wording for teachers to use in demonstrating a comprehension skill, the most effective way to correct students' errors, the number and range of examples necessary to ensure mastery of a new concept. While many researchers may treat these topics as separate strands, practitioners play them in concert.

This concern with precision in all details of instruction was particularly alien to educational thinking in the late '60s, when Follow Through originated. Developmental, Piagetian, and psychodynamic models of early childhood education were then in vogue. Many felt that the extremely structured teaching would stifle students' learning (Maccoby and Zellner 1970) or impede teachers' creativity and ultimate effectiveness (Resnick 1981a).

Yet independent evaluations of direct instruction in Follow Through showed that economically disadvantaged students made significant progress in reading comprehension as measured on standardized tests (Stebbins et al. 1977; Guthrie 1977). More recent research has indicated that these students have maintained their elementary school gains in comprehension through high school (Gersten et al. 1984).

Building on the Follow Through experience, a group of researchers at the University of Oregon began to examine the applicability of direct instruction for teaching reading comprehension to students at the intermediate and secondary levels.

CURRENT PROBLEMS IN COMPREHENSION INSTRUCTION

There have been several investigations of how comprehension is actually taught in classrooms. After observing over 600 hours of reading instruction in grades 3 through 6, Durkin concluded:

> Practically no comprehension instruction was seen. Comprehension *assessment*, carried on for the most part through interrogation, was common. Whether children's answers were right or wrong was the big concern . . . time spent in giving, completing, and checking assignments consumed a large part of the observed periods. (1983, p. 318)

Duffy and Roehler (1982) collected and analyzed audiotapes of actual comprehension lessons being taught in the primary grades. The majority of teachers in their study merely gave students the right answer without offering explanations or suggesting strategies by which students could reach the right answer.

For example, the following excerpt chronicles a teacher's attempt to instruct students in how to select an appropriate title for a story:

Teacher: Listen to the story I read you, and I will give you three possible titles. Listen really closely. See if you can pick out a good title for it. (Teacher reads the story aloud.) All right. Now here are some possibilities: "A Trip Downtown," "A New

Shirt," "The Shirt That Didn't Fit." Of those three possibilities, which one goes best? Angela?

Angela: "A Trip Downtown."

Teacher: Okay. Tom, what do you think?

Tom: "The New Shirt."

Teacher: Andy, what was your choice?

Andy: "The New Shirt."

Teacher: Susie, how about you?

Susie: "The Trip Downtown."

Teacher: Joe, how about you?

Joe: "The New Shirt."

Teacher: I think the girls decided on "The Trip Downtown," and the boys liked "The New Shirt." Mainly, what was the story about?

Child: A trip downtown.

Child: Getting a new shirt.

Teacher: Getting a new shirt, wasn't it?

Examples like this led Duffy and Roehler to conclude that a typical teacher "only asks for answers . . . her responses to pupil answers *do not create an understanding of either the main idea or strategy for figuring out the main idea*. Apparently, students are expected to come up with both the answer and the strategy (on their own)" (p. 135). Although some students are unable to develop their own strategies, few teachers can spontaneously think up ways to help them (Durkin 1984), and teachers' guides attached to basal series do not provide the necessary guidance.

EXPLICIT STRATEGY INSTRUCTION

In contrast, the distinguishing characteristic of the approach we examined in the 16 experimental studies is the use of *explicit, step-by-step training* in comprehension strategies. When this was not possible, students were provided with models of appropriate performance followed by extensive practice with immediate feedback.

The purpose in articulating and demonstrating a step-by-step strategy is to show students how a thinking process can lead to accurate solutions, or to demonstrate reasonable attempts at deducing an acceptable answer to a question. In demonstrating a strategy for solving a particular type of problem, the teacher makes each step clear to the student. This overt demonstration and guidance appears to be most important for low-performing students, who do not intuitively devise ways to answer comprehension questions. These students learn to copy the steps modeled by the teacher, however, and later will modify or personalize them. Duffy and Roehler (1982) found that teachers needed the most help with this crucial step of articulating and modeling explicit strategies.

Rather than present a detailed overview of the instructional model (see fig. 1), I think one can get a sense of the model by examining the actual teaching methods used in three experimental studies. The studies involved three different types of com-

FIGURE 1 Components of Direct Instruction

1. Instruction on *explicit* step-by-step strategy. (When this is not possible or necessary, model effective performance.)
2. Student mastery of each step in the process.
3. Strategy (or process) corrections for student errors.
4. *Gradual* fading from teacher-directed activities toward independent work.
5. Adequate, systematic practice for students—using a range of examples.
6. Cumulative review.
7. Teaching formats that anticipate ("pre-correct") potential errors.

prehension skills: the ability to draw inferences in the context of distracting information, knowledge of story grammar (a technique for comprehending narrative), and the ability to detect faulty arguments (a critical reading skill). The first two studies involved low-achieving students: the third involved average and above-average students. Teaching strategies in these three studies range from the highly detailed approach used in the "distracting information" study, to the looser approach used in the metacognitive story grammar study. Each study focused on teaching students a specific procedure or strategy for dealing with the comprehension.

DRAWING INFERENCES IN THE CONTEXT OF DISTRACTING INFORMATION

In a study by Carnine, Kameenui, and Woolfson (1982), students were taught to draw an inference based on relevant information. Rather than *teach* an explicit strategy, teachers *modeled* its appropriate use by a series of prompting questions. We felt that with a good deal of detailed guided practice and teacher feedback, students' performance could improve dramatically.

To select students for the study, we gave a screening test consisting of a series of passages that contained distracting information. Only students who failed, scoring less than 65 percent on the test, were included in the study. These students were then randomly separated into three groups to receive either direct instruction, corrective feedback only, or no intervention. Those who received corrective feedback were given a series of comprehension passages containing distracting information, asked to answer questions, and told whether they were right or wrong. The average score for the corrective feedback group was 23 percent. The control group, at 20 percent, scored only a little lower. The average score for students taught with direct instruction, however was 63 percent.

A sample passage from the study (fig. 2) ends with a question for the reader: "Which carrots did John buy?" In the first paragraph, John states his criterion for buying food: having lots of vitamins. A sophisticated reader would be able to relate the rule in the second paragraph—"the fresher the food, the more vitamins it has"—to John's criterion to draw the correct inference. Intentionally distracting facts, however, make an inappropriate choice appear attractive. The sweet, tasty carrots from California look inviting (and they are cheap), but they're not as fresh as the smaller, local carrots. If students do not carefully discriminate the distracting from the relevant information, they're likely to respond incorrectly. The direct instruction teaching sequence in figure 3 illustrates the level of detail necessary to improve the performance of low-achieving students.

The teaching format in figure 3 shows that the teacher assists and directs the child in crucial steps of the thinking/analysis process. The teacher points out the small steps in the strategy so that children (1) see how a successful step-by-step solution to the problem works, and (2) can correct errors immediately. Teachers, for their part, can see *exactly* where breakdowns occur and can solve particular comprehension problems more easily. If, for example, a child tends to interject inappropriate background knowledge (e.g., "Everyone wants cheaper carrots because my mom says you should always try to buy things that are the cheapest"), the teacher can direct the child back to the exact sentence in the text where John states what he wants. If students inappropriately put themselves in the protagonist's place (e.g., "John wants the sweet carrots 'cause *I* know they're the best"), the teacher can again direct the child back to the text. If, on the other hand, the student has difficulty making the inference from the given information, the teacher can work on that specific problem. With this kind of step-by-step breakdown, teaching becomes more analytical and precise.

Pearson's (1984) synthesis of research on comprehension instruction concluded that "younger and poorer readers benefit from *conscious explicit attempts to alter comprehension strategies* . . ." (p. 229, emphasis added). In contrast, teachers in situations that Duffy and Roehler observed tended to ask the same question repeatedly until someone in the group came up with a correct answer.

Almost as crucial as helping students with their mistakes is gradually withdrawing teacher guidance until students can apply a strategy independently. The teacher continually assesses how the child is doing and, when the child is performing well, slowly reduces the external structure, using increasingly subtle prompts until the students can perform on their own.

Students who move easily through all the steps in a teaching sequence don't need the teacher's prompts for very long. After successfully using the procedures three or

FIGURE 2 Sample Passage: "Drawing Inferences in the Context of Distracting Information" Study

John is recovering from a bad cold. His doctor told him to change his eating habits and eat good foods. John went to the local health food store and told the clerk about his problem, "I am tired of being sick all the time. All I care about is eating good food with lots of vitamins."

"I had colds all the time until I started eating fresh foods," the clerk said. "Fresh foods taste so much better than canned foods and have a lot more vitamins. We have the best vegetables in town—they are all organic. Look at these nice carrots. Did you know that carrots have more vitamin A than any other vegetable, as well as being high in Vitamins D, C, and K. You know, the fresher the food, the more vitamins it has. This batch of carrots just arrived from the largest farm in California. Have you ever seen such big carrots? They had a great growing season down there, so they are especially sweet and tasty. Also, the price is really low. They are only 29¢ a pound. They are a week-and-a-half old and a great buy. Carrots can be prepared in different ways. You can eat them raw or cooked. It wouldn't take many of these big ones to make a nice carrot cake.

"These smaller ones are nice, too. But they are just from a little garden around the corner. They were picked yesterday. Because it rained so much this summer, these carrots are small and don't have as much taste. But they would make good carrot juice. They cost 52¢ a pound. Last year carrots from the same garden were 10¢ a pound, but I guess everything costs more today."

Which carrots do you think John bought—the big carrots or the small carrots?

FIGURE 3 Example of a Teaching Format: "Drawing Inferences in the Context of Distracting Information"

Introduction

Teacher:	Read this story carefully; you're going to answer the question at the end. [The subject read the entire story orally. The teacher assisted with any decoding errors.]

1. *Statement of the Problem:* Student reads the question at the end.

Teacher:	Now let's go back to the beginning of the story so we can figure out the answer to the question at the end of the story. First, what does John want?
Student:	Not to be sick all the time.
Teacher:	Right. What's most important to him?
Student:	To eat good food with lots of vitamins.

2. *Discrimination Questions*

Teacher:	Is getting big carrots most important to him?
Student:	No.
Teacher:	Is getting sweet and tasty carrots most important to him?
Student:	No.
Teacher	Is getting cheap carrots most important to him?
Student:	No.

3. *Review of Problem Statement*

Teacher:	What's most important to John?
Student:	To get food with lots of vitamins.

4. *Identification of Rule*

Teacher:	What does it tell you in the story about getting lots of vitamins?
Student:	The fresher the food, the more vitamins it has.
Teacher:	Good. So what do you have to find out now to tell which carrots John will choose?
Student:	Which carrots are fresher.

5. *Locating and Converting Indirect Information*

Teacher:	Find out how fresh the big carrots are.
Student:	A week-and-a-half old.
Teacher:	Now find out how fresh the small carrots are.
Student:	One-day old.

6. *Making the Text-Based Inference*

Teacher:	How fresh are the big carrots?
Student:	A week and a half old.
Teacher:	How fresh are the small carrots?
Student:	One-day old.
Teacher:	What does that tell you about which carrots John will choose?
Student:	The small carrots.

Adapted from Carnine, Kameenui, and Wolfson (1982)

four times, these students can generally use them without assistance. On the other hand, students who are easily distracted, or who have not developed analytical strategies, need the teacher's assistance with the step-by-step models until they are ready for independent work. Neither group of students, however, should aimlessly guess at a story title.

Another important aspect of the strategy-teaching process is preemptive teaching. In figure 3 the student has just told the teacher that John really wants carrots with a lot of vitamins. The teacher then asks: "Is getting big carrots important? Sweet and tasty carrots? Cheap carrots?" These questions ensure that the student *maintains the correct focus* and doesn't get sidetracked by a lingering thought such as, "My mom always said to buy cheap food" or "I like sweet things." This step is especially important for weak readers. Rather than let a student make an error and then deal with it, the steps in the teaching format try to *preempt* errors.

STORY GRAMMAR

One focus of recent reading research has been *story grammar*, a student's awareness of the components of typical narratives and the relationships among these components. Most people acquire the essentials of story grammar from reading and listening to stories. Singer and Donlan (1982) devised an instructional system for teaching story grammar to students with insufficient knowledge of the basic structure of fiction.

More recently, Carnine and Kinder (1985) attempted to merge Singer and Donlan's approach with explicit instruction. The subjects were 13 intermediate-level students with poor comprehension skills, most of whom were receiving remedial instruction in reading. All of these children could read the experimental passages with at least 95 percent word recognition accuracy, yet all scored lower than 60 percent on an experimenter-designed comprehension test. For instructional purposes, the Singer and Donlan framework was simplified to four questions.

1. Who is the story about?
2. What does he or she want to do?
3. What happens when he or she tries to do it?
4. What happens in the end?

Each 20–30 minute training session involved three stories. The teacher read the first story and asked the group the four questions. Then the teacher asked individual students in the group to read the second story aloud, asking each story grammar question when appropriate. She immediately corrected any student errors and then asked the students to summarize the story according to the story grammar questions. The students read the third story silently. The teacher told them to ask themselves each question as they read, answering the fourth question when they finished the story. Only when all students had completed the reading and the questions did the teacher ask the class a series of comprehension questions.

Instruction, using a range of narrative stories from basal and remedial reading texts, lasted for ten days. Students received two short-answer comprehension tests based on two short passages; in addition, three independent judges taped and rated students' summaries of the stories. The team administered maintenance tests two and four weeks later to determine students' retention skills.

Presenting low-performing students with an understandable, systematic approach to narrative material led to significant increases in performance. The average student's performance increased from 53 to 75 percent. The fact that students maintained gains over a four-week period showed that they had integrated this approach into their reading.

Students seemed to internalize these four questions, using them to pinpoint what was important. The teaching sessions incorporated several key principles of our model: (1) teacher modeling of explicit strategies; (2) immediate correction of student errors, (3) gradual shift from teacher-directed activities to independent work, and—perhaps most important—(4) sustained, supervised work on the strategy until students demonstrate that they are using the strategy independently.

THE ABILITY TO DETECT FAULTY ARGUMENTS: AN EXAMPLE OF CRITICAL READING

The third study was conducted with above-average ability students in the domain of critical reading and critical thinking (Patching et al. 1983). This study examined the effectiveness of systematically teaching students one aspect of critical reading—the detection of potentially faulty arguments. A review of some publications of the Institute for Propaganda Analysis (Smith 1974) helped us identify three categories of commonly used invalid arguments. We then developed an instructional procedure to teach students to identify these types of invalid arguments. Figure 4 is a sample teacher's guide for the lesson that trains students to detect what is often called "invalid testimonial."

First the guide stated a clear rule to help students recognize instances of invalid testimonial: "Just because someone important in one area says something is good or bad in another area, you can't be sure it's true" (step 1, fig. 4). Students practiced distinguishing between a person's being important or competent in one area and being an expert in all areas of knowledge. They practiced with a set of examples—comedians may not be experts on nutrition, and high school principals may not know everything about sex or emotion. As in the *rule-based inference* example discussed earlier, teachers used a detailed, step-by-step analysis during the early stages of instruction.

Unlike the other studies, students in this study were reading at or above grade level. Nonetheless, 39 percent of the 5th graders failed the screening test (i.e., were unable to detect invalid arguments more than 50 percent of the time). This is not so surprising when one realizes that advertisers and politicians commonly use invalid testimonials to confuse adults.

Students were randomly assigned to one of three groups: (1) direct instruction with an adult teacher, (2) workbook practice using the direct instruction teaching ma-

FIGURE 4 Critical Reading: Sample Teaching Format

1. Teacher:	Listen. Here's a rule. Just because someone important in one area says something is good or bad in another area, you can't be sure that it's true.
2. Teacher:	When someone important in one area says something is good or bad in another area, can you be sure that it's true?
3. Student:	No.
4. Teacher:	No, just because someone important in one area says something is good or bad in another area you can't be sure that it's true.
5. Teacher:	OK, listen. Dr. Smith is a very good doctor, and everyone likes him. He tells people why they are sick and helps them get better quickly. One day I saw Dr. Smith at Ben's Hardware Store. I wanted to buy a lawnmower. Dr. Smith told me that I shouldn't buy a Victor mower because they are the worst around. Since he's a good doctor, he should know.
6. Teacher:	In what area is Dr. Smith important?
7. Student:	Being a doctor.
8. Teacher:	And what is Dr. Smith saying?
9. Student:	Victor mowers are the worst around.
10. Teacher:	So what is the other area that Dr. Smith is talking about?
11. Student:	Mowers.
12. Teacher:	Since we're learning to judge what people say, can you be sure what a doctor says about Victor mowers is true?
13. Student:	No.
14. Teacher:	Why not? (Or prompt with, "What can you say when someone important says something good or bad?")
15. Student:	You can't be sure it's true, and doctors may not know very much about mowers.

terials and exercises (with corrective feedback from an adult), or (3) a control group (workbook practice or general comprehension exercise). After only three days of teaching, the mean score for the direct instruction group was 90 percent: scores for the other two groups were both at 58 percent. The study shows that students with the greatest gains had the benefit of direct instruction and guided workbook practice as well as work with a teacher who modeled the steps, asked questions, and provided immediate feedback.

These three examples from recent research suggest how explicit strategies work and what level of detail is necessary for most students to acquire new learning. In addition, the majority of the studies cited in figure 5 support the use of direct

EFFECTIVENESS OF THE APPROACH

As recently as 1981, Resnick concluded her review of instructional psychology with this remark: "For the moment, cognitive instructional psychology is largely descriptive science, intent upon analyzing performance but not upon making strong suggestions for improving it" (1981b, p. 692). Pearson was more blunt in his summation,

FIGURE 5 Research Conducted to Date on Direct Instruction in Reading Comprehension Strategies

General Comprehension
1. Story grammar (Carnine and Kinder 1985)
2. Study skills (Adams, Carnine, and Gersten 1982)
3. Reading for meaning: oral reading errors (Carnine 1984)

Inference
1. Critical reading (Patching et al. 1983)
2. Rule-based deductions (Carnine, Kameenui, and Woolfson 1982, Carnine and Gersten, Carnine, Kameenui, and Maggs 1982, Ross and Carnine 1982)
3. Logical deductions (Collins 1985)
4. Character motives (Carnine et al. 1982)

Specific Skills (Vocabulary, Syntactic)
1. Learning vocabulary from context (Carnine, Kameenui, and Coyle 1984)
2. Vocabulary drill (Kameenui, Carnine, and Freschi 1982)
3. Computer-assisted vocabulary instruction (Johnson, Carnine, and Gersten 1985)
4. Syntax—pronoun constructions, clauses, passive voice (Kameenui, Carnine, and Maggs 1980; Kameenui and Carnine 1982)
5. Anaphoric structures (Dommes, Gersten, and Carnine 1984)

Text Structure
1. Visual displays (Darch and Carnine in press)

Comprehension in the Content Areas
1. Mathematics word problems (Darch, Carnine, and Gersten 1984)
2. Legal concepts (Fielding, Kameenui, and Gersten 1983)
3. Science concepts (Darch and Gersten in press)

---

declaring that throughout the '70s "our knowledge about *teaching* reading comprehension advanced very little, if at all" (1982, p. 11).

An assumption underlying the design of our research agenda was that teachers need precise guidance in how to teach comprehension to low-performing students. Virtually all the strategies used in the research led to significant improvements in the targeted comprehension skill. A meta-analysis of the studies (White, Gersten, and Carnine 1983) revealed a mean magnitude of effect of .97 standard deviation units, well above levels usually set for educational significance. The meta-analysis demonstrated significant effects for retention of the skills as well.

In their review of the research on strategy training, Belmont and Butterfield (1977) concluded, "Children can be trained to use effective strategies, but once trained, they frequently revert to their immature strategies when no longer explicitly constrained to play the instructor's program" (p. 465). In the studies presented here, the consistent effects on *maintenance measures administered one or two weeks after the intervention* suggest that students are still using strategies even though no one is present to monitor or remind them to use them.

CASES WHERE INTENSIVE INSTRUCTION WAS NOT NECESSARY

Up to now, our implicit assumption has been that modeling an explicit, overt strategy leads to higher performance. However, our research has shown that this is not always the case. Sometimes providing extensive systematic practice on the skill (accompanied by corrective feedback) is as effective as teaching step-by-step strategies. It appears that for relatively simple comprehension skills—such as using context clues to learn the meaning of unfamiliar vocabulary words (Carnine, Kameenui, and Coyle 1984), or determining real (versus apparent) character motive in a story (Carnine et al. 1982)—teachers may not need to model or explain an overt process. By receiving extensive practice (with feedback), even low-achieving students appear to learn not to trust everything characters say, but to evaluate their motivation by their actions, as well.

In these studies, the amount of practice differs radically from the amount found in most conventional teaching (Durkin 1984). In the study teaching students to identify character motives, for example, students were given 14 practice examples spread over a three-day period. In a basal reader, that much practice on such a skill might be spread over three years.

In most studies, however, explicit step-by-step instruction by an adult was necessary. In the two studies discussed in detail—learning to analyze arguments (Patching et al. 1983) and learning to draw inferences to analyze arguments (Carnine et al. 1982)—students who received extensive practice on the skill performed no better than students who received no practice at all. For these fairly difficult abstract skills, the teacher's role may be to provide successful models, offer immediate feedback, and systematically correct errors. This observation could have significant implications for how teachers use their time during the reading lesson. If research can indicate which topics and skills seem to require concerted, active teaching in reading—as well as in other disciplines—teachers could allocate instructional time accordingly.

STRATEGIES WITH LIMITED UTILITY

Even extensive practice and teacher feedback on purportedly critical comprehension skills do not necessarily ensure improvements in comprehension. For example, a large body of research on pronoun constructions (e.g., Bormuth et al. 1970) has suggested that confusion about the meaning of antecedent pronouns impairs students' comprehension. Yet, intensive training in how to identify pronoun antecedents in typical social studies passages did not enhance overall comprehension skill (Dommes et al. 1984). Although systematic instruction improved students' ability to identify pronoun antecedents, this ability did not significantly enhance students' comprehension of passages containing pronoun antecedents. The lack of an effect for direct instruction on this pronoun subskill highlights the importance of the relationship between an intervention and its intended effect. Strategy teaching, if done well, might improve performance on a targeted behavior, but not on other seemingly related domains of behavior.

A major advantage of explicit step-by-step procedures is that they allow teachers to provide specific feedback to students when they make errors. The work of Duffy and Roehler indicates, though, that most teachers don't know how to correct comprehension "errors." Our own observations as part of a naturalistic study of reading in intermediate grades support this contention (Gersten and Carnine 1984).

The explicit strategies create a shared language between teachers and students, which teachers can use when correcting errors. Without this shared language many teachers simply don't know what to say (as the Duffy-Roehler audiotapes reveal); when students have difficulty with a comprehension item, teachers merely ask the child to think again, call on another student, or give the answer themselves.

"RIGIDITY" OF STRATEGIES

Some educators are concerned that teaching a step-by-step strategy will produce students who "think" in exactly the same way. An investigation of teaching study skills (Adams, Carnine, and Gersten 1982) demonstrated that many students personalized the study process by omitting one of the steps they had been taught. Others integrated the new procedure (which did not call for taking notes) with their own ideas of note-taking. Students who adapted the procedure were no less accurate. These observations demonstrate that only in the early stages of instruction need the strategy be explicit: thereafter, students will adapt and modify a strategy so that it works well for them. Providing their performance remains accurate, these adaptations are fine.

DRAWING EXPLICIT MAPS FOR LEARNING

To know exactly which strategies to use, for which skills, and with which children requires more applied research as well as informal field-testing and discussion. Our research indicates that some skills may not be worth much investment of time because transfer effects are so weak. In most cases, however, explicit strategy instruction produces positive results. Furthermore, while some components of the explicit strategy model (such as providing extensive practice) have received a good deal of attention recently, other components (provision of detailed step-by-step models, fading of those models, and type of discrimination practice provided in the rule-based inference and legal concepts examples) have received scant attention.

The real power of teaching strategies comes when students can build broad mental maps that integrate a wide range of examples. Then students learn more than the particular lessons. They learn different ways of organizing and relating information. Thus the four "story grammar" questions become powerful to the extent that students can improve in their comprehension of a number of different stories.

This highly structured approach goes against the grain of what many educators feel comprehension instruction should be—an opportunity for students to spontaneously develop and articulate perceptions. Classroom observations, however, reveal that elementary (and probably middle school) teachers need guidance in teaching students to make sense of what they read. The research demonstrates that the type of questions, the detailed step-by-step breakdowns, and the extensive practice with a range of examples illustrated in our three studies will significantly benefit students' comprehension. The next step is integrating these procedures into reading series and into teacher training programs.

The quotation at the beginning of this article, from a poem by Charles Olson, was written soon after the destruction of Hiroshima and Nagasaki in World War II. When many poets and humanists attacked science, blaming it for nuclear destruction and the beginning of the arms race. Olson offered a different view. Refuting the superficial conflict between humanism and science, Olson concluded, "We can be precise."

Many of the dichotomies that have plagued education are equally superficial. The goal of precise instruction in comprehension strategies—no less than the goal of educational humanists—is for students to be capable of independent, intelligent analysis of writing. To accomplish this goal, we need only to build on what we know from research and technology about making our instruction more precise.

REFERENCES

Adams, A., D. Carnine, and R. Gersten. "Instructional Strategies for Studying Content Area Texts in the Intermediate Grades." *Reading Research Quarterly* 13, 1 (1982): 27–55.

Anderson, R. C., E. H. Hiebert, J. A. Scott, and I. A. Wilkinson. *Becoming a Nation of Readers*. Champaign, Ill.: Center for the Study of Reading, 1985.

Becker, W. C. "Teaching Reading and Language to the Disadvantaged—What We Have Learned from Field Research." *Harvard Educational Review* 47 (1977): 518–543.

Belmont, J. M., and E. C. Butterfield. "The Instructional Approach to Developmental Cognitive Research." In *Perspectives on the Development of Memory and Cognition*, pp. 437–481, edited by R. Kail and J. Hagen. Hillsdale, N.J.: Erlbaum, 1977.

Bormuth, J. R., J. C. Manning, J. W. Carr, and P. D. Pearson. "Children's Comprehension of Between and Within-Sentences Syntactic Structures." *Journal of Education Psychology* 61 (1970): 349–357.

Carnine, D., E. J. Kameenui, and G. Coyle. "Utilization of Contextual Information in Determining the Meaning of Unfamiliar Words." *Reading Research Quarterly* 14, 2 (1984): 188–204.

Carnine, D., E. J. Kameenui, and A. Maggs. "Components of Analytic Assistance: Statement Saying, Concept Training, and Strategy Training." *Journal of Educational Research* 75 (1982): 374–377.

Carnine, D., E. J. Kameenui, and N. Woolfson. "Training of Textural Dimensions Related to Text-Based Inferences." *Journal of Reading Behavior* 14, 3 (1982): 335–340.

Carnine, D., and D. Kinder. "Teaching Low-Performing Students to Apply Generative and Schema Strategies to Narrative and Expository Material." *Remedial and Special Education* 6, 1 (1985): 20–30.

Carnine, D., C. Stevens, J. Clements, and E. Kameenui. "Effects of Facilitative Questions and Practice on Intermediate Grade Students' Understanding of Character Motives." *Journal of Reading Behavior* 14, 2 (1982): 179–190.

Carnine, L. M., D. Carnine, and R. Gersten. "Analysis of Oral Reading Errors Made by Economically Disadvantaged Students Taught with a Synthetic-Phonics Approach." *Reading Research Quarterly* 19, 3 (1984): 343–356.

Collins, M. T. "The Effectiveness of Computer Correction Procedures on Secondary Students' Reasoning Skills." Paper presented at Association for Behavior Analysis, Columbus, Ohio. May 1985.

Creeley, R., ed. *Selected Writings of Charles Olson*. New York: New Directions, 1966.

Darch, C., and D. Carnine. "Approaches to Teaching Learning Disabled Students Literal Comprehension During Content Area Instruction." *Exceptional Children* (in press).

Darch, C., D. Carnine, and R. Gersten. "Explicit Instruction in Mathematics Problem Solving." *Journal of Educational Research* 77, 6 (1984): 350–359.

Darch, C., and R. Gersten. "Direction-Setting Activities in Reading Comprehension." *Learning Disabilities Quarterly* (in press).

Dommes, P., R. Gersten, and D. Carnine. "Instructional Procedures for Increasing Skill Deficient Fourth Graders' Comprehension of Syntactic Structures." *Educational Psychology* 4, 2 (1984): 155–165.
Duffy, G. G. "From Turn-Taking to Sense Making: Broadening the Concept of Reading Teacher Effectiveness." *Journal of Educational Research* 76, 3 (1983): 134–139.
Duffy, G., and L. Roehler. "A Study of Teacher Explanation Behavior." Paper presented at the annual meeting of the International Reading Association, Chicago, April 1982.
Durkin, D. "What Classroom Observations Reveal About Reading Comprehension Instruction." In *Reading Research Revisited*, edited by L. M. Gentile, M. L. Kamil, and J. S. Blanchard. Columbus, Ohio: Charles Merrill, 1983.
Durkin, D. "Do Basal Reader Manuals Provide for Reading Comprehension Instruction?" In *Learning to Read in American Schools: Basal Readers and Content Texts*, edited by R. Anderson, J. Osborn, and R. Tierney. Urbana: University of Illinois, Center for the Study of Reading, 1984.
Englemann, S., and D. W. Carnine. *Theory of Instruction*. New York: Irvington, 1982.
Fielding, G., E. Kameenui, and R. Gersten. "A Comparison of Inquiry and Direct Instruction Approaches Towards Teaching Legal Concepts and Applications to Secondary Students." *Journal of Educational Research* 76 (1983): 287–293.
Gersten, R., and D. Carnine. *Administrative Support of School Improvement: Interim Report*. Report submitted to National Institute of Education, 1984.
Gersten, R., D. Carnine, and T. Keating. "The Lasting Impact of the Direct Instruction Follow Through Program: Preliminary Findings of a Longitudinal Study of 1500 Students." Paper presented at American Educational Research Association. New Orleans, April 1984.
Gersten, R., D. Carnine, and P. Williams. "Measuring Implementation of a Structured Educational Model in an Urban Setting: An Observational Approach." *Educational Evaluation and Policy Analysis* 4 (1982): 67–79.
Guthrie, J. "Follow Through: A Compensatory Education Experiment." *The Reading Teacher* 3 (1977): 240–244.
Johnson, G., D. Carnine, and R. Gersten. "Computer-Assisted Vocabulary Instruction: Effects of Set Size and Review Cycles." Manuscript submitted for publication. Eugene: University of Oregon, 1985.
Kameenui, E., and D. W. Carnine. "An Investigation of Fourth-Graders' Comprehension of Pronoun Constructions in Ecologically Valid Texts." *Reading Research Quarterly* 17, 4 (1982): 556–580.
Kameenui, E., D. Carnine, and R. Freschi. "Effects of Text Construction and Instructional Procedures for Teaching Word Meanings on Comprehension and Recall." *Reading Research Quarterly* 17, 3 (1982): 367–388.
Kameenui, E., D. W. Carnine, and A. Maggs. "Instructional Procedures for Teaching Reversible Passive Voice and Clause Construction to Three Mildly Handicapped Children." *Exceptional Child* 27, 2 (1980): 29–40.
Maccoby, E. E., and M. Zellner. *Experiments in Primary Education: Aspects of Project Follow Through*. New York: Harcourt Brace Jovanovich, 1970.
Meyer, L. A. "Long-Term Academic Effects of the Direct Instruction Project Follow Through." *Elementary School Journal* 84, 4 (1984): 380–394.
Palincsar, A. S., and A. L. Brown. "Reciprocal Teaching of Comprehension-Fostering and Comprehension-Monitoring Activities." *Cognition and Instruction* 1 (1964): 117–175.
Patching, W., E. Kameenui, R. Gersten, and G. Colvin. "Direct Instruction in Critical Reading." *Reading Research Quarterly* 18, 4 (1983): 406–418.
Pearson, D. P. "Direct Explicit Teaching of Reading Comprehension." In *Comprehension Instruction: Perspectives and Suggestions*, 222–223, edited by G. G. Duffy, L. R. Roehler, and J. Mason. New York: Longman, 1984.
Resnick, L. "Discussion of 'Entry IQ and Yearly Achievement Gains with Direct Instruction.'" Presented at American Educational Research Association. Los Angeles, April 1981a.
Resnick, L. "Instructional Psychology." In *Annual Review of Psychology*, edited by M. R. Rosenweig and L. W. Porter. Palo Alto: Annual Review, 1981b.
Ross, D., and D. W. Carnine. "Analytic Assistance: Effects of Example Selection, Subjects' Age, and Syntactic Complexity." *Journal of Educational Research* 75 (1982): 294–298.
Singer, H., and D. Donlan. "Active Comprehension: Problem Solving Schema with Question Generation for Comprehension of Complex Short Stories," *Reading Research Quarterly* 2 (1982): 166–186.
Smith, B. "Critical Reading for Propaganda Techniques." Master's thesis. Rutgers University, 1974 (ERIC No. ED098530).

Stebbins, L. R., G. St. Pierre, W. C. Proper, R. B. Anderson, and T. R. Cerva. *Education as Experimentation: A Planned Variation Model, Vols. IVA-D*. Cambridge, Mass.: ABT Associates, 1977.

White, W. A. T., R. Gersten, and D. Carnine. "A Quantitative Analysis of Direct Instruction Interventions in the Intermediate and Secondary School Content Areas." Paper presented at the annual conference of the American Educational Research Association. Montreal, Quebec, April 1983.

Authors' Note: We wish to thank John Woodward, Bruce Shortland Jones, and Lynne Anderson-Inman for thoughtful, incisive feedback on earlier drafts of this manuscript, and John Lawrence for his assistance in the preparation of the dozen or so drafts of the manuscript.

Russell Gersten and Douglas Carnine are with the College of Education, University of Oregon.

From *Educational Leadership*, 1986, April, pp. 70–77. Used by permission.

Harth builds on his own research in applying Feuerstein's theory to teaching. This selection provides a review of Feuerstein's work with particular attention to the theory of *mediated learning experiences*, the Learning Potential Assessment Device, and *instrumental enrichment*. Harth carefully integrates applied examples into his theoretical discussion of Feuerstein's work.

The Feuerstein Perspective On the Modification of Cognitive Performance

Robert Harth

Education of exceptional children, particularly the mildly handicapped, is going through major changes. A new era of optimism is gradually taking hold. Feuerstein (1979) has brought this transition into perspective by describing the old and new approaches. The old approach, which he labels "passive-acceptant," is based on the assumption that low functioning individuals are not modifiable, that their present level of functioning is considered to be an adequate reflection of their potential. Educational programs based on this approach are primarily designed to prepare an individual to function at this low level. These programs mold the requirements and activities of the educational setting to fit the student's level of functioning. Thus, the student's educational program prepares him or her to function in a marginal, perhaps semi-dependent, environment.

The approach toward which we are moving is termed by Feuerstein as "active-modification." This approach looks at the exceptional individual as an open system, amenable to considerable modification under appropriate social, cultural, and educational policy. The observed low level of performance is accepted neither as status quo nor as a fixed ceiling of an individual's capacity. The emphasis with this approach is to move the individual toward increasingly higher levels of functioning.

Over the past 30 years, Feuerstein has been working toward the development of procedures to facilitate active-modification programs for exceptional students. This article will focus on four related topics. The first is the theory of *Mediated Learning Experience*, which is the theoretical base for Feuerstein's work. Second, we will look at the *Learning Potential Assessment Device,* Feuerstein's unique approach to the assessment of learning potential. Third, we will take a look at Feuerstein's curriculum for remediating cognitive deficits—*Instrumental Enrichment*. Finally, the article will discuss the implications of Feuerstein's work for the teaching of academic subjects.

THEORY OF MEDIATED LEARNING EXPERIENCE

Proper understanding of Dr. Feuerstein's work requires a discussion of his theory of mediated learning experience (MLE). The theory argues that development of cognitive structures in an individual is a function of an organism interacting with the environment in two ways.

The first of these interactions involves direct exposure to sources of stimuli that impinge on the organism, starting from the earliest stages of its development. This mode of interaction is the more universal of the two since it tends to be characteristic of most living organisms. Exposure to sources of stimuli affects the organism behaviorally and cognitively. This, in turn, affects its interaction with the environment.

The second type of interaction is the mediated learning experience. MLE is much less universal and more characteristic of man. It refers to the way in which a mediating agent transforms stimuli emitted by the environment for the growing organism. The mediating agent, usually a parent, sibling, or other caregiver:

> . . . guided by his intentions, culture and emotional investment, selects and organizes the world of stimuli for the child. The mediator selects stimuli that are most appropriate and then frames, filters, and schedules them: he determines the appearance or disappearance of certain stimuli and ignores others. (Feuerstein, 1980, p. 16)

By this mediating process, a child acquires behavior patterns and learning sets that eventually make it easier for him or her to become modified by direct exposure to stimuli. This becomes, of course, an extremely important process for the developing child. Direct exposure to stimuli constitutes the greatest part of the organism's experience. Thus, the existence of behavior patterns and learning sets (acquired through mediation) allows the child to learn from direct exposure to stimuli. With mediation individuals are able to frame, filter, and schedule direct stimuli themselves.

The MLE theory requires us to look at alternative ways of conceptualizing the etiology of retarded cognitive performance. Feuerstein (1980) has distinguished between what he calls the "distal etiology" and the "proximal etiology." The distal etiology includes things we traditionally assume to be the causes of retarded cognitive performance—hereditary/genetic factors, organicity, reduced environmental stimuli, socioeconomic status, emotional problems of child/parents, and so on. Feuerstein argues that these are not necessarily the direct causes of retarded performance. Rather than triggering the retarded performance, they instead trigger the proximal etiology—a lack of MLE. The lack of MLE is directly responsible for the cognitive deficit, regardless of the nature of the distal etiology. The important notion here is that if we can apply appropriate mediated learning experiences that can overcome or bypass the factors preventing mediation (distal etiologies), we can restore normal cognitive growth.

A lack of MLE means that a child has not had the environment intentionally mediated to him or her. As a result, the child will not be modified by direct exposure to stimuli. He or she will have limited ability to become modified by life situations and exposure to new situations. The child is bound to fail because there is no way of relating an event to what has preceded or to what will follow. The impact of this will be felt most in areas requiring cognitive behavior (i.e., academic work in school).

The performance of individuals who have not received MLE is characterized by a deficiency in the cognitive functions considered to be prerequisites to operational, internalized representational thinking. Over many years of clinical experience, Feuerstein has identified a number of these deficient functions. Table 1 represents a listing of the deficient functions identified thus far; the impaired deficient functions are categorized into the input, output, and elaboration levels.

At the input level, the impaired cognitive functions represent the things that affect the quality and quantity of data gathering as an individual begins to solve a given problem. The elaboration level includes deficient functions that prevent individuals from making efficient use of the data available to them. At the output level are factors that lead to inadequate communication of the results of an elaborative process.

Although these levels overlap considerably, distinguishing between them is important for diagnostic and prescriptive purposes. Failure to do this often results in mistakenly identifying a cognitive deficiency as a problem of elaboration when it may actually be a problem of input or output.

Feuerstein considers input and output as peripheral determinants of the cognitive

TABLE 1
Deficient Cognitive Functions

Input Level

1. Blurred and sweeping perception.
2. Unplanned, impulsive, and unsystematic exploratory behavior.
3. Lack of, or impaired, receptive verbal tools that affect discrimination.
4. Lack of, or impaired, spatial orientation.
5. Lack of, or impaired, temporal concepts.
6. Lack of, or impaired, conservation of constancies.
7. Lack of, or deficient, need for precision and accuracy in data gathering.
8. Lack of capacity for considering two or more sources of information at once; this is reflected in dealing with data in a piecemeal fashion, rather than as a unit of organized facts.

Elaboration Level

1. Inadequacy in the perception of the existence and definition of an actual problem.
2. Inability to select relevant vs. non-relevant cues in defining a problem.
3. Lack of spontaneous comparative behavior or limitation of its application by a restricted need system.
4. Narrowness of mental field.
5. Episodic grasp of reality.
6. Lack of, or impaired, need for pursuing logical evidence.
7. Lack of, or impaired, interiorization.
8. Lack of, or impaired, inferential-hypothetical thinking.
9. Lack of, or impaired, strategies for hypothesis testing.
10. Lack of, or impaired, ability to define the framework necessary for problem solving.
11. Lack of, or impaired, planning behavior.
12. Nonelaboration of certain cognitive categories, because the verbal concepts are not a part of the individual's verbal repertoire on a receptive level.

Output Level

1. Egocentric communication modalities.
2. Difficulty in projecting virtual relationships.
3. Blocking.
4. Trial-and-error responses.
5. Lack of, or impaired, tools for communicating adequately elaborated responses.
6. Lack of, or impaired, need for precision and accuracy in communicating one's responses.
7. Deficiency of visual transport.
8. Impulsive, acting out behavior.

Note: This table represents only a listing of the deficient functions. Readers are encouraged to read Chapter 4 of Feuerstein's *Instrumental Enrichment* (Baltimore: University Park Press, 1980), pp. 71–105, for a more complete description of the deficient cognitive functions.

processes and elaboration as a more central determinant. Elaboration is more essential for appropriate cognitive functioning. Deficiencies of input or output do not impair the child as much as do elaborational deficiencies. Because of difficulties at the input and output level, we often fail to see that elaboration is intact. In many instances, the elaboration problems we see are nothing more than the result of faulty input or output.

Central to Feuerstein's work is his concept of modifiability. Feuerstein notes that the deficient functions are not fixed. The MLE theory proposes that these deficient functions are amenable to change, regardless of the individual's age or developmental level.

THE LEARNING POTENTIAL ASSESSMENT DEVICE

The functioning of retarded performing individuals represents a problem in trying to assess these individuals' true capacities. Most approaches to assessing capacity focus on manifest functioning; that is, a series of cognitive tasks are presented to an individual in a structured way, making assumptions about capacity based upon the performance. Feuerstein (1979) argues that in assessing retarded performing individuals, one must abandon the focus on manifest functioning. He advocates, instead, an approach that looks at modified performance. In this "modificational assessment" one controls the deficient functions (see Figure 1), then observes performance.

Feuerstein's approach to this type of assessment is his *Learning Potential Assessment Device* (LPAD). The LPAD has five purposes: (1) to assess general learning modifiability, (2) to assess the extent of modifiability, (3) to assess the amount of teaching investment necessary to bring about changes, (4) to assess the probability of transfer of new learning to other areas, and (5) to determine appropriate strategies to bring about change in the individual.

The LPAD is typically administered on an individual basis (although a group version has been developed as well). In its administration a student is taught a series of problem-solving strategies and then is asked to use those strategies on a series of new and more difficult tasks. Central to the assessment is the identification of deficient cognitive functions and, then, the control of them in the teaching process.

Because of the nature of this device, Feuerstein has introduced four major changes in testing procedure. The first of these is a change in the examiner-examinee relationship. With the LPAD, the examiner becomes a teacher and the examinee becomes a learner. The examiner teaches problem-solving strategies and helps the examinee apply them to increasingly difficult tasks. The examiner does not have a rigidly defined script to be used during administration. Rather, the examiner has a set of guidelines that define the parameters of the task. From this point on the examiner uses whatever strategies are available to assure that the individual learns the principles inherent in the task.

The second change is in the structure of the test. The test instruments are similar to appropriately graduated, well sequenced educational curricula.

Another important change is a shift from a product to a process orientation. In most traditional tests the product of a cognitive process is what is important. The examiner is interested in determining if the student can come up with the correct answer to a problem. The LPAD is not concerned with what the student knows. It is more concerned with how an individual learns—what he or she does and does not do when trying to solve a problem. Perhaps even more important than either of the above is whether the student can be induced to do something different and thus come up with a more appropriate product.

The final change has to do with interpretation of test results. The LPAD is less concerned with scores than are most traditional tests. It tends to be more interested in a description of how the child learns. The focus of a typical testing report is on a narrative of the deficient cognitive functions, functions that are not deficient, and the individual's response to modification procedures.

The LPAD, then, involves a teach-test procedure. The child is taught a number of problem-solving strategies and then is tested to determine the extent to which he or she can become modified by instruction. Upon completion of the testing, several kinds of data are available. First, data is available on the extent of modifiability. Did the student learn? Did the student systematically apply what was taught? Related to the above is the issue of amount of investment. This is important not only to determine whether or not the student learned but also to determine how much instructional effort was necessary to produce successful learning. A third type of data available after testing is a description of the child's unique pattern of deficient functions. The examiner can identify these functions and describe how they impacted on the student's learning. After the assessment the examiner has a notion of the types of approaches to instruction that proved most useful.

INSTRUMENTAL ENRICHMENT

To remediate the deficient cognitive functions Feuerstein (1980) has developed a specific curriculum called *Instrumental Enrichment*. The aim of the program, as described by Feuerstein, is to:

> . . . change the overall cognitive structure of the retarded performer by transforming his passive and dependent cognitive style into the characteristic of an autonomous and independent thinker. (Feuerstein, 1980, p. 1)

The specific goals and objectives of Instrumental Enrichment are presented in Table 2.

Instrumental Enrichment is a paper-and-pencil curriculum administered three to five times a week over a two- to three-year period. Each lesson lasts about one hour and is typically used as part of the school program. The more than 500 pages of exercises are divided into 15 instruments. Each instrument focuses on a specific deficient cognitive function but addresses other cognitive functions as well. When typically applied as part of a large school program, it is taught to whole-class groups in a prescribed sequence. For prescriptive remedial purposes a clinician may select particular instruments to match the deficient functions of the pupil under treatment.

Each of the instruments is content-free; it does not address any specific curricular skill or content area. Rather, it focuses on the process of learning directly. The content

TABLE 2
Goals and Objectives of Instrumental Enrichment

Major Goal: To increase the capacity of the human organism to become modified through direct exposure to stimuli and experiences provided by encounters with life events and with formal and informal learning opportunities.

Major Subgoals:

1. The foremost subgoal is correction of the deficient cognitive functions.
2. Acquisition of basic concepts, labels, vocabulary, operations, and relationships necessary for instrumental enrichment.
3. Production of intrinsic motivation through habit formation.
4. Production of reflective, insightful processes in the student as a result of his confrontation with both his failing and succeeding behaviors.
5. Creation of task-intrinsic motivation.
6. A shift from the role of a passive recipient and reproducer of information to the role of a generator of information.

Note: From Feuerstein's *Instrumental Enrichment* (Baltimore, MD: University Park Press, 1980).

around which the instruments are built serve only as vehicles for development of the prerequisites of thinking.

Perhaps the best way to express the nature of the program is to describe the IE lesson. Although teacher's manuals are available, each lesson does not have a script. The teacher has to clearly define the objectives and scope of each lesson based upon the needs of the particular group of students. The manual gives guidelines and suggestions.

The lesson begins with an introductory discussion lasting about 10 minutes. The purpose is to define the problem in the lesson and to stimulate interest and motivation. As much as possible, definition of the problem is drawn from the students rather than being presented by the teacher.

The introductory discussion is followed by about 25 minutes of independent activity in which the students work on the problem. During this time the teacher circulates around the room offering individualized assistance, reinforcing successful mastery of the task, and preventing frustration or repetition of errors.

The independent work leads into a discussion and insight development period that lasts about 10 minutes. In this period the teacher and the students explore various thought processes and alternative responses used in the activity. Also, difficulties that were faced are analyzed, as well as ways in which the difficulties were overcome. An important element of this phase of the lesson is what Feuerstein calls "bridging." In bridging, the principles and processes learned are discussed in terms of their relevance to the real world. This, of course, becomes a critical determinant of generalization and transfer.

The lesson ends with a five-minute summary including a review of the lesson and an assessment of the degree to which the goals were achieved. When first using IE, the teacher does the summary. Later, this becomes the students' responsibility.

APPLICATION TO THE TEACHING OF ACADEMICS

As indicated earlier, typical application of the Feuerstein model is through *Instrumental Enrichment*. The procedures to be discussed were developed by the author (Harth, 1981) in two special education classes in Sedalia, Missouri.

Feuerstein is skeptical about the use of curricular content learning for enhancing and modifying cognitive performance. In fact, he has identified a number of problems associated with this (Feuerstein, 1980, pp. 120–133). The first has to do with the nature of disabled learners who tend to be action-oriented and unwilling to operate beyond the solution of content activities. Once the problem is solved, students like this are unwilling to enter into a discussion of the material or into an analysis of its various components and the relationship existing between them. The second set of problems relates to the nature of content material itself. Curricular content has its own structure and sequence that do not always coincide with that needed for producing cognitive changes. A third problem relates to the teacher. Teachers tend to not be trained in the area of recognizing prerequisites of cognitive behavior. Consequently, they have difficulty recognizing cognitive deficiencies when they occur. Finally, Feuerstein is concerned about previous failure. Most of these children have histories of failure with curriculum content, which produces resistance to full involvement.

These problems identified by Feuerstein certainly make the challenge of producing cognitive changes more difficult if one is to use curricular content materials. Even so, it was felt that if one were to use *Instrumental Enrichment*, change could be facilitated if similar procedures for teaching could be used for dealing with academics.

In applying the Feuerstein model to teaching curriculum content, the *Learning Potential Assessment Device* proved quite useful. This is because the LPAD offers a structured approach for teaching cognitive material. Through this approach one is able to respond to the deficient cognitive functions, as well as to other aspects of cognitive problem solving. Teaching in the LPAD is directed not only at teaching specific content, but it also tries to establish the prerequisites to cognitive functioning and the necessary behaviors for problem solving.

In translating the LPAD approach to classroom teaching, one major adjustment must be made. The LPAD is an individually administered device. The examiner, who is always in contact with the student, can adjust the teaching and respond directly to each student's specific needs. In classroom teaching, teachers tend to deal with groups of students. As a result, they are not always in direct one-to-one contact with students. This requires the introduction of mediation directly into the written assignments presented to the students. (This will be discussed more fully later in the article.)

Feuerstein (1979) has described five aspects of the teaching process in the LPAD: (1) regulation of behavior through inhibition and control of impulsivity, (2) improvement of deficient cognitive functions, (3) enrichment of the repertoire of mental operations, (4) enrichment of the task-related contentual repertoire, and (5) creation of reflective, insightful thought processes. These five points also form the basis for teaching academics under the Feuerstein model.

Regulation of Behavior through Inhibition and Control of Impulsivity

This deficient cognitive function tends to be a major problem with many retarded performing students. It is the most frequently noted of the deficient functions, and the first to which a teaching response is required. This impulsivity, seen at the input, elaboration, and output levels, is a major source of errors in the problem-solving behavior of these students. One of the major ways of controlling impulsivity is for the teacher to impose a latency in responding.

An example of this procedure occurred in the work in Sedalia. In a group lesson the teacher would ask a question and the students would immediately blurt out answers. To initially counter this, the teacher required the students to write out their answers before orally responding. This imposed a time lapse between presentation of the problem and discussion of the response. The result was a tendency to reduce some of the impulsivity and increase more thoughtful behavior.

When some control of impulsivity through this procedure was observed, the teacher began to phase out the procedure and to introduce the use of cue words to regulate behavior. After asking a question, the teacher would initially say "stop," then "think," then "raise your hand." These words were eventually put on a sign in the classroom and the teachers would point to them at appropriate times.

Improvement of Deficient Cognitive Functions

The second aspect of the teaching process involves improvement of deficient cognitive functions. Impulsivity is not the only deficient function seen in retarded performing students. Each student has a unique pattern of deficient functions.

Deficient functioning tends to be a far greater problem when the students are working by themselves. Without the teacher's constant vigilance, problem-solving behavior tends to break down. In this situation a whole complex of deficient functions commonly begin to show up. This complex can be defined by the following deficient functions.

At the Input Level

1. Blurred and sweeping perception.
2. Unplanned, impulsive, and unsystematic exploratory behavior.

At the Elaboration Level

3. Inadequacy in the perception of the existence and definition of an actual problem.
4. Inability to select relevant versus non-relevant cues in defining a problem.
5. Lack of, or impaired, ability to define the framework necessary for problem solving.
6. Lack of, or impaired, planning behavior.

At the Output Level

7. Trial-and-error responses.
8. Impulsive, acting-out behavior.

The result of all of this is that the student presents a disorganized approach to the task, reflecting a lack of investment in the task. To counter this kind of problem solving, a rather elaborate procedure must be applied to the variety of independent seatwork activities presented to the students. Table 3 gives an example of one way in which this problem can be handled. The example comes out of the work in Sedalia mentioned earlier.

In the figure, two versions of a seatwork assignment are presented. The first is the assignment in its traditional form. This is usually presented to a group of students following an introductory activity introducing the task. The second is the modified version designed to control the complex of deficient functions identified earlier. The modified version contains two sets of directions. The first set consists of instructions typically included on the top of the page. The second set is written specifically for each item on the worksheet. These appear below each item.

Data were collected on the use of this particular assignment to determine if it would promote better performance. The traditional assignment was given on one day, followed by the modified assignment on the next day. Two days later the students were given the traditional assignment again, this time with new sentences. Each assignment had 20 sentences. The results, shown in Table 4, clearly reveal that the strategy was effective in helping the students increase their effectiveness on those assignments.

These are not the only deficient functions seen in retarded performing students. A lack of spontaneous comparative behavior tends to be a rather common deficiency. In most cases, these students *can* compare, but they do not do so spontaneously. The curriculum is rich in possibilities for using comparative behavior. Science, social studies, current events, math, and so on all provide opportunities for comparison. The teachers should make sure that comparative behavior is required.

Lack of planning behavior, a deficient function identified earlier, also tends to create problems. Often, students jump into a task without planning ahead of time what they are going to do. A number of activities can facilitate planning behavior. Before starting a task the teacher must assist the students in identifying their plan of attack. One useful activity is to have students plan out their day when they arrive in school.

TABLE 3
Examples of Traditional and Modified Assignment

WRITING TITLES (Traditional)

Titles of complete books are usually underlined when handwritten. Titles of parts of books (chapters, songs, poems, stories) are usually in quotation marks. All important words are capitalized. Use capitals where needed. Underline or put titles in quotes.

1. Mark Twain wrote the book tom sawyer.
2. Who wrote the song the star-spangled banner?
3. . . . .

WRITING TITLES (Modified)

Titles of complete books are usually underlined when handwritten. Titles of parts of books (chapters, songs, poems, stories) are usually in quotation marks. All important words are capitalized. Use capitals where needed. Underline or put titles in quotes.

1. Mark Twain wrote the book tom sawyer.
   A. Find the title.
   B. Will you underline it or put quotation marks around it?
   C. What words will you capitalize?
2. Who wrote the song the star-spangled banner?
   A. Find the title.
   B. Will you underline it or put quotation marks around it?
   C. What words will you capitalize?
3. . . . .

Note: See R. Harth, R. Johns, C. Cloud, & C. Campbell, "Mediation: How it can improve problem solving skills" *Academic Therapy,* 1981, 17, 225–230.

The teacher can start by just assisting them in planning the school day. Eventually, this can extend to planning after-school and evening activities—which is much more complicated because more choices are available; students have to balance things such as play, chores, eating, and television in their plans.

The above are only a few examples of the kinds of activities that can be done in response to deficient functions. In the project in Sedalia, these and other strategies were generated through a process of observing poor problem solving, identifying the deficient function, and brainstorming strategies that might control the behavior. These strategies were tested and their impact was determined. The example presented earlier, "Writing Titles," was derived from this process.

TABLE 4
Percentage of Correct Responses on Each of the Three Assignments

Student	Traditional	Modified	Follow-up (Traditional)
	(%)	(%)	(%)
A	37	88	87
B	52	91	89
C	42	100	81
D	35	80	88
E	32	100	87
F	63	83	94
G	84	88	90

Two additional issues require discussion. The first has to do with the permanence of changes produced. Retarded performers have developed a number of ineffective approaches to problem solving. The procedures defined above should facilitate a change. For the change to be meaningful, however, it has to become habitual. The student has to use the approach regularly without a need for teacher reminders. The only way this will occur is if the teacher consistently requires the use of appropriate strategies over time. For instance, planning behavior will become habitual only if the teacher constantly requires the student to plan.

The second issue is independence. The techniques described above are, for the most part, imposed by a teacher on a student. For example, in the task "Writing Titles," the teacher essentially imposed an effective problem-solving structure on the students. This has to be seen as only a starting point. Eventually the students need to be able to impose their own structure on a task. This issue, and procedures for addressing it, are discussed in the section, "The Creation of Reflective, Insightful Thought Processes."

Enrichment of the Repertoire of Mental Operations

The third aspect of the teaching process involves enrichment of the student's repertoire of mental operations. By including this as part of the teaching process, Feuerstein (1979) is saying that the LPAD responds not only to the deficient functions but also tries to enrich the student's mental operations. Here, use of the Feuerstein model to teach content differs from teaching in both the LAPD and in Instrumental Enrichment. In both the LPAD and Instrumental Enrichment, the appearance of mental operations such as analogies, categorization, progressions, seriation, and so on are highly structured. They appear in systematic ways and can be dealt with in systematic ways. When the medium of intervention is curriculum content, the appearance of these operations is not as structured. Curriculum content has its own structure, and we can respond to the operations only when they occur. This is not to say that one cannot respond to the mental operations, but the intensity of response will not be at the same level as with the LPAD or with Instrumental Enrichment. This is a strong argument for the combined use of Instrumental Enrichment and these content teaching procedures.

Enrichment of the Task-Related Contentual Repertoire

The next aspect of the teaching process is enrichment of the task-related contentual repertoire. Essentially, what Feuerstein is talking about is that certain concepts must be present for efficient problem solving to take place. Specifically, such content can be grouped into three categories.

The first category is made up of *orientation* concepts. This refers to things such as left, right, up, down, before, after, vertical, horizontal, and so forth. The second category is formed by concepts dealing with *relationships between objects and events*. These include concepts such as identical, opposite, common, similar, different. For any type of relational thinking, these concepts are required. The final category involves *labels for specific objects or events and their characteristics*. This includes not only the ability to label but to describe characteristics as well.

Without sufficient background in these three areas, students have tremendous difficulty in solving curricular problems. It means that the teacher must be checking constantly to see that these concepts are accessible to the student and be prepared to provide specific instruction if they are not.

Creation of Reflective, Insightful Thought Processes

Perhaps the most important aspect of the teaching process is the creation of reflective, insightful thought processes. Insight is defined as an awareness of one's own problem-solving behaviors. It is essential for generalization and transfer, particularly for processes that are newly learned and, therefore, vulnerable. Throughout teaching, the teacher continually strives to provoke reflective thinking in the student.

Reflective thinking is encouraged by having students analyze behaviors that have led to a given outcome, whether that outcome was a success or a failure. When confronted with failure, the individual should be able to isolate the particular causes, and even relate them to the deficient functions—for instance, "I got the problem wrong because I didn't look at the whole problem" (blurred and sweeping perception). When the student is successful, he/she should be able to do the same thing.

Reflective, insightful thinking is also facilitated by having students identify the process they used to solve a particular problem. Initially, the teacher may identify the process for them, but eventually they must identify the process for themselves. Fig. 1

presents an example of an arithmetic assignment in which the process is presented to the student. Figure 2 gives an example of an assignment in which the student must identify the process himself/herself.

Some additional techniques for creating reflective, insightful thought are:

1. Questioning reasons for responses.
2. Discussing how the correct answer was attained.
3. Comparing present performance with how a student used to approach similar problems.
4. Discussing systematic ways to approach a problem.
5. Questioning and discussing sources of error.
6. Distinguishing between correct and incorrect parts of answers.
7. Generating similar examples for generalization.

The creation of reflective, insightful thinking is directed not only at the problem-solving process but also the curriculum content itself. In teaching, the concern is not only with the correct answer but also with having students think about their work. Teacher questioning must go beyond the "right" answer. Students must be asked to do a number of things: to speculate about implications of certain events, to discuss the application of information learned in various subject areas, to project the meaning of events into the future. Students must be asked what they think led to a certain event—i.e., what may have caused something to happen. In summary, students are asked to put themselves into situations that arise in the content of the curriculum.

Figure 3 presents an excerpt from a worksheet designed to encourage reflective, insightful thinking. The worksheet is from a lesson used in the project in Sedalia. Some of the items on the worksheet are simple, direct questions that require nothing more than finding the answer in the newspaper. Items 5, 6, and 10, however, can be answered only by reflection and insight. The figure contains one of these, Item 5.

FIGURE 1 Worksheet With Process Written Out

Math — Reducing Fractions

1. Write all of the factors.
2. Write all of the common factors.
3. Circle the largest common factor.
4. Divide by the largest common factor.

		N	D	Common factors	Divide
Example:	3/6 = 1/2	1,3	1,6,2,3	1,3	3/6 ÷ 3 = 1/2
		N	D	common factors	Divide

1. 2/4 = ______
2. 3/9 = ______
3. 2/10 = ______
4. 6/8 = ______
5. 6/12 = ______
6. 4/12 = ______

FIGURE 2 Worksheet for Identifying the Process

Math

1. Work the problem

$$\begin{array}{r} 24\text{-}4/5 \\ +\ 17\text{-}1/2 \\ \hline \end{array}$$

2. Write the process

1.
2.
3.
4.
5.
6.
7.
8.
9.
10.
11.
12.
13.
14.

Mediated Learning Experience

The previous sections of this article have essentially defined a mediated learning experience approach to teaching curriculum content. Before leaving this topic, the three major criteria for this approach to teaching (Feuerstein, 1980) are briefly discussed below.

The first criterion is *intentionality*. Mediation is an intentional act in which both teacher and student are aware of what is happening. When the teacher, for instance, points out a sequence of events to the student, it is done intentionally to convey to the student the idea that it is important. Thus, this criterion creates in the student the appropriate orientation to the task, the readiness to attend to the task, and the ability to focus and persevere.

The second criterion is *transcendence*. With any instructional interaction the teacher is trying to do at least two things. First, of course, the teacher is trying to teach the particular task. But the teacher should be doing more than that. The teacher should also be teaching strategies that transcend the immediate task. He/she should be developing skills that are useful not only for the immediate task, but that can be used in solving other problems as well. In controlling the deficient functions, in sensitizing the student to the process, the teacher is transcending the immediate task. Transcendent goals determine the nature of intervention in a mediated learning experience. This second criterion—transcendence—allows the student to use the acquired principles, rules, and functions for more remote types of tasks. This becomes a major factor in the generalization and transfer of learning.

FIGURE 3 Excerpts from a Worksheet Requiring Reflective, Insightful Teaching

Reading the Newspaper

Page Two

Find the headline, "Officials Say Chapman Planned Slaying."

Circle paragraphs one through five.

1. Who was John Lennon? (tell two things about him) ____________________

A. Read the question.
B. Circle the key words.
C. Find the key words on the board.
D. Think about the discussion.

4. What do most killers do after they shoot someone? ____________________

A. Read the question.
B. Circle the key words.
C. Think.
D. What would you do?

5. Why do you think Chapman did what he did after killing Lennon? ____________________

A. Read the question.
B. Circle the key words.
C. Think.
D. Why would he just sit down?

7. How many months had Chapman been working for Liva? ____________________

A. Read the question.
B. Circle the key words.
C. Find the key words in the article.
D. Think. You will have to do a little math.

The third criterion of mediated learning experience is the mediation of *meaning*. Performance on a task should be a response to a need. One of the characteristics of retarded performing students is that they are not motivated to perform cognitive tasks. As a result, the teacher must create and reinforce the need for performance. To the extent that the teacher is successful here, the student's need system will be enlarged and the potential for higher levels of motivation and achievement need will be created.

SUMMARY AND CONCLUSIONS

A mediated learning experience approach offers possibilities for the education of retarded performing students. An approach to assessment and two instructional approaches were discussed in this article. The question at this point is whether one should use both approaches to instruction or whether one will suffice.

Instrumental enrichment, as it is traditionally taught, pays little attention to the teaching of content. Similarly, content approaches most often do not attend to the cognitive processes. Instrumental enrichment, combined with the kinds of content teaching procedures identified in this paper, appear to offer the best chance for producing the most in the way of cognitive redevelopment. Both make unique contributions to the other. This is not to say that one, by itself, will not produce change but that combined, the possibility of change is expanded.

REFERENCES

Feuerstein, R. (1979). *The dynamic assessment of retarded performers*. Baltimore, MD: University Park Press.

Feuerstein, R. (1980). *Instrumental enrichment*. Baltimore, MD: University Park Press.

Harth, R. (1981). *The Sedalia project*. Unpublished manuscript.

Harth, R., Johns, R., Cloud, C., & Campbell, C. (1981). Mediation: How it can improve problem solving skills. *Academic Therapy, 17*, 225–230.

Robert Harth is Chairperson of the Department of Special Education, National College of Education, Evanston, Illinois.

The authors discuss the complex process of developing communication through non-traditional communication systems for severely and multiply handicapped students. They stress the importance of interdisciplinary teams in the development and initiation of auxiliary communication programs. A seven-step decision-making model is presented in a manner that is easily understood. The authors provide guidelines for selecting commercially produced automated communication systems and for developing teacher-made systems.

Selection and Initiation of a Nonvocal Communication Program for Severely Handicapped Students

Paul A. Alberto, Elizabeth Garrett, Thomas Briggs, and Forrest Umberger

As the public schools assume responsibility for the education of more severely and multiply handicapped students, special education teachers and speech pathologists increasingly encounter students for whom traditional verbal language programming is not appropriate. With these students the challenge is to develop functional communication through nontraditional communication systems. These systems are referred to as auxiliary (nonvocal) language programs; they include manual communication, communication aids, and communication codes (Nietupski & Hamre-Nietupski, 1979).

The decision to initiate an auxiliary communication program cannot be made by a single teacher or clinician. Integrated consideration must be given to the language, cognitive, social, emotional, and physical characteristics of the student. It is a decision, therefore, requiring complex professional judgment based on input from members of a variety of disciplines (e.g., special education, speech pathology, physical therapy, occupational therapy, and psychology) and the student's parents.

THE SEVEN-STEP DECISION-MAKING SEQUENCE

We are proposing here a seven-step sequence for decision making to assist the interdisciplinary team in making a systematic and logical communication programming decision (Fig. 1 diagrams this process). This decision sequence will guide the team from the initial consideration of a student's verbal potential, through the selection of an appropriate alternative nonvocal program, and finally to the procedure necessary for successful program initiation.

FIGURE 1 Steps in Consideration and Implementation of Nonvocal Language Programming

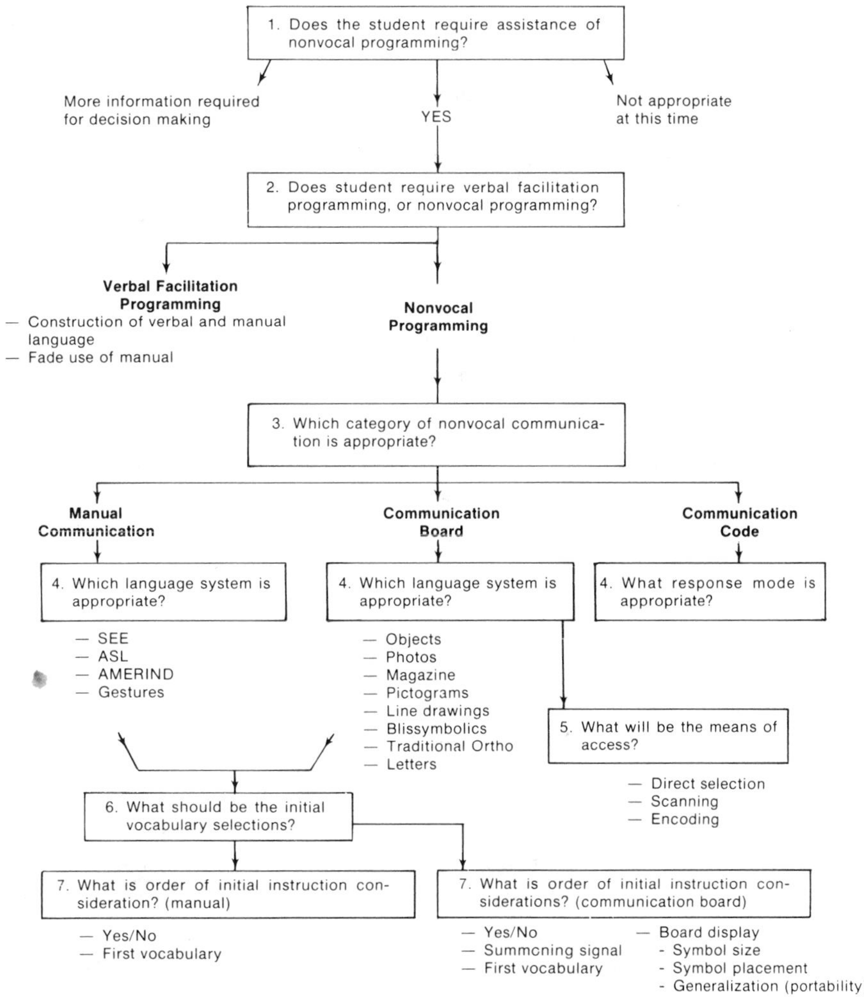

Decision Step 1: Should a Nonvocal System be Considered?

The first decision to be made upon a student's referral for auxiliary communication training is whether a nonvocal system is appropriate for the student at this time. For some students trial speech therapy or cognitive instruction may be considered prior to, or in conjunction with, nonvocal programming. To assist in making this decision, six factors should be considered.

1. *Evaluation of the vocal mechanism*. When evaluating a student, consideration must be given to the structure of the vocal mechanism and the nature of the student's oral reflexes. Are there physiological impediments to successful vocal production? An abnormality of the vocal mechanism that prevents phonation or production of intelligible speech is an immediate indicator that a nonvocal system is necessary. Examples of *mechanism abnormalities* include paresis of the tongue that impairs the timing of the rapid ballistic movement, contractions or atrophy of the palate, and mandibular facet slip (Achilles, 1955).

Evaluative attention must also be given to the student's oral reflexes. Uncontrolled release of primitive reflexes may interfere with voluntary and selective control of the speech mechanism. Mysak (1963) has listed the following as indicators of these *uncontrolled reflexes:*

- Cephalic reactions: irregular movement of head upon stimulation of facial area.
- Facial response: pouting protrusion of lips upon tapping around lips.
- "Rooting" reactions: movement of face toward side of tactile stimulus of lips and mouth.
- Biting reflex: biting action upon placing stimulus object between teeth or gums.
- Suckling reflex: forward upward and backward movement of tongue upon touching stimulus to teeth, tongue, gums, or hard palate.
- Chewing reflex: chewing movements resulting from placing stimulation object between teeth.

2. *Quality of the student's current communication*. Although a student may be vocalizing, the quality of communication may not be sufficiently functional in all current or future settings. If the intelligibility of a student's present communication abilities is limited to a select, familiar audience (e.g., teacher, parent), communication is not truly functional. When addressing the question of *functional quality of communication,* it should be required that the student's communication be understood by at least three people who are unfamiliar with the student, in at least three settings (Vanderheiden, 1981). This is especially important when considering a student's need to move between educational placements (e.g., special education class to regular education class) and to participate in vocational and community experiences outside the school setting.

When evaluating the quality of speech production of students exhibiting neuromuscular handicaps, it should be remembered that a majority of these children's speech is dysarthric. Specifically, the student's capacity to produce smooth, coordinated motor responses affecting potential intelligibility is inhibited by a group of motor disorders affecting articulation, respiration, and voice (Nicolosi, Harryman, & Kresheck, 1978). Evaluation of these components of production may lead to an interim decision for speech therapy, prior to a final decision for a nonvocal program.

The articulation of neurologically impaired children reflects deficits in sounds that require fine coordination and ballistic movements of the tongue and other musculature. The speech sounds of a student with cerebral palsy, for example, may be distorted because of the slow rate and laborious movements of the speech musculature. Some sounds may be omitted because of the time element; paralysis or sounds that can be produced with less effort may be substituted. Irwin's (1961) articulation test for use with cerebral palsied children may provide useful information in deciding whether a student should be considered for a nonvocal system.

Observation of respiration during speech may reveal inadequate breathing caused by weak musculature, opposition of the muscles of inhalation and exhalation, or improper coupling of the breath stream to the nasal passages as a result of palatal paresis. If the student lacks control of breathing or breath-stream management because of release phenomena or inability to inhibit primitive reflexes, the physical therapist may be able to select reflex inhibiting postures that will allow the student to exert voluntary control over the breathing mechanism. The objective is for the student to eventually inhibit the interfering reflex phenomena in the absence of the reflex inhibiting postures.

According to Mecham, Berko, Berko, and Palmer (1966), voice difficulties require only the ability of the examiner to recognize normal voice patterns and quality. To assess adequacy of voice for communication purposes, they have suggested the following questions:

- Are intensity and intensity-change adequate to meet the needs of the average speaking situation?
- Is the pitch flexible and appropriate for the age and sex of the individual?
- Is the quality unusually nasal or hoarse, etc.?
- Can a steady tone be prolonged at least 10 seconds?
- Are variations in the voice pitch and intensity smooth and controlled or jerky and irregular?
- Do prosodic aspects of the voice sound normal, or does the student sound like he/she has a peculiar accent?
- Can the student coordinate voice with articulation (i.e., produce appropriate voice for voiced sounds and eliminate voice on voiceless sounds)?
- Does the voice sound metallic or raspy?
- Does voice pitch break into a falsetto occasionally?

The primary question to answer when evaluating voice production is not whether the voice quality is within "normal" limits as measured against the general population, but whether the voice quality deviates sufficiently to mask out intelligibility of speech articulation. A student who may sound strange as a result of a voice quality deviation, but who is still intelligible to naive listeners, would probably not be a candidate for a nonvocal communication system. For students exhibiting voice qualities that interfere with speech articulation intellibility, a period of trial voice therapy would be the probable choice before making a decision regarding a nonvocal communication system.

3. *Current cognitive functioning*. The relationship of the emergence of an individual's intentional communication (i.e., gestures and holophrastic speech) with the attainment of Stage V of the sensorimotor period (Piaget, 1952) continues to receive the attention of language researchers (Bates, 1976; Bates, Camaioni, & Volterra, 1975; Ingram, 1981; Reichle & Yoder, 1979). Chapman and Miller (1980) have suggested that mastery of Stage V is a prerequisite to successful use of an auxiliary communication system. With mastery of Stage V the student has developed a number of cognitive abilities. The abilities of attending, imitation, and an understanding of causality are of primary importance to the coordination of communication and are considered to be prerequisite to effective communication programming.

Attending is a basic cognitive function that involves the ability to focus upon an object in space visually, auditorially, or tactually, and track the object as it changes position. Attending is essential for the instruction of a nonvocal system. For example, in the case of a manual system, the student must be able to visually attend to the individual who performs a sign. In the case of a communication board system, the student must be able to attend to the symbols that appear on the board. Furthermore, nonvocal systems with deaf-blind students require attention to tactile stimuli.

Associated with the prerequisite ability to attend is the ability to perform successful *imitation*. Prior to auxiliary communication instruction, the student must be able to imitate motor responses. These may be either the motor responses necessary for imitation of a manual sign, or imitation of the movements used in selecting a symbol on a communication board.

Although attending and imitation are practiced during earlier sensorimotor levels, the higher order language prerequisite of *recognition of causality* does not come into place until mastery of Stage V (Piaget, 1952). Causality is the ability to understand the relationship between cause and effect. With mastery of Stage V, the student not only understands that his/her behavior will have a consequence that alters the environment, but also realizes that tools may be used as part of his/her behavior to produce a desired effect. For example, the child pulls a small rug to retrieve an out-of-reach object resting on the rug (Flavell, 1977); the child understands that a spoon can be used to get pudding from a bowl to his/her mouth. Similarly, gestures and holophrastic speech must be understood by the child as tools (the means) to produce a desired effect (e.g., pointing to or saying "cookie" prompts another person to give the child a cookie). This recognition of the use of language as a tool for change is essential to intentional communication.

Complex or expanded language ability (i.e., beyond the one-word stage) is associated with mastery of Stage VI of the sensorimotor period (Bates et al., 1975; Ingram, 1981). Stage VI is the culmination of the student's ability to "reproduce an absent model through memory" (Robinson & Robinson, 1978). This ability is characterized as an *understanding of object permanence*. Object permanence is demonstrated by a student's understanding that when a stimulus disappears from the visual, auditory, or tactual field, it still has existence. Language becomes the symbolic representation of absent objects or concepts. The understanding that a concept exists in the absence of an immediate referent enables the student to use language representationally to effect environmental change. With the understanding of object permanence, the student's verbalizations and gestures are no longer stimulus-bound.

Coincident with mastery of sensorimotor Stage VI, breadth of vocabulary and length of utterance increase (Ingram, 1981). Therefore, to consider whether a communication system should involve expanded vocabulary and multi-word utterances, the degree of a student's understanding of object permanence should be considered.

4. *Previous verbal training attempts, student age, and remaining instructional time*. Before initiating nonvocal training, one must evaluate the data resulting from prior instructional attempts at verbal language training. The teacher and the speech pathologist must make a determination that, after good faith efforts at verbal language instruction over time, the student has not made expected progress (Scheuerman, Baumgart, Spisma, & Brown, 1976). Within the analysis, the teacher and clinician must decide if they also have been able to deal effectively with *interfering behaviors*, such as stereotypic behaviors, to validate that these have not been the cause of delayed language acquisition. Elimination of interfering behavior should be addressed prior to a change in language training approaches.

It is also necessary to determine whether lack of progress or attempts at communication may be attributed to inhibition for *emotional* rather than cognitive/language or production reasons. If so, intervention to meet the social/emotional needs of the student may be necessary before beginning a nonvocal program.

Consideration of chronological age in relationship to developmental age or cognitive level is necessary. A reasonable delay in acquisition of verbal language should be expected as a function of the student's diminished level of cognitive functioning. The student may reach a chronological age or grade level at which the expectation of verbal competence is not reasonable given that the time remaining in the educational setting is so limited. At this point, the immediate need for functional communication takes precedence over continued emphasis on verbal language training and requires initiation of an alternative communication program.

5. *Analysis of current expressive and receptive language levels*. If a significant discrepancy between expressive and receptive vocabulary exists, a nonvocal system should be considered. That a student understands a larger vocabulary than he/she uses is not unexpected. But a comparative assessment of receptive and expressive vocabulary that reveals a significant expressive lag may indicate the presence of *production obstacles*, particularly when the lag is as much as two years. A nonvocal system can circumvent product impediment. Thus, for students with significant expressive/recep-

Phillips Memorial
Library
Providence College

tive discrepancy, a nonvocal system should be considered as a means toward recognizing language potential indicated by the higher receptive measure.

6. *Recognition of the student's current attempts at communication.* Prerequisite to initiation of a nonvocal program is the student's recurrent attempts to communicate (Vanderheiden, 1981). These attempts may be recognized by the presence of metacommunication, functional-motor communication, or differentiated vocalizations.

Metacommunication is evidenced when the student responds in recognizable, consistent patterns to changes in his/her environment. These responses may be vocalizations such as crying when in discomfort and laughing when being tickled. Metacommunication indicates expressive communication at the most elementary level.

Functional-motor communication is evidenced when the student uses motor behavior to indicate wants or needs. This may be represented by students' pointing to desired objects or pulling the teacher in their direction.

Differentiated vocalizations are consistent pairings of nonstandard phonations with objects and experiences. Because of their pattern of association, they become recognizable as expressive cues for environmental referents.

Decision Step 2: Should a Verbal Facilitation Program be Initiated?

An augmentation program of nonvocal techniques is a temporary support system. Its purpose is to facilitate verbal communication for a student with an intact vocal mechanism. The primary instructional goal, therefore, remains that of verbal competence.

Selection of a facilitation approach rather than a full nonvocal approach may be considered if current verbal language usage is limited as a result of (a) poor articulation or other intelligibility problems, (b) minimal vocabulary pool, (c) discrepancy between receptive and expressive capability, (d) minimal degree of language generalization, and (e) inhibition because of emotional problems.

Manual signing is a frequently used facilitation approach. Current data suggest that use of a signing system will not inhibit development of verbal language (Harris-Vanderheiden, Brown, MacKenzie, Reiner, & Scheibel, 1975). In fact, recent studies have reported that signing may enhance development of verbal language (Grinnell, Detamore, & Lippke, 1976; Kahn, 1975; Kotkin & Simpson, 1976; Reich, 1978). Speculation on the facilitative role of manual communication involves several theories. Initiation of a sign may serve as a supplementary discriminative stimulus for making an oral response. The sign may give the student a constant feedback loop for verbal expression, or formation of the sign may provide a pacing monitor as a guide for production of verbal language as the sign user pairs verbalization with the sign. Production of the sign may serve to distract the student from anxiety he/she has developed or associated with production of the verbalization.

Because manual systems have been demonstrated to facilitate the emergence of language, manual communication is the nonvocal program of choice to enhance a student's skills in verbal expression. As verbal responses increase, manual augmentation is progressively faded (Schaeffer, 1980; Schaeffer, Kollinzas, Musil, & McDowell, 1977).

Decision Step 3: Which Nonvocal Category Should be Selected?

After deciding that the student is indeed a candidate for nonvocal communication training, the next determination is which of the three categories of nonvocal communication—*manual communication, communication board,* or *communication code*—would best suit the needs and capabilities of this particular student. To make this decision, the following information should be gathered and considered.

1. *Does the student currently gesture?* When the student is making attempts at communication, is this gesturing to indicate some item that he/she wants or some feeling about himself/herself? Indications that the student does consistently use gestures in this way support a decision for a manual system.

2. *What is the student's degree of visual acuity?* A student with poorer visual acuity is more likely to be a candidate for a communication board system. A teacher cannot alter the size of the signing hand to accommodate visual impairment, but one can easily alter the size of symbols placed on a communication board or raise symbols using clay or wooden cutouts similar to a Braille concept.

3. *What is the efficiency of the student's imitation skill?* The more efficient the student is at imitating, the more one would lean toward a manual system. Because of the complex patterns of movement involved in producing a sign, the student's imitation ability must be efficient and consistent to ensure accuracy and intelligibility. Alternatively, if the student is less efficient at imitating, one would lean toward a communication board. The only imitation required if the student is going to be a board user is the ability to imitate the single-symbol selection response the teacher models.

4. *What is the student's fine-motor capability and range of motion?* The more proficient the student is in fine-motor skills, the more likely a candidate he/she is for a manual system, as he/she will be able to make the intricate fine-motor movements necessary for forming signs. In the case of the motorically limited student, a board system requires a single operant response by the student to select the appropriate symbol. In most instances this response will be a pointing response or a movement to depress a switch. Technological aids can enhance a simple response (e.g., head movement, puff of air, slight finger movement) and couple that response with an electronic board system. While a signing system may require expansive use of the upper extremities, and therefore a wide range of motion, a board system may incorporate technology and prosthetic devices to facilitate symbol selection.

5. *What is the degree of the student's memory deficit?* The greater the memory deficit, the more is the indication for a board system. When the student uses a communication board, the symbols are static and in constant view. A board system presents ready recognition memory cues. A signing system requires the student to maintain all the signs and all their referents in memory without concrete retrieval or recall

memory cues. Thus, a board system best assists students who have difficulty with memory and retrieval skills.

6. *What is the degree of necessity, current or potential, for naive communicators to have access to the student's communication system?* The more diverse the group of individuals with whom the student comes in contact, the greater is the need for a nonvocal system that can be immediately engaged and understood. The need for access to a large, diverse community supports implementation of a communication board system. Regardless of symbol choice on a board, the printed word always appears in conjunction with the symbol. Conversely, a manual system is efficient only with another person who is equally fluent in that particular sign system.

7. *To what degree will the student be able to conform to a traditional system with only minor modifications?* A manual system that must be significantly tailored to the student's production capacity is probably not the system of choice. A manual system requires that the student learn and maintain a predetermined set of signs. Modification of a traditional sign system reduces the universality of understanding of the student's vocabulary. Individuals who are unfamiliar with the student's modifications cannot understand his/her particular language. Thus, the audience is severely limited. The pairing of printed words with symbols on a communication board, however, enables symbol modification to the maximum extent necessary for the board user without masking meaning. When the need for extensive modification presents itself, a board system is preferable.

8. *Do the parents have preferences?* Parental agreement and involvement in decisions concerning the nonvocal system to be used are important. Parental preference should be taken into account to ensure that use of the nonvocal system is generalized beyond the classroom into the home.

Decision Step 4:
Within the Chosen Category, Which Language System Should be Selected?

Once the interdisciplinary team has selected which of the three major categories of nonvocal communication is most appropriate for the student, a determination of the language system within the chosen category must be made.

Category of Manual Communication

If manual communication has been selected as the most appropriate category for the student, the team may then select from several manual language systems: *idiosyncratic gesturing* (Hamre-Nietupski et al., 1977), *American Indian Sign* (Skelley, 1977; Skelley, Schinsky, Smith, Donaldson, & Griffin, 1975; Tomkins, 1969), *American Sign Language* (Fant, 1972), or *Signing Exact English* (Gustason, Pfetzing, & Zawolkow, 1972). To assist in making a selection among these systems, two questions may be asked:

1. *Is one of the language systems currently being used by an essential community?* Is one of these systems already in general use by the people with whom the student will come in contact most frequently? Consideration should be given to the system currently being used by the parents and by teachers and peers in the school setting. Additionally, consideration should be given to the system that may be in use in future vocational and community settings. The functional advantage of an immediate audience supports use of a locally popular system.

2. *What is the student's functional level?* The degree of sign *iconicity* and *grammatic complexity* of the language system should be matched to the student's functional level. Iconicity of a sign refers to how much the sign resembles the item/action it represents. The lower the functioning level of the student, the greater is the iconicity that may be required for him/her to understand and reproduce a sign. If idiosyncratic gesturing is selected, these gestures derived from current student usage will probably have the most meaning for the student (Nietupski & Hamre-Nietupski, 1979).

Of the standard sign systems, American Indian Sign (Amerind) operates at a very reduced symbolic level and is therefore highly iconic (Skelley, 1977). Observers can interpret Amerind with over 80% comprehension without previous instruction, suggesting a high degree of iconicity (Skelley, Schinsky, Smith, & Fust, 1974). American Sign Language (ASL), used by a large number of deaf persons in the United States, retains a higher degree of iconicity than Signing Exact English (SEE) (Babbini, 1974). ASL signs represent concepts in contrast to representation of isolated or individual words as is the case in SEE.

The second consideration is the degree of grammatic complexity within the signing system. Amerind "has no required grammatical or structural rules" (Skelley, 1977). SEE is complex in that it resembles spoken English and includes inflections of tense and linear syntax paralleling verbal language structure. Because of its close parallel with spoken and written English, SEE may be the system of choice for potential readers. ASL constitutes a separate language from English (Stokoe, 1970). ASL is a system that uses signs to represent whole concepts, and it has its own grammatic rules and structures.

Category of Communication Boards

Within this category of nonvocal communication are a variety of specific language systems from which to select. Arranged in a hierarchy from the most concrete to the most abstract, these systems include the use of objects, photographs, magazine pictures, commercially made picture drawings (Maharaj, 1980), line drawings, Blissymbolics (Bliss, 1965), traditional orthography (words), and letters. Selecting from among these systems should consider the following questions.

1. *What degree of representation (iconicity) does the student need?* Moving up the hierarchy, the symbols become more abstract and, therefore, more representational. A student who has not mastered the concept of object permanence may have difficulty with symbols that do not "mimic" what they represent. For cognitively de-

layed students, highly concrete symbols (e.g., objects, photographs, magazine pictures, pictograms) may be more appropriate.

2. *What is the need for extended vocabulary and for a vocabulary that can make discrete differences of meaning?* A student with receptive language and cognitive potential to attain extensive vocabulary and complex, multi-word communication is a candidate for Blissymbols, traditional orthography, letters, or a combination of these. This type of system allows students to create a large number of concepts as language needs arise. The structure of these systems enables the combination of symbols to express new concepts, thereby freeing cognitively able students from the constraints of more fixed, concrete systems.

3. *How much time is required to instruct the student in use of the system?* Two studies have investigated the amount of teacher time required for instruction and the number of trials to mastery of symbol systems. When pictograms were compared with Blissymbols, the results suggested that the iconic pictures are more readily acquired, maintained, and generalized (Hurlbut, Iwata, & Green, 1982). When comparing pictograms, Blissymbols, and traditional orthography, pictograms were found to be the most efficient and effective for instruction, followed by Blissymbols and then traditional orthography (Briggs, 1983).

Although a team may select one symbol system, a student might be able to utilize more than one system as the board develops. A student might begin with photographs, but as he/she becomes a more fluent communicator and as cognitive skills develop, the student may gradually transfer to more abstract, flexible symbols.

Category of Communication Codes

Use of a communication code should be selected when no other alternative is available. Communication codes are usually employed with only the most physically disabled students, or with individuals in a rehabilitative setting who need a temporary means to express their needs until recuperation. Codes should be considered for use only if physical impairments preclude all but the most rudimentary motor movements.

Codes are transmitted as response modes in the form of eye blinking or finger and foot tapping, for example. With mentally handicapped students the language content may be as limited as allowing for a yes/no response, or as complex as using the Morse code with higher functioning students. Because codes require the listener to be the initiator of any communication exchange, and knowledgeable in the deciphering technique, the use of codes is extremely limited and, therefore, the most restrictive means of nonvocal communication.

The determination as to what type of code to train is based on the topography of response the student is capable of making. Technological advances have made communication codes unnecessary for most students. Scanning and encoding systems linked to micro-switches have expanded what was thought at one time to be limits prescribed by physical disability. For example, a puff of breath can now activate an elaborate communication system. For a more complete discussion of codes and technological alternatives, refer to Silverman (1980) and Vanderheiden and Grilley (1975).

Decision Step 5: What Will Be the Means of Access?

When the decision has been made to utilize a particular communication symbol/board system, the means by which the student will be able to access the language elements must be determined. The three basic techniques of access are: direct selection, scanning, and encoding (Vanderheiden & Grilley, 1975).

1. *Direct selection* occurs under the complete control of the communicator. Pointing to a specific symbol site on the communication array, the individual initiates and completes symbol selection independently. Pointing may be done by using a body part (e.g., finger), prosthetic device (e.g., head wand), or technical aid (e.g., light beam). The appropriateness of a direct selection system is judged by the student's accuracy and time efficiency allowed by the pointing method.

2. *Scanning* relies on the assistance of someone else or something else to move a pointing signal across the communication board. As the signal device moves across the array of symbols, the communicator issues the command to indicate when the signal should stop. The position at which the pointing signal is stopped indicates what the communicator is saying. Scanning may be as simple as having the teacher run a finger across the rows of a communication board until the communicator indicates "stop" or it may involve a technical aid such as a light pulse that moves automatically across the board until the communicator flips a stop switch.

When motoric limitations prevent direct selection, scanning is an option because it requires only minimal motor response. Any consistently recognizable signal can be used to "say when." Although scanning does accommodate severe physical involvement, it also requires some cognitive skill beyond direct selection and is a slower procedure.

3. *Encoding* uses a limited number of communicator initiated signals that are combined in order to locate the coordinates of a specific site on the communication board. Thus, the communicator indicates the code for the intended word, not the actual word itself. A simple example of encoding is a board with numbered rows and color-coded columns. The communicator first indicates the number of the row of interest and then the color of the column containing the intended symbol. The intersection of number and color gives the location of the symbol of interest. Encoding is useful for individuals with limited range of motion who can use a large expressive vocabulary. The advantages of expanded vocabulary offered by encoding are balanced by the cognitive demands on the communicator to understand and use the procedure.

Selection of a symbol accessing technique is based on the motor function, cognitive capacity, and vocabulary needs of the student. Any method—direct selection, scanning, or encoding—can be facilitated through use of technological aids (Vanderheiden, 1978). Before selecting a commercially produced, automated system, one must determine that the student can interact with its basic format. Therefore, experimentation and practice with teacher-made access systems are beneficial. Simple arrays and accessing techniques can always be made more complex as the student indicates the need and aptitude for a more sophisticated communication system.

Vanderheiden and Grilley's (1975) book provides a detailed survey of the realm of accessing possibilities available to teachers. As long as the student evidences a consistent operant response, some sort of access technique apparently can be devised. Motor imitation training may be used to teach students who initially lack consistent response.

Decision Step 6: Selection of Initial Vocabulary

When choosing either a manual system or a communication board system, the following criteria will assist in selecting an initial pool of vocabulary words.

1. Words should reflect the student's *functional needs* in various settings. Functional words may be determined by taking an inventory of essential daily activities the student encounters most frequently, as well as determining which vocabulary items the student finds reinforcing. Language elements necessary for an instructional exchange (e.g., give me, I don't know) also should be included (Grinnell, Detamore, & Lippke, 1976; Hamre-Nietupski et al., 1977; Richardson, 1975).

2. Words that allow the student to express *basic human needs* are necessary. Vocabulary items enabling communication of pain, hunger, and toileting needs are taught to enable the student to alert others and thereby help to reduce inappropriate behavior. Including "feeling words" (e.g., happy, sad, angry) allows the student the basic human dignity of self-expression.

3. The student should be provided with an *expressive mode* for his/her current receptive vocabulary.

4. Inclusion of preferred items will allow a *motivational element* for communication. The teacher should observe whether the student indicates preferences for certain objects such as a favorite toy.

5. One of the criteria that should be taken into account for sign selection should be the actual *motor requirements* of sign production. Words that are represented easily help the student experience successful initial language efforts. Although use of functional or motivational objects is essential in determining which signs to train, it should not be the only factor in initial sign selection (Stremel-Campbell, Cantrell, & Halle, 1977).

Research has identified motor dimensions of signs that are significant to initial learning. These dimensions are *iconicity,* or how much the movement looks like what the sign represents; *taction,* or whether there is contact with the body in making the sign; and *symmetry,* or whether symmetrical or asymmetrical movement of the hands is required to produce the sign. To promote faster acquisition, initial signs should be symmetrical, have taction, and be iconic (Kohl, 1981).

6. Words representing *general concepts* rather than discrete definitions may be desirable. Initially, generic terms may be selected when specific item terms are too difficult to produce either cognitively or motorically (e.g., one sign or symbol to represent all cookies).

7. An initial vocabulary should take advantage of a skill or activity the student already has in his/her *behavioral repertoire* in terms of conceptualization and production. For example, initial verbs in any system should be based on activity that the student has already mastered, eliminating the need to teach the concept with the new sign or symbol.

When using a manual system, initial signs should take advantage of motor responses already in the student's movement repertoire, thus eliminating the need to teach a new movement pattern with the new sign. For example, the sign for "drink" mimics the actual movement of drinking from a glass. A student who drinks independently has mastered this movement and, therefore, should not have difficulty producing the movement signifying "drink."

Decision Step 7: What Is the Order of Initial Instruction?

After the decision for steps 1 through 6 have been made, instruction can be initiated using the communication system that has been selected.

1. A student's first experience with language should give him/her an immediate degree of *environmental control* to clearly demonstrate the function of language. Alberto, Briggs, Sharpton, and Goldstein (1981) have suggested that the first phase of instruction should be that of building in an appropriate yes/no response. Yes/no instruction is appropriate in both manual and communication board systems. Starting with a yes/no response allows the student (a) experiences in which the functional utility of appropriate communication is made concrete and may be appropriately reinforced, (b) a language content that may be immediately generalized across settings and agents, (c) means to transfer nonstandard communication of yes (e.g., smiling) or no (e.g., crying) into a more acceptable format, (d) the functional ability to indicate wants and needs appropriately, thus promoting social and emotional control skills, and (e) a method to discriminate between choice items at a basic response level, thereby developing cognitive skills through appropriate decision making. The instruction of yes and no responding may be quickly and efficiently conducted through the basic instructional technology of physical guidance procedures and appropriate reinforcement techniques (Alberto et al., 1981).

2. If the student is using a board system, the second phase of instruction builds in an *attention summoning signal*. An attention summoning signal is a device that is easily accessible to the student and is used to indicate to others that the student wants to

communicate. For example, the nonverbal student may tap a bell to attract the teacher's attention. The method chosen as a signaling source, however, must be used exclusively for that purpose. The signaling device helps the student understand from the beginning of instruction that his/her system may be used to initiate conversation as well as to respond.

3. Instruction of the first vocabulary item is critical. At this initial encounter, when the sign or symbol is first presented, the student must learn to make the connection between representation of the sign or symbol and the reality of its referent. Nouns are introduced first because they have the most *concrete referents*. We suggest that the first noun introduced be the referent for an item that was used as a reinforcer in yes/no instruction. If during "yes training," the item used to occasion yes from the student was a particular toy, that toy should be represented by the first sign or symbol selected for instruction.

4. If a language board system has been selected, three additional considerations must be taken into account in planning for its use by the student:

a. *Size of the symbol*. Considering the visual acuity of the student, one must determine the appropriate size of the symbols to be placed on the board. A procedure patterned after the Parson's Visual Acuity Project (Cress et al., 1981) might be followed. This involves teaching the student a simple discrimination task using a symbol card for "correct" (a known picture) paired with an "incorrect" distractor. Starting with relatively large cards, the student is asked to point to the correct card. The size of the stimulus cards is systematically reduced as this task continues. The point at which the student is no longer able to make the appropriate response indicates the point at which the card becomes too small. Therefore, the size of symbols should be the size of the last correctly identified "correct" card.

b. *Symbol placement and order of instruction*. The general organization of the board is based on the Fitzgerald Key (1949). Figure 2 presents suggested sequences for placement of symbols on an initial communication board.

1. *Yes*, the first symbol to be taught, is placed in the upper lefthand corner.
2. *No* is placed in the upper righthand corner.
3. *Nouns* are placed on the righthand side of the board. Five nouns should be chosen from the pool of initial vocabulary developed during Step 6. As previously indicated, the first noun should be the object used as a reinforcer in yes/no instruction. The second and third nouns should be two more concrete objects; and nouns four and five should be two places, such as toilet and home.
4. Five *verbs* are selected from the initial vocabulary pool. The first verb selected should be "want" (Keogh & Reichle, 1982). The inclusion of "want" gives the student a means to differentiate between object identification and object requests (i.e., "apple" identification is differentiated from "I want apple").

   The second verb suggested is "go." "Go" may be taught as the motoric oppo-

FIGURE 2 Sequence for Initial Placement of Symbols on a Communication Board

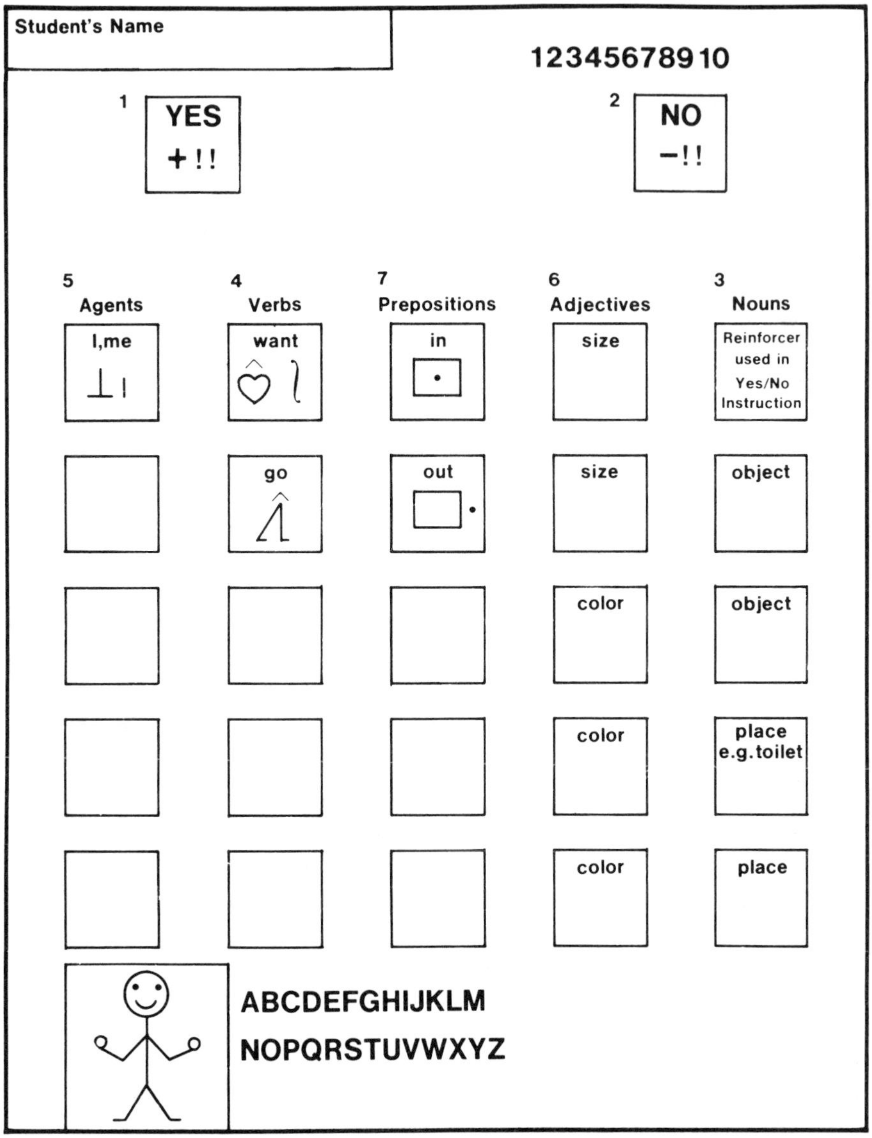

site of "want." "Want" indicates bringing an object to the speaker; "go" indicates movement toward an object. Instruction may center on discriminating between these two actions, matching the actions with the symbols. Further support of "go" comes from the finding that "go" is the most frequent mover-location action verb produced by children at the initial stages of language acquisition (Bloom, Miller, & Hood, 1978).

5. *The next item instructed is a list of agents.* Agent symbols are placed on the extreme lefthand side of the board. We suggest that the first agent listed be "I, me." The student may then be taught to communicate sentences such as "I want . . ." The remaining four agents should be persons most frequently in contact with the student, such as the parent, teacher, speech pathologist, and paraprofessional.
6. Placement of *adjectives* follows next. Initial adjectives should refer to size and color, as they are two of the three relevant dimensions to which children first attend when considering new stimuli (Gruen & Berg, 1973; Lovaas, Schreibman, Koegel, & Rehm, 1971).
7. Next is placement of *prepositions*. The first prepositions suggested for instruction are "in" and "on." These are the first prepositions to emerge in normal language acquisition (Brown, 1973) and are clearly discriminate opposites.

Following this initial symbol instruction, the student has a basic 25-word vocabulary selected from the initial vocabulary pool. This vocabulary contains all the basic grammatic elements. The symbols are placed so that the student will be able to move from left to right, making a grammatically correct sentence.

No matter which symbol system is used, the printed word should appear directly above the symbol on each symbol card. As vocabulary is increased, columns of symbols may be extended or doubled depending on the size of the board. Color coding word categories (e.g., agents—yellow, verbs—red) will assist the student's rate of scanning the board for a particular symbol.

Figure 2 is a standard starting format in a communication board design. Though this figure represents a typical format, the student's range of motion must be taken into account when planning specific symbol placement. A board should always be arranged to facilitate the student's ease of selection. For example, if a student has a pointing response that is functional solely in the lower right quadrant of the board, symbols should be placed in that quadrant only. If a student is using eye pointing for symbol selection, the space between symbols may be exaggerated for greater clarity.

When adapting the symbol layout, care should be taken not to reinforce any inappropriate primitive reflexes (e.g., asymmetric tonic neck reflex). A student should not be asked to use a primitive reflex to point.

Additional functional symbols may be added to a student's board. One example is to include a representational stick figure in the lower lefthand corner (note Figure 2). By pointing to arm, leg, etc. on the stick figure, the student is able to talk about specific body parts. This symbol, therefore, provides a space-efficient means for identifying body parts quickly (McDonald, 1980). Also, a number line placed across the top of the board and an alphabet across the bottom allows a student information to use in the communication process or can serve the teacher as instruction continues. Cognitively capable students will use the number line in academic as well as informal responses. Using the letters to spell new words vastly increases the number of concepts a higher functioning student can generate.

c. *Portability.* A major consideration in the development of a communication board is to make sure the student can handle it without difficulty. Limited portability reduces the student's opportunities for functional use of the board. Ready access to symbols is necessary to ensure spontaneous, continuous, and generalized use of communication.

To devise the most functional design, the team should consider the student's manipulation and mobility skills. Popular arrangements include fixing the board to the lap tray of a wheelchair, adding a shoulder strap to the board so it can be turned easily, or enclosing the board within a file folder. For students who are unable to position the board themselves, the attention summoning signal may be used to express, "I want to talk; please place my board so that I may use it." Ensuring that students can use their boards whenever they wish is necessary not only to increase their desire to use the board, but also to encourage others to interact with their special language programs.

As the student comes to use an increasing number of symbols, specific mini-boards may be developed to increase portability. For example, the student may carry a card in his/her wallet displaying only the symbols required in using public transportation. Mini-boards may also be developed to accommodate unique vocabulary requirements for a particular setting. For example, the student may have a board that displays symbols needed in the vocational setting or for grocery shopping.

AUTOMATED COMMUNICATION

Technology supplies an extensive variety of access and output modes that may be combined to create a fully automated communication system. Matching the appropriate system to the student is essential to ensure that (1) the system is functional and (2) the cost is justified.

Before considering an automated system, the student's positioning needs must be determined and accommodated. After functional positioning has been developed, the teacher/clinician should experiment with the accessing techniques described in Step 5. Prior to investigation of commercial products, an accessing technique based on the student's cognitive ability and response mode should be identified and trained so that the student is proficient with some form of teacher-made communication system. This assures that functional communication is not delayed while awaiting a specific technology, and it provides a basis for choice among the broad spectrum of commercial products.

Factors in Evaluating Commercial Systems

When evaluating commercial systems, several factors must be taken into account. The system should be *adaptable* to accommodate the customized positioning, accessing, and symbol array required by the student. The system should be *flexible* to keep pace with expansion of the student's vocabulary. And it should be *applicable* to a variety of uses (e.g., peer interaction, telephone conversation, written message recording).

Also, *portability* is essential to ensure that the system has generalized utility. The user must be able to transport it to a variety of settings. Systems that may be mounted on a wheelchair have an obvious advantage to nonambulatory students. In addition, a system that has a built-in *call signal* increases its interactive potential across settings.

Durability is mandatory. A system should be resistant to damage from moisture and impact. This feature is required by users who experience uncontrolled drooling and involuntary movement. Several systems offer additional protective coverings to enhance durability.

Related to durability is the requirement of *appropriate service and warranty*. If a system is damaged, the distributor/manufacturer must have reasonable repair and replacement guarantees to establish that the system will be useful over time.

Expense is a significant factor. Careful analysis is required to determine whether the specific features made available through technology are necessary. In many cases, a totally functional communication system can be constructed without having to resort to commercial communication packages and, thus, without the expense of current automated systems.

Most importantly, the student must recognize the advantage of automation. A system that the student views as neither desirable nor functional will not be used optimally. Therefore, the student's input and attitude are controlling factors throughout the decision process.

Examples of Commercially Produced Automated Communication Systems

This sampling of products indicates the variety of sources available.

Both Voc Aide (Texas Instruments) and Handivoice (Phonic Mirror) provide a fixed array of vocabulary items. Mode of access is by direct selection, and output is auditory. Because the vocabulary items are predetermined, the expressive repertoire may not match the user's level or needs. The feature of auditory output, however, enables users to interact with any listeners who are not hearing impaired. Therefore, these devices facilitate peer interaction since output is heard and not read, removing the requirement of normal vision and reading ability.

Versa Scan (Prentke Romich Company) and Zygo Model 16 (Zygo Industries) provide a format for access by scanning. The user determines the vocabulary array. Both systems utilize a light pattern to scan. Versa Scan employs a circular scan; Zygo Model 16 utilizes row/column scanning. Vocabulary items are superimposed over each device and may appear in any form (pictures, symbols, words, letters). The receiver identifies the output as that item which corresponds to the light cue. Thus, these systems are functional only for communication with individuals who have adequate vision and cognitive skills to interpret the illuminated symbol. At the same time, however, the scanning and flexible vocabulary features enable Versa Scan and Zygo Model 16 to be utilized as an expressive system for students with significantly impaired motor and cognitive ability.

The Canon Communicator (Canon USA) and Sharp Memorywriter (Sharp Electronics) utilize direct selection of letters on a keyboard to produce printed communication, which is displayed on a tape printout. The Sharp Memorywriter also includes a calculator dimension. The requirement of generating words and sentence structure limits these two systems to individuals without significant cognitive impairment. The permanent printout of communication is certainly a useful feature for those who are able to use these systems.

The Autocom (Prentke Romich) and Express 3 (Prentke Romich) offer a selection of access modes (direct or scanning), a flexible vocabulary (programmed by the user), and a variety of output modes (auditory, printed tape, or liquid crystal display). An additional feature is that these systems may be linked to a computer (Apple) to program input or receive output. Not surprisingly, the significantly increased versatility and sophistication of these systems is accompanied by significantly increased expense.

When to Invest

In some cases, the expense of a commercial communication system is balanced by its benefits to the user. But first, the student should have mastered some teacher-made system demonstrating that positioning and potential accessing technique have been addressed. The family must be able and willing to maintain and reprogram an automated system when the student leaves the school environment. The communication skill of the student should have reached a level of maturity to ensure that the automated system will not become obsolete soon after its adoption. The student's vocabulary needs should have exceeded the limits of what is available using teacher-made systems.

Finally, at some point the student's need for interaction with others or with information processing equipment may be met only by an automated system. When the student's needs exceed what the teacher or clinician can accommodate, a commercial automated system may be considered.

REFERENCES

Achilles, R. (1955). Communicative anomalies of individuals with cerebral palsy. *Cerebral Palsy Review, 16,* 15–24.

Alberto, P., Briggs, T., Sharpton, W., & Goldstein, D. (1981). Teaching a nonverbal yes/no response to severely handicapped students. *Journal of Childhood Communication Disorders, 5,* 90–103.

Babbini, B. (1974). *Manual communication: Finger-spelling and the language of signs.* Urbana: University of Illinois Press.

Bates, E. (1976). *Language and context: The acquisition of pragmatics.* New York: Academic Press.

Bates, E., Camaioni, L., & Volterra, V. (1975). The acquisition of performatives prior to speech. *Merrill-Palmer Quarterly, 21,* 205–266.

Bliss, C. K. (1965). *Semantography.* Sydney, Australia: Semantography Publishing Co.

Bloom, L., Miller, P., & Hood, L. (1978). Variations and reduction as aspects of competence in language development. In L. Bloom (Ed.), *Readings in language development*. New York: John Wiley.
Briggs, T. (1983). *An investigation of the efficiency and effectiveness of three nonvocal communication systems with severely handicapped students*. Unpublished doctoral dissertation, Georgia State University.
Brown, R. (1973). *A first language: The early stages*. Cambridge, MA: Harvard University Press.
Chapman, R., & Miller, J. (1980). Analyzing language and communication in the child. In R. L. Schiefelbusch (Ed.), *Nonspoken language and communication: Acquisition and intervention*. Baltimore: University Park Press.
Cress, P., Spellman, C., DeBriere, T., Sizemore, A., Northam, J., & Johnson, J. (1981). Visual screening for persons with severe handicaps. *Journal of the Association for the Severely Handicapped, 6*, 41–49.
Fant, L. (1972). *Ameslan: An introduction to American Sign Language*. Silver Spring, MD: National Association of the Deaf.
Fitzgerald, E. (1949). *Straight language for the deaf*. Washington, DC: Alexander Graham Bell Association for the Deaf.
Flavell, J. (1977). *Cognitive development*. Englewood Cliffs, NJ: Prentice-Hall.
Grinnell, M., Detamore, K., & Lippke, B. (1976). Sign it successful—Manual English encourages expressive communication. *Teaching Exceptional Children, 8*, 123–125.
Gruen, G., & Berg, B. (1973). Visual discrimination learning in familial retarded and non-retarded children. *American Journal of Mental Deficiency, 78*, 63–69.
Gustason, G., Pfetzing, D., & Zawolkow, E. (1972). *Signing Exact English*. Rossmoor, CA: Modern Signs Press.
Hamre-Nietupski, S., Stoll, A., Holtz, K., Fullerton, P., Ryan-Flottum, M., & Brown, L. (1977). Curricular strategies for teaching selected nonverbal communication skills to severely handicapped students. In L. Brown, J. Nietupski, S. Lyon, S. Hamre-Nietupski, T. Crowner, & L. Gruenewald (Eds.), *Curricular strategies for teaching nonverbal communication, functional object use, problem solving and mealtime skills to severely handicapped students* (Vol. 7, Part 1). Madison, WI: University of Wisconsin-Madison and Madison Metropolitan School District.
Harris-Vanderheiden, D., Brown, W., MacKenzie, P., Reiner, S., & Scheibel, C. (1975). Symbol communication for the mentally handicapped. *Mental Retardation, 13*, 34–37.
Hurlbut, B., Iwata, B., & Green, J. (1982). Nonvocal language acquisition in adolescents with severe physical disabilities: Blissymbol versus iconic stimulus formats. *Journal of Applied Behavior Analysis, 15*, 241–258.
Ingram, D. (1981). The transition from early symbols to syntax. In R. L. Schiefelbusch & D. D. Bricker (Eds.), *Early language: Acquisition and Intervention*. Baltimore: University Park Press.
Irwin, O. (1961). An integrated articulation test for use with children with cerebral palsy. *Cerebral Palsy Review, 22*, 3–20.
Kahn, J. (1975). Relationship of Piaget's sensorimotor period to language acquisition of profoundly retarded children. *American Journal of Mental Deficiency, 79*, 640–643.
Keogh, W., & Reichle, J. (1982, November). *Teaching "want."* Paper presented at the national conference of The Association for the Severely Handicapped, Denver.
Kohl, F. (1981). Effects of motoric requirements on the acquisition of manual sign responses by severely handicapped students. *American Journal of Mental Deficiency, 5*, 396–403.
Kotkin, R., & Simpson, S. (1976). A sign in the right direction: Language development for the non-verbal child. *AAESPH Review, 1*, 75–81.
Lovaas, O., Schreibman, L., Koegel, R., & Rehm, R. (1971). Selective responding by autistic children to multiple sensory input. *Journal of Abnormal Psychology, 77*, 211–222.
McDonald, E. (1980). *Teaching and using Blissymbolics*. Toronto: Blissymbolics Communication Institute.
Maharaj, S. (1980). *Ideogram communication*. Saskatchewan, Canada: George Reed Foundation.
Mecham, M., Berko, M., Berko, F., & Palmer, M. (1966). *Communication training in childhood brain damage*. Springfield, IL: Charles C Thomas.
Mysak, E. (1963). Dysarthria and oropharyngeal reflexology: A review. *Journal of Speech & Hearing Disorders, 28*, 252–260.
Nicolosi, L., Harryman, E., & Kresheck, J. (1978). *Terminology of communication disorders*. Baltimore: Williams & Wilkins.

Nietupski, J., & Hamre-Nietupski, S. (1979). Teaching auxiliary communication skills to severely handicapped students. *AAESPH Review, 4,* 107–124.

Piaget, J. (1952). *The origins of intelligence in children.* New York: Norton.

Reich, R. (1978). Gestural facilitation of expressive language in moderately and severely retarded preschoolers. *Mental Retardation, 16,* 113–116.

Reichle, J., & Yoder, D. (1979). Communication behavior for the severely and profoundly mentally retarded: Assessment and early stimulation strategies. In R. York & E. Edgar (Eds.), *Teaching the severely handicapped* (Vol. 4). Columbus, OH: Special Press.

Richardson, T. (1975). Sign language for the severely mentally retarded and profoundly mentally retarded. *Mental Retardation, 13,* 17.

Robinson, C., & Robinson, J. (1978). Sensorimotor functions and cognitive development. In M. Snell (Ed.), *Systematic instruction of the moderately and severely handicapped.* Columbus, OH: Charles E. Merrill.

Schaeffer, B. (1980). Teaching signed speech to non-verbal children: Theory and method. *Sign Language Studies, 26,* 20–63.

Schaeffer, B., Kollinzas, G., Musil, A., & McDowell, P. (1977). Spontaneous verbal language for autistic children through signed speech. *Sign Language Studies, 17,* 287–328.

Scheuerman, N., Baumgart, D., Spisma, K., & Brown, L. (1976). Toward the development of a curriculum for teaching nonverbal communication skills to severely handicapped students: Teaching basic tracking, scanning and selection skills. In N. Scheuerman, L. Brown, & T. Crowner (Eds.), *Toward an integrated therapy model for teaching motor, tracking, and scanning skills to severely handicapped students* (Vol. 6, Part 3). Madison, WI: Madison Metropolitan School District.

Silverman, F. (1980). *Communication for the speechless.* Englewood Cliffs, NJ: Prentice-Hall.

Skelley, M. (1977). Indian sign (Amerind), distinctive characteristics differentiating it from other sign systems. *ASHA, 19,* 746–747.

Skelley, M., Schinsky, L., Smith, R., Donaldson, R., & Griffin, J. (1975). American Indian Sign: A gestural communication system for the speechless. *Archives of Physical Medicine, 56,* 156–160.

Skelley, M., Schinsky, L., Smith, R., & Fust, R. (1974). American Indian (Amerind) as a facilitator of verbalization for oral verbal apraxic. *Journal of Speech & Hearing Disorders, 39,* 445–456.

Stokoe, W. (1970). Sign language diglossia. *Studies in Linguistics, 21,* 27–41.

Stremel-Campbell, K., Cantrell, D., & Halle, J. (1977). Manual signing as a language system and as a speech initiator for the nonverbal severely handicapped student. In E. Sontag (Ed.), *Educational programming for the severely and profoundly handicapped.* Reston, VA: Council for Exceptional Children.

Tomkins, W. (1969). *Indian Sign Language.* New York: Dover.

Vanderheiden, G. (Ed.). (1978). *Nonvocal communication resource book.* Baltimore: University Park Press.

Vanderheiden, G. (1981). *The practical applications of high and low technologies to aid communication in non-vocal severely physically handicapped individuals.* Paper presented at the regional conference of the Southeast Regional Coalition for Personnel Preparation to work with the Severely/Profoundly Handicapped, Atlanta.

Vanderheiden, G., & Grilley, K. (Eds.). (1975). *Non-vocal communication techniques and aids for the severely physically handicapped.* Baltimore: University Park Press.

The authors are all affiliated with Georgia State University, where Paul Alberto is Associate Professor and Program Director-Severely Handicapped, Elizabeth Garrett and Thomas Briggs are graduate students in Special Education, and Forrest Umberger is Associate Professor and Program Director-Speech Pathology.

Brantlinger and Guskin couch their discussion of educational implications of social and cultural differences in a comparison of handicapped groups with other minorities. The significance of discrimination in education is presented in terms of how discrimination is operationalized by the schools. In offering suggestions for teachers, the authors are careful to document their suggestions by references to the literature.

Implications of Social and Cultural Differences for Special Education

Ellen A. Brantlinger and Samuel L. Guskin

Programs for multicultural, nonsexist, and handicap awareness share a number of common characteristics and goals. All three focus on diminishing the stereotypes of their respective groups and on increasing their power. Their goals are to enhance academic performance and general student competence and to improve interaction among diverse groups of students, enabling these students to work together for a future they all share.

DEFINITIONS AND IMPLICATIONS

Smith (1983) explores the similarities and intertwinings of the "isms" (racism, sexism, heterosexism) as a productive way of examining prejudice and showing how systems of oppression interconnect. Holding negative stereotypes of low-income people and of handicapped groups can fittingly be added to Smith's list. These minorities constitute political categories representing persons who, for no reason other than some biological, physical (ethnocultural or social-psychological) difference, are negated, denied, discriminated against, and oppressed (Tinney, 1983).

These groups are defined as minorities not because they are few in numbers (for example, females in fact outnumber males), but because they are politically excluded from proportionate roles and responsibilities in the major institutions of power. Too, they receive less than their share of goods, services, values, rewards, power, prestige, and prerogatives (Tinney, 1983). All are groups that majority, or dominant, groups define as deviant, difficult, inferior, or wrong (Lorde, 1983). Ogbu (1974) uses the term "subordinate subgroups" to describe oppressed minorities.

Belief in the inherent superiority of one pattern over others justifies the powerful group's right to dominance (Lorde, 1983). Competence, then, is not so much a matter of individual ability as it is a matter of who has the power (such as public school teachers) to define and judge competence (Burnett, 1976). Cultural attributes are determined by dominant classes in a capitalist society and are transmitted differentially to school children, reproducing in school the inequitable power relations characteristic of the larger society (Giroux, 1983). In fact, Berman (1984) asserts, school may be the most visible arena in which capitalist hegemony is disseminated to a captured clientele. Thus, the public school, being a mechanism for cultural transmission, is boundary maintaining rather than boundary breaking, in structuring ranked social groups (Singleton, 1974).

Forms of Discrimination

Tinney (1983) has distinguished three different levels of discrimination: institutional, collective, and individual. *Institutional discrimination* prevents equal participation in associations or the bestowal of equal benefits by those associations. Institutional discrimination (i.e., educational, social, legal) has been rampant regarding handicapped individuals. Until 1975, handicapped children could be legally excluded from the public school—an institution requiring mandatory attendance for nonhandicapped individuals. Laws requiring involuntary sterilization or incarceration of handicapped people were in effect in most states during this century. Rights to sexual behavior, marriage, and parenthood have been denied handicapped people simply because they had been classified as handicapped.

Regarding present policies, McKnight (1982), for example, questions the existence of a "disorder" with learning disabled students, claiming that the label is instead an effort to justify the school's failure to educate a segment of the school population. Similarly, rights of racial or ethnic minorities related to schooling, as well as other domains of life, have been—and in many ways still are—restricted. Thus, "Rights have been and remain the prerogative of only one group consistently." (Tinney, 1983, p. 5).

Collective discrimination refers to "those discriminations which result from collective norms, values, and mores that work within society to legitimize oppressions" (Tinney, 1983, p. 5). For example, there is a general, or collective, denial of minority culture. White, Anglo-Saxon, middle-class values predominate in school, and cultural traditions of minority groups are perceived as obstructions. Minority students are expected to renounce the unique aspects of themselves and assimilate to the dominant culture in school. Most school evaluation systems are set up so that only one group—academically-advanced students—can really succeed. Collective (i.e., normed), very limited interpretations exist regarding intelligence, achievement, and success in school, and these interpretations favor the dominant majority.

Individual discrimination, or personal prejudice, based on stereotypes and misinformation is the easiest form of discrimination to notice and combat, in Tinney's (1983) opinion. Perhaps most of the present effort to eradicate discrimination focuses on individual discrimination in the form of multicultural, nonsexist, and handicap-sensitive teacher training.

Discrimination in Education

Among the most pressing challenges of public education is to provide quality education to children of various personal characteristics in integrated settings. Oden (1976) contends that school desegregation and mainstreaming are the most urgent moral imperatives facing the American people. In addition to between-school segregation, such as racial segregation, attention has been focused on within-school segregation, such as tracking students according to ability or providing separate special education services.

Numerous books on the subject of racial desegregation have been published in the past decade (e.g., Crain, Mahard, & Narot, 1982; Orfield, 1978; Patchen, 1982; Rist, 1979; St. John, 1975; Schofield, 1982). At the same time, mainstreaming of handicapped children has been the focus of attention of many special educators (e.g., Gottlieb, 1982; Jones & Wilderson, 1976; MacMillan, 1976; Polloway, 1984). Although social class desegregation has not been a widely acknowledged goal, many have written about the influence of social class membership on schooling (e.g., Anyon, 1980; Apple, 1982; Bowles & Gintis, 1976; Brantlinger, 1985a; Jencks, 1972; Lightfoot, 1981; Sieber, 1982). Social class segregation in education, in fact, is intimately and intricately related to racial segregation, special class segregation, and tracking segregation.

Intelligence and Achievement Scores

It has long been documented that low-income and minority students' IQ and achievement scores are lower than high-income and majority children. Ramey and Campbell (1979) claim that social class has a pronounced effect on scores on developmental tests. Children of higher socioeconomic classes show progressive gains in their rate of development beginning in infancy, while lower SES children show progressive decline relative to norms. In a study of approximately 26,000 black and white 4-year-olds, Broman, Nichols, and Kennedy (1975) found that SES was the best single predictor of IQ. Kushlick and Blunder (1974) claim that the relationship between social class and retardation is so strong that no parents of higher socioeconomic groups have children with IQs of less than 80 unless they have a pathological condition, as demonstrated cross-culturally by a series of epidemiological studies. Mare (1981) projects that the dependence of educational attainment on social origins will continue to increase.

Racial and ethnic status are similarly correlated with achievement and cognitive measures. Yet, Levine, Kukuk, and Meyer (1979) wrote that the correlation of race and achievement does not mean that racial composition is independently related to achievement apart from SES. Results of their analysis indicated that racial composition generally added nothing to the prediction. Thus, when SES is controlled, racial differences in test results tend to disappear.

Even when IQ is held constant, achievement scores fluctuate according to race and social class. Gordon (1976) reported on a study involving 1,102 Chicago-area fifth and sixth graders who were aggregated into seven cohorts of approximately equal IQ scores (95–104.9); whites scored higher on achievement tests than blacks of the same sex and race. Gordon concluded that "overachievement" and "underachievement" among children with similar IQ scores were consistently related to race and class.

Placement and Services

Proportionately more blacks and other minority children are placed in special classes (Anderson & Anderson, 1983; Argulewicz, 1983; Educational Testing Service, 1980; Ford, Mongon, & Whelan, 1982; Pink, 1982; Polloway & Smith, 1983; Ysseldyke, Algozzine, & Richey, 1982). Linguistically different children are even more disproportionately represented (Aguirre, 1979; Argulewicz, 1983; Bernal, 1983; Ochoa, Pacheco, & Omark, 1983; Wright & Santa Cruz, 1983). Bernal (1983) maintains that many "normal" LEP (limited English-proficient) children are placed in special classes in systems that have resisted bilingual programming. Gerber (1984) expressed concern about erroneous classification and inequitable treatment of children labeled as handicapped in the educational system. Algozzine, Ysseldyke, and Christenson (1983) found that between 1977 and 1980 the rate of new cases of children referred and placed with special education services (i.e., incidence) increased at a rate of 3% per year.

Moran (1984) recommends that special, remedial, and compensatory education join together to claim a place for low achievers in the mainstream. She feels that separate administrators, teachers, materials, and accountability work against chances of integration. Gardner (1982) concurs, stating that special education has been diverting too much staff time toward determining which category of exceptionality is appropriate to serve low-achieving students.

Special education has been perceived as a special case of tracking (Madden & Slavin, 1983). Parents tend to accept professional judgment as legitimate authority and assume they are doing what is best for their children. Parents of children in lower tracks have been led to believe that their children are less capable and less intelligent than other children. Drummond (1982) maintains that to suggest that a handicap, such as mental illness, resides solely within the individual is the power elite's lie. Oden (1976) states that special education in isolation is a vicious form of segregation with negative effects on children. Such a statement sounds remarkably similar to one made by Charles Sumner before the Massachusetts Supreme Court in 1849: "Segregation injures the child who is white as well as the minority child . . . their hearts, while yet tender with childhood, are necessarily hardened by this conduct, and their subsequent lives, perhaps, bear enduring testimony to this legalized uncharitableness" (Harris, 1978, p. 53).

In accordance with most desegregation and mainstreaming ideologies, the position taken in this article is that inclusion of diverse children in schools and classrooms is desirable. Like Crosland (1974), we argue for a sense of community and social cohesion that may result in a nation composed of people who understand and care about each other.

RECOMMENDATIONS FOR INSTRUCTION OF HETEROGENEOUS GROUPS

Class Size

Glass (1980) recommends that federal funds be spent for extra teachers to reduce teacher/pupil ratios and permit mixed groupings of high, average, and low achievers in smaller classes instead of segregating special education students for special services. Clark, Lotto, and McCarthy (1980) summarized research on urban schools, and among their recommendations was to reduce teacher/pupil ratios. But Longo (1982) cautions that merely reducing class size will not necessarily improve the academic rate of low achievers. Other facilitating strategies have to be adopted.

Individualized Instruction

According to Longo (1982), differentiated or individualized instruction is a necessary strategy for teaching diverse groups. His plan for integration is to: (1) retrain and reorient teachers and administrators; (2) provide direct support to teachers as they initiate integration; (3) allow long-term planning by building teams; and (4) encourage a variety of instructional mechanisms and environments (pp. 164, 176).

Similarly, Wang (1976) developed the Individually Prescribed Instruction program, which allows students choices of time and sequence for doing prescribed activities independently. A later report (Reynolds & Wang, 1983) described the Adaptive Learning Environment Model (ALEM), based on a systems approach to program development. ALEM includes a highly structured, hierarchically organized prescriptive environment, maximization of use of time and classroom resources, multi-age grouping and instructional teaming support systems, a systematic staff development program, and a family participation component. Wang's approach is consistent with reviews of work on instructional effectiveness by Brophy (1982), Rosenshine and Berliner (1978), and Rosenshine (1979), all of whom advocate a structured environment in which students are actively engaged in mastering correctly sequenced basic academic skills.

In contrast to Wang, who recommends pupil choice, Rouck's (1980) strategies, while centering on individualized assignments, suggest that low SES students learn more when activities are at a low level of complexity without pupil initiative. These suggestions are open to criticisms of stereotyping and oversimplification of curriculum for low-achieving, low-income children, which Meier (1984) claims is a recent trend among some educators.

Multidimensional Classrooms

Meier (1982) contends that schools should acknowledge a broad conception of human intelligence. Similarly, Rosenholtz and Wilson (1980) and Rosenholtz and Simpson (1984) stress the likely negative impact of "unidimensional classrooms" that narrowly define academic abilities and have a tendency to increase the amount of social stratification within them. By assigning uniform tasks in which peers can judge performance superiority, the effect is to produce inequality among students' perceptions of their own and others' abilities. Rosenholtz contends that students' feelings about school are closely associated with their academic ability levels and suggests that classrooms be organized in a multidimensional manner in which a number of attributes are valued and students select from a wide variety of tasks. Judgments about performance superiority are more difficult and less likely as tasks become more varied.

Wang (1981) might concur with Rosenholtz's hypothesis, claiming that in a class with a wide continuum of academic and social learning goals, a student is less likely to develop perceptions of exception or failure. Jencks (1972), too, stresses the importance of diversity and choice. Roper and Roper (1979) suggest shifting more courses to an elective basis. Meier (1982) recommends that methods be used to stimulate curiosity and widen visions. Activities must be perceived as purposeful by the learner (Jencks, 1972). Hendricks (1981), in *The Centered Teacher,* suggests a variety of "nonacademic" activities, such as learning about feelings, building responsibility, and increasing self-awareness, to broaden the curriculum.

Student Self-Management

Students adept in self-management are able to discover independently how to use previously learned concepts to solve problems without much teacher assistance (Pines & Julian, 1972). Wang and Lindvall (1984) claim that students' sense of personal control affects classroom behavior and the learning process. They believe that students' feelings can be modified through instructional intervention including students' opportunity to select activities from a choice of learning options. Wang (1976) emphasizes the importance of pupil choice in increasing the completion of work. Hollins (1982) suggests fostering leadership among pupils by encouraging children to think for themselves and take charge of their own destinies and helping students see the relationship between instructional content and personal aspirations.

Individualized Incentives and Goal Structures

Attribution theories postulate that students use information to arrive at causal ascriptions for outcomes primarily in terms of ability, effort, task difficulty, and luck (Weiner, 1979). Of these, effort is the only factor under students' volitional control amenable to change. If students believe that increased effort will result in success, they persist longer at a task and increase their level of performance. In contrast, individuals who find themselves unable to control aversive stimuli (i.e., negative evaluation) perceive themselves as helpless. Weiner maintains that classroom situational factors affect subsequent student behaviors (i.e., persistence, cognitions of success or failure, expectancies for future learning).

Under competitive conditions, Ames and Ames (1981) report, students perceive ability as a more salient cause of their successes or failures. They maintain that failing students are more self-punitive and perceive themselves as less capable of competition. On the other hand, a magnified positive affect is associated with success for successful students. Ames and Ames recommend individual goal-setting and contract learning in which students and teachers jointly develop plans to overcome learning obstacles, thus strengthening the effort/performance linkage and promoting realistic goal-setting and constructive interpretations of failure.

Monitoring Pupil Progress

Teachers in effective schools emphasize completion and mastery of curricular objectives. They also make efforts to monitor and assess students' academic progress (Brookover & Lezotte, 1979).

Personalized Grading

Crain, Mahard, and Narot (1982) assert: "We subject children to a form of competitive grading which we would not tolerate for ourselves as adults. Public school is the last bastion of cutthroat competition. Teachers grade students, but they bitterly resist outside evaluation of their work" (p. 209). Block (1984) and Nicholls (1979) suggest that the motivational aspect of evaluation is more successful if it is based on task mastery rather than on social comparison. A task mastery grading strategy avoids the informational cues of single-dimensional judgments of relative ability found in social comparison (i.e., curve or normed) grading.

The grading done in special education classrooms often has been linked to personalized Individual Education Program goals and may be negotiated through teacher/pupil contracts. There is no reason why similar strategies cannot be implemented in regular heterogeneous classrooms. Personalized curriculum and grading are likely to result in experiences of school success for pupils which, in turn, are likely to result in a cycle of continuing academic achievement (i.e., prevention of the learned helplessness syndrome) and vocational or career success (Gottfredson, 1980).

According to self-worth theory (Covington, 1984), success should cause feelings of high self-esteem, especially if students perceive their efforts and abilities to be responsible for their achievement, whereas failure causes a sense of worthlessness and social disapproval. Ornstein (1978) emphasizes the importance of minimizing failure situations and nurturing positive self-definitions. Cohen and Lazerson (1977) caution, however, that grades be based on objective criteria rather than subjectively based on personal characteristics.

Maximizing Engaged Time

Academic achievement depends on a high-powered academic emphasis in classrooms (Brophy, 1982). Instead of offering a worklike curriculum phrased in businesslike terminology ("time on task," "better products"), Block (1984) maintains that children prefer playlike, voluntary, personally meaningful activities. Children seem to better concentrate on these types of activities and feel more competent and in control in the classroom. Another method used to maximize engaged time is classwide peer tutoring (Reynolds & Wang, 1983).

Opportunity to Respond

In a recent investigation, Stanley and Greenwood (1983) found that a high-achieving group had significantly more time for academic response than did low achievers, which those authors believe was caused by different instructional procedures used with the two levels. They suggest that instructional programs and teaching formats be designed to engage low-achievers in order to ameliorate below grade level achievement deficits. In setting goals for a comprehensive program for responsible citizenship, Brown (1977) emphasizes development of a value system compatible with principles underlying democratic institutions, as well as development of self-esteem to fully participate in civil life. A high level of student participation in class activities and opportunity to respond are correlated with achievement.

Opportunity to Learn

Of hundreds of variables surveyed, aside from home background, Walberg and Rasher (1979) found that opportunity to learn was most closely related to achievement. Opportunity to learn can include hours of instruction, hours of homework, cumulative years of study in the subject, and curricular emphasis and challenge. Brophy and Good (1974) found that teacher communication toward children from lower socioeconomic classes and racial and ethnic minority backgrounds is more likely to be aimed at controlling or managing behaviors, while communications to majority middle class children are more likely to be relevant to the content or skills of instruction. Although the results of expectancy studies vary considerably, Taylor (1979) found that teachers' interactions with their students in a lab situation varied with implanted expectations; more support, challenge, and encouragement were given to the high-expectations students. Clearly, interaction with minority children should be more instructionally oriented and should result in increased opportunity to learn.

Continuity Between Teaching and Learning Styles

According to Edgerton (1981), "Because we know that subcultural differences can be important, we may be lulled into the belief that we have adequately taken them into account," but "our knowledge of subcultural factors is so inadequate that we can not have provided for differences" (p. 320). Witkin, Moore, Goodenough, and Cox (1977) maintain that when cognitive styles of students and teachers are matched, they view each other more positively and evaluations of students' performances are higher. Most school environments reflect a field-independent style (Cohen, 1969), characterized by an "analytic approach to a stimulus context that is reflected in the ability to restructure a perceptual field and extract the salient features from the embedded context" (Witkin et al., 1977, p. 3). In contrast, a field-dependent cognitive style is represented by a global mode of perception manifested by "the inability to separate part of a perceptual field from the field as a whole" (Witkin et al., 1977, p. 4).

Some minority groups have been described as field-dependent (i.e., blacks, by Shade, 1982; Mexican-Americans, by Cohen, 1969). School socialization or acculturation usually influences a transition from field-dependent to field-independent cognitive style (Berry, 1983). Field-independence is associated with Westernization. Although researchers in cognitive styles generally assume the position of cultural relativism, they search for systematic relationships among patterns of abilities and elements of cultural contexts (Berry, 1983). Nevertheless, success in mainstream school culture is associated with field-independent styles.

Secondary students classified as learning disabled often plateau at fourth or fifth grade, a level at which basic skill instruction ceases and students move on to a new level of cognitive functioning that requires integrating and applying what is learned (Sheinker, Sheinker, & Stevens, 1984). Sheinker et al. maintain that academic achievement requires students to know *how* to learn rather than just what to learn. Gerber (1983), however, suggests that learning disabled students are not necessarily strategy-deficient (connoting absence of strategy use) but are strategy-inefficient or strategy-inflexible. Deliberately teaching cognitive strategies associated with improved academic performance has been recommended by Peterson and Swing (1982). They suggest that teachers can get information about effective learning strategies by questioning students about their thought processes at various times during instruction.

Using microethnography and context analysis, Mehan (1979) studied a class of low-income black and Mexican-American children in a school in San Diego. He concluded that classroom competence involves matters of form as well as content. Students must learn the appropriate *form* in which to cast their academic knowledge in school. Competent classroom membership involves employing interactional skills and abilities such as when, with whom, and where they can speak and act. Mehan distinguishes between *general socialization,* which he defines as the interactional and symbolic process involved in the transmission of general skills and abilities that everyone needs to know to be a competent member of a society, and *formal education,* which is concerned with the transmission of specialized skills, logical operations, and abstract systems.

Sullivan (1979) differentiates between structural and cultural assimilation, or acculturation. *Structural assimilation* requires the ability to deal with members of other groups in instrumental transactions and is necessary for success in school. Basically, students share with the school certain assumptions about schooling; however, they are able to maintain their ethnic or cultural uniqueness. In contrast, *acculturation* requires students to give up their cultural uniqueness.

There are different perspectives on acculturation. Those who take a cultural or cognitive deficit perspective would structure the school environment so as to modify the home or minority style. Those who adhere to a cultural relativity position, and who see cognitive variations as not only acceptable but valued, often recommend that teaching styles be adapted to accommodate minority learners who have unique styles. They believe that in a pluralistic, democratic society schools should go to the community to discern if a specific cultural identify is valued and desired or if acculturation and assimilation into the dominant culture is desired (Berry, 1983).

In an ethnographic study of a bicultural-bilingual classroom, Cazden, Carrasco, Maldonado-Guzman, & Erickson observed that successful teachers matched their teaching with minority pupil styles and adapted their interaction to fit local customs. Cazden's conclusion was that effective bilingual/bicultural education resulted in better achievement, psychic well-being and adjustment to both worlds. Hollins (1982) wrote that Marva Collins's success in teaching inner-city black children was attributable to the consistency between instructional style and interaction patterns commonly found in traditional black family settings, friendship groups, and religious settings.

American Indian children that Philips (1982) studied are enculturated in their preschool years into modes of organizing the transmission of verbal messages that are culturally different from those of Anglo middle-class children, she contends. The difference makes it difficult for them to comprehend verbal messages conveyed through schools' Anglo middle-class modes of organizing classroom interaction. Eventually Native American children don't participate verbally in classroom interactions because the social conditions for participation to which they have become accustomed in the Indian community are lacking. Philips calls the cultural differences "invisible" because school personnel working with the American Indian children do not notice them.

Saville-Troike (1978) summarizes the findings of a number of studies that have found that visual perception and visual memory of Native American children are higher than their Anglo age-mates. Sando (1973) analyzes how a difference in time orientation affects school performance: (1) It lowers attendance, particularly when school bus schedules are inflexible; (2) it is harder to command children's attention according to teacher-designed schedules; (3) it lowers scores on timed tests and assignments; and (4) American Indian children are unwilling to plan ahead. Sando claims, more generally, that the value structure of affluent-oriented teachers alienates poor children. Their reaction is often social withdrawal in and from school.

Social withdrawal also has been observed by Wax, Diamond, and Gearing (1971), who report that the Sioux who do not conform to and adopt the Anglo culture of the school experience almost inevitably fail in school and are pushed out of school because of subcultural rather than academic reasons. Sioux children who do (marginally) succeed in school are characterized by their peers as lacking independent thought, spontaneity, and creativity—all highly prized Sioux traits. Dumont and Wax (1969) observed a nonresponsiveness in the reservation classroom, which was interpreted as the manner in which students protect themselves from cultural assault. Indians apparently see education as an Anglo intrusion. What is more, they find that the Cherokee do not believe that success in school will have an impact on the quality and character of their lives on the reservation.

Fuchs and Havighurst (1973) contend that American Indian children perceive their subordinate status and thus lose self-confidence and deny motivation for school success. Those authors found that only 11% of Bureau of Indian Affairs teachers were of Native American ancestry and the majority of teachers did not have a good understanding of, sensitivity to, and respect for the Indian community.

Positive and Accepting Climate

Contrary to the conclusions of the report on educational opportunity by Coleman and his colleagues (1969), there is evidence that certain classroom environments have a differential impact on various students and that they produce recognizable patterns of behavior (Forness, Guthrie, & MacMillan, 1982). In England, Rutter, Maugham, Mortimore, and Ouston (1979) and Rutter (1983) found a significant effect of school climate on achievement test results in secondary schools. Even if a teacher/pupil style match is not possible, the creation of a warm, responsive climate in which diverse children are valued can be effective. Research indicates that low-income pupils are particularly sensitive to school climate (Spady, 1973).

Teacher socialization style has a powerful impact on children's social cognition and reported interpersonal classroom behavior, especially with younger children (Rohrkemper, 1984). Students appear to internalize the underlying principles of their teacher's strategies for dealing with peers. Halperin (1976) also observes that teachers' goals and beliefs influence classroom activities, children's behaviors, and children's perceptions of school. Certain ideologies produce environments that children find anxiety-arousing.

According to Lightfoot (1983), "Good schools are places where students are seen as worthy of respect" (p. 350). Crain, Mahard, and Narot (1982) found that respect for students was influential in creating a positive school climate. Jencks (1972) suggested that school life be thought of as an end in itself. He observed that some schools are dull, depressing—even terrifying—places, while others are lively, comfortable, and reassuring. He recommended that children be offered diversity and choice and that schools be enjoyable, with children feeling that they are doing something purposeful.

Regarding social-psychological environments, Haertel, Walberg and Haertel (1979) conclude that learning gains are positively associated with student-perceived cohesiveness, satisfaction, task difficulty, formality, goal-directedness, and a good material environment, and negatively associated with frustration, cliques, apathy, and disorganization. Walberg and Rasher (1979) add that student involvement in school and student perceptions of democratic practices are also related to achievement.

Acceptance of Child's Language

Among the functions of language are those of serving as a symbol and identifier of group membership and as the principal medium for mediating and manipulating social relationships (Saville-Troike, 1980). Language is unique in its dual role as an intrinsic component of culture and as a medium through which other aspects of culture, including the content of formal education, are expressed and transmitted. Language is an intricate part of selfhood, and the way others respond to it affects the child's self-concept and feelings toward others.

Teachers' perceptions of limited-English proficient children or children with minority dialects are often negative. Teachers may categorically type the child without being sensitive to details of the language performance (Williams, 1976). Labov (1972) has written of the richness, fluency, and general competence of speakers of black English. Clearly, teachers should learn to appreciate language differences and make use of them creatively in the classroom.

Increasing Tolerance for Diverse Students

Regular class teachers tend to believe that the welfare of the larger group is their responsibility. Thus, among problem behaviors, disruptiveness, with the possibility of being "contagious" or having a ripple effect on other students' behaviors, is least acceptable because it is perceived as interfering with the general well-being of the group (Safran & Safran, 1985). Teachers perhaps can be taught to broaden their range of tolerance for behavioral and academic differences (Oden, 1976). Through preservice or inservice training, they might also learn more effective behavior management strategies. A third possibility is to provide more classroom support or technical assistance in helping teachers deal with problematic behaviors.

Morton and Hull (1976) described a school where children simply were not referred for special education and the principal welcomed all. Mitman (1985) found that teachers who showed more concern for lower-achieving students tended to have more flexible and accurate perceptions of students—but unfortunately they were rated lower on their quality of teaching. Feree (1985) believes that to know students, teachers must be able to put themselves in the student's place.

Handicap Awareness

Stevens and Allen (1984) summarize strategies for improving attitudes toward handicapped individuals. These include classroom instruction, role play (disability simulation), increased contact, media presentations, and social participation in structured social situations. Salend and Knops (1984) contend that some models tend to instill "well-meaning but overly sympathetic" views toward handicapped people. They recommend a cognitive approach, whereby students learn about realistic classroom problems of handicapped students, to facilitate constructive, equal-status relationships.

Dealing with Conflict

According to Crain, Mahard, and Narot (1982), in desegregated settings "no open conflict is a bad sign" (p. 67). They, as well as Hilliard (1978) and Coleman (1978), advocate an open, communicative atmosphere where conflicts are brought into the open, discussed, and resolutions planned.

Liss and Robinson (1978) have described a number of specific methods for dealing with intergroup conflicts: (1) Sponsor student retreats with representatives from a variety of student groups; (2) conduct leadership training in racial/ethnic awareness, understanding, and problem solving; (3) select committees of students to work toward problem resolution; (4) utilize faculty to seek solutions to racial strife; (5) have a separate disciplinary policy for dealing with racial incidents (they used a review board to hear cases involving alleged racial conflicts); (6) initiate a faculty/student human relations committee; (7) encourage "trouble-makers" to get involved with constructive solutions to the school's problems; and (8) provide more social and recreational activities in the school. Removing police from the school facilities was found to have a positive impact in the Liss and Robinson and the Crain, Mahard, and Narot situations.

Parent/Community Involvement in Schools

Walker and Perez (1980) emphasize the importance of local community schools in enhancing parental attitudes toward schools. They suggest that the school be a catalytic agent by providing leadership to mobilize community resources to solve identified community problems. Although Walker and Perez prefer small schools because they reduce anonymity and invite alliances between urban schools and the community, other sources have suggested creating long-term subgroups of students or within-school clusters, to involve students and give them a sense of belonging and being known in school (Crain, Mahard, & Narot, 1982). The consensus is that attempts should be made to actively involve parents in schools. Walberg (1984) distinguishes various roles for family partnerships in schooling: audience for child's work, home tutor, co-learner, supporter of school programs, advocate before school board and other officials, committee members, and paid school workers.

Conscious Involvement of Diverse Children

Steps should be taken to involve mainstreamed handicapped students in the daily routine; otherwise they are unlikely to become accepted members of the regular class (Gottlieb & Leyser, 1981). Gresham (1982), too, claims that benefits do not occur with mainstreaming unless active programmatic interventions are implemented.

Social Skills Training

Maheady, Maitland, and Sainato (1984) report that mildly mentally handicapped children engage in behavior associated with social perception deficits more often than their nondisabled peers. Gresham (1982), too, argues that mainstreaming efforts do not increase social interaction with most handicapped students because they lack the social skills needed to interact with their peers. Elias and Maher (1983) report that their television-based instructional format for teaching social-cognition, problem-solving skills is valuable in teaching social skills.

Peer tutoring has been advocated as an effective technique for improving social adjustment. The technique used by Custer and Osguthorpe (1983) was unique: having handicapped students tutor their nonhandicapped peers in sign language for 8 weeks—which gave the handicapped students a superior social advantage. They found that social interaction between handicapped and nonhandicapped individuals during free time rose from 5% to 46%, and nonhandicapped students reported that the handicapped were "fun to be with." Powell and Lindeman (1983) utilized "free play" periods to teach social interaction skills. They suggest that teachers prompt, model, and physically assist handicapped children to share, assist peers, and initiate and maintain an activity. Dodge (1983) and Odom and McConnell (1985) report success in studies of different strategies for promoting social competence in children with social problems to increase and improve social relations.

Grouping Strategies

Allport (1954) suggests that common goals be held for all students and that a cooperative atmosphere is conducive to positive peer interaction. A multitude of studies about cooperative grouping arrangements have been conducted of late. Although there are a variety of models for cooperative grouping, they all seem to involve some form of heterogeneous pupil grouping (variety of ability or achievement levels, handicapped and nonhandicapped, members of different races and ethnic groups, males and females) that works together toward a common goal.

Cooperative grouping can be as simple as peer tutoring or as complex as a group investigation with individualized assignments. For example, Aronson, Blaney, Stephen, Sikes, & Snapp (1978) developed a "Jigsaw Classroom," involving five- to six-member groups in which each member is assigned a portion of the total assignment, masters that material, and then teaches the group. Thus, students depend on each other for the total picture. After 6 weeks of use, those authors claimed students: (1) had a stronger liking of peers, (2) believed they could learn from classmates, (3) liked school better, (4) had more positive self-concepts, (5) improved academically, and (6) showed improved racial behavior.

In comparison with competitive or individualistic arrangements, a number of reviews have concluded that cooperative learning techniques can achieve both cognitive and affective goals (Johnson, Maruyama, Johnson, Nelson, & Skon, 1981; Sharan, 1980; Slavin, 1980). Team learning can have a positive effect on motivation (Slavin & Karweit, 1984) and self-concept of ability (Ames, 1981). It also promotes cross-handicap interaction during instruction and during post-instruction free time (Johnson & Johnson, 1981), has a positive impact on race relations (DeVries & Slavin, 1976; Slavin & Madden, 1979), promotes cross-sex and cross-ethnic relationships (Warring, Johnson, Maruyama, & Johnson, 1985), and creates favorable attitudes toward school and academic success.

Cooperative grouping arrangements can create a sense of mutual concern and group membership (DeVries & Slavin, 1976; Slavin, 1980), improve student perceptions of degree of cooperation in their learning environment (Talmadge & Pascarella, 1984), increase the accuracy of daily work and post-instructional retention (Yager, Johnson, & Johnson, 1985), and improve reading achievement (Talmadge & Pascarella, 1984). Combined with individualized instruction (i.e., in the Team Assisted Instruction program), cooperative grouping can increase mathematics achievement (Slavin & Karweit, 1984). Slavin (1984) emphasizes that student achievement in the use of cooperative methods results from the use of cooperative *incentives,* not cooperative tasks.

Teacher Characteristics

Rosenholtz (1985) emphasizes the importance of recruiting outstanding teachers, monitoring their actions, and supplying technical assistance, to improve student achievement in inner-city schools. Others contend that teachers of diverse groups of children must value different types of people (Love, 1977), have positive expectations for all children (Dotts, 1975), and encourage all children to excel (Love, 1977).

These teachers must be dedicated to the principles of integrated education (Braziel, 1978) and be advocates for low-income and minority children (Fuchs, 1973). They need to eradicate residual prejudice from their language (Hilliard, 1978). Gallagher (1985) and Baum and Frazita (1979), among others, have documented positive changes in teacher attitude toward mainstreaming following training.

Leadership

An Educational Testing Service (1976) study of 118 elementary and 93 high schools concluded that good race relations among students resulted at schools where both black and white teachers gave principals high ratings as "supportive." In aggregating the results of approximately 1,200 studies of urban schools, Clark, Lotto, and McCarthy (1980) rank leadership—particularly that of school principals—and teacher attitudes toward education and the expected success of educational programs at the top of their list. Walter (1981) calls for vigorous leadership at all levels, and administrators who are well-versed in program content and who give feedback effectively. Further, he contends that administrators must be willing to take risks, or make changes in the face of substantial opposition, and articulate and implement policies that have new programs, role changes, and different organization. Walter believes that effective implementation requires time, personal interaction and contacts, inservice training, and people-based support.

CONCLUSION

Serow and Solomon (1979) found a majority of parents to be in favor of racial-desegregation. In interviews with low-income parents, Brantlinger (1985b) found that the majority preferred social-class integrated schools for their children. A multitude of writers (e.g., Gardner, 1982; Moran, 1984; Oden, 1976; Strang, Smith, & Rogers, 1978) emphasize the potential benefits of mainstreaming for mildly handicapped children. But simply desegregating diverse populations without adopting effective methods of teaching them can have a negative impact on the minority student.

REFERENCES

Aguirre, A. (1979). Chicanos, intelligence testing and the quality of life. *Educational Research Quarterly, 4*, 3–12.

Algozzine, B., Ysseldyke, J. E., & Christenson, S. (1983). The masses are burgeoning. *Journal of Special Education, 17*(2), 141–146.

Allport, G. (1954). *The nature of prejudice*. Reading, MA: Addison-Wesley.

Ames, C. (1981). Competitive versus cooperative reward structures: The influence of individual and group performance factors on achievement attributions and affect. *American Educational Research Journal, 18*, 273–287.

Ames, C., & Ames, R. (1981). Competitive versus individualistic goal structures: The salience of past performance information for causal attributions and affect. *Journal of Educational Psychology, 73*, 411–418.

Anderson, G. R., & Anderson, S. K. (1983). The exceptional native American. In D. R. Omark & J. G. Erickson (Eds.), *The bilingual exceptional child* (pp. 163–180). San Diego: College-Hill Press.

Anyon, J. (1980). Social class and the hidden curriculum of work. *Journal of Education, 62*, 67–92.

Apple, M (1982). *Education and power*. Boston: Routledge/Kegan Paul.

Argulewicz, E. N. (1983). Effects of ethnic membership, socioeconomic status, and home language on LD, EMR, and EH placements. *Learning Disabilities Quarterly, 6*, 195–200.

Aronson, E., Blaney, N., Stephen, C., Sikes, J., & Snapp, M. (1978). *The jigsaw classroom*. Beverly Hills, CA: Sage Publications.

Baum, R. B., & Frazita, R. F. (1979). Educating the exceptional child in the regular classroom. *Journal of Teacher Education, 30*(6), 20–21.

Berman, E. H. (1984). State hegemony and the schooling process. *Journal of Education, 166*(3), 239–253.

Bernal, E. M. (1983). Trends in bilingual special education. *Learning Disabilities Quarterly, 6*, 424–431.

Berry, J. W. (1983). Comparative studies of cognitive styles. In R. J. Samuda & S. L. Woods, *Perspectives in immigrant and minority education* (pp. 247–257). Lanham, MD: University Press of America.

Block, J. H. (1984). Making school learning activities more playlike: Flow and mastery learning. *Elementary School Journal, 85*(1), 64–75.

Bowles, S., & Gintis, H. (1976). *Schooling in capitalist America*. New York: Basic Books.

Brantlinger, E. A. (1985a). Low-income parents' perceptions of favoritism in the schools. *Urban Education, 20*(1), 82–102.

Brantlinger, E. A. (1985b). Low-income parents' opinions about the social class composition of schools. *American Journal of Education, 93*(3), 389–408.

Brazziel, W. (1978). Quality integrated education. *Theory Into Practice, 17*(2), 93.

Broman, S. H., Nichols, P. L., & Kennedy, W. A. (1975). *Preschool IQ: Prenatal and early developmental correlates*. Hillsdale, NJ: Erlbaum Press.

Brookover, W. B., & Lezotte, L. (1979). *Changes in school characteristics coincident with changes in student achievement*. East Lansing: Michigan State University, Institute for Research in Teaching.

Brophy, J. (1982). Successful teaching strategies for the inner-city child. *Phi Delta Kappan, 63*, 527–530.

Brophy, J. E., & Good, T. (1974). *Teacher-student relationships: Causes and consequences*. New York: Holt, Rinehart & Winston.

Brown, B. F. (1977). *Education for responsible citizenship* (Report) Washington, DC: National Task Force on Citizenship Education.

Burnett, J. H. (1976). Commentary: Paradoxes and dilemmas. *Anthropology & Education Quarterly, 7*, 37–38.

Cazden, C. B., Carrasco, R., Maldonado-Guzman, A. A., & Erickson, F. (1980). The contribution of ethnographic research to bicultural-bilingual education. In J. E. Alatis (Ed.), *Current issues in bilingual education* (pp. 64–80). Washington, DC: Georgetown University Press.

Clark, D. L., Lotto, L. S., & McCarthy, M. M. (1980). Factors associated with success in urban elementary schools. *Phi Delta Kappan, 61*, 467–470.

Cohen, D., & Lazerson, M. (1977). Education and the corporate order: Merit and equality. In J. Karabel & A. H. Halsey (Eds.), *Power and ideology in education*. New York: Oxford University Press.

Cohen, R. A. (1969). Conceptual styles, cultural conflict and nonverbal tests of intelligence. *American Anthropologist, 71*, 828–856.

Coleman, J. M. (1978). The intergroups relations specialist: Change agent for public schools. *Theory Into Practice, 17*(2).

Coleman, J. S., et al. (1969). *Equal educational opportunity*. Cambridge, MA: Harvard University Press.

Covington, M. V. (1984). The self-worth theory of achievement motivation: Findings and implications. *Elementary School Journal, 85*(1), 4–20.

Crain, R. L., Mahard, R. E., & Narot, R. E. (1982). *Making desegregation work: How schools create social climates*. Cambridge, MA: Ballinger Publishing Co.

Crosland, C. A. R. (1974). Comprehensive education. In *Socialism now and other essays* (pp. 193–210.). London: Cape Press.

Custer, J. D., & Osguthorpe, R. T. (1983). Improving social acceptance by training handicapped students to tutor their nonhandicapped peers. *Exceptional Children, 50*(2), 173–174.

DeVries, D. L., & Slavin, R. E. (1976). *Teams-games tournament: A final report on the research*. Baltimore: Center for Social Organization of Schools, Johns Hopkins University.

Dodge, K. A. (1983). Promoting social competence in school children. *Schools & Teaching, 1*(2).

Dotts, W. (1975). Black and white teacher attitude toward disadvantage and poverty. *Education, 99*, 48–54.

Drummond, H. (1982). Power, madness and poverty. *Behavior Disorders, 7*, 101–109.

Dumont, R., Jr., & Wax, M. L. (1969). Cherokee school society and the intercultural classroom. *Human Organization, 28*, 217–226.

Edgerton, R. B. (1981). Another look at culture and mental retardation. In M. J. Begab, H. C. Haywood, & H. L. Garber, *Psychosocial influences in retarded performance* (Vol. 1) (pp. 309–323). Baltimore: University Park Press.

Educational Testing Service. (1976). *Conditions and processes of effective desegregation*. Princeton, NJ: Educational Testing Service.

Educational Testing Service. (1980). New vistas in special education. *Focus, 8*, 1–20.

Elias, M. J., & Maher, C. A. (1983). Social and affective development of children: A programmatic perspective. *Exceptional Children, 49*(4), 339–344.

Ferree, G. (1985). The epistemology of knowing how students feel. *American Journal of Education, 93*(2), 240–251.

Ford, J., Mongon, D., & Whelan, M. (1982). *Special education and social control: Invisible disaster*. London: Routledge/Kegan Paul.

Forness, S. R., Guthrie, D., & MacMillan, D. L. (1982). Classroom environments as they relate to mentally retarded children's observable behavior. *American Journal of Mental Deficiency, 87*(3), 259–265.

Fuchs, E. (1973). How teachers learn to help children fail. In N. Keddie (Ed.), *The myth of cultural deprivation* (pp. 75–85). London: Penguin Education.

Fuchs, E., & Havighurst, R. J. (1973). *To live on this earth*. New York: Anchor/Doubleday.

Gallagher, P. (1985). Inservice: A mandated special education course and its effects on regular classroom teachers. *Teacher Education & Special Education, 8*(2), 59–65.

Gardner, W. I. (1982). Why do we persist? *Education & Treatment of Children, 5*, 369–378.

Gerber, M. M. (1984). Learning disabilities and cognitive strategies: A case for training or constraining problem solving? *Journal of Learning Disabilities, 16*(5), 255–260.

Giroux, H. A. (1983). Theories of reproduction and resistance in the new sociology of education: A critical analysis. *Harvard Educational Review, 53,* 257–293.

Glass, G. V. (1980). On criticism of our class size/student achievement research. *Phi Delta Kappan, 62,* 242–244.

Gordon, M. T. (1976). A different view of the IQ-achievement gap. *Sociology of Education, 49,* 4–11.

Gottfredson, G. D. (1980). *Schooling and delinquency prevention: Some practical ideas for educators, parents, program developers and researchers* (Report Number 303). Baltimore: Johns Hopkins University Center for Social Organization of Schools.

Gottlieb, J. (1982). Mainstreaming. *Education & Training of the Mentally Retarded, 17,* 79–82.

Gottlieb, J., & Leyser, Y. (1981). Facilitating the social mainstreaming of retarded children. *Exceptional Education Quarterly, 1*(4), 57–69.

Gresham, F. M. (1982). Misguided mainstreaming: The case for social skills training with handicapped children. *Exceptional Children, 48,* 422–435.

Haertel, G. D., Walberg, H. J., & Haertel, E. H. (1979, April). *Socio-psycological environments and learning: A quantitative synthesis.* Paper presented at the annual meeting of the American Educational Research Association, San Francisco.

Halperin, M. S. (1976). First grade teachers' goals and children's developing perceptions of school. *Journal of Educational Psychology, 68,* 636–648.

Harris, J. J., III (1978). Impact of desegregation: A historical and legal analysis. In F. Aquila (Ed.), *School desegregation: A model at work* (pp. 53–68.). Bloomington, IN: Training Institute, School of Education.

Hendricks, G. (1981). *The centered teacher: Awareness activities for teachers and their students.* New Jersey: Prentice-Hall.

Hilliard, A. G., III (1978). Straight talk about school desegregation problems. *Theory Into Practice, 17*(2), 100–106.

Hollins, E. R. (1982). The Marva Collins story revisited: Implications for regular classroom instruction. *Journal of Teacher Education, 33*(1).

Jencks, C. (1972). *Inequality, a reassessment of the effect of family and schooling in America.* New York: Harper & Row.

Johnson, D. W., Maruyama, G., Johnson, R., Nelson, D., & Skon, L. (1981). Effects of cooperative, competitive and individualistic goal structures on achievement: A meta-analysis. *Psychological Bulletin, 89*(1), 47–62.

Johnson, R. T., & Johnson, D. W. (1981). Building friendships between handicapped and non-handicapped students: Effects of cooperative and individualistic instruction. *American Educational Research Journal, 18,* 415–423.

Jones, R. L., & Wilderson, F. B., Jr. (1976). Mainstreaming and the minority child: An overview of issues and a perspective. In R. L. Jones (Ed.), *Mainstreaming and the minority child* (pp. 1–13), Reston, VA: Council for Exceptional Children.

Kushlick, A., & Blunder, R. (1974). The epidemiology of mental subnormality. In A. M. Clark & A. B Clarke (Eds.), *Mental deficiency: The changing outlook* (3rd ed.). New York: Free Press.

Labov, W. (1972). *Language in the inner city: Studies in Black English vernacular.* Philadelphia: University of Pennsylvania Press.

Levine, D. U., Kukuk, C., & Meyer, J. K. (1979). Poverty in big cities. In H. J. Walberg (Ed.), *Educational environments and effects.* Berkeley: McCutchan Publishing Corp.

Lightfoot, S. L. (1983). The good high school: Portraits of character and culture. New York: Basic Books.

Liss, M., & Robinson, J. C. (1978). The Carteret story: The peer group deals with racial conflict. *Phi Delta Kappan, 57,* 169–172.

Longo, P. (1982). Mainstreaming: The promise and the pitfalls. *Urban Education, 17,* 157–180.

Lorde, A. (1983). There is no hierarchy of oppressions. *Interracial Books for Children, 14*(3 & 4), 9.

Love, B. J. (1977). Desegregation in your school: Behavior patterns that get in the way. *Phi Delta Kappan, 56,* 168–170.

MacMillan, D. L. (1976). *Mental retardation in school and society.* Boston: Little, Brown.

Madden, N., & Slavin, R. E. (1983). Mainstreaming students with mild handicaps: Academic and social outcomes. *Review of Educational Research, 53,* 519–569.

Maheady, L., Maitland, G. & Sainato, D. (1984). The interpretation of social interactions by mildly handicapped and non-disabled children. *Journal of Special Education, 18*(2), 151–159.

McKnight, R. T. (1982). The learning disability myth in American education. *Journal of Education, 164*(4), 351–359.

Mare, R. D. (1981). Change and stability in educational stratification. *American Sociological Review, 46*, 72–87.

Mehan, H. (1979). *Learning lessons: Social organization in the classroom*. Cambridge: Harvard University Press.

Meier, D. (1982). Planning to keep them in their place. *In These Times*, May 26.

Meier, D. (1984, Winter). "Getting tough" in the schools. *Dissent*, pp. 61–70.

Mitman, A. L. (1985). Teachers' differential behavior toward higher and lower achieving students and its relation to selected teacher characteristics. *Journal of Educational Psychology, 77*(2), 149–161.

Moran, M. R. (1984). Excellence at the cost of instructional equity: The potential impact of recommended reforms upon low achieving students. *Focus on Exceptional Children, 16*(7), 1–12.

Morton, K. A., & Hull, K. (1976). Parents and the mainstream. In R. L. Jones (Ed.), *Mainstreaming and the minority child* (pp. 37–52). Reston, VA: Council for Exceptional Children.

Nicholls, J. G. (1979). Quality and equality in intellectual development: The role of motivation in education. *American Psychologist, 34*, 1071–1084.

Ochoa, A. M., Pacheco, R., & Omark, D. R. (1983). Addressing the learning disability needs of limited-English proficient students: Beyond language and race issues. *Learning Disabilities Quarterly, 6*, 416–423.

Oden, C. W., Jr. (1976). Desegregation and mainstreaming: A case of deja vu. In R. L. Jones, *Mainstreaming and the minority child* (pp. 53–64). Reston, VA: Council for Exceptional Children.

Odom, S. L., & McConnell, S. R. A performance-based conceptualization of social competence of handicapped preschool children: Implications for assessment. *Topics in Early Childhood Special Education, 4*(4), 1–19.

Ogbu, J. U. (1974). *The next generation: An ethnography of an urban neighborhood*. New York: Academic Press.

Orfield, G. (1978). *Must we bus? Segregated schools and national policy*. Washington, DC: Brookings Institute.

Ornstein, A. C. (1978). *Education and social inquiry*. Itasca, IL: F. E. Peacock Publishers.

Patchen, M. (1982). *Black-white contact in schools: Its social and academic effects*. West Lafayette, IN: Purdue University Press.

Peterson, P., & Swing, S. (1982). Beyond time on task: Students' reports of their thought processes during classroom instruction. *Elementary School Journal, 82*, 481–491.

Philips, S. U. (1982). *The invisible culture: Communication in classroom and community on the Work Springs Indian Reservation*. New York: Longman Press.

Pines, H. A., & Julian, J. W. (1972). Effects of task and social demands on locus of control differences in information processing. *Journal of Personality, 40*, 407–416.

Pink, W. T. (1982). School effects, academic performance, and school crime. *Urban Education, 17*, 51–72.

Polloway, E. A. (1984). The integration of mildly retarded students in the schools: A historical review. *Remedial & Special Education, 5*(4), 18–28.

Polloway, E. A., & Smith, J. D. (1983). Changes in mild mental retardation: Population, programs, and perspectives. *Exceptional Children, 50*, 149–159.

Powell, T. H., & Lindeman, D. P. (1983). Developing a social interaction teaching program for young handicapped children. *Exceptional Children, 50*(1), 72–74.

Ramey, C. T., & Campbell, F. A. (1979). Compensatory education for disadvantaged children. *School Review, 87*, 1711–1789.

Reynolds, M. C., & Wang, M. C. (1983). Restructuring "special" school programs. *Policy Studies Review, 2*(1), 189–212.

Rist, R. C. (Ed.) (1979). *Desegregated schools: Appraisals of an American experience*. New York: Academic Press.

Rohrkemper, M. M. (1984). The influence of teacher socialization style on students' social cognition and reported interpersonal classroom behavior. *Elementary School Journal, 85*(2), 244–275.

Roper, D., & Roper, S. (1979). The accountable school: Elective courses, competition and cost effectiveness. *Phi Delta Kappan, 62*, 527–528.

Rosenholtz, S. J. (1985). Effective schools: Interpreting the evidence. *American Journal of Education, 93*(3), 352–388.

Rosenholtz, S. J., & Simpson, C. (1984). Classroom organization and student stratification. *Elementary School Journal, 85*(1), 21–37.
Rosenholtz, S., & Wilson, B. (1980). The effect of classroom structure on shared perceptions of ability. *American Educational Research Journal, 17,* 75–82.
Rosenshine, B. V., & Berliner, D. C. (1978). Academic engaged time. *British Journal of Teacher Education, 4,* 3–16.
Rosenshine, B. V. (1979). Content, time and direct instruction. In P. Peterson & H. Walberg (Eds.), *Research on teaching: Concepts, findings and implications* (pp. 28–56). Berkeley: McCutchan Press.
Rouck, U. (1980). What makes an effective teacher? Research confirms the complexity of the teacher's job. *American Educator, 4*(3), 14–17.
Rutter, M. (1983). School effects on pupil progress: Research findings and policy implications. *Child Development, 54,* 1–29.
Rutter, M., Maugham, B., Mortimore, P., & Ouston, J. (1979). *Fifteen thousand hours: Secondary schools and their effect on children.* Cambridge, MA: Harvard University Press.
Safran, S. P., & Safran, J. S. (1985). Classroom context and teachers' perceptions of problem behaviors. *Journal of Educational Psychology, 77*(1), 20–28.
St. John, N. (1975). *School desegregation: Outcomes for children.* New York: John Wiley & Sons.
Salend, S. J., & Knops, B. (1984). Hypothetical examples: A cognitive approach to changing attitudes toward the handicapped. *Elementary School Journal, 85,* 228–235.
Sando, J. (1973). Educating the native American: Conflict in values. In L. Branford, L. Baca, & K. Lane, *Cultural diversity and the exceptional child* (pp. 58–65). Reston, VA: Council for Exceptional Children.
Saville-Troike, M. (1978). *A guide to culture in the classroom.* Roslyn, VA: National Clearing House for Bilingual Education.
Saville-Troike, M. (1980). Cross-cultural communications in the classroom. In J. E. Alatis, (Ed.), *Current issues in bilingual education.* Washington, DC: Georgetown University Press.
Schofield, J. W. (1982). *Black and white in school: Trust, tension or tolerance?* New York: Praeger Publishers.
Serow, R. C., & Solomon, D. (1979, June). Parents' attitudes toward desegregation: The proximity hypothesis. *Phi Delta Kappan,* pp. 752–753.
Shade, B. J. (1982). Afro-American cognitive style: A variable in school success? *Review of Educational Research, 52,* 219–244.
Sharan, S. (1980). Cooperative learning in small groups: Recent methods and effects on achievement, attitudes and ethnic relations. *Review of Educational Research, 50*(2), 241–271.
Sheinker, A., Sheinker, J. M., & Stevens, L. J. (1984). Cognitive strategies for teaching the mildly handicapped. *Focus on Exceptional Children, 17*(1), 1–15.
Seiber, R. T. (1982). The politics of middle-class success in an inner-city public school. *Journal of Education, 164,* 30–47.
Singleton, J. (1974). Implications of education as culture transmission. In G. Spindler (Ed.), *Education and cultural process: Toward an anthropology of education.* New York: Holt, Rinehart, & Winston.
Slavin, R. E. (1980). Cooperative learning. *Review of Educational Research, 50*(2), 315–342.
Slavin, R. E. (1984). Students motivating students to excel: Cooperative incentives, cooperative tasks, and student achievement. *Elementary School Journal, 85*(1), 53–63.
Slavin, R. E., & Karweit, N. L. (1984). Mastery learning and student teams: A factorial experiment in urban general mathematics classes. *American Educational Research Journal, 21*(4), 725–736.
Slavin, R. E., & Madden, N. A. (1979). School practices that improve race relations. *American Educational Research Journal, 16,* 169–180.
Smith, B. (1983). Homophobia: Why bring it up? *Interracial Books for Children, 14*(2 & 4), 7–8.
Spady, W. G. (1973). The impact of school resources on students. In F. Kerlinger (Ed.), *Review of Research in Education* (Vol. 1). Itasca, IL: F. E. Peacock Publishers.
Stanley, S. O., & Greenwood, C. R. (1983). How much "opportunity to respond" does the minority disadvantaged student receive in school? *Exceptional Children, 49*(4), 370–373.
Stevens, R. N., & Allen, R. F. (1984). Strategies for improving attitudes toward handicapped students. *Social Studies, 75,* 220–223.
Strang, L., Smith, M. D., & Rogers, C. M. (1978). Social comparison, multiple reference groups and the self-concept of handicapped children before and after mainstreaming. *Journal of Educational*

Psychology, 70, 487–497.

Sullivan, M. L. (1979). Desegregation in a polyethnic New York City high school. In R. C. Rist (Ed.), *Desegregated schools: Appraisals of an American experience* (pp. 201–240). New York: Academic Press.

Talmage, H., & Pascarella, E. T. (1984). The influence of cooperative learning-strategies on teacher practices, student perceptions of the learning environment and academic achievement. *American Educational Research Journal, 12*(1), 163–179.

Taylor, M. C. (1979). Race, sex and the expression of self-fulfilling prophecies in a laboratory teaching situation. *Journal of Personality & Social Psychology, 37,* 897–912.

Tinney, J. S. (1983). Interconnections. *Interracial Books for Children, 14*(3 & 4), 4–6 + .

Walberg, H. J. (1984). Families as partners in educational productivity. *Phi Delta Kappan, 65*(6), 397–400.

Walberg, H. J., & Rasher, S. P. (1979). Achievement in fifty states. In H. J. Walberg (Ed.), *Educational environments and effects* (pp. 353–368). Berkeley: McCutchan Publishing Corp.

Walker, J. E., & Perez, R. L. (1980). Improving public confidence in education. *Clearing House, 53,* 394–396.

Walter, J. E. (1981). Successful program implementation in urban schools. *Educational Leadership, 38,* 635–638.

Wang, M. C. (1976). *Maximizing the effective use of school time by teachers and students.* Pittsburgh: Learning Research & Development Center, University of Pittsburgh.

Wang, M. C. (1981). Mainstreaming exceptional children: Some instructional design and implementation considerations. *Elementary School Journal, 81,* 194–221.

Wang, M. C., & Lindvall, C. M. (1984). Individual differences and school learning environments. In E. W. Gordon (Ed.), *Review of research in education* (Vol. 2). Washington, DC: American Educational Research Association.

Warring, D., Johnson, D. W., Maruyama, G., & Johnson, R. (1985). Impact of different types of cooperative learning on cross-ethnic and cross-sex relationships. *Journal of Educational Psychology, 77*(1), 53–59.

Wax, M. L., Diamond, S., & Gearing, F. O. (Eds.). (1971). *Anthropological perspectives on education.* New York: Basic Books.

Weiner, B. (1979). A theory of motivation for some classroom experiences. *Journal of Educational Psychology, 71,* 3–25.

Williams, F. (1976). *Explorations of the linguistic attitudes of teachers.* Rowley, MA: Newbury House.

Witkin, H. A., Moore, C. A., Goodenough, D. R., & Cox, P. W. (1977). Field-dependent and field-independent cognitive styles and their educational implications. *Review of Educational Research, 47,* 1–64.

Wright, P., & Santa Cruz, R. (1983). Ethnic composition of special education programs in California. *Learning Disabilities Quarterly, 6,* 387–394.

Yager, S., Johnson, D. W., & Johnson, R. T. (1985). Oral discussion, group-to-individual transfer, and achievement in cooperative learning groups. *Journal of Educational Psychology, 77*(1).

Ysseldyke, J. E., Algozzine, B., & Richey, L. (1982). Judgment under uncertainty: How many children are handicapped? *Exceptional Children, 48.*

Ellen Brantlinger and Samuel Guskin are affiliated with the Special Education Department, Indiana University.

The authors describe the *optimal learning environments model* developed at Vanderbilt University. They use their experience in implementing the model with infants and toddlers as a basis for helping readers understand the training and curricular implications of the program. The authors provide an excellent review of the research literature on early intervention of preschool children with disabilities.

An Optimal Learning Environment for Infants and Toddlers with Severe Handicaps

Steven F. Warren, Cathy L. Alpert, and Ann P. Kaiser

Infants and toddlers with severe handicaps have immense needs. During the period when normal children develop most rapidly, the multiple deficits of children with handicaps prevent them from interacting with the environment in ways that are critical to subsequent development of motor, cognitive, communicative, and social skills. They are doubly limited by their delayed physical development and by their limited ability to engage with the environment in ways that can stimulate development. Young children with severe cerebral palsy, for example, may be so motorically impaired that they must have assistance to engage in even rudimentary self-directed exploration of the environment. Deaf-blind babies' motor, social, and communicative behaviors are limited dramatically by their lack of auditory and visual input from the environment. Many children with severe handicaps are chronically ill during early childhood (Batshaw & Perret, 1981) and spend considerable time hospitalized. The characteristics of this particular environment, the illness itself, and the effects of the illness on mother-child interaction may further impede the child's developmental progress (Horowitz, 1982).

Current programs for infants and toddlers with severe handicaps are often inadequate (Garland, Stone, Swanson, & Woodruff, 1981). Few teachers and support staff have appropriate and sufficient training to design and deliver the range of services this population requires. Although advances have been made in therapeutic and instructional procedures, most current techniques have been adapted from those developed for older and less handicapped children (Tjossem, 1976). The service delivery systems available for providing treatment to infants are often problematic. Home-based intervention, which has many attractive aspects, may not provide intensive enough training to promote a child's interaction with the environment. Traditionally organized early childhood intervention settings and typical therapy models may result in low rates of child-teacher contact when implemented with severely handicapped toddlers (Hart, 1982), who may require one-to-one or two-to-one child-teacher ratios (Ramey & Trohanis, 1982). When staff-child ratios are higher, children may spend a great deal of time waiting for therapy and stimulation while the crucial period of early development slips away (Sailor & Guess, 1983).

Because programs for very young children with severe handicaps have been initiated only recently, service delivery and treatment model problems are not surprising. Nevertheless, the need to design models for more effective and efficient treatment for these children is pressing (Garland et al., 1981). Simply increasing teacher-child ratios—even if such a solution were affordable—would not necessarily guarantee a higher quality of individual services. The challenges in providing quality services to handicapped children are fourfold: (a) to provide sufficient individualized training in each area of development; (b) to ensure that this training generalizes to functional contexts; (c) to promote self-directed exploration and engagement with the environment as a means of supplementing directly programmed training; and (d) to provide these services in a cost-effective manner. To address all of these issues, intervention programs must be designed to include specialists from several disciplines, a curriculum that is adaptable to children with a range of needs across all domains, an environment that supports child engagement and includes incidental teaching interactions to facilitate naturalistic learning, procedures to promote generalization of newly learned behaviors, and a strategy for doing all of these things with finite resources.

THE OPTIMAL LEARNING ENVIRONMENTS MODEL

Recent developments in microcomputer technology, environmental design, and service delivery models may offer some solutions to the basic problems that face providers of infant interventions. The model presented here for the education and treatment of toddlers with severe handicaps integrates these developments. The resulting model program is based on the premise that increasing teacher-child contact and child engagement and improving the quality of instruction can be accomplished through application of the principles of environmental design and use of computer technology when applied in the framework of a transdisciplinary, consultant-therapist model. Use of an Individual Curriculum Sequencing approach in combination with other components of the model can effectively address the issues of functional use and generalization by infants and toddlers with severe handicaps. We call the resulting center-based intervention approach the Optimal Learning Environments model. We have been developing and refining this model at the John F. Kennedy Experimental School at Vanderbilt University over the past 3 years. During this time we have served over 20 children and their families. Students in the program have ranged from infants to 3-year-olds (average age, 14 months). All children were multiply handicapped with some degree of mental retardation.

We have attempted to effectively address the individual needs of very young children with severe handicaps by designing an environment that optimizes learning opportunities within a service delivery system that minimizes logistical constraints on providing quality services. Children in the program have made substantial progress, as demonstrated by gains in tests of cognitive and motor functioning and attainment of IEP objectives in multiple areas of development.

As primary consumers of the program, parents consistently have indicated strong satisfaction with the type and quality of services provided to them and to their children. Along with the evidence on effectiveness of the model, evidence also exists on its replicability. Key components and major activities related to the model already have been systematically and effectively replicated across two early intervention programs. Further replication of the model at other sites in Tennessee and across the nation is ongoing.

COMPONENTS OF THE MODEL

Prerequisites for fully implementing the model are:

1. The classroom must be data-based.
2. The staff must be competent in basic teaching tactics (e.g., shaping, task analysis).
3. A program must have a 1:3 staff-to-child ratio, or better.
4. The staff must be willing to try innovative approaches.
5. The staff must be committed to effective teaching as its *first priority*.
6. Administrative and supervisory personnel must be fully supportive.

The Optimal Learning Environments model has five basic components: environments designed for severely handicapped infants and young children, enhanced quality of instruction through technology, a transdisciplinary consultant-therapist approach, individualized curriculum sequencing, and services to families.

Component 1: Environments Designed for Severely Handicapped Infants and Young Children

Infants and toddlers with severe/multiple handicaps require intensive support and individual attention for learning and environmental interaction. When this support is not available, children are often passive, or at least not engaged in stimulating activity. During the last 10 years, guidelines for designing settings have been offered for normal infants and toddlers (Herbert-Jackson, O'Brien, Porterfield, & Risley, 1977; O'Brien, Porterfield, Herbert-Jackson, & Risley, 1978), moderately handicapped preschoolers (Rogers-Warren, 1982; Rogers-Warren & Wedel, 1979), and severely handicapped adolescents (Hursh, Sayre, & House, 1982), and adults (Kernan, Begab, & Edgerton, 1983). The principles implicit in these guidelines have been similar and have focused on ways to increase interaction between individuals and the persons, objects, and events comprising the immediate setting. These principles, which when translated into practice increase engagement with the physical and social environments and optimize conditions for learning, are applicable to settings for very young children who have severe and multiple handicaps (Hart, 1982).

The Optimal Learning Environments model utilizes principles of environmental design to develop a setting that maximizes teacher-child and therapist-child teaching interactions, while minimizing management and custodial tasks. The classroom is divided into zones for activities, and specific staff-student arrangements are assigned to each zone throughout the day. Decisions about zones and staffing arrangements are based, in part, on research by LeLaurin and Risley (1972) indicating that dividing a classroom into zones for specific activities and assigning the staff to zones are more efficient strategies than having staff members move with individual children across areas.

Zones are designed by room dividers that are carpeted on both sides to minimize classroom noise. As recommended by Hart (1982), the dividers are high enough to prevent children from becoming visually distracted by activities in other zones but low enough to allow staff members to view the entire classroom and communicate with one another. Shelves for required training materials are located within each zone. Allowing teachers to readily find, access, and manage materials reduces non-teaching time spent searching for materials. Moreover, specifically arranging the environment so that children have access only to particular materials facilitates attention to the task.

Two other important features of the classroom include: (a) placing emphasis on programming during transitions between activities, and (b) using a modular daily schedule. To encourage children to move from activity to activity using whatever means of mobility is available to them, the classroom is designed to include unobstructed areas between zones. The classroom schedule is designed to reflect the specific programming and care needs of individual children. The modular, individualized schedule allows children with various abilities and needs to spend appropriate but different amounts of time in various activities. The "Premack Principle" (Premack, 1969) is applied to facilitate and maintain child interest and attention. In addition, generalization is programmed by scheduling a variety of adults (teachers, therapists, parents, practicum students) to work with individual children and to provide training in a variety of locales both within and outside of the classroom. A sample daily schedule is presented in Figure 1.

FIGURE 1 Sample Daily Schedule

January 6, 1986 (Monday)

	CAREN	CARYN	MARK	CINDA	ELLEN	OTHER
8:30–9:00	AREA 2 Terri	Work On Computer		AREA 3 David & Angela	BUS: Jason & Alethea	
9:00–9:15	GOOD MORNING GROUP	Work On Computer	Work On Computer	PROMPTER	PROMPTER	
9:15–9:45	AREA 2 David and Angela	AREA 3 Alex and Alethea	Work On Computer	AREA 1 Jason & Terri	AREA 1 Assist Cinda	
9:45–10:00		GO TO GYM	Set Up Snack		GO TO GYM	
10:00–10:30		SNACK David and Terri	SNACK Alex and Alethea		SNACK Jason and Angela	
10:30–11:00		AREA 2 Alethea	AREA 3 Jason & Alex			
11:00–11:15	BUS: PROMPTER	MUSIC GROUP	PROMPTER			
11:15–11:45	AREA 3 Chad & Tyree	AREA 1 Mark and Jason	AREA 2 LaKecia & Melissa			
11:45–12:15	A-1: JJ/MW Set Up Lunch	A-2: LC/MT GYM/OUTSIDE	A-3: CS/TR GYM/OUTSID			
12:15–12:30		LUNCH Chad and Tyree	LUNCH Jason & Mark	LUNCH LaKecia & Melissa		
12:30–12:45		Finish Lunch and Diapering	Finish Lunch and Diapering	Finish Lunch and Diapering		
12:45–1:00		Clean-Up	Clean-Up	Clean-Up		

Component 2: Enhanced Quality of Instruction Through Technology

The second key component of the Optimal Learning Environments approach involves innovative use of microcomputer technology for enhancing the quality of instruction, as well as maximizing service delivery and teacher-child contact with severely handicapped students. Existing and emerging microcomputer technology is used in two unique applications. First, the microcomputer is used to assist teachers in IEP development, instructional decision-making, data collection and analysis, report writing, development of daily classroom schedules, and other administrative tasks. Second, the microcomputer is used to assist in direct instruction of gross motor skills.

In recent years special education teachers and researchers have demonstrated the importance of collecting data on the learning performance of students with severe handicaps (Cooper, 1981; White & Haring, 1980). By collecting and graphing these data, teachers can determine when an instructional program is ineffective so that the program can be changed before it adversely affects the student. Until recently, however, the literature contained few specific guidelines describing exactly how to use performance data as an aid in instructional decision making.

Data-Based Decision Rules

New research has led to development of a set of guidelines, known as "data-based decision rules," that enable teachers to use performance data as a basis for instructional decision making. The effectiveness of using data-based decision rules for selecting instructional strategies that result in improved rates of learning by persons with severe handicaps was reported by Haring, Liberty, and White (1980a, 1980b, 1981). Although Haring et al. (1981) found that teachers who used decision rules spent less time in planning their programs than teachers who did not, the decision rules have not been widely used. The process of using decision rules may not be practical for teachers with limited support services (Wehman, 1979), and the graphing and use of flowcharts necessary for applying data-based decision rules is perceived as a complex and time-consuming endeavor (Howell, Kaplan, & O'Connell, 1979).

AIMSTAR

Our colleagues Hasselbring and Hamlett (1982) developed an integrated set of computer programs, titled AIMSTAR, that allows teachers to easily implement the decision-rule process in the classroom. AIMSTAR allows our teachers to develop detailed individualized education plans, manage student performance data, and implement data-based decision rules to enhance the instructional decision-making process. Graphs and monthly summary reports on student programs are produced, as in Figure 2. During the first 2½ years of the model demonstration project, teachers collected data on child programs by hand and later entered the data into the AIMSTAR decision-making program. In the third year of the project, a system was developed whereby teachers entered data directly into a TRS-80 Model 100 portable computer as they worked with students. At the end of the school day, the data were transferred electronically into the AIMSTAR program. Development of this system eliminated the time teachers previously had spent entering hand-collected data into the AIMSTAR program.

FIGURE 2 AIMSTAR Graph for ITLP Student's Knee-Walking Program

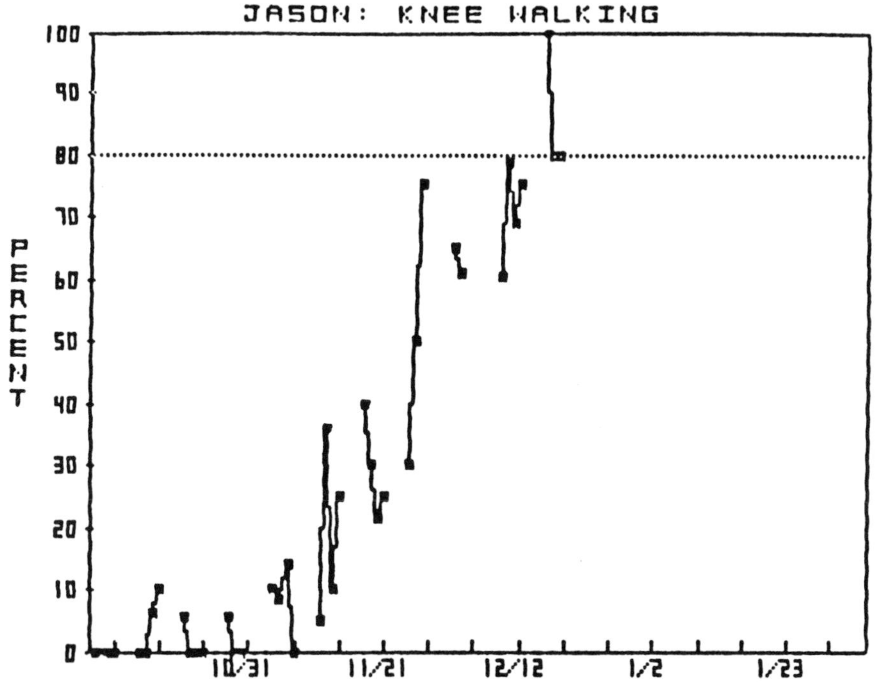

In addition to the AIMSTAR software, Hasselbring and Hamlett developed software that allows teachers to easily and efficiently design modular classroom schedules (see Component 1). These are individualized daily according to the adults and children present, type and length of activities, staff-student assignments, and assignment of activities and persons to zones.

Direct Instruction

Microcomputers also are used for purposes of direct instruction with children (Hooper & Hamlett, 1985; Warren, Hooper, & Hill, in press). Teachers construct switches that connect to the computer and a battery-operated toy. Design of the individual switches is based on a child's physical limitations and the nature of the motor or cognitive skill to be trained. Hand switches, mercury switches, and lightbeam switches have been developed to train a variety of motor skills (e.g., head erect; maintaining a hands-and-knees position; using two hands simultaneously). The computer records frequency and duration data on child responses.

In conjunction with these data, the computer also records prompt data that the trainer enters on a "touch pad." Teachers access computerized data from direct instruction in the form of trial data, summary data, and graphic presentations. The data are entered into AIMSTAR to determine when a child reaches criterion on a goal and when changes in instructional procedures are in order.*

Component 3: Transdisciplinary Consultant-Therapist Approach

To realize their developmental potential, infants and toddlers with severe multiple handicaps require intensive intervention efforts from a variety of disciplines, as well as support from parents. The traditional model of therapy, in which a therapist provides treatment in the area of his or her expertise, often has been ineffective with children having the range and degree of needs of the severely handicapped (Holm & McCartin, 1978).

Traditional Specialist Approach

Shortcomings associated with the traditional specialist approach are that: (a) the amount of time treatment is provided in a specific area is limited because only the specialist works with the child; significant others who interact with the child frequently in natural contexts (e.g., parents and teachers) do not participate in treatment within specialty areas; (b) the specialist seldom obtains detailed information from the teacher and parents concerning the child's problems or progress outside the specialist's treatment setting; (c) assessment, remediation, and evaluation typically are conducted in a single "therapeutic setting" that bears little resemblance to the child's normal environments; moreover, little thought is given to the importance of skills trained for the child's day-to-day functioning; (d) generalization of trained skills to appropriate non-training contexts often is limited because skills are taught by a single individual, in a very specific context, often under highly predictable circumstances; and (e) training of skills from one specialty domain is isolated from training of skills in other domains. Complex interdependencies exist between superficially distinct skills (Hayden & McGinness, 1977) and, hence, an integrated training approach in which skills from different areas of development are trained concurrently may enhance the functionality and generalized use of trained skills by children (Guess & Noonan, 1982).

A New Model

Empirical evidence of the ineffectiveness of the traditional specialist approach led a number of innovators in special education to propose (and in some cases demonstrate) the use of a transdisciplinary, consultant-therapist model (Hanson, 1981; Guess, Jones, & Lyon, 1981; McCormick & Goldman, 1979). This model is based on the transdisciplinary team approach to service delivery and the concept of "role release" (Lyon & Lyon, 1980) by therapists, teachers, and other personnel. The consultant-therapist model differs from the specialist approach in that the specialist,

---

The software and hardware applications described here were developed in cooperation with Expert Systems Software, 923 Van Leer Dr., Nashville, TN.

teachers, and parents share responsibility for conducting planned remediation. The consultant-therapist designs the instructional program so that teachers, parents, paraprofessionals, and other therapists can implement portions of it.

The consultant-therapist also assesses the child's behavior in a range of contexts typical of the child's natural environments and obtains teacher and parental input to identify absent skills or maladaptive behaviors that limit the child's ability to function. Skills targeted for training are those that will improve the child's functioning in day-to-day activities. Generalization is facilitated because the consultant-therapist approach involves integrated skill training, training of functional skills, and training by a number of persons in a variety of meaningful contexts.

In the consultant-therapist approach, then, the specialist is involved in identification and remediation of the child's problems in one area defined as the "specialty." The specialist additionally "releases" his or her role by training teachers, parents, therapists, and paraprofessionals to provide the prescribed intervention. The specialist observes these persons as they work with children and provides feedback and additional training as needed. He or she also develops procedures for data collection and modifies individual child programs as indicated by the data.

The Optimal Learning Environments model utilizes a transdisciplinary consultant-therapist approach. A transdisciplinary team consists of special education teachers, a speech/language therapist-consultant, a physical therapist-consultant, and a parent trainer. Other specialists, such as a nutritionist and a vision specialist, may be consulted on an individual child basis. Consultant-therapists are responsible for: (a) analyzing each child's problems and educational needs in the area defined as the specialty; (b) designing individualized instructional plans to meet the needs identified; (c) training teachers, teacher aides, parents, and other therapists to implement various components of the instructional plans; (d) specifying data relevant to evaluation of the instruction; and (e) assessing the effectiveness of, and modifying accordingly, the instructional efforts and the learning environments.

A transdisciplinary team meeting is held on a weekly basis. Topics discussed include individual child needs, program plans and modifications, data collection procedures, and so on. Specialists also train classroom personnel, as necessary, during the weekly team meetings. In addition to these formal meetings, team members meet informally on a daily basis.

Component 4: Individualized Curriculum Sequencing

Two concerns influenced the selection of a curriculum approach to be implemented in this model. The first concern was in providing truly individualized training sequences that would adequately reflect the composite of needs displayed by infants and toddlers who have severe and multiple handicaps. The second concern was for teaching skills that would be immediately functional for the children. To meet these concerns, the curriculum would have to be specific, yet adaptable to a range of developmental levels across domains within the same child and across a group of children. It also should facilitate skill integration and generalization of newly learned skills to everyday contexts.

The Individualized Curriculum Sequencing (ICS) model (Brown, Holvoet, Guess, & Mulligan, 1980; Holvoet, Guess, Mulligan, & Brown, 1980; Mulligan & Guess, 1984) is utilized in our Optimal Learning Environments approach because it addresses the concerns for functional use and integration of skills into new behavior patterns. Implementation of the ICS begins with a thorough evaluation of a child's skills in all domains (gross and fine motor; social development; communication; self-help; and cognitive) using formal and observational assessment procedures. Target skills in each domain are identified using the dual criteria of *appropriateness* to the developmental sequence and *functionality* in the child's typical environments. Individual target skills then are assigned to classroom activities and events that offer appropriate opportunities for the behaviors to be trained in a functional and natural manner.

Four or five target skills typically are assigned to an activity. These skills are sequenced or "clustered" into logical sets. Clustering is based on the functional occurrences of behavior such that one behavior or response logically leads to the next behavior in the training sequence. For example, a skill cluster may teach a child to: (a) imitate the word "up" (communication); (b) pull to stand and maintain standing (gross motor); (c) discriminate between two toys (preacademic); (d) imitate the name of the object selected (communication); and (e) manipulate the object appropriately with another child (social). This cluster approximates a natural sequence of events.

A series of clusters, each consisting of four or five related, functional, child-appropriate behaviors can be identified and presented several times across the classroom day. In this way, single skills across content areas are distributed within and across sequences so that skill integration is programmed and mass trials of the same skill rarely occur in succession. This distribution across functional contexts facilitates acquisition and programs for generalization by providing training in multiple settings with several trainers.

The ICS interfaces well with other key components of the Optimal Learning Environments model. Specifically, assignment of activities to zones, use of a modularized schedule with age-appropriate activities, involvement of a transdisciplinary team, and use of computer-managed decision making and record keeping systems form an excellent base for ICS application.

Component 5: Services to Families

The birth of a child with handicaps impacts the family system in a variety of ways. Parents must attend to the child's medical and therapeutic needs and, at the same time, deal with their own and other family members' emotional responses (Wikler, 1981). Parental needs may range from assistance with planning to meet new financial demands, to learning new skills that address the child's health, therapeutic, and educational needs. Without considerable professional help and support, parents may struggle for years to meet their basic emotional and child management needs.

From a more positive perspective, parents have a great deal to offer their children in the way of teaching. Young children normally learn far more from their mothers and fathers than from any preschool program. Most fundamental conceptual, communicative, and self-help skills are learned in the context of the home. Although this may be less true in the case of a child with severe handicaps, parents still must be recognized as a great source of teaching for their child, and incorporated into their child's education program in ways that are advantageous for the child, the parents, and the education program. Parent involvement in early education of children with severe and multiple handicaps is essential if these children are to reach their developmental potential (Linder, 1983).

The Optimal Learning Environments model includes a comprehensive range of training and support services for parents. Parent needs are assessed regularly (every 4 to 6 months) through a written needs assessment, informal observation by team members, and discussion between team members and parents. Following the identification of parent needs, an individualized family plan (IFP) is developed; it takes into account the needs and dynamics of each family situation. In developing the IFPs, efforts are made to meet the support, training, and informational needs of parents, plan for father involvement, and address the needs of nonhandicapped siblings.

Development of IFPs is based on the notion of "evolving needs" of parents of children with handicaps (Turnbull, 1984). The notion of "evolving needs" maintains that the needs of individual parents change over time and are affected by a variety of factors including the child's health and developmental status, responses to the child and family by relatives, friends, and professionals, the availability of support services, financial constraints on the family, and so on. Given the individual and fluctuating nature of parents' needs, IFPs are developed and reviewed jointly by the parent and parent trainer on a regular and frequent basis.

The model of parent involvement, then, includes identifying individual parent needs and providing a variety of training and support options to address those needs. The classroom staff does not prescribe the specific nature of each parent's involvement in the child's early intervention. Rather, the parent and parent trainer determine this jointly. Services to families that are available through the model demonstration project are described in the following paragraphs.

Classroom Participation

All parents are involved in developing their child's individualized education program (IEP) and participating in the IEP meetings. Parents who indicate an interest, and who are not hindered by time constraints, participate in the classroom program for a few hours each week. During this time the parents observe the child's educational program, actively participate in various aspects of the training program (e.g., feeding, motor skill training, toileting), and receive instruction in procedures for teaching the child and collecting data. Some of the parents also are taught to enter their child's data into the AIMSTAR data management program.

Parent Support Group Meeting

Parent support group meetings are held every other week. These meetings provide a forum for parents to share feelings and experiences, exchange information, and learn about topics relevant to rearing a child with special needs. Parents often suggest topics for discussion, and the parent trainer organizes the meetings and makes arrangements for guest speakers, as necessary. Recent topics include estate planning (the guest speaker was a professor of law from Vanderbilt University) and preparing for the child's enrollment in public school (the guest speaker was a special education teacher from the Nashville Metro School District). Parental emotional needs also are addressed in the parent support group meetings. When individual support or counseling needs cannot be met in this context, parents are referred to the Kennedy Center Family and Child Study Center, where individual therapy and family and marital counseling are provided.

Home Visits

Individual team members visit families at home once a month or every 2 months, depending on the nature and extent of family needs. Home visits often involve training parents how to use specific interactional, intervention, and management skills. The education and management of a young child with severe and multiple handicaps also can be facilitated in the home through application of the same principles of environmental design that are utilized in the classroom. Therefore, home visits also focus on assisting parents in the arrangement of home environments to facilitate child learning and care of the child. Emphasis is placed on low-cost, flexible, arrangements that can be modified as the child's and family's needs change.

Training Parents in Management and Treatment Strategies

The parent trainer, teachers, and consultant-therapists provide parents with training, as needed, in child management and treatment skills. Training is offered in behavior management, physical therapy, strategies for teaching self-help skills, and incidental language teaching procedures. Parent management and treatment skill training is provided both in the classroom and during home visits.

Information and Support Services

A variety of support networks and services is available to families with handicapped children in the Nashville area. The parent trainer provides parents with information about many of these services and facilitates contact between parents and organizations/services as desired and needed by individual families. The family component also makes available to parents a resource library containing books, articles, pamphlets, and other material on handicapping conditions, intervention procedures, programs for children with special needs, and so forth. In addition, a respite care file containing names of persons who are interested in providing temporary child care was compiled and is available to parents.

EVALUATION OF THE MODEL

The Optimal Learning Environments model integrates the five components discussed into an intensive data-based intervention program. The most basic assumption underlying this model is that child engagement with the environment is a critical characteristic of an optimal learning environment (Hart, 1982; McWilliam, Trivette, & Dunst, 1985). Infants and toddlers with severe and multiple handicaps often are characterized by a lack of self-directed exploratory behavior. Thus, an intervention must, at the minimum, increase the child's engagement with persons and objects as a requisite condition for increasing learning and facilitating development.

Pragmatic Assumptions

In addition to this philosophical assumption, pragmatic assumptions about the characteristics of an effective program are:

1. The intervention should address the goals identified for each child during the IEP process.
2. A high percentage of the staff's time should be spent in non-caretaking activities with the children.
3. Transition time between activities should be minimal.
4. Teaching should occur in all activities during the school day.

Observation Coding

Based on these assumptions, we designed and implemented a classroom observation code to measure: (a) the kinds of activities ongoing in the classroom; (b) teacher-child contact time in terms of occurrence and content of the interactions; (c) child engagement with materials and teachers; (d) teacher activity; (e) monitoring of child performance; and (f) teacher-child ratios.* In addition to the information obtained from the code, IEPs were reviewed to generate a list of specific treatment goals for each child so that treatment in the classroom could be coded as goal-related or general. To determine major activity codes, observations of several infant classrooms were made.

The protocol for coding is based on a scanning system. A scan is a 35-second interval in which the observer watches and records behavior for a single subject for 30 seconds, then locates the next subject during seconds 31–35. At the beginning of the observation, the children and teachers are assigned a sequence for scanning. This sequence is followed until each subject has been observed at least six times. Total reliability for the code averaged 88% (range = 81%–97%). Careful analyses of the code showed the reliability for each category to be well above 85%.

**This observation code is available from the authors upon request, c/o Dept. of Special Education, Box 328, George Peabody College for Teachers, Vanderbilt University, Nashville, TN 37203.*

Analysis of Data

Data are presented on *teacher behavior,* the *delivery of treatment across time and activities,* and *child engagement.* For purposes of comparison, data related to teacher behavior and the delivery of treatment across time and activities are provided from the model demonstration project (School A), as well as from two other classrooms for infants and toddlers with severe and multiple handicaps. School B has 10 children enrolled in a full-day intervention program and follows a fairly traditional preschool schedule. School C is a full-day program with six children enrolled. Teacher-child ratios for the three settings are typically: School A—1:2; School B—1:3; School C—1:3. Data on child engagement are provided from two time periods (with approximately 15 observations per time period) at Schools A and B.

As shown in Fig. 3, the Optimal Learning Environments model (School A) clearly differed from the other two sites in terms of time devoted to treatment (treatment was defined as teaching related to specific IEP goals). Teachers in this setting devoted 65% of their observed time to training related to IEP goals, while teachers in the other two settings spent slightly less than 20% of their time in treatment. Teachers in School A generally spent less time in non-teaching activities (passive, material, unoccupied, and other) than did teachers in the other two settings.

Teachers in School A distributed their treatment across all activities in the classroom, as shown in Fig. 4. School B teachers provided treatment primarily during Manipulative and Doing activities. School C teachers provided the most treatment during an Exercise period, when they worked on physical therapy goals.

As shown in Fig. 5, analyses of treatment across time periods confirmed that teachers in School A were teaching across activities; treatment was observed during 60% to 70% of the intervals observed across the day. Teachers in School B also delivered treatment throughout the day; however, the level of treatment was significantly lower than for teachers in School A, averaging less than 25% of the observed intervals. Teachers in School C provided treatment during the first 2 hours of the day, but the intensity of treatment was much higher during the first hour than during the second (50% vs. 9%). Since levels of treatment might vary according to teacher-child ratios, a comparison was made using a subset of data in which the same teacher-child ratio occurred in each setting. The pattern of differences was nearly identical to the one described in Fig. 3, suggesting that the difference in distribution of teacher activity was not a function of number of adults in the setting.

With regard to child engagement, children at the model demonstration program were engaged with teachers or materials during 90% of the observed intervals at Time 1 and 86% of the observed intervals at Time 2. Children at School B were engaged with teachers or materials during 53% of the observed intervals at Time 1 and 63% of the observed intervals at Time 2.

Comparison of the Optimal Learning Environments model classroom with two other classrooms indicates that the model resulted in: (a) much more actual teaching time and less time in non-teaching activities; (b) skills being taught across the day and across different types of activities; (c) higher levels of teaching within specific ac-

FIGURE 3 Teacher Behavior Observed During Morning Session

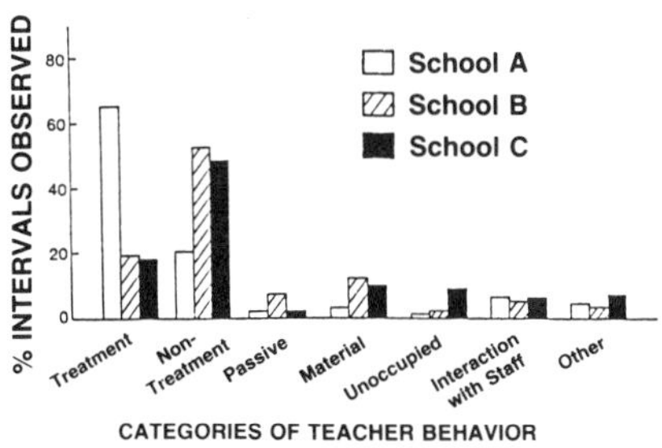

FIGURE 5 Teachers' Treatment Behavior Across Different Times

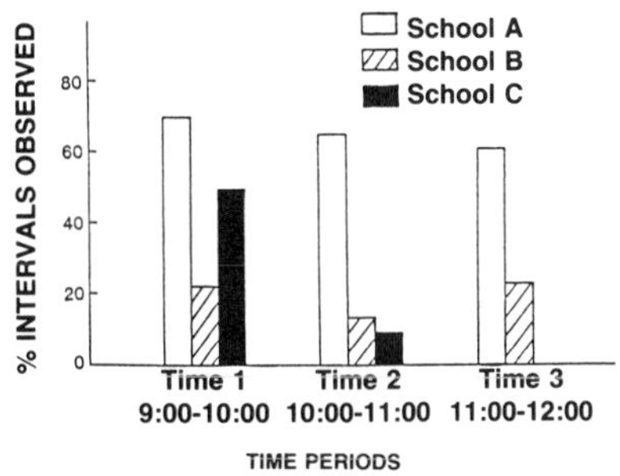

FIGURE 4 Teachers' Treatment Vs. Other Behavior Across Various Activities

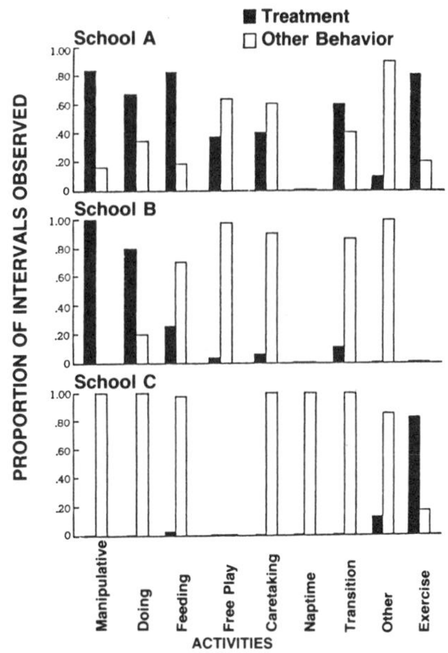

tivities; and (d) higher child engagement levels. In short, the model resulted in more teaching and higher levels of child engagement. Over the long-term these two variables should facilitate optimal child outcome.

CONCLUSION

The need for effective early intervention programs to meet the needs of infants and toddlers with severe handicaps is critical. Efforts to identify children with handicaps have been successful; each year more children are screened and evaluated before the age of 3. Nevertheless, with the increasing birthrate, the survival of more babies with severe handicaps, and the decreasing federal and state support for prenatal care, the next decade likely will see a record number of children requiring intervention in the first three years of life.

These increasing numbers of children are not likely to be matched with increasing support for very early intervention. Most states have not yet extended the mandate of PL94–142 to the education of children between birth and 3 years (Cohen, Semmel, & Guralnick, 1979; Linder, 1983), and downward extension appears unlikely in the next five years. Two pieces of evidence might be persuasive in encouraging states to assume responsibility for the education of very young handicapped children. The first is evidence of *immediate child progress* and *long-term effects* resulting from intervention in the first three years of life, particularly for children with moderate to severe handicaps. The second is evidence that positive results can be obtained in ways that are *cost-efficient*. The demonstration of an effective model for early intervention and the analysis of costs of each component of that model could contribute important information on these issues.

For educators who are interested in very young children, the immediate challenge is to develop and refine educational and service delivery strategies that fully meet the needs of this special population and their families. The requirements of intensive, multidisciplinary programming for children who have a limited range of skills are considerable. Meeting individual needs effectively and maximizing the benefits of intervention are primary concerns.

The Optimal Learning Environments model seeks to address the individual needs of very young children with severe handicaps by designing an environment that maximizes learning opportunities within a service delivery system that minimizes logistical constraints on quality services. Initial evaluation suggests that this model results in a qualitatively and quantitatively positive educational experience for young children with very severe handicaps. Long-term systematic replication, combined with comprehensive evaluation, is needed now to determine the true efficacy of this model.

REFERENCES

Batshaw, M. L., & Perret, Y. M. (1981). *Children with handicaps: A medical primer.* Baltimore: Paul Brookes Publishing.

Brown, F., Holvoet, J., Guess, D., & Mulligan, M. (1980). The individualized curriculum sequencing model (III): Small group instruction. *Journal of the Association of the Severely Handicapped, 5,* 352–367.

Cohen, S., Semmel, M., & Guralnick, M. Public Law 94–142 and the education of preschool handicapped children. *Exceptional Children,* 1979, *45,* 279–285.

Cooper, J. O. (1981). *Measuring behavior.* Columbus, OH: Charles E. Merrill.

Garland, C., Swanson, J., Stone, N. W., & Woodruff, G. (Eds.). (1981). *Early intervention for children with special needs and their families.* Seattle: WESTAR.

Guess, D., Jones, C., & Lyon, S. (Eds.). (1981). *Developing an intervention program for severely/multiply handicapped preschool children: A transdisciplinary approach.* Unpublished manuscript, University of Kansas, Lawrence.

Guess, D., & Noonan, M. J. (1982). Curricula and instructional procedures for severely handicapped students. *Focus on Exceptional Children, 14*(5), 1–12.

Hanson, M. J. (1981). A model for early intervention with culturally diverse single and multi-parent families. *Topics in Early Childhood Education, 1,* 37–44.

Haring, N. G., Liberty, K. A., & White, O. R. (1980a). *Data-based decision rules for instructional programs.* Unpublished monograph, University of Washington Child Development and Mental Retardation Center, Seattle.

Haring, N. G., Liberty, K. A., & White, O. R. (1980b). Rules for data-based decisions in instructional programs: Current research and instructional implications. In W. Sailor, B. Wilcox, & L. Brown, (Eds.), *Methods of instruction for severely handicapped students*. Baltimore: Paul Brookes Publishing.

Haring, N. G., Liberty, K. A., & White, O. R. (1981). *An investigation of phases of learning and facilitating instructional events for the severely and profoundly retarded*. Unpublished monograph, University of Washington, College of Education, Seattle.

Hart, B. (1982). So that teachers can teach: Assigning roles and responsibilities. *Topics in Early Childhood Special Education, 2,* 1–9.

Hasselbring, T. S., & Hamlett, C. (1982, May). Using the microcomputer to apply data-based decision rules for assisting in the selection of instructional strategies for the handicapped. *Proceedings of the Twentieth Annual Association for Education Data-Systems Conference,* Orlando, FL.

Hayden, A. H., & McGinness, G. D. (1977). Bases for early intervention. In E. Sontag (Ed.), *Educational programming for the severely and profoundly handicapped*. Reston, VA: Council for Exceptional Children.

Herbert-Jackson, E., O'Brien, M., Porterfield, J. & Risley, T. (1977). *The infant center: A complete guide to organizing and managing infant day care*. Baltimore: University Park Press.

Holm, V. A., & McCartin, R. E. (1978). Interdisciplinary child development team: Team issues and training in interdisciplinariness. In K. E. Allen, V. A. Holm, & R. L. Schiefelbusch (Eds.), *Early intervention—A team approach*. Baltimore: University Park Press.

Holvoet, J., Guess, D., Mulligan, M., & Brown, F. (1980). The individualized curriculum sequencing model (II): A teaching strategy for severely handicapped students. *Journal of the Association of the Severely Handicapped, 5,* 325–336.

Hooper, E. H., & Hamlett, C. (1985, June). *Microcomputer applications for young children with severe handicaps*. Paper presented at the Council for Exceptional Children National Software Conference, Alexandria, VA.

Horowitz, F. D. (1982). Infant environments. In A. Rogers-Warren (Ed.), *Final Report of the Kansas Early Childhood Institute*. University of Kansas, Lawrence.

Howell, K. W., Kaplan, J. S., & O'Connell, C. Y. (1979). *Evaluating exceptional children: A task analysis approach*. Columbus, OH: Charles E. Merrill Publishing.

Hursh, D., Sayre, T., & House, D. (1982, May). *PUSH: Evaluating the design process*. Paper presented at the annual meeting of the Association for Behavior Analysis, Milwaukee, WI.

Kernan, K., Begab, M., & Edgerton, R. (Eds.). (1983). *Environments and behavior: The adaptation of mentally retarded persons*. Baltimore: University Park Press.

LeLaurin, K., & Risley, T. R. (1972). The organization of day care environments: "ZONE" versus "man to man" staff assignments. *Journal of Applied Behavior Analysis, 5,* 225–232.

Linder, T. (1983). *Early childhood special education*. Baltimore: Paul Brookes Publishing.

Lyon, S., & Lyon, G. (1980). Team functioning and staff development: A role release approach to providing integrated educational services to severely handicapped students. *Journal of the Association for the Severely Handicapped, 5,* 250–263.

McCormick, L., & Goldman, R. (1979). The transdisciplinary model: Implications for service delivery and personnel preparation for the severely and profoundly handicapped. *AAESPH Review, 4,* 152–161.

McWilliam, R. A., Trivette, C. M., & Dunst, C. J. (1985). Behavior engagement as a measure of the efficacy of early intervention. *Analysis and Intervention in Developmental Disabilities, 5,* 59–72.

Mulligan, M., & Guess, D. (1984). Using an individualized curriculum sequencing model. In L. McCormick & R. L. Schiefelbusch (Eds.). *Early language intervention*. Columbus, OH: Charles E. Merrill Publishing.

O'Brien, M., Porterfield, J., Herbert-Jackson, E., & Risley, T. (1978). *The Toddler Center: A practical guide to day care for one- and two-year olds*. Baltimore: University Park Press.

Premack, D. (1969). Reinforcement theory. In *Nebraska symposium on motivation*. Lincoln: University of Nebraska Press, pp. 123–128.

Ramey, C. T., & Trohanis, P. L. (Eds.). (1982). *Finding and educating high-risk and handicapped infants*. Baltimore: University Park Press.

Rogers-Warren, A. K. (1982). Behavioral ecology in classrooms for young, handicapped children. *Topics in Early Childhood Special Education, 2,* 21–22.

Rogers-Warren, A., & Wedel, J. (1979). The physical ecology of preschool classrooms for the handicapped. In J. Gallagher (Ed.), *New directions for exceptional children* (Vol. 1). San Francisco: Jossey-Bass.

Sailor, W., & Guess, D. (1983). *Severely handicapped students—An instructional design*. Boston: Houghton Mifflin.

Tjossem, T. D. (Ed.). (1976). *Intervention strategies for high risk infants and young children*. Baltimore: University Park Press.

Turnbull, A. (1984, November). *Research in family systems*. Paper presented in the Department of Special Education, Peabody College of Vanderbilt University, Nashville, TN.

Warren, S. F., Hooper, E. H., & Hill, E. W. (in press). Some innovative educational applications of advanced technologies. In D. Guess, L. Goetz, & K. Stremel-Campbell (Eds.), *Innovative program design for individuals with sensory impairments*. Baltimore: Paul Brookes Publishing.

Wehman, P. (1979). *Curriculum design for the severely and profoundly handicapped*. New York: Human Services Press.

White, O. R., & Haring, N. G. (1980). *Exceptional teaching* (2nd ed.). Columbus, OH: Charles E. Merrill.

Wikler, L. (1981). Chronic stresses of families of mentally retarded children. *Family Relations, 30*, 281–288.

The contributions of our colleagues Ted S. Hasselbring, Caren Millen, Eva Hooper, Joji Colond, Kris Derer, and Carol Hamlett are gratefully acknowledged.

Steven Warren is an Associate Professor of Special Education and Psychology, Cathy Alpert a Research Assistant Professor of Special Education, and Ann Kaiser (formerly Ann Rogers-Warren) an Associate Professor of Special Education and Psychology, all at George Peabody College for Teachers of Vanderbilt University.

Placement in the least restrictive environment for the education of children and youth with severe disabilities is not easily achieved. If integration of severely disabled students with nondisabled students is to occur, attention must go beyond attitudinal and organizational concerns to focus on curriculum. Noonan and Hemphill discuss curricular consideration as an introduction to reviewing three specific curriculums: "The Social Skills Curricular Strategy for Students with Severe Disabilities" by Noonan, Hemphill and Levy, "The Special Friends Program: A Trainer's Manual for Integrated School Settings" by Voeltz et. al., and "The Smallest Minority: Adapted Regular Education Social Studies Curriculum for Understanding and Integrating Severely Disabled Students" by Hemphill and Voeltz; Brown, Fruehling, and Hemphill; and Hemphill, Zukas, and Brown. In addition, the authors emphasize the importance of community involvement, inservice training for school staff, and parent participation.

Comprehensive Curricula for Integrating Severely Disabled And Nondisabled Students

Mary Jo Noonan and Norma Jean Hemphill

Integration, from an educational perspective, means that all students have equal access to the total school environment for the purpose of achieving their educational goals. The legal, social, and educational rationales for integrating severely disabled and nondisabled students have been delineated in numerous publications (cf., Bricker, 1978; Brown et al., 1979). Federal funding of large-scale demonstration projects (e.g., Hawaii Integration Project, Kansas Integration Project) and research institutes (e.g., San Francisco State University and University of Minnesota) demonstrates governmental support of integration efforts. And a major professional organization, The Association for Persons with Severe Handicaps, has adopted a deinstitutionalization resolution proclaiming the rights of disabled students to access integrated environments in the public schools ("TASH Adopts Resolution," 1980).

Integration is more than a special education trend; it is an expression of a broader concern for safeguarding the constitutional rights of all citizens on the basis of the equal protection doctrine. Equal protection is rooted in the values of self-fulfillment and disregard of unalterable traits (H. R. Turnbull, personal communication, 1981). Self-fulfillment implies that an individual is free from unnecessary restrictions and limitations to his/her liberty. Disregard of unalterable traits means that an individual is not discriminated against (or restricted) on the basis of inborn characteristics such as sex, race, ancestry, and disability. Integration of severely disabled students addresses the values of self-fulfillment and disregard of unalterable traits by providing *equal* and *shared* access to environments, programs, and events available to nonhandicapped students.

Equal access in an educational environment has three elements: (a) physical accessibility, (b) programmatic accessibility, and (c) affective accessibility (Stodden, 1980). Physical accessibility requires that all areas within the environment accommodate disabled students. Modifications such as ramps, rails, signs (e.g., pictures), elevators, braille markers, and so on may be necessary to accomplish physical accessibility. Programmatic accessibility requires that the same variety of school programs (e.g., homeroom, recess, lunch periods, intramurals, drama, music, art) and the same types of educational materials (e.g., library books, gym equipment, microcomputers) be available to disabled students. Affective access means that personal beliefs of stereotypes about a student or group of students do not prevent that individual or group from utilizing school environments or program resources. An affective access barrier exists if nondisabled students are never observed interacting with disabled students during shared lunch periods. Comprehensive efforts to integrate severely disabled students with their nondisabled peers must consider all three types of accessibility: physical, programmatic, and affective.

THE ROLE OF CURRICULA IN INTEGRATION

Curricula generally provide the scope of instructional content, a delineation of goals and objectives, and in some instances strategies/procedures for meeting the goals and objectives. Integration curricula can address programmatic and attitudinal accessibility by providing guidelines, lessons, or activities illustrating when, where, and how to integrate severely disabled and nondisabled students. Persons involved indirectly with integration efforts (e.g., ancillary staff, parents) should be included in integration activities to enhance their respect for individual differences, improve their understanding of integration purposes, and support the generalization of positive attitudes developed through integration.

Although curricula can assist some aspects of integration, curricula cannot make an environment physically accessible to disabled persons. Physical accessibility, as mandated by law (Section 504 of PL 93–380), requires administrative decisions.

The location of classrooms for severely disabled students is one physical accessibility concern that cannot be remedied by curriculum. Classrooms for disabled students must be adjacent to or in close proximity to classrooms for regular education students of the same age. Special education classrooms should not be at the end of a hallway, in a distant wing, in a separate building, or in a remote area of the school campus.

Activities such as homeroom, lunch, recess, and extra-curricular programs will be accessible to all students (disabled and nondisabled) only if they are scheduled at the same time. Scheduling barriers to integration are a physical and programmatic accessibility issue and are a function of administration rather than curriculum. Unless advanced planning for integration occurs when the school's overall schedule is developed, incompatible special education and regular education schedules may create unnecessary barriers to integration.

PARAMETERS OF APPROPRIATE INTEGRATION CURRICULA

Valued Roles

In proposing that the term *social role valorization* be adopted in place of *normalization*, Wolfensberger (1983) has argued that the ultimate goal "must be the creation, support, and defense of valued social roles for people who are at risk of social devaluation" (p. 234). Integration curricula must allow students with severe disabilities to assume valued social roles and participate meaningfully with their nondisabled peers. Valued roles are created by enhancing a person's social image and social competence through the use of natural settings, relationships and groups, and programs and activities.

Integrative, Not Additive, Procedures

Integrative procedures influence *how* something is done rather than *what* is done. They modify or expand upon events already occurring within the school community, whereas additive procedures are supplemental to the regular activities (Hemphill, 1981). Integrative curricula are more desirable than additive curricula because they provide a normalizing context for activities.

A 2-hour inservice training session on how to integrate severely disabled students would be an additive procedure and, therefore, less appropriate than an inservice meeting on extracurricular activities that would include recommendations and strategies for facilitating integration. Some schools provide an orientation program and booklet to incoming regular education students and their parents. Expanding the program and booklet to include disabled students and their parents is another example of a possible integrative procedure.

Age-Appropriate Interactions

Special education classes should be located on age-appropriate campuses to provide the natural environment for teaching age-appropriate social skills (Brown et al., 1979; Hamre-Nietupski & Nietupski, 1981). Observational data of social interactions among severely disabled students and their peers indicate that peer relationships are qualitatively different from teacher-child relationships.

In an analysis of joint object orientation, joint object use, and joint intentional behaviors, Noonan & Hemphill (1983) found that teachers are more effective than peers in getting disabled students to interact with objects (reflecting the educational nature of the interaction). Peers, however, do a much better job of maintaining students' attention to an activity. The higher frequency of joint attention with peers suggests that the friendship relationship is more social than the teacher-student dyad and may be contributing to the disabled student's social development.

Communication/Interaction, Not Information

One of the most important skills that disabled and non-disabled students can learn is to communicate with one another. Personalized learning situations have been demonstrated to result in greater acceptance by nondisabled students than information-focused procedures (Voeltz et al., 1983). Although information about disabilities may be interesting and helpful in certain respects (e.g., satisfying curiosity or discrediting unfounded stereotypes), it does not contribute to the development of positive peer interactions or attitudes.

Reciprocal Relationships

Integration curricula should foster joint and complementary participation that benefits both individuals (e.g., giving and taking, shared decision making). Friendships provide reciprocal experiences for acquiring the social and communication skills necessary to engage in mutually rewarding relationships.

In contrast, peer tutoring is a unidirectional relationship; the tutor is a helper and decision maker, and the tutee is a passive receiver. A tutoring relationship results in inequitable benefits. Once a helping relationship has been established between individuals, that relationship is difficult to change to a reciprocal one (Hemphill, 1981).

SOCIAL SKILLS TRAINING

Social skills are a significant factor in predicting the success of disabled individuals in normalized environments such as kindergarten (Vincent et al., 1980), vocational settings (Johnson & Mithaug, 1978; Niziol & DeBlassie, 1972), and community group homes (Crawford, Aiello, & Thompson, 1979; Jacobson & Schwartz, 1983; Schalock, Harper, & Genung, 1981). Integration efforts should be supported by teaching appropriate social skills to severely disabled students in the context of natural, integrated environments. As Brown and his colleagues have pointed out, functional objectives cannot be taught in segregated environments because segregated environments are unlike any natural environments (Brown et al., 1983).

The Interactive Curricular Model

The Social Skills Curricular Strategy for Students with Severe Disabilities (Noonan, Hemphill, & Levy, 1983) is designed for implementation in integrative contexts. The curriculum is based on the Interactive Curricular Model for Life Planning

(Hemphill, Noonan, & Levy, 1983), a model consisting of three interactive components: roles, environments, and basic human needs. Figure 1 shows these dimensions graphically. Within the Interactive Curricular Model, the curriculum focuses on the social skills needed to participate in a variety of valued roles, such as work, friend, maintenance, student, and recreational/leisure roles. Social skills are learned in environments natural to the role, including domestic, vocational, educational, and community environments. Providing access to these valued roles and normalized environments through integrative curriculum can create opportunities for all students to meet the full range of human needs.

Although social skills are emphasized, social-related and task-related skills are inherent in the successful performance of every routine and activity (Hemphill, Noonan, & Levy, 1983). These social and task skills are so intertwined that separating them is often difficult. For example, when going to the movies, one needs the task-related motor skills to move forward in the ticket line, the expressive communication skills to ask for a ticket, and the money skill to buy the ticket. But how one waits in the line with other people and the tone of voice one uses to address the ticket seller are the social skills of the routine. Figure 2 illustrates the complexity of this differentiation of skills.

FIGURE 1 Interactive Curricular Model for Students with Severe Disabilities

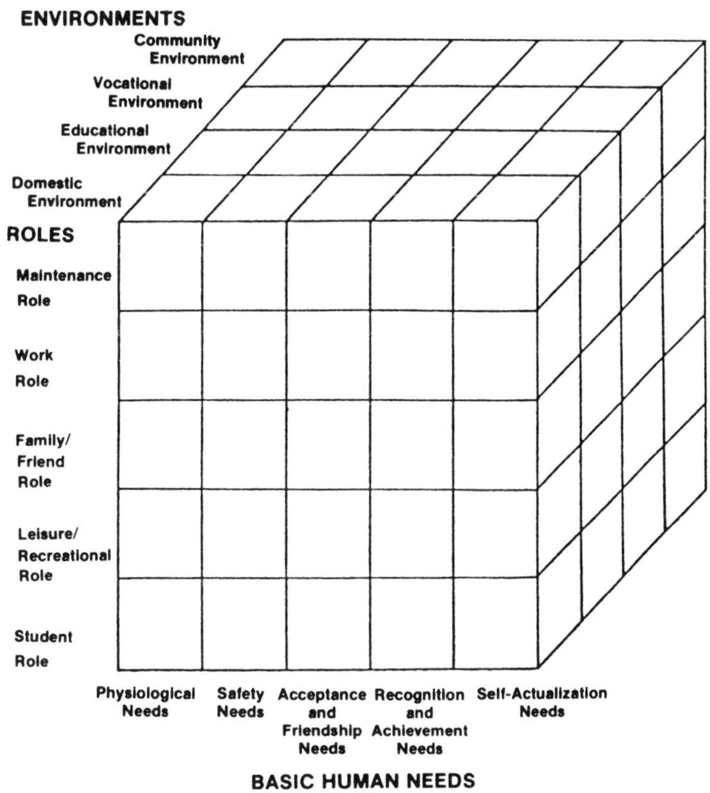

FIGURE 2 Differentiation of Social-Related and Task-Related Skills

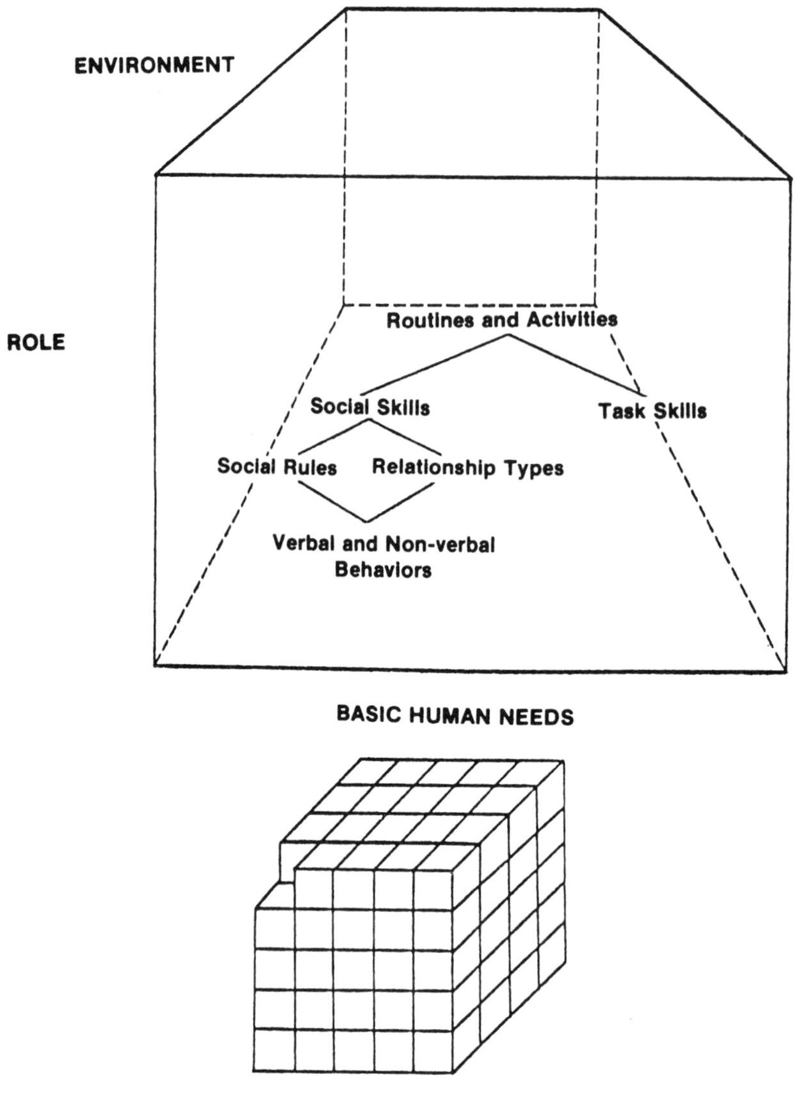

Assessment of Social Skill Needs

The curriculum strategy provides a step-by-step process for assessing social skill needs and deriving appropriate objectives through consideration of valued roles, natural environments, and basic human needs (the components of the Interactive Curricular Model). The process entails:

1. Identification of present and future roles and environments desired and valued by the disabled student, his/her parents/guardians, teacher, and society;
2. Observation of the student's present routines and activities;
3. Discrepancy analysis between the desired and the present routines and activities;
4. Selection of critical routines and activities;
5. Behavioral assessment of the social skills embedded in the critical routines and activities, and identification of appropriate instructional objectives.

Steps 1 through 4 of the assessment process narrow down and prioritize routines and activities specific to the student's needs in present and future environments. In step 5, social skill requirements are differentiated from the task skills of the priority routines and activities, and the social skills are assessed through direct observation. Figure 3 is an example of a completed social skills behavioral assessment for a priority routine of toileting. During an observation period (Part I) all behaviors are coded according to topography (e.g., formal sign language = s) and categorized according to social skill functions (e.g., gains entry/greetings, initiates question/statement/preference). The appropriateness of the response (or skill deficits) is noted in the "Post-Observation" column. Based on the post-observation comments and teacher judgments concerning the quality and nature of the observation (Part II), the assessment is summarized, and the student's major social skill needs for the routine/activity are listed (Part III).

Functional Methods of Instruction

Following the assessment process, the Social Skills Curricular Strategy describes and provides examples of how to utilize functional methods of instruction with the objectives identified through the final step of assessment. A matrix, such as the example in Figure 4, is recommended for identifying natural situations within the ongoing routines and activities for social skills instruction. The matrix is filled in by indicating the relationship of each social skill objective (listed across the top of the matrix) and each daily routine/activity (listed down the left side of the matrix). An "X" is placed in the cell if the social skill is not relevant to the corresponding routine/activity.

Social skills instruction is then implemented in conjunction with other instructional programs during each routine/activity, or the social skills identified for each routine/activity can be arranged in logical skill sequences and taught during the routine/activity. The Social Skills Curricular Strategy provides detailed procedures for teaching social skills in skill sequences, a curriculum approach developed by Doug Guess and his colleagues at the University of Kansas (Guess & Noonan, 1982; Holvoet, Guess, Mulligan, & Brown, 1980; Mulligan & Guess, 1984).

Special Friends Program

The Special Friends Program: A Trainer's Manual for Integrated School Settings (Voeltz et al., 1983) is a transitional training program to assist social interaction

FIGURE 3 Sample Behavioral Assessment of a Student's Social Skills Associated with the Priority Routine of Toileting

HAWAII INTEGRATION PROJECT

Social Skills Assessment

Date: 9/20/83

Student: C # Peers Present: 3 # Adults: 1 Rater: MJN

Setting: School bathroom Routine/Activity: toileting Time Period: 9¹⁰am - 9²⁰am

PART I

a) In the Observation column below, code the student's social interaction behaviors in the context of the identified setting and routine/activity.

b) In the Post-Observation column, write comments about behaviors that were not observed (or not observed at an appropriate frequency) but would be useful and/or adaptive to the setting and routine/activity. If behaviors were socially inappropriate, note the reason(s).

BEHAVIOR CODE
- v: vocalization or verbalization
- s: formal sign language
- g: gesture/facial expression/non-verbal communication
- e: social eye contact
- ...: preceding coded behavior occurred repeatedly
- —: preceding coded behavior was socially inappropriate

SOCIAL SKILL	OBSERVATION	POST-OBSERVATION
Gains entry/greetings	e— e—	should greet familiar person
Initiates question/statement/preference		NA
Responds to question/statement	g— e — g	no response to question
Chooses among materials, activities, etc. presented		NA
Imitates model		NA
Follows directions	g—e— g—e—	instructions were repeated with physical assistance
Follows activity's rules	g—	must recognize indications of vacancy
Accepts assistance	v, g, v, g	O.K.
Requests/offers assistance	g—	should request help w/soap dispenser
Takes exit/farewells		NA

PART II

	CIRCLE ONE		
1. Was the social nature of the routine/activity passive or active?	(passive)		active
2. Rate the student's level of social participation in the activity?	(low)	medium	high
3. Was the student's social behavior "typical" of him/her?	(yes)		no
4. Did the student demonstrate the necessary task-related skills (motor, cognitive, affective) to engage in the activity?	yes	(partially)	no

PART III

Summary - major social skill needs of routine/activity:

1. greet familiar peers encountered in the bathroom
2. goes to toilet without assistance (i.e., walks directly to stall and locates vacant one and enters)
3. recognizes vacant stall
4. verbally requests assistance with soap dispenser.

among severely disabled and nondisabled students. The program has two major goals: (a) to develop positive, mutually rewarding relationships that generalize across environments and maintain across time, and (b) to support the development of social competence such that disabled and nondisabled children function successfully in integrated environments.

To achieve these goals, the Special Friends Program integrates opportunities for the development of friendships during recess and other shared activities. Not only does the program make the socially valued friendship role available to severely disabled students who would otherwise be unlikely to engage in friendship relationships, but Special Friends is also an integrative program utilizing existing school programs (e.g., recess). Extensive field testing of the Special Friends Program in Hawaii and a replication of the program in Kentucky indicate that participation in the program results in significantly more positive behaviors and attitudes among nondisabled students toward their disabled peers (Hemphill, 1983; Voeltz, 1980a, 1980b, 1982).

Nondisabled students, as well as severely disabled students, need assistance in learning how to interact with one another successfully. This issue is not resolved by simply reassuring the nondisabled students with philosophical discussions about individual differences. The Special Friends Program allows students to express their concerns through discussions of this nature, but the program emphasizes skill development.

FIGURE 4 Sample Curriculum Sequencing Matrix Describing the Relationship Between Social Skill Objectives and Daily Routine/Activities

HAWAII INTEGRATION PROJECT

Social Skills Objectives

Routines/ Activities	Greets familiar persons	Recognizes vacant toilet	Goes to toilet w/o assistance	Verbally requests assistance	Attend to speaker when spoken to	Indicate choice
Hygiene	Greets peers	Recognizes vacant toilet	Goes to toilet without assistance	Requests assistance w/removal of tight caps	Attends to teacher	Selects personal items, prefers cologne
Street Crossing				Requests assistance stepping up/down curbs	Attends to teacher	
Making Purchases	Greets familiar store clerks			Requests assistance with counting change	Attends to clerk at checkout	Selects items to purchase
Food Preparation	Greets home economic teacher assistants			Requests assistance with jar lids	Attends to teacher and teaching assistants	Selects preferred ingredients, seasonings
Lunch	Greets familiar schoolmates	Recognizes vacant toilet in restroom	Goes to vacant toilet without assistance	Requests assistance to open container	Attends to conversation at lunch table	Selects type of milk, vegtable and dessert
Gym	Greets gym teacher and new classmates	Recognizes vacant toilet in restroom	Goes to vacant toilet without assistance	Requests assistance shoe tying & clothes changing	Attends to gym teacher or peers	Selects teammates
Prevocational	Greets vocational teacher and new classmates			Requests assistance if task unknown	Attends to vocational teacher	Selects among three work tasks
Afternoon Leisure (home)	Greets parent and sibling	Recognizes vacant toilet at home	Goes to vacant toilet without assistance	Requests assistance changing clothes	Attends to conversation with parent or sibling	Selects leisure activity
Dinner (home)					Attends to dinner time conversation	Selects preferred foods and quantity

Some of the Special Friends activities for nondisabled students are preparatory for the integrated activities. These elements of the curriculum explore topics such as communicating with nonverbal children, basic sign language, and feelings of empathy. A session illustrating how prostheses are used as tools begins by presenting the students with a cartoon of a child who sees apples in a tree but cannot reach them. The students are asked to generate creative approaches, particularly involving the use of tools, to obtain the apples. Following a discussion of their answers, the concept of tool use is expanded to include modes of transportation. The students are guided to two major conclusions: (a) tools help us do something we couldn't otherwise do on our own, and (b) tools can help us do things more quickly or more efficiently. Finally, the term *prosthesis* is introduced, and a variety of prostheses used by disabled students (e.g., wheelchairs, communication boards, prone standers) are shown and discussed.

Social, play, and leisure interchanges are the primary foci of the Special Friends Program. The integration activities usually involve turn-taking so that the activities (e.g., pinball, electronic or video games, blowing and catching bubbles) are mutually reinforcing. Because the severely disabled student's behavioral repertoire is probably quite unlike that of most of the nondisabled student's friends, the nondisabled student must learn how to interact, communicate, and play with the disabled peer. These skills must be specific to each disabled peer so that successful interactions can take place.

For the nondisabled student, this social skill training is primarily vicarious. Only initial instruction from a teacher is required; the natural cues and consequences provide the student with information to make the necessary adjustments to maintain the interaction. For the disabled participants, these didactic interactions are ideal contexts for the severely disabled participant to generalize social, communication, and leisure skills that he/she is learning.

SOCIAL STUDIES CURRICULA FOR NONDISABLED STUDENTS

A major objective of social studies is to learn about self and others in a societal context—an objective that is easily adapted for supporting integration within a school environment. For example, the following global objectives are included in *The Smallest Minority: Adapted Regular Education Social Studies Curricula for Understanding and Integrating Severely Disabled Students* (Brown, Hemphill, & Voeltz, 1982; Brown, Fruehling, & Hemphill, 1982; Hemphill, Zukas, & Brown, 1982):

1. Development of responsibility to self and others;
2. Development of a positive self-concept;
3. Development of decision-making and problem-solving skills;
4. Development of effective communication skills.

An integrative curriculum is developed by infusing these objectives into the regular social studies lessons.

The Smallest Minority is a series of three curriculum guides for lower elementary, upper elementary, and secondary grades. They focus on learning about self and other individuals in the school—particularly those other students who are severely disabled. The curricula do *not* teach students about types, causes, or symptoms of disabilities. Rather, the activities help students learn that disabled students are students like themselves, with similar needs and feelings (even though they may require adaptive equipment or specialized instruction/materials to have their educational needs met). The integration activities emphasize that students can learn about individual differences through interactions with other students in the school. The appendix of each curriculum guide includes two sections of supplementary information: Etiquette with People [who have disabilities] and Integrated Recreational Activities for Disabled and Nondisabled Peers.

The Lower Elementary Grades: Understanding Self and Others (Brown, Hemphill, & Voeltz, 1982) has three units: (a) similarities and differences, (b) problem-solving skills and alternative methods (e.g., using prostheses as tools), and (c) alternative methods of communication (e.g., communication with sign language or communication boards).

The Upper Elementary Grades (4–6): Understanding Prejudice (Brown, Fruehling, & Hemphill, 1982) explores the dynamics of groups and group membership. The roots of prejudice (judgments on the basis of assumption) are examined, and the privileges and responsibilities of group membership are discussed. The curriculum includes a unique role-playing activity in which the students experience actual discrimination or preferential treatment solely on the basis of whether they choose a red or black card.

The final curriculum guide in the series, *The Secondary Grades (7–12): Understanding Alienation* (Hemphill, Zukas, & Brown, 1982) focuses on the examination of self and the alienation of disabled persons. One activity involves a short script in which three students assume the roles of school newspaper reporters and three students portray physically disabled students who are interviewed by the reporters. In addition to learning about personal alienation, physical and programmatic barriers that contribute to the alienation of disabled persons are studied. For a final project, students evaluate the barriers and alienation in their school and design possible solutions.

Special Alternatives: A Learning System for Generating Unique Solutions to Problems of Special Education in Integrated Settings (Fruehling, Hemphill, Brown, & Zukas, 1981) is another example of an integrative social studies curriculum for nondisabled students. *Special Alternatives* is a small-group activity that instructs through the process and the content of the activity. Participation enhances the student's ability, as an individual and as a group member, to generate a large number of unique solutions to a variety of problem situations. Students confront issues and problems faced by children in special and regular education, parents, and school administrators. The curriculum guide outlines 11 categories of problems. The following are examples of questions from some of the categories:

- Name things that students can do in school that make them feel good about themselves.
- The parents of disabled children complain that their children are not allowed to eat lunch with the regular education children. The principal replies that disabled children slow down the lunch line (can't carry their own trays, move slowly, can't give the right amount of money, etc.). What can parents and the school personnel do so that the children can all eat together?
- A child's wheelchair breaks down at school. What can the child and his/her friends do?

The learning activities are designed to teach students that problems can be solved. Generating alternatives for problem solving is helpful in developing and supporting reciprocal friendships with severely disabled students. Finding new ways to play old games so that disabled students can participate is one example.

SCHOOL PERSONNEL INSERVICE CURRICULA

The most typical method of imparting new ideas and skills to administrators, teachers, therapists, and other ancillary personnel is through inservice training. Although this may be an effective method, care should be taken to develop an integrative rather than additive inservice program. Special education teachers and regular education personnel should participate together in inservice training that addresses the needs and interests of both groups. The following inservice training modules are examples of this recommendation: *The Art of Being with One Another* (Yoneshige, 1983b), *School Climate* (Levy & Yoneshige, 1983), *Advocacy Skills* (Yoneshige, 1983a), and *Starting a Special Friends Program in Your School* (Voeltz et al., 1983). Each of the four modules consists of four instructional hours with follow-up activities implemented by each participating teacher in his/her own classroom.

The Art of Being with One Another was designed primarily for regular education teachers but is applicable to special education teachers also. The module describes how to develop or select effective instructional materials and techniques to facilitate the acceptance of individual differences among students.

The *School Climate* module addresses the integration of minority or disabled students as issues that affect the total school environment. For example, the case study included in the module describes a problem situation created by a teacher's attempt to integrate severely disabled students into a regular education music class. The competencies of the module include: (a) understanding the concept of school climate, identifying its components, and analyzing its relationship to educational goals; (b) developing an awareness of one's level of influence, one's capacity to effect change, and the influence level of others; and (c) understanding how to engage others in effecting change and how to utilize systematic strategies for change.

Advocacy Skills were developed for an audience with a variety of school-related roles and the common goal of improving skills for asserting and defending student rights. The four competencies are: (a) developing an understanding of advocacy, (b) recognizing factors essential for effective advocacy in education, (c) demonstrating effective advocacy skills, and (d) recognizing factors needed for developing an integration program for severely disabled students in a regular school. Participants focus on integration and other issues that are of immediate concern to them and their school.

Starting A Special Friends Program is appropriate for teachers, related service providers, or administrators who are interested in beginning the Special Friends Program in their school. The module follows a "how to" approach, and the only requisite is that classrooms for severely disabled students be located on the regular education campus.

Inservice training activities focusing on integration often have been based on the assumption that regular education teachers need their "poor" attitude toward disabled students changed to a "good" one. When teachers interviewed in the Hawaii Integration Project were asked if they would promote integrated activities among severely disabled students and their nondisabled students, however, they indicated that they were willing to do so (Hemphill, 1983). Further, teachers seemed to prefer integrated activities initiated by other school personnel (librarian, physical education teacher, and special education teacher) occurring outside of the regular teacher's classroom. One integration activity, however, that regular teachers appear to feel comfortable enough to initiate on their own and in their classrooms is art.

Programs such as Special Friends and the adapted social skills curricula build in integration experiences and provide the teachers with supportive strategies. The result is increased interactions among disabled and nondisabled students and among special and regular education teachers. The "best" integrative learning situation for teachers may be to learn *with* their students as the students participate in integrated activities.

PARENT PARTICIPATION

The ultimate success or failure of integrating severely disabled and nondisabled students in the public schools may rest with parent participation. Parents of special education and regular education students should be informed of the purposes and goals of integration and should be active participants in planning integration activities. The development of positive parent attitudes toward integration can reinforce and support the development of positive attitudes among the students. Failure to include parents may cause misunderstandings between the school and parents and may result in opposition to integration efforts. A case study reported in the school climate curriculum (Levy & Yoneshige, 1983) describes an actual incident in which poor planning for integration in a music program created low morale among faculty and confusion among parents.

In the earlier discussion of parameters of integration curricula, activities such as joint special education/regular education school orientation programs and booklets are suggested for integrative parent participation. A parent manual developed by the Regular Education for All Children with Handicaps (REACH) project recommends that parents of disabled students join their school's PTA group (Halvorsen, no date). The REACH parent manual outlines several integration presentations and activities that parents of special education students can use with PTA groups. Parent presentations may be preferable to professional presentations because parents have high credibility with other parents and are more likely to speak without jargon. "Hearing that a parent of a severely handicapped child wants his child to have the chance to learn from friends her age who are not handicapped may mean more to the average PTA member than hearing about structured social programs to increase interaction" (p. 98).

INTEGRATION CURRICULA IN THE COMMUNITY

Full integration of severely disabled and nondisabled students requires community support. Participation by parents of disabled students in the PTA is one way to address integration in the community because diverse community involvement is likely to be reflected in its membership. Specific community agencies, facilities, and programs that are particularly appropriate or interesting to disabled students may be identified for direct integration efforts (e.g., public library, neighborhood swimming pool, zoo). Community integration curricula should include awareness and information about disabled individuals, specific skill training to facilitate integration (e.g., how to communicate with persons who use communication boards), and several suggestions for appropriate integrative activities.

Honolulu Zoo Docent Training: Enhancing Integrated Zoo Experiences for Disabled and Nondisabled Children/Youth (Hemphill, Fruehling, Takemoto, Yamate, & Zukas, 1982) is an inservice training procedure designed to help zoo docents provide integrative zoo experiences for nondisabled and disabled children/youth. The program consists of a series of activities requiring approximately 4½ hours to complete. The activities are designed to help individuals examine their ideas about persons with disabilities, differentiate between a disability and a handicap, enhance their verbal descriptions of zoo experiences, learn simple sign language relevant to zoo tours, and rapidly generate alternative solutions to problematic situations that might arise in integrated settings. The manual can be easily adapted to other docent groups, such as those that serve museums, aquariums, and so on.

Many community organizations offer support to disabled persons by sponsoring parties, trips, sports events, and the like. Although these events are well-intended, the result is segregation of disabled individuals from their nondisabled peers. Community organizations should be encouraged to redirect their efforts to further community integration of disabled individuals through activities such as building a ramp into an inaccessible public library or developing a public park.

SUMMARY

Integration of severely disabled students in the public schools should involve a comprehensive curriculum approach for disabled and nondisabled students, regular and special education teachers, related service personnel, school administrators, and the community. Preparatory curriculum might include social skills training for severely disabled students or learning about individual differences in social studies for nondisabled students, but the focus of integration should be on actual integration experiences (such as Special Friends).

Curricula that are appropriate for integration must create valued roles for disabled students, provide integrative rather than additive experiences, be age-appropriate, focus on communication and interaction, and facilitate the development of reciprocal relationships. Implementing a comprehensive curriculum approach and adhering to these parameters will contribute to providing equal access for all students in school and in the community.

REFERENCES

Bricker, D. D. (1978). A rationale for the integration of handicapped and nonhandicapped preschool children. In M. J. Guralnick (Ed.), *Early intervention and the integration of handicapped and nonhandicapped children* (pp. 3–26). Baltimore: University Park Press.

Brown, L., Branston, M. B., Hamre-Nietupski, S., Johnson, F., Wilcox, B., & Gruenewald, L. (1979). A rationale for comprehensive longitudinal interactions between severely handicapped students and non-handicapped students and other citizens. *AAESPH Review, 4,* 3–14.

Brown, L., Ford, A., Nisbet, J., Sweet, M., Donnellan, A., & Gruenewald, L. (1983). Opportunities available when severely handicapped students attend chronological age-appropriate regular schools. *Journal of the Association for the Severely Handicapped, 8,* 16–24.

Brown, S., Fruehling, R., & Hemphill, N. J. (1982). *The smallest minority: Adapted regular education social studies curricula for understanding and integrating severely disabled students. Upper elementary grades: Understanding prejudice.* Honolulu: University of Hawaii/Manoa, Hawaii Integration Project.

Brown, S., Hemphill, N. J., & Voeltz, L. (1982). *The smallest minority: Adapted regular education social studies curricula for understanding and integrating severely disabled students. Lower elementary grades: Understanding self and others.* Honolulu: University of Hawaii/Manoa, Hawaii Integration Project.

Crawford, J. L., Aiello, J. R., & Thompson, D. E. (1979). Deinstitutionalization and community placement: Clinical and environmental factors. *Mental Retardation, 17,* 59–63.

Fruehling, R., Hemphill, N. J., Brown, S., & Zukas, D. (1981). *Special alternatives: A learning system for generating unique solutions to problems of special education in integrated settings.* Honolulu: University of Hawaii/Manoa, Hawaii Integration Project.

Guess, D., & Noonan, M. J. (1982). Curricula and instructional procedures for severely handicapped students. *Focus on Exceptional Children, 14*(5), 1–12.

Halvorsen, A. T. (no date). *P.A.C.T.: Parents and community together.* San Francisco Unified School District and San Francisco State University, Project REACH.

Hamre-Nietupski, S., & Nietupski, J. (1981). Integral involvement of severely handicapped students within regular public schools. *Journal of the Association for the Severely Handicapped, 6,* 30–39.

Hemphill, N. J. (October, 1981). *Application of an integrated inservice model to promote social interactions between severely handicapped and regular education students in public school settings.* Paper presented at the 8th Annual Convention of the Association for the Severely Handicapped, New York.

Hemphill, N. J. (1983). *Promoting the integration of severely handicapped children into school/community social systems: Final report* (U.S. Department of Special Education Contract No. 300-80-0746). Honolulu: University of Hawaii/Manoa.

Hemphill, N. J., Fruehling, R., Takemoto, K., Yamate, S., & Zukas, D. (1982). *Honolulu zoo docent training: Enhancing integrated zoo experiences for disabled and nondisabled children/youth.* Honolulu: University of Hawaii/Manoa, Hawaii Integration Project.

Hemphill, N. J., Noonan, M. J., & Levy, G. (May, 1983). *HIP Interactive Curriculum Model.* Paper presented at the Assessment and Improvement of Related Services Workshop. Honolulu.

Hemphill, N. J., Zukas, D., & Brown, S. (1982). *The smallest minority: Adapted regular education social studies curricula for understanding and integrating severely disabled students. The secondary grades: Understanding alienation.* Honolulu: University of Hawaii/Manoa, Hawaii Integration Project.

Holovoet, J., Guess, D., Mulligan, M., & Brown, F. (1980). The individualized curriculum sequencing model II: A teaching strategy for severely handicapped students. *Journal of the Association for the Severely Handicapped, 5,* 337–357.

Jacobson, J. W., & Schwartz, A. A. (1983). Personal and service characteristics affecting group home placement success: A prospective analysis. *Mental Retardation, 21,* 1–7.

Johnson, J. L., & Mithaug, D. E. (1978). A replication survey of sheltered workshop entry requirements. *AAESPH Review, 3,* 116–122.

Levy, I., & Yoneshige, D. (1983). *School climate: Applied to integration and access of special education children in full learning environments. A Ho'okoho module.* Honolulu: University of Hawaii/Manoa, Hawaii Integration Project.

Mulligan, M., & Guess, D. (1984). Using an individualized curriculum sequencing model. In L. McCormick & R. L. Schiefelbusch, *Early language intervention* (pp. 299–323). Columbus, OH: Charles E. Merrill.

Niziol, O. M., & DeBlassie, R. R. (1972). Work adjustment and the educable mentally retarded adolescent. *Journal of Employment Counseling, 9,* 158–166.

Noonan, M. J., & Hemphill, N. J. (1983). Differences among joint and SPED interactions with teachers and peers. In N. J. Hemphill, *Promoting the integration of severely handicapped children into school/community social systems: Final report* (U.S. Department of Education Contract No. 300-80-0746) (p. 113). Honolulu: University of Hawaii/Manoa.

Noonan, M. J., Hemphill, N. J., & Levy, G. (1983). *Social skills curricular strategy for students with severe disabilities.* Honolulu: University of Hawaii/Manoa, Hawaii Integration Project.

Schalock, R. L., Harper, R. S., & Genung, T. (1981). Community integration of mentally retarded adults: Community placement and program success. *American Journal of Mental Deficiency, 85,* 478–488.

Stodden, R. A. (1980). *Occupational skills training materials.* Boston: Commonwealth of Massachusetts, Department of Occupational Education.

TASH adopts resolution calling for abolition of institutions (1980, January). *The Association for Severely Handicapped Newsletter,* p. 1.

Vincent, L. J., Salisbury, C., Walter, G., Brown, P., Gruenewald, L. J., & Powers, M. (1980). Program evaluation and curriculum development in early childhood/special education. In W. Sailor, B. Wilcox, & L. Brown (Eds.), *Methods of instruction for severely handicapped students* (pp. 303–328). Baltimore: Paul H. Brookes.

Voeltz, L. M. (1980a). Children's attitudes toward handicapped peers. *American Journal of Mental Deficiency, 86,* 455–464.

Voeltz, L. M. (1980b). Special Friends in Hawaii. *Education Unlimited, 2.* 10–11.

Voeltz, L. M. (1982). Effects of structured interactions with severely handicapped peers on children's attitudes. *American Journal of Mental Deficiency, 86,* 380–389.

Voeltz, L., Hemphill, N. J., Brown, S., Kishi, G., Klein, R., Fruehling, R., Levy, G., Collie, J., & Kube, C. (1983). *The Special Friends program: A trainer's manual for integrated school settings.* Honolulu: University of Hawaii/Manoa, Hawaii Integration Project.

Wolfensberger, W. (1983). Social role valorization: A proposed new term for the principle of normalization. *Mental Retardation, 21,* 234–239.

Yoneshige, D. (1983a). *Advocacy skills: Applied to integration and access of special education children in full learning environments. A Ho'okoho module.* Honolulu: University of Hawaii/Manoa, Hawaii Integration Project.

Yoneshige, D. (1983b). *The art of being with one another: Applied to integration and access of special education children in full learning environments. A Ho'okoho module.* Honolulu: University of Hawaii/Manoa, Hawaii Integration Project.

Dr. Noonan is an Assistant Professor, Special Education, University of Hawaii at Manoa. Dr. Hemphill is affiliated with the Center for Human Growth, Honolulu.

Employment is a primary goal in the process of assisting persons with disabilities to attain independence. For persons with severe handicaps, intense training is required to attain a level of self-sufficiency that will sustain them in a work setting. Rusch and Chadsey-Rusch offer practical suggestions in implementing what they refer to as a *community-referenced approach*—for curriculum development and for the coordination of resources.

Employment for Persons With Severe Handicaps: Curriculum Development and Coordination of Services

Frank R. Rusch and Janis Chadsey-Rusch

One of the primary outcomes of education is preparation for adulthood. With adulthood come certain responsibilities and roles that we are all expected to assume. One of these roles is that of "contributor to society," which can be achieved in various ways, including finding and maintaining employment. Employment is also important to the individual. Through employment one derives monetary rewards, which can be used to purchase desired goods and services; employment also provides intangible rewards such as the opportunity to interact with others, the development of self-worth, and the chance to contribute to society (Turkel, 1972). Employment is tantamount to our daily lives because it structures our individual adjustment and influences our residential and recreational opportunities.

Assistant Secretary of the Office of Special Education and Rehabilitative Services Madeline Will (1984) also has suggested that employment is critical to the lives of most Americans regardless of whether their work is specialized (e.g., banking, computer science, medicine), entry-level (e.g., maid services, janitorial services, food services), or supported (e.g., work crews, enclaves). Will's statement has important implications for persons with severe handicaps because these individuals are likely to be employed in entry-level or supported employment positions. Unfortunately, prevailing educational and adult services in this country have resulted in few employment opportunities to persons with severe handicaps.

Recently the U.S. Commission on Civil Rights (1983) reported that the percentage of all persons with disabilities who are unemployed is between 50% and 80%. These data suggest that a disproportionately large number of disabled persons, and practically all those labeled severely handicapped by the schools, do not obtain meaningful jobs. Several recent follow-up studies conducted in Vermont (Hasazi, Preskill, Gordon, & Collins, 1982), Virginia (Wehman, Kregel, & Zoller, 1984), and Colorado (Mithaug, Horiuchi, & Fanning, 1985) reflect similar employment figures. For example, Wehman et al. (1984) indicated that less than 12% of all severely handicapped individuals are employed in Virginia and all of these persons are underemployed.

Although considerable attention has been focused upon elementary and secondary education over the past few years, these resources have not resulted in meaningful employment outcomes for graduating students who are severely handicapped. Consequently, we are at a crucial point in our education of persons with severe handicaps. It is time to implement the current "best practices" in order to prepare students who are severely handicapped for adulthood, particularly if adulthood includes employment. Undoubtedly, more research and development must occur to further refine and clarify the "best practices" in employment preparation. In fact, with the exception of a single text (i.e., Wilcox & Bellamy, 1983) and a few chapters and articles, educational "best practices" related to employment for students who are severely handicapped appear to have not attained a level of universal adoption that results in meaningful outcomes—i.e., employment.

All students with severe handicaps should be prepared for employment. Further, this preparation should take place when the student is between the ages of 13 and 21. Not only should preparation for employment begin in the schools, but school personnel also must assume a leadership role in enhancing students' meaningful transition from school to work. This article provides curriculum guidelines that will enable school personnel to assume this role. It also describes the need for coordinated services that will result in an effective, efficient transition from school to work.

GUIDELINES FOR CURRICULUM DEVELOPMENT

The following guidelines focus upon four interrelated steps suggested by Rusch (1983), Wehman (1981), and others that have been shown to result in *meaningful employment outcomes**. These steps form a model whereby the community is first surveyed to identify possible job placement and their associated social and vocational survival skills (Rusch, 1979). Next, community-based (nonsheltered) training sites are established within actual community work settings, and the student is trained in the work setting (the nonsheltered training site). Third, a job is found for the student and the student is placed. Finally, training and supervision are provided to the student on the job during initial placement and later at regular intervals to ensure that acquired skills are maintained and the student successfully adjusts to employment.

**Meaningful employment refers to working in integrated settings whereby all employees work for mutual outcomes—production of useful services or valued goods for monetary reward.*

This curriculum model is important because it provides the blueprint for teachers to consider when establishing a program's philosophical commitment. The commitment includes establishing a curriculum that is (a) community-referenced, (b) integrated, (c) longitudinal, and (d) community-based.

Community-Referenced Approach

Community-referenced curricula answer the "what to teach" question by identifying the behaviors students must be able to perform in employment settings in which they are going to be placed. The community-referenced approach does not follow more traditional approaches to curriculum development that are organized along academic sequences (e.g., language, reading, math). Instead, this approach focuses upon the basic demands of adult life (e.g., employment, leisure, community participation). This guideline has opened a new arena for curriculum planning that may prove to be as influential to students with handicaps as was the identification of goals and objectives in the 1960s and the formation of individualized education plans in the 1970s.

Briefly, in developing a community-referenced curriculum, the local community is surveyed to determine (a) the types of jobs available and (b) the requirements of the jobs identified. Bates (1986) has described six methods for determining available community jobs: (a) listing previously successful employment options of past graduates, (b) keeping a record of the frequency with which specific types of jobs appear in classified ads, (c) obtaining a list of employment openings from local rehabilitation counselors, (d) conducting surveys of local businesses, (e) utilizing personal contacts with community leaders (e.g., principals, small business operators), and (f) visiting other successful programs. Jobs that have been identified as potential employment options for students in the Champaign-Urbana (Illinois) area are:

Assembly Line Worker
Baggage Transporter
Bakery Assistant (doughnut filler/finisher)
Candy-Striper
Concession Stand Worker
Copy Shop Assistant
Dishwasher
Doctor or Dentist Office (cleaning instruments)
Gardener/Greenskeeper (planting and tagging shrubs, small trees)
Grocery Store/Supermarket Bagger, Carryout
Linen Room Assistant
Meter Maid (emptying meters)
Painter's Assistant
Pet Care Assistant (Humane Society)
Plugger (cabinet company)
Postal Worker (mail sorter)
Surgical Instrument Wrapper
Vending Room Supplier/Attendant

Once a listing of potential jobs has been generated, the specific "survival skills" required in each of the potential job sites is identified. *Survival skills* are generally thought of as those behaviors that facilitate functioning in the community (Martin, Rusch, & Heal, 1982). In relation to employment, survival skills are those that, when acquired, increase the likelihood of employment and job maintenance (Rusch, 1979). Survival skills usually are divided into two categories—social survival skills and vocational survival skills. *Social survival skills* are those that require interaction with other persons—e.g., exchanging greetings and following directions. *Vocational survival skills* refer to the nonsocial skills required on the job—e.g., completing a task assignment and moving from one task to another throughout the work day.

Identifying social and vocational survival skills is important because this information results in a better understanding of what students should learn in school. Teachers then can use the identified survival skills (the actual requirements of the job) as a basis for selecting instructional objectives. These objectives, when taught, will likely result in meaningful employment outcomes for students with severe handicaps when they leave school.

Survival skills can be identified by (a) verbal reports or (b) direct observation. Verbal reports usually involve an interview with an employer, a job supervisor, or even an employee, who describes the requirements for a specific job (Rusch & Mithaug, 1980). Often, employers have difficulty identifying survival skills because few employers have ever really described the specific behaviors necessary to get and maintain a job. For example, rather than saying that an employee should be able to ask for help when needed, an employer may state that an employee needs to be a "good worker." These broad, general statements are not helpful for formulating instructional objectives. Thus, teachers must structure the interview so that employers specify the important requirements for the job, as well as the possible standards and criteria that go along with the job requirements.

Often, using a questionnaire to solicit specific survival skills information may be helpful. For example, one of the items on a questionnaire administered by Rusch, Schutz, and Agran (1982) asked employers to indicate how long they expected employees to work continuously (0–15 minutes, 15–30 minutes, 30–60 minutes, 1–2 hours, or more than 2 hours).

Another method that can be used for determining social and vocational survival skills is through direct observation of workers performing targeted jobs (Rusch & Mithaug, 1980). Teachers, however, must have some direction about the behaviors they are going to observe before they begin to collect information, or else they may spend time observing behaviors that are not necessarily essential to job functioning. Guidance on the valued job skills to observe can again come from the employer, supervisor, or other employees. Direct observation of workers performing jobs has one advantage over getting this information strictly through verbal reports or questionnaires: It allows the teacher to see first-hand what types of job skills are critical for success rather than relying on verbal reports, which may over- or underestimate, or even misrepresent the actual requirements for the job.

After teachers have compiled a list of potential jobs and identified the critical vocational and social survival skills needed for job success, they must still decide which type of job is most appropriate for individual students. This decision can be facilitated by assessing parent and student preference for the specific jobs available in the community and by determining how well the student's skills match the social and vocational skills needed for the job.

Again, a community-referenced curricula consists of specific behaviors, or survival skills, that students must be able to perform in employment settings in which they are going to be placed. Local communities are surveyed for the types of jobs available and the requirements for the jobs (i.e., social and vocational survival skills) are identified by verbal report and/or direct observation.

Integrated Settings

The traditional occupational choice for students who are severely handicapped has been the sheltered workshop or similar segregated settings, such as adult day care centers and work activities centers. Usually, these segregated settings offer limited work opportunities. Consequently, little training for specific jobs occurs. If work is available, it most often represents work performed in nonsheltered settings in the community by persons who are not handicapped. This work then is subcontracted to segregated settings for persons who are handicapped. Typically, sheltered workshop employees work at subminimum wages, completing tasks such as assembling, packaging, or sorting "widgets," for periods of less than 2 to 3 hours per day. From a rehabilitative perspective this work is viewed as therapeutic. From our perspective this work is viewed as demeaning and does not contribute to the individual's growth and development.

Students with severe handicaps should be prepared to work in settings with nonhandicapped persons. Employment preparation in integrated settings allows the student to have exposure to and experience with the demands and expectations of these environments. Integrated settings also provide employers and co-workers opportunities to interact with students who have handicaps. Through this symbiotic relationship the student can more easily learn appropriate social and vocational skills needed for the job, and the employer and co-workers can learn of the student's potential as a reliable employee and friend. Often, as a consequence of integrated teaching environments, students may also earn a more competitive wage.

Longitudinal Instruction

As students with severe handicaps move from one instructional level to the next (e.g., from intermediate to secondary classrooms), they should acquire a range of skills that will eventually lead to employment. For example, if working continuously at a job for 1- to 2-hour intervals has been identified as a survival skill needed to enter a community work situation, curricula should be developed so that this skill is in the students' repertoire by the time they leave high school.

One way to ensure that this objective is reached is to begin work on the skills early in the educational sequence of classes. Thus, preschool through high school experiences should include instruction that develops identified survival skills. Regarding the goal "work continuously at the job for 1- to 2-hour intervals," preschool students might be required to participate in direct instruction for at least 15 minutes per day. This would be extended to increasingly longer periods as the students grow and progress through the educational sequence of classes. Eventually they would work continuously for at least 30- to 60-minute periods in community job stations.

Each teacher's major responsibility is to teach skills required in future placements. Acquiring a list of the social and vocational skills potential employers believe are critical for job entry allows the teacher to develop a coordinated, longitudinal curriculum. Preschool, elementary, and intermediate classroom teachers should develop instructional programs that advance students from general applications of each skill to employer-specific task applications, which is the responsibility of the secondary classroom teacher.

Instructional content should be based on goals that are sequenced and on what is functional for each student. *Functionality* within the context of employment preparation refers to teaching relevant, age-appropriate applications of survival skills identified as important for eventual job entry. For example, a student might learn to move independently around the classroom, from the classroom to the cafeteria for lunch, then to the playground, and eventually from home to work. At the secondary level all skills should be taught on placement-specific tasks, such as riding the bus to and from a community-based employment training station.

Community-Based Training Stations

One of the significant learning problems students with severe handicaps possess is that they often do not generalize, or transfer, skills they have acquired across settings, people, behaviors, and/or time. Educational efforts to date reflect the assumption that what is learned in the classroom or during simulated work stations will also be performed outside of the school or in real work situations. Since this assumption is frequently faulty, teachers must establish and provide instruction in community-based training stations.

Establishing community-based training stations in actual employment settings is one way of providing realistic and functional training for employment. A community-based training station is a vocational training site within an ordinary community work setting (e.g., in dishwashing rooms in restaurants, in industrial plants) (Stainback, Stainback, Nietupski, & Hamre-Nietupski, 1986). One of the major implications of community-based instruction is that students will receive less and less instruction in the classroom. In fact, when a student reaches the age of 12, instruction in the community should occur for extended periods. This means that school personnel will have to provide instruction on job sites in the community outside of the classroom. Community-based job sites also must be *community-referenced*; they must be established where there is a potential market for employment. Since students will likely hold more than one job in their lifetime, they must learn skills that are useful across jobs.

Community-based training sites have been successfully established and maintained by special education teachers (Alper, 1981; Nietupski, Hamre-Nietupski, Welch, & Anderson, 1983). Compared to sheltered, segregated, and simulated work settings, community-based training stations offer many advantages, some of which are listed below.

1. Training of vocational survival skills is ensured.
2. Opportunities to learn social survival skills are provided.
3. Co-workers serve as role models.
4. Co-workers begin to understand persons who are severely handicapped.
5. Direct service personnel become familiar with employment.
6. A more normalized learning experience is offered.
7. Community members' expectations are influenced positively.
8. The likelihood of employment is enhanced.

As much as possible, special educational personnel should capitalize on these advantages by trying to establish community work stations as primary settings for vocational training of students who are severely handicapped.

Summary of Curriculum Guidelines

Guidelines that have resulted in meaningful employment outcomes for students who are severely handicapped include the development of a community-referenced, integrated, longitudinal, and community-based curriculum. A community-referenced curriculum focuses upon the "actual" demands of the local communities and jobs and pinpoints objectives that guide the development of students' IEPs. The integrated guideline is important because it directs attention toward equitable opportunities for training and placement. Longitudinal and community-based guidelines refer to skills being taught in the community that are functional and that share some commonality throughout the student's school years.

When students with severe handicaps graduate from school, many will still need specialized services after job placement, including continued job training, through follow-up. Unfortunately, when the student is severely handicapped, few agencies provide post-school services along the guidelines just discussed. Coordination of services between school and rehabilitation personnel is needed to enhance the transition from school to work.

COORDINATION OF SERVICES

Consider the case of Bob. Bob is a student with severe mental retardation who was educated in a local public school system and had received vocational training ever since he was in junior high school. Bob was taught to ride the bus with assistance, learned to express himself with the use of a communication book (e.g., he pointed to pictures when he was hungry, had to go to the bathroom, was sick, or needed help), could use the restroom independently, and was able to bus tables (he could pick up dirty dishes from a table and then wipe the table clean). When Bob left the public school system, he was referred to the local rehabilitation agency and was placed in an adult day care center.

When Bob's teachers learned of his placement, they were furious! Why, they asked, had they bothered to educate Bob using a curriculum that was community-referenced, integrated, longitudinal, and community-based if Bob was going to be placed into an adult day care center? Similarly, the local rehabilitation staff was angry. Why, they asked, had not the school system contacted them before Bob graduated so they could have worked together to make certain Bob was continued in the job for which he was trained? Had they known about Bob and his skills, they could have worked actively with the schools, Bob, and his parents to ensure that the transition from school to work was efficient, appropriate, and mutually agreed upon.

Unfortunately, the above scenario happens all too frequently in communities in the United States. Even more unfortunately, individuals like Bob and his family are the ones who suffer the most from lack of communication and coordination between and among service providers. Educational and rehabilitation programs cannot effectively serve students who are severely handicapped until both service providers make an effort to plan and coordinate their services. Coordinated services (a) provide a more efficient, effective, and meaningful continuum of services for students, (b) help reduce duplicative efforts, and (c) offer service personnel additional knowledge and appreciation for each other's roles in service delivery (Hall, 1980).

Transition is a term that has been used for several years (Brown et al., 1981). Recently, Wehman (1984) defined vocational transition as:

> . . . a carefully planned process, which may be initiated either by school personnel or adult service providers, to establish and implement a plan for either employment or additional vocational training of a handicapped student who will graduate or leave school in three to five years. Such a process must involve special educators, vocational educators, parents and/or the student, and an adult service system representative, and possibly an employer. (pp. 23–24)

According to Wehman's definition, vocational transition must be: (a) a well-planned and systematic process, which (b) occurs well before the student reaches 21 years of age, and combines the efforts of (c) individuals from numerous disciplines and service agencies, and (d) parents or students, or both. This coordination is achieved by developing and implementing a vocational transition plan. Like the IEP, a vocational transition plan helps to ensure that educational and rehabilitation personnel meet and pool their resources so that students will obtain employment or additional vocational training after leaving high school.

The Transition Planning Team

Several individuals can be involved in planning for transition, including parents, students, school personnel, rehabilitation personnel, and employers.

Parents

Parents are crucial to the transition team because they usually make the ultimate decision regarding which employment options are the most desirable for their children. Parental choices vary depending upon their personal values, expectations for their children, and information they possess about program options (McDonnell, Sheehan, & Wilcox, undated). So that the best decisions can be made for students, parents have to be well informed regarding the employment options existing in their communities. Employment options that are common to many communities include work activity centers, sheltered workshops, supported employment, and competitive employment.

Work Activity Centers. Work activity centers are day programs in which 20 to 60 individuals with handicaps spend their day performing activities that bear little if any relation to employment (e.g., coloring, dressing a doll, sitting quietly). Few work activity centers offer employment training or wages; most centers focus their training efforts on leisure activities such as arts and crafts. If wages are offered, they generally are quite low (e.g., less than $300 a year).

Sheltered Workshops. Although the goal of sheltered workshops is to prepare individuals for competitive employment, actual placement out of the workshop seldom occurs. If work is offered and wages are paid, the wages are often low (about $700 a year). Sheltered workshops, like work activity centers, are segregated and employ large numbers of individuals with handicaps (50–100). Few persons who are severely handicapped attain sheltered workshop status; most workshops employ individuals who are mildly or moderately handicapped.

Supported Employment. Supported employment options include work crews and enclaves, which exist in only a few communities. Work crews generally consist of small groups of individuals who are handicapped and under the supervision of an individual who is not handicapped. Work crews perform jobs according to specified contracts that are bid upon (e.g., yard work or janitorial services at an office building). *Work crews* usually move from one job to another job throughout a work day. *Enclaves* are located within a single business or industry performing light industrial or electronic assembly tasks. Similar to work crews, enclaves consist of a group of individuals with handicaps who are trained and supervised by a nonhandicapped individual. Both employment options assume that the individual worker will require continuing support throughout the tenure of employment. Thus, this option is a viable one for individuals who are severely handicapped. Supported employment options most often occur in integrated settings and offer competitive wages for full- or part-time work.

Competitive Employment. An individual who is competitively employed performs work that is valued by an employer in an integrated setting and earns minimum wage or better. Traditionally, competitive employment options exist in most communities. Agencies such as Vocational Rehabilitation offer job placement services to eligible clients. These services are usually offered to individuals who require little training to learn job-related tasks and, once placed on the job, require little if any follow-up. Individuals served by Vocational Rehabilitation are placed into competitive and integrated settings. Many individuals utilizing these services are not mildly handicapped but, rather, are considered disadvantaged or displaced workers (nonhandicapped workers who have lost their jobs).

Competitive employment is also a viable alternative for persons who are severely handicapped if each of the four curriculum guides introduced earlier (community-referenced, integrated, longitudinal, community-based) is followed. Rusch (1986) suggests that competitive employment should include intensive job-site training and advocacy, ongoing evaluation, and extended follow-up services. In competitive employment, ongoing services are not necessarily needed for the duration of employment (in contrast to the supported employment option) and, in fact, services are gradually withdrawn as soon as the individuals show that they can maintain employment on their own.

Although not all employment options may exist in all communities, parents should be aware of innovative employment programs occurring in other communities. The lack of various options also should not stop parents from requesting services that they think would be appropriate for their child. If parents want an employment option that does not yet exist, McDonnell et al. (undated) have suggested that parents choose an alternative that should be regarded as temporary with the understanding that a more appropriate option will be available at a later date.

Students

Students should be involved in planning their transition from school to work. As much as is possible, their interests and needs regarding various employment options should be considered.

Schools

As has been stated, schools have the responsibility to prepare students for employment. Classroom teachers should work together with the local rehabilitation agency staff to conduct surveys of communities for potential job training sites as well as permanent employment positions. It makes little sense for classroom teachers and rehabilitation personnel to conduct independent job surveys or to establish independent job training sites. These duplicative efforts—which often exist in communities—could be eliminated by early coordination of services. This coordination of efforts with the local rehabilitation agency ensures that parents will be well informed of the various employment options available for their children when the children leave the school system.

Adult Service Agencies

Adult rehabilitation agency personnel (and/or employees) should be represented on the transition planning team. Reasons for involving these personnel include their need to inform teachers, parents, and students about employment options existing in the community and their need to work closely with the teachers and parents to facilitate entry into desired employment placements. Also, adult service providers should work continually to improve employment options. Expanding their access to community references is important to the continual development of their programs.

In summary, several individuals should be involved in planning the transition from school to work for individuals with severe handicaps. Parent participation is necessary because parents usually make the ultimate decision regarding the most desirable employment option for their children. The students themselves should be involved, when possible, so their vocational interests are known. The school is essential because it prepares the student for employment; and adult service agencies facilitate entry into desired employment placements and may provide further training or follow-up services. The transitional process is further enhanced by formulating a written transitional plan.

The Vocational Transition Plan

The vocational transition plan is a formal mechanism for making certain that recommendations for employment occur. Essentially, vocational transition plans should be individualized and delineate the necessary steps or procedures (e.g., type of training, materials) needed for entry into the employment option selected. The plans should specify the recommended employment option selected and designate the person(s) responsible for implementing the procedures within a specified time period. An example of a transition plan suggested by McDonnell et al. (undated) is provided in Figure 1. The vocational transition plan ensures that the parents are aware of employment options and adult services, enables the student to acquire adult services with few disruptions, and gives school personnel and adult service agency representatives a set of procedures and timelines to follow.

FIGURE 1
Vocational Transition Plan

Date ____________

Student's Name ____________ Age ______ Date of Graduation ____________

High School ____________

Participants ____________

Employment Placement	Recommendations	RESPONSIBILITIES					
		Parent/Guardian		School		Adult Service Provided	
		Action	Time Line	Action	Time Line	Action	Time Line

REFERENCES

Alper, S. (1981). Utilizing community jobs in developing vocational curriculum for severely handicapped youth. *Education & Training of the Mentally Retarded, 16,* 217–221.

Bates, P. E. (1986). Competitive employment in southern Illinois: A transitional service delivery model for enhancing competitive employment outcomes for public school students. In F. R. Rusch (Ed.), *Competitive employment: Service delivery models, methods, and issues.* Baltimore: Paul H. Brookes Publishing Co.

Brown, L., Pumpian, I., Baumgart, D., VanDerventer, L., Ford, A., Nisbet, J., Schneider, J., & Gruenwald, L. (1981). Longitudinal transition plans in programs for severely handicapped students. *Exceptional Children, 47,* 624–630.

Hall, H. B. (1980). The intangible human factor: The most critical coordination variable. In J. O. Elder & P. R. Magrab (Eds.), *Coordinating services to handicapped children: A handbook for interagency collaboration* (pp. 45–62). Baltimore: Paul H. Brookes Publishing Co.

Hasazi, S., Preskill, H., Gordon, L., & Collins, C. (1982). *Factors associated with the employment status of handicapped youth.* Paper presented at the American Educational Research Association, New York, NY.

Martin, J. E., Rusch, F. R., & Heal, L. W. (1982). Teaching community survival skills to mentally retarded adults: A review and analysis. *Journal of Special Education, 16*(3), 243–267.

McDonnell, J., Sheehan, M., & Wilcox, B. (undated). *Effective transition from school to work and adult services: A procedural handbook for parents and teachers.* Eugene, OR: University of Oregon.

Mithaug, D. E., Horiuchi, C. N., & Fanning, P. M. (1985). A report on the Colorado statewide follow-up survey of special education students. *Exceptional Children 51*(5), 397–404.

Nietupski, J., Hamre-Nietupski, S., Welch, J., & Anderson, R. (1983). Establishing and maintaining vocational training sites for moderately and severely handicapped students: Strategies for community/vocational trainers. *Education & Training of the Mentally Retarded. 18,* 169–175.

Rusch, F. R. (1979). Toward the validation of social/vocational survival skills. *Mental Retardation, 17*(3), 143–145.

Rusch, F. R. (1983). Competitive vocational training. In M. Snell (Ed.), *Systematic instruction of the moderately and severely handicapped* (2nd ed.). Columbus, OH: Charles E. Merrill Publishing Co.

Rusch, F. R. (1986). *Competitive employment: Service delivery models, methods, and issues.* Baltimore: Paul H. Brookes Publishing Co.

Rusch, F., & Mithaug, D. (1980). *Vocational training for mentally retarded adults: A behavior analytic approach.* Champaign, IL: Research Press.

Rusch, F. R., Schutz, R. P., & Agran, M. (1982). Validating entry-level survival skills for service occupations: Implications for curriculum development. *Journal of the Association for the Severely Handicapped, 7,* 32–41.

Stainback, W., Stainback, S., Nietupski, J., & Hamre-Nietupski, S. (1986). Establishing community-based training stations. In F. R. Rusch (Ed.), *Competitive employment: Service delivery models, methods, and issues.* Baltimore: Paul H. Brookes Publishing Co.

Turkel, S. (1972). *Working.* New York: Pantheon.

U.S. Commission on Civil Rights. (1983). *Accommodating the spectrum of disabilities.* Washington, DC: Author.

Wehman, P. (1981). *Competitive employment: New horizons for the severely disabled.* Baltimore: Paul H. Brookes Publishing Co.

Wehman, P. (1984). Transition for handicapped youth from school to work. In J. Chadsey-Rusch (Ed.), *Conference proceedings document: Enhancing transition from school to the workplace for handicapped youth* (pp. 22–39). Champaign, IL: University of Illinois, Office of Career Development for Special Populations.

Wehman, P., Kregel, J., & Zoller, K. (1984). *A follow-up of mentally retarded graduates' vocational and independent living skills in Virginia.* Manuscript in preparation, Richmond, VA.

Wilcox, B. & Bellamy, G. T. (Eds.). (1982). *Design of high school programs for severely handicapped students.* Baltimore: Paul H. Brookes Publishing Co.

Will, M. (1984), March/April). Bridges from school to working life. *Programs for the Handicapped, 2.*

Frank Rusch is Professor of Special Education and Director of the Secondary Transition Intervention Effectiveness Institute at the University of Illinois at Urbana-Champaign, where Janis Chadsey-Rusch is Assistant Professor, Department of Special Education.

Two
Teaching Presentation

Glenn A. Vergason

This section deals with teaching presentation, or the status of instructional practices and technology in special education. It covers definitive changes that have occurred in instructional practices over the last few years. This introduction should provide a roadmap for understanding this section, as well as to point out diverse factors that are pulling special education in different directions or, as some people even say, pulling it apart.

Some of the elements of change were apparent, in a previous collection of essays, with topics such as thinking skills and coping skills (Vergason, 1983). Special education at that time had come through a period in which it had separate curricula and operated out of separate special classes. Within special education there were indications of a theoretical relationship between the various curricula and the delivery system. Most articles on curriculum content appeared under traditional curriculum topics. In the last 15 years, as special education moved to the resource model, there has been a major shift away from curriculum, or what to teach, toward how to teach, or how to present instruction. This shift has continued as special and regular educators continue to develop a working relationship, to examine the appropriateness of various delivery systems and to identify the most effective ways to educate the mildly handicapped.

At the present time most mildly handicapped students are in regular education with what has been referred to as the "pullout model" (Will, 1986). The pullout model is what special education calls the resource room or resource teacher model. Will and a number of her associates have mounted an attack on the way special education for the mildly handicapped is organized and have proposed changes in the delivery models, as well as in the special education funding base. Will wants to accomplish the "regular education initiative," or the education of mildly handicapped individuals in the regular classroom. Funds presently used for special education would be used to provide instructional support for these students in regular education classes. These handicapped students would belong to regular education, and the school principal would be the program leader.

Whether the regular education initiative will become reality is a matter that only time, and perhaps, politics, will tell. Ms. Will, assisted by a group of people, describes an instructional approach to handicapped students wherein the instruction occurs almost totally in regular classrooms (Wang & Birch, 1984; Stainback & Stainback, 1984; Stainback, Stainback, Courtnage, & Jaben, 1985; Wang, Walberg & Randolph 1985; Reynolds, Wang, & Walberg, 1987).

The articles in this section discuss how to teach special students and, in some respects, how to transcend educational settings while acknowledging that the regular classroom may not address learning handicaps or the time factors needed to accomplish instruction. It also can be noted that the regular classroom and mainstreaming do not appear to have been beneficial for mildly handicapped students (Hasazi, Gordon, & Roe, 1985; Edgar, 1987).

As Edgar noted in his studies, 30% of the special education students dropped out of such programs, and less than 18% of the special education graduates obtained positions of employment above the minimum wage. When Edgar removed individuals with behavior disorders and learning disabilities, the percentage dropped to 5% who were employed. One could then say that students who have been mainstreamed since 1975 are graduating after having been in regular education the majority of their school life. These students were in resource rooms three or fewer periods, with a curriculum that was basically that of regular education, but watered down. Certainly 12 or more years of mainstreaming has not resulted in life skills and employment success (Edgar, 1987).

Special education is in turmoil, and the attacks upon it come from within the field rather than outside of it. In regular education the contrary has been true, with National Commissions, study groups, and Governors' Study Commissions calling for reform. In regular education these commissions often have representatives from business and legislators as part of their membership. In special education the attacks have come almost exclusively from within the field, especially from those in higher education. If the reader goes back 20 years, the same type of voices came from Dunn (1968) and Lilly (1970). The names of Wang, Birch, Reynolds, Stainback, Walberg, and others, who already have been referred to in connection with the regular education initiative, are also professors in higher education.

PRESENTATION APPROACHES

The term *instruction* could be used for this section, but *presentation* is broader. The approaches described here are varied but have many common threads. One researcher or writer may use one term; another may use a slightly different term. Thus, cognitive training, cognitive behavior modification, self-instructional training, and a variety of terms used in this section may have similar histories or meanings. This results from a basic change in the way handicapped students are viewed as learners. Instead of emphasizing differences in student characteristics, student learning handicaps, and what to teach, the newer approaches have perceived handicapped and nonhandicapped students as being similar, except that the handicapped are more passive in their approach to learning (Feuerstein, 1983). Gerber (1983) believes these students are strategy inefficient. The article by Schuler and Perez indicates that the deficits are in metacognition.

In the area of behavior disorders, the students are perceived as being limited in the regulation of their own emotional state, as well as in the ability to reflect upon the relationship between their own behavior and external events. These concepts of handicaps are very different from some of the ideas of retardation resulting from deficits and of learning disabilities resulting from perceptual handicaps, to say nothing of the perception of behavior disorders as being mentally ill. These new conceptions are far more treatable from an instructional point of view.

One amazing factor is that the field of special education, while having certain concepts about the way these children learn, is nevertheless not theory-driven. For some reason, special education has been short on developing theories of instruction and theories of learning relating to handicaps. And no person or group appears to exercise an "executive function" over the terminology or practice in the field. For this reason, no one has said, "Let's call this construct A when referring to one type of training and refer to construct B when certain other functions are to be communicated." As a result, the special education literature has a lack of consistency. For example, cognitive training may be referred to as cognitive strategies or cognitive behavioral training.

The advantages of a field with theories and a common vocabulary are obvious. A theory-driven field generates research to prove or disprove its own theories. As time goes on, theories are modified or lead to new theories that explain certain learning phenomena better than previous attempts.

ORGANIZING APPROACHES

Some elements of organizational grouping are arbitrary. One might say that all of the approaches could be grouped under "cognitive approaches," or what is referred to as "effective instruction." I have chosen to discuss them under the headings of:

Learning strategies
Cognitive training/Cognitive behavior modification
Self-control/Cooperative planning
Direct instruction
Effective instruction
Peer tutoring
Curriculum-based assessment (measurement)

Learning Strategies

In looking at teaching presentation in the field of special education for the mildly handicapped, learning strategies were probably the first to develop. The big influences came from the University of Kansas and the University of Virginia Institutes for

Learning Disabilities (Deshler, Schumaker, Alley, Warner, & Clark, 1982; Hallahan, Hall, et al., 1983). Those centers were established at the time when the major expansion in special education was in secondary programming for mildly handicapped. Secondary teachers, both regular and resource, were calling for help. At that time, certain theoretical considerations had not developed and learning strategies took less of a cognitive emphasis. They asked, "How can we help these students cope in the regular curriculum?"

These strategies, as they are discussed in this section, involve rules for summarization (Brown & Day, 1983) and note taking (Taylor, 1982); summarizing, paraphrasing, note taking, study skills, listening skills, and test taking. The effectiveness of these strategies has been well documented. Deshler, Schumaker, Lenz, and Ellis (1984) demonstrated specific strategies that resulted in improved classroom grades, and regular education teachers' perception of these students improved.

One strategy that has received considerable use is SQ3R, which stands for "survey, question, read, recite, review" (Robinson, 1975). This procedure, restructured and renamed *Multipass,* was demonstrated to be effective with learning disabled adolescents by Schumaker, Deshler, Alley, and Warren (1983). Learning strategies has been a valuable addition to the repertoire of skills that assist mildly handicapped in coping.

Cognitive Training/Cognitive Behavior Modification

Cognitive training is probably a more comprehensive concept than *cognitive strategies*, which refers to the actual practices used to help improve the attention, memory, and academic skills of mildly handicapped students. In any event, metacognition and metamemory (Palincsar, 1986) have been central in this movement. Both these terms relate to the self-awareness of how one learns or memorizes materials. Improvements along these dimensions can make students with learning handicaps show improved academic skills.

One of the first strands of this movement came out of the behavior modification movement of the 1970s, adding the element of cognition. The first descriptions of cognitive behavior modification came from Meichenbaum and Goodman (1971). These have been considerably expanded by Harris and by Sheinker, Sheinker, and Stevens, whose articles are contained in this section. A step-by-step review of cognitive behavior modification is given by Schuler and Perez in this section. The latter emphasizes how this procedure employs modeling, overt behavior, and finally covert behavior. Associated with this technique is the concept of self-control, or self-instruction. Others have extended this as cognitive-behavioral training (Brown & Alford, 1984; Lloyd, 1980).

Self-Control/Cooperative Planning

Some of the same principles have been employed in attempts to teach students how to become independent learners (Paris & Oka, 1986), to assist learners in self-instruction in math (Leon & Pepe, 1983), and to assist in the development of self-control in students with behavior disorders (Fagen, Long, & Stevens, 1975; Hallahan, Hall, et al., 1983). Hallahan's work (Kneedler & Hallahan, 1981; Hallahan & Sapona, 1983) shows the effectiveness of self-monitoring and recording on attention and gains in academic production. Wang, Walberg, and Randolph (1985) have suggested that cooperative planning through provisions for appropriate student-choice facilitates student learning. Fagan, Long, and Stevens (1975) even have a curriculum to assist in the development of self-control. Emphasis on self-control without emphasis on academic production may not result in academic improvement. Therefore, the self-control approach includes elements of both cognitive and affective skills, as discussed by Edwards and O'Toole in their article in this section.

Direct Instruction

Direct instruction is another effective instructional practice. It also has been an integral part of much of the cognitive training and cognitive behavior modification practices. Direct instruction comes out of the work of Engelmann and Carnine (1982). Its research and advocates stem mainly from Ohio State University (Stephens, 1977; Stephens, Hartman, & Lucas, 1983) and the University of Oregon (Gersten & Carnine, 1986). The components of direct instruction include explicit step-by-step teaching strategy, student mastery of each step, strategy correction for student errors, gradual fading from teacher direction, adequate systematic practice, cumulative review, and a teaching format that anticipates potential errors.

The benefits of this approach are well documented. Becker and Carnine (1981) showed that students involved in direct instruction make more overall academic gains. Slow/immature learners are helped by direct instruction (Doyle, 1983). Also, improvements were demonstrated in targeted comprehension skills (Singer & Dolan, 1982), and direct instruction was far more effective than traditional approaches in teaching math word problems (Darch, Carnine, & Gersten, 1984). Some researchers favor direct instruction because the methods are closer to those of regular education (Wang, Walberg, & Randolph, 1985).

Effective Instruction

Although this whole book relates to effective instructional practices, the emphasis under the above heading is on the movement called *effective instruction*. This movement is characterized by careful measurement of instructional practices that produce the greatest academic learning. These highly effective methods have emphasized rapid introduction of content to students, importance of time on task, and many other variables. The best overall review of this literature is found in articles by Carol Englert (e.g., 1984). In their article in this section, Ellis and Sabornie also examine the principles of effective instruction in relation to microcomputer use; and Isaacson presents the literature on effective instruction in written composition. Peters et al. (1987) examines the relevance of this instruction to the teaching of math. Gersten and Carnine (see Part One of this book) apply effective instruction to the teaching of reading.

Probably no body of literature offers more promise for special and regular education than effective instruction. Most of the technology has been developed on both populations. Even seemingly small factors, such as the teacher explaining the goals of the lesson and concluding with a summary of what has been taught, have a measurable impact on academic learning (Englert, 1984).

Peer Tutoring

Another educational practice with highly effective results is peer tutoring, as described by Jenkins and Jenkins in their article. This practice may have been injured by the educational reform movement, which emphasizes keeping students in class and requiring greater numbers of Carnegie Units for graduation. In spite of this, administrators should carefully weigh the use of students, cross-age tutors, and even adult volunteers. The results are impressive and cost-effective. Armstrong, Colon, Pierson, and Stahlbrand (1979) demonstrated that high school tutors were equally effective as paraprofessionals at one third the cost of paraprofessionals. Mayhall and Jenkins (1977) showed highly effective results in tutoring periods as short as one half hour. In fact, Cohen, Kulik, and Kulik (1982) indicated that shorter duration programs had larger gains.

Peer tutoring and effective instruction have some close parallels. Stallings and Kaskowitz (1974) demonstrated that teachers who devote considerable time to individual students are less effective overall. Peer tutoring is one of the most effective ways of increasing time in instruction without the teacher having to change grouping methods. It also increases the amount of time a student is involved in instruction. Another consideration is the use of gifted tutors. Cohen and Stover (1981) demonstrated that these students not only could tutor, but they also were capable of shortening, simplifying vocabulary, inserting diagrams, and removing irrelevant information in instructional materials for retarded students. This extends the use of tutors beyond what was already an effective procedure.

Curriculum-Based Assessment (or Measurement) (CBA or CBM)

In recent years the CBA or CBM movement in regular and special education has begun to have an effect on judging the effectiveness of program selection practices in special education and what has been referred to as *pre-assessment* in special education (Deno, Marson & Mirkin, 1982; Deno, Mirkin, & Chiang, 1982). Though some special educators may view this as an assessment tool, in actuality the procedure provides a valid means for judging instructional materials (Deno, Mirkin, & Chiang, 1982), for making management decisions (Deno, Marston, & Tindal, 1986), and for evaluating the effectiveness of IEP goals (Fuchs, Wesson, Tindal, Mirkin, Deno, 1981).

The article by Deno and Fuchs, in Part Three of this book, does give a basic introduction to CBA, along with an extensive list of references. The reader will be able to develop an appreciation of this method, which some professionals believe is criterion-referenced instruction and others view as an extension of precision teaching. In any event, CBA offers one method of systematically monitoring and graphing what is taught and determining how effective that instruction is with individual students, schools, and systems.

SUMMARY

The literature in this section represents special education's educational technology at this time. The effective methods that have been reviewed all have interlocking relationships. In this case, the methods have different elements of cognition, whether in the area of memory, attending, self-regulation, self-instruction, or self-awareness of the importance of how we learn. These methods, if they had been employed consistently, would no doubt have led to less speculation on the effectiveness of special education. After about 1972, most mainstreamed students essentially received tutoring in basic skills when they received instruction in the resource room. Certainly that approach might be no more effective than regular education.

I encourage the field to adopt the techniques discussed in this section because they have a theoretical rationale and a track record for effective instruction with mildly handicapped learners. These practices can only lead to better special education and greater effectiveness with students.

REFERENCES

Armstrong, S. B., Colon, M. F., Pierson, P. M., & Stahlbrand, K. (1979). *The cost effectiveness of peer and cross-age tutoring*. Paper presented at the Annual Meeting of the Council for Exceptional Children, Dallas, TX.

Becker, W. C., & Carnine, D. W. (1981). Direct instruction: A behavior theory model for comprehensive educational intervention with the disadvantaged. In J. W. Bijou & R. Ruiz (Eds.), *Behavior modification: Contributions to education*. Hillsdale, NJ: Erlbaum.

Brown, R. T., & Alford, M. (1984. Ameliorating attentional deficits and concomitant academic deficiencies in learning disabled children through cognitive training. *Journal of Learning Disabilities, 17*,(1), 20–26.

Brown, A. L., & Day, J. D. (1983). *Macrorules for summarizing: The development of expertise* (Tech. Rep. No. 270). Urbana-Champaign: University of Illinois.

Cohen, P. A., Kulik, J. A., & Kulik, C. C. (1982). Educational outcomes of tutoring. *American Educational Research Journal, 19*, 237–248.

Cohen, S. A., & Stover, G. (1981). Effects of teaching sixth grade students to modify format variables of math word problems. *Reading Research Quarterly, 16*, 175–199.

Darch, C., Carnine, D., & Gersten, M. (1984). Explicit instruction in mathematical problem solving. *Journal of Educational Research, 4*, 155–165.

Deno, S., Marston, D., & Mirkin, P. (1982). Valid measurement procedures for continuous evaluation of written expression. *Exceptional Children, 48*, 368–371.

Deno, S., Mirkin, P., & Chiang, B. (1982). Identifying valid measures of reading. *Exceptional Children, 49*, 36–45.

Deno, S., Marston, D., & Tindal, G. (1986). Direct and frequent curriculum-based measurement: An alternative for educational decision making. *Special Services in the Schools, 2*, 5–27.

Deshler, D. D., Schumaker, J., Alley, G. R., Warner, M. M., & Clark, F. (1982). Learning disabilities in adolescent and young adult populations: Research implications. *Focus on Exceptional Children, 15*,(1), 1–12.

Deshler, D., Schumaker, J., Lenz, B. K., & Ellis, E. (1984). Academic and cognitive interventions for L. D. adolescents (Part II). *Journal of Learning Disabilities, 17*(3), 170–179.

Doyle, W. (1983). Academic work. *Review of Education Research, 53*(2), 159–199.

Dunn, L. (1968). Special education for the mildly retarded: Is much of it justifiable? *Exceptional Children, 38*, 5–22.

Edgar, E. (1987). Secondary programs in special education: Are many of them justifiable? *Exceptional Children, 53,* 555–561.
Englert, C. S. (1984). Effective direct instruction practices in special education settings. *RASE, 5*(2), 38–47.
Engelmann, S. E., & Carnine, D. W. (1982). *Theory of instruction.* New York: Irvington.
Fagen, S. A., Long, N. J., & Stevens, D. J. (1975). *Teaching children self control: Preventing emotional and learning problems in the elementary school children.* Columbus, OH: Charles Merrill.
Feuerstein, R. (1983). *Instrumental enrichment.* Baltimore, MD: University Park Press.
Fuchs, L., Wesson, C., Tindal, G., Mirkin, P., & Deno, S. (1981). *Teacher efficiency in continuous evaluation of IEP goals* (Research Report No. 53). Minneapolis: University of Minnesota Institute for Research on Learning Disabilities.
Gerber, M. (1983). Learning disabilities and cognitive strategies: A case for training or constraining problem solving? *Journal of Learning Disabilities, 16*(5), 255–260.
Gersten, R. & Carnine, D. (1986, April). Direct instruction in reading comprehension. *Educational Leadership*, pp. 70–78.
Hallahan, D. P., Hall, R. J., Ianna, S. O., Kneedler, R. D., Lloyd, J., Loper, A. B., & Reeve, R. E. (1983). Summary of research findings at the University of Virginia Learning Disabilities Resource Institute. *Exceptional Education Quarterly, 4*(1), 85–114.
Hallahan, D. P., & Sapona, R. (1983). Self-monitoring of attention with learning-disabled children: Past research and current issues. *Journal of Learning Disabilities, 16*(10), 616–620.
Hasazi, S. B., Gordon, L. R., & Roe, C. A. (1985). Factors associated with the employment status of handicapped youth exiting high school from 1979 to 1983. *Exceptional Children, 51,* 455–469.
Kneedler, R. D., & Hallahan, D. P. (1981). Self-monitoring on task behavior with learning disabled children: Current studies and directions. *Exceptional Education Quarterly, 2,* 73–78.
Leon, J. H., & Pepe, H. J. (1983). Self-instruction teaching: Cognitive behavior modification for remediating arithmetic deficits, *Exceptional Children, 50*(1), 54–60.
Lilly, S. M. (1970). Special education: A teapot in a tempest. *Exceptional Children, 37,* 43–48.
Mayhall, W. F., & Jenkins, J. R. (1977). Scheduling daily or less-than-daily instruction: Implications for research programs. *Journal of Learning Disabilities, 10*(3), 159–163.
Meichenbaum, D., & Goodman, J. (1971). Training impulsive children to talk to themselves: A means of developing self-control. *Journal of Abnormal Psychology, 77,* 115–126.
Palincsar, A. S. (1986). Metacognitive strategy instruction. *Exceptional Children, 53,* 118–124.
Paris, S. G., & Oka, E. R. (1986). Self-regulated learning among exceptional children. *Exceptional Children, 53,* 103–108.
Peters, E., Lloyd, J., Hasselbring, T., Goin, L., Bransford, J., & Stein, M. (1987). Effective instruction in math. *Teaching Exceptional Children, 19,* 30–35.
Reynolds, M. C., Wang, M. C., & Walberg, H. (1987). The necessary restructuring of special and regular education. *Exceptional Children, 53,* 391–398.
Robinson, K. A. (1975). *Teaching reading and study strategies.* Boston: Allyn & Bacon.
Schumaker, J. B., Deshler, D. D., Alley, G., & Warren, M. M. (1983). Toward the development of an intervention model for learning disabled adolescents: The University of Kansas Institute. *Exceptional Education Quarterly, 4*(1), 45–74.
Singer, H., & Dolan, D. (1982). Active comprehension: Problem solving scheme with question generalization for comprehension of complex short stories. *Reading Research Quarterly, 2,* 166–186.
Stainback, W., & Stainback, S. (1984). A rationale for the merger of special and regular education. *Exceptional Children, 51,* 102–111.
Stainback, W., Stainback, S., Courtnage, L., & Jaben, T. (1985). Facilitating mainstreaming by modifying the mainstream. *Exceptional Children, 52,* 144–152.
Stallings, J. A., & Kaskowitz, D. (1974). *Follow-through classroom observation evaluation,* 1972–3. Stanford, CA: Stanford Center for Research & Development in Teaching.
Stephens, T. (1977) *Teaching skills to children with learning and behavior disorders.* Columbus, OH: Charles Merrill.
Stephens, T. M., Hartman, A. C., & Lucas, U. H. (1983). *Teaching children basic skills: A curriculum handbook* (2nd ed.). Columbus, OH: Charles Merrill.
Taylor, B. M. (1982). Text structure and children's comprehension and memory for expository material. *Journal of Educational Psychology, 74*(3), 323–340.
Vergason, G. A. (1983). Curriculum content. In E. Meyen, G. Vergason, & R. Whelan, (Eds.), *Promising practices for exceptional children: Curriculum implications* (pp. 127–142). Denver: Love.

Wang, M. C., & Birch, J. W. (1984). Effective special education in regular classes. *Exceptional Children, 50*(5), 391–397.

Wang, M., Walberg, H., & Randolph, R. (1985). *Classroom processes and outcomes of exemplary adaptive instruction programs*. Pittsburgh: Learning Research & Development Center.

Will, M. C. (1986). Educating children with learning problems: A shared responsibility. *Exceptional Children, 52*, 411–415.

In recent years cognitive training has been at the forefront of special education methodology. This article reviews the research and provides numerous practical applications for teachers. Three main cognitive approaches are examined across a variety of constructs and academic areas. The three overlapping strategies are *cognitive behavior modification, comprehension monitoring,* and *metacognition*. The authors note the extensive research demonstrating the effectiveness of these approaches.

Certain areas of caution are offered so that teachers will be encouraged not to abandon successful areas such as direct instruction. The authors also note that most cognitive training works best with students who have basic academic skills, and that students must be at least at the concrete level of cognitive development. A variety of approaches are offered for improving generalization and memory attention, along with suggestions for improving academic learning.

Cognitive Strategies for Teaching the Mildly Handicapped

Alan Sheinker, Jan M. Sheinker, and Linda J. Stevens

As recently as 2 years ago researchers were speculating about the applications of cognitive training to the classroom and warning that although this area of investigation had yielded promising results, the lack of careful research on actual applications was cause for caution in utilizing such approaches (Cavanaugh & Perlmutter, 1982; Gerber, 1983; Kendall & Mason, 1982). In her review of the research on cognitive behavior modification, Harris (1982) outlined the course that research has taken and the implications of that research for future application in the classroom. Since that review, significant progress has been made through research applying cognitive strategies to areas such as attention and memory, academic achievement, and strategic learning (Keogh, 1983).

For several reasons, the results of this classroom-related research are of interest to the practitioner working with mildly handicapped students. First, teachers have long been aware of students' lack of success in applying what they were taught in the resource room to the regular classroom and in generalizing those skills from one task to another (Schumaker, Deshler, Alley, & Warner, 1983). Some researchers believe that this inability to transfer learning results from an inherent passivity in learning disabled (LD) students' approach to academic tasks (Torgesen, 1979; Wong, 1982), and from lack of systematic planning for skills application activities to facilitate generalization (Meichenbaum, 1983). Several investigators advocate the inclusion of metacognitive training in the instructional program as a critical element of such planning (Brown & Smiley, 1978; Meichenbaum, 1983; Sheinker, Sheinker, & Stevens, 1983).

Second, researchers have noted that LD students appear to reach a learning plateau in high school that is equivalent to about a fourth or fifth grade achievement level (Deshler, Schumaker, Alley, Warner, & Clark, 1982; Schumaker, Deshler, Alley, & Warner, 1983). Interestingly, this achievement level is the point at which basic skills instruction generally ceases and students move on to apply those skills to inferential reading comprehension, math applications, expository writing, and extensive use of content textbooks for learning in science and social studies (Deshler, Warner, Schumaker, Alley & Clark, 1984). A new level of cognitive functioning is required for students to integrate and apply what they have learned. Academic achievement at this level requires that students know *how* to learn rather than just *what* to learn; strategic learning is essential to successful, efficient functioning in the regular classroom and to successful learning from content materials (Schumaker et al., 1983; Sheinker, Sheinker, & Stevens, 1983). Although more research is needed, a number of studies completed over the past few years indicate that cognitive strategies instruction can be an effective tool to help students achieve beyond the basic skills level.

Finally, one goal that has been too seldom attained is the successful reintegration of special students in regular content classes (Deshler et al., 1982; Schumaker et al., 1983). Cognitive strategies training may hold the greatest promise for spanning the distance between learning settings (Pearson, 1982). Many researchers (Brown & Alford, 1984; Hallahan, Hall, Ianna, Kneedler, Lloyd, Loper, & Reeve, 1983; Maier, 1980) have asserted that the results of their studies demonstrate that special students can master these strategies. Some (Hall, 1980; Harth, 1982) believe that although most special students possess cognitive and metacognitive skills, they require training in order to apply them appropriately. Gerber (1983) noted that LD children are not necessarily strategy deficient (connoting the absence of strategy use) but, rather, are strategy inefficient or strategy inflexible.

AREAS OF RESEARCH IN COGNITIVE STRATEGIES INSTRUCTION

Research in teaching cognitive strategies has addressed three amorphous and frequently overlapping concepts: cognitive behavior modification, comprehension monitoring, and metacognition. Different researchers frequently assign the same behaviors to two or more of these categories. To better communicate the nature and cognitive demands of the strategies to be discussed, definitions are suggested for each item.

- *Cognitive behavior modification* refers to the manipulation of covert thought processes to modify overt behavior (Hallahan & Sapona, 1983). It involves a combination of behavior modification techniques and self-treatment methods such as self-monitoring, self-instruction, and self-evaluation (Hresko & Reid, 1981).
- *Comprehension monitoring* involves the act of evaluating one's comprehension processes. Actions to regulate comprehension and resolve comprehension failure, included by some (Bos & Filip, 1984) as part of comprehension monitoring, might more suitably be termed comprehension fostering activities (Palincsar & Brown, in press). The combination of monitoring and regulation functions comprises metacomprehension (Fitzgerald, 1983).
- *Metacognition* involves knowing about and controlling one's own thinking and learning (Armbruster, Echols, & Brown, 1983). Some theorists also refer to these processes as executive functioning (Forrest-Pressley & Waller, 1984).

The difficulty in distinguishing among those areas is apparent in the above definitions. To recognize, however, that metacognition extends beyond the somewhat narrower limits of the other two categories, and in some sense subsumes them, may be important in practice.

CAUTIONS

The concerns of the early 1980s about application of cognitive strategies to the classroom are being addressed by researchers who have applied these techniques to instruction. With growing documentation of the effectiveness of these strategies and the pressing need for the academic progress these strategies may foster, practitioners are beginning to incorporate cognitive strategies into their arsenal of instructional tools. Some cautions should be considered in the implementation of these strategies:

- Don't abandon methods already in use that have proven effective for improving the academic performance of mildly handicapped students. For example, the cognitive strategies approach is not a substitute for direct instruction, which has been demonstrated to be effective in teaching basic reading and math skills (Adams, Carnine, & Gersten, 1982; Carnine, 1983).
- Don't use cognitive strategies techniques as merely an add-on to what you are already doing (Palincsar & Brown, 1984). Cognitive strategies should be a distinct, well organized, integral part of the instructional sequence.
- Before attempting to implement cognitive strategy training in a classroom, be thoroughly versed in the aspects found by research to be effective (Peterson & Swing, 1983). Haphazard use may result in unpredictable and possibly negative outcomes.
- Use cognitive teaching strategies appropriately; these strategies are not a substitute for basic skills instruction.

— Research suggests that cognitive strategy training may not be effective with students below the concrete operational stage of cognitive development (Nichol,

Cohen, Meyers, & Schleser, 1982). Many children do not attain this stage until third to fourth grade (Adams, Carnine, & Gersten, 1982).

— Mastery of basic skills is prerequisite to acquisition and use of generalized cognitive strategies (Brown & Alford, 1984; Lloyd, Saltzman, & Kauffman, 1981). In most cases, students with achievement levels below mid-third to fourth grade will have difficulty generalizing the use of formally taught cognitive strategies (Brown & Smiley, 1978).

- Choose applications of cognitive strategy instruction logically:

— Teach inferential comprehension as well as literal comprehension. Although direct instruction is effective in teaching literal skills, cognitive strategy instruction may be more effective in teaching inferential skills (Maier, 1980).

— Teach regrouping as well as basic facts in math. Preskills are necessary for successful cognitive strategy training (Lloyd, Saltzman, & Kauffman, 1981). Direct instruction, drill, and precision teaching methods may be more efficient for basic facts (Carnine, 1983).

— Teach expository writing as well as mechanics and syntax (Harris & Graham, 1985). There is a variety of effective methods for teaching mechanics, but few validated techniques for teaching expository writing.

— Teach strategies for managing and recalling content materials as well as comprehending them. Distilling and organizing content for later recall are essential for successful studying, and require more than simply understanding what has been read (Armbruster, Echols, & Brown, 1983).

With these cautions in mind, the current state of the art in classroom application of cognitive strategies is discussed here. By no means should this review be considered an exhaustive compilation of relevant research, or the applications discussed here be construed as the only appropriate ones for teaching cognitive strategies. Rather, we have selected recent studies that represent promising practices with documented effectiveness that appear to have immediate relevance for the practitioner. These include cognitive strategies instruction to enhance performance in memory and attention, academic learning (mathematics, written language, and reading comprehension), and studying content material. Future directions in cognitive strategy training and research are also discussed.

GENERALIZATION

A primary reason for the current interest in teaching cognitive strategies is the assertion of several researchers that strategy training may constitute a key ingredient in achieving generalization (Loper, 1980; Meichenbaum, 1983; Wong, 1985). Many have theorized about the components of instructional practice necessary for ensuring generalization; yet, research on the accuracy of these hypotheses has been conducted only in the past few years. Guidelines for achieving generalization have been provided by Baer (1981) and by Meichenbaum (1983). Meichenbaum's recommendations are discussed below, documented by findings of recent research on achieving generalization.

1. *Analyze target behaviors.*

Know what you want to teach. The importance of careful goal setting and systematic task analysis in determining components of the desired behavior has long been documented (Carnine, 1983).

2. *Listen to the student.*

In designing appropriate interventions, one must determine the student's current use of strategies and detect individual differences that may inhibit strategic learning. Swanson (1984) notes that traditional assessment tools were not designed to evaluate children's specific processing strengths and weaknesses. Consequently, teachers must conduct systematic observations and collect formative data concerning baseline strategy use to design effective training programs.

3. *Select training tasks carefully.*

Training tasks teach skills we intend to instill. If we wish students to make general use of a skill, we must design training tasks to encourage use of the strategies necessary for general application of that skill. Kendall (1981) found that impulsive 8- to 12-year-olds who received conceptual self-instruction training (using globally-worded directions that applied to a variety of problem situations) showed significantly better recall of training material on a 1-year follow-up than students who received more task-specific self-instruction training.

Student characteristics should dictate the nature of the tasks. For example, teachers of handicapped students initially may have to provide mediating questions for tasks that provide a model of strategy use while encouraging students to develop their own mediating strategies. Harth (1982) described a study in which the experimenters observed students' poor problem-solving behaviors, identified their strategic deficiencies, and formulated methods of compensating for them through mediation of the task (e.g., the insertion of mediating questions).

4. *Collaborate.*

When generalizing skills to new situations and settings, students must be able to control application of their strategies. If training did not provide the student with experience in assuming responsibility for his/her own learning, the ability to appropriately apply those strategies may not develop. For example, Brown and Palincsar (1982) found that seventh grade poor comprehenders initially experienced significant difficulty in leading a dialogue concerning text segments—an activity that required them to generate questions and formulate hypotheses. Teachers initially found it necessary to model their own strategies, but as training progressed, students' ability to lead the discussion improved dramatically. Students continued to use the strategies 2 months after training was concluded.

Collaboration can also take the form of discovery learning. Schleser, Meyers, Cohen, and Thackwray (1983) found that an experimental group of third and fourth grade non-self-controlled children who were taught academic skills using a Socratic dialogue approach to discovery learning generalized those skills significantly better than did a control group or two self-instruction groups trained in task-specific and general problem-solving skills.

5. *Train.*

Skill generalization calls for well planned training based on mastery of prerequisite skills and incorporating metacognitive skills instruction. Neilans and Israel (1981) used direct and vicarious learning procedures to teach elementary school behaviorally handicapped students to monitor and evaluate their progress in math and reading; students observed the teacher self-goal-set, self-instruct, and self-evaluate after he or she described each skill. These students were better able to remain on task than students who were trained in a more conventional token economy system and also were able to generalize the self-regulation skills in their reading class. Palincsar and Brown (1984) found that intensive training of seventh grade poor comprehenders in the rationale, generality, range of utility, and self-regulation of comprehension monitoring activities resulted in sizable gains on laboratory and standardized comprehension tests, maintenance of those gains, and generalization of the strategies to both classroom comprehension tests and novel laboratory tasks.

6. *Provide feedback.*

Students should receive explicit feedback to show that using the strategy improves performance. Ringel and Springer (1980) provided one treatment group of elementary students with feedback about how their use of a sorting strategy increased the number of pictures they could recall. These third grade students applied the strategy to a transfer task and recalled more than third graders who were merely taught how to implement the strategy.

7. *Generalize.*

Students need to be prompted to identify other opportunities to utilize strategies that are being learned. Palincsar and Brown (1984) found that explicitly training seventh grade poor comprehenders concerning the range of utility for a strategy facilitated its generalization. Students were taught several comprehension strategies. Throughout instruction, the students were told that the strategies applied to other comprehension tasks and would improve their performance. The students later used the strategies in a social studies class although strategy use was not cued.

8. *Train in multiple settings.*

To foster generalization, training should occur in more than one setting or with more than one trainer or task. The ideal situation would be to provide all three, since different students require different combinations in order to generalize skills across settings. Schumaker et al. (1983) found that the opportunity to apply the strategies to a variety of regular classroom materials within the training setting enabled some LD adolescents to generalize strategy use outside the training setting; others required practice in other settings before generalization was evident.

9. *Prevent relapse.*

Safeguards are necessary to ensure that students do not regress to inefficient behaviors. Schumaker et al. (1983) accomplished relapse prevention by consulting with regular teachers in whose classes learning disabled adolescents were to apply the strategies taught in a resource room. Regular teachers were given the rationale for strategy use information about student performance before and after strategy training, cue cards listing the strategy steps to give the students as reminders, possible applications of the strategies in their classrooms, and methods for cuing the student to use the strategies in those situations. This approach resulted in significant improvement in regular class grades and greater teacher satisfaction with students' performance.

10. *Terminate training appropriately.*

Completion of training should depend upon student mastery of the strategy and demonstrated ability to apply the trained skill to a variety of tasks. Booster sessions should be provided as needed to prevent regression of strategy use to pre-training levels, and to quickly and effectively bring the skill back to post-training levels if regression occurs over time. Brown and Palincsar (1982) found that although seventh grade poor comprehenders maintained comprehension monitoring strategies at approximately a 60% level after training was concluded, reintroduction of strategy training produced an increase to a 90% performance level.

The evidence presented here strongly supports the effectiveness of systematic planning for generalization. Although this planning may initially require substantial effort, the results in improved prognosis for mildly handicapped students justify the expenditure of time and effort.

MEMORY AND ATTENTION

Considerable research has been conducted on the effects of cognitive strategy training on handicapped learners' performance in the areas of memory and attention. Unfortunately, most of the research on memory has been conducted in laboratory settings with relatively few applications to classroom instruction (Pressley, Levin &

Bryant, 1983). Nevertheless, some of the hypotheses emerging from this research appear relevant to the selection and design of memory training tasks for mildly handicapped students. Although the volume of research on attention strategies is somewhat smaller, such research more frequently has been conducted in classroom settings, and thus has greater relevance for the practitioner.

Hagen and Barclay (1982) proposed four related periods of change in the strategic development of memory skills. The first period involves a "mediation deficiency" characterized by an inability to use a mnemonic strategy even when trained to do so. Newman and Hagen (1981) conducted a study in which primary and upper elementary LD students were trained in sorting and clustering strategies to assist free recall of 25 pictures. Although older students recalled more items after training, younger students did not improve, demonstrating a failure to spontaneously produce the trained strategy.

In the second period, students are capable of learning strategies but improvement in recall is minimal. Ringel and Springer (1980) found that training first graders in a sorting strategy did not improve recall on later sorting tasks. Students were able to use the strategy in a task-specific manner but could not adequately apply the strategy to assist them on subsequent tasks.

The third period is one of production deficiency during which training can elicit an effective strategy. Newman and Hagen (1981) found that training in sorting improved the performance of upper elementary LD children in recalling a series of pictures. They hypothesized that these children had the sorting strategy in their repertoire but failed to apply it prior to training because they lacked awareness of the strategy's efficacy.

In the fourth period, students make appropriate spontaneous use of mnemonic strategies. In a study by Kurtz and Borkowski (1984), an experimental group of first and third graders who initially exhibited good metamemory skills and were taught rehearsal, clustering, and checking profited more from metacognitive skills training (selection, monitoring, and modification) than similarly trained children who initially demonstrated poorer metamemory skills. The children with better metamemory skills also were able to generalize the strategies more effectively to new tasks.

Despite the evidence cited here, some disagreement is apparent concerning the adequacy of the production deficiency hypothesis in explaining children's failures. Borkowski and Buchel (1983) have suggested that poor results may be attributed more to inadequate or inappropriate instruction than to the child's deficiency. Similarly, in their review of efforts to teach learning disabled students memorization skills, Gelzheiser, Solar, Shepherd, and Wozniak (1983) noted that most investigators have not taught integrated study plans with potential for generalization or trained skills to the point of automaticity. Instead, lower level, task-specific component skills have been taught. Those efforts, though often successful in meeting their limited goals, have not resulted in generalized application. As a result, this body of research does not provide a clear direction for determining either the content or sequence of memory strategy instruction in the classroom.

In contrast, recent research provides some excellent examples of methods to improve attention that can be used in the classroom. The relevance of these training techniques for the teacher of the mildly handicapped stems from evidence that such students may be unaware of factors necessary for maintaining attention. Loper, Hallahan, and Ianna (1982) noted that although they found a relationship between awareness of attention and achievement for normal 7- to 11-year-old children, the relationship did not hold for LD children of the same age except after successful academic intervention.

Results of a line of research conducted at the University of Virginia Learning Disabilities Research Institute (Hallahan et al., 1983; Hallahan & Sapona, 1983) guided the development of procedures for designing classroom interventions to increase attention. Self-recording of on-task behavior by LD elementary school students with attentional problems has resulted in increased on-task behavior and, to a lesser degree, improved academic productivity. Although student monitoring of on-task behavior had to be cued initially, attending behavior was maintained even after self-recording and cuing were faded. Student self-assessment of on-task behavior was found to result in greater gains than teacher assessment, regardless of the accuracy of that self-assessment. These techniques were used successfully during both individual seatwork and group activities.

The self-monitoring procedure also was taught successfully to LD and non-LD students in a second grade classroom. Reinforcement for correct use of the procedure (e.g., recording their behavior each time the tone sounded) led to even higher levels of attention (Rooney, Hallahan, & Lloyd, 1984). Similarly, when Rhode, Morgan, and Young (1983) trained behaviorally handicapped elementary school students in self-evaluation procedures in the resource room and then implemented a less intense procedure (which was subsequently faded) in the regular classroom, students generalized their improved behaviors to the new setting. As with other cognitive strategy training, prerequisite academic skill knowledge is necessary for effective modification of attending behaviors (Lloyd, Saltzman, & Kauffman, 1981).

Several studies from the Virginia Institute (Hallahan, Lloyd, Kosiewicz, Kauffman, & Graves, 1979; Hallahan, Marshall, & Lloyd, 1981; Hallahan & Sapona, 1983; Lloyd, Hallahan, Kosiewicz, & Kneedler, 1982) yielded a consistent set of procedures for increasing attending behaviors in the classroom.

1. The teacher operationally defined attending and nonattending behaviors for the student.
2. The teacher modeled the procedures to be followed by the student in self-assessing and self-recording on-task behaviors: A signal (supplied by a tape recorder or wrist counter) sounded at random intervals; when the signal sounded, the student asked him/herself, "Was I paying attention?"; the student recorded his/her evaluation of on-task behavior according to the definitions provided by the teacher.
3. The procedure was implemented. If necessary (as indicated by frequent inaccurate evaluations), the teacher intermittently verified the accuracy of the self-assessment.
4. Self-recording and cuing signals were faded as attending behavior became well established.

A complete description of the procedure is given in *Improving Attention with Self-Monitoring: A Manual for Teachers* (Hallahan, Lloyd, & Stoller, 1982).

ACADEMIC LEARNING

An early contribution to the application of cognitive behavior modification techniques to academic instruction was provided by Meichenbaum and Burland (1979). Elements of this approach have been incorporated into the work of several individual researchers and that of the University of Kansas and University of Virginia learning disabilities research institutes (Hallahan et al., 1983; Schumaker et al., 1983). This body of research has yielded considerable evidence concerning the efficacy of this approach, as well as specific guidelines for implementing such strategies in classroom settings.

Researchers at the University of Kansas (Deshler, Schumaker, Lenz, & Ellis, 1984) found that not only could LD adolescents be taught task-specific strategies but that strategy learning resulted in improved classroom grades, regular teachers' perceptions of students' performance, and scores on district competency examinations. Ellis (1983) reported that LD adolescents who were taught an executive strategy for developing task-specific strategies improved their performance in the regular classroom. Students were taught to assess setting and task demands, to generate their own task-specific strategies, to monitor strategy effectiveness, and to make necessary modifications, resulting in improved grades and teacher perceptions of product quality.

Research at the University of Virginia (Hallahan et al., 1983) has yielded some important findings concerning effective procedures for teaching cognitive strategies in classrooms. Investigators found that elementary LD students could be trained to apply attack strategies to a variety of academic tasks and that the training required little time when prerequisite skills were present. Students also were able to generalize those strategies to related tasks for which prerequisite skills had been learned. When prerequisite skills were the same for two new academic skills, mastery of attack strategies for one academic skill facilitated learning attack strategies for the second.

Mathematics

Researchers have devised other applications of cognitive strategy training. Genshaft (1982) used cognitive behavior modification with adolescent girls to reduce math anxiety. Although the students were not labeled handicapped, their math achievement was at least 1 year below their reading achievement. Students were taught to use covert self-instruction to talk themselves through math tasks they found anxiety-producing. Training resulted in both significant improvement on a standardized computation measure and more favorable attitudes toward math.

Leon and Pepe (1983) used self-instruction procedures to teach upper elementary LD and educable mentally handicapped students basic math computation skills. Self-instruction training was effective not only in teaching the computation skills but also in achieving generalization to similar skills that were taught directly. Students in the experimental group correctly completed 48 more modules covering skills not yet taught than students in the control group who received only skills training. Special education teachers provided individualized instruction using the following procedure:

1. *Model*. The teacher modeled overt self-instruction as she/he computed the math problem.
2. *Reproduce the model*. The teacher and student together computed a problem, with the student using self-instruction.
3. *Self-instruct overtly*. The student used outloud self-instruction to guide him/herself as she/he computed problems while the teacher assumed a monitoring role.
4. *Fade self-instruction*. The student whispered self-instruction statement as she/he computed problems while the teacher monitored the process.
5. *Self-instruct covertly*. The student used covert (nonverbal) self-instruction as she/he computed problems.

Lloyd et al. (1981) formulated a more task-specific application of this procedure. In a study to determine whether attack strategy training could facilitate generalization of math computation skills, 8- and 9-year-old learning disabled boys were taught a four-step strategy to help them solve multiplication problems. For a given problem (e.g., 6×2), the student first pointed to the number in the problem by which she/he could count ("I can count by 2s"). Next the student made hashmarks for the other number (//////) and counted by the number to which she/he was pointing ("2, 4, 6, 8, 10, 12"). Finally, the student wrote the last number (12) in the answer space. The instructional process included the same elements—teacher modeling, student reproduction of the model, and fading of overt self-instruction—proposed by Meichenbaum and Burland (1979), and used by Leon and Pepe (1983).

Written Language

Harth, Johns, Cloud, and Campbell (1981) reported a study in which cognitive strategies based on Feuerstein's theory of mediated learning experience were applied to written language instruction. Experimenters constructed activities to teach written language mechanics that included mediating directions and questions designed to focus sixth grade LD students' attention on the strategies necessary to select a correct response. Students were provided items requiring them to capitalize and punctuate sentences containing titles (e.g., "Michael Jackson wrote the song beat it."). Mediating directions and questions were provided (e.g., "A. First, I locate the title. B. What do I need to do—underline or use quotation marks? C. Which words should I capitalize?"). The skills acquired through use of this mediating strategy generalized to improve performance on traditional language arts assignments.

Investigators at the University of Kansas Institute for Research in Learning Disabilities (IRLD) developed four strategies that students used successfully to improve their ability to express information in reports, essays, tests, and assignments (Schumaker et al., 1983). LD students were taught a sentence writing strategy to construct four basic types of sentences, a paragraph writing strategy to organize and write coherent paragraphs, a theme writing strategy to organize and write an integrated multi-paragraph theme, and an error monitoring strategy to detect and correct errors in capitalization, punctuation, spelling, and overall appearance of written work.

Harris and Graham (1985) developed a strategy training approach to teach composition to upper elementary LD students using instructional procedures adapted from those of Meichenbaum (1977) and the University of Kansas IRLD (Schumaker et al., 1983). The stories students wrote after training received significantly higher quality ratings than those they wrote before training, and students maintained and generalized these gains over a 6-week period. The procedure consisted of six basic steps:

1. *Teacher modeled and student practiced a task-specific strategy*. The teacher provided a definition and example of a specific language skill (e.g., use of action words). The student practiced applying the skill.
2. *Current performance level and training goals were reviewed*. Use of the targeted skill (e.g., use of action words) was charted, and the training goals and rationale for skill improvement were discussed.
3. *Strategy steps and self-statements were introduced*. A five-step strategy included looking at a stimulus picture and recording action words, generating a story idea to incorporate these action words, writing the story, evaluating the story and use of action words, and improving the story (e.g., adding more action words). The teacher modeled and the student practiced generating appropriate self-statements.
4. *The teacher modeled the learning strategy and self-instruction*. Using a new stimulus picture, the teacher modeled four types of self-instruction: problem definition, planning, self-evaluation, and self-reinforcement. The student identified the four types and recorded examples of each.
5. *Strategy steps and self-instruction types were memorized*. The student memorized strategy steps and examples of the four self-instruction types.
6. *Strategy steps and self-instruction were practiced*. The student set a goal for the number of action words she/he would use, practiced the learning strategy and self-instruction with new stimulus pictures (initially using outloud thinking and fading to covert self-instruction), and charted the number of action words used.

A follow-up after several months indicated that students maintained knowledge of the task strategies and use of self-instruction over time and across settings, but strategy implementation was less consistent. The authors suggested that booster sessions should be provided following termination of training to ensure long-term maintenance of strategy use.

Cognitive strategy instruction also has been applied with some success to handwriting (Graham, 1983; Kosiewicz, Hallahan, Lloyd & Graves, 1982). Researchers using this approach trained students in self-instruction and self-correction procedures. Booster sessions following termination of training were found to improve short-term performance (Kosiewicz et al., 1982).

Reading Comprehension

In recent years researchers have focused efforts increasingly on the area of comprehension monitoring. *Comprehension monitoring refers to the metacognitive process involved in determining whether comprehension occurs and is influenced by person, task, and strategy variables.* An individual's ability to evaluate his/her comprehension significantly affects his/her reading competency (Wagoner, 1983).

Although most of the research in this area has contrasted good and poor readers, a few recent studies have examined comprehension monitoring skills of learning disabled students. Bos and Filip (1984) found that LD seventh graders demonstrated a deficiency in comprehension monitoring when evaluating texts with specific inconsistencies, whereas average readers used comprehension monitoring skills to detect the text inconsistencies. When LD students were cued concerning the existence of an inconsistency, however, they were able to apply comprehension monitoring skills and to detect text confusions. Taylor and Williams (1983) found that LD students and nondisabled upper elementary students with similar reading achievement who were approximately 2 years younger performed comparably when asked to read paragraphs and to detect deviant sentences. A comparable group of LD students who read the passages silently while the examiner read them aloud, however, detected the deviant sentences with significantly greater accuracy.

Another study (Forrest-Pressley & Waller, 1984) examined the relationships among knowledge of comprehension skills, monitoring, and performance on comprehension tasks of poor, average, and good readers in third and sixth grades. Younger and poor readers demonstrated a high rate of acceptance of incorrect sentences and were less able to predict their own comprehension accuracy than older and better readers. Comprehension scores and use of comprehension strategies increased with age and reading achievement. Forrest-Pressley and Gillies (1983) suggested that younger and poor readers may not possess knowledge of the range of appropriate strategies and may not monitor their strategy use.

The relationship between strategy training, comprehension monitoring, and student performance on comprehension tasks was further examined by Short and Ryan (1984) in a study of fourth grade boys who were skilled and less-skilled readers. Implementation of a metacognitive intervention program, consisting in part of story grammar training to improve comprehension monitoring, resulted in dramatic increases in comprehension, as well as maintenance and generalization of strategy use.

Researchers at the University of Kansas IRLD developed several strategies that successfully increased the reading comprehension of high school LD students. The visual imagery strategy required the student to read a passage and form visual images representing the passage content. With the self-questioning strategy, the student formed questions about the passage during reading in order to maintain interest and improve recall (Clark, Deshler, Schumaker, Alley, & Warner, 1984). In the paraphrasing strategy, the student paraphrased the main idea and important details of each paragraph. Another strategy, interpreting visual aids, helped the student gain information from charts, tables, pictures, diagrams, and maps (Schumaker et al, 1983).

Pearson and Gallagher (1983) developed a procedure that successfully taught elementary level poor readers to apply background knowledge and prediction strategies to comprehension tasks. In a number of studies with elementary school good, average, and poor readers (Gordon, 1980; Gordon & Pearson, 1983; Hansen, 1981; Hansen & Pearson, 1983) using various forms of this procedure, trained students out-performed control group students on both standardized and informal inferential reading comprehension measures. The following procedure was used:

1. Prior to reading a story, students were given alternative story introductions. They were asked to relate the circumstances to their own experiences and predict what they thought might happen in two or three critical incidents from the story.
2. Students recorded their prior knowledge experiences and predictions separately and then integrated them on a third page.
3. Students read the story and compared their predictions to story events.
4. Students were then helped to change their conceptions of the reading process by becoming aware of the "known" (experience) to "new" (story) principle by examining their comparisons. Hansen (1984) suggested that a questioning procedure may be used to help students discern these relationships.

From the results of their studies, Hansen and Pearson (1983) concluded that poor readers' inferential comprehension can be improved through strategy training.

In a more comprehensive procedure, Palincsar and Brown (1984) taught seventh grade poor readers summarizing, questioning, clarifying, and predicting strategies. Their results indicated that the most effective approach involved teaching prerequisite skills before attempting to teach the actual strategies, collaborating with the student in helping him/her to develop strategies, and making the general applicability of the strategies explicit to the student. The procedure included the following steps:

1. *Locate the information*. Students read a passage and answered 10 comprehension questions. The instructor praised correct answers and redirected the student to the appropriate portion of the passage to find responses for incorrect answers.
2. *Define the strategies*. Students were informed about the strategies they would use—summarizing, questioning, predicting, and clarifying.
3. *Teach reciprocally*. The instructor and students discussed the story to be read and predicted passage content, decided who would act as teacher (the student and instructor took turns in this role), and read a portion of the passage. The "teacher" asked questions, summarized, and offered predictions and clarifications for the next portion of the passage. The instructor used outloud thinking to model improved strategy use ("I might ask—," "Did this seem unclear?").
4. *Explicate the need and means for generalization*. Throughout the lessons, students were informed of the rationale for use of these strategies in silent reading and were given explanations of how paraphrasing text and anticipating questions that might be asked can be helpful in understanding what is read.

Informal measures of reading comprehension indicated the efficacy of these procedures. In addition, gains were maintained over a 2-month period following two booster sessions, and were generalized to comprehension tasks in a social studies classroom for a majority of the subjects.

STUDYING CONTENT MATERIAL

Research on the application of cognitive strategies to reading comprehension tasks has shown some promising results. Strategies that extend beyond those necessary for comprehension, however, are needed for meeting the goals of students' reading for study purposes in social studies, science, and other types of content (Baker & Brown, 1980). Studying puts increased task demands on the student; in addition to simply understanding what was read, she/he must be able to focus attention upon the ideas and relationships within the material that have to be remembered to obtain good test grades. Anderson and Armbruster (1982) described this strategic behavior as selection and retention of "high pay-off" ideas and relationships from textbook chapters.

According to recent research findings, these strategic behaviors appear to be lacking among poor readers. Carlson and Alley (1981) found that when compared to high-achieving high school students, LD high school students were deficient in note taking, monitoring writing errors, knowledge of test taking, scanning a textbook passage for information, and listening comprehension. Winograd (1983) concluded from his research on summarization with eighth graders that poor readers' difficulties with higher-order comprehension may relate to strategy deficits. Although poor readers were as aware as good readers of the purpose of summarizing, poor readers did not reflect that awareness through the information included in their summaries.

Moreover, the points of the passage that poor readers identified as important bore little relationship to the information contained in their summaries. Poor readers tended to draw almost half of their summary information from the first quarter of the passage; good readers drew one third from the first quarter, almost one fourth from the last quarter, and the remainder from the middle. This finding may relate to the tendency reported by Maria and MacGinitie (1982) for LD students to fix their attention on the first major topic discussed in a passage that related to their own prior knowledge. Lacking strategic behavior, these students may have difficulty attending to subsequent information.

Strategy instruction for mildly handicapped students may have a double benefit. Alvermann (1984) noted that the result of teaching strategies in content material is not only enhanced strategy use but increased content learning as well. In addition, Armbruster and Anderson (1981) observed that study strategies are taught most effectively through specific application to text materials. Instruction in "general" study strategies may be hindered by the need to adapt those general strategies to the specific characteristics of particular text. Students need to know more than the steps of the strategies; they need to know *how, when*, and *why* to apply them in specific situations.

Knowing how, when, and why to apply strategies requires the use of metacognitive skills. Alvermann and Ratekin (1982), however, found that even average seventh and eighth grade readers tended to use a limited range of passive strategies for studying. They speculated that this behavior may have resulted from a failure to recognize when other strategies were needed. Hare and Smith (1982) found that sixth and seventh grade students' accounts of their strategy use correlated significantly with their reading achievement. This finding suggests that the students' metacognitive awareness of their strategy use may relate to their ability to understand what they read. Forrest-Pressley and Gillies (1983) reported that older and better readers demonstrated greater metacognitive knowledge about comprehension fostering strategies, were better able to evaluate their success in comprehending, and were more likely to adapt strategies to meet task demands than younger and poorer readers.

Several attempts have been made to formulate effective study strategies instruction. Among the earliest of these efforts was the SQ3R method—survey, question, read, recite, review (Robinson, 1975). Although based on sound theoretical assumptions, this procedure has been used with disappointing results. In their reviews of the research on the effectiveness of this method, Graham (1982) and Johns and McNamara (1980) reported that SQ3R appeared to be no more effective than traditional study methods.

The University of Kansas IRLD developed several SQ3R strategies that successfully enhanced content learning by LD adolescents (Schumaker, Deshler, Alley, Warner, & Denton, 1983). In the Multipass strategy, students went through a content chapter three times to familiarize themselves with the main ideas and organization of the passage, to gain specific information, and to test themselves on the chapter material. Other strategies included S.O.S.—an adaptation of Multipass in which selected portions of textbook chapter were marked and audiotaped for use by lower achieving LD students, and the listening-notetaking strategy, in which students were taught to listen for and identify cues in order to note and outline key words. A test preparation strategy, a test-taking strategy, and an assignment completion strategy were also developed.

Other study strategy approaches combine direct instruction and metacognition. Adams, Carnine, and Gersten (1982) developed a method for systematic instruction in study strategies. They used explicit definitions of the strategies, rationales for and teacher prompting of strategy use (subsequently faded), structured lessons requiring frequent student responses, and correction procedures, including methods for students to monitor their studying. A social studies text was used to teach fifth grade students the method, which was based, in part, on the SQ3R approach; instructors adhered to the restraints children normally encounter in the classroom (restrictions concerning timelines and writing in textbooks). The experimental group studied longer and performed significantly better than two comparison groups on an immediate short-answer test and maintained performance on a delayed test despite studying for a significantly shorter time.

Sheinker, Sheinker, and Stevens (1983) described another method that organizes study strategies instruction into a sequence consisting of skimming, summarizing, note taking, and outlining and uses regular content textbooks for training materials. The procedure, which has been used with LD (in groups of five to seven) and regular students (entire classrooms) in grades four through twelve, involved an initial use of direct instruction methods followed by training in metacognitive skills through discussion of rationales, use of questioning and outloud thinking techniques, and fostering of self-evaluative processes. The following procedures (Sheinker & Sheinker, 1982a) were used.

1. *Determine current performance level.* Before beginning instruction in each of the four strategies, the group was directed to read a textbook passage and execute the strategy (e.g., summarizing). Students graded their product by comparing it to the teacher's example.
2. *Teach the skill.* The teacher defined the strategy, introduced the strategy steps, and presented a rationale for each step. Students read a second textbook passage and independently executed the strategy.
3. *Model strategy use through collaboration.* With the teacher acting as facilitator, the group followed the strategy steps (brainstorming key points, combining related items, eliminating less important information, and rechecking). The teacher fostered self-evaluation of student contributions through a questioning procedure (e.g., "Why did you make that choice?" "How did you arrive at that conclusion?")

   After students had made their contributions, the teacher modeled her/his own strategies through an outloud thinking process (e.g., "At first, I thought the main point was rising interest rates, but as I read further, I noticed that more space was devoted to discussing inflation. So I decided that the interest rates demonstrated only one aspect of inflation. What do you think?"). Students gradually assumed a more active role in the discussions, questioning and challenging each other to explain choices, thus stimulating further self-evaluation. In addition, students began to offer explanations for their choices without teacher questioning.
4. *Explicate the need for and means of generalization.* The teacher explained how the strategy (e.g., summarizing) helped students efficiently extract information from the textbook passage and that the strategy could be used with most textbooks (e.g., "Now that we have combined related key points into fewer sentences, we have fewer units of information to study and remember. Most textbook passages include discussions of points that can be combined to reduce the number of items to be studied").
5. *Apply the strategies to a variety of materials.* After the group mastered the strategy using the same textbook, students selected other texts and practiced the strategy individually. The teacher monitored progress and facilitated strategy use through the questioning techniques described earlier.
6. *Monitor student progress and promote mastery.* The teacher monitored performance by examining daily progress charts kept by each student. When students reached the mastery criterion (e.g., 80% accuracy of summary statements as compared to the group summary), the group moved to the next stage of instruction (individual practice or the next strategy).

An experimental group of tenth and eleventh grade LD students trained in this procedure performed significantly better on a standardized reading text than a comparison group taught decoding and reading comprehension skills using direct instruction procedures in alternative materials (Sheinker & Sheinker, 1982b). Students in the experimental group, who received no other reading instruction, were trained to use study strategies in their social studies and science texts.

CONCLUSIONS

The instructional methods described here provide the practitioner with validated procedures for teaching cognitive strategies to mildly handicapped students. Several issues related to classroom applications, however, require further research and explanation: appropriateness of group versus individual instruction, position of strategy training along the instructional continuum, and the role of such training in achieving generalization of skills taught in the resource room to regular classroom content materials.

Many of the investigations reviewed here were conducted with individual students and utilized single-subject designs. Although Sheinker and Sheinker (1982b) worked originally with groups, a number of other investigators also have recently taught cognitive strategies to groups of from two to seven handicapped students (Deshler, Warner, Schumaker, Alley, & Clark, 1984; Palinscar & Brown, 1984; Rooney, Hallahan, & Lloyd, 1984). Group instruction may provide some important benefits resulting from student interaction. Pearson (1982) noted that group (particularly small group) instruction consistently has been associated with achievement gains and appears to be more effective than individualized seatwork-oriented instruction. Group interactions may produce higher rates of academic responding; those higher rates, in turn, increase academic productivity (Hallahan & Sapona, 1983).

Cognitive strategy training should not be regarded as a panacea for the skill deficits of handicapped students. Monitoring skills such as planning, self-testing, and predicting, however, may account for substantial differences between LD and non-LD learners (Wong, 1985) and also may apply to other mildly handicapped students. Because cognitive strategy instruction may be an essential part of an instructional sequence directed toward reintegration of handicapped students into regular classrooms, more specific information about its relationship to other techniques and its position along an instructional continuum would clarify some important issues for practitioners. Once students have been taught basic skills for each academic area (word attack and literal comprehension in reading, basic facts for each operation in math, mechanics and usage in written language), cognitive strategies may be a necessary part of the generalized use of those skills to foster mastery of inferential comprehension, math regrouping and reasoning, and expository writing.

Cognitive strategy training also may be essential in the final stage of special instruction, which has as its objective the successful reintegration of the handicapped student into the regular classroom. This stage, in which metacognitive skill training may play a key role, requires even broader generalization of inferential comprehension and expository writing skills to the study and interpretation of content material. If future investigations continue to validate the effectiveness of cognitive strategy instruction, this technique may hold promise for mildly handicapped students who have been unable thus far to apply skills taught in the resource room to task demands in the regular classroom. If that promise is fulfilled, a vital component may be added to the instructional process for these students.

REFERENCES

Adams, A., Carnine, D., & Gersten, R. (1982). Instructional strategies for studying content area texts in the intermediate grades. *Reading Research Quarterly, 18*(1), 27–55.

Alvermann, D. E. (1984). Helping the LD learner read in the content areas. *Topics in Learning & Learning Disabilities, 3*(4). 41–51.

Alvermann, D. E., & Ratekin, N. H. (1982). Metacognitive knowledge about reading proficiency: Its relation to study strategies and task demands. *Journal of Reading Behavior, 14*(3), 231–241.

Anderson, T. H., & Armbruster, B. B. (1982). Reader and text-studying strategies. In W. Otto & S. White (Eds.), *Reading expository material* (pp. 219–241). New York: Academic Press.

Armbruster, B. B. & Anderson, T. H. (1981). Research synthesis on study skills. *Educational Leadership, 39*(2). 154–156.

Armbruster, B. B., Echols, C. H., & Brown, A. L. (1983). *The role of metacognition in reading to learn: A developmental perspective* (Reading Education Report No. 40). Champaign: University of Illinois at Urbana-Champaign, Center for the Study of Reading.

Baer, D. M. (1981). *How to plan for generalization*. Lawrence, KS: H & H Enterprises.

Baker, L., & Brown, A. L. (1980). *Metacognitive skills and reading* (Tech. Rep. No. 188). Champaign: University of Illinois at Urbana-Champaign, Center for the Study of Reading. (ERIC Document Reproduction Service No. 195 932).

Borkowski, J. G., & Buchel, F. P. (1983). Learning and memory strategies in the mentally retarded. In M. Pressley & J. R. Levin (Eds.), *Cognitive strategy research: Psychological foundations* (pp. 103–128). New York: Springer-Verlag.

Bos, C. S., & Filip, D. (1984). Comprehension monitoring in learning disabled and average students. *Journal of Learning Disabilities, 17*(4), 229–233.

Brown, A. L., & Palincsar, A. S. (1982). Inducing strategic learning from texts by means of informed, self-control training. *Topics in Learning & Learning Disabilities, 2*(1), 1–17.

Brown, A. L., & Smiley, S. S. (1978). The development of strategies for studying. *Child Development, 49*, 1076–1088.

Brown, R. T., & Alford, N. (1984). Ameliorating attentional deficits and concomitant academic deficiencies in learning disabled children through cognitive training. *Journal of Learning Disabilities, 17*(1), 20–26.

Carlson, S. A., & Alley, G. R. (1981). *Performance and competence of learning disabled and high-achieving high school students on essential cognitive skills* (Research Rep. No. 53). Lawrence, KS: University of Kansas, Institute for Research in Learning Disabilities.

Carnine, D. (1983). Direct instruction: In search of instructional solutions for educational problems. In Society for Learning Disabilities and Remedial Education (Ed.), *Interdisciplinary voices in learning disabilities and remedial education* (pp. 1–60). Austin, TX: Pro–Ed.

Cavanaugh, J. C., & Perlmutter, M. (1982). Metamemory: A critical examination. *Child Development, 53*, 11–28.

Clark, F. L., Deshler, D. D., Schumaker, J. B., Alley, G. R., & Warner, M. M. (1984). Visual imagery and self-questioning: Strategies to improve comprehension of written material. *Journal of Learning Disabilities, 17*, 45–149.

Deshler, D. D., Schumaker, J. B., Alley, G. R., Warner, M. M., & Clark, F. L. (1982). Learning disabilities in adolescent and young adult populations: Research implications. *Focus on Exceptional Children, 15*(1), 1–12.

Deshler, D. D., Schumaker, J. B., Lenz, B. K., & Ellis, E. (1984). Academic and cognitive interventions for LD adolescents: Part II. *Journal of Learning Disabilities, 17*(3), 170–179.

Deshler, D. D., Warner, M. M., Schumaker, J. B., Alley, G. R., & Clark, F. L. (1984). The learning strategies intervention model: Key components and current status. In J. D. McKinney & L. Feagans (Eds.), *Current topics in learning disabilities* (pp. 245–284). Norwood, NJ: Ablex.

Ellis, E. S. (1983). *The effects of teaching learning disabled adolescents an executive strategy to facilitate self-generation of task specific strategies*. Unpublished doctoral dissertation, University of Kansas, Lawrence.

Fitzgerald, J. (1983). Helping readers gain self-control over reading comprehension. *Reading Teacher, 37*(3), 249–253.

Forrest-Pressley, D. L., Gillies, L. A. (1983). Children's flexible use of strategies during reading. In M. Pressley & J. R. Levin (Eds.), *Cognitive strategy research: Educational applications* (pp. 133–146). New York: Springer-Verlag.

Forrest-Pressley, D. L. & Waller, T. G. (1984). Knowledge and monitoring abilities of poor readers. *Topics in Learning & Learning Disabilities, 3*(4), 73–79.

Gelzheiser, L. M., Solar, R. A., Shepherd, M. J., & Wozniak, R. H. (1983). Teaching learning disabled children to memorize: A rationale for plans and practice. *Journal of Learning Disabilities, 16*(7), 421–425.

Genshaft, J. L. (1982). The use of cognitive behavior therapy for reducing math anxiety. *School Psychology Review, 11*(1), 32–34.

Gerber, M. M. (1983). Learning disabilities and cognitive strategies: A case for training or constraining problem solving? *Journal of Learning Disabilities, 16*(5), 255–260.

Gordon, C. J. (1980). *The effects of instruction in metacomprehension and inferencing on children's comprehension abilities*. Unpublished doctoral dissertation, University of Minnesota, Minneapolis.

Gordon, C. J., & Pearson, P. D. (1983). *The effects of instruction in metacomprehension and inferencing on children's comprehension abilities* (Tech. Rep. No. 277). Champaign: University of Illinois at Urbana-Champaign, Center for the Study of Reading.

Graham, S. (1982). Comparing the SQ3R method with other study techniques for reading improvement. *Reading Improvement, 19*(1), 45–47.

Graham, S. (1983). The effect of self-instructional procedures on LD students' handwriting performance. *Learning Disability Quarterly, 6*(2), 231–234.

Hagen, J. W., & Barclay, C. R. (1982). The development of memory skills in children: Portraying learning disabilities in terms of strategy and knowledge deficiencies. In W. C. Cruickshank & J. W. Lerner (Eds.). *Coming of age: Vol. 3. The best of ACLD* (pp. 127–141). Syracuse, NY: Syracuse University Press.

Hall, R. J. (1980). Cognitive behavior modification and information-processing skills of exceptional children. *Exceptional Education Quarterly, 1*, 9–15.

Hallahan, D. P., Hall, R. J., Ianna, S. O., Kneedler, R. D., Lloyd, J. W., Loper, A. B., & Reeve, R. E. (1983). Summary of research findings at the University of Virginia Learning Disabilities Research Institute. *Exceptional Education Quarterly, 4*(1), 95–114.

Hallahan, D. P., Lloyd, J., Kosiewicz, M. M., Kauffman, J M., & Graves, A. W. (1979). Self monitoring of attention as a treatment for a learning disabled boy's off-task behavior. *Learning Disability Quarterly, 2*(3), 24–32.

Hallahan, D. P., Lloyd, J. W., & Stoller, L (1982). *Improving attention with self-monitoring: A manual for teachers*. Charlottesville, VA: University of Virginia, Learning Disabilities Research Institute.

Hallahan, D. P., Marshall, K. J., & Lloyd, J. W. (1981). Self-recording during group instruction: Effects on attention to task. *Learning Disability Quarterly, 4*(4), 407–413.

Hallahan, D. P., & Sapona, R. (1983). Self-monitoring of attention with learning-disabled children: Past research and current issues. *Journal of Learning Disabilities, 16*(10), 616–620.

Hansen, J. (1981). The effects of inference training and practice on young children's comprehension. *Reading Research Quarterly, 16*, 391–417.

Hansen, J. (1984). The role of prior knowledge in content area learning. *Topics in Learning & Learning Disabilities, 3*(4), 66–72.

Hansen, J., & Pearson, P. D. (1983). An instructional study: Improving the inferential comprehension of fourth grade good and poor readers. *Journal of Educational Psychology, 75*, 821–829.

Hare, V. C., & Smith, D. C. (1982). Reading to remember: Studies of metacognitive reading skills in elementary school-aged children. *Journal of Educational Research, 75*(3), 157–164.

Harris, K. (1982). Cognitive-behavior modification: Application with exceptional students. *Focus on Exceptional Children, 15*(2), 1–16.

Harris, K. R., & Graham, S. (1985). Improving learning disabled students' composition skills: A self-control strategy training approach. *Learning Disability Quarterly, 8*(1), 27–36.

Harth, R. (1982). The Feuerstein perspective on the modification of cognitive performance. *Focus on Exceptional Children, 15*(3), 1–12.

Harth, R., Johns, R., Cloud, C., & Campbell, C. (1981). Mediation: How it can improve problem solving skills. *Academic Therapy, 17*(2), 225–230.

Hresko, W. P., & Reid, D. D. (1981). Five faces of cognition: Theoretical influences on approaches to learning disabilities. *Learning Disability Quarterly, 4*, 238–243.

Johns, J. L., & McNamara, L, P. (1980). The SQ3R study technique: A forgotten research target. *Journal of Reading, 23*(8), 705–708.

Kendall, P. C. (1981). One-year follow-up of concrete versus conceptual cognitive-behavioral self-control training. *Journal of Consulting & Clinical Psychology, 49*, 748–749.

Kendall, J. R., & Mason, J. M. (1982). Metacognition from the historical context of teaching reading. *Topics in Learning & Learning Disabilities, 2*(2), 82–89.

Koegh, B. K. (1983). A lesson from Gestalt psychology. *Exceptional Education Quarterly, 4*(1), 115–127.

Kosiewicz, M. M., Hallahan, D. P., Lloyd, J. & Graves, A. W. (1982). Effects of self-instruction and self-correction procedures on handwriting performance. *Learning Disability Quarterly, 5*(1), 71–78.

Kurtz, B. E., & Borkowski, J. G. (1984). Children's metacognition: Exploring relations among knowledge, process, and motivational variables. *Journal of Experimental Child Psychology, 37*(2), 335–354.

Leon, J. A., & Pepe, H. J. (1983). Self-instructional training: Cognitive behavior modification for remediating arithmetic deficits. *Exceptional Children, 50*(1), 54–60.

Lloyd, J. W., Hallahan, D. P., Kosiewicz, M. M., & Kneedler, R. D. (1982). Reactive effects of self-assessment and self-recording on attention to task and academic productivity. *Learning Disability Quarterly, 5*(3), 216–227.

Lloyd, J., Saltzman, N. J., & Kauffman, J. M. (1981). Predictable generalization in academic learning as a result of preskills and strategy training. *Learning Disability Quarterly, 4*, 203–215.

Loper, A. B. (1980). Metacognitive development: Implications for cognitive training. *Exceptional Education Quarterly, 1*(1), 1–8.

Loper, A. B., Hallahan, D. P., & Ianna, S. O. (1982). Meta-attention in learning disabled and normal students. *Learning Disability Quarterly, 5*(1), 29–36.

Maier, A. S. (1980). The effect of focusing on the cognitive processes of learning disabled children. *Journal of Learning Disabilities, 13*(3), 34–38.

Maria, K., & MacGinitie, W. H. (1982). Reading comprehension disabilities: Knowledge structures and non-accommodating text processing strategies. *Annals of Dyslexia, 32*, 33–59.

Meichenbaum, D. (1977). *Cognitive behavior: An integrative approach.* New York: Plenum Press.

Meichenbaum, D. (1983). Teaching thinking: A cognitive-behavioral approach. In Society for Learning Disabilities and Remedial Education (Ed.), *Interdisciplinary voices in learning disabilities and remedial education* (pp. 127–150). Austin, TX: Pro–Ed.

Meichenbaum, D. & Burland, S. (1979). Cognitive behavior modification with children. *School Psychology Digest, 8*(4), 426–433.

Neilans, T. H., & Israel, A. C. (1981). Toward maintenance and generalization of behavior change: Teaching children self-regulation and self-instructional skills. *Cognitive Therapy & Research, 5*(2), 189–195.

Newman, R. S., & Hagen, J. W. (1981). Memory strategies in children with learning disabilities. *Journal of Applied Developmental Psychology, 1*(4), 297–312.

Nichol, G., Cohen, R., Meyers, A., & Schleser, R. (1982). Generalization of self-instruction training. *Journal of Applied Developmental Psychology, 3*(3), 205–215.

Palincsar, A. S., & Brown, A. L. (1984). Reciprocal teaching of comprehension-fostering and comprehension monitoring activities. *Cognition and Instruction, 1*(2), 117–125.

Pearson, P. D. (1982). *A context for instructional research on reading comprehension* (Tech. Rep. No. 230). Champaign: University of Illinois at Urbana-Champaign, Center for the Study of Reading.

Pearson, P. D., & Gallagher, M. C. (1983). The instruction of reading comprehension. *Contemporary Educational Psychology, 8*, 317–344.

Peterson, P. L., & Swing, S. R. (1983). Problems in classroom implementation of cognitive strategy instruction. In M. Pressley & J. R. Levin (Eds.), *Cognitive strategy research: Educational applications* (pp. 267–289). New York: Springer-Verlag.

Pressley, M., Levin, J. R., & Bryant, S. L. (1983). Memory strategy instruction during adolescence: When is explicit instruction needed? In M. Pressley & J. R. Levin (Eds.), *Cognitive strategy research: Psychological foundations* (pp. 25–49). New York: Springer-Verlag.

Rhode, G., Morgan, D. P., & Young, K. R. (1983). Generalization and maintenance of treatment gains of behaviorally handicapped students from resource rooms to regular classrooms using self-evaluation procedures. *Journal of Applied Behavior Analysis, 16*(2), 171–188.

Ringel, B. A., & Springer, C. J. (1980). On knowing how well one is remembering: The persistence of strategy use during transfer. *Journal of Experimental Child Psychology, 29*, 322–333.

Robinson, H. A. (1975). *Teaching reading and study strategies*. Boston: Allyn & Bacon.

Rooney, K. J., Hallahan, D. P., & Lloyd, J. W. (1984). Self-recording of attention by learning disabled students in the regular classroom. *Journal of Learning Disabilities, 17*(6), 360–364.

Schleser, R., Meyers, A. W., Cohen, R., & Thackwray, D. (1983). Self-instruction interventions with non-self-controlled children: Effects of discovery versus faded rehearsal. *Journal of Consulting & Clinical Psychology, 51*(6), 954–955.

Schumaker, J. B., Deshler, D. D., Alley, G. R., & Warner, M. M. (1983). Toward the development of an intervention model for learning disabled adolescents: The University of Kansas Institute. *Exceptional Education Quarterly, 4*(1), 45–74.

Schumaker, J. B., Deshler, D. D., Alley, G. R., Warner, M. M., & Denton, P. H. (1982). Multipass: A learning strategy for improving reading comprehension. *Learning Disability Quarterly, 5*(3), 295–304.

Sheinker, J., & Sheinker, A. (1982a). *Study strategies: A metacognitive approach*. Rock Springs, WY: White Mountain Publishing Co.

Sheinker, J., & Sheinker, A. (1982b). [The effects of study strategies training on reading comprehension]. Unpublished raw data.

Sheinker, J., Sheinker, A., & Stevens, L. (1983). *Study strategies: A metacognitive approach (teachers'/trainers' manual)*. Rock Springs, WY: White Mountain Publishing Co.

Short, E. J., & Ryan, E. B. (1984). Metacognitive differences between skilled and less skilled readers: Remediating deficits through story grammar and attribution training. *Journal of Educational Psychology, 76*(2), 225–235.

Swanson, H. L. (1984). Process assessment of intelligence in learning disabled and mentally retarded children: A multidirectional model. *Educational Psychologist, 19*(3), 149–162.

Taylor, M. B., & Williams, J. P. (1983). Comprehension of learning-disabled readers: Task and text variations. *Journal of Educational Psychology, 75*(4), 743–751.

Torgesen, J. K. (1979). Factors related to poor performance on memory tasks in reading disabled children. *Learning Disability Quarterly, 2*(3), 17–23.

Wagoner, S. A. (1983). Comprehension monitoring. What it is and what we know about it. *Reading Research Quarterly, 18*(3), 328–346.

Winograd, P. N. (1983). *Strategic difficulties in summarizing texts* (Tech. Rep. No. 274). Champaign: University of Illinois at Urbana-Champaign, Center for the Study of Reading.

Wong, B. Y. L. (1982). Strategic behaviors in selecting retrieval cues in gifted, normal achieving and learning-disabled children. *Journal of Learning Disabilities, 15*(1), 33–37.

Wong, B. Y. L. (1985). Metacognition and learning disabilities. In T. G. Waller, D. Forrest, & E. MacKinnon (Eds.), *Metacognition, cognition, and human performance: Vol. 2. Instructional practices* (pp. 137–180). New York: Academic Press.

Alan Sheinker is Director of Research and Development for Sweetwater County School District Number One, Rock Springs, Wyoming. Jan Sheinker is a private educational consultant with background in direct service, diagnostic testing, and teacher training in public schools. Linda Stevens is a doctoral candidate in the Department of Educational Psychology at the University of Minnesota and has provided technical assistance to federally funded learning disabilities projects.

Cognitive behavior modification, or CBM, has become fashionable for instructing deficient learners in recent years. Yet, when one examines the literature, few constructive articles really review how to use this technique to its best advantage. The present article is probably the single best reference for special educators. It goes beyond theory, showing the teacher how to use cognitive modeling, self-instructional training (SIT), and other aspects of CBM.

Cognitive-Behavior Modification: Application with Exceptional Students

Karen R. Harris

> "When I use a word," Humpty Dumpty said, "it means just what I choose it to mean—neither more nor less." "The question is," said Alice, "whether you *can* make words mean so many different things." "The question is," said Humpty Dumpty, "which is to be the master—that's all."
>
> Lewis Carroll
> *Through The Looking Glass*

Interest in the application of cognitive-behavioral interventions with exceptional students is increasing among both researchers and practitioners. Cognitive-behavioral models for teaching and learning represent an integrated, eclectic approach influenced by behaviorism, social-learning theory, cognitive psychology, developmental psychology, and instructional theory (Craighead, Wilcoxon-Craighead, & Meyers, 1978; Mahoney, 1977a). Teachers of exceptional children have received training in these areas, and many report the use of an eclectic approach—choosing and combining what appears to be the best from diverse sources. Kendall and Hollon (1979), however, have noted the dangers of unguided, unselective eclecticism and the need for empirical support. Research on a variety of cognitive-behavioral interventions, collectively labeled cognitive-behavior modification (CBM), helps to provide both the guidance and empirical support needed.

ORIGINS, DEVELOPMENT, AND DEFINITION

The origins and development of CBM present a complex picture. Trends in the field of behavior modification, including development of social-learning theory and research on self-regulation, are discussed first. Contributions from the areas of cognitive psychology, private speech, and instruction are then noted.

Behavior Modification

Behaviorists have traditionally explained human behavior through environmental antecedents and consequences, limiting research and procedures to readily observable and measurable overt behaviors. The focus of behavior modification is on establishing a behavior, increasing or maintaining a behavior, or reducing or eliminating a behavior (Mahoney & Thoresen, 1974). Maladaptive behaviors are identified, and incompatible, adaptive behaviors are taught. The assumption underlying the behavioral approach is that "the best way to change thoughts and feelings is to change behavior directly; changes in thoughts and feelings will then follow" (Ledwidge, 1978, p. 371). To the radical behaviorist, cognitions have no place in the science of behavior. Although more moderate behaviorists do not deny the existence of the mind, cognitive components of behavior change are considered either irrelevant or trivial (Kendall & Hollon, 1979; Ledwidge, 1978).

Sabatino, Miller, & Schmidt (1981) noted that behavior modification procedures with exceptional students have helped to increase academic response rates, talking, instruction following, positive prosocial interactions, attendance, achievement, and grades. Behavior modification procedures have also helped to establish the importance of a performance orientation, methodological rigor, empirical evaluation, and observable behavioral change (Kendall & Hollon, 1979; Mahoney & Thoresen, 1974).

Nonetheless, there has been a growing dissatisfaction with traditional behavioral interventions over the years. Part of this dissatisfaction arose from the limited scope and effectiveness of behavioral interventions, which used discrete procedures to change certain restricted behaviors (Kendall & Hollon, 1979; Mahoney, 1977a, 1977b) and part arose from frequent failure to obtain durable and generalizable effects after treatment (Abikoff, 1979). This dissatisfaction is evident within the field of special education. Based on their work with hyperactive children, Douglas and her colleagues (Douglas, 1975; Douglas, Parry, Marton, & Garson, 1976) have suggested that relying solely on operant techniques in developing interventions is unwise, as long-term effects and resistance to extinction have not been established.

In addition, the use of reinforcement may result in unique responses among hyperactive children—disrupting their performance, decreasing their attention to the task, and increasing impulsivity. The use of task-extrinsic rewards, especially to motivate learning, may have widespread undesirable effects (cf. Meichenbaum, 1979a). Sabatino et al. (1981) noted that emphasizing behavior modification procedures may preclude exceptional children from learning how to learn, and that special education has become overdependent on intervention strategies unrelated to cognitive development.

Concurrent with the growing dissatisfaction with traditional behavior modification techniques, the behavioristic model has gradually expanded (Kanfer & Karoly,

1972). Behavior modification has "gone cognitive." The view that behavior modification involves cognitive processes, and that cognitive factors are involved in the learning process (Craighead et al., 1978) has slowly been accepted and integrated into behavioral interventions. This movement was expressed in the following statement:

> The predominant conceptualization of the "Behavior Therapies as conditioning techniques involving little or no cognitive influence on behavior change is questioned. It is suggested that current procedures should be modified and new procedures developed to capitalize upon the human organism's unique capacity for cognitive control. (Goldfried, cited in Kendall & Hollon, 1979, p. 7)

Some of the new ingredients that have found their way into behavior modification include the use of self-reports for assessment and treatment, attempts to alter thinking, imagery, and attitudes, and an emphasis on involving individuals in their own treatment (Kanfer & Phillips, 1970; Ledwidge, 1978).

Social-Learning Theory

Covert, or internal, processes are viewed among social-learning theorists as crucial elements in understanding human behavior (Thoresen, 1974). Environmental antecedents and consequences are seen as mediated by cognitions such as internal dialogue, perceptions, and beliefs (Craighead et al., 1978). Moreover, cognitions, or the "internal environment," may act as antecedents and consequences (Mahoney & Thoresen, 1974). Bandura (1978) advanced the concept of reciprocal determinism—that environmental, person, or behavioral variables may act on, and interact with, one another over time. He also demonstrated the importance of self-efficacy and the role of modeling in learning and development (Bandura, 1977a, 1977b). Modeling has become an integral part of many CBM procedures (Denney, 1973; Harris, 1980, 1981a; Harris & Brown, 1982).

Mahoney (1977a) listed several factors that social-learning theory indicates are relevant to the modification of cognition, including: motivation and incentives, demand characteristics, performance and outcome expectancies, a rationale for performance, graduated performance tasks, adequate and relevant perceptual focusing, optimal information processing, and the individual's biological state. Consideration for these variables has been incorporated into various CBM procedures, and researchers have begun to evaluate their individual importance and effectiveness (Harris, 1981b; Keogh & Glover, 1980; Meichenbaum, 1980).

Self-Regulation

Behavioristic research on the development of self-control and the process of self-regulation has also been a major contributor to the development of CBM procedures (researchers have also investigated self-control from a cognitive perspective—cf. Pressley, 1979). Craighead et al. (1978) described self-regulation as a general cognitive strategy, in which the child or adult determines a criterion and then observes his/her own performance, compares the two, and appropriately self-reinforces or self-punishes. Cognitive processes and individual characteristics such as motivation level and learning history are intricately involved in the process of self-regulation. The development of self-regulation is seen as a gradual process in which the child takes over the communicative and regulative responsibilities formerly assumed by the adult (Wertsch, 1979a, 1979b). Calling it a "behavioristic excursion into the lion's den," Kanfer and Karoly (1972) developed a model of self-regulation that includes three basic steps: self-monitoring, self-evaluation, and self-reinforcement.

Cognitive Psychology

Cognitive psychology and interventions, as opposed to behavioral interventions, begin with the view that behavior is influenced by unobservable, and sometimes unconscious, covert operations. Training regimens and interventions are aimed at cognitions, including private speech, thoughts, imagery, perceptions, beliefs, expectancies, and attributions (cf. Harris, 1981a; Kendall & Hollon, 1979; Meichenbaum, 1977). Cognitive therapists believe that "the critical determinants of human behavior lie *within* the individual" (Mahoney, 1977a, p. 6). Although environmental events are seen as important, they are not of primary importance (Meichenbaum, 1977, 1980b). Most cognitive interventions focus on systematically replacing nonfunctional, inappropriate cognitions with effective, organized, and task (or situation) relevant cognitions and behaviors.

Cognitive interventions, however, often incorporate behavioral components. Cognitive therapists view cognitions as *behaviors,* subject to the same laws of development, modification, and extinction as overt behaviors. Therefore, cognitive training procedures frequently apply operant principles (e.g., shaping, positive reinforcement, response cost, elimination of eliciting cues, extinction, controlled practice, and arranging for a high percentage of correct responses) to covert behaviors, including private speech and imagining. Cognitive therapists may also manipulate environmental factors and events in order to affect cognitions (Craighead et al., 1978; Pressley, 1979). In fact, determining where cognitive training ends and CBM begins is sometimes difficult. Keogh and Glover (1980) noted that differentiating between CBM and cognitive training may be unnecessary from a practical standpoint.

Although the behavioral and cognitive viewpoints at first appeared to be fundamentally incompatible, and have resulted in antagonism and bitter dispute (Mahoney, 1977a), they actually share several similarities. Both cognitive and behavioral interventions are "ahistorical" in that they do not focus on traditional, semantic therapy constructs such as the unconscious, infantile sexuality, and so on (Hollon & Kendall, 1979; Ledwidge, 1978). Both viewpoints emphasize a structured approach, methodological rigor, and empirical support.

Private Speech: A Cognitive-Developmental Perspective

Postulated relationships between private speech, thought, and behavior have also been an influential force in the development of CBM procedures and on the application of CBM with exceptional children. Private speech refers to speech that is directed to the self, ". . . not intended for, or not effectively adapted for, communication with others" (Zivin, 1979, p. 9). Private speech is self-regulating, may be either overt (out loud) or covert (internal), and may operate on motor activity, cognitive processing, or perceptual processing.

Soviet researchers were the first to explore the cognitive-developmental functions of private speech. Vygotsky 1934/1962) saw private speech as serving the cognitive functions of orienting, organizing, and structuring behavior. He believed that children used private speech to consciously understand or focus on a problem or situation and to overcome difficulties. Based on his research, Vygotsky reported that overt private speech increases until the age of 6 or 7, declining and becoming primarily covert by the age 8 to 10. As private speech becomes covert, changes occur in its semantic, structural, and grammatic form. Covert private speech is seen as one step removed from thought, where, in Vygotsky's terms, "Words die as they bring forth thought" (p. 149). Individuals at any age, however, may resort to "thinking out loud" when faced with a difficult problem or situation (Zivin, 1979).

Luria (1960, 1961a, 1961b) demonstrated three stages in the development of verbal self-regulation. In the first stage (age 1½–2½), the speech of others controls and directs the child's behavior to some extent, while the child's own speech is ineffective in controlling his/her behavior. The child's overt private speech can initiate behavior to some extent in the second stage (age 3–4), but cannot inhibit behavior. During the third stage (4½–5½), the child's private speech, overt or covert, is able to initiate, direct, and inhibit behavior. Luria believed that language regulated behavior through neurophysiological relationships, and hypothesized that language could help to develop, modify, or maintain behaviors among individuals with developmental or behavioral problems. His research with children having a syndrome similar to hyperactivity supported this hypothesis (Luria, 1961a).

Western researchers have investigated the occurrence of spontaneous verbalizations and strategies, and their ability to mediate behavior, under the labels "mediational deficiency" and "production deficiency" (Kendler, Kendler, & Wells, 1960; Kuenne, 1946; Maccoby, 1964; Reese, 1962). Flavell and his colleagues (Flavell, Beach, & Chinsky, 1966; Keeney, Cannizzo, & Flavell, 1967) explained production deficiency as a failure to produce task relevant verbalizations and/or strategies. They found that production deficiencies occur among students who have the intellectual capabilities, components, and strategies required for a task. Mediational deficiencies occur when verbalizations and strategies are produced but fail to affect behavior.

The way in which private speech and self-regulation work together can be clarified by an example. Consider the private speech that may occur while a teacher prepares a lesson. The hypothetical teacher is experienced, and gets the material needed to plan the lesson almost automatically. With little or no private speech (overt or covert), the teacher gets the plan book, related books, and materials, then gets situated in the best work environment, with adequate lighting, several pencils, and minimal distractions. In becoming involved in the work, the teacher engages in several cognitive processes, including private speech, self-regulation, imagining, and anticipating. The internal dialogue runs something like this: "What do I need in order for them to understand?" "They should be able to . . ." "I'll try . . ." "Last year . . ." "I can use. . . ."

When a problem is encountered, the teacher begins to think more in full sentences, asking: "How am I going to get *this* across?" After beginning to work out an idea, the teacher mutters out loud, "No, no, that isn't going to work." Evaluating the plan and imagining the students' reactions, the teacher thinks, "This is too hard, I've got to break it down into smaller steps." In working out the problem, self-evaluation and self-reinforcement messages include, "I've got it" ". . . This is going to be a good lesson." Upon reaching a point at which the teacher would really rather be doing something else, coping messages enable staying on task: "If I get this done, I can later relax and won't have to worry about it." The teacher found that this thought is usually effective.

Although private speech has rarely been directly investigated among exceptional students, Harris (1981b, 1982) found that young learning disabled children working on a problem-solving task produced significantly more task-irrelevant private speech (word play, descriptions of irrelevant stimuli, general and affective statements) than normally achieving children, and very little task-relevant private speech. After CBM training, this pattern was reversed; task performance and persistence significantly increased.

Instructional Theory and Research

Instructional research offers valuable contributions to the construction of CBM procedures for use with children in classroom settings. Tobias (1982) noted that time on task alone is not enough for learning; how the student uses that time and what the student is thinking while working are important variables. Students with low prior achievement need a good deal of instructional support and stimulation, and may need assistance in improving cognitive processing of instruction. Research indicates that learning is facilitated when the learner is active and involved (Henker, Whalen & Hinshaw, 1980); when the task requires understanding, meaningful processing, and the development of cognitive representations of new behaviors rather than task-specific response sets (Anderson, 1970; Denney, 1975); and when a demonstration-prompt-practice format and sufficient practice are provided (Stevens & Rosenshine, 1981).

Analyses of both the task and the learner, as well as teacher direction, an academic focus, and individualization are also characteristic of effective instruction (Case, 1978; Stevens & Rosenshine, 1981). In addition, researchers are increasingly indicating that teaching exceptional students *how* to think is at least as important as teaching them *what* to think (Borkowski & Cavanaugh, 1979; Deshler, Alley, Warner, & Schumaker, 1981; Maier, 1980; Meichenbaum & Asarnow, 1979). Emphasis is placed on learning to learn, on "improving students' self-control and self-awareness of their own learning processes" (Brown, Campione, & Day, 1981, p. 14.).

Several recently developed eclectic procedures for teaching and learning combine the results of CBM and instructional research. Over the past five years a learning strategies model has been developed at the University of Kansas Institute for Research in Learning Disabilities (Deshler et al., 1981). And Lloyd (1980) has set forth the steps involved in applying attack strategy training to academic instruction. The University of Virginia Learning Disabilities Research Institute is evaluating training techniques that fall under the general rubric of CBM for use with impulsive and hyperactive children (Hallahan, 1978).

Brown et al. (1981) reported on techniques for enhancing learning to learn among EMR and remedial students. The "turtle technique" (Robin, Schneider, & Dolnick, 1977; Schneider, 1974) and a "think aloud" program (Camp, Blom, Hebert, & Van Doorninck, 1977) have been developed to teach delayed responding and social problem solving to aggressive children. Self-instructional training has been applied to a host of behavioral and academic problems among both normal and exceptional students (Meichenbaum, 1977; Meichenbaum & Asarnow, 1979).

CBM: Rationale and Definition

Having traced the historical development of and some major contributors to the CBM perspective, one can see that CBM is based on belief in the interactive, reciprocal nature of cognitions, feelings, and behaviors. Though cognitive, affective, and behavioral viewpoints are each necessary for an understanding of human behavior and the development of interventions, none alone is sufficient (Craighead et al., 1978; Kendall & Finch, 1979; Mahoney, 1977a). Thus, a purposeful, integrated intervention approach should prove superior when children face significant difficulties (Kendall & Hollon, 1979). Although further validation is needed, evidence supporting this tenet is increasing (Hollon & Kendall, 1979). Furthermore, CBM emphasizes the active role children play in their own development and learning, rather than "reshaping" controlled by the teacher (Henker et al., 1980). Deficits are addressed, but the focus is on desired skills and behaviors, developmental capabilities, and ultimately placing the child in control (McKinney & Haskins, 1980; O'Leary, 1980).

The widespread interest in cognitive-behavioral interventions has led to a variety of methods and labels. The eclectic nature of the approach prompted Craighead et al. (1978) to use the phrase "cognitive-social-developmental behavioral approach to child-clinical intervention" (p. 161); they noted that this approach has generally been labeled CBM. CBM is a generic term, encompassing numerous procedures and formats based on a common rationale and goals (Hollon & Kendall, 1979; Kendall, 1977; Keogh & Glover, 1980; Mahoney, 1977a, 1977b; Meichenbaum, 1977, 1979b). The terms *CBM*, *general strategy training*, and *self-instructional training* (among others) are frequently used synonymously. Actually, general strategy training and self-instructional training are procedures that fall under the CBM umbrella; they are sometimes used alone and are often incorporated into more complex training regimens.

CBM training regimens number almost as many as researchers and practitioners working within the CBM philosophy. Meichenbaum (1979a) has noted that the content and format of CBM training regimens can be thought of as falling along continua from concrete to abstract, and from directive to generally didactic teaching. The picture is not likely to get any clearer, as CBM is a dynamic field. New and coming contributors to CBM interventions include metacognition; information processing; attribution theory; research on perception, attention, and memory; expectancy formation; and existential-gestalt psychology (Hollon & Kendall, 1979; Mahoney, 1977a;

Meichenbaum, 1979a). Kendall and Hollon (1979) noted that this multidimensional process should be encouraged and stated that, "It may be somewhat premature to go any further in attempting to categorize the approach, to define its components, or to outline its methods" (p. 3).

Therefore, a flexible definition is needed. The term CBM is used in this article to refer to *the selective, purposeful combination of principles and procedures from diverse areas into training regimens or interventions, the purpose of which is to instate, modify, or extinguish cognitions, feelings, and/or behaviors*. The principles and procedures chosen may be either partially or fully integrated; cognitive and/or behavioral techniques may be directed at any combination of cognitive and/or behavioral targets (Hollon & Kendall, 1979). Whether the procedures and targets are cognitive, affective, or behavioral should depend on characteristics of the problem, the individuals involved and the setting. These decisions, however, often seem to depend on the allegiance(s) of the designer.

CBM may be particularly appropriate for exceptional students, as they exhibit characteristics such as learned helplessness, an external locus of control, production and mediation deficiencies, and deficits in inhibition, self-regulation, problem solving, and means-ends thinking (cf. Brown, 1974; Brown et al., 1981; Denney & Turner, 1979; Havertape & Kass, 1978; Kendall & Finch, 1979; Reid & Hresko, 1980). Exceptional students may not make use of verbal mediation processes or may not have developed an effective linguistic control system (Camp, 1977; Craighead et al., 1978; Meichenbaum, 1976). Classroom procedures can be readily modified to include CBM approaches (Deshler et al., 1981; Meichenbaum & Asarnow, 1979), and CBM can be tailored to individuals of all ages (Meichenbaum, 1980a). The use of some CBM procedures, however, may be inappropriate with severely and profoundly retarded individuals, and some students may need careful pretraining in prerequisite skills and CBM components (Kendall, 1977).

COMPONENTS, PROCEDURES, AND APPLICATIONS

Although CBM regimens vary, several typical components have been identified (Abikoff, 1979; Lloyd, 1980). Students learn to control their own behavior through processes such as self-instruction, self-monitoring, self-assessment, and self-reinforcement. Verbalizations, often overt at first and later covert, are used to guide the student through a series of task-analytic steps aimed at producing effective behavior. Modeling is a common and effective method of teaching the learner to verbalize through these steps. Additionally, many cognitive procedures incorporate teaching students to delay responding in order to evaluate various alternatives.

Some research comparing various components has been done (cf. Denney & Turner, 1979; Keogh & Glover, 1980; Meichenbaum & J. Goodman, 1971; O'Leary, 1980), but further study of the relative effects of singular or combined components is needed. Recent reviews of research in this area have indicated that programs using abbreviated steps or differing components can significantly affect behavior (Abikoff, 1979; Finch & Spirito, 1980; Meichenbaum, 1979a).

Two CBM regimens, sometimes used alone and often incorporated into other regimens are illustrated in this section. The first is Meichenbaum's self-instructional training regimen. Meichenbaum has been credited with providing the major rationale underlying CBM (Abikoff, 1979), though Ledwidge (1978) viewed self-instructional training as a descendent of Rational-Emotive Therapy (Ellis, 1963). Problem-solving training is then discussed.

Self-Instructional Training

Self-instructional training is a particularly relevant method of developing verbally mediated self-control. It has been noted as one of the most promising CBM approaches for use with children (Kendall, 1977). Recent reviews credit self-instructional training as demonstrating the most promising results with attentional problems and with the development of nonimpulsive behavior (Craighead et al., 1978; Kendall & Finch, 1979). Self-instructional training is also seen as an especially viable intervention to alleviate learned helplessness, develop self-esteem, and improve maintenance of treatment effects (Borkowski & Cavanaugh, 1979; Canino, 1981).

The behavioral components of self-instructional training include modeling, successive approximations, graduated difficulty, prompts, feedback, and social reinforcement. Self-regulation is stressed, and students are trained explicitly in the use of task-relevant private speech and the inhibition of task-irrelevant private speech. The natural development of private speech is used as a guide; control over behavior is gradually faded from overt verbalizations by an adult to covert verbalizations by the student. Training is built around four basic steps (Meichenbaum & S. Goodman, 1979):

1. *Cognitive modeling:* The adult model performs a task while talking aloud; the child observes.
2. *Overt guidance:* The child performs the task using the same verbalizations, assisted by the adult at first, then alone.
3. *Faded self-guidance:* The child whispers the instructions (often in an abbreviated form) while going through the task.
4. *Covert self-instruction:* The child performs the task, guided by covert self-speech.

These four steps represent only the bare bones of self-instructional training. Six basic types of self-statements are modeled by the adult and rehearsed by the child (cf. Meichenbaum & J. Goodman, 1971; Meichenbaum & S. Goodman, 1979): (a) problem definition (What is it I have to do?); (b) focusing of attention (I have to concentrate, think only about my work); (c) planning and response guidance (Be careful . . . look at one at a time); (d) self-reinforcement (Good—I got it!); (e) self-evaluation (Am I following my plan . . . did I look at each one?); and (f) coping and error-correcting options (That's ok . . . even if I make an error I can back up and go slowly). These different types of statements are directed at alleviating deficits in comprehending the nature of the problem, producing task-relevant strategies and verbalizations, and using these strategies and verbalizations to directly and effectively mediate behavior (cf. Bem, 1970; Flavell et al., 1966; Reese, 1962).

In addition to these six types, self-statements can be divided into two levels (cf. Brown et al., 1981; Kendall, 1977; Meichenbaum, 1979a; Meichenbaum & Asarnow, 1979): task-approach and task-specific. Task-approach statements refer to global metacognitive, cognitive, and behavioral strategies that are relevant across a variety of related tasks, as well as the task at hand. Task-approach statements can be aimed at components of the task and/or characteristics of the learner. An example of a task-approach statement aimed at the task (and of the problem definition type) is: What am I supposed to do here? . . . What is my first step? Task-approach statements can also be aimed at characteristics of the learner that may interfere with performance, such as impulsivity, external locus of control, or a helpless attitude. Examples include: I must remember to go slow and think first . . . It's up to me how well I do . . . What's important is that I do *my best*. On the other hand, task-specific statements are relevant to the specific task at hand. An example of a task-specific statement (also of the problem definition type) is: I have to put this puzzle together . . . First, I have to turn all the pieces up.

All six types of self-statements can be developed at either the task-approach or task-specific level. Kendall and Finch (1979) reported that general, global task-approach statements result in greater treatment effects and facilitate generalization. Lloyd (1980), however, suggested that task-specific strategies have a better chance of being successful on academic tasks. More research is needed on the differential effects of task-approach and task-specific strategies and self-statements across varying tasks. A combination of the two levels may prove to be most effective, or a gradual transition from task-specific to task-approach statements may prove superior (Kendall, 1977; Meichenbaum, 1979a).

Self-instructional training also emphasizes the importance of the student playing an active, collaborative role in the design, implementation, and evaluation of training regimens (Meichenbaum, 1977). First, the student should help identify any negative, maladaptive, or ineffective cognitions and self-statements that occur. Then, the instructor and the learner should engage in what Meichenbaum terms a Socratic dialogue; the instructor might ask the student how he/she would do the task, then provide feedback and build on the student's advice. The purpose of the task, appropriate strategies, and how to effectively execute the strategy(ies) should be discussed. As training progresses, the instructor should gradually fade support so that the student is spontaneously generating and answering these questions on his/her own. The instructor might occasionally falter in the use of verbalizations and strategies and permit the student to catch the errors.

Self-instructional training should be long-term, occurring across tasks of graduated difficulty and in different settings. Reinforcing and coping statements should be modeled throughout training; all statements should be modeled with appropriate inflection and feeling and should be appropriate for the student's language level. Superficial imitation or mimicry should be discouraged. The child could be asked to re-word or abbreviate self-statements as long as the meaning is preserved. Imagery might also be incorporated; the young, impulsive child might imagine a slow, careful turtle and say, "I will not go faster than a slow turtle." In short, self-instructional training "should not be viewed as regimented or austere but, rather, individually tailored and highly responsive to each child" (Meichenbaum, 1977, p. 98). Many investigators, however, have failed to follow the guidelines and parameters initially presented by Meichenbaum & J. Goodman (1971) and later elaborated by Meichenbaum (1977).

Problem-Solving Training

Successful problem solving is an important factor in adjustment and mental health; problem solving increases coping skills, independence, and self-regulation, and helps to prevent future social and emotional problems (Craighead et al., 1978). Training in problem solving can be done in the classroom and has been effective in reducing behavior problems and aggression, controlling impulsivity, and increasing social interaction among shy, inhibited children (Craighead et al, 1978; Spivack & Shure, 1974). Cognitive-behavioral approaches for training problem solving help meet the need for teaching exceptional students how to learn, may increase generalization, and may help prevent students from adopting strategies as blind rules (Meichenbaum, 1980b). Problem solving has been investigated from a number of perspectives, three of which are briefly discussed here.

Meichenbaum (1980b) noted that a number of general problem-solving strategies have been taught successfully via CBM. These strategies include self-interrogation, self-checking, analyzing tasks and breaking problems into manageable steps and proceeding through these steps, and scanning strategies within one's abilities to find those that match the demands of a task. To master such strategies, the student must become more aware of his/her cognitive processes and abilities, and must learn to deautomatize the learning process. Then the student can learn when and how to employ problem-solving strategies and can develop a sense of efficacy in their use.

D'Zurilla and Goldfried (1971), after reviewing the literature, presented five general steps applicable to teaching problem solving:

1. *General orientation:* Help the student learn to recognize problems and to realize that problems can be dealt with in appropriate ways.
2. *Problem definition:* Operationally define the problem, consider the history of the problem, and identify antecedents and consequences controlling or related to the problem.
3. *Generate alternatives:* Brainstorming. All ideas should be accepted, and the student (and instructor) should think of as many solutions as possible, perhaps writing them down.
4. *Decision making:* Carefully examine the alternatives generated in step 3 in terms of their acceptability and short-term and long-range effectiveness. Then devise a plan for carrying out the selected alternative(s).

5. *Implementation and evaluation:* Implement the plan and carefully monitor it. If it does not solve the problem, start the sequence again.

Gordon (1974) has illustrated the use of these procedures in the classroom.

Spivack, Platt, & Shure (1976) identified five skills involved in social problem solving, which emerge and differ in significance at different ages: (a) an awareness that problems or potential problems may exist when humans interact; (b) the ability to generate alternative solutions to problems; (c) means-end thinking—being able to specify the steps necessary to carry out the solutions to problems; (d) understanding the consequences of behavior on self and others; and (e) cause-effect thinking—realizing that social interaction is a reciprocal, interactive process among those involved. Spivack and Shure (1974) found that children with behavior problems fail to consider possible consequences of their behavior and to generate alternative solutions and possibilities. They used approximately 30 lessons, in a game format, to help children with behavior problems learn to identify emotions, consider the feelings of others, generate alternative solutions to social problems, and evaluate cause-effect relationships. Training, whether by teachers or parents, resulted in significant and durable positive effects on social behavior with peers.

Applications

CBM has been applied to a host of social, emotional, and academic behaviors (Harris, 1981a). Target areas with exceptional students are given in Table 1. Comprehensive reviews noting both the successes and failures of CBM are offered by Abikoff (1979), Craighead et al. (1978), and Meichenbaum (1979a).

Researchers have begun to study the efficacy of CBM procedures in classroom settings. Two of these studies are briefly presented here, to illustrate the use of CBM in the classroom.

Study #1

Douglas et al. (1976) developed a training program for hyperactive children that has been termed the most comprehensive program to date for the treatment of attentional problems (Craighead et al., 1978). Eighteen hyperactive boys (age 6 years, 1 month to 10 years, 11 months) with attentional and impulsivity problems participated in 24 one-hour training sessions over a three-month period (two sessions per week). Parents and teachers observed and participated in these training sessions whenever possible. In addition, at least six consultation sessions with each child's teacher and 12 sessions with one or both parents were held. During these sessions, teachers and parents were taught cognitive and contingency management training techniques and ways to implement these techniques at home and school, as well as how to encourage and reinforce the child for using their new strategies in real-life situations. Cognitive modeling, self-verbalization, and self-reinforcement procedures were developed following self-instructional training guidelines presented by Meichenbaum and his colleagues.

TABLE 1
Applications of CBM

Target Areas	References
• Attentional deficits and impulsivity	Douglas, Parry, Marton, and Garson (1976) Kendall and Finch (1976; 1978; 1979) Keogh and Margolis (1976) Messar (1970)
• Reattribution and motivational training	Canino (1981) Diener and Dweck (1978) Henker, Whelan, and Hinshaw (1980) Thomas (1979)
• Problem solving	McKinney and Haskins (1980)
• Development of social skills and control of aggression and behavioral problems	Abikoff (1979) Craighead, Wilcoxon-Craighead, and Meyers (1978) Gresham (1981) Kneedler (1980)
• Memory	Brown (1974) Campione and Brown (1977)
• Metacognition	Brown, Campione, and Day (1981) Loper (1980; in press)
• Training of Intelligence	Sabatino, Miller, and Schmidt (1981) Sternberg (1981)
• Development of self-regulation and self-management skills	Karoly (1977) Kneedler and Hallahan (in press) Nelson (1977) Pressley (1979)
• Academic skills	
Reading comprehension	Abikoff (1979) Douglas, Parry, Marton, and Garson (1976) Lloyd, Kosiewicz, and Hallahan (in press)
Handwriting	Graham (1982) Kosiewicz, Hallahan, Lloyd, and Graves (1982)
Arithmetic instruction	Cullinan, Lloyd, and Epstein (1980)

These procedures were then used to teach general and specific strategies for coping effectively and independently "with cognitive problems and social situations in which care, attention, and organized planning are required; closely related to this goal was the need to help them achieve better inhibitory control" (Douglas et al., 1976, p.

393). Contingency management techniques were used only when a student was particularly unmanageable, and only minor emphasis was placed on limiting movement and decreasing distractors.

General, task-approach problem-solving strategies were taught, including: defining a problem and the various steps within it, generating and evaluating possible solutions before acting, self-checking and calmly correcting errors, staying with a problem until everything possible had been tried to solve it correctly, and self-reinforcement for work well done. The task-specific strategies taught included: searching, focusing, and attention deployment, planning ahead and thinking sequentially, organizing ideas and work materials, rehearsal and memory strategies, and strategies for cooperating with a peer on a task or game. These general and specific strategies were taught across a variety of cognitive tasks, academic assignments, and social situations. Students were trained in pairs part of the time. Training time on each activity was gradually extended as the sessions progressed.

Significant improvement was found on several measures, both immediately after training and at a three-month follow-up. Areas of improvement included increased persistence, control of impulsive responding, coping with frustration, oral reading, and oral and listening comprehension. Little evidence for effects of training were found on the *Bender-Gestalt Test,* an arithmetic test, and on teacher ratings of hyperactive behaviors. Although training initially occurred outside of the classroom in this study, special educators could design and conduct similar training sessions within the classrooms.

Study #2

Hallahan, Marshall, and Lloyd (1981) taught three learning disabled boys to self-monitor their on-task behavior while participating in oral reading tasks. Self-monitoring consisted of two components: self-assessment and self-recording. All training was conducted by the classroom teacher and an aide. A tape recorder placed behind the students emitted tones at random intervals. During the first phase of training, students were taught to ask themselves: "Was I paying attention?" at the sound of each tone. If students judged themselves to be on task (looking directly at the aide), they pressed a button on the wrist counters they wore; if not, they did nothing. The question, "Was I paying attention?" was written on the blackboard at the beginning of each lesson, as a cue. During initial training, the aide verbally corrected students when they made an incorrect recording.

After a three-week period, the cues for self-monitoring were gradually faded. For the next two weeks the wrist counters were not used. For the next three months the tape recorder was also removed, but the question, "Was I paying attention?" was left on the blackboard. All three students made and sustained substantial gains in on-task behavior. This study illustrates a creative, relatively simple procedure that classroom teachers can easily use.

Space does not permit further examples. Interested readers are referred to Thomas and Pashley's (1982) classroom training on task persistence and attributions.

CONSTRUCTING AND IMPLEMENTING COGNITIVE-BEHAVIORAL INTERVENTIONS

Task Analysis

The cognitive-behavioral approach requires more than an analysis of hierarchical component skills and the development of sequential learning activities designed to take the student through the steps in the task analysis. The psychological demands of the task and the sequential, organized cognitions that the student must engage in to perform adequately on the task must also be analyzed (Meichenbaum, 1976). The component cognitive strategies and the cognitive capacity required by each step in the task analysis must be identified (Brown, 1974; Meichenbaum & Asarnow, 1979). As the cognitive processes required for performance become more numerous and complex, task difficulty increases and greater cognitive capacity is required (Carroll, 1981).

To determine the cognitions and strategies necessary for successful performance, the teacher or an "expert" (adult or student) might do the task, examining and reporting his/her strategies. The teacher might also observe and interview both those who do well and those who perform poorly, in order to speculate on what leads to poor performance. Cognitions involved in comprehension of the problem or task, the production of appropriate strategies, and the application and monitoring of these strategies should be considered. Both Case (1978) and Meichenbaum (1976) have detailed how this can be done.

Input and output modalities required by the task should be analyzed; training tasks should facilitate generalization of the strategies taught to problems requiring various modalities (Douglas et al., 1976). Materials used should be analyzed in terms of their logical structure, form, and content; they may provide cues and assistance for performance (Brown et al., 1981). The results of this cognitive-behavioral task analysis will be combined with results of the learner analysis in selecting CBM components and designing training procedures.

Learner Analysis

Analysis of the learner is a complex process, one that must go beyond data gathered from standardized and criterion-referenced tests. Characteristics and predilections that the learner brings to the task may include: age, cognitive capacity and capabilities, language development, attributions and beliefs, motivational level, learning style, internal dialogue, initial knowledge state, spontaneously produced strategies, and responses to behavioral antecedents, consequences, contingencies, and medication (when appropriate). Each of these characteristics, and any others relevant to the goal of training and the task(s) involved, should be carefully considered.

Task and training requirements must be compatible with the learner's cognitive capacity, chronological age, and mental age. Cognitive capacity influences the form, content, and rate of training (Meichenbaum 1980b). Kendall (1977) noted that slow learners may need careful pretraining in the use of self-instructions (e.g., rote memorization of several self-statements), on component task skills (e.g., holding a pencil), and on attending to and copying a model. Young students and those with severe learning problems may be incapable of dealing with more than a few items of information at one time, because of limited memory or information processing abilities. Too, they may produce strategies that are reasonable but oversimplified (Case, 1978). Overt verbalizations, concrete, externally based training, and frequent, salient reinforcement may be necessary and more effective with younger children and those with greater deficits (Henker et al., 1980; Loper, 1980).

Brown et al. (1981) concluded that the more severe the learner's problem is, the more explicit the training must be; procedures must be developed to help the learner integrate general training, self-management training, and strategy training. Older, more intelligent students may respond readily to simpler procedures such as modeling, cognitive modeling, or instructions (Wagner, cited in Craighead, et al., 1978).

Language development is another variable to be examined (Kendall, 1977; Keogh & Glover, 1980). The learner's receptive and expressive vocabulary, language style, and idiosyncratic preferences should be monitored. Self-statements and instructions used in CBM can then be matched to the individual's verbal style and language ability level. A language sample can also provide a measure of cognitive development (Maier, 1980).

An integral part of CBM design is assessment and understanding of the learner's cognitions. The student's attributions, belief systems, and expectancies can all interact with training components and approaches. Although modifying an individual's belief system is not easy (Mahoney, 1977b), CBM with exceptional students must often contain components aimed at modifying maladaptive, inappropriate, or ineffective cognitions. Holland (1982) identified *motivation, persistence, responsibility,* and *structure* as four elements crucial to learning and noted that students high in these characteristics perform more effectively and require significantly less structure. CBM procedures should be aimed at positively affecting these characteristics. And, since interventions create attributions (Craighead et al., 1978; Henker et al., 1980), the student's feelings about both the training program and his/her performance should be carefully monitored and assessed.

Cognitive assessment is not an easy task and is therefore often neglected (Sternberg, 1981). Cognitive assessment must focus on the dynamic processes involved in thinking and learning. Intraindividual differences and the interaction of the learner with materials and information to be learned should be examined (Sabatino et al., 1981). Though a great deal of interest and growth is evident in this area, relatively few cognitive or cognitive-behavioral instruments exist. Also lacking is readily available information on the cognitive strategies effective with academic and learning tasks among students of differing ages and abilities (Thomas & Pashley, 1982).

Various procedures have been recommended for assessing cognitions. Interviews, post-performance questionnaires, thought listing, think aloud, and other verbal report measures may provide valuable information on both the presence of maladaptive cognitions and the absence of appropriate, adaptive cognitions and strategies (Case, 1978; Meichenbaum, 1979a). Caution should be exercised in tapping self-reports of cognitions, however, because the reliability and validity of such self-reports are often unknown, a student may have difficulty communicating cognitions verbally, and self-awareness is a skill that must be acquired (Meichenbaum, 1979a; O'Leary, 1980).

Observation and daily record keeping on responses to questions, approaches, and probes may also be helpful (Reid & Hresko, 1980). Since the way in which questions are asked may affect the answers, listening to spontaneous conversations and informal, open-ended discussions may help provide objective information (Henker et al., 1980). Further information on the presence or absence of skills and cognitions may be gained by manipulating characteristics of the task (modality or presentation, rate of stimulus presentation, support available, and so on) and by creating modified versions of the task that help to identify the student's task approach (Case, 1978; Meichenbaum, 1976).

Establishing the learner's initial knowledge state is important, including both the spontaneous strategies the learner produces in the learning situation and the strategies the learner is capable of using but does not produce. This information can help to determine cognitive capacity and to establish what the learner is doing or failing to do that interferes with performance (Meichenbaum, 1976). Knowledge of these things is critical in setting the goal of training, choosing training tasks, and establishing the sequence of learning activities that lead to the established goal. The learner's metacognitive skills must also be assessed, including self-awareness and the learner's ability to assess a situation, identify available, relevant strategies, choose among alternatives, develop a plan, monitor performance, and modify cognitive activities as necessary (Loper, 1980; Henker et al., 1980). Training must often be aimed at deficits in metacognition.

Lastly, relevant aspects of the learner's cognitive and learning style should be considered, and task demands altered if the student's learning style, information-processing pattern, or cognitive style is not compatible with the task (Holland, 1982). For example, field-dependent students can learn more rapidly when cue salience and structure are increased (Holland, 1982). Students who are both field-dependent and impulsive often have severe learning problems and require special consideration (Keogh & McG. Donlon, 1972). The student's locus of control, whether the problem is seen as internally or externally controlled, may also interact with training and task requirements (Henker et al., 1980). Holland (1982) has discussed elements of cognitive and learning styles.

If task and training requirements are not matched to the learner's characteristics and predilections, problems can occur. Students may learn to use a strategy and yet show no improvement in performance. For example, training an impulsive child to delay responding, adopt a more reflexive style, and stay on-task will have little effect if the child does not know what to do with the time gained. The child must also be taught to utilize cognitive strategies appropriate to the task, such as effective scanning, matching to standard, reviewing and checking solutions, and so on (Craighead et al., 1978).

Moreover, if current abilities are not well understood, the learner may be taught a strategy less efficient or no better than the one he/she is already using (Loper, 1980), or one that is beyond his/her cognitive-developmental abilities. Students with a helpless attitude, feelings of anger or dislike for learning, a low self-concept, negative expectancies, a low need for achievement, or a low motivational level may exert little or no effort to learn new skills or to use the skills they do learn to improve performance. Other students simply may not believe that their new skills are more efficient or effective than their current behaviors.

Development and Implementation

In conjunction with a careful, thorough analysis of task and learner, operationally defined goals of training are established. Then the teacher (or researcher) selects CBM components and procedures appropriate to the task, learner, and goals. Simple procedures, such as explaining a strategy or providing a model, may be all that is necessary when the task is simple or the learner's problems are relatively minor. As the goals of training become more involved (e.g., development of effective problem solving and metacognitive skills) and the learner's deficits more significant, training becomes more complex, requiring multiple training tasks, components, and stages.

In designing the CBM intervention, the teacher must keep in mind the purpose of training and tailor learning activities to the desired outcomes (Brown et al., 1981). Is the purpose to learn a specific skill, to teach the use of a certain strategy(ies), or both? Training should focus on the operationally defined goals and not on some abstract dimension or presumed underlying deficit (Craighead et al., 1978; Meichenbaum & Asarnow, 1979).

The teacher must determine whether self-instructions, imagery, modeling, shaping, successive approximations, contingencies such as reinforcement or response-cost, and so on will be used. Task-approach and task-specific strategies must be identified and, if appropriate, corresponding verbalizations developed. Strategy instructions must be well formulated and appropriate for learners' cognitive and developmental levels. Learners should be as actively involved as possible in the design, implementation, and evaluation of CBM training.

Once the CBM regimen is developed, training is initiated. Training can be facilitated if the student is first made aware of any negative or ineffective self-statements and strategies he/she is producing, if the advantages of the strategy(ies) to be taught are made clear, and if the student desires the training (Case, 1978; Meichenbaum, 1976). A favorable relationship with the student and an enthusiastic attitude on the part of the trainer are also important (Kendall, 1977).

If multiple components and procedures are to be used in training, it may be helpful to begin on tasks at which the learner is somewhat proficient, gradually introducing new components and procedures. One should begin with a simple set of self-statements, self-instructions, or self-controlled consequences and gradually work toward more complex sets. Task difficulty and length of training sessions should be gradually increased. Sufficient practice should be provided, using interesting and varied materials. Learner management and control of strategies should be emphasized. External control, prompts, and cues should be gradually decreased. The student should be allowed to abbreviate verbalizations and steps after demonstrating mastery of a skill. The effects of training should be monitored, and revised as necessary.

Overt Verbalizations

Self-instructions, at first overt and later covert, have generally been found to be an effective, important part of training (Craighead et al., 1978; Douglas et al., 1976; Kendall, 1977; Meichenbaum & Asarnow, 1979; Pressley, 1979). Researchers who have employed overt verbalizations as a part of the CBM training have made several suggestions. Meichenbaum (1977) noted that students may respond more favorably when they are asked to "think aloud" rather than to "talk out loud to yourself."

Optimal use of overt and covert verbalizations should be considered, as overt verbalizations may interfere with behaviors that are timed, require reflexive reactions, or involve complex processing (Harris, 1981a; Meichenbaum & J. Goodman, 1969). For example, Robin, Armel, and O'Leary (1975) found overt verbalizations cumbersome and difficult to shape while teaching a group of naive kindergartners to print. Kosiewicz et al. (1982) reported no difficulties with self-instructions used to improve one student's cursive writing. Douglas et al. (1976) noted that problems with overt verbalizations are most likely to occur when self-verbalization is taught in a mechanical, rote-learning manner. Problems can be avoided if the student is involved in the development of verbalizations and encouraged to verbalize strategies in his/her own words. If students resist the use of overt verbalizations or find it embarrassing, they might be allowed to practice in isolation, whisper, or speak into a microphone. A tape recorder might also be used to monitor the precision and consistency of the self-instructions modeled by the trainer and copied by the student.

Correspondence Between Saying and Doing

When verbalizations are used, correspondence between saying and doing should be carefully monitored. Merely saying the right things or a doing-saying sequence does not have as significant an effect on behavior (Craighead et al., 1978; Kendall, 1977). Some time may have to be spent in shaping and developing correspondence between verbalizations and the behaviors they are to control (Meichenbaum, 1980b).

Modeling

When a live model is used in CBM training, this model should be carefully selected. To be effective, the model must be viewed favorably (i.e., seen as competent, attractive, rated high on a sociometric scale, and so on) and have a positive relationship with the student (Bandura, 1977a; Craighead et al., 1978). Teachers, parents, paraprofessionals, and peers can be effective models. The model should be enthusiastic and use self-statements with appropriate phrasing and inflection. In some cases, allowing the target student to serve as a model for another student can improve performance (Pressley, 1979).

In addition, modeling of self-instructions and self-regulation can be done on an impromptu basis, during games, discussions, instruction, and everyday occurrences. Although live models are often preferable and more effective (Kendall, 1977; Ledwidge, 1978), other alternatives have been used successfully. Examples include a permanent model or written list of steps and statements, tape-recorded statements, the combination of a written model and tape-recorded statements, videotapes, and cartoons or drawings (cf. Harris, 1980, 1981a, 1982; Lloyd, 1980; Meichenbaum, 1977).

Individual vs. Group Training

Although individual training is frequently preferable and more efficient, it may not be practical for all problems or classroom settings. While CBM training can be conducted effectively in small groups, special considerations are warranted. Developing self-instructions compatible with several students' individual styles may pose a problem (Kendall, 1977). To handle this problem, the teacher might model a statement and then encourage each student to express the same idea in his/her own words. An aide or peer may be needed to help monitor consistent and proficient usage of self-statements. Individual students should be allowed to progress through training activities at their own rate. Even within a group setting, training should be as individualized as possible.

Durable and Generalizable Results

If the results of CBM training are to be significant, they must be durable and generalizable to new tasks, settings, and conditions. Brief, short-term interventions should not be expected to show long-term, generalizable effects. Durability appears easier to obtain than generalization, although reports of generalization are increasing as CBM regimens become more sophisticated in design and implementation (cf. Brown et al., 1981; Douglas et al., 1976; Hollon & Kendall, 1979; Meichenbaum, 1979a; Seabaugh & Schumaker, 1981).

The ability to generalize may be related to age, readiness, and metacognitive maturity, as generalization requires changes in metacognitive development and abilities (Loper, 1980; Meichenbaum & Asarnow, 1979). Young children may be more likely to maintain and generalize skills when the training and generalization tasks are concrete and familiar. Blankenship & Baumgartner (1982) noted that differentiating between students who can't generalize and those who can but won't may be necessary. The former may require more intensive instruction, while contingent reinforcement may prove effective with the latter.

Although the "train and hope" approach to obtaining generalization may be the most frequent method used, maintenance and generalization should be planned and programmed (Stokes & Baer, 1977). The following suggestions for enhancing durability and generalization have been offered by various researchers (cf. Borkowski & Cavanaugh, 1979; Deshler et al., 1981; Douglas et al., 1976; Kendall, 1977; Kendall & Finch, 1979; Meichenbaum & Asarnow, 1979; Stokes & Baer, 1977):

1. Develop training procedures and behaviors that can be maintained by natural contingencies after transfer to a new environment or situation.
2. Provide training that is prolonged and in depth, and conducted by several individuals across a variety of tasks, materials, modalities, settings, and conditions.
3. Make sure that stimuli common to the generalization setting(s) are also present in the training setting.
4. If distractors will be present in the generalization setting, include in the training gradual innoculation against distractors and coping strategies for handling distraction.
5. Tell students to generalize, and reinforce instances of generalization.
6. In training, emphasize the development of metacognitive, self-regulatory skills.
7. Gradually fade cues and prompts during training, to facilitate transfer of control to the student.
8. Make use of delayed and intermittent reinforcement during training, to strengthen learned skills and behaviors. Durability is necessary but not sufficient for generalization.
9. Require similar (but not necessarily identical) cognitions and skills in the training and generalization tasks.
10. Gradually adapt training materials and setting to the terminal goal. Training a child to cope with frustration on a maze task is not likely to improve aggressive tendencies with peers without intermediate steps.
11. Provide feedback about the purpose and usefulness of the strategy(ies) taught, as well as feedback on the learner's performance.
12. Gradually increase the demand for mental involvement in the training tasks.
13. Actively involve the student in the development of training and the acquisition of new strategies and skills.
14. Emphasize consistency and precision in strategy use during the initial phase of strategy instruction, then train loosely.
15. Facilitate generalization by attributing observed changes to the student's own efforts.

Caveats

CBM is not a panacea or a remedy for all the problems facing exceptional students and their teachers. Academic and learning proficiency represent a composite of many skills. As Sabatino et al. (1981) noted, no one intervention can affect all aspects of behavior and performance. Knowledge of CBM components and procedures allows teachers to expand the scope of their intervention and classroom approaches and provides guidance in the use of eclectic interventions. CBM should be used when it meets the learner's needs and characteristics, is appropriate for the problem, and is likely to be more effective than alternative interventions. For example, Keogh and Glover (1980) reported that CBM has improved problem-solving performance, decreased impulsiveness, and increased attention to various tasks, but has not been as effective as medication in reducing activity level, or as effective as behavior modification in increasing specific on-task behavior during academic tasks.

Direct training and modification of task demands may be as effective as CBM and more cost-effective with some problems (Craighead et al., 1978; McKinney & Haskins, 1980). Global cognitions and behaviors (e.g., aggression) or those that are well instated may be particularly difficult to modify and require extended intervention. In addition, cognitive changes may take some time to result in improved academic performance or behavioral changes (Abikoff, 1979; Craighead et al., 1978).

Research and Advances Needed

Design flaws and simplistic, naive conceptualization and construction of CBM interventions has characterized many research studies (Meichenbaum, 1979a, 1979b; Meichenbaum & Asarnow, 1979; Sabatino et al., 1981). CBM prodecures and research design must be carefully evaluated when drawing conclusions about the effectiveness of CBM regimens. Well designed, carefully formulated studies have proven the viability and superiority of cognitive-behavioral interventions across a range of populations and problems (Hollon & Kendall, 1979). Nevertheless, a great many questions remain to be answered.

One, further substantiation of durable and generalizable effects is needed. Two, researchers must turn their attention to identifying the necessary and sufficient components for lasting and generalizable results among different types of learners. In group studies in which CBM does not result in significant long-term effects for the majority of subjects, lasting effects may occur for some individuals (cf. Harris, 1980). Researchers should investigate predictors of sustained effects among these individuals. Three, more data are needed on the use of CBM in classroom settings, on the relationship between developmental level and treatment, on matching treatment to the learner, and on the relative and combined effects of specific skill training and training general, metacognitive skills (Abikoff, 1979; Craighead et al., 1978; Meichenbaum, 1979b; O'Leary, 1980). Four, acceptable, reliable measures of cognitive processes have to be developed to assist in the design and evaluation of CBM regimens. Finally, we need to know more about the causal links between cognitive phenomena and behaviors and what factors influence the development, maintenance, or change of cognitions (Mahoney, 1977a).

In summary, CBM must remain open to diligent and critical examination to help assure proper application and successful results. Caution should be taken to avoid inappropriate proliferation of CBM techniques and the use of CBM merely because it represents a current fad (Kendall, 1977).

The Teacher

The use of cognitive-behavioral interventions creates many demands on classroom teachers. Considerable time is necessary for the analyses, planning, and implementation procedures required for success. CBM requires teachers to keep up with a dynamic area and be diversified in skills and knowledge. To paraphrase Mahoney (1977a), the teacher must be aware of students' physical, cognitive, and social environment, a good listener, an accurate observer, and an effective problem solver. The teacher has to adopt a metacognitive perspective and develop an understanding of the demands of learning (Brown et al., 1981). Tasks and activities that require students to use metacognitive skills must be developed and opportunities for the use of metacognitive skills identified (Meichenbaum & Asarnow, 1979).

The teacher has to establish the credibility of CBM in the classroom and obtain student cooperation and support (Meichenbaum, 1979a). An academic focus must be maintained, and CBM procedures should not be used to the point of boredom, fatigue, or carelessness (cf. Tobias, 1982). The natural development of behavioral regulation is a slow process keyed to developmental stages. The teacher should act as a model of self-regulation, problem solving, and coping with difficulties and failures. The success of CBM depends on the teacher's understanding of all of these points, and not on the casual "throwing in" of verbalizations with existing instructional procedures.

CONCLUSION

Cognitive-behavioral interventions appear to be a promising approach with exceptional students. Special educators should carefully monitor research findings, advances, and new contributors in this area. Though further work is needed to establish the parameters of CBM interventions and their relationships to desired effects, the selective, empirically based combination of principles and procedures from diverse areas offers a viable alternative for dealing with the problems of exceptional students.

REFERENCES

Abikoff, H. (1979). Cognitive training interventions in children: Review of a new approach. *Journal of Learning Disabilities, 12,* 65–77.

Anderson, R. (1970). Control of student mediating processes during verbal learning and instruction. *Review of Educational Research, 40,* 349–369.

Bandura, A. (1977a). *Social learning theory.* Englewood Cliffs, NJ: Prentice-Hall.

Bandura, A. (1977). Self-efficacy: Toward a unifying theory of behavioral change. *Psychological Review, 84,* 191–215.

Bandura, A. (1978). The self system in reciprocal determinism. *American Psychologist, 33,* 344–358.

Bem, S. (1970). The role of comprehension in children's problem solving. *Developmental Psychology, 2,* 351–358.

Blankenship, C. S., & Baumgartner, M. D. (1982). Programming generalization of computational skills. *Learning Disability Quarterly, 5,* 152–162.

Borkowski, J. G., & Cavanaugh, J. C. (1979). Maintenance and generalization of skills and strategies by the retarded. In N. R. Ellis (Ed.), *Handbook of mental deficiency: Psychological theory and research* (2nd ed.). Hillsdale, NJ: Erlbaum.

Brown, A. L. (1974). The role of strategic behavior in retardate memory. In N. R. Ellis (Ed.), *International review of research in mental retardation* (Vol. 7). New York: Academic Press.

Brown, A. L., Campione, J. C., & Day, J. D. (1981). Learning to learn: On training students to learn from text. *Educational Researcher, 10,* 14–21.

Camp, B. W. (1977). Verbal mediation in young aggressive boys. *Journal of Abnormal Psychology, 86,* 145–153.

Camp, B. W., Blom, G. E., Herbert, F., & Van Doorninck, W. J. (1977). Think aloud: A program for developing self-control in young aggressive boys. *Journal of Abnormal Child Psychology, 5,* 157–169.

Campione, J. C., & Brown, A. L. (1977). Memory and metamemory development in educable retarded children. In R. V. Kail, Jr., & J. W. Hagen (Eds.), *Perspectives on the development of memory and cognition*. Hillsdale, NJ: Erlbaum.

Canino, F. J. (1981). Learned-helplessness theory: Implications for research in learning disabilities. *Journal of Special Education, 15,* 471–484.

Carroll, J. B. (1981). Ability and task difficulty in cognitive psychology. *Educational Researcher, 10,* 11–21.

Case, R. A. (1978). A developmentally based theory and technology of instruction. *Review of Educational Research, 48,* 439–463.

Craighead, W. E., Wilcoxon-Craighead, L., & Meyers, A. W. (1978). New directions in behavior modification with children. In M. Hersen, R. M. Eisler, & P. M. Miller (Eds.), *Progress in behavior modification* (Vol. 6). New York: Academic Press.

Cullinan, D., Lloyd, J., & Epstein, M. (1980). Strategy training: A structured approach to the arithmetic instruction. *Exceptional Education Quarterly, 1,* 41–49.

Denney, D. R. (1973). Modification of children's information processing behavior through learning. *Child Study Monographs, 1,* 1–22.

Denney, D. R. (1975). The effects of exemplary and cognitive models and self-rehearsal on children's interrogative strategies. *Journal of Experimental Child Psychology, 19,* 476–488.

Denney, N. W., & Turner, M. C. (1979). Facilitating cognitive performance in children: A comparison of strategy modeling and strategy modeling with overt self-verbalization. *Journal of Experimental Child Psychology, 28,* 119–131.

Deshler, D. D., Alley, G. R., Warner, M. M., & Schumaker, J. B. (1981). Instructional practices for promoting skill acquisition and generalization in severely learning disabled adolescents. *Learning Disability Quarterly, 4,* 415–421.

Diener, C. I., & Dweck, C. S. (1978). An analysis of learned helplessness: Continuous changes in performance, strategy, and achievement cognitions following failure. *Journal of Personality & Social Psychology, 36,* 451–462.

Douglas, V. I. (1975). Perceptual and cognitive factors as determinants of learning disabilities: A review paper with special emphasis on attentional factors. In R. M. Knights & D. J. Bakker (Eds.), *Neuropsychology of learning disorders: Theoretical approaches*. Baltimore: University Park Press.

Douglas, V. I., Parry, P., Marton, P., & Garson, C. (1976). Assessment of a cognitive training program for hyperactive children. *Journal of Abnormal Child Psychology, 4,* 389–410.

D'Zurilla, T. J., & Goldfried, M. R. (1971). Problem solving and behavior modification. *Journal of Abnormal Psychology, 78,* 107–126.

Ellis, A. *Reason and emotion in psychotherapy.* New York: Lyle Stuart, 1963.

Finch, A. J., Jr., & Spirito, A. (1980). Use of cognitive training to change cognitive processes. *Exceptional Education Quarterly, 1,* 31–39.

Flavell, J. H., Beach, D. R., & Chinsky, J. M. (1966). Spontaneous verbal rehearsal in a memory task as a function of age. *Child Development, 37,* 283–299.

Gordon, T. (1974). *Teacher effectiveness training*. New York: Peter W. Wyden.

Graham, S. (1982). *The effects of cognitive and behavioral procedures on the handwriting performance of LD students*. Manuscript submitted for publication.

Gresham, F. (1981). Social skills training with handicapped children: A review. *Review of Educational Research, 51,* 139–176.

Hallahan, D. P., Gajar, A., Cohen, S., & Tarver, S. (1978). Selective attention and locus of control in learning disabled and normal children. *Journal of Learning Disabilities, 11,* 47–52.

Hallahan, D. P., Marshall, K. J., & Lloyd, J. W. (1981). Self-recording during group instruction: Effects on attention to task. *Learning Disability Quarterly, 4,* 407–413.

Harris, K. R. (1980). The sustained effects of cognitive modification and informed teachers on children's communication apprehension. *Communication Quarterly, 28,* 47–56.

Harris, K. R. (1981a). *Self-speech, language, and cognitive training: A review of theory and practice*. Paper presented at the meeting of the International Communication Association, Minneapolis.

Harris, K. R. (1981b). *The effects of cognitive training on self-speech and task performance during problem solving among learning disabled and normally achieving children*. Unpublished doctoral dissertation, Auburn University.

Harris, K. R. (1982, March). *The effects of cognitive training on private speech and task performance during problem solving among learning disabled and normally achieving children*. Paper presented at the meeting of the American Educational Research Association, New York.

Harris, K. R., & Brown, R. (1982). Cognitive-behavior modification and informed teacher treatments for shy children. *Journal of Experimental Education, 50,* 137–143.

Havertape, J. F., & Kass, C. E. (1978). Examination of problem solving in learning disabled adolescents through verbalized self-instructions. *Learning Disability Quarterly, 1,* 94–100.

Henker, B., Whalen, C. K., & Hinshaw, S. P. (1980). The attributional contexts of cognitive intervention strategies. *Exceptional Education Quarterly, 1,* 17–30.

Holiand, R. P. (1982). Learner characteristics and learner performance: Implications for instructional placement decisions. *Journal of Special Education, 16,* 7–20.

Hollon, S. D., & Kendall, P. C. (1979). Cognitive-behavioral interventions: Theory and procedure. In P. C. Kendall & S. D. Hollon (Eds.), *Cognitive-behavioral interventions: Theory, research, and procedures*. New York: Academic Press.

Kanfer, F. H., & Karoly, P. (1972). Self-control: A behavioristic excursion into the lion's den. *Behavior Therapy, 3,* 398–416.

Kanfer, F. H., & Phillips, J. S. (1970). *Learning foundations of behavior therapy*. New York: Wiley.

Karoly, P. (1977). Behavioral self-management in children: Concepts, methods, issues and directions. In M. Hersen, R. M. Eisler, & P. M. Miller (Eds.), *Progress in behavior modification* (Vol. 5). New York: Academic Press.

Keeney, T. J., Cannizzo, S. R., & Flavell, J. H. (1967). Spontaneous and induced verbal rehearsal in a recall task. *Child Development, 38,* 953–966.

Kendall, P. C. (1977). On the efficacious use of verbal self-instructional procedures with children. *Cognitive Therapy & Research, 4,* 331–341.

Kendall, P. C., & Finch, A. J. (1976). A cognitive-behavioral treatment for impulse control: A case study. *Journal of Consulting & Clinical Psychology, 44,* 852–857.

Kendall, P. C., & Finch, A. J. (1978). A cognitive-behavioral treatment for impulsivity: A group comparison study. *Journal of Consulting & Clinical Psychology, 46,* 110–118.

Kendall, P. C., & Finch, A. J. (1979). Developing nonimpulsive behavior in children: Cognitive-behavioral strategies for self-control. In P. C. Kendall & S. D. Hollon (Eds.), *Cognitive-behavioral interventions: Theory, research and procedures*. New York: Academic Press.

Kendall, P. C., & Hollon, S. D. (1979). Cognitive-behavioral interventions: Overview and current status. In P. C. Kendall & S. D. Hollon (Eds.), *Cognitive-behavioral interventions: Theory, research, and procedures,* New York: Academic Press.

Kendler, J. S., Kendler, H. H., & Wells, D. (1960). Reversal and nonreversal shifts in nursery school children. *Journal of Comparative & Physiological Psychology, 53,* 83–88.

Keogh, B. K., & Glover, A. T. (1980). The generality and durability of cognitive training effects. *Exceptional Education Quarterly, 1,* 75–82.

Keogh, B. K., & Margolis, J. (1976). A component analysis of attentional problems of educationally handicapped boys. *Journal of Abnormal Child Psychology, 4,* 349–359.

Keogh, B. K., & McG. Donlon, G. (1972). Field dependence, impulsivity, and learning disabilities. *Journal of Learning Disabilities, 5,* 331–335.

Kneedler, R. D. (1980). The use of cognitive training to change social behaviors. *Exceptional Education Quarterly, 1,* 65–73.

Kneedler, R. D., & Hallahan, D. P. (In press). Self-monitoring of on-task behavior with learning disabled children: Current studies and directions. *Exceptional Education Quarterly.*

Kosiewicz, M. M., Hallahan, D. E., Lloyd, J., & Graves, A. W. (1982). Effects of self-instruction and self-correction procedures on handwriting performance. *Learning Disability Quarterly, 5,* 71–78.

Kuenne, M. K. (1946). Experimental investigation of the relation of language to transposition behavior in young children. *Journal of Experimental Psychology, 36,* 471–490.

Ledwidge, B. (1978). Cognitive behavior modification: A step in the wrong direction? *Psychological Bulletin, 85,* 353–375.

Lloyd, J. (1980). Academic instruction and cognitive behavior modification: The need for attack strategy training. *Exceptional Education Quarterly, 1,* 53–63.

Lloyd, J., Kosiewicz, M. M., & Hallahan, D. P. (In press). Reading comprehension: Cognitive training contributions. *School Psychology Review.*

Loper, A. B. (1980). Metacognitive development: Implications for cognitive training. *Exceptional Education Quarterly, 1,* 1–8.

Loper, A. B. (In press). Metacognitive training to correct academic deficiency. *Topics in Learning & Learning Disabilities*.

Luria, A. R. (1960). Verbal regulation of behavior. In M. A. B. Brazier (Ed.), *The central nervous system and behavior.* New York: Josiah Macy, Jr., Foundation.

Luria, A. R. (1961a). *The role of speech in the regulation of normal and abnormal behavior* (J. Tizard, trans.). New York: Liveright.

Luria, A. R. (1961b). The genesis of voluntary behavior. In N. O'Connor (Ed.), *Recent Soviet psychology.* New York: Liveright.

Maccoby, E. E. (1964). Developmental psychology. *Annual Review of Psychology, 15,* 203–250.

Mahoney, M. J. (1977a). Reflections on the cognitive learning trend in psychotherapy. *American Psychologist, 32,* 5–13.

Mahoney, M. J. (1977b). Cognitive therapy and research: A question of questions. *Cognitive Therapy & Research, 1,* 5–16.

Mahoney, M. J., & Thoresen, C. E. (1974). *Self-control: Power to the person*. Monterey, CA: Brooks/Cole.

Maier, A. (1980). The effect of focusing on the cognitive processes of learning disabled children. *Journal of Learning Disabilities, 13,* 34–38.

McKinney, J. D., & Haskins, R. (1980). Cognitive training and the development of problem-solving strategies. *Exceptional Education Quarterly, 1,* 41–51.

Meichenbaum, D. (1976). Cognitive factors as determinants of learning disabilities: A cognitive-functional approach. In R. M. Knights & D. J. Bakker (Eds.), *The neuropsychology of learning disorders: Theoretical approaches*. Baltimore: University Park Press.

Meichenbaum, D. (1977). *Cognitive behavior modification: An integrative approach*. New York: Plenum.

Meichenbaum, D. (1979a). *Cognitive-behavior modification newsletter* (No. 4). Waterloo, Ontario: University of Waterloo.

Meichenbaum, D. (1979b). Cognitive behavior modification: The need for a fairer assessment. *Cognitive Therapy & Research, 3,* 127–132.

Meichenbaum, D. (1980a). Cognitive behavior modification with exceptional children: A promise yet unfulfilled. *Exceptional Education Quarterly, 1,* 83–88.

Meichenbaum, D. (1980b). *Teaching thinking: A cognitive-behavioural perspective*. Paper presented at the NIE-LRDC Conference on Thinking and Learning Skills, Pittsburgh.

Meichenbaum, D., & Asarnow, J. (1979). Cognitive-behavioral modification and metacognitive development: Implications for the classroom. In P. C. Kendall & S. D. Hollon (Eds.), *Cognitive-behavioral interventions: Theory, research, and procedures*. New York: Academic Press.

Meichenbaum, D., & Goodman, J. (1969). The developmental control of operant motor responding by verbal operants. *Journal of Experimental Child Psychology, 7,* 553–565.

Meichenbaum, D., & Goodman, J. (1971). Training impulsive children to talk to themselves: A means of developing self-control. *Journal of Abnormal Psychology, 77,* 115–126.

Meichenbaum, D., & Goodman, S. (1979). Clinical use of private speech and critical questions about its study in natural settings. In G. Zivin (Ed.), *The development of self-regulation through private speech*. New York: Wiley & Sons.

Messar, S. B. (1970). Reflection-impulsivity: Stability and school failure. *Journal of Educational Psychology, 61,* 487–490.

Nelson, R. O. (1977). Assessment and therapeutic functions of self-monitoring. In M. Hersen, R. M. Eisler, & P. M. Miller (Eds.), *Progress in behavior modification* (Vol. 5). New York: Academic Press.

O'Leary, S. G. (1980). A response to cognitive training. *Exceptional Education Quarterly, 1,* 89–94.

Pressley, M. (1979). Increasing children's self-control through cognitive interventions. *Review of Educational Research, 49,* 319–370.

Reese, H. W. (1962). Verbal mediation as a function of age level. *Psychological Bulletin, 59,* 501–509.

Reid, D. K., & Hresko, W. P. (1980). Thinking about thinking about it in that way: Test data and instruction. *Exceptional Education Quarterly, 1,* 47–58.

Robin, A., Armel, S., & O'Leary, K. D. (1975). The effects of self-instruction on writing deficiencies. *Behavior Therapy, 6,* 178–187.

Robin, S., Schneider, M., & Dolnick, M. (1977). The turtle technique: An extended case study of self-control in the classroom. In K. D. O'Leary & S. G. O'Leary (Eds.), *Classroom management: The successful use of behavior modification* (2nd ed.). New York: Pergamon.

Sabatino, D. A., Miller, P. F., & Schmidt, C. (1981). Can intelligence be altered through cognitive training? *Journal of Special Education, 15,* 125–144.

Schneider, M. (1974). Turtle technique in the classroom. *Teaching Exceptional Children, 7,* 22–24.

Seabaugh, G. O., & Schumaker, J. B. (1981, April). *The effects of self-regulation training on the academic productivity of LD and NLD adolescents* (Research Report No. 37). Lawrence: University of Kansas Institute for Research in Learning Disabilities.

Spivack, G., Platt, J. J., & Shure, M. B. (1976). *The problem-solving approach to adjustment.* San Francisco: Jossey-Bass.

Spivack, G., & Shure, M. B. (1974). *Social adjustment of young children: A cognitive approach to solving real-life problems.* San Francisco: Jossey-Bass.

Sternberg, R. J. (1981). Cognitive-behavioral approaches to the training of intelligence in the retarded. *Journal of Special Education, 15,* 165–183.

Stevens, R., & Rosenshine, B. (1981). Advances in research on teaching. *Exceptional Education Quarterly, 2,* 1–9.

Stokes, T., & Baer, D. (1977). An implicit technology of generalization. *Journal of Applied Behavior Analysis, 10,* 349–367.

Thomas, A. (1979). Learned helplessness and expectancy factors: Implications for research in learning disabilities. *Review of Educational Research, 49,* 208–221.

Thomas, A., & Pashley, B. (1982). Effects of classroom training on LD students' task persistence and attributions. *Learning Disability Quarterly, 5,* 133–144.

Thoresen, C. E. (1974). Behavioral means and humanistic ends. In M. J. Mahoney & C. E. Thoresen (Eds.), *Self-control: Power to the person.* Monterey, CA: Brooks/Cole.

Tobias, S. (1982). When do instructional methods make a difference? *Educational Researcher, 11,* 4–9.

Vygotsky, L. S. (1962). *Thought and language* (E. Hanfmann & G. Vakar, Eds. and trans.). Cambridge, MA: MIT Press. (Originally published 1934)

Wertsch, J. V. (1979a). From social interaction to higher psychological processes, a clarification and application of Vygotsky's theory. *Human Development, 22,* 1–22.

Wertsch, J. V. (1979b). The regulation of human action and the given-new structure of private speech. In G. Zivin (Ed.), *The development of self-regulation through private speech.* New York: Wiley & Sons.

Zivin, G. (Ed.). (1979). *The development of self-regulation through private speech.* New York: Wiley & Sons.

Karen Harris is an Assistant Professor of Special Education, University of Maryland.

During the 1980s a much overworked word has been "transition." Too often the term has been loosely applied—generally implying a need for a bridge between high school and the world of work. In this article the authors examine the skills that students must have when they move from elementary to junior high school. They also discuss at length how the absence of these same skills can be devastating to the learning disabled. Most of the deficit skills are academic, self-management, and social adaptive in nature. Specific skills are addressed under topics such as note taking, summarizing, paraphrasing, listening skills, following directions, and test taking. It is hoped that this form of instruction will result in more successful mainstreaming.

Preparing Dysfunctional Learners to Enter Junior High School: A Transitional Curriculum

Suzanne M. Robinson, Catherine Trefz Braxdale, and Steven E. Colson

Literature in the field of special education continues to reflect the growing movement toward an ecological view of the learner, the environment, and the teacher—resulting in concentrated focus on their interactions (Adelman, 1983; Hardin, 1978; Heron, 1982; Ysseldyke, 1983). Special educators finally are embracing a paradigm that stresses not only the uniqueness of each dysfunctional learner but also that of individual settings. This view proposes that dysfunctional learners often fail because of a mismatch between the learning environment and the learner's present level of functioning. Awareness of students entering a learning environment unprepared has prompted interest in directly facilitating effective transitions to reduce this mismatch (Will, 1985).

Festinger's (1957) view of cognitive dissonance can help educators see the potential for disruption of the teacher-learner match. Environmental demands upon students may disrupt their equilibrium, forcing them to display avoidance behaviors that can lead to a state of dissonance or level of discomfort for learning. Students who experience continual frustration with new settings demands may "shut down," thus preventing any viable flow of questioning and discussion for the purpose of learning.

Most attempts to conceptualize and develop transition curricula have focused on the abrupt and often devastating transition from high school to the world of work (Edgar, 1985; Halpern, 1985; Hasazi, Gordon, & Roe, 1985; Will, 1985). Armed with limited basic skills, high school seniors with learning handicaps find themselves ill-equipped to function in the workplace. Recently, attempts to expand the concept of transition have included the move from nursery to school. But few educators have explored the need for a curriculum to address the transition from elementary school to junior high school.

We will delineate the differences in school demands between the elementary and junior high settings and address how the transition from the former to the latter could be made smoother for exceptional students through planned instruction. To that end, a proposed transitional program will be discussed. The curriculum to be described is conceptual, drawn from an integration of research on the setting demands of secondary schools, effective intervention, and best instructional practices.

THE JUNIOR HIGH SCHOOL SETTING

Students about to enter junior high school often are at a difficult time in their young lives. Most of them are experiencing physical changes and concomitant emotional upheaval. The school environment within which they have learned from kindergarten to the present is about to change. These environmental changes will include a new and bigger school building with greater numbers of students, new content material, a large number of teachers, and increased expectations of independent behavior (Schumaker, Deshler, Alley, & Warner, 1983). Over the course of 3 summer months, these students lose the status and esteem of having been in the oldest and most knowledgeable group and become the youngest and least respected group.

All of these experiences are magnified for learning disabled (LD) students. Most junior high LD students have a history of receiving special services, and most inevitably have experienced a degree of failure in school (Mercer, 1979). This pattern typically persists. Given the accelerating content demands, LD students are faced with new and greatly increased opportunities for failure (Smith, Robinson, & Voress, 1982).

Changes in existing elementary special education programs might alleviate this situation. Most programs for elementary LD youngsters concentrate on teaching basic skills, but this does not appear enough to prepare LD students for junior high school. Programs might better help these students move into secondary schools by also offering them instruction in compensatory skills, as well as task approach (or learning) strategies that will enable them to master mainstream curriculum demands more independently.

We propose that educators begin to introduce task approach or learning strategy instruction in the upper elementary grades. Research (Schumaker, Deshler, Alley, & Warner, 1983; Alley, Deshler, Clark, Schumaker & Warner, 1983) has demonstrated that secondary-age students profit from learning strategy instruction with a resulting improved performance in mainstream settings. Teacher reports and observation, however, have convinced educators that this type of instruction (teaching students how to learn) must begin earlier than junior high school.

First, students in upper elementary school can learn and profit from knowing independent learning strategies. Second, more secondary-aged LD students would likely be able to be maintained in mainstream settings if they were to have prior knowledge of the learning demands. If the LD student enters the secondary system with no skills with which to compensate for deficits, and thus is unable to function somewhat effectively in mainstream settings, junior and senior high school resource teachers are left with little time and few options. Either they must tutor the student so that a course can be passed or teach basic strategies at the expense of direct tutorial assistance. Neither of these options offers the LD student maximum benefit of time spent with the learning specialist.

If some initial preparation were to take place prior to entering the secondary system, junior high LD teachers could focus immediately on helping students apply learned strategies in mainstream settings, instruct students in more sophisticated learning techniques, and not have to rely solely on tutorial instruction to keep students afloat. Thus, a preventive approach toward future learning problems underlies the proposed curriculum as well as encourages a continuum of learning strategies instruction across elementary and secondary schools.

The following sections address areas in which development of curriculum earlier in the LD student's educational life is needed. Junior high curriculum demands differ from those of the elementary school in many areas. These demands/expectations are grouped here as (1) academic, (2) self-management/study skills, and (3) social/adaptive behaviors. The descriptive categories are defined in the following way:

1. *Academic* demands refer to behaviors associated with successful performance in the classroom for completion of a course with a passing grade or better.
2. *Self-management/study skills* are behaviors that lead to successful preparation for learning, maximizing reception of actual instruction and appropriate reporting of the material learned in a test situation.
3. *Social/adaptive* demands are defined here as behaviors that lead to acceptance by peers balanced by respect for authority and the structure of school.

These groupings are made merely for the purpose of explanation. In actuality, the discrete behaviors interact and affect one another. For example, a student who is receiving a failing grade in social studies (academic demand) because that student did not prepare appropriately for the tests (self-management/study skills) may not be allowed to join the football team with all of his friends (social) and possibly acts inappropriately during social studies class as a result of frustration caused by the lack of success (adaptive behavior). Skill deficits in any of these areas impede success.

Academic Demands

Junior high school teachers assume that their students have acquired at least a minimum level of competency in basic skills prior to entering junior high classrooms. Therefore, the teacher begins instruction using a lecture format, assigning independent reading from the text, presenting further lectures to integrate text material, and then testing over the material covered. Thus, the instructional format changes dramatically from that of elementary school.

The academic subjects presented in content areas (e.g., history, social studies, science, government) all require mastery of basic reading skills. Recent research by several authorities (Johnson, 1977; McClenaghan, 1979; Schumaker & Beals, 1983; Todd & Curti, 1982) has indicated that junior high school text readability typically exceeds the grade level at which that text is used. Thus, one of the demands at the junior high school level is reading above grade level or having a proficient strategy for dealing with these accelerated materials. Armbruster (1984) noted an added burden for students: Many texts are poorly organized and poorly written, warranting the description "inconsiderate text." These demands obviously present serious problems for the typical LD student who is already below grade placement in reading.

Reading also is an integral part of mathematics at the secondary level. No longer is mastery of computation skills the only requirement. Students must read and understand syntactically complex passages (Larsen, Parker, & Trenholme, 1978). Story problems, presentation of concepts, directions for working sample problems, and explanations of examples must be assimilated to perform nightly homework assignments.

In addition to substantial reading demands in all content areas, proficiency in writing is necessary for academic success. Skills in handwriting, spelling, punctuation, and sentence structure are integrated and generalized to tasks such as creative writing, book reports, thematic and term papers, and testing (Smith, Robinson, & Voress, 1982). LD students have extreme difficulty with written production, compounded by a lack of skill in detecting errors in their work. Without the ability to proofread or monitor errors, they have little chance of improving a poor product (Deshler, Ferrell, & Kass, 1978).

Self-Management Demands/Study Skills

The junior high setting demands more independence and self-control than does the elementary school (Nesselroade & Reese, 1973). Students are expected to have developed study habits, to be able to complete assignments without reminders, and to request assistance when it is needed (Schumaker, Deshler, Alley, & Warner, 1983). Albeit difficult, after only a few weeks or even months normally achieving students begin to develop a system for note taking, recording assignments, completing homework in a timely manner, and preparing for tests. These new demands all emphasize skills in which most LD and underachieving students are deficient (Link, 1980; Mercer, 1979; Schumaker et al., 1983).

The demand for more independent learning behavior is further evidenced by the instructional format of junior high school classrooms. Lecture is the predominant teaching style, and students have few opportunities during class to provide the teacher with feedback pertaining to degree of understanding (Moran, 1980). Tests or written products constitute the predominant means of student evaluation (Schumaker et al.,

1983). Smith, Robinson, and Voress (1982), however, noted that most junior high-age LD students were deficient in comprehending, evaluating, and acting on oral information, as well as evidencing difficulty in self-questioning, self-monitoring, or self-testing behaviors. These students undoubtedly will have difficulty functioning well in the junior high setting.

Social/Adaptive Demands

LD adolescents surely must find junior high school frustrating. Their approach to learning is largely unsuccessful. Their deficiencies in reading directly affect academic success. These problems are compounded by social or interaction demands for which they are unprepared. Following classroom rules presents a particular problem for LD adolescents. Many LD youngsters are handicapped by poor social perceptions, visual and auditory misinterpretations of social cues, gestures, affective states, and verbal messages (Bryan, 1978; Cook, 1979; Kronick, 1978).

As the spoken and written requirements for success in each classroom vary with each teacher, students must try to adjust behavior to meet the demand. Brown (1982) explained that one environment may require a great amount of verbal exchange (language experience or group discussion) and another may require silence (study hall). Thus, the need for interactive learning skills (understanding nonverbal cues of behavioral expectations, responding appropriately to feedback, asking for clarification, participating effectively in group discussions, etc.) becomes evident.

The transition from elementary school to junior high school is difficult for most LD students. Students struggling to meet the academic demands of sixth grade in May probably will not be able to cope with the academic, self-management, and social demands of the junior high setting in September. If special education programs at the elementary level would direct some attention to the compensatory skills and learning strategies discussed here, LD students would be better prepared for the accelerating demands of the secondary setting.

THE TRANSITION CURRICULUM—WHAT TO TEACH

The elementary school LD teacher typically has a multitude of goals that guide instruction for each LD student served. Therefore, a program designed to facilitate students' transitions from elementary to middle school settings must be limited (there already is much to teach within the elementary program), yet it must target skills most problematic to LD youngsters upon entry into junior high school.

Skills selected for the transitional curriculum should be those not typically taught in elementary school, yet necessary for success in junior high settings. Therefore, both preparing for success in junior high school and acknowledging the existent demands of the elementary setting guided (as well as limited) skill selection for the proposed curriculum. Mehl (1984) surveyed junior high school teachers about skills in which LD students were least prepared and caused them most difficulty upon entering junior high settings. From this study and a review of the literature, the following skill list was developed to serve as the core of the transition curriculum. It is not assumed to be a list of all skills necessary for success in junior high school. Instead, it identifies critical areas that cause significant problems for a predominant number of LD youngsters. Other skills not included in the core curriculum but which might be of particular concern in regard to specific students could be added. Table 1 delineates each skill under the categories of *academic skills, self-management/study skills,* and *social/adaptive behavior.* A final category, *general orientation to junior high,* also is discussed briefly.

TABLE 1
Skills Taught in the Transition Curriculum

SKILL	WHEN TAUGHT 5th Grade	6th Grade
Academic Skills		
1. Reading for the purpose of content comprehension (Deemphasis on decoding)		
1.1 Paraphrasing/Summarizing		
1.1.1 Oral paraphrasing	x	
1.1.2 Written paraphrasing/ taking notes from text	x	
1.2 Text analysis		x
Self-Management/Study Skills		
2. Listening		
2.1 Following oral directions	x	
2.2 Note taking from lectures		x
3. Self-Management		
3.1 Planning Work Time		
3.1.1 Planning time use at school	x	
3.1.2 Planning study time at home	x	x
3.1.3 Organization of materials		x
3.2 Record-Keeping Techniques		
3.2.1 Assignment record keeping	x	
3.2.2 Assignment completion	x	
3.2.3 Self-evaluation of assignments before submission		x
4. Test Taking		
4.1 Test preparation		x
4.2 Test taking		x
Social/Adaptive Behavior		
5. Interactive Learning		
5.1 Appropriate questioning	x	
5.2 Interpreting feedback	x	
5.3 Group discussion skills		x
General Orientation to Junior High School Setting		x

Academic Skills Featured in the Transition Curriculum

As noted earlier, reading often ceases to be a subject in and of itself in junior high schools. Rather, it becomes a tool by which content material is assimilated. Therefore, LD students must become proficient at extracting meaning from difficult-to-read material if they are to succeed in mainstream junior high settings. Comprehending content material, then, becomes an important instructional goal.

Research in reading (Capelli & Markman, 1982; Markman, 1981) demonstrated that a skill crucial to understanding and remembering text is the ability to accurately summarize information in one's own words. This cognitive process facilitates the integration of information through continual review of what was read. Furthermore, researchers (Brown & Palincsar, 1982; Capelli & Markman, 1982; Wong & Jones, 1982) successfully taught LD youngsters both at the elementary and junior high school levels to monitor their reading comprehension in this manner. Thus, the transitional curriculum would include teaching students to paraphrase the main idea and selected details of paragraphs and longer reading selections (Schumaker, Denton, & Deshler, 1984).

The ability to paraphrase and summarize information also is important in notetaking (Saski, Swicegood, & Carter, 1983). Because taking notes from texts and lectures is a significant new demand of the junior high school setting, students would be taught to apply the skill of paraphrasing main ideas and key details to taking notes.

Knowledge about textbook organization is another skill not typically taught in the elementary school years, but it is extremely helpful in gaining information from texts. The ability to identify how a chapter fits into a book section, how boldface print and italics indicate main ideas, key details, and important vocabulary, and how illustrations are used to reinforce and restate important information can help LD youngsters better comprehend information in textbooks (Larkin & Reif, 1976; Alley & Deshler, 1979). Therefore, youngsters in the transitional curriculum would learn basic skills of text analysis.

Self-Management/Study Skills

Listening and Note Taking

Students at the junior high school level must be able to listen well. More class time is spent listening to lectures than was the case in elementary school (Moran, 1980), and students must be able to follow oral directions given by six or seven different teachers each day. Yet, students receive little instruction in how to listen well (Robinson & Smith, 1981).

Therefore, a component of the transitional curriculum would be instruction in strategies students could use to remember and follow oral directions and to listen to lectures and take notes. Robinson (1983) demonstrated that upper elementary LD students could successfully apply a rehearsal strategy to the task of following oral directions after a minimum amount of instruction. Another researcher (Seager, 1985) found that LD students could learn to identify important information in lectures and note it in a manner that could be deciphered and studied later, thereby increasing their comprehension of lecture material as measured by delayed comprehension tests. Both skills are critical to success in the junior and senior high school settings and, in both, LD teachers perceive students to be woefully inadequate (Mehl, 1984).

Self-Management

LD students find the increasing demand to work independently a source of great difficulty. No longer are one or two solicitous teachers on hand to help students complete work over the course of a day or a week. Instead, LD youngsters are faced with the differing demands of six or seven teachers whose ability to assist students in completing work is limited by the short time in which teacher and student are in contact and by the fact that each teacher is attempting to meet the demands of 150 or so students each day. Indeed, independent work skills are necessary for success in junior high schools.

Self-management requires students to become actively involved in managing their own educational programs. Research (Dickerson & Creedon, 1981; Seabaugh & Schumaker, 1981; Smith, 1984) has demonstrated that when instructional methods require the learners' active participation in planning the use of their time, most students increase their independent work and seem to change their motivational levels, thereby doing and learning more. Planning one's own work time has been taught successfully to elementary-aged LD students, with a resulting increase in productivity (Lovitt, 1973).

Getting the work done is not enough, though. Work usually is evaluated on the basis of quality. Therefore, it is recommended that students also be taught self-evaluation procedures. Researchers (Hallahan, Marshall, & Lloyd, 1981; Kneedler & Hallahan, 1981; Lloyd, Hallahan, Kosiewicz, & Kneedler, 1982; Schumaker et al., 1981) found that self-recording of performance quality on an evaluative checklist (e.g., Did I do what I was supposed to do? Did I find all the punctuation errors? etc.) produced positive performance changes. The ability to evaluate the quality of one's work prior to submission to a teacher should increase a student's success in independent learning situations. Thus, time management, assignment completion, and self-evaluation would be included in the transitional curriculum.

Test Taking

Another study skill that gains in importance during junior high school is test taking. Knowledge of course content often is measured through one's performance on tests. Yet, elementary students often have minimal experience with the objective or essay test formats commonly used in junior and senior high settings. Knowledge about study techniques, terminology used on tests, test preview procedures, scheduling time for completion and review, use of clue words, and how to estimate or "guess" on difficult questions can help LD students perform better in evaluation situations. Therefore, test preparation techniques, as well as strategies to use while taking a test, would be included in the study skills section of the curriculum.

Social/Adaptive Behaviors

Learning in an interactive manner (talking with others in a class discussion, asking questions, receiving feedback from teachers and peers) is important in both elementary and junior high school settings. Teachers' perceptions change, however, as students progress into higher grades; teachers believe that their students are fairly proficient in these interactive learning behaviors by the time they reach junior high school. Yet, the social deficiencies of the LD adolescent are well documented (Hazel, Schumaker, & Sheldon-Wildgen, 1981; Schumaker et al., 1983). Specifically, the teachers surveyed by Mehl (1984) noted class discussion skills, the ability to ask appropriate questions, and acception feedback as areas in which LD youngsters entering junior high school were deficient and in need of instruction.

Orientation to Junior High School

Parents and teachers report that the specter of junior high creates anxiety for most students. Therefore, a thorough orientation to the junior high setting, informing incoming students of what they will encounter, is necessary. This often is a component of the last semester of elementary school for all students.

Successful components of an orientation process include counselors from the junior high school visiting the elementary students to talk about courses, requirements, and scheduling; going on a tour of the new school; and holding orientation meetings for parents and new students (Bent, 1976; Allan & McKean, 1984). However thorough this orientation process might be, the likelihood that LD youngsters will need more information is great. Junior high school demands (moving from class to class within a time limit, organizing and retrieving needed materials from lockers, working a combination lock, coping with more than one teaching style, following a schedule, and so forth) require explicit clarification and discussion for students with learning disabilities. Possible repeat visits from junior high school counselors to answer new questions that students might have after thinking and talking about the junior high setting would aid this process. Providing explicit information about the new and upcoming environmental changes has the potential of circumventing considerable confusion for LD youngsters (Allan & McKean, 1984; Quattropani, 1982).

A curriculum designed to ease the transition from elementary to junior high school must meet two goals:

1. It must be effective, including skills most crucial to success in the new school setting.
2. It must be efficient.

The needs of LD youngsters at the end of elementary school often are many, and certainly varied. Basic skill instruction must continue. Thus, a transitional curriculum must be limited in both scope and necessary time to implement. The proposed curriculum was designed to meet both goals.

A TRANSITION CURRICULUM—HOW TO TEACH

Intervention success can be attributed to a constellation of variables that has been orchestrated well. For example, skills necessary for school success have been identified, student need for each skill has been validated, development of prerequisite skills has occurred, and teachers have adhered to effective teaching practices. In other words, a combination of knowing *what* to teach and *how* to teach will increase the likelihood of successful instruction.

Assessment of the learner's present level of performance is crucial in choosing what skills to teach. Equally important is to limit instruction to only those skills that appear deficient after a preliminary assessment. Observing and interviewing both teacher and student can provide invaluable information in compiling a list of deficit areas in need of remediation.

We suggest that a checklist similar to that of Figure 1 be used before placing any student in a transition curriculum. Furthermore, it is advantageous to delineate specifically at what level of understanding each skill has been integrated into the student's daily performance. In evaluating a student's skill usage, checking either "yes" or "no" gives little insight into the learner's readiness to learn that or any skill. An instructional hierarchy both for assessing the student's present level of performance and to what extent each skill is needed for a particular grade or course is recommended. Checking "no knowledge of this skill" would indicate a more intensive approach to remediating this deficit. "Skill emerging—teacher assistance required" would warrant an instructional approach that can build on the student's existing knowledge in this area. Indicating that a student has "mastery of this skill/can train other students" would require only minimal spot-checks by the teacher while also denoting a possible peer tutor for other students in the curriculum.

The teacher effectiveness literature has confirmed the utility of specific teaching practices to ensure student achievement (Bloom, 1984; Englert, 1984; Rosenshine, 1983). Providing structure and systematic instruction, using modeling and guided practice, maximizing time in which students are actively engaged in learning activity, and applying mastery learning principles are all techniques that researchers have proved to be highly effective.

Deshler and his colleagues (Deshler, Alley, Warner, & Schumaker, 1981; Schumaker, Deshler, Alley, & Warner, 1983) developed and validated, through numerous replications, a sequence of instructional steps that incorporates the previously mentioned effective teaching tactics to promote the acquisition of new learning behaviors. Others (Hazel, Schumaker, & Sheldon-Wildgen, 1981; Robinson, 1982; Seager, 1985) also have found these instructional steps effective in teaching LD youngsters listening skills, notetaking, comprehension techniques, and other academic and social skills. For the purpose of this discussion and the subsequent example lesson plan, the eight-step instructional sequence developed by Deshler et al. (1981) will be used. In this instructional sequence:

Step 1 consists of evaluation of a student's current learning style. If inefficient or ineffective, the need for a new approach to the task is confirmed and discussed with the student.

FIGURE 1 Pre-Assessment of the Learner

Student:________ Grade:________ Date:________

Teacher:________ Subject:________

SCORING: (1) No knowledge of this skill
(2) Awareness only of this skill
(3) Skill emerging—teacher assistance required
(4) Semi-independence for this skill—teacher assistance rarely needed
(5) Mastery of this skill/can train other students

Student can:	Student's present level	Level of skill needed for this grade/course	Comments
LISTENING			
• Follow multiple-step oral directions			
• Take appropriate, readable notes from lectures			
SELF-MANAGEMENT			
• Plan time needed for reading assignments			
• Plan time needed for written assignments			
• Bring appropriate materials to class			
• Attend class regularly			
• Arrive to class promptly			
RECORD KEEPING			
• Keep records of assignments due			
• Complete assignments on time			
• Self-evaluate potential grade of assignments/tests			
READING CONTENT FOR COMPREHENSION			
• Paraphrase in written form			
• Paraphrase orally			
• Take accurate and appropriate notes from texts			
• Read/interpret graphs			
• Read/interpret illustrations			
• Take advantage of boldfaced/italicized words			
• Take advantage of chapter prefaces/summaries			
• Use a table of contents			
• Use a glossary			
• Interpret maps			
TEST TAKING			
• Prepare for tests			
• Succeed on true/false tests			
• Succeed on multiple-choice tests			
• Succeed on matching tests			
• Succeed on essay tests			
INTERACTIVE LEARNING			
• Ask appropriate questions			
• Ask for teacher assistance for assignment clarification/additional information in an appropriate manner			
• Accept criticism/praise			
• Participate in class discussions using complete thoughts, staying on current topic with appropriate comments/questions			

Step 2 involves describing the new strategy or method of approaching the task.

Step 3 consists of the teacher's modeling the new learning behavior, which may include "thinking aloud" while doing the task.

Step 4 requires the student to rehearse verbally what he or she is to do, ensuring that the student knows what to do and can self-instruct at a later point.

Step 5 requires the student to practice the skill in controlled materials (e.g., ability level reading material, a role play situation) so that mastery of the new learning behavior is assured before asking the student to apply it to a "real" demand (for example, taking notes in a regular classroom lecture, reading a grade level text, taking a final exam in geography class).

Step 6 consists of student practice in grade-appropriate materials.

Step 7 is a posttest and discussion of the need to generalize newly learned skills to other settings.

Step 8 consists of tactics to assure generalization through review of the new learning behavior, discussion of where it best can be applied, and supervised practice of the new technique in the generalization settings.

Concurrent with all steps is the use of specific corrective feedback to inform students how they are doing and what they must do to master the task. (Please refer to Deshler, Alley, Warner, & Schumaker, 1981, or Schumaker, Deshler, Alley, & Warner, 1983, for further discussion of this instructional procedure). Figure 2 is an example

FIGURE 2 Lesson Plan for Instruction in Record Keeping

Skill: Self-Management
Subskill: Record-Keeping Techniques
Component Skill: Assignment Record Keeping
Daily Time Requirements: 5 minutes in the resource room. This unit is supplemental to any selected area of study. These presentations can be made in tandem with other assignments in the resource room.

Day 1
Objective:
- Initiate acquisition of Assignment Record-Keeping Strategy.

Step #1
Analysis of Current Learning Habit

Procedure:
- Discuss how the student is currently recording assignments in the regular classroom.
- Discuss how knowing *what* was assigned is the first step in correctly completing homework.
- Ask whether the student's current strategy for recording assignments is working.
- Ask the student how accurate recording of assignments could help his or her grades.

Day 2
Objective:
- Initiate acquisition of Assignment Record-Keeping Strategy.

Procedure:
- Assist the student in identifying subject area(s) in which assignment recording is crucial.
- Discuss all subjects that require homework.
- Explore with student the subject in which he or she has the lowest grade or in which he or she has the *most* trouble.

Day 3
Objective:
- Assist the student in developing a form for recording assignments.

Step #2
Describe the New Strategy

Procedure:
- Assist the student through discussion in identifying what information should be recorded in order to correctly complete an assignment.
- Discuss how the student could keep this chart available for easy access.
- Assist the student in making the chart simple to maintain.

Example:

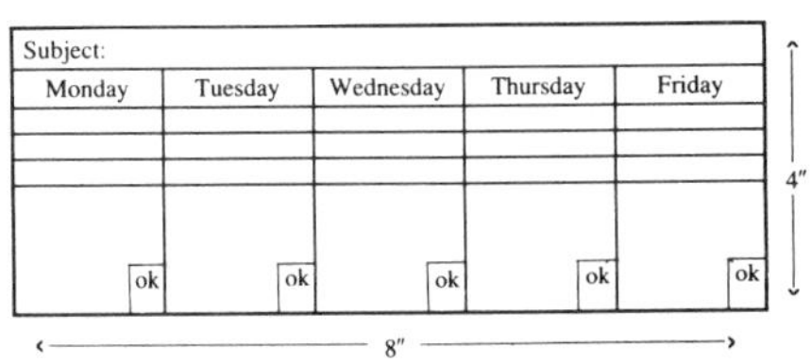

From Deshler et al. (1981). Used by permission.

(continued)

(Figure 2, cont.)

Day 4

Objective:

- Initiate use of the chart.

Step #3
Model the New Strategy

Procedure:

- Provide practice for the use of the chart. Using two examples, copy an assignment from the board and write it down as teacher gives it orally.
- Role play with the student. Act as the student checking with the regular classroom teacher to clarify the assignment.
- Role play with the student. Have the student give an assignment and the teacher copy it.

Step #4
Verbal Rehearsal of the Strategy's Steps

Procedure:

- Provide practice situation wherein the student will verbalize all the steps required for correctly recording the assignment..
  a. Chart (or paper) is available.
  b. Pencil (or pen) is available.
  c. Correct date is written.
  d. Correct subject name is written.
  e. Page numbers are written.
  f. Type of assignment (read, write, answer, etc.) is noted.
  g. Date due is included.

Day 5

Objective:

- Continue verbal rehearsal of the strategy, and provide practice for its use.

Procedure:

- Provide practice in developing a chart for keeping track of all assignments correctly recorded.
- Discuss with the student when he or she will mark this chart during the time in the resource room.
- Agree upon a student-selected reward for 5 correct recordings of assignments.

Example:

#1	#2	#3	#4	#5	Reward
					popcorn

Days 6 through 10

Objective:

- Provide a controlled situation in which the student can practice the new strategy.

Step #5
Student Practices in Controlled Situation

Procedure:

- Throughout the week give assignments as usual. Provide feedback to the student, through use of the student-developed check chart, as to whether the student has correctly recorded the assignment.
- Provide corrective feedback to the student if the student has not correctly recorded the assignment.

Day 11 through 15

Objective:

- Provide the student with the opportunity to use the assignment chart in a selected regular classroom.

Steps #6-8
Student Practices in Grade-Appropriate Practice and Generalization

Procedure:

- Through interview, discuss again what subject requires the most homework. Review how the strategy can be used in that setting.
- Practice record keeping in mainstream setting with regular corrective feedback.
- Continue to chart correct recordings of homework assignments in the resource room, with subsequent rewards.
- Continue maintenance check after mastery is reached.

lesson plan for the way in which the time management skill of record keeping might be taught.

The transitional curriculum described here was conceptualized with an awareness of pre-existing instructional obligations. Obviously, many students have learning deficits that require immediate attention and remedial instruction. Therefore, the skills included in the curriculum would be taught over a 2-year period. Skill introduction in fifth of sixth grade is suggested (and noted in Table 1) with possible utilization in existing elementary settings in mind. Individual settings and student needs, however, must determine the actual skills sequence for a given student.

CONCLUSION

Broadening the existing concept of transition and transition curricula can help narrow the cognitive dissonance between dysfunctional learners and the junior high school. With a growing body of research supporting a learning strategies curriculum (Alley, Deshler, Clark, Schumaker, & Warner, 1983; Deshler, Schumaker, Alley, Warner, & Clark, 1982; Robinson, 1983; Schumaker, Deshler, Alley, & Warner, 1983; Seager, 1985), special education now must focus on the efficacy of adapting strategic learning instruction for dysfunctional learners entering the junior high school setting. Waiting until the student has entered the junior high setting before initiating transitional efforts can only prolong the period of cognitive dissonance, resulting in a losing game of catch-up. Adopting an effective curriculum that prepares dysfunctional students before entry into the junior high school setting can facilitate smooth educational transitions from elementary school to the accelerating demands of secondary programs.

REFERENCES

Adelman, H. (1983). *Learning disabilities in perspective*. Glenview, IL: Scott, Foresman.

Allan, J., & McKean, J. (1984). Transition to junior high school: Strategies for change. *School Counselor, 5*, 43–48.

Alley, G., & Deshler, D. (1979). *Teaching the learning disabled adolescent: Strategies and methods*. Denver, CO: Love Publishing.

Alley, G., Deshler, D., Clark, F., Schumaker, J., & Warner, M. (1983). Learning disabilities in adolescents and young adult population: Research implications (Part II). *Focus on Exceptional Children, 15*(1), 1–16.

Armbruster, B. B. (1964). The problem of "inconsiderate text." In G. Duffy, L. Roehler, & J. Mason (Eds.), *Comprehension instruction: Perspectives and suggestions*. New York: Longman.

Bent, A. (1976). Orientation and the transfer student. *Clearing House, 49*, 350–352.

Bloom, B. B. (1984). The search for methods of group instruction as effective as one-to-one tutoring. *Educational Leadership, 41*, 4–17.

Brown, A. L., & Palincsar, A. S. (1962). Inducing strategic learning from texts by means of informed, self-control training. *Topics in Learning & Learning Disabilities, 2*, 1–17.

Brown, L. (1982). Evaluating and managing classroom behavior. In D. D. Hammill & N. R. Bartel (Eds.), *Teaching children with learning and behavior problems* (3rd ed.). Boston: Allyn & Bacon.

Bryan, T. H. (1978). Social relationships and verbal interactions of learning disabled children. *Journal of Learning Disabilities, 11*, 107–115.

Capelli, C. A., & Markman, E. M. (1962). Suggestions for training comprehension monitoring. *Topics in Learning & Learning Disabilities, 2*, 89–96.

Cook, L. D. (1979). The adolescent with a learning disability: A developmental perspective. *Adolescence, 14*, 697–707.

Deshler, D. D., Alley, G., Warner, M., & Schumaker, J. B. (1981). Instructional practices for promoting skill acquisition and generalization in severely learning disabled adolescents, *Learning Disability Quarterly, 4*, 415–421.

Deshler, D. D., Ferrell, W. K., & Kass, C. E. (1978). Error monitoring of schoolwork by learning disabled adolescents. *Journal of Learning Disabilities, 11*, 401–414.

Deshler, D. D., Schumaker, J., Alley, G., Warner, M., & Clark, F. (1982). Learning disabilities in adolescents and young adult population: Research implications (Part 1). *Focus on Exceptional Children, 15*(9), 1–12.

Dickerson, E. H., & Creedon, C. F. (1981). Self-selection of standards by children: The relative effectiveness of pupil-selected and teacher-selected standards of performance. *Journal of Applied Behavior Analysis, 14,* 425–433.

Edgar, E. (1985). How do special education students fare after they leave school? A response to Hasazi, Gordon, and Roe. *Exceptional Children, 51*(6), 470–473.

Englert, C. S. (1984). Effective direct instruction practices in special education settings. *RASE, 5,* 38–47.

Festinger, L. A. (1957). *A theory of cognitive dissonance.* Stanford, CA: Stanford University Press.

Hallahan, D. P., Marshall, K. J., & Lloyd, J. W. (1981). Self-recording during group instruction: Effects on attention to task. *Learning Disability Quarterly, 4,* 407–413.

Halpern, A. (1985). Transition: A look at the foundations. *Exceptional Children, 51*(6), 479–486.

Hardin, V. (1978). Ecological assessment and intervention for learning disabled students. *Learning Disability Quarterly, 1,* 15–20.

Hasazi, S., Gordon, L., & Roe, C. (1985). Factors associated with the employment status of handicapped youth exiting high school from 1975 to 1983. *Exceptional Children, 51,* 455–469.

Hazel, J. S., Schumaker, J. B., & Sheldon-Wildgen, J. (1981). *Application of a social skill and problem-solving group training program to learning disabled and non-learning disabled youth* (Research report #30). Lawrence, KS: University of Kansas Institute for Research in Learning Disabilities.

Heron, T., & Heward, W. (1982). Ecological assessment: Implications for teachers of learning disabled students. *Learning Disability Quarterly, 5,* 117–125.

Johnson, R. E. (1977). The reading level of elementary social studies textbooks is going down. *Reading Teacher, 30,* 901–906.

Kneedler, R. D., & Hallahan, D. P. (1981). Self-monitoring of on-task behavior with learning disabled children: Current studies and directions. *Exceptional Education Quarterly, 2,* 73–82.

Kronick, D. (1978). An examination of psychosocial aspects of learning disabled adolescents. *Learning Disability Quarterly, 1,* 86–93.

Larkin, J. H., & Reif, F. (1976). Analysis and teaching of a general skill for studying a scientific text. *Journal of Educational Psychology, 68,* 431–440.

Larsen, S. C., Parker, R. M., & Trenholme, B. (1978). The effects of syntactic complexity upon arithmetic performance. *Learning Disability Quarterly, 1,* 80–85.

Link, D. P. (1980). *Essential learning skills and the low achieving student at the secondary level: A rating of the importance of 24 academic abilities.* Unpublished master's thesis, University of Kansas, Lawrence.

Lloyd, J. W., Hallahan, D. P., Kosiewicz, M. M., & Kneedler, R. D. (1982). Reactive effects of self-assessment and self-recording on attention to task and academic productivity. *Learning Disability Quarterly, 5,* 216–227.

Lovitt, T. C. (1973). Self-management projects with children with learning disabilities. *Journal of Learning Disabilities, 6,* 138–150.

Markman, E. M. (1981). Comprehension monitoring. In W. P. Dickson (Ed.), *Children's oral communication skills.* New York: Academic Press.

McClenaghan, W. A. (1979). *Magruder's American government.* Boston: Allyn & Bacon.

Mehl, K. A. (1984). *Teacher's perceptions of student preparedness and the skills necessary for success in the junior high classroom.* Unpublished master's thesis, University of Kansas, Lawrence.

Mercer, C. D. (1979). *Children and adolescents with learning disabilities.* Columbus, OH: Charles E. Merrill.

Moran, M. R. (1980). *An investigation of the demands on oral language skills of learning disabled students in secondary classrooms* (Research report #1). Lawrence: University of Kansas Institute for Research in Learning Disabilities.

Nesselroade, J. R., & Reese, H. W. (1973). *Life span development psychology: Methodological issues.* New York: Academic Press.

Quattropani, D. J. (1982). Smoothing the transition to secondary school. *Principal, 61,* 55.

Robinson, S. M. (1983). *A study of the efficacy of instruction in two strategies, rehearsal and self-questioning, to increase listening skills of learning disabled students.* Unpublished doctoral dissertation, University of New Mexico, Albuquerque.

Robinson, S. M., & Smith, D. D. (1981). Listening skills: Teaching learning disabled students to be better listeners. *Focus on Exceptional Children, 13*(8), 1–15.

Rosenshine, B. (1983). Teaching functions in instructional programs. *Elementary School Journal, 83*, 335–351.

Saski, J., Swicegood, P., & Carter, J. (1983). Notetaking format for learning disabled adolescents. *Journal of Learning Disabilities, 6*, 265–272.

Sattler, J. M. (1982). *Assessment of children's intelligence and special abilities*. Boston: Allyn & Bacon.

Schumaker, J. B., & Beals, V. (1983). *An analysis of readability of commonly used textbooks at the secondary level* (Research monograph). Lawrence: University of Kansas Institute for Research in Learning Disabilities.

Schumaker, J. B., Denton, P. H., & Deshler, D. D. (1984). *The paraphrasing strategy*. Lawrence, KS: University of Kansas.

Schumaker, J. B., Deshler, D. D., Alley, G. R., & Warner, M. W. (1983). Toward the development of an intervention model for learning disabled adolescents: The University of Kansas. *Exceptional Education Quarterly, 4*, 45–74.

Schumaker, J. B., Deshler, D. D., Nolan, S., Clark, F. C., Alley, G. R., & Warner, M. M. (1981) (Research report #32). *Error monitoring: A learning strategy for improving academic performance of LD adolescents*. Lawrence: University of Kansas Institute for Research in Learning Disabilities.

Seabaugh, G. O., & Schumaker, J. B. (1981). *The effects of self-regulation training on the academic productivity of LD and non-LD adolescents* (Research report #37). Lawrence: University of Kansas Institute of Research on Learning Disabilities.

Seager, P. (1985). *Teaching sixth grade LD students LINKS: A listening/notetaking strategy*. Unpublished master's thesis, University of Kansas, Lawrence.

Smith, D. D. (1984). *Effective discipline*. Austin, TX: Pro-Ed.

Smith, D. D., Robinson, S., & Voress, J. (1982). The learning disabled: The transition from dependence to independence. *Topics in Learning and Learning Disabilities, 2*, 27–39.

Todd, L. C., & Curti, M. (1982). *Rise of the American nation*. New York: Harcourt, Brace.

Will, M. (1985). Let us pause and reflect—but not too long. *Exceptional Children, 51*(1), 11–16.

Wong, B. L., & Jones, W. (1982). Increasing metacomprehension in learning disabled and normally achieving students through self-questioning training. *Learning Disability Quarterly, 5*, 226–240.

Ysseldyke, J. (1983). Generalizations from five years of research on assessment and decision making: The University of Minnesota Institute. *Exceptional Education Quarterly, 4*, 75–94.

The authors are affiliated with the University of Kansas, where Suzanne Robinson is an Assistant Professor of Special Education, Catherine Braxdale is a Supervisory Teacher, Clinical Classroom for Learning Problems, and Steven Colson is Associate Director of the Clinical Classroom for Learning Problems.

This article examines a number of theoretical issues related to cognitive development, learning, thinking skills, and social interaction. In addition, the authors discuss a number of current instructional practices in special education and point out relationships not readily available to practitioners. Some of the practices examined are self-regulation, metacognitive skills, cognitive behavior modification (CBM), cognitive training, instrumental enrichment, and mediation. The authors also examine changes in perceptions regarding mildly handicapped students. These handicaps are increasingly being viewed as cognitive handicaps revolving around poor planning, organization, self-checking, and problem-solving skills.

The Role of Social Interaction In the Development of Thinking Skills

Adriana L. Schuler and Linda Perez

The last two decades undoubtedly will go into history as the heyday of teaching technology. Through task analysis, special educators and educators at large have become increasingly capable of devising ingenious lesson plans, reducing complex tasks to carefully sequenced series of operationally defined subskills. This focus on observable behavior has lent itself to remarkably precise measurement, and thereby program fine-tuning through ongoing evaluation of teaching efforts, assuring high rates of correct responding and, ultimately, task mastery. The premise of this evolving technology has been precise operational description and measurement of small segments of observable behavior—a premise that may prove to be its ultimate limitation.

Within the context of a nationwide growing dissatisfaction with the quality of education, dissatisfaction with the long-term outcome of special education efforts has been increasingly voiced. Concerns tend to revolve around limited generalization, lack of functional use of skills taught in school, and limited problem-solving skills. Frustration often is expressed as to whether many of these students will ever learn to think independently.

Teaching special education students introduces extra challenges. Limitations in teaching outcome are not necessarily a reflection of poor teaching, because many special education students are handicapped by sensory and physical conditions that may seriously thwart their cognitive development. Moreover, the bulk of invisible handicaps, such as learning handicaps, perceptual handicaps, behavior disorders, emotional disturbances, and so on, are viewed increasingly as cognitive handicaps revolving around poor planning, organization, self-checking, and problem-solving skills. These limitations in self-regulatory behaviors often are associated with limitations in social-cognitive knowledge, as evidenced by a lack of understanding of others' perspectives and of cause/effect relationships that pertain to their own as well as other people's behavior.

This article examines current views on cognitive development and learning pertinent to the needs of special education students. Emphasis is given to the role of language in the form of "self-talk" in planning, behavior organization, and problem solving, and on the importance of social interaction. To put it differently, the self-regulatory functions of language are examined, highlighting the intricate interrelations between language and thinking.

To further clarify this relationship, the discussion of self-regulatory skills is preceded by a brief overview of the interactions of early communicative and cognitive development. In this context the notion of *mediation* is introduced and then elaborated upon in later sections.

Second, a closely related matter—the role of social interaction in developing thinking skills—is discussed. Because social interaction is viewed as a critical mediating force in communicative development and development in general, its impact on the development of self-regulation and thinking skills in general deserves close attention. Despite the fact that social interaction has been the major mode through which our species has transmitted culture to its younger members, social interaction has not been viewed as a critical force in prevalent views of learning and development. Major theorists who have impacted educational practices in this country, such as Piaget and Chomsky, typically have expressed little interest in social interaction as a developmental force. This neglect, interestingly, has been paralleled by a similar neglect within behavioral circles. For instance, operant learning principles such as those articulated by Skinner only touch upon other people, as dispensers of reinforcement rather than having interactional qualities.

DEFINITION OF TERMS

Any discussion of thinking and cognition runs risks of becoming entangled in terminological confusion as well as unresolved controversies such as those pertaining to the effects of language on cognition, and its reciprocal, the effects of cognition on language. The term *communication* is used here in reference to behavior of one individual that serves to effect behavior of others, involving verbal as well as nonverbal behaviors of varying levels of intentionality and abstraction. The term *language* is used in reference to a highly formalized system of communication characterized by communicative intent, symbolic reference, and grammatical organization, thereby allowing for the communication of decontextualized meaning.

The term *cognition* is used in reference to unobservable mental processes applied to stimulus input, providing for interpretation and categorization, and for the creation of mental representations rather than sensory images guiding intentional action. The term *social cognition* refers to the understanding of own and others' feelings, agendas, and perspectives, and of the causality of human behavior at large.

EARLY COMMUNICATIVE AND COGNITIVE DEVELOPMENT

Developmentally, communication and cognition both are linked critically to the establishment of intentionality. Both involve the anticipation of behavior sequences on the basis of previously established behavior outcome or inferences about observed contiguity of events. Early communication and cognition both involve the active prediction of subsequent behavior(s) and event(s). The mere act of predicting a next occurrence introduces a mental activity over a physical reality, even when only highly routinized and predictable events are involved. In fact, the latter provide the basis for intentional communication, as the violation of anticipated occurrences provides the motivation to act in such a fashion that the anticipated sequence of events is restored. For instance, an infant may learn to extend his or her arms to make an adult continue an interrupted tickling motion.

The desire to communicate thus is rooted within cognitions about event sequences, activated by the desire to confirm hypothesized sequences of events and to take corrective action when hypothesized scripts are violated, allowing for a sense of control. In this view, both early communicative and cognitive development arise from the desire to detect and maintain contingencies. In more cognitive terms, the need to postulate and test rules regarding the relationships between people, objects, and events provides the core of communicative development. What is emphasized here is the active nature of the learning involved, as currently emphasized by researchers in infant development (for a discussion of this issue, see Lewis, 1985), and as opposed to common assumptions underlying special education practices (e.g., De Ruiter & Wansart, 1983).

Differentiations can be made between thinking that involves people and thinking that involves objects. While predictions about action sequences (i.e., causality) in the physical world may be made void from social interaction, inferences about the social world, involving the cause/effect relationships of own and others' actions, depend highly on apparent consistencies in social interaction. In fact, social cognition is deeply entrenched in interpersonal communication as similar skills are involved (e.g., understanding others' perspectives). In contrast, as discussed in Hoffman (1981), object cognition is not so dependent upon consistencies in social interaction as upon consistencies observed in the rules and regularities within the physical world.

Nevertheless, caregivers may yet arrange for the discovery of these consistencies by arranging an infant's physical environment—thereby imposing a structure that is salient to the infant involved. For instance, in response to an infant's initial attempts to do so, an adult may provide an infant with a number of opportunities to remove lids from receptacles, starting with the easiest ones first. Adults are able to do so on the basis of a keen appraisal of that infant's current interest and agenda, guided by close observation of that infant's behavior, as well as emotional state.

Behaviors of co-interactants are most pertinent to an infant's emerging social and communicative knowledge, as they are the very scope of the infant's investigations of social cause/effect relations. Erratic behavior that is out of line with an infant's focus of attention and action is not conducive to the infant's security and sense of efficacy and ultimately may lead to a sense of powerlessness in the infant. Of interest here is that developmental growth is not viewed as the final outcome of accumulated experience and stimulation but, rather, as the active product of the child's mental processes. Motivation thus is viewed as more than a matter of external reinforcement. The desire to predict, be correct, or, rather, to impose order may be as powerful as the desire to be fed, held, and physically comforted.

As acknowledged in an increasingly growing body of literature pertaining to the role of social interaction in early development, closely attuned and contingent actions of others are a mediating force in early communicative (Snow, 1984) as well as overall cognitive development (Lewis, 1985). Snow (in Snow & Ferguson, 1977) used the term *semantic contingency* in descriptions of parents' reference to and interpretation of their children's early actions such as reaching, laughing, smiling, and vocalizing. Similarly, infants' subsequent object manipulations become the topic of caregivers' verbalizations when they become capable of manipulating objects in a more sustained manner. Apparently, caregivers' utterances shift gears, making accommodations for that child's current focus of interest (Snow, 1986). These caregiver behaviors apparently are guided by that caregiver's appraisal of the child's perspectives and interests and by the desire to see the child demonstrate competence.

What is critical here is for the child to learn that what he or she does matters. Contingent responses, such as topic acknowledgment and elaboration, imitation, and the provision of consequences, which teach the child that his or her actions will work to produce desired effects, are at the core of children's early communicative development. Similarly, Watson (1966) has claimed that adult responses that are contingent upon some prior infant behavior facilitate early cognitive development.

The subsequent need for mediation in learning new skills and acquiring new concepts at later points in development is not easily evaluated. Nevertheless, lack of mediation has been reported as a major cause of cognitive breakdown in mildly retarded adolescents (Feuerstein et al, 1981). Furthermore, theorists such as Smith (1983) and Rogoff (1985) have pointed toward the important role of social interaction in the development of literacy. According to Smith, students need "active encouragement to predict, understand, to enjoy" (Smith, 1982, p. 83).

Gains in reading result from collaborative interactions with adults who do not penalize students for reading failure but who instead provide for success by structuring the learning environment in accordance with the student's needs. As further argued by Smith (1982, 1983), typically used remedial reading programs tend to transfer control from the teacher to sources outside the classroom. Hence, they fail to provide for mediation because the predetermined curriculum cannot anticipate what a particular child might be interested in at any given point.

THE INTERPLAY BETWEEN LANGUAGE AND COMMUNICATION

With early communication and cognition both stemming from the desire to make predictions about observed events, their lifetime interdependence is not surprising, nor is the close interrelation of both with language. Language grows out of nonverbal communication when more diversified communicative functions demand communication beyond the physical restraints of the "here and now" along with advances in abstraction skills. As discussed earlier, a formalized language system allows for the communication of ideas, needs, feelings, and so on, without reliance on situational context. For a more detailed discussion of the emergence of language as an integral part of more generalized symbolic capabilities, see Bates (1979) and Wolff and Gardner (1982).

Paradoxically, the early prediction of action sequences in highly predictable, routinized contexts sets the stage for the emergence of more abstract reference and grammar, allowing for the gradual decontextualization of meaning. Though the combined forces of established communicative and cognitive advances provide the roots of linguistic development, the subsequent reciprocal impact of language on cognitive and communicative functioning can hardly be underestimated. Communication and cognition mutually impact on each other. When examining the intricate interrelations between social interaction, communication, language, and cognition, the social functions of language have to be differentiated from the more cognitive functions. Although language and thinking are intricately interwoven in a non-linear fashion, discussion of the interdependence of language and cognition is fruitless if no distinctions are made in the range of functions that language may serve. For instance, a language function such as initiating interactions with currently present individuals does not require a notion of object permanence, while a request for invisible objects does.

One major function of language—self-regulation—is of utmost relevance to cognition. This close interplay between language and cognition is the focus of the remainder of this article.

Although the importance of language for purposes of behavior organization and self-regulation has long been recognized by psychologists (e.g., Vygotsky, 1976), this function has only recently received attention in the United States. This recent interest reflects growing dissatisfaction with a mostly structural perspective on the study of language—which has led to the adoption of a more functional perspective, emphasizing the use of language for a range of social as well as cognitive purposes. This is as evident in the proliferation of studies dealing with the *pragmatics* of language (its use in social context).

Second, a greater interest has been displayed recently in nonobservable dimensions of behavior that are not easily captured in precise operational definitions. Third, at a more applied level and as pointed out earlier, long-term results of the implementation of precise instructional technology, characterized by minute task breakdown, have left many disappointed.

THE DEVELOPMENT OF SELF-REGULATORY AND METACOGNITIVE SKILLS

Increased interest in self-regulatory processes has been voiced from a number of perspectives. Researchers within the domain of developmental cognitive psychology have investigated so-called metacognitive processes, defined as "thinking about thinking." Major researchers such as Brown (1978) and Flavell (1976) have investigated the when, how, and why of normal children learning to reflect on and direct their own thinking. These metacognitive processes are related to self-regulatory behaviors, as each one involves the deliberate use of reflective strategies. In part, self-regulatory skills emerge out of social interactions and require an awareness of social conventions.

According to Luria (1960, 1961), not until ages 4 and 5 do language and cognition play a major role in self-regulatory functions. The beginning of self-regulation involves the internalization of overt caregiver requests, as manifested in the infant's compliance with commands such as "no." Not until children internalize previous overtly repeated adult instructions does covert self-talk play a critical role in self-regulation. At this time self-regulation is intertwined with metacognition at large. For a more extensive discussion of these intertwined developments, see Addison-Stone and Wertsch (1984) and Wertsch (1985).

The basic thinking skills of metacognition have been defined as including the prediction and subsequent checking of results of an action or event, the monitoring of ongoing activity, reality testing, and other controlling and coordinating behaviors (Bondy, 1984). To put it in more educational terms, metacognition is a matter of "one's awareness and one's systematic use of efficient learning strategies" (Wiens, 1983), which can be further divided into two basic categories—those dealing with (a) what an individual knows about his or her cognitive abilities, and (b) the ability to control these processes by planning, choosing, and monitoring. Within the domain of information processing theory and artificial intelligence, the term *executive function* has been applied to top-level management of more basic processes such as memory and attention, introducing a construct predicated upon metacognitive knowledge.

In terms of special education practices, interest in metacognition has been further raised through the investigation of information processing abilities of students commonly labeled as learning disabled. It has been reported that many of these students are not lacking so much in memory or attention span (basic information-processing capabilities) as in the strategic, goal-directed use of these abilities (Hallahan et al., 1983). Learning disabled students thus are viewed increasingly as having deficits in metacognition rather than in attention, perception, and memory, and have become referred to as passive learners, lacking in the effective use of active problem-solving strategies (Torgeson, 1982). Similarly, students labeled as behavior disordered or emotionally disturbed may be viewed as limited in the regulation of their own emotional state as well as in reflection upon the relationships between their own behavior and external events and the perspectives of others.

Therefore, it has been argued that traditional treatment approaches such as stimulus reduction, medication, and behavior modification may be counterproductive, as they all treat the child as a passive organism—"someone you do something to" (Kneedler & Hallahan, 1981). The old techniques of shielding, manipulating, or medicating the child have merely reinforced the passivity that is at the root of the learning disabled students' problems (Hallahan et al., 1983).

COGNITIVE BEHAVIOR MODIFICATION

The practice of cognitive behavior modification (CBM) has been suggested as an antidote for problems commonly exhibited by learning disabled students, such as impulsivity, distractibility, and haphazard responding (Meichenbaum, 1980). One of the goals of cognitive behavior modification is to encourage the student to assume an internal locus of control and take responsibility for his or her own learning. This is to be accomplished by equipping the student with effective problem-solving and self-monitoring strategies through application of principles of direct instruction.

As pointed out by Lloyd (1980), cognitive behavior modification practices all share some common features. *First,* the student is actively involved in the learning process and may increasingly become his or her own teacher, therapist, or trainer. *Second*, overt or covert forms of verbalization often are part of the teaching procedure, so that behavior may increasingly become regulated by some form of "self-talk," which relates to the *third* feature—extensive use of modeling. Initially, overt teacher verbalizations are gradually substituted by covert student verbalizations that serve to regulate the behaviors of the student involved, analogous to common assumptions about the development of covert self-talk, as discussed earlier. *Fourth*, the identification of a series of steps through which students are to proceed to solve a range of problems is often a core ingredient of this type of training. *Fifth*, many CBM techniques have focused on teaching students to delay their responses in an uncertain situation until alternatives have been considered.

Self-monitoring techniques, such as those described by Kneedler and Hallahan (1981), provide a relatively straightforward example of cognitive behavior modification. Here, students learn to monitor their own on-task behavior. After initially being asked to record their on- or off-task behavior in response to some arbitrary external cue (e.g., a beep), students eventually are to be weaned from this external structure and to monitor themselves through more covert self-checking processes. These types of procedures reportedly have resulted in considerably increased on-task behavior, but the results have not been as impressive when academic productivity is applied as a criterion for evaluation.

Other examples include self-instructional training, as described by Meichenbaum and Goodman (1971), in which students are taught to direct their own behavior through self-interrogation, involving phrases such as "remember to go slow," "back up again," "that's okay," and so on. Despite the fact that these types of teaching procedures typically produce gains in the specific training contexts used, maintenance and transfer have been limited. Classroom applicability may be limited as well because of the focus on behavior rather than on skill acquisition or learning in more general terms (Torgeson, 1982). Although students may be taught successfully to stop themselves and think, they also need to learn what they should be thinking.

COGNITIVE TRAINING

In response to the apparent limitations of cognitive behavior modification in the classroom, more specific cognitive strategies have been promoted for precisely attacking specific academic problems. Examples of cognitive training have been reported by Cullinan, Lloyd, and Epstein (1980) in the context of teaching basic multiplication facts (a straightforward example of basic arithmetic computations) and by Atwell and Rhodes (1984) in the less tangible context of reading comprehension. An effective combination of cognitive behavior modification and specific attack strategy training was provided by Brown and Alford (1984) in an effort not only to increase time on-task but also to use specific strategies to analyze a problem. Again, encouraging results were reported in the context of related tasks but limited generalization across tasks.

Apparently, transfer to other tasks may be obtained as long as similar stimulus and response properties are involved but not if tasks employ different materials and responses (McKinney & Haskins, 1980). Portable coping strategies adapted to a range of problems encountered in school and other domains of life evidently are not that easily taught. Of course, goals as ambitious as generalized coping and problem solving, which normally take a lifetime, may not be taught in one series of training sessions.

The other question that obviously is of relevance here is whether critical periods should be postulated in the development of self-regulation and metacognition. Furthermore, cognitive behavior modification and specific strategy training, which exemplify application of the principles of direct instruction, may not go far enough. As Torgeson (1982) stated, cognitive training will fail unless it can teach not only specific task strategies but also more general academic strategies and, last but not least, reflective skills implying the domains of metacognition and motivation at large.

INSTRUMENTAL ENRICHMENT

When teaching a broad array of skills, as implied in metacognitive knowledge, the paradigm of direct instruction may not suffice. The unavoidable question that demands closer scrutiny pertains to what type of learning is involved in the acquisition of more generalized, conceptual and abstract knowledge and to what extent nurture rather than nature is involved. Encouraging examples of the positive effects of nurture are provided by alternative cognitive training practices described as *instrumental enrichment* by Feuerstein (1980) and his co-workers (Feuerstein et al., 1981). Feuerstein's position that intellectual functioning is modifiable is supported by his work with so-called culturally deprived individuals who initially demonstrated mild levels of retardation as measured by traditional IQ tests.

Feuerstein has generated a comprehensive body of work, which includes not only an information processing model of intelligence upon which a program of remediation is based but also an assessment device and an explanation for the individual differences that occur in cognitive development. Instrumental enrichment consists of 15 curriculum packages (called "instruments"), which are paper-and-pencil tests grouped according to presumed areas of cognitive deficit. The packages supply materials for 1-hour lessons, three to five times a week, for a period from 2 to 3 years.

Although these paper-and-pencil exercises, designed to systematically teach thinking skills, provide the centerpiece of instrumental enrichment, the essence of Feuerstein's teaching philosophy is not so much in the paper as in what the classroom teacher can do with it. The materials are merely the tools that a teacher uses to sample and modify students' thinking, with mediated social interaction constituting the process of cognitive change. The interactions in which the teacher engages the students are not of the directive type so typical of common instructional packages, and answers are not simply dichotomized as right versus wrong. Of greatest interest to the teacher is to determine which strategies, if any, students are capable of initiating and to assist these students in developing more effective strategies.

Specific "cognitive deficiencies" may be demonstrated in the way a problem-solving task is approached during one or more phases of the problem-solving process: the *input* phase (that is, while gathering needed information), the *elaboration* phase (while operating on the input), or the *output* phase (dealing with communication of the solution) (Messerer, Hunt, Meyers, & Lerner, 1984). At the input level, Feuerstein has identified seven specific deficiencies, including problems in labeling, gathering complete information, and systematic searching. At the elaborative level, 10 deficiencies have been identified, such as poor planning, use of irrelevant cues, and comparative thinking. Four types of deficiencies have been identified at the output level—e.g., impulsive behavior and egocentric communication.

Many of these problems typify those commonly encountered in learning disabled students. Feuerstein attributes them to a passive attitude, analogous to the view of learning disabled students as passive learners (Torgeson, 1982). According to Feuerstein, this passive attitude is caused by a lack of past mediated learning experiences. Although the learners may have been engaged in many social interactions, systematic instruction about these interactions is lacking, so they remain unmediated. Feuerstein believes that interaction by itself does not guarantee optimal development. What is critical is *the deliberate actions of relevant others serving to frame and organize learning experiences* for children. Good mediation is viewed as a conglomerate: (a) It is intentional; (b) it is transcendent, moving beyond the here and now in explanations of current events; (c) it assigns meaning to stimuli and interactions; (d) it encourages competence and confidence; and (e) it is concerned with the regulation of behavior, helping the child to gain self-control.

COGNITIVE TRAINING AND THE NOTION OF MEDIATION

When comparing instrumental enrichment with current cognitive behavior modification practices, the overlap between the two warrants comment. Both capitalize on the need to teach unobservable mental processes in a systematic way, and both are designed to increase self-control and problem-solving ability. The difference lies in the instructional methodology applied. Cognitive behavior modification has adopted principles of direct instruction, whereas instrumental enrichment is more interactive and focuses on student variables pertaining to the specific types of cognitive deficiencies encountered. The latter also is more student-centered in the sense that it starts with students' current thought processes. It is less judgmental in that interactions between teacher and students are more of a reciprocal than a directive nature, avoiding highly directive and didactic interactions.

In terms of the variables involved in design of instructional programs, instrumental enrichment operates on student variables as well as those that pertain to student responses and context, whereas cognitive behavior modification revolves merely around the breakdown of desirable student responses. Nevertheless, comparisons between various cognitive approaches to teaching should examine the role of task and student variables. Differentiations may have to be made between tasks that are more rather than less conducive to direct instruction and specific strategy training.

For instance, though hypothesis testing and self-checking are extremely critical to fluent reading and comprehension, these types of cognitive, self-regulatory activities should be complemented by more automatic decoding processes. Direct instruction thus may be most conducive to the latter, but mediation-based cognitive training may be more conducive to the former, as it emphasizes student initiation and analysis of the student's current thinking patterns, avoiding regurgitation of externally imposed behaviors.

What makes instrumental enrichment different from enrichment practices as commonly observed within the field of special education is that mere exposure to external stimuli is viewed as insufficient. The adult has to provide the needed structure to allow the child to make sense out of what is experienced, to interpret it, to assimilate it with past experience, and to provide the basis for accurate predictions about future actions and events. The adult arranges for and filters stimulus input in such a way that it provides the child with a basis for detecting contingencies—for the abstraction of rules. As pointed out recently by Gerber (1986), "Good instruction" provides or elicits the amount of structure most likely to maximally reduce response uncertainty, with the amount of structure being provided relating inversely to the cognitive maturity of perspective learners. Provision of the optimum amount of structure is not unique to instrumental enrichment but, rather, is an implicit yet not explicitly specified element of quality teaching.

Feuerstein's view of mediation as a critical mechanism in the transmission of culture invites comparison with notions of "scaffolding," as introduced by developmental theorists such as Bruner (1975). By carefully structuring young children's events, a scaffold is provided for generating accurate predictions about the outcome of one's own and other people's actions and about the ways in which events are related. The importance of interpersonal exchange, and social interaction in general, as currently stressed in the literature on early communicative development, is remarkably in line with Feuerstein's notion of mediation. Furthermore, the positive effects of caregiver responsiveness and communicative style on language development have been documented in a number of studies (Ainsworth & Bell, 1974; Cross, 1977; Barnes, Gutfreund, Satterly, & Wells, 1983; Ellis & Wells, 1980; Furrow, Nelson, & Benedict, 1979; Newport, 1977; Mervis, 1984; Peck, 1985.)

Although the long-term results of these linguistic and interactive variables are not easily determined, some intriguing findings were reported recently by Schlesinger (1986, 1987, in press). On the basis of her longitudinal study of outcomes relating to early parent-child interaction, she reported that deaf children whose parents had interacted through responsive, mediated dialogue ended up doing significantly better than those exposed to directive monologues. Schlesinger argued that parents who are overwhelmed by the experience of having a child with a disability tend to display a highly directive and restrictive linguistic stance toward controlling their child. Coping parents, on the other hand, use language more frequently with the intent to communicate.

SUMMARY AND IMPLICATIONS

A number of alternatives and supplements to direct instruction of carefully operationally defined instructional objectives has been proposed. All of them are cognitive in orientation insofar as nonobservable mental processes are the focus. This cognitive orientation appears to come from a growing dissatisfaction with the long-term results of traditional approaches to special education as well as from the growing realization that many of the problems of special needs students are of a cognitive rather than a perceptual nature. More specifically, metacognitive limitations have been implied in many students commonly described as learning disabled, behaviorally disordered, or emotionally disturbed.

Even though cognitive behavior modification is an extension of direct instruction in that the instructional content is expanded to include less observable processes, the other alternatives described offer a further departure from established teaching practices. The training of specific cognitive strategies goes beyond cognitive behavior modification because it focuses on training specific thinking skills rather than overall behavior. Instrumental enrichment, as promoted by Feuerstein, also is cognitive in orientation, but it is different insofar as instruction is more student-centered, less directive and, above all, social interaction-based, congruent with the notion of teachers as mediators of learning.

What remains to be determined is how these various cognitive approaches compare in relation to both student and task variables. For instance, are direct instruction and specific strategy training most useful when tasks require automaticity such as sight word recognition and basic numerical computations? In contrast, are interactive and less externally controlled approaches more conducive to generalized problem solving, inquisitiveness, and positive attitudes about learning and perceptions of self? Also, are these types of approaches more appealing to students who resist highly directive teaching styles? As pointed out by Ellis (1986), highly organized and tightly structured classrooms may inadvertently increase students' dependency on external cues and decrease opportunities for development and use of the metacognitive skills of self-structuring and monitoring.

The Role of Mediation

The focus on social interaction as a vehicle for problem solving and learning in general concurs with a more widespread interest in the notion of mediation. For instance, social interaction is viewed increasingly as a powerful mediating force in the context of early communicative development, more advanced linguistic development, and cognitive development at large. Rather than being merely a matter of exposure to other people, mediated social interaction is viewed as a matter of active perspective taking—an interpretation that capitalizes on the child's initiations and interests. Through mediated social interaction children are provided with opportunities to postulate and test rules and be successful at affecting their environment.

This is accomplished through the help of keenly observant adults who are attuned to the child's initiations and perspectives. These adults thereby are capable of creating contexts that allow the child to hypothesize correctly and shield that same child from contexts that present insufficient structure and predictability. Thus, the child is provided with opportunities to make correct predictions and successfully affect his or her immediate environment, increasing his or her sense of efficacy and thereby the likelihood of future initiations, hypothesis testing, and problem solving.

Social mediation is viewed as a mechanism designed to mobilize motivational and cognitive forces within the child through the provision of child-centered structure and predictability. If social mediation is viewed as the root of children's evolving sense of control over their surroundings, its consequences pertain to both affective and cognitive domains. Lack of such control thus may be reflected in a lack of initiation, low self-esteem, depression, and overall passivity, analogous to the construct of "learned helplessness," as articulated by Seligman (1975). If caregivers act to enhance a child's sense of predictability and efficacy, that child is protected from a feeling of powerlessness and ultimately of lethargy and depression, which could easily arise when actions and events experienced are perceived as unrelated to one's own actions. Schlesinger's (1987) claim that low socioeconomic status, depression, or parenting of a child with a disability can all through different routes contribute to powerlessness is of interest here.

Nature Versus Nurture

The notion of mediation invites reevaluation of longstanding controversies regarding the relative contributions of nature versus nurture on development and learning. Although Feuerstein claims that instead of being a fixed entity, intelligence is modifiable through mediation, learning cannot be explained without the postulation of biological correlates; perceived connections between stimuli have to be registered and retrieved at some level of biological organization through some type of learning mechanism. No matter what the environment can supply in terms of responsivity and staging of contexts conducive to motivation and success, actions and their precipitated outcomes have to be associated through some physiological mechanism, determining the ease with which associations are made and how well they are retained over time. These basic physiological processes may have most to do with mental acuity, but so-called executive processes may be more a reflection of nurture—i.e., mediation and experience.

A related question pertains to whether mediation should be viewed as a major developmental force in all cases or as a powerful compensatory mechanism in individuals developmentally at risk. Sameroff and Chandler (1975) have argued for the increased importance of nurture when biological risk factors are involved. They introduced the notion of a "continuum of caretaking casualty," describing the range of deviant outcomes attributed to poor parenting. According to them, the environment has the potential of maximizing or minimizing early developmental complications.

Of particular interest in this discussion is the interaction between development of self-regulation and cognitive development at large. Early neurological status and newborn behavior apparently are poor predictors of developmental outcome past 3 years of age (Drage, Berendes, & Fisher, 1969; Graham, Ernhart, Thurston, & Craft, 1962), but social status variables become increasingly important predictors of outcome. As pointed out by Sameroff and Chandler (1975), parenting behavior apparently serves to modulate the effects of perinatal factors.

The question that has to be addressed in accounting for apparent non-linear developmental trends and signs of major behavior reorganization around ages 4 and 5 is the extent to which these changes are a reflection of the emergence of self-regulatory mechanisms. It is just about the age most children demonstrate remarkable gains in self-regulatory abilities. If these types of skills are relatively more susceptible to nurture than earlier acquisitions that are more reflective of relatively constant biological forces, this relative unpredictability indeed could attest to the impact of nurture and explain why socioeconomic status is such a powerful determinant of developmental outcome.

Development of Communicative Behaviors

The importance of nurturant interactions with adults raises some questions about language use and communicative style in relation to the complexity of child-directed adult talk (see Blank, Rose, & Berlin, 1978, for a discussion of these complexities) and the functional qualities of that talk. Adult and child discourse should be discussed in terms of its semantic and pragmatic features. As extensively discussed by Wolf Nelson (1985), this emphasizes the need for critical analysis of teacher and parent discourse in terms of which attributes make it most facilitative of communicative and cognitive growth.

A related topic of critical importance pertains to teaching pre- or emerging linguistic students and more generally to the perspectives of cognitive training in the most severely handicapped students, who often are nonverbal. In this context alternative symbol or signal systems, of course, could take the place of speech. Although the use of alternative and augmentative communication systems has been well documented for purposes of requesting and commenting, their use for self-regulatory functions remains largely unexplored. Particularly when dealing with individuals who have pronounced speech and language deficits, self-regulatory functions may well be served through nonverbal means such as pictorial sequences or any other systems or combination of systems incorporating a variety of alternatives to spoken language or even nonverbal precursors of speech. Even though intentional behavioral self-regulation does not emerge until ages 4 to 5, behavioral precursors of those abilities appear to control behavior at earlier points (see Kopp, 1982, for an extensive discussion of this issue).

Furthermore, self-regulatory functions may appear in children's behavioral repertoires before the emergence of a fully diversified symbol system. For instance, self-regulatory functions of echoing behavior have been reported in the communication of delayed individuals before they established symbolic reference and grammar (Prizant, 1983; Schuler & Prizant, 1985). Also, the increased interest in multiple intelligence (Gardner, 1983) invites the exploration of other than verbal modes of thinking.

Even when self-regulation as such may not be an explicit instructional goal, the notions of mediation and scaffolding are pertinent to even the most severely involved students. By staging a highly motivating context and by capitalizing on the student's initiations and perspectives, effective communicative behaviors involving the use of non-speech modes of communication can be promoted (e.g., see Schuler, 1985).

Role of the Teacher

Probably the most pertinent issues raised by the social origin of self-regulatory skills and the related notion of mediation have to do with the teacher's role and with teacher-student communication. The prevalence of direct instruction practices and programmed instruction may have created an image of a teacher as a technically skilled designer and dispenser of educational programs. Notions of mediation, however, impose a different image of a teacher. Because adoption of the perspective of individual students and the ability to respond contingently are involved in being an effective mediator, more dynamic interactional qualities are implied.

In fact, social cognitive skills such as affective and cognitive perspective taking (which naturally grow out of social interaction), in conjunction with effective communication skills, may be more critical to effective teaching than is generally assumed. Excellence in teaching may be predicated upon the imposition of the types of skills described by Gardner (1983) as "intra and inter-personal intelligences" upon analytical and inferential skills germane to the provision of task breakdown and sequencing. *Gains in learning are the compound results of effective management of task content as well as learner variables* (for a further discussion of these critical determinants of learning, see Ross, 1980).

The type of skills that have been attributed to mediation and positive social experiences may be exactly those that provide for effective interactions with students who are limited in these areas and, therefore, could be invaluable to effective teaching. Reappraisal of some of the social-cognitive skills that teachers so easily take for granted seems in order.

REFERENCES

Addison-Stone, C., & Wertsch, J. (1984). A social interaction analysis of learning disabilities. *Journal of Learning Disabilities, 17,* 194–198.

Ainsworth, M. D. S., & Bell, S. M. (1974). Mother-infant interaction and the development of competence. In K. J. Connolly & J. S. Bruner (Eds.), *The growth of competence.* New York: Academic Press.

Atwell, M. A., & Rhodes, L. K. (1984). Strategy lessons as alternatives to skills lessons in reading. *Journal of Reading, 27*(8), 700–705.

Barnes, S., Gutfreund, M., Satterly, D., & Wells, G. (1983). Characteristics of adult speech which predict children's language development. *Journal of Child Language, 10,* 65–84.

Bates, E. (1979). *The emergence of symbols: Cognition and communication in infancy.* New York: Academic Press.

Blank, M., Rose, S., & Berlin, L. (1978). *The language of learning.* New York: Grune & Stratton.

Bondy, E. (1984). Thinking about thinking: Encouraging children's use of metacognitive processes. *Childhood Education, 6*(4), 234–238.

Brown, A. L. (1978). Knowing when, where, and how to remember: A problem of metacognition. In R. Glaser (Ed.), *Advances in instructional psychology.* Hillsdale, NJ: John Wiley.

Brown, R. T., & Alford, N. (1984). Ameliorating attentional deficits and concomitant academic deficiencies in learning disabled children through cognitive training. *Journal of Learning Disabilities, 17*(1), 20–26.

Bruner, J. S. (1975). The ontogenesis of speech acts. *Journal of Child Language, 2,* 1–20.

Cross, T. (1977). Mothers' speech adjustments: The contributions of selected child listener variables. In C. Snow & C. Ferguson (Eds.), *Talking to children.* Cambridge, England: Cambridge University Press.

Cullinan, D., Lloyd, J., & Epstein, M. (1980). Strategy training: A structured approach to arithmetic instruction. *Exceptional Education Quarterly, 2,* 41–50.

DeRuiter, J. A., & Wansart, W. L. (1983). *The psychology of learning disabilities.* Rockville, MD: Aspen Systems Corp.

Drage, J. S., Berendes, H. W., & Fisher, P. D. (1969). The Apgar score and four-year psychological examination performance. In *Perinatal factors affecting human development.* Proceedings, Pan American Health Organization WHO (Scientific Publication No. 185), pp. 222–226.

Ellis, S. E. (1986). The role of motivation and pedagogy on the generalization of cognitive strategy training. *Journal of Learning Disabilities, 19*(2), 66–70.

Ellis, R. & Wells, G. (1980). Enabling factors in adult-child discourse. *First Language, 1,* 46–82.

Feuerstein, R. (1980). *Instrumental enrichment.* Baltimore, MD: University Park Press.

Feuerstein, R., Miller, R., Hoffman, M. B., Rand, Y., Mintzker, Y., & Jensen, R. J. (1981). Cognitive modifiability in adolescence: Cognitive structure and the effects of intervention. *Journal of Special Education, 15,* 273.

Flavell, J. (1976). Metacognitive aspects of problem solving. In L. Resnick (Ed.), *The nature of intelligence.* Hillsdale, NJ: Lawrence Erlbaum Assoc.

Furrow, D., Nelson, K., & Benedict, H. (1979). Mothers' speech to children and syntactic development: Some simple relationships. *Journal of Child Language, 6,* 423–442.

Gardner, H. (1983). *Frames of mind.* New York: Basic Books.

Gerber, M. M. (1986). Cognitive-behavioral training in the curriculum: Time, slow learners, and basic skills. *Focus on Exceptional Children, 18*(6), 1.

Graham, F. K., Ernhart, C. B., Thurston, D. L., & Craft, M. (1962). Development three years after perinatal anoxia and other potentially damaging newborn experiences. *Psychological Monographs, 76*(3). (Series no. 522).

Hallahan, D., Hall, R. J., Ianna, S., Kneedler, R. D., Lloyd, J., Loper, A. B., & Reeve, D. J. (1983). Summary of research findings at the University of Virginia Learning Disabilities Research Institute. *Exceptional Education Quarterly, 4,* 95–115.

Hoffman, M. L., (1981). Perspectives on the difference between understanding people and understanding things: The role of affect. In J. H. Flavell & L. Ross (Eds.), *Social cognition*. Cambridge, MA: Cambridge University Press.

Kneedler, R. D., & Hallahan, D. P. (1981). Self-monitoring of on-task behavior with learning disabled children: Current studies and directions. *Exceptional Education Quarterly, 2*, 73–78.

Kopp, C. B. (1982). Antecedents of self-regulation: A developmental perspective. *Developmental Psychology*, 18, 199–214.

Lewis, M. (1985). Developmental principles and their implications for at-risk and handicapped infants. In M. Hanson, *Atypical infant development*. Austin, TX: PRO-ED.

Lloyd, J. (1980). Academic instruction and cognitive behavior modification: The need for attack strategy training. *Exceptional Education Quarterly, 4*, 53–63.

Luria, A. R. (1960). Verbal regulation of behavior. In M. A. B. Brazier (Ed.), *Conference on central nervous system and behavior*. New York: Josiah Macy Foundation.

Luria, A. R. (1961). *The role of speech in the regulation of normal and abnormal behavior.* London: Pergamon Press.

McKinney, J. D., & Haskins, R. (1980). Cognitive training and the development of problem-solving strategies. *Exceptional Education Quarterly, 4*, 41–51.

Meichenbaum, D. (1980). A cognitive behavioral perspective on intelligence, *Intelligence, 4*, 271–283.

Meichenbaum, D., & Goodman, J. (1971). Training impulsive children to talk to themselves: A means of developing self-control. *Journal of Abnormal Psychology, 77*, 115–126.

Mervis, C. (1984). Early lexical development: The contributions of mother and child. In C. Sophian (Ed.), *Origins of cognitive skills*. Hillsdale, NJ: Erlbaum.

Messerer, J., Hunt, E., Meyers, G., & Lerner, J. (1984). Feuerstein's instrumental enrichment: A new approach for activating intellectual potential in learning disabled youth. *Journal of Learning Disabilities, 17*(6), 322–325.

Nelson, W. N. (1985). Teacher talk and child listening—Fostering a better match. In C. S. Simon (Ed.), *Communication skills and classroom success*. San Diego: College-Hill Press.

Newport, E. (1977). Motherese: The speech of mothers to young children. In N. J. Castellan, D. Pisoni, & G. Potts (Eds.), *Cognitive theory* (Vol. 2), Hillsdale, NJ: Erlbaum.

Peck, C. A. (1985). Increasing opportunities for social control by children with autism and severe handicaps: Effects on student behavior and perceived classroom climate. *Journal of the Association for Persons with Severe Handicaps, 10*(4), 183–193.

Prizant, B. (1983). Language acquisition and communicative behavior in autism. Toward an understanding of the whole of it. *Journal of Speech & Hearing Disorders, 48*.

Rogoff, B. (1985). Adult assistance of children's learning. In T. E. Raphael & R. E. Reynolds (Eds.), *Contexts of literacy*. New York: Longman.

Ross, A. (1980). *Learning disability unreal*. New York: McGraw Hill.

Sameroff, A., & Chandler, M. J. (1975). Reproductive risk and the continuum of caretaking casualty. In F. D. Horowitz (Ed.), *Review of child development research* (pp. 187–244). Chicago: University of Chicago Press.

Schlesinger, H. S. (1986). Reliance on self and others: Autonomy and the lessening of dependency of young deaf adults. In D. H. Ashmore (Ed.), *Proceedings of the Regional Conference on Postsecondary Education for Hearing Impaired Persons*. Knoxville, TN: University of Tennessee, Postsecondary Education Consortium.

Schlesinger, H. S. (1987). Effects of powerlessness on dialogue and development: Disability, poverty and the human condition. In B. Heller, L. Flohr, & L. Zegans (Eds.), *Psychosocial interventions with sensorially disabled persons*. New York: Grune & Stratton.

Schlesinger, H. S. (In press). Dialogue in many worlds: Adolescents and adults—hearing and deaf. In G. Anderson (Ed.), *Proceedings of the Second Conference on Deaf Adolescents*. State University, AR: Research and Training Center.

Schuler, A. L. (1985). Selecting augmentative communication systems on the basis of current communicative means and functions. *Australian Journal of Human Communication Disorders, 13*(2), 99–116.

Schuler, A. L., & Prizant, B. (1975). Echolalia. In E. Schopler & G. Mesibov, (Eds.), *Communication problems in autism*. New York: Plenum.

Seligman, M. E. P. (1975). *Helplessness: On depression, development and death.* San Francisco: Freeman.

Smith, F. (1982). *Understanding reading, A psycholinguistic analysis of reading and learning to read* (3rd ed.). New York: Holt, Rinehart & Winston.

Smith, F. (1983). *Essays into literacy, selected papers and some afterthoughts*. Exeter, London: Heinemann.

Snow, C. (1984). Parent-child interaction and the development of communicative ability. In R. L. Schiefelbusch & D. Pickar (Eds.), *The acquisition of communicative competence*. Baltimore: University Park Press.

Snow, C. (1986). Conversations with children. In P. Fletcher & M. Garman (Eds.), *Language acquisition* (2nd ed.). New York: Cambridge University Press.

Snow, C. & Ferguson, C. (1977). *Talking to children: Language input and acquisition*. Cambridge, England: Cambridge University Press.

Torgeson, J. K. (1982). The learning disabled child as an inactive learner: Educational implications. *Topics in Learning Disabilities, 2*, 45–52.

Vygotsky, L. S. (1976). Play and its role in the mental development of the child. In J. S. Bruner, A. Jolly, & K. Sylva, *Play: Its role in development and evaluation*. New York: Basic Books. (Original work published 1933).

Watson, J. (1966). The development and generalization of contingency awareness in early infancy: Some hypotheses. *Merrill-Palmer Quarterly, 12*, 123–135.

Wertsch, J. V. (1985). *Vygotsky and the social formation of mind*. Cambridge, MA: Harvard University Press.

Wiens, J. W. (1983). Metacognition and the adolescent passive learner. *Journal of Learning Disabilities, 16*, 144–149.

Wolff, R., & Gardner, H. (1982). Structure of early symbolization. In D. Bricker & R. Schiefelbusch, *Early language*. Baltimore: University Park Press.

We thank Marci Hanson, Cheri Hamilton, Charles Peck, Barry Prizant, and James Podratz for their input and support in the preparation of this manuscript.

Dr. Schuler is Professor of Special Education, San Francisco State University, where Linda Perez is a doctoral candidate.

Many students have problems that extend beyond reduced achievement. This has led to programs emphasizing the affective dimensions of instruction. One of the more systematic programs is called the *self-control curriculum*. Edwards and O'Toole describe this program, and the research on its effectiveness. The curriculum involves instruction in four cognitive and four affective areas or, as the authors call them, "skill clusters."

Examination of the curriculum units leads one to believe that the cognitive skill areas are similar to "learning strategies," and what have been referred to in the literature as metamemory and metacognition or "learning how you think and how you memorize." In the affective areas, emphasis is on the child's learning ways to control his or her feeling, relaxation, accepting feelings, developing positive feelings, and similar emphasis areas. Such an approach, when combined with cognitive behavior modification, may be a valuable resource in the teachers repertoire.

Application of the Self-Control Curriculum With Behavior Disordered Students

Linda L. Edwards and Barbara O'Toole

Among the problems that beset the field of educating behavior disordered children, one issue involves the focus of special classroom intervention. For comparison, some consensus has been reached about what happens or what ought to happen in classrooms for learning disabled, mentally retarded, hearing impaired, and gifted students. Though educators in those fields do not always agree with each other or adhere to the same model, curriculum models and specific materials have been developed in each of these areas. A possible reason that a clear curricular approach (or at least clearer than in behavior disorders) has begun to emerge may be that in those categories of special education, children are identified and taught according to their learning characteristics. Or, as Rezmierski and Rubinstein (1982) pointed out, the locus of the problem in these areas is clear and understandable, not confused by its existence within the context of the adult/child interaction, as is so often the case in the educational treatment of behavior disordered students. An unresolved issue in our basic philosophy about education for this population of children has been the "unclear role of the schools vis-a-vis the affective domain . . ." (Morse & Ravlin, 1979).

Behavior disordered students may be performing academically at expected grade level, though most of those identified probably do not. These students are ones whose behaviors interfere with their own learning or that of others, or both. How they learn what they learn has been thought to be so highly individualistic and, therefore, diverse that no common set of learning characteristics has been attempted. Because behavior disordered students have been identified for the most part according to their social/emotional characteristics, emphasis historically has been upon *how* to teach rather than *what* to teach. Therefore, until recently curriculum has been left to vary widely among classrooms and programs within districts and agencies delivering education to this population.

HISTORICAL OVERVIEW OF CURRICULAR APPROACHES

Haring and Phillips (1962) wrote *Educating Emotionally Disturbed Children*, probably the first organized approach to educational methodology in this field. Within this book a chapter titled "Educational Methods and Materials" comprises 15 pages of a total of 322. This chapter did not mention specific materials; rather, it gave a general statement to the effect that curricula similar to traditional subject matter should be taught. The emphasis was on method, with primary focus on directives such as reduction of group participation, reduction of stimuli, immediate scoring, and consistency.

This approach is consistent with what existed in the field for some time, with the significant and almost immediate addition of behavior modification principles, and their refinement, to educational methodology. Contingency contracting, modeling, point systems, and parent-school reporting systems all arose as specific procedures for helping behavior disordered children learn traditional subject matter. Under this approach, children's learning was individualized, consistent consequences were applied, and academic learning was emphasized. Social/behavioral adjustment was the goal, to be accomplished by increasing the probability of academic success.

In the early 1970s this emphasis began to shift slightly. In an article entitled "Current Behavior Modification in the Classroom: Be Still, Be Docile, Be Quiet." Winett and Winkler (1972) challenged the preoccupation of both special and regular educators with external locus of control. Others began to analyze whether focusing on the stimulus variable (i.e., curriculum) might not be just as important as focusing on the response/consequence dimension (Edwards, 1980). Again, however, the emphasis was upon adapting material and changing the stimulus so that standard, traditional curricula could be taught more effectively. As a result of successful learning, it was postulated, problematic behavior would decrease as students began to feel better about themselves.

Another shift occurred toward the end of the 1970s. This time, materials themselves were the focus as educators began to direct their attention toward specific, direct teaching of affective and social skills to behavior disordered youngsters who all along had been so deficient in these areas. Materials aimed toward social learning continue to proliferate. That special educators seized them so readily is perhaps symptomatic of their eagerness to match at least some teaching content with the presenting characteristics of the children they taught.

Now the field is confronted with challenges related to teaching social/affective skills: how to choose from and evaluate the wealth of materials available, how to integrate affective teaching into an already full course of study with children who are sometimes severely academically deficient, how to measure the program's success (i.e., how to ensure that skills learned in the classroom transfer to real life situations), and how to convince others of the value of affective curricula. This article concerns application of a specific affective material, the Self-Control Curriculum (Fagen, Long, & Stevens, 1975), with behavior disordered students, in an attempt to address some of these concerns.

THE SELF-CONTROL CURRICULUM: A BRIEF DESCRIPTION

Teaching Children Self-Control (Fagen et al., 1975) evolved from the psychoeducational approach to teaching behavior disordered children. To a large extent, the developers have combined and integrated affective and cognitive tasks in this curriculum. Self-control, defined by these authors as the child's capacity to "direct and regulate personal action flexibly and realistically in a given situation," however, is derived from teaching a number of *skill clusters* that are arranged in a hierarchical, skill development manner. Thus, some authors consider the curriculum as belonging to a developmental approach (Swanson & Reinert, 1984).

Table 1 presents an overview of the eight curricular areas (skills) and corresponding teaching units within each area. The text discusses each area in detail and gives a variety of suggested activities for each unit within an area. The first four skills—Selection, Storage, Sequencing and Ordering, and Anticipating Consequences—are cognitive in orientation. The last four—Appreciating Feelings, Managing Frustration, Inhibition and Delay, and Relaxation—are considered affective.

Although *Teaching Children Self-Control* was designed primarily as a preventive curriculum for use in regular elementary grades, it can be readily adapted for use in special classrooms for behavior disordered children and for use with secondary students as well. A placement instrument, the Self-Control Behavior Inventory (SCBI) (Long, Fagen, & Stevens, 1971), is included in the material to aid the teacher in an individualized, prescriptive approach. The eight items correspond to the eight skill areas composing the curriculum. Fagen et al. (1975) have formulated 10 guidelines to assist the user in implementing the Self-Control Curriculum; these include starting at or below the child's functioning level, placing the tasks in a developmental sequence, maintaining enjoyment, preparing for real life transfer of training, and emphasizing short, frequent, regular teaching sessions.

USE OF THE SELF-CONTROL CURRICULUM

Teachers of children with behavior disorders have a unique instructional responsibility: to combine remediation of the child's primary behavioral problems while continuing to provide basic academic instruction. Acting out or withdrawn behaviors such

TABLE 1
The Self-Control Curriculum:
Overview of Curriculum Areas and Units

Curriculum Area	Curriculum Unit		Number of Learning Tasks
Selection	1. Focusing and Concentration	9	
	2. Figure-Ground Discrimination	4	
	3. Mastering Distractions	3	
	4. Processing Complex Patterns	3	
			(19)
Storage	1. Visual Memory	11	
	2. Auditory Memory	12	
			(23)
Sequencing and Ordering	1. Time Orientation	8	
	2. Auditory-Visual Sequencing	7	
	3. Sequential Planning	8	
			(23)
Anticipating Consequences	1. Developing Alternatives	11	
	2. Evaluating Consequences	7	
			(18)
Appreciating Feelings	1. Identifying Feelings	4	
	2. Developing Positive Feelings	8	
	3. Managing Feelings	10	
	4. Reinterpreting Feeling Events	4	
			(26)
Managing Frustration	1. Accepting Feelings of Frustration	2	
	2. Building Coping Resources	9	
	3. Tolerating Frustration	22	
			(33)
Inhibition and Delay	1. Controlling Action	13	
	2. Developing Part-Goals	5	
			(18)
Relaxation	1. Body Relaxation	5	
	2. Thought Relaxation	5	
	3. Movement Relaxation	3	
			(13)

as temper tantrums or self-imposed isolation make instruction of any kind problematic. Educators have become increasingly convinced, however, that these students have not serendipitously learned various kinds of socially valuable skills, such as self-control, through modeling or example, as have most normal learners. Therefore, the need to teach these skills directly has become a primary responsibility of the teacher of behavior disordered children. This is not an easy task, but it can be accomplished when approached in an organized manner and by using a well designed affective curriculum.

Teachers who have used the Self-Control Curriculum have found it to be a practical and organized approach because: (a) it provides a theoretical framework for understanding the goals of the curriculum, (b) it provides a wide variety of classroom activities to achieve these goals, (c) its activities are designed to remediate the skill deficits of many behavior disordered students, (d) it provides a measurement instrument for entering the curriculum and for evaluating its success, and (e) it is a relatively inexpensive program to implement. *Teaching Children Self-Control* enables both the experienced and novice teacher to integrate sequentially organized affective content into the ongoing, existing curriculum.

The curriculum consists of the textbook *Teaching Children Self-Control* (the text can be translated in a more easily accessible format, as discussed later in this article), which is composed of three parts. Part One, "Foundations of the Self-Control Curriculum," provides the reader with an understanding of disruptive behavior, the struggle children have to master self-control, and a justification for helping students gain this capacity in an educational setting. An operational definition of self-control is spelled out, as well as the authors' view of the construct as a "centralizing function comprised of discrete, teachable skills" (Fagen et al., 1975, p. 34.).

Part Two, the major content of the book, provides a chapter for each of the eight curriculum areas and the units within these areas. Each chapter includes a rationale for teaching, goals and objectives for the area, and detailed teaching activities for reaching the goals. Materials necessary for completing each activity are also listed.

The third portion of the text consists of a brief discussion of issues pertaining to the curriculum, such as transfer of learning, and the research bases for development of self-control. Methods of individualizing the curriculum are outlined.

Implementation

Teaching self-control or other affective skills to behavior disordered children can be accomplished in much the same way that academic skills are taught. A first priority here, too, becomes determining the child's present level of functioning, this time in self-control. Deficits have to be identified and prioritized just as in any academic area. When the self-control program is employed, this can be accomplished through use of the SCBI (Long et al., 1971), as is represented in Figure 1. This inventory can be completed by the classroom teacher and other personnel who work with the child on a regular basis, such as a teacher's aide or child care worker.

After the SCBI forms are completed, the teacher can develop a plan for organizing the curriculum to best meet identified student needs during the school year. The authors (Fagen et al., 1971) have identified several different time frames for teaching the areas and units. Teachers of behavior disordered students who have had experience using this curriculum seem to prefer presenting all eight areas within either one academic year or one semester since students they teach usually are deficient to some degree in all areas.

The only sequential caution the authors have suggested is that the Appreciating Feelings area precede teaching activities in the Managing Frustration area. Practical experience from teacher use additionally suggests that the exercises in Relaxation be taught early in the curriculum, especially before the Appreciating Feelings area. This has been found to be beneficial since children can use the relaxation techniques during more stressful lessons.

FIGURE 1 Self-Control Behavior Inventory (SCBI)

Name of Pupil ____________________ Teacher ____________________

School ____________________ Date ____________________

Grade ____________________ County ____________________

	A Rarely Does 0	B Sometimes Does 1	C Usually Does 2	D Almost Always Does 3
1. Pays attention to teacher's directions or instructions.				
2. Remembers teacher's directions or instructions.				
3. Organizes self to perform assignments.				
4. Anticipates the consequences of own behavior.				
5. Manages external frustration while working on assignment.				
6. Can delay actions even when excited.				
7. Expresses feelings through acceptable words and behavior.				
8. Thinks positively about self.				
Column Score	X			

Total SCBI Score ____________________

Scoring Values:

Rarely Does - 0 points
Sometimes Does - 1 point
Usually Does - 2 points
Almost Always Does - 3 points

Developing a Management System

When the skills to be taught are identified and prioritized and a sensible sequence has been developed, the teacher then is free to present these skills in any organized fashion compatible with his or her teaching style. Many teachers have found it helpful to implement a management system with everything necessary to facilitate a smooth presentation readily available. This system consists of a file box with 5″ × 7″ cards divided into the eight curricular areas. Each card might contain: (a) curriculum area, (b) teaching unit, (c) name of the activity or task, (d) a brief description, (e) materials needed, (f) any special problems noted in teaching the activity, (g) methods for facilitating generalization of the activity to a setting other than the classroom, (h) date(s) completed, and (i) a brief evaluative statement. Figure 2 gives one example. Developing a management system has proved to be worth the time it takes since it imposes additional structure on the program and makes it easier to implement.

Methods of Presentation

A major concern with the Self-Control Curriculum is that children have fun while mastering the various activities leading to internal impulse control. Though most of the tasks can be adapted to individualized instruction, the curriculum appears to be intended for small-group presentation. The three basic methods of activity presenta-

FIGURE 2 Card File Management System

Curriculum Area: Selection

Teaching Unit: #1—Focusing and Concentrating

Task: #1—Slow Motion Tasks

Description: Start with a simple task (e.g., walking), and progress to a more complicated task (e.g., slow motion baseball game).

Materials Needed: None

Special Problems: Can be a difficult activity for children who have fantasies.

Generalization: Encourage children to use the slow motion technique when they are getting angry in other settings (e.g., on the playground). Parents can use these skills to defuse angry outbursts at home.

Date(s) Completed: 10/20/84 **Evaluation:** Excellent

---

tion—games, role playing, and lesson/discussion—are obviously designed to involve the participation of several students. Teachers of behavior disordered students have found that the groups should not be larger than five to eight for maximum effectiveness.

The two most commonly employed methods of implementing affective curriculum within the ongoing classroom structure are: *subject teaching,* or presenting the material during a separate period of instruction, and *theme teaching,* blending the affective curricular instruction with academic basic skill teaching (Fagen, 1983). Theme teaching may require slightly more initial planning and practice, as well as familiarity with the content of the Self-Control (or any affective) Curriculum. This method, however, can be used in conjunction with nearly any academic subject and is preferred by many teachers, especially on grounds of facilitating generalization.

As one example of theme teaching using the Self-Control Curriculum, blending language arts (academic subject) with Appreciating Feelings (affective area) might involve the student writing a story from a point of view of a character other than the main character (e.g., how the wolf felt in *Little Red Riding Hood).* Another example, using mathematics as the academic area and Sequencing and Ordering (following plans) as the self-control task, would be for the students to prepare a dessert by following a recipe. The task labeled "Bill of Rights and Freedoms" under the area of Appreciating Feelings could be easily incorporated into a social studies lesson. The possibilities for integration and blending are many, but each must be carefully planned.

Subject teaching requires setting aside a separate period during the day to teach or reinforce affective skills. The activities in *Teaching Children Self-Control* are perhaps most easily adapted to this method. "Cool-Off Signals" in the curricular area of Appreciating Feelings is one example of many tasks that might be difficult to infuse into the regular academic tasks utilizing the theme approach. It requires the child to develop an individual cool-off signal to notify the teacher that he or she might lose control. When the teacher acknowledges the signal, the child is able to follow a prearranged plan that defuses the child's frustration and anger, thereby allowing resumption of the original activity. Ease of teaching the Self-Control Curriculum through the separate subject method is further enhanced in that most of the activities require only a short time, 5 to 15 minutes, to complete. Additionally, the activities can be dispersed throughout the school day.

Each of these two approaches has its own set of advantages and disadvantages. Most teachers who employ an affective curriculum seem to use a combination of the two methods (Fagen, 1983). A thorough knowledge of the components of one or several curricula of that nature is beneficial in all cases. A systematic approach, regularly offered to students, is the most important ingredient in successful affective teaching.

Difficulties in Implementation

Several obstacles that might hinder successful integration of the Self-Control Curriculum—or any other affective curriculum—are: teacher/administrator resistance, time restrictions, and a lack of comfort or feeling of inadequacy in presenting affective materials. Many educators believe that their major responsibility lies in teaching basic skills or other academic subject content and that effective education is not part of the job description.

A secondary public school teacher of behavior disordered students related an incident in which a student arrived in his fifth hour class displaying an array of objects she had shoplifted that morning from a local discount store. The girl showed them to the teacher and other students and bragged about having stolen only "color coordinated" items. The teacher discarded a prepared science lesson for the time being and began a discussion of shoplifting about the time an administrator stopped by his classroom. Later in the day the teacher was called upon to explain why he wasn't teaching the scheduled academic material.

Many concerned educators assume that students will or should learn values and other affective curricular objectives in the home or in other nonacademic settings. One of the tasks of the special educator of behavior disordered children is to present convincing evidence that with these students other settings have failed to accomplish important affective tasks and, for this reason, these students have been labeled as having this particular handicapping condition. An analogy to denying affective curricula to a behavior disordered student might be to deny large print books to a visually impaired student.

An assumption made in the preceding paragraphs is that teachers themselves believe in the value of affective curricula for behavior disordered students, and most probably do. Teacher resistance usually stems from lack of knowledge about, access to, and practice with using affective materials. Such discomfort can be significantly reduced through effective inservice or preservice training, enhanced by providing hands-on use of many materials, and including practice with matching materials to student characteristics and long- and short-term behavioral goals and objectives.

Scheduling time for yet another lesson in an already crowded curriculum is a concern that should not be minimized and is one that may also contribute to teacher resistance. In the case of the self-Control Curriculum, this difficulty is at least partly overcome through the combination of the theme teaching method and short, direct subject (affective) lessons.

Although the authors of the Self-Control Curriculum consistently discuss the importance of generalizing skills mastered to settings other than the classroom, they offer no concrete suggestions about how this can be accomplished. The task of developing appropriate activities is left up to the teacher's ingenuity. One approach might be to incorporate at least one generalization strategy on each activity card (as illustrated in Figure 2.) The importance of attention to generalization methods cannot be overemphasized.

Evaluation

As in all other content areas that are taught, the teacher must develop a plan to measure the effectiveness of teaching children self-control or any other affective curriculum. The process of evaluation is most readily structured through the student's individualized education program (IEP) by using the goals and objectives of the curriculum as measured by the Self-Control Behavior Inventory (SCBI). For example, a student's present level of performance might be described on the IEP as: difficulty staying in seat; problems with completing assignments and listening to teacher directions. Administration of the SCBI provides further support of these descriptors as the student rates low on following directions (Item #1) and organizing self to perform tasks (Item #3).

Using this information the teacher can develop long-term goals to increase the student's attention span and behavioral objectives to reach the goal. Methods and materials to accomplish the goal and corresponding short-term objectives are found in the Selection skill area of the Self-Control Curriculum. This approach allows the teacher to treat the student's behavior or emotional problems in a systematic way and to be accountable for the results of the intervention method. Additionally, measurement procedures should be developed to be completed by individuals who see the students in other than classroom settings, to assess the effects of generalization attempts.

RESEARCH CONCERNING EFFECTIVENESS OF THE SELF-CONTROL CURRICULUM

The Vaden Study

Fagen, Long, and Stevens (1975) have described an initial research effort at evaluating the impact of the Self-Control Curriculum among regular classroom, inner city second-graders carried out by Vaden (1972). This study found that "self-control program was significantly related to general school adjustment (based on teacher ratings of learning progress, self-control skills, and self-concept as a learner) at the .01 level of confidence" (Fagen et al., 1975, p. 250). Although a trend toward improved classroom behavior was evident, however, no significant differences occurred between the experiental and control groups in academic achievement. The authors suggested that further research is greatly needed in a number of areas including: the extent to which changes in pupil behavior are temporary or enduring, the most effective mode of instruction for the curriculum, and whether various skills comprising the self-control program contribute equally or differentially to changes in pupil adjustment.

Edwards' and O'Toole's Studies

We have conducted two studies attempting to assess the effects of application of the self-control program with groups of elementary and secondary behavior disordered, residentially placed students. The first study, done with 22 elementary-aged students, employed a simple pre-post treatment measurement strategy. The four teachers of these students rated their pupils on the SCBI in September, prior to using the Self-Control Curriculum, and again in May, after the curriculum had been employed for the 9-month academic year. Teachers were free to develop their own strategies for implementing the curriculum; however, all four chose the subject matter teaching approach. Gains in self-control as measured by the SCBI were significant at the .05 level of confidence. These gains may or may not be related to use of the Self-Control Curriculum, as no control group was available for comparison and many other interventions were going on simultaneously in the treatment milieu. Nevertheless, gains of two or more rating scale points on individual SCBI items were made by over half (12) of the 22 students participating in the program.

Edwards' and Watson's Research

The second study involved a more complicated design and attempted to assess effects on academic achievement as well as self-control behavior across several settings in a residential treatment environment (Edwards & Watson, 1982). It also entails adapting the Self-Control Curriculum for use with a high school aged population (Watson, 1981). In this study, boys were given instruction in groups of eight for 30 minutes per day each week day of a 10-week summer session. These 64 adolescents received instruction in the subject matter format also. Prior to instruction using the self-control program, several measures were obtained for students: The SCBI was completed for each pupil by his usual classroom teacher (in all cases this involved a special class teacher other than the one teaching the self-control instruction), by his dorm staff member, by his therapist, and finally, by the student himself. Achievement measures in the form of the Peabody Individual Achievement Test (PIAT) (Dunn & Markwardt, 1970) scores were available for 11 of the students for three different time periods—September, March, and the end of August. The curriculum was implemented by one teacher during June, July, and the first two weeks of August.

Achievement results from September to March (prior to the self-control intervention) showed an average (non-significant) gain of 3 months during a 6-month time span for these 11 students. The mean achievement gain from March to August (times corresponding roughly to pre- and post-treatment) was 9 months during a 5-month period. These gains were significant at the .05 level of confidence. As students were administered the PIAT on a rotating schedule, data corresponding to the time periods needed were unavailable for the other 53 students.

Three of the four groups measuring behaviors using the SCBI showed significant differences in a positive direction at the .05 level of confidence. In descending order of magnitude of difference, the dorm staff, teachers, and boys themselves rated student behavior as significantly improved after instruction in the Self-Control Curriculum. The therapists noted no significant differences pre- and post-treatment. Having the various groups rate pre- and post-behaviors was an attempt to assess generalization skills across settings. It seems apparent that learning transferred from the classroom into the student's living environment. Individuals encountering the boys in one-to-one situations (therapists), however, might have been unable to perceive changes as measured by the SCBI.

After the study was conducted, an attempt was made to investigate gains on the SCBI made by students with various types of presenting problems or diagnostic labels. A consistent finding was that the highest gains were made by students labeled "adjustment reaction to adolescence"—in this institution a term used for undersocialized, passive, rejected students. Moderate gains were made by students with hyperactive tendencies—impulsivity, short attention span, and low frustration tolerance. Small or no gains were made by students labeled sociopathic or character disordered and by students who were substance abusers.

SUMMARY

A characteristic common to most behavior disordered students is lack of effective social and affective skills. This very deficit in fact promotes their identification as handicapped and interferes with successful school achievement and life adjustment. Carefully implemented classroom intervention in this area, therefore, appears to be not only justifiable but mandatory.

This article discusses one curricular approach to intervention by the special classroom teacher in the area of increasing self-control. Its purpose has been to illustrate, by using the self-control program as an example, how affective teaching might be applied in classroom settings and how the effectiveness of this teaching might be evaluated. Vigorous research efforts to obtain immediate and long-term effects of this and other affective curricular approaches should be continued.

REFERENCES

Dunn, L. M., & Markwardt, F. C. (1970). *Peabody individual achievement test*. Circle Pines, MN: American Guidance Service.

Edwards, L. L. (1980). Curriculum modification as a strategy for helping regular classroom behavior disordered students. *Focus on Exceptional Children, 12,* 1–12.

Edwards, L. L., & Watson, K. (1982, February). Giving adolescents choices using the self-control curriculum: Application and research. In S. Braaten (Conference coordinator), *Programming for the developmental needs of adolescents with behavior disorders.* Symposium conducted by the Council for Children with Behavior Disorders, Minneapolis.

Fagen, S. A. (1983, February). *Curriculum.* Midwest symposium for leadership in behavior disorders, Kansas City, MO.

Fagen, S. A., Long, N. J, & Stevens, D. J. (1975). *Teaching children self-control: Preventing emotional and learning problems in the elementary school.* Columbus, OH: Charles E. Merrill.

Haring, N. J., & Phillips, E. L. (1962). *Educating emotionally disturbed children.* New York: McGraw-Hill.

Long, N. J., Fagen, S. A., & Stevens, D. J. (1971). *A psychoeducational screening system for identifying resourceful, marginal, and vulnerable pupils in the primary grades.* Washington, DC: Psychoeducational Resources.

Morse, W. C., & Ravlin, M M. (1979). Psychoeducation in the school setting. In S. I. Harrison (Ed.), *Basic handbook of child psychiatry* (Vol. 3). New York: Basic Books.

Rezmierski, V., & Rubinstein, M. F. (1982). To punish or to heal: The issues and dynamics of educating emotionally disturbed children. In C. R. Smith & B. J. Wilcots (Eds.), *Iowa monograph: Current issues in behavior disorders.* Des Moines: Iowa State Department of Public Instruction.

Swanson, H. L., & Reinert, H. R. (1984). *Teaching strategies for children in conflict* (2nd ed.). St. Louis: C. V. Mosby.

Vaden, T. B., with Long, N., Stevens, D., & Fagen, S. (1972). *An evaluation of a psychoeducational approach to the concept of self-control.* Washington, DC: Psychoeducational Institute, Hillcrest Mental Center.

Watson, K. (1981). *The self-control curriculum adapted for secondary aged behavior disordered students.* Unpublished manuscript, University of Missouri-Kansas City.

Winett, R. A., & Winkler, R. C. (1972). Current behavior modification in the classroom: Be still, be docile, be quiet. *Journal of Applied Behavior Analysis, 5,* 499–504.

Linda Edwards is Associate Professor, Special Education, University of Missouri-Kansas City. Barbara O'Toole is Director of Special Education, the Gillis Center, Kansas City, Missouri.

Written language appears to be a near lost art in the United States. Isaacson discusses what is known about teaching written language and examines the literature on effective instruction. Some common myths such as "written composition does not have to be taught" and "the best way to teach writing is to write more" are discussed. Suggestions are given for teaching written language effectively, and recommendations are offered for some variables related to teaching writing: clear objectives, student motivation, good models, guided practice, and selective feedback.

One conclusion that can be drawn from reading this article is that more time in writing instruction is needed, planning is necessary, and writing instruction must be guided. Though a great deal of research is still to be done, some of the effective instruction literature appears to be relevant. The amount of time on task, frequent use of praise, a high success rate, and modeling are all instructional practices with research support.

Effective Instruction In Written Language

Stephen L. Isaacson

Among the many skill deficiencies of mildly handicapped students, written expression is an often overlooked problem. Many learning disabled (LD) students are deficient in written language skills, as measured both by norm-referenced tests of written language (Poplin, Gray, Larsen, Banikowski, & Mehring, 1980) and by criterion-based analyses of their writing products (Anderson, 1982; Deno, Marston, & Mirkin, 1982; Morris & Crump, 1982; Nodine, Barenbaum, & Newcomer, 1985). Although reading, math, and spelling skills are emphasized in remedial programs, written expression has been given insufficient attention both in the curriculum and in educational literature (Roit & McKenzie, 1985).

As in regular education, special education has a need to identify and apply methods for effectively teaching written expression. In keeping with that aim, this article sets out to (a) identify current problems with existing instructional practices, (b) recommend a thorough model of written language on which curriculum should be based, and (c) discuss approaches and techniques that have been shown to be effective with both handicapped and nonhandicapped students.

PROBLEMS IN CURRENT INSTRUCTIONAL PRACTICE

The teaching of written expression suffers from three problems. First, educators give insufficient attention to writing in the curriculum. Second, written language instruction is based on an incomplete model of written language. Third, teachers have inadequate information regarding effective approaches to teaching written language and the ineffective techniques to avoid. Each of these problems contributes to the lack of impact that traditional instruction has had on the writing abilities of both handicapped and nonhandicapped students.

Insufficient Attention to Writing

Several authors (Hughes, 1978; Bridge & Hiebert, 1985; Shanahan, 1980) have documented the extent to which writing is overlooked in the curriculum. In a comparison study of 19 pairs of classrooms in the United Kingdom and the U.S., matched according to socioeconomic status, Hughes found that British children spent an average of 9½ hours per week composing, while U.S. children spent an average of only 1½ hours per week, with some classrooms spending as little as 1½ hours *per month*. The compositions of British children were twice as long, syntactically more mature, and better organized than those of U.S. children. Leinhart, Zigmond, and Cooley (1980) found that LD students observed in the U.S. also spent less than ½ hour per day in writing, and 75% of that time was spent copying.

The insufficient amount of time devoted to written language instruction in special education occurs because of two misconceptions among teachers. The *first* misconception is that writing does not have to be taught. It often is thought to be an outgrowth of oral language development and exposure to written language through reading. Although writing is positively correlated to both of the other language dimensions (Dyson, 1983; Shanahan, 1980, 1984) correlations are not high enough to assume that one necessarily will follow from the other. Each must be taught.

The *second* misconception centers on *when* written expression should be introduced. Many teachers believe that writing necessarily must wait until a child is proficient in reading. Myklebust (1965) described language development along a hierarchy of language skills in which expressive written language (writing) follows its receptive counterpart (reading). Other authors (Chomsky, 1976; Dyson, 1983; Graves, 1983) have suggested that development of literacy does not necessarily follow in that order. Most children attempt to write before they attempt to read. Writing is a means of becoming familiar with words and grapheme-phoneme correspondence. Waiting for the special education student to become proficient in reading before introducing writing may limit the growth of both literacy skills.

Incomplete Theoretical Model

Writing instruction also suffers from an inadequate theoretical model of written language. Shuy (1981) wrote of the need for a "template" to provide a guide for assessment, diagnosis, and prescription. Too frequently, teachers look only at the more obvious, surface aspects of writing. When Shuy compared current instructional practices with his model of language development, the comparison revealed two problems: (a) Early writing skills are taught far longer than they should be, and (b) later strategies seldom are taught at all.

The National Council of Teachers of English defined writing as "the process of selecting, combining, arranging and developing ideas in effective sentences, paragraphs, and, often, longer units of discourse" (U.S. Department of Health, Education, & Welfare, 1979, p. 12). A model of writing instruction, therefore, should take into account the *process* ("selecting, combining, arranging, and developing ideas"), as well as the *product* dimensions of written language ("sentences, paragraphs, and . . . longer units"). In addition, the *purpose* of writing is important in determining the appropriate mode of written communication (letter, poem, narration, etc.) and choosing related writing assignments.

Inadequate Information

Finally, writing instruction suffers from the lack of information that teachers have about validated teaching approaches and techniques. In his integrative review of studies on written language instruction, Hillocks (1984) concluded that the dimensions of effective instruction were quite different from what is commonly practiced in schools. What little research exists regarding writing instruction does not reach teachers in the field. When teachers in one district were asked to rate their teacher education programs in effectively preparing them to teach writing on a scale from 0 (poor) to 3 (excellent), teachers gave their undergraduate preparation a mean rating of 1 and their graduate preparation a mean rating of .8 (Bridge & Hiebert, 1985).

BEGINNING FROM A MODEL OF WRITTEN LANGUAGE

Planning written language instruction requires that teachers understand and consider all facets of the domain. A complete model of written language includes the dimensions of *process, product,* and *purpose*.

Process

First, teachers must teach the writing process. Models of composing vary as to the number of steps or stages the process includes, from only two (Elbow, 1981) to five (Glatthorn, 1981). But most authors (Emig, 1971; Hayes & Flower, 1980; Nold, 1981) agree to variations of a three-step model that begins with a prewriting stage (sometimes referred to as *planning*) and includes a writing stage (*transcribing*) and a rewriting stage (*revising*). As Humes (1983) pointed out, the process does not move in a straight line from planning to transcribing to revising. Writers move back and forth among these subprocesses. The difference between skilled and unskilled writers throughout the process is summarized in Table 1.

During the writing process a struggle goes on throughout each of the recursive stages between two simultaneous roles of the writer. Smith (1982) described the two roles as *author* and *secretary.* The author has to get ideas, organize his or her thoughts, and select and arrange words and phrases. The secretary, on the other hand, deals with the physical effort of writing and is concerned with mechanical aspects of the writing task. In the *planning* stage the author has to get ideas while the secretary tries to remember the rule about paragraphs. During *transcribing* the author keeps the message and audience in mind while the secretary worries about spelling, punctuation, and legibility. When reviewing and *revising* what has been written, the author should review globally as the secretary proofreads at the word and sentence level. Mildly handicapped writers have difficulty with both roles, but educators do not agree as to which should be emphasized first in instruction.

TABLE 1
The Writing Process of Skilled and Unskilled Writers

Stage	Unskilled Writer	Skilled Writer
Planning	Does not participate in prewriting discussions.	Explores and discusses topic.
	Spends little time thinking about topic before beginning composition.	Spends time considering what will be written and how it will be expressed.
	Makes no plans or notes.	Jots notes; draws diagrams or pictures.
Transcribing	Writes informally in imitation of speech.	Writes in style learned from models of composition.
	Is preoccupied with technical matters of spelling and punctuation.	Keeps audience in mind while writing.
	Stops only briefly and infrequently.	Stops frequently to reread. Takes long thought pauses.
Revising	Does not review or rewrite.	Reviews frequently.
	Looks only for surface errors (spelling, punctuation).	Makes content revisions, as well as spelling and punctuation corrections.
	Rewrites only to make a neat copy in ink.	Keeps audience in mind while rewriting.

Product

Teachers also must consider all aspects of the written product. When various theories of written language are compared (Isaacson, 1984), five principal components seem to emerge: *fluency*—the amount written (number of words in the composition); *syntax*—complexity of the sentences; *vocabulary*—degree of sophistication in the student's choice of words; *content*—originality of ideas, organization of thought, maturity of style; and *conventions*—the mechanical aspects, such as margins, verb endings, spelling, and punctuation, that teachers expect students to use.

Purpose

Finally, writing must be taught across different purposes. Britton (1978) proposed just three functions of writing: expressive, transactive, and poetic. *Expressive* writing is relatively unstructured, relating the speaker's thoughts and feelings in a personal voice. *Transactional* discourse is language to get things done; it directs, persuades, and instructs. *Poetic* writing is patterned, verbalizing the writer's feelings and ideas within a superimposed structure (not restricted to poems). Awareness of purpose pervades all decisions the writer makes at both the global and the sentence level.

Britton believes that the starting point for developing content should be expressive writing focusing on the writer's experiences and feelings. A functional curriculum, however, requires that transactional writing tasks also be introduced, since future job-related writing may include writing letters, progress reports, requisitions, technical descriptions, resumes, contracts, advertisements, brochures, and project proposals (Phelps, 1986).

The three dimensions of writing are interdependent. One dimension cannot be addressed without affecting the other dimensions. For example, the purpose of the writing will determine the style and voice the author takes while transcribing (process). Careful planning and revising of the composition (process) will greatly enhance the quality of its content (product).

Taking into account all three dimensions, the task of writing obviously is complex and difficult. As Nold (1981) and Daiute (1984) pointed out, the demands for focal attention in each subprocess, across product components, and between the author and secretary roles place an enormous load on short-term memory. Flower and Hayes (1980) described writing as something of a juggling act. The writer must retrieve knowledge of the topic, use the linguistic conventions unique to written texts, take into account the audience and the constraints of the rhetorical problem itself while managing the motor skills required for putting it all on paper (or computer screen). The writer's challenge is to keep all the balls in the air given the limits of short-term memory. Even a skilled writer must employ strategies to handle the overload—such as using index cards to organize and sequence content material. To teach the beginning writer how to write, the task must be simplified somehow, giving the teacher time to introduce processes gradually and teach the necessary control strategies.

DESIGNING A CURRICULUM

Teachers should not rely on basal texts to provide a complete writing program with sufficient and appropriate activities. Harrington-Brogan (1983) evaluated first, third, and fifth grade language arts textbooks and found that writing was not treated as a three-stage process; the texts neglected reviewing and revising activities almost entirely. Teacher strategy suggestions were few and often inconsistent with authoritative opinion. Content was not considered a major concern. Bridge and Hiebert's (1985) analysis revealed that by far the greatest number of textbook writing activities involved verbatim copying, focusing on the mechanics of grammar and punctuation.

Should instruction focus on the secretary's role or the author's role or both? Martin (1983) recommended that the two processes be separated and worked on at different times. Barenbaum (1983) advocated a focus on composition from the beginning of writing instruction, postponing the emphasis on mechanics until writers would gain confidence in their ability to express their thoughts. Humes (1983) argued that higher level skills, such as sentence variation and figures of speech, are not possible until lower level skills—e.g., handwriting, spelling, word usage, punctuation—become automatic after years of practice.

As Scardamalia (1981) pointed out, a teacher's lack of emphasis on correctness does not necessarily free students from that concern. Students who are frustrated with the mechanics of writing will still go on worrying about them. Mastering the secretary functions of writing, however, does not ensure that the student will do a good job as author. Scardamalia found that removing concerns for correctness through, for example, dictation to the teacher does not appear to lower the demands of idea coordination or result in coherent ideas, at least among average sixth graders. MacArthur and Graham's (1986) findings were different for sixth grade LD students: Dictated stories were significantly longer, were of higher quality, and had fewer grammatical errors than handwritten stories or those composed on a word processor. A reasonable approach, therefore, seems to be the one proposed by Roit and McKenzie (1985), who advocated the development of parallel skills—concept development and basic writing skills—taught concurrently rather than sequentially.

Teaching a variety of composition structures is important. Studies of mildly handicapped students (Anderson, 1982; Harris & Graham, 1985; Nodine, Barenbaum, & Newcomer, 1985) have investigated the abilities to write descriptive or narrative compositions. Learning expository text structures such as *comparison, causation, taxonomy,* and *persuasion* is also important (Giordano, 1983; Stewart, 1985), as these skills are important for report writing. Glatthorn (1981, pp. 39–40) includes *applied writing* (letters, memos, applications, resumes) as an important part of the writing curriculum.

A writing curriculum should address all facets of the written product as it incorporates all the stages of the writing process. Skilled writers produce good compositions, as detailed in Table 2. They usually write more words than writers who are less skilled (Deno et al., 1982), using longer, more complex sentences (Hunt, 1965; Loban, 1976; Morris & Crump, 1982). Skilled writers use mature words and fewer high-frequency,

TABLE 2
The Writing Products of Skilled and Unskilled Writers

Component	Unskilled Writer	Skilled Writer
Fluency	Writes few words in allocated time. Writes incomplete sentences.	Writes many words in allocated time. Writes complete sentences.
Syntax	Writes in simple S-V or S-V-O sentences.	Writes in longer, complex sentences with embedded clauses and phrases.
Vocabulary	Uses high-frequency words. Uses favored words repetitiously.	Uses mature words. Avoids repeating favorite words.
Content	Shows disregard of audience. Includes irrelevant information. Has poor organization and structure.	Uses style appropriate to topic and audience. Keeps to topic with good cohesion from sentence to sentence and overall. Produces compositions that have good beginning, logical development, and clear conclusion.
Conventions	Spells many words incorrectly. Omits punctuation or uses incorrectly. Writes illegibly. Errs in use of verb inflections and/or choice of pronouns.	Spells adequately. Uses correct punctuation. Writes legibly. Presents reasonably neat paper. Uses correct verb endings and pronouns.

undistinguished words (Chatterjee, 1983; Finn, 1977; Deno et al., 1982). Their compositions are rated higher in terms of quality of ideas, awareness of audience, cohesiveness, and organization (Cooper, 1977; Irwin, 1982; North, 1981; Robinson, 1984). In addition, skilled writers are better at the mechanics of writing, such as spelling, punctuation, and correct verb endings (Videen, Deno, & Marston, 1982). Producing compositions with these qualities requires the direct teaching of necessary subskills.

Fluency

The first goal for the remedial teacher is fluency—getting students to write simple declarative sentences and elaborate their thoughts into compositions of gradually increasing length. First writing attempts of young children may consist only of labeling the people or objects portrayed in their drawings (Dyson, 1982). Beginning fluency also develops as children write simple messages to each other and the teacher, reinforcing the function of written communication. Dyson reported that preschool children's "letters" do not always communicate any particular message but are written to initiate and maintain social contacts.

Sentence writing can be taught to beginning writers through sentence maps or patterned guides, such as the SIMS Written Language Program (Minneapolis Public Schools, 1977) or the Phelps Sentence Guide Program (Phelps-Terasaki & Phelps, 1980). In the *Expressive Writing* program, Englemann and Silbert (1983) attempt to develop basic writing skills in highly structured tasks that limit content demands on the author. Children begin the program by copying sentences and short paragraphs while learning how to indent and use capitals and periods. Instruction quickly follows in writing simple declarative sentences describing picture scenes. Students are told how to begin their sentences, are told what the sentences should express, and are given the spelling of necessary vocabulary.

Syntax

As the student masters the spelling of frequently used words and writes compositions of gradually increasing length, another instructional goal is for the student to use expanded, more complex sentences. Sentence combining exercises are an effective way to increase a student's syntactic maturity. The purpose of sentence-combining exercises is to make students more conscious of the transformational choices available to them for expressing their ideas (Mellon, 1981). For example, these two sentences

The man is in the kitchen
He likes ice cream

can be combined into this longer sentence:

The man who likes ice cream is in the kitchen.

Studies conducted from the mid-1960s until the present have consistently shown the beneficial effects of sentence-combining exercises on students of various ages and ability levels (Doyle, 1983; Hillocks, 1984; Isaacson, 1985; Stotsky, 1975). In addition to increasing syntactic maturity, sentence combining has been shown to improve the overall quality of written expression. Mellon (1979) wrote, "I don't know of any component in our arsenal of literacy-teaching methods that is better supported empirically than sentence combining" (p. 35).

Although sentence-combining texts often are written for use with students at the secondary level, Ney (1975) and Isaacson (1985) have demonstrated that simple combining tasks can be taught successfully to second and third grade students, even those with learning problems. Cooper (1973) and Lawlor (1983) outlined sequences for sentence combining according to the difficulty of the required transformation. Nutter and Safran (1984) have described ways in which sentence combining can be introduced to LD students using the students' own reading and spelling vocabulary.

Vocabulary

An important component of good writing is choosing correct and effective words. The direct way to address the problem is to teach synonyms for overused words (e.g., *said* or *awesome*). Synonym and antonym charts can be hung in the room for reference during writing periods. Mercer and Mercer (1985, p. 444) have recommended giving the student a short passage in which several words are underlined. The teacher then asks the student to substitute for the underlined word a more colorful or interesting word or phrase.

Giordano (1984, pp. 49–52) proposed a method for use with LD students that incorporates sentence writing, sentence transformation, and vocabulary practice in one activity. The CATS exercise has four steps, as described below:

*C*opy:	The student says a sentence, the teacher writes it, and the student copies it on paper.
*A*lter:	The teacher circles a content word in the sentence, and the student substitutes another word for it.
*T*ransform:	The student changes the sentence into a question, present tense into past, or singular forms into plural.
*S*upply:	The teacher asks a question that the student can answer by writing an original sentence using familiar words and phrases.

Content

Young writers often are too preoccupied with the mechanics of writing to give thought to the prospective reader (Fontaine, 1984). Perl (1983) and Phelps-Terasaki, Phelps-Gunn, and Stetson (1983, pp. 371–372) have recommended group interaction and feedback for remediating a writer's difficulty in attending to audience and mode. Various group members offer different audience responses to compositions shared in the group and provide the impetus for the student to rearrange and rewrite the composition. Perl (1983) recommended an "active listening" procedure whereby one student would respond to another's shared composition by paraphrasing what he or she thought the author intended to say. The listener's interpretation helps the author evaluate his or her writing and make necessary revisions to accommodate the audience.

Teacher-directed inquiry activities are an extremely effective way to increase students' expository writing skills (Hillocks, 1984). The teacher provides sets of data (e.g., tools used by pioneers, boats for different uses, sources of energy) and teaches students strategies for dealing with the data in order to write something about it. Steps include observation, recording details, interpretation and, finally, writing. All are directed by the teacher as structured problem-solving activity. In group instruction, data often are organized on a grid or chart. In Hillock's integrative review of writing instruction research, inquiry activities had the highest mean effect size for any instructional focus aimed at improving the quality of content—including writing models, revision scales, and free writing.

Harris and Graham (1986) demonstrated that strategy training in identifying and using elements of a story schema can significantly increase the quality of narrative compositions by LD students. Posttraining stories included more story elements and were judged by independent raters to be superior to pretraining stories. The simplest stories contain just three elements: state, event, state (Prince, 1973):

e.g., John was sad. He found his lost dog.
Then he was happy again.

Harris and Graham taught a story grammar composed of seven elements using the mnemonic "W-W-W, What = 2, How = 2." The mnemonic stands for the following questions: *Who* is the main character? *W*hen does the story take place? *Where* does the story take place? *W*hat does the main character want to do? *W*hat happens when he or she tries? *How* does the story end? *How* does the main character feel? Thomas, Englert, and Morsink (1984) recommended a simplified four-part structure for special needs students: setting (which includes introduction of the character), problem, response, and outcome.

Conventions

Spelling, punctuation, correct word usage, and handwriting are the writing factors most frequently taught by special education teachers, but they also are factors that should be approached most cautiously in the context of composition. Students in writing programs that emphasize mechanics and grammar achieve significantly lower qualitative gains in writing than students receiving instruction in which mechanics and grammar are considered irrelevant (Hillocks, 1984).

This is not to say that a remedial teacher should not teach spelling, punctuation, and handwriting; they are among the factors that most influence judgments of quality (Brown, 1981). Initially, however, they should be taught separately, on a parallel track, and not interfere with or discourage beginning writers in their composition attempts. During composition the secretary should not compete with the author for the writer's attention. As fluency develops, conventions should be introduced as an editing task. Editing for writing conventions should begin with structured materials provided by the teacher and then, as editing skills become proficient, applied to the student's own work in the postwriting stage.

There is no evidence whatsoever that the teaching of grammar rules has any significant effect on either oral or written language (deVilliers & deVilliers, 1978; Glatthorn, 1981; Hillocks, 1984; Lash, 1970; Straw, 1981). Grammar is best learned indirectly through practice in expression and exposure to good language models.

COMPOSITION STRATEGIES

Because writing is a complex task, the writer needs to learn ways to organize and monitor the process. The *metacognitive* skills required in writing—self-monitoring of task-related behavior, detection of contextual inconsistencies, and examination of alternatives—are aspects of being a writer that are routinely ignored by special educators (Roit & McKenzie, 1985). Few researchers have explored the teaching of metacognitive strategies as a means of increasing writing quality.

Scardamalia and Bereiter (1983) taught a control strategy to students in grades 4, 6, and 8 aimed at eliciting evaluative and tactical decisions during the composing process. The process involved three steps: compare, diagnose, operate (CDO). First, students were trained to compare what they intended to say with what they actually wrote, using a list of evaluative phrases reflecting probable reader reaction and their own personal satisfaction. Second, the students had to explain how the descriptor applied to what they had written. Finally, they did a self-evaluation, choosing a revision tactic and making the text change. Some of the students used the CDO strategy sentence by sentence as they wrote. Others employed it upon completion of the composition.

Most students reported that the strategy made the process easier, but their text revisions did not always result in better compositions. Scardamalia and Bereiter speculated that this may have been the result of concern with small units of language rather than overall text. When students were unable to rewrite a sentence, they often settled for minor word changes. Sentence combining and sentence transformation might have been appropriate prerequisite skills to teach before the CDO strategy.

A simpler and more effective strategy was taught to 12-year-old mildly handicapped students in a study by Harris and Graham (1985). The goal of the strategy was to increase the number of action words, action helpers ("how" adverbs), and describing words in the students' compositions. The steps in the strategy were: (a) Look at the picture and write down good action words (or action helpers or describing words); (b) think of a good story idea to use the words in; (c) write the story—it should make sense and use action words; (d) read the story—is it good? Did I use action words? (e) fix the story if it requires changes. The strategy was taught using a modification of methods developed at the University of Kansas Institute for Research in Learning Disabilities (Schumaker, Deshler, Alley, Warner, & Denton, 1982).

Table 3 outlines the steps in the teaching procedure. Not only was the student's application of the strategy successful in increasing the rate of target words used but also in increasing the mean number of total words produced and ratings of story quality. Most of all, treatment effects generalized from the experimental setting to the resource room.

Similar instructional procedures were used by Moran, Schumaker, and Vetter (1981) to teach a paragraph organization strategy to LD adolescents. All students improved in their paragraph organization scores and successfully transferred use of the strategy to a text structure not used in training.

ELEMENTS OF GOOD INSTRUCTION

Because educators give insufficient attention to writing in the curriculum, the *first* important function of the teacher is to establish sufficient time for writing to be taught and practiced. Research on effective teaching practices (Englert, 1984; Rosenshine, 1983) has revealed the primary importance of allocated instruction time and student engaged time in increasing pupil achievement. Engaged time is measured in terms of the student's active interaction with the teacher during direct instruction, as

TABLE 3
Seven-Step Procedure for Teaching a Control Strategy

Step 1	*Pretraining* The teacher defines the target concepts (e.g., action words). The teacher and student generate examples.
Step 2	*Review Performance Level* The teacher and student review the student's current level of performance and discuss the training goal.
Step 3	*Describe Strategy* The teacher describes the strategy using small chart to list the steps.
Step 4	*Model Strategy* The teacher models the strategy, writing a story while "thinking aloud" the steps.
Step 5	*Mastery of Strategy Steps* The student memorizes and rehearses the strategy steps.
Step 6	*Controlled Practice* The student applies the strategy while thinking aloud. The teacher prompts as necessary and provides feedback.
Step 7	*Data Collection* The student and teacher collect data on the student's performance.

Adapted from Graham and Harris (1987).

well as attention to academic materials during independent seatwork periods.

The teacher's *second* function is to plan instruction. Instructional planning must represent a complete model of written language that includes all aspects of process and product in their application across different purposes. Teachers cannot rely on basal texts or other commercial materials to provide a complete curriculum with sufficient writing activities.

Third, teachers must use theoretically sound and (when identified) empirically tested methods of teaching written language. Although studies of instructional variables are few, review of the literature reveals several components of writing instruction that have been shown to be important. They include those briefly described below.

Clear Objectives

The most effective instructional approaches are those with clear, specified objectives (Hillocks, 1984). Carefully chosen objectives ensure that all aspects of writing are considered and that instruction moves slowly and systematically from comprehension of written language structures to expression. Objectives written in behavioral terms separate out demands that are counterproductive to the instructional aim, such as penalizing the student for imperfect handwriting and spelling.

Student Motivation and Interest

Several authors (Dagenais & Beadle, 1984; Roit & McKenzie, 1985) have stressed the importance of motivating students to write. Although motivation alone will not lead to good writing skills, teachers must be sensitive to negative attitudes that mildly handicapped students bring to the act of writing.

Interest is generated through verbal discussions and prewriting activities. Part of the teacher's task is convincing students that they have within themselves an ample stock of ideas related to the topic. Choosing an appropriate topic is also a crucial task for the teacher. Writers with little knowledge about a topic tend to produce descriptive sequences that lack logical coherence (Stein, 1983).

Interest is increased through presentation of reasonable tasks appropriate to the student's current skills. Englemann and Silbert (1983, p. 4) pointed out that starting instruction by requiring children to make up imaginary stories carries many risks. The mechanical and vocabulary skills required may be well beyond their abilities. Myers (1978) proposed that instruction should begin with the sentence because it provides discrete boundaries within which the teacher and student can examine the basic principles of composition. The teacher can sustain interest by selecting activities that ensure high levels of student success while providing enough of a challenge for the student to feel that positive feedback is well earned.

Models

Models of good writing are important in providing students with opportunities to examine the structure of written language and the ways in which it differs from informal speech. Phelps-Terasaki, Phelps-Gunn, and Stetson (1983) stated that the first problem remediation programs must address is the student's reliance on speech structures as models for written expression (p. 363). Oral speech is characterized by false starts, vague vocabulary, and incomplete utterances, which would be unacceptable in written form. Models provide positive examples of appropriate *styles* and *text structures*. Selections from children's books and magazines or the teacher's own writing can serve as models. Marcus (1977, p. 150) and Myers (1978) pointed out the desirability of children borrowing heavily either the content or form of another's published work.

In addition to *product* models of written language, teachers must provide *process* models. The exclusive use of product models is less effective than methods that model evaluation, inquiry, and language problem solving (Hillocks, 1984). The process that is modeled should begin with the planning stage. Preparing to write is the most essential factor in helping students make decisions about content. Prewriting discussion can bring to the students' consciousness words and phrases necessary for shaping ideas and their expressions (Marcus, 1977, p. 146).

The teacher also should model *transcribing operations* to demonstrate the translation of idea material, notes, or planning charts into acceptable written sentences. One of the most important functions of the teacher is to teach the student *self-regulatory skills* that will assist in performing related skills. The teacher models self-instructions by thinking aloud while performing the task. Graham and Harris (in press) recommend that the model's script be worked out in advance and matched to the student's verbal style and language ability.

Finally, the teacher should model *reviewing and revising strategies*. For beginning readers a review strategy may consist only of rereading the sentence to verify correct word usage, spelling, and punctuation. Oral proofreading (reading aloud) is more effective for elementary students than silent proofreading, although both are beneficial (Van De Weghe, 1978). There seems to be no difference between the two methods for secondary students.

Guided Practice

As important as practice is to learning to write, the act of writing, in of itself, does not necessarily improve writing quality (Dagenais & Beadle, 1984). Careful development of a limited number of papers under teacher guidance is better than independent production of many, frequent compositions (Glatthorn, 1981, p. 8). Teaching students how to read and respond to a piece of writing in progress is one of the teacher's central tasks (Perl, 1983). Robinson (1983) found that *probing*—asking the student six to seven additional questions about the passage being written—significantly improves the quality of written expository tasks.

Student Interaction

Hillocks (1984) found that the most effective approaches to writing instruction were those that maintained high levels of student interaction in response to structured problem-solving tasks. In this approach brief teacher-led presentation or discussion is followed by small-group, problem-centered activities. Phelps-Terasaki et al. (1983, pp. 371–372) also advocate closely supervised group instruction. In addition to providing a variety of audience responses, group members can help each other construct new sentence patterns, find effective words or phrases, and offer ideas and encouragement.

Interactive groups are also effective for planning processes. Crealock, Sitko, Hutchinson, Sitko, and Marlett (1985) developed a group brainstorming procedure effective with 10th grade mildly handicapped students. In group discussion the students first listed seven components of a good story (setting, hero/heroine, climax, etc.). Then, beside each component they listed 10 words or phrases for each category, forming a large 7×10 grid. After choosing one word or phrase from each category, they discussed with a peer how they would integrate the seven elements into a story.

Using the elements, the students then wrote a draft of the story, writing each sentence on individual strips of paper. After talking with the teacher, who gave them feedback regarding the content, the sentence strips were arranged with large spaces between them for writing detail and transitions. After the teacher made suggestions for technical improvements, the students completed their final copy.

Selective Feedback

In regard to feedback on a student's composition, two principles apply. The first is to *praise* generously for description, ideas, or humor expressed and be cautious in giving criticism. Keeping the student's objective firmly in mind, correction should be provided only for aspects of the composition that have been taught. For example, if the objective is to increase fluency, the student should be reinforced for increasing the length of compositions, and spelling and punctuation errors should not be marked in red pencil. If the objective is to state an opinion and give two supporting facts, deficiencies in the student's choice of vocabulary should not be pointed out.

Although authors disagree as to whether praise and criticism significantly affect composition quality (Dagenais & Beadle, 1984; Glatthorn, 1981; Taylor & Hoedt, 1966; Van De Weghe, 1978), the consensus is that positive and negative feedback differentially affects student attitudes toward writing.

The second principle addresses the specificity of feedback. Barrs (1983) pointed out that with the lack of good pedagogical knowledge about writing, the teacher's model has been the hard-boiled editor who tells the young reporter, "This is a good try, Becky. . . . Try another beginning, okay?" Van De Weghe (1978) reported that among older students (ninth grade and above), text-specific comments have a greater positive effect on performance over longer periods of time than stock phrases such as, "Excellent! Keep it up" or, "Try to do better." It is reasonable to assume this holds true for beginning writers as well.

SUMMARY

Although written expression is an important component of literacy, it suffers from insufficient attention in the curriculum. Instruction that is provided is often not based on a complete model of language or validated teaching methods. Planning for instruction should take into account three dimensions of written language: process, product, and purpose.

Writing is an extremely complex cognitive task, requiring the writer to coordinate its various processes and subtasks: getting ideas, organizing and sequencing thoughts, selecting words and phrases, and managing the mechanical demands of putting words to paper. The task must be simplified for the beginning writer; processes must be introduced gradually, accompanied by teaching the necessary strategies. Especially important is for mildly handicapped students to learn a control strategy for organizing and monitoring the process of writing that will generalize to different writing tasks and environments.

The goals of writing instruction are based on the characteristics of good compositions. Components of the writing product that distinguish skilled from unskilled writers are fluency, syntax, vocabulary, content, and the conventions of standard grammar, spelling, punctuation, margins, and handwriting.

Three important functions of the teacher are: (a) establishing time for sufficient writing instruction and practice in the curriculum, (b) planning instruction that reflects all the dimensions of written language, and (c) using effective teaching methods. Although empirical studies of written language are few, several validated components of effective instruction can be found in the literature. They include:

clear objective
student motivation and interest
models of both the writing product and process
guided practice
student interaction throughout the process
selective feedback.

In Conally's (1983) words, "Education is inextricably linked with the capacity to produce visible language" (p. xi). Given the difficulty most handicapped students have in producing written language, teachers must begin to teach it often and teach it well.

REFERENCES

Anderson, P. L. (1982). A preliminary study of syntax in the written expression of learning disabled children. *Journal of Learning Disabilities, 15,* 359–362.

Barenbaum, E. M. (1983). Writing in the special class. *Topics in Learning & Language Disabilities, 3,* 12–20.

Barrs, M. The new orthodoxy about writing: Confusing process and pedagogy. *Language Arts, 60,* 829–840.

Bridge, C. A., & Hiebert, E. H. (1985). A comparison of classroom writing practices, teachers' perceptions of their writing instruction, and textbook recommendations on writing practices. *Elementary School Journal, 86,* 155–172.

Britton, J. (1978). The composing processes and the functions of writing. In C. R. Cooper & L. Odell (Eds.), *Research on composing: Points of departure* (pp. 13–28). Urbana, IL: National Council of Teachers of English.

Brown, R. (1981). National assessments of writing ability. In C. H. Fredericksen & J. F. Dominic (Eds.), *Writing: The nature, development, and teaching of written communication: Vol. 2. Process, development, and communication* (pp. 31–38). Hillsdale, NJ: Lawrence Erlbaum.

Cartwright, G. P. (1969). Written expression and spelling. In R. M. Smith (Ed.), *Teacher diagnosis of educational difficulties* (pp. 95–117).

Chatterjee, J. B. (1983). A comparative analysis of syntactic density and vocabulary richness in written language of learning-abled and learning-disabled children at third- and fifth-grade levels. *Dissertation Abstracts International, 44,* 2436A. (University Microfilms No. 83–28234)

Chomsky, C. (May, 1976). Approaching reading through invented spelling. Paper presented at the Conference on Theory and Practice of Beginning Reading Instruction, University of Pittsburgh. (ERIC Document Reproduction Service No. ED 155 630).

Connally, K. (1983). Foreword to M. Martlew (Ed.), *The psychology of written language: Developmental and educational perspectives*. Chichester, England: John Wiley & Sons.

Cooper, C. (1973). An outline for writing sentence combining problems. *English Journal, 62,* 96–102, 108.

Cooper, C. (1977). Holistic evaluation of writing. In C. R. Cooper & L. Odell (Eds.), *Evaluating writing: Describing, measuring, judging*. Buffalo, NY: National Council of Teachers of English.

Crealock, C. M., Sitko, M. C., Hutchinson, A., Sitko, C., & Marlett, L. (April, 1985). *Creative writing competency: A comparison of paper and pencil and computer technologies to improve the writing*

skills of mildly handicapped adolescents. Paper presented at Annual Meeting of American Educational Research Association. (ERIC ED 259 531).
Dagenais, D. J., & Beadle, K. R. (1984). Written language: When and where to begin. *Topics in Language Disorders, 4*(2), 59–85.
Daiute, C. A. (1984). Performance limits on writers. In R. Beach & L. S. Bridwell (Eds.), *New directions in composition research* (pp. 205–224). New York: Guilford.
Deno, S., Marston, D., & Mirkin, P. (1982). Valid measurement procedures for continuous evaluation of written expression. *Exceptional Children, 48,* 368–371.
deVilliers, J. G., & de Villiers, P. A. (1978). *Language acquisition*. Cambridge, MA: Harvard University Press.
Doyle, W. (1983). Academic work. *Review of Educational Research, 53,* 159–199.
Dyson, A. H. (1982). Talking with young children writing. *Childhood Education, 59,* 30–35.
Dyson, A. H. (1983). The role of oral language in early writing processes. *Research in the Teaching of English, 17,* 1–30.
Elbow, P. (1981). *Writing with power: Techniques for mastering the writing process*. New York: Oxford University Press.
Emig, J. (1971). *The composing processes of twelfth graders* (Research Report No. 13). Urbana, IL: National Council of Teachers of English.
Englemann, S., & Silbert, (1983). *Teacher presentation book: Expressive writing I*. Tigard, OR: C. C. Publications.
Englert, C. S. (1984). Measuring teacher effectiveness from the teacher's point of view. *Focus on Exceptional Children, 17*(2), 1–14.
Finn, P. A. (1977). Computer-aided description of mature word choices in writing. In C. Cooper & L. Odell (Eds.), *Evaluating writing: Describing, measuring, judging*. Buffalo, NY: National Council of Teachers of English.
Flower, L S., & Hayes, J. R. (1980). The dynamics of composing: Making plans and juggling constraints. In L. W. Gregg & E. R. Steinberg (Eds.), *Cognitive processes in writing* (pp. 31–50). Hillsdale, NJ: Lawrence Erlbaum.
Fontaine, S. I. (1984). *Writing for an audience: How writers at three age levels demonstrate an awareness of the audience and respond with two contrasting audiences*. Unpublished doctoral dissertation, University of California, San Diego.
Giordano, G. (1983). Metagrammars: A technique for disabled writers. *Academic Therapy, 18,* 499–505.
Giordano, G. (1984). *Teaching writing to learning disabled students*. Rockville, MD: Aspen.
Glatthorn, A. A. (1981). *Writing in the schools: Improvement through effective leadership*. Reston, VA: National Association of Secondary School Principals.
Graham, S., & Harris, K. R. (1987). Improving composition skills with self-instructional strategy training. *Topics in Language Disorders, 7*, 66–77.
Graves, D. (1983). *Writing: Teachers and children at work*. Exeter, NH: Heinemann Educational Books.
Harrington-Brogan, V. S. (1983). Instructional writing suggestions in elementary school language arts textbooks: An analysis based upon opinions of writing authorities. *Dissertation Abstracts International, 44,* 1332A–1333A.
Harris. K. R., & Graham, S. (1985). Improving learning disabled students' composition skills: Self-control strategy training. *Learning Disability Quarterly, 8,* 27–36.
Hayes, J. R., & Flower, L. S. (1980). Identifying the organization of writing processes. In L. W. Gregg & E. R. Steinberg (Eds.), *Cognitive processes in writing* (pp. 3–30). Hillsdale, NJ: Lawrence Erlbaum.
Hillocks, G., Jr. (1984). What works in teaching composition: A meta-analysis of experimental treatment studies. *American Journal of Education, 93,* 133–170.
Hughes, T. (1978). *What the British tell the U.S. about writing and reading*. Paper presented at the 3rd Great Lakes Regional Conference of the International Reading Association, Cincinnati, OH (ERIC Document Reproduction Service No. Ed 175 020)
Humes, A. (1983). Research on the composing process. *Review of Educational Research, 53,* 201-216.
Hunt, K. W. (1965). *Grammatical structures at three grade levels* (Research Report No. 3). Urbana, IL: National Council of Teachers of English. (ERIC Document Reproduction Service No. ED 113 735)
Irwin, J. W. (1982). A review of procedures for analyzing coherence in written language samples. *Diagnostique, 8,* 43–51.
Isaacson, S. (1984). Evaluating written expression: Issues of reliability, validity, and instructional utility. *Diagnostique, 9,* 96–116.

Isaacson, S. L. (1985). *Assessing the potential syntax development of third and fourth grade writers.* Unpublished doctoral dissertation, Arizona State University, Tempe.

Lash, H. (1970). *The effect of instruction in transformational grammar on basic writing skills.* Unpublished doctoral dissertation, University of Alabama.

Lawlor, J. (1983). Sentence combining: A sequence for instruction. *Elementary School Journal, 84,* 53–62.

Leinhart, G., Zigmond, N., & Cooley, W. W. (April, 1980). *Reading instruction and its effects.* Paper presented at the annual meeting of the American Educational Research Association, Boston.

Loban, W. (1976). *Language development: Kindergarten through grade twelve* (Research Report No. 18). Urbana, IL: National Council of Teachers of English.

MacArthur, C. A., & Graham, S. (May, 1986). *Learning disabled students' composing with three methods: Handwriting, dictation, and word processing.* Paper presented to the Annual Meeting of the American Educational Research Association, San Francisco.

Marcus, M. (1977). *Diagnostic teaching of the language arts.* New York: John Wiley & Sons.

Martin, N. (1983). Genuine communications. *Topics in Learning & Learning Disabilities, 31,* 1–11.

Mellon, J. (1979). Issues in the theory and practice of sentence combining: A twenty year perspective. In D. A. Daiker, A. Kerek, & M. Morenburg (Eds.), *Sentence combining and the teaching of writing* (pp. 1–38). Akron, OH: L & S Brooks.

Mellon, J. (1981). *Sentence-combining skills: Results of the sentence combining exercises in the 1978–79 National Writing Assessment* (Special Paper No. 10–W–65 prepared for the National Assessment of Educational Progress). (ERIC Document Reproduction Service No. ED 210 696).

Mercer, C. D. & Mercer, A. R. (1985). *Teaching students with learning problems* (2nd ed.). Columbus, OH: Charles E. Merrill.

Minneapolis Public Schools (1977). *SIMS written language program.* Minneapolis: Author.

Moran, M. R., Schumaker, J. B., & Vetter, A. F. (1981). *Teaching a paragraph organization strategy to learning disabled adolescents* (Research Report No. 54). Lawrence: University of Kansas Institute for Research in Learning Disabilities.

Morris, N. T., & Crump, D. T. (1982). Syntactic and vocabulary development in the written language of learning disabled and non-learning disabled students at four age levels. *Learning Disability Quarterly, 5,* 163–172.

Myers, M. (1978). Five approaches to the teaching of writing. *Learning, 6*(8), 38–41.

Myklebust, H. (1965). *Development and disorders of written language: Picture story language test.* New York: Grune & Stratton.

Ney, J. W. (1975). *Linguistics, language teaching, and composition in the grades.* The Hague, Netherlands: Mouton.

Nodine, B. F., Barenbaum, E., & Newcomer, P. (1985). Story composition by learning disabled, reading disabled, and normal children. *Learning Disability Quarterly, 8,* 167–179.

Nold, E. W. (1981). Revising. In C. H. Fredericksen & J. F. Dominic (Eds.), *Writing: The nature, development, and teaching of written communication:* Vol. 2. *Process, development and communication* (pp. 67–79). Hillsdale, NJ: Lawrence Erlbaum.

North, S. (1981). Toward system in a student-centered curriculum. *English Record, 32*(3), 6–10.

Nutter, N., & Safran, J. (1984). Improving writing with sentence combining exercises. *Academic Therapy, 19,* 449–455.

Perl, S. (1983). How teachers teach the writing process: Overview of an ethnographic research project. *Elementary School Journal, 84,* 19–24.

Phelps, T. O. (1986). What will they really write? *English Journal, 75*(3), 81–82.

Phelps-Terasaki, D., & Phelps, T. (1980). *Teaching written expression: The Phelps sentence guide program.* Novato, CA: Academic Therapy Publications.

Phelps-Terasaki, D., Phelps-Gunn, T., & Stetson, E. G. (1983). *Remediation and instruction in language: Oral language, reading, and writing.* Rockville, MD: Aspen.

Poplin, M., Gray, R., Larsen, S., Banikowski, A., & Mehring, T. (1980). A comparison of components of written expression abilities in learning disabled and non-learning disabled children at three grade levels. *Learning Disability Quarterly, 3,* 46–53.

Prince, G. (1973). *A grammar of stories.* The Hague, Netherlands: Mouton.

Robinson, S. F. (1983). *Coherence in student writing.* Unpublished doctoral dissertation, Harvard University, Cambridge, MA. (University Microfilms No. DA 8421221)

Roit, M. L., & McKenzie, R. G. (1985). Disorders of written communication: An instructional priority

for LD students. *Journal of Learning Disabilities, 19,* 258–260.
Rosenshine, B. (1983). Teaching functions in instructional programs. *Elementary School Journal, 83,* 335–351.
Scardamalia, M. (1981). How children cope with the cognitive demands of writing. In C. H. Fredericksen & J. F. Dominic (Eds.), *Writing: The nature, development, and teaching of written communication: Vol. 2. Process, development, and communication* (pp. 81–104). Hillsdale, NJ: Lawrence Erlbaum.
Scardamalia, M., & Bereiter, C. (1983). The development of evaluative, diagnostic, and remedial capabilities in children's composing. In M. Martlew (Ed.), *The psychology of written language: Developmental and educational perspectives* (pp. 67–95). Chichester, England: John Wiley & Sons.
Schumaker, J. B., Deschler, D. D., Alley, G. R., Warner, M. M., & Denton, P. H. (1982). Multipass: A learning strategy for improving reading comprehension. *Learning Disability Quarterly, 5,* 295–304.
Shanahan, T. (1980). The impact of writing instruction on learning to read. *Reading World, 19,* 357–368.
Shanahan, T. (1984). Nature of the reading-writing relation: An exploratory multivariate analysis. *Journal of Educational Psychology, 76,* 466–477.
Shuy, R. W. (1981). Toward a developmental theory of writing. In C. H. Fredericksen & J. F. Dominic (Eds.), *Writing: The nature, development, and teaching of written communication: Vol. 2. Process, development, and communication* (pp. 119–132). Hillsdale, NJ: Lawrence Erlbaum.
Smith, F. (1982). *Writing and the writer.* New York: Holt, Rinehart & Winston.
Stein, N. L. (1983). Methodological and conceptual issues in writing research. *Elementary School Journal, 84,* 100–108.
Stewart, S. R. (1985). Development of written language proficiency: Methods for teaching text structure. In C. S. Simon (Ed.), *Communication skills and classroom success: Therapy methodologies for language-learning disabled students* (pp. 341–364). San Diego: College Hill Press.
Stotsky, S. L. (1975). Sentence-combining as a curricular activity: Its effects on written language development and reading comprehension. *Research in the Teaching of English, 91,* 30–71.
Straw, S. B. (1981). Grammar and teaching of writing: Analysis versus synthesis. In V. Froese & S. B. Straw (Eds.), *Research in the language arts: Language and schooling* (pp. 147–161). Baltimore: University Park Press.
Thomas, C., Englert, C. S., & Morsink, C. (1984). Modifying the classroom program in language. In C. V. Morsink (Ed.), *Teaching special needs students in regular classrooms* (pp. 239–276). Boston: Little, Brown.
U.S. Department of Health, Education and Welfare. (1979) *What do we know about standards for effective skills programs?* Washington, DC: Office of Education, Basic Skills Improvement Program.
Van De Weghe, R. (1978). Research in written composition: Fifteen years of investigation (Research report). Las Cruces: New Mexico State University. (ERIC Document Reproduction Service No. ED 157 095).
Videen, J., Deno, S., & Marston, D. (1982). *Correct word sequences: A valid indicator of proficiency in written expression* (Research Report No. 84). Minneapolis: University of Minnesota, Institute for Research in Learning Disabilities.

Dr. Isaacson is an Assistant Professor in the Department of Special Education, State University of New York at Geneseo.

Educators have wondered about the extent to which achievement and self-concept are interrelated. This article, and the research reported, demonstrate a positive relationship between self-concept and achievement. Pupil scores are likely to be higher if self-concept is measured after achievement rather than visa versa. The relationship seems to be positive under most conditions, but self-concept appears to be fragile. It appears easy to improve achievement and self-concept, but the improvement requires work to maintain. The same type of gains can be obtained by parents, but they are also transitory. Research also indicates that programs emphasizing knowledge and skill acquisition are more successful than programs designed to raise feelings of self-worth. Teachers can readily apply the ideas in this article to improve the self-concept and achievement of disabled learners.

The Relationship Between Pupil Affect and Achievement

Richard J. Whelan, Lupe Mendez de Saman, and Dennis J. Fortmeyer

And so it was written: Achievement precedes adjustment. This simply means that our self-esteem, self-concept, or whatever label we use to describe how we feel about ourselves is a product of how well we succeed in managing tasks that confront us each day. Success results in good feelings about the self. Conversely, failure may result in feelings of worthlessness. But wait—isn't all this really a "chicken and egg" argument that has no beginning and no ending? Isn't it also true that feeling good about oneself promotes successful performances in school and in other environments? Indeed, both views are correct. To feel good inside usually means that outside performance is good. And when outside performance is good, good feelings usually bubble inside.

The relationship between achievement and self-worth is an issue that has confronted educators for years. It probably dates back to the very first time one person attempted to teach a concept, skill, or performance to another person. Of course, the dilemma for teachers resides in the best way to approach the issue. Do we build up pupils' self-worth first and let achievement follow, or do we ensure successful achievement and hope that increased self-worth will result? In the day-to-day practice of instruction, effective teachers do both. They provide and promote opportunities for successful performance, and they also confirm experiences of feeling good about accomplishments.

What exactly are teachers to do? We can measure pupil performance by administering periodic tests. We can ask a school psychologist or school counselor to give a test of self-concept. If our pupils are achieving, they should feel good about themselves. On the other hand, if our pupils aren't doing well, they probably also feel bad inside. If all this information is known, shouldn't we be able to maintain, change, or improve curriculum to better serve our pupils each and every day?

A complicating factor is that some days students feel great to begin with and then really get down as the day goes on. Other days they come to class feeling blue and leave with smiles and feelings of pride. Standardized tests of self-concept and achievement will provide some global scores, but these scores are static. They reflect a pupil's responses on the day and time the tests were administered, so we can't be sure that they really measure the dynamic day-to-day interaction between pupils and teachers on matters of achievement and feeling.

Isn't there another way—one that we can use each day or several times a week—to find out about this most important relationship between feelings and achievement? Yes, teachers, there is, and that is what this article is all about.

BACKGROUND

The relationship between achievement and feelings about the self has been the topic of investigations for many years. In general, feeling good about oneself is believed to lead to acceptable behaviors and adequate academic performance. Conversely, negative feelings about the self predispose a person to behave and perform poorly in school and other environments. If these beliefs are true, it logically follows that students' feelings about the self are closely linked to academic performance in school. Negative feelings will produce poor achievement, and positive feelings will result in satisfactory academic competence. It seems reasonable to conclude, then, that if educators were to focus efforts upon enhancing positive feelings about the self, a change in these feelings should be followed by improved academic performance. So instructing a pupil with the intent of making the self-worth more positive would seem to be an appropriate goal.

The assumption, logical or not, that instruction focused upon improving self-worth will produce higher achievement has been researched extensively. The results of that research are at best mixed. Scheirer and Kraut (1979) conducted an extensive review of previously published research on the issue of improving educational achievement by enhancing feelings of self-worth. In the 1960s researchers found correlations of about .40 between self-concept and achievement; that is, the higher the measure of self-worth, the higher was the measure of achievement. And low self-worth scores were associated with lower achievement scores. As Scheirer and Kraut (1979) pointed out, this research stimulated educators to initiate programs to improve pupils' feelings of self-worth, or self-esteem. In essence, the proposition advanced was that a pupil had to have a positive self-regard in order to perform successfully in school (Rubin, Dorle, & Sandidge, 1977).

The review of past research by Scheirer and Kraut (1979) resulted in several important findings or conclusions:

1. Although an intensive program designed to enhance self-worth can succeed in reaching that end and can produce small achievement gains, the gains in self-worth and achievement do not persist over time.
2. When parents are instructed to use positive communication and supportive statements of children's efforts in school, increases in self-concept and achievement result. But when parent instruction is withdrawn, gains in both variables are not maintained.
   The implication of this finding is that parents reverted to previous styles of relating to their children about their experiences in school. Thus, symbolically meaningful persons can change children's self-worth and, by doing so, increase academic achievement. For the gains to be maintained, though, meaningful persons, such as parents, must be consistent and persistent in their support of children's efforts to do well in school tasks or learning activities.
3. Correlational relationships between self-worth and achievement are influenced by the sequence used to measure both variables. When self-worth measures are obtained *after* measures of achievement, the correlation is higher than when self-worth is measured prior to achievement. This finding supports the contention that self-worth is probably an outcome rather than a producer of achievement.
4. Structured instructional programs that emphasize knowledge and skill acquisition produce greater gains in achievement and self-worth measures than do programs designed to focus efforts upon enhancing self-worth.
5. The basic assumption that enhancing pupils' self-worth will lead to increased academic achievement is not supported. Rather, the research to date backs the position that improved self-worth is a product of increased competence in successfully completing academic tasks.

The research would seem to support the assertion that low self-worth is probably influenced heavily by low academic achievement. This finding is consistent when exceptional and nonexceptional pupils are compared (Reid & Hresko, 1981). And individuals who play a significant role in a pupil's life, specifically parents, can have a positive impact upon children's academic performance in instructional settings (Kroth, Whelan, & Stables, 1970).

The message from this research is reasonably clear. Teachers can have a powerful, positive influence upon pupils' feelings of self-worth about their accomplishments by helping them successfully complete school-related tasks. So apparently achievement *does* precede adjustment. And who can better help pupils achieve than teachers? That is their area of expertise, competence, and professional preparation. Teachers can manipulate the variables that improve achievement. Appropriate instructional planning, acknowledgement of pupil performance, and attention to associated affective factors that influence achievement foster both effective intellectual and emotional responses, the most important aspects in promoting independent functioning by pupils (Fagen, Long, & Stevens, 1975).

PURPOSE AND RATIONALE

A basic purpose of the research reported in this article was to determine if self-reports of feelings regarding performance in academic areas were positively, negatively, or not at all associated with actual performance measures. The approach consisted of daily measurement of achievement on academic tasks and a simple daily measure of a pupil's feelings before and after completing an academic task. The procedure for obtaining information about feelings required little pupil time to complete and little teacher time to score.

Use of the term *associated* requires some additional explanation. Types of associations that could be observed are as follows:

1. No Association: Self-reports of feelings have no relationship to academic scores. Satisfactory academic performance is not predictive of more positive feelings, nor is poor academic performance predictive of negative feelings of self-worth. The association has no pattern. A high academic performance score is just as likely to result in negative feelings as positive feelings.
2. Negative Association: Based upon the reported research, this pattern is not likely to be observed. For a pupil to do well on a task and then report a negative self-evaluation would be unusual. This association *could* occur, however, so teachers should be alert to the possibility. An observed pattern of this type could mean, for example, that a pupil is trying to meet an impossible standard. It could also signal the need for counseling or other forms of intervention.
3. Positive Association: Self-reports of feelings follow the level of academic performance. A good performance results in positive feelings. Conversely, a poor performance results in negative feelings. In brief, if the association is positive, the self-report of feelings and the academic measures tend to rise or fall together.

Although published research data provide strong support for improving pupil self-worth via promoting increased academic accomplishments, the application of this information by classroom teachers is still a complex challenge. Teachers cannot administer numerous standardized and normed tests of achievement and self-worth to determine if their instructional programs are producing desirable results. If they were able to do so, little time would be left to them or their pupils for the business at hand—teaching and learning. Yet, how pupils feel, in terms of self-worth, about what they accomplish is obviously important. Feeling good about one's competence provides a positive set or approach tendency toward accomplishment of future tasks (Whelan, 1977).

Teachers need a procedure by which they can obtain some indication of how their pupils feel about themselves in relation to the pupils' levels of success with academic tasks. They need a procedure that is simple to use, can be administered frequently, will not detract from instructional time, and will yield useful information for future instructional planning and evaluation.

METHOD

Two studies were designed and conducted for the purpose of providing information about the relationship between achievement and self-reports of feelings. The first study was with pupils from the elementary grades. The second study focused upon pupils from the secondary grade levels.

Subjects

Pupils participating in the elementary-grade study were five girls and six boys, a total of 11. Their ages ranged from 7 through 9. Most of the pupils were performing below ability levels but were within the normal range of intelligence. All had displayed behavior problems to the extent that they were placed in a resource room for a portion of their instruction. Instruction in the resource room was individualized to increase the probability that each pupil would be successful in completing daily academic tasks.

The pupils in the secondary-grade study were in a self-contained classroom program. Six pupils, three boys and three girls, participated. Their ages ranged from 13 through 17. All were identified as exhibiting behavior disorders. Each had an individual, daily plan of study designed to promote task completion with acceptable accuracy.

Materials

In both the elementary and secondary studies, the materials used were simple to design and apply. For the elementary study the academic tasks were daily assignments in reading comprehension. For the secondary study daily arithmetic assignments were used. These types of assignments were selected because a pupil's response to the stimuli (i.e., a comprehension question or a problem requiring computation) could be measured and recorded in a reliable manner.

The pupils' self-reports of feelings were marked on circles divided into pie-shaped wedges. Figure 1 depicts the circle chart for the elementary study. It is divided into four wedges or parts. In each part are three faces—one with a smile, one with a frown, and one with a straight line. The pupil recorded a specific feeling in each of the four parts. One wedge was used to record emotional feelings. If a pupil felt really great inside, the smile face was checked; if the pupil felt down, the frown face was checked; if he or she felt somewhere between these extremes, the straight-line face was checked. Another wedge was used to record how the pupil felt physically. A third was used to record feelings about being in the special education resource room. The fourth wedge was used to record and compare feelings about task or work experiences completed, first, in the regular classroom and, second, in the resource room. A large circle chart was mounted on the bulletin board, to explain each wedge, the faces within the wedges, and instructions for marking.

Figure 2 illustrates the circle chart used in the secondary study. It is divided into eight wedges or parts, each with three items representing a range of feelings. Several types of feelings (e.g., emotional, physical, motivation, need for support from others) were included in the chart. This chart was enlarged and placed on the bulletin board, with instructions about how it was to be completed.

Procedures

The procedures used in the elementary and secondary studies were similar but had some variance, mostly in response to the age differences between the two groups. The chart for the elementary pupils had only four wedges, and the choices were among facial expressions representing feelings. The chart for the secondary pupils had eight wedges, with word choices from which the pupils selected and recorded their feelings.

As indicated previously, a large wall chart for each of the two study groups included instructions for completing the individual chart, which was identical to it. Upon coming into the classroom each day, and prior to beginning work in the classroom, the pupils were asked to record their feelings on all of the wedges of their individual chart. After the initial or *pre-charts* were completed, the teacher collected and stored them out of sight. Then the pupils began work on assigned academic tasks.

FIGURE 1 The Elementary Study Chart For Self-Report of Feelings

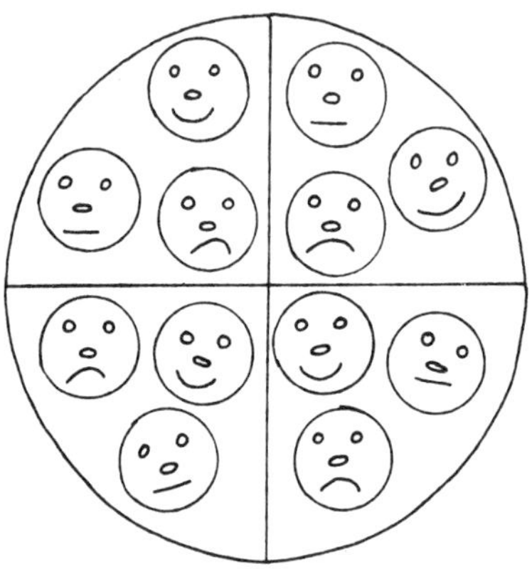

FIGURE 2 The Secondary Study Chart For Self-Report of Feelings

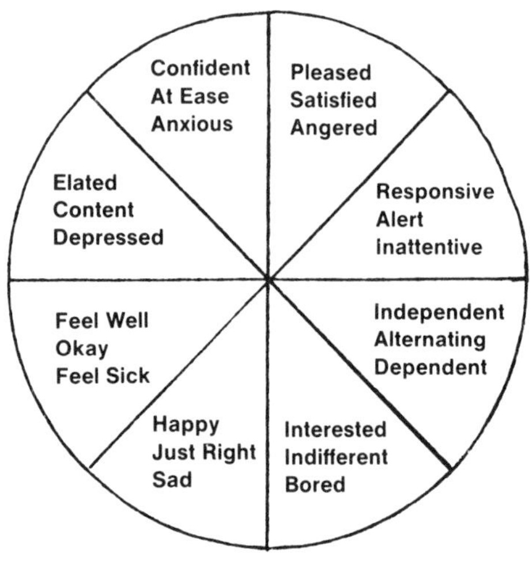

When the pupils signaled completion of the tasks, the teacher evaluated the work, calculated percent-correct scores, and gave these to the pupils—an example of immediate feedback, or immediate knowledge of results. After seeing their individual scores, the pupils completed a second or *post-chart* as a record of their feelings. The teacher collected the post-charts and stored them with the percent-correct scores and pre-charts.

Figure 3 illustrates the pre- and post-procedure used with the elementary group. Pupils selected their pre-charts from a large envelope, labeled *HI!,* on the bulletin board. After finishing a task and getting it graded, each pupil pulled a post-chart from the *BYE!* envelope and made one mark in every wedge. The teacher of the secondary pupils gave a chart to each pupil before the task and another blank form after the task was completed and graded.

RESULTS

The elementary and secondary studies were conducted over a 3-week period, encompassing 15 school days. Variation in the number of days that data were recorded for each pupil reflects absences, for a variety of reasons, from class.

As indicated previously, every pupil completed a chart before and after an academic task or assignment. The marks placed upon the charts became a record or self-report of feelings. For each day, every pupil had a pre- and post-feelings score and a percent-correct score for an academic task. Each smile face carried 3 points, each straight face 2 points, and each frown face 1 point. Thus, if an elementary pupil marked every smile face on his or her chart for the day, the total feelings score was 12; if all the straight faces were marked, the total score was 8; if all the frown faces were marked, the total score was 4. The scores for the elementary group, then, ranged from 4 through 12 per chart. The range in scores for the secondary group was 8 through 24 (because the charts contained eight wedges rather than four).

Data were collected and recorded each day for every pupil. The data on feelings could reflect three possible patterns. For each pattern, there was an associated

FIGURE 3 The Elementary Study Procedure For Pre and Post Self-Report of Feelings

percent-correct score for academic tasks. These examples, including sample scores of observed patterns, are:

1. Pre-feelings low/post-feelings high
   a. Elementary: Pre = 8 and Post = 11
   b. Secondary: Pre = 10 and Post = 16
2. Pre-feelings high/post feelings low
   a. Elementary: Pre = 12 and Post = 6
   b. Secondary: Pre = 20 and Post = 13
3. Pre-feelings tied with post-feelings
   a. Elementary: Pre = 11 and Post = 11
   b. Secondary: Pre = 22 and Post = 22

Obviously, number 3 above could include the full range of score possibilities. A pupil could begin the class feeling good and leave the same way. Or the same pupil could arrive feeling poorly and leave with the same feeling.

The Elementary Study

Table 1 displays data for the 11 pupils who participated in the elementary study. The three observed patterns described previously are listed on the table as column headings. The "Task % Correct" column for each pattern is the most important source of information because it provides a comparison of pupil performance among the patterns. For the pre low/post high pattern, the mean task-percent correct was 90. For the pre high/post low pattern, the mean task-percent correct performance was only 71. And for the pre-post ties pattern, the mean was 85.

TABLE 1
Comparison of the Relationship Between Feelings and Task Achievement: The Elementary Study

	Self-Reports of Feelings Patterns								
	Pre Low/Post High			Pre High/Post Low			Pre-Post Ties		
Pupil	No.	Amount of Increase	Task % Correct	No.	Amount of Decrease	Task % Correct	No.	Variance	Task % Correct
1	7	9	88	1	1	50	7	1	89
2	9	14	84	4	10	73	2	0	91
3	8	12	80	1	2	74	6	2	75
4	13	23	96	1	1	90	1	0	80
5	6	6	88	5	6	81	4	2	87
6	1	1	87	2	3	50	12	0	95
7	4	11	87	2	2	97	8	0	83
8	-	-	-	2	2	45	13	1	83
9	4	9	97	6	10	61	5	3	72
10	1	1	100	-	-	-	14	0	89
11	9	9	94	2	4	88	4	1	95
Total	62	95	901	26	41	709	76	10	939
Mean	6	10	90	3	4	71	7	1	85

Table 1 requires additional explanation. The "No." columns indicate the number of times the pattern was observed for each pupils. Columns labeled "Amount of Increase" and "Amount of Decrease" show the total point differences for the number of observed patterns. For examples, pupil 1 had seven pre low/post high patterns, and a 9-point increase from pre to post over the seven occurrences. The "Variance" column under the "Pre-Post Ties" pattern indicates the range of differences. For instance, pupil 9 showed a range of ties from 9 through 12. When a column does not indicate a number or task percent-correct score, as for pupils 8 and 10, this simply means that the pattern of feelings indicated in the column was not observed. Pupil 8, for instance, did not have any pre low/post high patterns.

In every instance except pupil 7, each pupil's task percent-correct score in the pre low/post high pattern exceeded the score in the pre high/post low pattern. A comparison of the "Pre Low/Post High" and "Pre-Post Ties" columns reveals that of 10 possible independent chances, the pre low-post high scores were higher in seven instances. And in eight of 10 instances, the "Pre-Post Ties" column percent-correct scores were higher than the pre high/post low scores.

The task percent-correct scores in Table 1 were analyzed using the *Friedman Two-Way Analysis of Variance* (Siegel, 1956). Vacant cells for pupils 8 and 10 were assigned a task percent-correct value equal to the mean of the other cells in the columns in order to have a score in each cell (Winer, 1971). The x_r^2 equaled 9, a value that is significant ($p < .02$); that is, the observed results would occur by chance only 2 times in 100 independent observations. However, the statistical analysis only confirms what can be observed in Table 1. The scores for the pre low/post high were significantly higher than for the pre high/post low pattern.

From the results, it is clear that when pupils in the elementary study did well in their assigned academic tasks, their feelings were affected in a positive manner, and when the pupils performed poorly on academic tasks, their feelings scores were in a negative direction. Stated another way, our feelings appear to result from or are the product of our experiences—in this case, achievement scores on academic tasks.

The Secondary Study

Table 2 provides a summary of the data for the secondary pupils. Similar to the elementary study, the task percent-correct average score for the pre low/post high pattern (92) exceeded the task percent-correct mean score for the pre high/post low pattern (84). In every instance the pupils in the pre low/post high pattern had higher scores than in the pre high/post low pattern.

Unlike the elementary group, however, the secondary pupils had a higher task percent-correct mean score, by one point, for the pre-post ties pattern than for the pre low/post high pattern. (This finding is elaborated upon in the next section.)

Task percent-correct scores were analyzed by the *Friedman Two-Way Analysis of Variance* (Siegel, 1956). The obtained x_r^2 was 9, which was significant ($p < .01$). Again, the statistical analysis confirms that under the pre low/post high pattern, pupils performed significantly better than they did under the pre high/post low pattern.

TABLE 2
Comparison of the Relationship Between Feelings and Task Achievement: The Secondary Study

	Self-Reports of Feelings Patterns								
	Pre Low/Post High			Pre High/Post Low			Pre-Post Ties		
Pupil	No.	Amount of Increase	Task % Correct	No.	Amount of Decrease	Task % Correct	No.	Variance	Task % Correct
1	6	9	91	3	6	79	6	7	90
2	8	45	86	5	18	72	2	3	94
3	2	2	94	2	2	92	5	3	97
4	2	2	90	4	8	79	6	7	91
5	3	13	93	4	7	86	3	2	94
6	9	16	95	3	6	93	3	6	93
Total	30	87	549	21	47	501	25	28	559
Mean	5	15	92	4	8	84	4	5	93

Internal feelings of worth for the secondary level pupils were affected by how successfully they performed tasks. When the performance was good, positive feelings resulted. When it did not meet individual expectations, the reported feelings were negative.

DISCUSSION

The obtained results from this study support the position that a relationship exists between how one performs and how one feels about that performance. Indeed, a strong case can be made for the statement that achievement precedes adjustment. It should be discerned that teachers—acknowledged experts in instruction—can influence a pupil's internal feelings, often referred to as self-concept or self-worth. That influence, of course, is a function of assisting a pupil to perform successfully in school-related tasks.

Another important finding is that the elusive, global variable called self-worth may be a collection of many, many experiences. The day-to-day experiences and interactions in school settings probably summate to a general, internal assessment of one's competence in relation to self and others' expectations. If pupils experience a preponderance of daily successes, these successes will likely be reflected by a generally positive self-concept. Conversely, of course, lack of achievement (failure) can produce a poor self-concept. Teachers, then, have unique yet important responsibilities to ensure that pupils do acquire success patterns of performance rather than orientations to failure.

Several additional comments will further explain the data in the tables. In Table 1, pupil 7 had a higher task percent-correct score on the pre high/post low patterns than on the other two patterns. This pupil was the only exception to the overall findings of the elementary and secondary studies. But inspection of this pupil's daily scores yields some possible explanations. First, this pupil had only two instances of the "No." pre high/post low pattern. The pre feelings scores were 11 and 12, the post scores were 10 and 11, and the academic scores were 100% and 93%. It seems that this pupil came to class feeling good, did well on tasks, and left feeling good, too. Perhaps the one-point drop in self-reports of feelings for each instance was simply due to random error. For the pre low/post high pattern, the pupil task percent-correct average would have been 91 except for one day of 75%. A notation in the teacher's record book indicated that a new lesson was introduced that day. Possibly the pupil believed that since the task was difficult and new, a task percent-correct of 75 was quite satisfactory and, therefore, felt quite good about it.

The "Pre-Post Ties" columns of Tables 1 and 2 also require additional explanation. For the elementary group (Table 1), the task percent-correct mean was 85, 5 points below the mean of the pre low/post high pattern. A pattern of ties between pre and post feelings can reflect considerable variance. For example, a pupil who enters class feeling good and does well may leave class at the same feelings level. The same relationship holds for pupils who come to class feeling down; if they do poorly on academic tasks, they probably leave with negative feelings. Task percent-correct scores for the elementary group ranged from 50% through 100%. The mean of 85 simply is a reflection that most pupils came in feeling fine, did fine, and left feeling fine.

For the secondary study (Table 2), the average task percent-correct score for the pre-post ties pattern was 93, one point better than the pre low/post high pattern mean of 92. This group of pupils had a great many days of coming to class feeling good, doing well in academics, and leaving with good feelings.

The data described in this article provide additional support for the position that feelings about one's behavior (hence, oneself) tend to follow performance. On the other hand, a history of mostly successful day-to-day functioning builds up confidence. A confident pupil approaches difficult tasks instead of avoiding them. Avoiding difficult tasks is a product of numerous failures to respond successfully to expectations. Approaching difficult tasks is a product of numerous successes.

IMPLICATIONS FOR TEACHING

One criticism often directed at teachers is that they are too oriented toward academics; they simply don't care about the emotional or inner life of pupils. Frankly, that criticism is not valid. Sure, teachers care about academics. Their job is to help pupils grow and progress in the knowledge and skills required of productive citizens. But teachers also care about feelings. Humans do not thrive by production alone. They may exist, but positive feelings of self-worth are necessary for thriving. Feelings, though, are intangible. They are difficult to grasp, manipulate, change, and measure—not at all like dealing with arithmetic instruction. As a result, teachers probably do not devote much time to helping pupils reach an understanding and appreciation of the role that feelings play in the development of a mentally healthy, competent human being. Teachers are aware that a positive self-concept is important but are unsure how to go about enhancing that elusive aspect of the human gestalt.

Teachers can use the simple technology described in this article to plan and evaluate instruction and to determine how pupils feel in relationship to it. Academic performance and feelings act as partners to enhance pupil growth and progress in cognitive and affective domains. Frequent measures of achievement and feelings can provide important feedback to teachers and pupils. For example, if pre high/post low feelings patterns and low task percent-correct performance scores become frequent, that is a signal to modify instructional planning. Perhaps a simple modification in instructional content or mode of presentation can be enough to reverse the pattern.

Relating feelings to and with achievement also provides opportunities to teach pupils that a few instances of low academic performance may make them feel badly for a brief time but that the condition is not permanent. By working together, pupils and teachers can turn failure patterns into success patterns and, by doing that, both achievement and self-concept will be strengthened.

So, teachers, and as promised, this article shows a way to deal with the relationship between feelings and achievement. The procedures described here do not offer any magic. They do, however, offer a way to help pupils—and teachers—deal with their ups and downs in a productive manner. Go ahead and try the procedures. We all may find that those feelings are indeed wonderful!

REFERENCES

Fagen, S. A., Long, N. J., & Stevens, D. J. *Teaching children self-control*. Columbus, OH: Charles E. Merrill Publishing Co., 1975.

Kroth, R. L., Whelan, R. J., & Stables, J. M. Teacher application of behavior principles in home and classroom environments. *Focus on Exceptional Children*, 1970, *2*(3), 1–10.

Reid, D. K., & Hresko, W. P. *A cognitive approach to learning disabilities*. New York: McGraw-Hill, 1981.

Rubin, R. A., Dorle, J., & Sandidge, S. Self-esteem and school performance. *Psychology in the Schools*, 1977, *14*, 503–507.

Scheirer, M. A., & Kraut, R. E. Increasing educational achievement via self-concept change. *Review of Educational Research*, 1979, *49*(1), 131–149.

Siegel, S. *Nonparametric statistics for the behavioral sciences*. New York: McGraw-Hill, 1956.

Whelan, R. J. Human understanding of human behavior. in A. J. Pappanikou & J. L. Paul (Eds.), *Mainstreaming emotionally disturbed children*. Syracuse, NY: Syracuse University Press, 1977, pp. 64–79.

Winer, B. J. *Statistical principles in experimental design* (2nd ed.). New York: McGraw-Hill, 1971.

Richard Whelan is Chairperson, Department of Special Education, University of Kansas; Lupe Mendez de Saman is affiliated with the North American School, Edo, Zulia, Venezuela; and Dennis Fortmeyer is with the Doniphan Country Education Cooperative, Bendina, Kansas.

With so much of the instruction of mildly handicapped students being accomplished in regular classes, the resource teacher must develop children's own management and teaching strategies that will allow them to survive and will enable instruction outside the regular class to be effective. The authors describe a program of responsibilities or tasks for the student and the teacher to use. Teacher tasks involve organization of materials, optimal work area, time constraints, and task transitions. Student task responsibilities are following directions, approaching tasks, obtaining assistance, giving feedback, and gaining reinforcement. If these areas of responsibility are developed by students and teachers, students should be more effective.

Teaching Children to be Independent Learners: A Step-by-Step Strategy

Sandra Cohen and Laurie de Bettencourt

The introduction and maintenance of mildly handicapped children in regular classrooms has pointed up the need for special education resource teachers to reconsider classroom management and teaching strategies. One aim of this article is to isolate and evaluate procedures that enable regular education teachers to provide the greatest amount of personalized attention to the greatest number of students. Considering the limitations of large regular class sizes, increasing curriculum scope, complex support service schedules, and specified academic programs, individualized teaching is no easy matter today.

The heterogeneity of today's classroom can result in an extremely frustrating situation for the classroom teacher who sincerely wants to help children function at their own level and pace. Common statements among teachers working in mainstreamed settings include:

—I need more time—The time passes by so quickly.
—I have added responsibility toward just one student, and that may take time (instruction) from others.
—Too much attention is given to the handicapped child at the expense of others.
—I now need to adjust strategies to meet each child's needs.
—I'm not trained to teach handicapped children or to deal with such a range of problems. (Schwartz, Schwartz & Cohen, 1979)

A thread that seems to run through these concerns is: "How can the teacher give each child the attention needed within a day's time limit?" In many cases, classroom teachers are turning to special educators for approaches that will allow them to resolve this problem. Resource teachers are beginning to help classroom teachers understand that the answer to this dilemma is in the management of individual students' behaviors—resulting in their becoming independent learners. The special educator should be able to instruct the classroom teacher in specific procedures that will enable all children, including slow learners, to work independently.

The special educator, in serving classroom teachers who are involved in mainstreaming, should provide consultative services including: (a) feedback on student progress, (b) information related to teaching skill development, (c) support for personal efforts, and (d) assistance in program development and documentation. Within the last category a wide range of services can be established, but the emphasis should be on creating organizational and programmatic components that will allow problem learners to fit within the functioning sphere of the regular classroom routine. A graphic illustration of this concept, given in Figure 1, depicts the ultimate goal of consultation: to include mildly handicapped learners within the regular classroom.

Children who are able to work without continuous supervision allow the teacher to spend time in more direct instruction. Becker and Carnine (1981) compared several instructional programs and found that students involved in direct instruction programs made the most overall academic gains. The direct instruction approach is built on the behavioral model of teaching, in which students are taught to work independently, allowing the teacher to spend more time on small group instruction. This arrangement enables a teacher to work with groups of children in initial skill training, to provide remedial assistance, and to facilitate learning programs while the individual child pursues his/her own assignments. Embedded within this structure are procedures to facilitate learning at various achievement levels.

FIGURE 1 Regular Classroom Inclusion Sphere

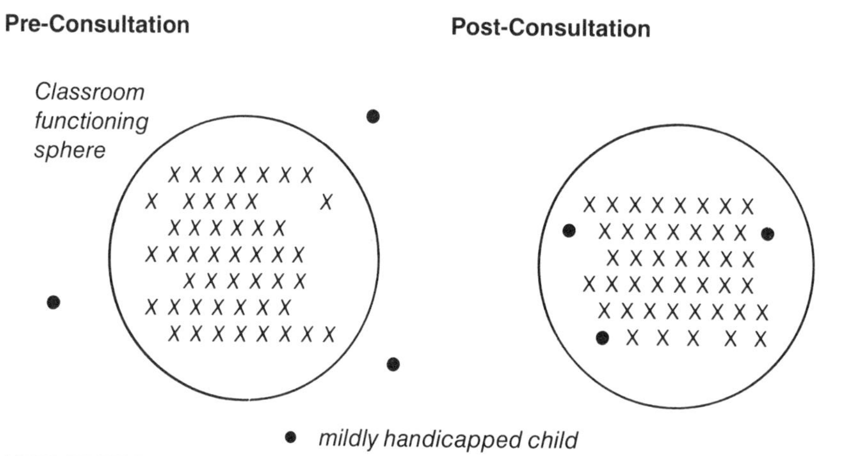

To reach the objective of managing a range of ability levels and to enable each child to function for specified time periods without direct teacher attention, a systematic approach toward developing independent learners is necessary. Independent learners reap the benefits of using time productively, developing a better self-image through personal management, and establishing learning strategies that will be helpful throughout school. Independent learning skills are not child-specific; they are not possessed only by children of certain personality traits, backgrounds, or intellectual levels. All children can be taught to work independently through a step-by-step strategy.

A MODEL FOR STUDENT AND TEACHER RESPONSIBILITIES

To establish an effective program, two sets of responsibilities must be considered: student task responsibilities and teacher task responsibilities. The two units of task responsibilities are interdependent and should develop concurrently. The teacher's segment creates the framework within which the student carries out the specific components leading to independent task completion.

1. *Student task responsibilities*
   a. Following directions
   b. Approaching tasks
   c. Obtaining assistance
   d. Gaining feedback
   e. Gaining reinforcement
2. *Teacher task responsibilities*
   a. Materials organization
   b. Work areas
   c. Time constraints
   d. Task transitions

Student Responsibilities

Following Directions

For the majority of independent learning activities, the child is expected to follow written directions—a complicated task for the youngster with reading difficulties. The most commonly used instructions incorporate approximately 15 key words or phrases. These appear over and over again in a wide variety of assignments, and a child's failure to decode them often underlies incompletely or inaccurately done tasks. Each of these terms and a simple rebus code are provided in Figure 2.

The direction words and their associated picture stimuli should be clearly posted in the room for quick reference whenever necessary. Other significant words may be added to the list whenever appropriate for class activities. The procedure specified for instruction would remain the same no matter what words were substituted. Through

FIGURE 2 Examples of Direction Words and Associated Pictures

	Direction Word	Picture Stimulus
1.	circle	
2.	cross out	
3.	book	
4.	read	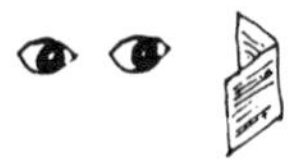
5.	page	
6.	cut	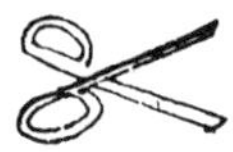
7.	color	
8.	look (at; over)	
9.	listen	
10.	underline	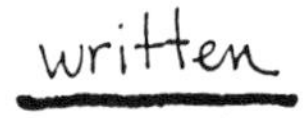
11.	do	
12.	write	
13.	think	
14.	tape (record)	
15.	remember	

this strategy the child learns to respond to a specific picture stimulus and to carry out the simplified directions.

The next step is to transfer the child's attention from the picture to the actual direction word. This is done through the systematic fading procedure given in Figure 3. The picture stimulus is gradually transferred to the word so the child can successfully read the printed direction. The directions should be kept simple until the child has mastered the basic elements.

Attention must also be given to adjusting commercially made materials so problem readers can follow the directions. By adapting materials, the teacher expands the range of consumers, individualizes instruction, and trains students to work more independently. Some suggestions for adapting commercial materials are:

1. *Use picture directions.* Teach key words in directions using rebus symbols until the child is able to follow these directions independently. Then gradually fade the pictures into actual word directions.
2. *Use a tape recorder.* Record directions on tape. The student can replay the tape to comprehend difficult directions.
3. *Simplify written directions.* Highlight or underline significant parts of the directions. Or rewrite the directions to include only the significant parts, expressed in a simpler form.
4. *Reduce extraneous stimuli.* Use line markers or page covers to block out unnecessary parts of the direction statement. This helps the child focus upon the essential components of the direction.
5. *Vary response forms.* Change a response mode that is difficult for a particular learner. For instance, ask a child who has trouble with handwriting to circle or underline to indicate the response.
6. *Clarify directions.* Following a directional sequence can be a problem for some learners.
   a. Have the child repeat the directions to check for understanding.
   b. Paraphrase the directions and provide an appropriate example.
   c. Repeat the directions while the child is working on an example.

Adhering to the simple rules listed below will allow the student to develop a more accurate expectation of the task:

1. Keep directions short.
2. Present directions clearly.
3. Highlight relevant information.
4. Specify what to do when finished.
5. Specify time limit.

Approaching Task

Often a student can perform a task but does not approach the task systematically, resulting in time lost while getting started on each assignment. If the teacher is working with a small group in another section of the room, it is distracting and time con-

FIGURE 3 Systematic Fading Procedure
Direction Word Teaching Sequence

Step 1: Introduce 2-4 oral word direction words and their picture stimuli (rebus) at a time.
Step 2: Practice rebus directions until the child is able to use them correctly in 10 successive trials.
Step 3: Use rebus symbol to give directions on student assignments.
Step 4: Associate rebus and written direction word in practice list.
Step 5: Associate rebus directions and written directions on assignments.
Step 6: Fade rebus while highlighting the written word direction.
Step 7: Present written directions but allow the child to find uncertain words on class rebus poster, if necessary.

Sample Step Fading Procedure

Step 1: Look

Step 2: Teacher: This word is (○) circle.
What is this word? (point to ○).
Class: Circle.
Teacher: Good—circle.
Again (point to ○).
Class: Circle.
Teacher: Yes.
Here are two words: △ ○
Teacher: Show me circle.
Class: (Points to circle.)
Repeat varying stimuli until class (child) can identify circle 10 times out of 10.

Step 3: ○ A words
Circle A words

Step 4: *Rebus* *Word*
○ .... circle
Teacher: Class, what is this word? (point to the word *circle*).
Class: Circle.
Teacher: Yes, this word is *circle*.

Step 5: p. 6+
Read page 6 and listen to tape.
○ words
Circle the words you hear on the tape in the book.
p. 6+
Read page 6 and listen to the tape.
○ words
Circle the words you hear on the tape.

---

suming to constantly cue a student for each response. Teaching the child a systematic task approach can be accomplished using a step-by-step sequence that helps the child structure behavior. The procedure consists of asking oneself a series of questions listed on a Job Card. Figure 4 gives an example. Before beginning a task, the independent worker figures out what has to be done to complete the task, where the necessary materials are, the appropriate place to do the assignment, how much time is available for the activity, and what should be done after completing the assignment.

Success in teaching the student to approach a task independently requires initial teacher time and consistent teacher behavior. Children who have always depended on teachers to lead them through the day will continue to solicit unnecessary assistance and will be reluctant to change old habits. Independent work skills have to be consistently reinforced.

In some cases getting together the necessary materials to begin a task is not the problem, but deciding what to do to perform the task independently and correctly is a problem. Strategy training procedures are designed to help students approach or attack school learning tasks in systematic ways (Lloyd, 1980). In strategy training students are taught to use simple, direct systems for approaching different tasks. Generally, a strategy training approach to instruction includes four steps:

1. Define a group of related problems that you want the student to be able to solve.
2. Identify a step-by-step procedure (strategy) for solving the problems.
3. Specify the skills required by each of the steps in the strategy.
4. Assess the student's performance in each of the component skills, and separately teach component skills not mastered.

The exact nature of the strategy will depend on the attributes of the learning task.

Strategy training has been found to be an effective means of teaching essential academic skills and an effective means of building independent skills in students (Carnine, Prill, & Armstrong, 1978; Kameenui, Carnine, & Maggs, 1980; Lloyd, Saltzman, & Kauffman, 1981). To employ strategy training procedures in your classroom requires extra initial time in setting up the tasks, but it will save a great deal of time over the long term.

FIGURE 4 Job Card

DO I KNOW THESE THINGS?

__________ 1. What do I need?
__________ 2. Where is it?
__________ 3. Where should I work?
__________ 4. How much time do I have?
__________ 5. What do I do with my work and myself when I'm done?

Obtaining Assistance

Before the student can work independently, a support system must be developed to provide assistance and prevent or reduce frustration. The assistance component is of primary importance during the initial independent learning period when a new skill is being introduced and practiced.

Situations in which children may need assistance are:

—assistance in decoding a word.
—explanation of an uncertain concept.
—clarification of a response that differs from the provided answer key, and stimulus cues or prompts.
—reminder of appropriate problem strategy.

The student could select from several alternative approaches to gain assistance when a task problem arises. One procedure is to sign up for a *teacher-pupil conference*. Figure 5 shows a sample sign-up sheet. This is most successful when the child does not need immediate help. For example, if the child has checked his or her responses using a self-correction device and is somewhat confused in applying a concept (e.g., regrouping), the teacher-pupil conference offers time for further one-to-one teaching of the concept. Using this approach, assistance is aimed at eliminating confusion and preventing future failure.

Another alternative, one that can provide more immediate help for preventing frustration as the task continues, is *peer tutoring*. In this approach the child consults with another pupil who has previously mastered the skill or concept. When using peer tutors, the teacher must assume responsibility for the instructional plan. The teacher determines the skills to be reviewed, the materials to be used, and the instructional

FIGURE 5 Conference Sign-Up Sheet

NEED HELP??? — GET ASSISTANCE!!!

Date	Time	Student
11/2	9:30 - 9:45	Julie J.
	9:45 - 10:00	Robin S.
	10:45 - 11:00	Danny Court
	12:15 - 12:30	Patrick C.
	12:30 - 12:45	
	2:00 - 2:15	

activity to be employed. The teacher must also have a system for monitoring its progress so that problems can be swiftly identified and solved (Gerber & Kauffman, 1981).

Some guidelines for the use of peer tutoring are outlined below.

1. Create the proper mental set: "Everyone needs help sometime." This will reduce competition (peer tutoring is a support program, not a competitive sport).
2. Work out procedural details such as:
   —time periods.
   —specific assignments.
   —tutoring dyads that last one to two weeks so that pairs do not become too entrenched in their roles.
   —never having tutors administer real tests.
   —starting off slowly.
   —planning so that everyone can be a tutor at some time.
   —carefully selecting tutoring pairs (don't put best friends or worst enemies together).
   —training tutors to use reinforcement and to provide feedback.
   —informing parents of program development.
3. Organize by:
   —giving clear directions to each tutor.
   —establishing rules to be followed by each participant.
   —presenting planned activities for the tutoring sessions.

Still another approach that allows the independent learner to gain assistance is for the teacher to provide *materials* that *cue a correct response* when the child is uncertain. An example would be a number triangle, as show in Figure 6, for children who are learning simple computation, or a material that cues left and right sides of the room for children who are learning directionality.

The *cloze procedure,* when applied to instruction rather than diagnosis, is another technique that can aid the problem learner in selecting an appropriate response. Some examples are:

> The boy wanted __________ mother to come home early.
> When are you ____________ your report?
> (writing, righting)
> The bl __________ is very big.

Prompts provided within the learning material can be removed gradually as the problem learner gains competency in the skill.

Gaining Feedback

Children who work independently on completing a task should have a means to check their work. Immediate feedback has the advantage of providing opportunities for self-correction. Research (e.g., Graham & Miller, 1979) has shown that structured

FIGURE 6 Addition and Subtraction Number Triangle

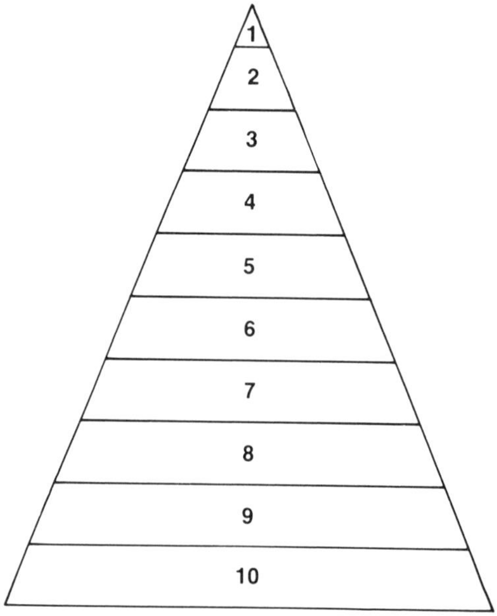

When adding two digits, the student puts a marker under the smaller digit and moves down the same number of spaces as the second addend. For subtraction, the student places the marker under the larger number and moves up the number of spaces designated by the smaller digit. This device is similar to the number line, but it has the added advantages of showing size relationships and providing an alternative for children who have had trouble with traditional number lines.

self-correction is an extremely important factor in learning rote memory tasks. Feedback can be gained independently through self-checking materials.

To the extent that material provides instruction and allows the child to determine correct versus incorrect responses, it can be considered a teacher substitute. Mercer and Mercer (1978) have suggested that feedback devices:

—Provide immediate response confirmation.
—Reduce failure experiences by reducing the chance of incorrect response practice.
—Maintain the child's attention to the task longer.

A brief listing of self-correcting techniques is provided below:

Flash cards. A problem is presented on one side of a stimulus card, and the answer is placed on the other side.

Matching picture cards. Sets of cards are prepared with the problem on one card and the answer on another card. The back of the set of cards contains a picture. When the student chooses an answer, he or she turns over the cards. If the appropriate answer is chosen, the pictures on the back of the cards fit together to complete a scene.

Puzzle. Pieces of material fit together to indicate a match or correct answer. The top or side of each puzzle shows an object or problem, and the bottom or the other side provides the name of the object or the answer to the problem. The sections will interlock only if they belong together.

Pockets. Pockets may be made easily of envelopes stapled to the back of the learning material (e.g., game board). Pockets may hold the answer key or may be coded to provide feedback.

Cards with holes. Problems are written on one side of a card or sheet, and a hole is punched beside or underneath each item. The answer to each problem is written on the back of the card next to or under the hole. Students may use this learning material in pairs. The student who supplies the answer sticks a pencil through the hole, and the other student checks to see if it corresponds with the correct answer.

Flap. A flap may be made of paper or other material and affixed to the page or sheet. The student can check his or her response by lifting the flap to reveal the answer.

Windows. Small squares may be cut in materials, leaving one side uncut so the window may be open or closed. The correct answer appears in the open window.

Overlays. The correct response is clearly marked on a transparency. The child places the transparency on top of his or her work to check the answer. This is especially use for written letter forms, designs such as dot-to-dot puzzles, and structured worksheets with specific spaces for answers.

Answer tapes. The child listens to a cassette or Language Master tape with the correct answers while checking his or her own answers on paper. This is a good means of providing an alternative mode of input.

The often heard criticism of using self-correcting materials is that, contrary to becoming independent learners, children begin to rely on the answers and do not progress in achievement. This is a strong allegation but not necessarily well-founded. Self-correcting material as a means of providing corrective feedback has been documented recurrently as an effective procedure (Kazdin, 1980).

In most cases, children use answer sheets and other correction devices in much the same way adults use dictionaries to confirm spellings of uncertain words. Finding the correct answer when it is unknown or checking accuracy is an intelligent learning procedure, especially for *initial* skill learning and during early *practice*.

The teacher should be alert, however, to children who seem uncertain of their ability over an extended period of time and confirm each response before going on to the next problem. Perhaps the material is too difficult and the teacher should check the child's prerequisite skill level. If this seems to be clearly established, the child should be taught the skill under a different approach. Other children who seem overly reliant upon the checking procedure may need only to gain confidence in themselves. Many mildly handicapped children are so doubtful about their learning ability that they may erase or cross out a spelling word many times, trying a variety of letter patterns and being confident in none.

Gaining Reinforcement

Upon completing the assigned task, the independent learner should receive reinforcement that does not require direct teacher interaction. Like the other steps in the independent learning sequence, reinforcement should be predetermined and child-initiated. All reinforcement should be based upon an acceptable reinforcement *menu*—a list of appropriate reinforcements created by the teacher with student input—and should be accessible to the student upon completion of the task. If reinforcement is part of a task routine (e.g., a math worksheet), the learner must understand the reinforcement format (e.g., progress graph) before beginning the task.

A student who has progressed to administering self-reinforcement evidences a level of self-evaluation, motivation, and confidence. In the end, the self-reinforcer is able to instigate and sustain task orientation and to achieve great satisfaction.

A variety of alternative reinforcement systems can be instituted at the culmination of student-directed assignments. A few of the possibilities for student reinforcement are:

—using tokens governed by specific rules for dissemination (see Sulzar-Azaroff & Mayer, 1977).
—charting a progress graph (see Lloyd & deBettencourt, 1982).
—plotting a student profile (see White & Liberty, 1976).
—initiating instructional contract rewards (e.g., free time).

Summary of Student Task Responsibilities

Frequently, students are unable to initiate even the simplest beginning steps of a task; or they begin a task appropriately but do not persist long enough to complete assignments. These students need to become independent workers capable of self-monitoring behavior. By learning to monitor behavior, students will remain on-task and, thus, will improve their attending skills. A summary of steps for training independent work skills is given below.

1. Create a specific time for training.
2. Set aside two blocks of time, 30 minutes each.
3. Provide a folder of seatwork that can be completed with 100% accuracy. (Initially the focus is on teaching students to work independently, not teaching the students new academic skills.)
4. Explain to the students what "working hard" means.
5. Post five or six class rules as a reminder of how a student works hard (e.g., starting work right away, minding your own business, keeping at work, raising your hand if you have a question).
6. Model what a good worker should do.
7. Differentially reinforce the desired behavior.
8. Gradually increase the amount of time the children are expected to work independently without pause.

9. Initially break the 30-minute time period into smaller segments that vary in length (e.g., Session 1: 3 min., 5 min., 7 min., 4 min., 6 min., 5 min.).
10. Set a timer for the first small segment, and have the children begin their work.

The first step in training independent work habits and self-monitoring of these habits is to set aside a specific time for skill development. The most ideal time is early in the day, as this will eventually be the time when teachers most often want students to work independently. An estimated time frame of approximately 30 minutes is appropriate.

The teacher must establish what is meant by "working hard" in the classroom. This can be done by explaining it verbally while modeling the behaviors for the students. Behaviors that indicate "working hard" may include *starting work* and *eyes on your own desk*.

In training the student to attend to independent tasks, the desired independent work habits must be reinforced. At first this should be on a continuous schedule, and then intermittently.

Teacher Task Responsibilities

The teacher must create the framework within which the student carries out the independent learning task. In doing this, the teacher focuses upon establishing the appropriate structured environment and training and supervising the independent learner. Structuring features to be considered include: designation of materials and their location; optimal work space; time constraints; and task transitions from one activity to the next. Preparation of the classroom environment and materials may at first seem time-consuming and tedious but, once again, the initial time investment is small in comparison to the time saved in direct teacher attention.

Materials Organization

Each learning activity or task should be clearly labeled so that the child knows exactly what materials are needed to successfully complete it. This eliminates unnecessary teacher interruptions and student talk. Less time is needed to complete tasks if all the materials required have been located before attempting to begin the work.

Teacher-made activity cards or spirit duplicating masters can be permanently marked to specify the necessary materials. Figure 7 shows this. Likewise, commercially obtained materials can be easily adapted by systematically adding a "Materials Needed" section to each kit or component. Duplicate lists of commonly used materials can be cut and clipped to various worksheets, learning activity cards, or student contracts. By circling the needed materials for each activity, the master list eliminates the repetitive labeling of similar materials.

crayon	counting sticks	paper
scissors	glue	markers
pencil	dice	dot board
	spinner	worksheet no. ______

FIGURE 7 Sample Marking of Worksheets

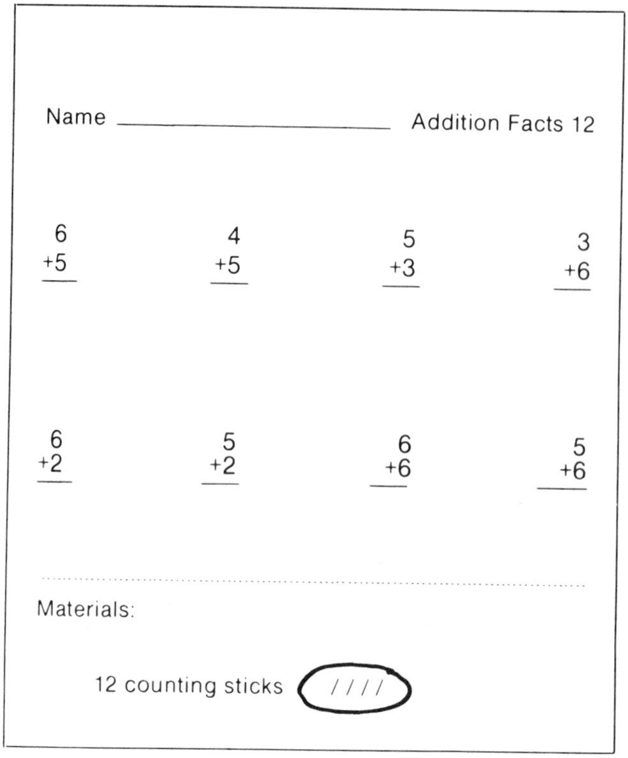
Name ______________ Addition Facts 12

6 +5	4 +5	5 +3	3 +6
6 +2	5 +2	6 +6	5 +6

Materials:

12 counting sticks ////

Materials needed to complete independent tasks can be made easily accessible by devising a system for coding and grouping materials in the classroom. Here are some ideas:

1. Use a small file box to categorize all classroom materials. This serves as the master file, with each card specifying a material, the objectives, the approximate level, and possible adaptations.
2. Develop a material code to specify the type of activity. For example: ▲ Workbook; ● spirit duplicating sheet; ★ group name; and ■ tape. Label each material with the appropriate code.
3. Divide materials according to levels, and assign the level number along with the material code. Example: ● ***4*** (ditto, level 4).
4. Organize materials in separate locations for various skill areas (e.g. math, spelling). This also may be done by color coding different subjects.
5. Use the codings and material labels to assign work tasks. A student needing to do a reading cassette tape might be given an assignment sheet with a red (for reading) ■ 6.2 (tape) and ● 6.3 (supplemental ditto).

Children cannot be expected to work independently if they have to depend on teacher assistance before getting started on a task. Books about learning centers are excellent sources for ideas or techniques for logically arranging materials for easy accessibility.

Work Areas

For almost every learning activity there is an optimal place in the classroom for each child to accomplish the task. In most instances, children can make the choice based on their own experiences or on classroom rules. An activity that requires a tape player, for example, may be limited to an area in the classroom where this can be set up and used without distraction. Other activities may require a large table where construction paper, glue, and scissors are kept and work space is ample. Independent reading or writing tasks may suggest the use of a carrel or desk set apart from the other students. Movable shelves or bookcases are sometimes used to separate work spaces from the main area of instruction. Children's expressed preferences for a work area may also include working on the floor in a carpeted area, leaning against a wall, writing their responses on the chalkboard rather than a worksheet, and opting to work in the library or other school designated space.

Classroom rules that the class has agreed upon may limit the choices of where children can work. For example, if the class has agreed that all cutting and pasting is to be done only at a certain table, the best place to do this activity has already been determined. Ideally, children should be able to make the decision on work space for themselves as they become more independent learners.

Time Constraints

Before they begin work, children need to know the time constraints for completing activities. This encourages the independent learner to self-pace and prioritize work. Labeling each learning activity with the time estimated for completion gives children a sense of what self-pacing means. Setting time limits slows down impulsive workers while making the slower workers aware that time is passing.

Time structuring can be achieved by stamping each activity with a set time or by scheduling the completion of several activities at the end of a larger time block. The method selected depends on teacher/student preference, amount of independence previously demonstrated, and scheduling demands.

Task Transitions

Self-structuring of behavior as an independent learner does not end with completion of a task. The final steps are (1) to place the completed work in a designated area and (2) to prepare for the next activity. Valuable classroom learning time is lost as children make unstructured transitions between activities. Children who have to be reminded what to do next disrupt the classroom activity flow. Transitions can be managed through methods such as by specifying directions, charting movements, and assigning students to act as task monitors.

The teacher should be sure to include these last two steps in the independent learning program. To stress the importance of placing completed work in the proper place, misplaced work should not be graded. Daily instructional time is wasted if desks, folders, and baskets have to be searched for missing work. To avoid having to remind children of what to do next, the teacher should present clear directions and check to be certain that each child knows what activity to turn to upon completing each task.

Summary of Teacher Task Responsibilities

The classroom teacher's responsibilities involve training the student to become an independent learner and structuring the environment in which the student carries out each learning task. By structuring the environment, the teacher prevents the student from wasting valuable instructional time in transition from one task to another.

Components involved in arranging the classroom environment include organizing materials, determining work areas, designating time constraints, and programming transitions. These features should be clearly introduced and explained to each student. As in any other training, students should be reinforced for following the structure provided. By incorporating the above components into a classroom routine, the teacher is programming for efficient, independent learning.

REFERENCES

Becker, W. C., & Carnine, D. W. (1981). Direct instruction: A behavior theory model for comprehensive educational intervention with the disadvantaged. In J. W. Bijou & R. Ruiz (Eds.), *Behavior modification: Contributions to education*, Hillsdale, NJ: Erlbaum.

Carnine, D. W., Prill, N., & Armstrong, S. (1978). *Teaching slower performing students general case strategies for solving comprehension items*. Eugene: University of Oregon Follow Through Project.

Gerber, M., & Kauffman, J. M. (1981) Peer tutoring in academic settings. In P. S. Strain (Ed.), *The utilization of classroom peers as behavior change agents*. New York: Plenum.

Graham, S., & Miller, L. (1979). Spelling research and practice: A unified approach. *Focus on Exceptional Children, 12*, 2, 1–16.

Kameenui, E. J., Carnine, D. W., & Maggs, A. (1980). Instructional procedures for teaching reversible passive voice and clause constructions to three mildly handicapped children. *Exceptional Child, 27*(1), 29–41.

Kazdin, A. E. (1980). *Behavior modification in applied settings* (2nd ed.). Homewood, IL: Dorsey.

Lloyd, J. (1980). Academic instruction and cognitive behavior modification: The need for attack strategy training. *Exceptional Education Quarterly, 1*(1), 53–63.

Lloyd, J. W., & deBettencourt, L. J. U. (1982). *Academic strategy training: A manual for teachers*. Charlottesville: University of Virginia Learning Disabilities Research Institute.

Lloyd, J. W., Saltzman, N. J., & Kauffman, J. M. (1981). Predictable generalization in academic learning as a result of preskills and strategy training. *Learning Disability Quarterly, 4*, 203–216.

Mercer, C. D., & Mercer, A. R. (1978). The development and use of self-correcting materials with exceptional children. *Teaching Exceptional Children, 11*(1), 6–11.

Schwartz, T. A., Schwartz, R., & Cohen, S. B. (1980, April 10). *Teacher dissatisfaction and alienation as related to mainstreaming in education*. Paper presented at the annual meeting of the American Educational Research Association, Boston, MA.

Sulzar-Azaroff, B., & Mayer, G. R. (1977). *Applying behavior-analysis procedures with children and youth*. New York: Holt, Rinehart & Winston.

White, O. R., & Liberty, K. A. (1976). Behavioral assessment and precise educational measurement. In N. J. Haring & R. L. Schiefelbusch (Eds.), *Teaching special children*. New York: McGraw-Hill.

Sandra Cohen is an Associate Professor, Department of Special Education, University of Virginia. Laurie de Bettencourt is an Adjunct Research Associate, Department of Special Education, University of Pittsburgh.

All teachers face the challenge of making enough time to teach children, and especially to help slower children reach mastery. This article discusses probably the most effective and cost-efficient program to provide assistance to the teacher. It moves the resource teacher to serving as a program manager and trainer of tutors. The research clearly demonstrates the effectiveness of tutoring as an approach to increase academic learning and to increase the academic engaged time. Studies also demonstrate achievement by tutors comparable to paraprofessional aides at one third the cost. Tutors, while assisting other students (tutees), have been shown to profit from this strategy themselves.

Peer Tutoring in Elementary And Secondary Programs

Joseph Jenkins and Linda Jenkins

The task facing professionals who teach students with handicaps is clear enough—how to raise achievement rates and thereby reduce the discrepancy between handicapped children and their peers. Teachers with whom we have talked are confident they could teach almost anything to almost anyone, if they had the time. A student who requires 80 repetitions of a rule before applying it consistently has a problem only if the teacher does not have enough time to provide the repetitions. Of course, time spent with this student is probably time taken away from other students who already have learned the rule, or who are at an earlier spot in the curriculum. Whether, or when, a particular student learns a rule will probably not be determined by the teacher's ability to teach but, rather, by the teacher's available time. The problem of having sufficient time for teaching is a function of class size and of the varieties of human differences found in schools.

Data gathered in elementary classrooms have identified "academic engaged time" as a highly significant correlate of achievement—one that distinguishes classrooms that produce above and below average achievement levels. Berliner, Fisher, Filby, and Marlieve (1976) have described academic learning time as the time a student spends engaged in academically relevant tasks that are moderately difficult. Academic engaged time is not the same as allotted instructional time. A typical elementary classroom allots from 90 minutes to 2 hours daily to language arts instruction. Observations of what the students do during this period, however, reveal that far fewer minutes are actually spent engaged in a learning task.

Academic engaged time is highly related to content coverage, which itself has been shown to be consistently and significantly related to student achievement gain. In summarizing research on effective classrooms, Rosenshine and Berliner (1978) concluded:

> A fairly consistent pattern emerges from the studies cited. The primary finding is that time spent engaged in relevant content appears to be an essential variable for which there is no substitute. Teachers who make a difference in students' achievement are those who put students into contact with curriculum materials and find ways to keep them in contact. (p. 12)

> Within the area of instruction in basic skills in primary grades, the major skill needed by a teacher is that of obtaining "sufficient" content coverage and academic engaged minutes per day. (p. 13)

THE RATIONALE FOR TUTORING

Because every skill cannot be taught simultaneously, a sequence of instructional objectives is usually developed. Ideally, a student should be able to concentrate on mastering one objective at a time before facing the next objective in the sequence. Grouping students for instruction, however, usually prevents individuals from making maximum progress. Ordinarily a student who is instructed in a group will be forced either to proceed to the next objective before attaining mastery of the current objective or to remain on an objective he or she has already mastered while waiting for the peer group to attain adequate performance.

As long as individual students' learning rates vary, small-group instruction will produce less than optimum rates of progress through an instructional sequence, because, by its nature, grouping for instruction guarantees that some children will not receive instruction on an objective appropriate for them. Thus, even though a well designed group format can produce high levels of task engagement, the academic engaged time for an individual student (learning-relevant content) will be less than the total instructional time for the group. From this analysis, it appears that academic engaged time could be augmented by substituting one-to-one instruction for some small-group sessions and private seatwork assignments.

Unfortunately, teachers are not themselves able to provide much individual instruction, as evidenced by the amount of group instruction and private work observed in classrooms. Teachers who devote much time to individual students are overall *less* effective (Stallings & Kaskowitz, 1974), presumably because attention to the individual detracts from the time available for other class members. If teachers desire to increase academic engaged time through one-to-one instruction, they must expand their reserve of instructional personnel. They need not look far. Some of the best helpers are other students who can be recruited from inside their own school.

RESEARCH SUPPORT FOR TUTORING

A meta-analysis of 65 tutoring programs was recently reported (Cohen, Kulik, & Kulik, 1982). The effects of tutoring programs on the tutees' academic performance were greater in well structured and more cognitively oriented programs. Tutoring programs of a shorter duration had larger student gains. Tutors had a better understanding of the subject matter in which they were tutored, and student attitudes toward subject matter were more positive in classrooms with tutoring programs. This effect was shared by tutor and tutee.

Several studies have contrasted the effects of tutorial and small-group instruction. Jenkins, Mayhall, Peschka, and Jenkins (1974) compared teacher-led small-group instruction with one-to-one instruction delivered by cross-age tutors. The tutored children were learning disabled and mentally retarded youngsters receiving service in special education resource rooms, and the tutors were regular third and fourth grade students who had undergone training and had worked as tutors for several months. Across several tasks including work recognition, oral reading, spelling, and math facts, learning was greatest in the tutorial condition, with one-to-one instruction from a peer exceeding teacher-led small-group instruction.

Program cost is another factor that deserves attention because public education is expensive and becomes more so every year. A group of special educators in Vermont conducted a cost effectiveness study in which they compared two forms of service delivery to handicapped children, one of which involved cross-age tutoring (Armstrong, Conlon, Pierson, & Stahlbrand, 1979). For several years school districts in Vermont had employed paraprofessional teacher aides to tutor handicapped students. The aides were trained and supervised by a special education consulting teacher who designed and monitored individualized teaching programs for each special education student.

Working within this context, Armstrong et al. designed an alternative means of service delivery. They recruited and trained high school seniors to work with consulting teachers in tutoring special education students who were failing to master regular education curriculum objectives. Throughout the school year these high school students tutored three periods a week and conferred with the consulting teacher one additional period weekly. Their students, who came from first through fourth grade classrooms, gained an average of 1.7 months for each month tutored—exactly the same gain registered by equivalent students who were tutored by paraprofessional aides.

Complete data were maintained on the costs associated with training and supervising both the high schoolers and the aides, and the additional cost of salaries for the latter. Expenses associated with the paraprofessionals were over three times greater than those for the high school tutors, even though both groups were equally effective in facilitating student achievement. The high school students acquired useful teaching, measuring, and managing skills and rated their experience as highly rewarding.

The most recent evidence on cost effectiveness comes from a study by Levin, Glass, and Meister (1984). They compared four common interventions for improving reading and math achievement in elementary schools. Cross-age tutoring, using student tutors, was more than twice as cost effective as the next strongest intervention—computer assisted instruction—which in turn was more effective than reducing class size or increasing instructional time.

In summary, several lines of research suggest that one-to-one tutoring has much to offer even when it is conducted by another student. Among the apparent benefits of tutoring are: increased academic engaged minutes, more learning within a single lesson, and more optimum progressions through curriculum sequences for the individual learner. In addition to these benefits, tutoring at the secondary level can also provide an opportunity for students to acquire study skills necessary for learning information in courses required for graduation.

CRITICAL COMPONENTS OF SUCCESSFUL PEER TUTORING PROGRAMS

We have attempted to pinpoint characteristics of tutoring programs that contribute to success. These characteristics have been identified from research and from 13 years of experience with peer tutor programs. The following pages delineate each of the critical components in implementing a successful tutor program.

Lesson Formats

Tutoring proceeds more smoothly when tutors have a lesson format that enables them to function without asking teachers, "What do I do today?" With *highly structured and carefully prescribed lessons,* tutors know what to do.

Structured lessons are also advantageous to the teacher. When teachers don't have to explain each lesson to their tutors, they can assume a managerial role, monitoring several tutoring projects simultaneously. They can plan in advance for new lessons, devote time to problem lessons needing revision, and attend to individual crises without interrupting the progress of other tutoring pairs.

After tutoring has begun, changes in lesson formats may be needed to maximize individual student progress. In our experience the basic format of the lesson remains the same for 90% of the students. What may change is the amount of time spent on a particular task or on motivational procedures.

Content of Instruction

Some common-sense notions support correlating tutoring content with classroom content. In the first place, the concepts of normalization and least restrictive environment imply that services for students with learning problems should be designed in ways that will help them maintain enrollment in regular class settings. When students with learning problems cannot keep up with their classmates, some teachers are inclined to dispatch them to another setting (e.g., a self-contained special education class). In secondary schools, students who do not keep up are given failing grades, jeopardizing their chances of graduation. Thus, the challenge for special and remedial education teachers is to help students remain in the mainstream.

Because teachers define objectives in terms of their classroom curricula, they tend to judge a student's competence in relation to success or failure in those materials. Remedial services based on the student's classroom curriculum will more likely improve performance in that curriculum. In contrast, services based on another curriculum, even if they effectively teach that curriculum's objectives, are less likely to teach the "right" skills—i.e., those the classroom teacher uses as his/her criterion. To teach the same curriculum, adaptations in presentation style may be needed to create a structured lesson format.

In most situations tutoring provides the opportunity for *extra instruction, practice, repetition,* or *clarification* of a concept that enables students to succeed in the classroom curriculum. Improved performance on academic objectives selected by the regular teacher can be recognized by both teachers and students.

If tutoring does not help improve students' progress, the curriculum may have a major design inadequacy. For example, in schools that use beginning reading with a sight-word emphasis, supplemental phonics instruction may be required. Teachers in one such district trained cross-age tutors to teach from a phonics-based curriculum (DISTAR I) while the teachers continued using the district curriculum. Another teacher in this school district taught a group of low-performing third graders using a non-district, phonics-based program (*Corrective Reading*) and used third grade peers to tutor in the district's adopted curriculum.

In secondary level tutoring programs the program manager must monitor whether tutoring content matches the real demands of classroom teachers. Is information from reading assignments and lectures tested? What is the testing format—true-false, matching, multiple-choice, short answer, or essay? What are the teachers' criteria for grading—test scores, number of assignments turned in, class discussion? Is the student complying with attendance and make-up policies?

Mastery Learning

Closely related to the issue of instructional content is the degree to which a tutoring program approximates a mastery learning model. In a mastery model, any skills targeted for instruction are considered to be of sufficient importance to require that students demonstrate mastery of them. *In a mastery-based tutoring model, a skill is identified and instruction in that skill occurs every day until students master it.*

Conventional wisdom suggests the importance of carefully selecting tutoring content and of guaranteeing that students master the content. Programs that focus on the "wrong" content will not help the students much, even if they succeed in teaching that content. Likewise, tutoring programs emphasizing the "right" content will also fail if they do not guarantee that students master this content.

Tutors' satisfaction with and sense of accomplishment from their jobs are affected by observing their students actually master the instructional content. One of the more potent intrinsic reinforcers connected with teaching is the sense of accomplishment that comes with having discernibly helped someone.

Frequency and Duration of Tutoring Lessons

One of the first considerations in implementing a tutoring program is the scheduling of instructional sessions. How long should each session last, and how many days per week should tutoring occur? Time available for tutoring may be greatly affected by schedule conflicts such as whole-school grouping for reading and math, the numbers of periods available in which secondary students can earn credits for graduation, and competing opportunities for extracurricular or service activities.

In tutoring programs at the secondary level, students are usually scheduled daily for one period. In middle schools, which have more varied class schedules, scheduling a tutoring class for fewer than 5 days per week is possible. No research on frequency of tutoring at the secondary level has been done, as most secondary schools are locked into set schedules. Two studies, however, investigated the scheduling factor in elementary tutoring programs using a pull-out model (Ellson, Harris, & Barber, 1968; Mayhall & Jenkins, 1977). Tutoring was more effective when scheduled daily and for sessions that lasted approximately half an hour.

Regular education teachers who wish to incorporate tutoring into their own classrooms can schedule tutoring periods of briefer duration and still obtain substantial effects. One study (Hall, Delquadri, Greenwood, & Thurston, 1982) found that a 15-minute peer tutoring period within a regular classroom markedly improved the performance on weekly spelling tests for a group of low-performing third graders.

Other considerations, although not data-based, favor scheduling daily sessions of moderate length. One consideration is the classroom disruption produced by setting changes, movement, and so forth, and the additional teacher energies consumed in organizing this extra transition. To justify this, tutoring sessions should last long enough to have an effect and not just result in extra bother. Another consideration is especially pertinent in programs using cross-age tutors. Classroom teachers often prefer a fixed time, a regular (daily) period when their students will be out of the room for tutoring. This allows them to plan for and concentrate exclusively on the remaining students. In most secondary tutoring programs tutoring is a regularly established class period.

To imply that for a tutoring program to be effective, it *must* be scheduled daily for half-hour sessions would be misleading. On the contrary, a number of successful tutoring programs employ a less than daily schedule, or one with individual sessions lasting under 30 minutes. Our point is that when temporal factors were studied experimentally, results favored the more *continuous programs of moderate duration*. These findings in combination with nuisance factors, such as interruption of classroom schedules and transition time, point to daily sessions of moderate length as the preferred organization as long as other factors, such as availability of tutors, do not dictate otherwise.

Tutor Training

The last situation teachers want to create is an unpleasant, negative interpersonal experience for children. Researchers have observed that if left to their own, older children occasionally show impatience with, or boss and ridicule, younger students whom they are "helping" (Lippitt, 1968). *Tutors have to be trained in appropriate interpersonal behaviors that result in comfortable, satisfying experiences for both members of the tutoring dyad.*

Behaviors that tutors should be trained to perform include giving clear directions, encouraging and praising learners for their efforts, confirming correct responses, correcting errors in a non-punitive fashion, and avoiding overprompting. Interestingly, children who tutor appear not to engage in these behaviors spontaneously (Niedermeyer, 1970). Fifth and sixth grade students who had received no specific tutor training tended during tutoring sessions to confirm correct responses less than 50% of the time, rarely gave corrective feedback, did not praise their tutees, nor did they engage in friendly, non-instructional conversation before or after the tutoring sessions. In contrast, tutors who had received training in these behaviors exhibited high rates of appropriate instructional and interpersonal behavior.

Efficiency considerations suggest that tutors be trained in gathering and replacing instructional materials, measuring and recording student performance, allocating time to specific tasks, and possibly monitoring or participating in post-tutoring games. Other tutoring tasks, such as teaching letter sounds, sound blending, arithmetic algorithms, specialized correction procedures, literal or inferential questioning, note taking, organization of notes around main ideas, and the like, require specific training if a tutor is assigned to teach them.

Tutor training should match the lesson format developed by the tutor trainer. Moreover, training should not end once actual tutoring begins. As to the content of the continued training, careful supervision of the tutors will alert teachers to additional training needs.

In an elementary or secondary setting tutoring might occur four times per week with one day a week scheduled for continued training or teacher conferencing with the tutor. In the secondary program, the first 5–10 minutes of each tutoring class can be used to provide a mini-lesson on tutorial procedures. If the tutees are assigned to the same classroom as the tutors, they can be included in the training. If the tutees choose not to participate, they can work independently on other assignments.

Class Climate and Active Supervision

School climate is positively correlated with student achievement and with student and staff satisfaction, and it is a significant factor in tutoring programs. The tutoring center or class should be a place where caring and a commitment to personal growth are obvious features. *Respect and mutual concern* should be explicitly encouraged and shaped between tutors, tutees, and the teacher. The teacher and students should *establish high expectations* for all involved in the program. Is the tutor yawning, inattentive, or crabby? Is the tutee complaining or being unkind to the tutor? Signs of boredom and non-compliance should be recognized early, and a positive, task-oriented pattern should be established.

We recommend that teachers interact daily with every dyad. *Active supervision helps keep tutors and tutees interested.* Some days the teacher may spend most of the lesson with one or two pairs, but teachers should try to "visit" every tutoring pair at least once during each session.

Finally, teachers should model the positive reinforcement, enthusiasm, interest, and commitment to high expectations that they want tutors to demonstrate. Active involvement by the teacher sends a message that he/she is interested in the students' daily achievements and successes.

Staff and Administrative Support

Tutoring programs interface with the total school program and require support from a number of individuals. Teachers who manage a tutoring program need well-refined interpersonal skills because they must relate to a large number of students and staff, frequently negotiating solutions to problems. They serve as advocates for the tutee and occasionally the tutor, and they consult with regular teachers as necessary. The *advocate role is a key in peer tutoring programs*. Often, students who are tutored do not have a parent who is able or willing to assume an advocacy role. Many secondary students do not want their parent "interfering" with their life at school.

Because teacher referral is most important in recruiting prospective tutors, the teaching staff must support peer tutoring as an integral component of the school curriculum. Principals must approve the program so that teachers can release tutors from class. At the secondary level they must arrange for tutors to receive credit for their participation.

Program Organization

How can a school organize to provide the tutor training and supervision necessary for a successful program? There are several possibilities. One organization for an elementary setting places a special education resource teacher or a remedial teacher in the *program manager role*. This individual might devote three or four periods daily to peer- or cross-age tutoring programs. The program manager is responsible for recruiting tutors from various classrooms within the school or, if geographically feasible, from a nearby secondary school. Ordinarily special education and remedial teachers have sufficiently flexible schedules at the beginning of the school year to accomplish this task.

Another organizational framework for an elementary school places the school librarian in the program manager position. For example, the librarian might, in collaboration with several classroom teachers, organize and monitor tutoring for 10–15 low-performing students.

As an alternative to the program manager type of organization, regular elementary classroom teachers could organize a tutoring program within their own classrooms or collaborate with one or more of their colleagues to develop a *cross-classroom program*. One instructional period such as sustained silent reading time, the independent work time, or the round robin reading time can be set aside daily for tutoring. Several schedule variations are possible within these frameworks, ranging from daily tutoring to a combination of tutoring and teacher-led instruction on separate days. In one elementary school the principal assigned an aide for 20 minutes daily for 2 weeks so that a teacher of 25 low-performing first grade readers could train 25 fifth and sixth grade tutors during her language arts block. The tutors monitored the children's oral reading, allowing the teacher to spend her time introducing new skills and developing comprehension and language skills.

In secondary schools several program organizations are possible. The special education teacher might coordinate tutoring services for students assigned to *resource rooms,* rather than attempt to instruct 11–15 mainstreamed students in the various content classes (e.g., world history). Instead of devoting several minutes to multiple content areas, the resource teacher can train and supervise tutors to supplement content areas instruction.

Similarly, remedial teachers in reading and math can organize their services on a tutoring model. Typically students' entry-level skills vary widely in these classes, and *individualized instruction* by tutors is one means of addressing the needs of a diverse student population.

Finally, a teaching position could be established specifically for managing a tutoring program. Creating a *full-time teacher position* enables a school to schedule tutoring every period during the day. Although this option appears to be expensive, it is actually cost-effective compared to other remedial models because it results in serving 50 to 80 tutees and as many tutors.

A tutor manager position in one school district was staffed by using teachers from several departments—special education, ESL, basic skills, and regular education. Using staff members from various departments helped to define the program as one for *all* students, not just those in special education. Having a regular education teacher as a part of the tutoring team helped in recruiting tutors; the regular teachers had personal contact with a larger number of students and, thus, were better known by the student body.

In our most successful secondary experiences about one-third of the students have been from special education and the rest from the remedial or general population of students. This class is the only "special education" class that some handicapped students take, and IEPs are written to reflect this intervention. Inclusion of nonhandicapped students makes sense because in most classrooms one to three youngsters need help, and with 150 students per day teachers are unable to provide extra instruction to help those students succeed. Providing service to low-achieving students not only helps them, but it also broadens the impact of the tutoring program and gains wider staff cooperation and support.

Measurement of Progress

One obvious disadvantage of turning over instructional duties to another person is the loss of information about how students are progressing. One means of compensating for this information loss is observing the teaching-learning activities (Mayhall et al., 1975). Teachers can also keep in touch with learner progress by *keeping daily performance data on instructional objectives*.

Teachers who have access to the daily measures are better able to adjust tutoring programs to achieve greater learning (Jenkins, Mayhall, Peschka, & Townsend,

1974). Decision making improves when people have access to better information, a proposition that is as true in classrooms as it is in government and industry. In addition to their contribution to decision making, good data systems can have other beneficial effects as well. When students recognize that their progress toward specific objectives will be measured at the end of every day's lesson, they are less likely to drift off task.

We have found that tutors can collect daily performance data on each teaching objective. Within a reading lesson that includes instruction on letter sounds, isolated words, reading in context, and comprehension questions, the tutor can measure each element separately and display the results visually on a chart. By inspecting these charted performances, the tutor manager determines how each child is progressing, when instructional procedures have to be changed, and when the child is ready for a new task.

Measurement at the Elementary Level

Below are two examples of measurement procedures used for tutoring reading in elementary settings.

Simple Monitoring. Third grade peer tutors have used the data sheet shown in Figure 1. The classroom teacher establishes a rule that to continue, a tutee must make two or fewer reading errors.

Daily Performance Chart. The daily performance chart monitors the student's functioning on behaviors that are directly taught. Figure 2 gives an example of a daily performance chart showing aspects of a student's reading performance. Using the bands on this performance chart, the teacher monitors comprehension accuracy (first band), letter sound accuracy (second band), oral reading rate (third band), and reading accuracy (fourth band). The reading accuracy and rate data are based on a 100-word passage drawn from the story being read. If the student reads a sample with less than 95% accuracy, he/she must work on that story another day. Comprehension data are

FIGURE 1 Format and Example for Simple Monitoring: Elementary Level

READING RECORD

Student: Donald **Tutor:** Jessica
Book: Riding Rainbows

Date	Page No.	Error Tally	Errors	Comments
9-24	8	3	what, him, why	
	8	2	that, what	worked
	9	1	pigeon	hard!
10	0			
9-25	11	2	what, why	
etc.				

FIGURE 2 Example of Daily Performance Chart

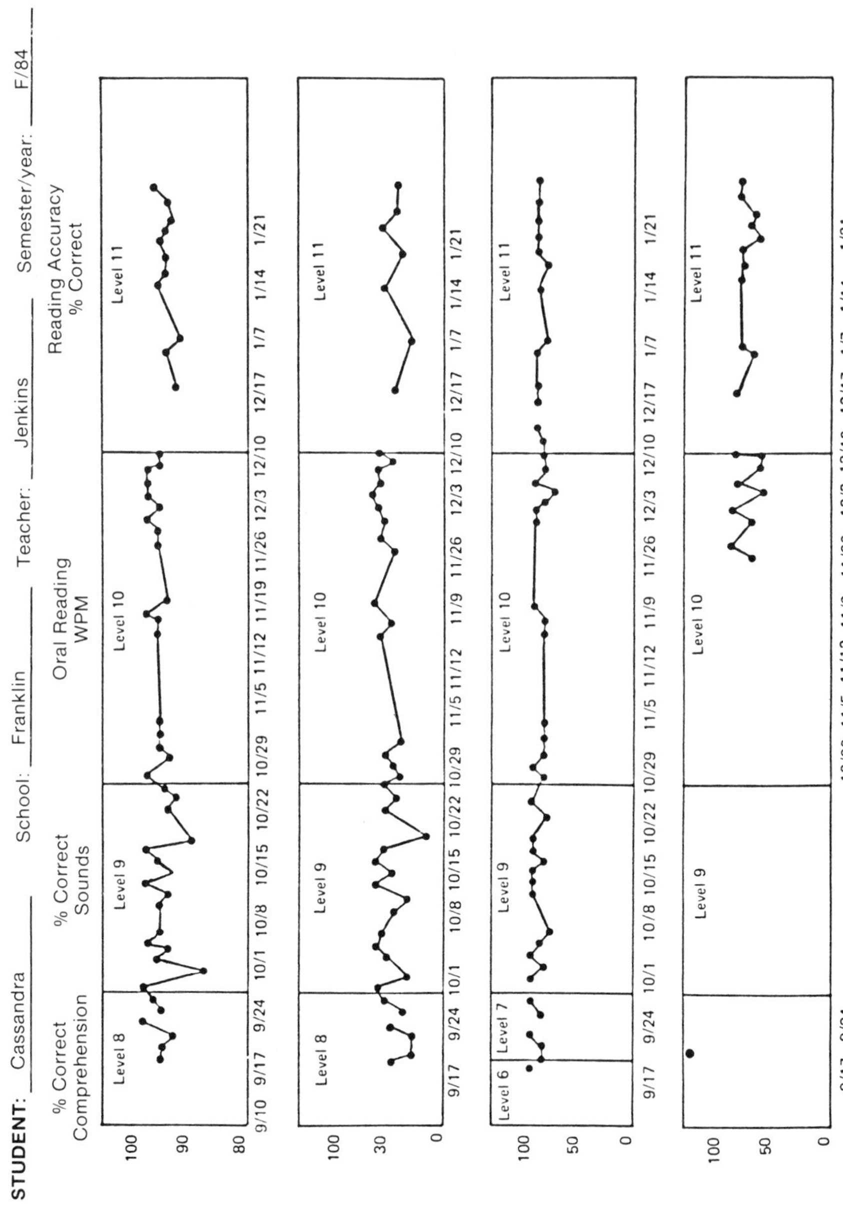

based on answers to several questions covering the story's content. At least 80% comprehension of each story is required.

Measurement at the Secondary Level

Tutorial programs at the secondary level are based on content from mainstream classes. This places regular classroom teachers in a prominent role in evaluating the success of tutoring, because the primary data on program effects come from performance in their classes. Several type of records are kept to help the tutor teacher monitor assignments, tests, and classroom performance.

Daily Assignment Record. Each tutee keeps a daily record of class assignments. The tutor cross-checks these with the notetaker's record (described later). When the program manager visits the dyad, he/she checks to see that the tutee is keeping an accurate record.

Monthly Calendar. The tutor maintains a calendar that lists future tests, quizzes, major assignments, projects, term papers, and the like. The tutor and program manager use this to determine if adjustments in daily goals are required.

Log of Daily Goals and Accomplishments. The tutoring dyad establishes goals for each day's session. At the end of the period, tutor and tutee evaluate their accomplishments and establish a tentative goal for the next day. A notebook containing these goals is kept open on the desk, allowing the teacher to check them as he/she monitors each group. In that way, the teacher can make suggestions about the number and quality of goals and participate in rating the effectiveness of the pair.

Weekly Progress Check. Each week the tutor visits briefly (3–5 minutes) with the content teacher at a prearranged time. The tutor inquires about assignments completed by the tutee, test or quiz scores, attendance, and participation in discussion or labs, and solicits suggestions to help the tutee succeed in the course. Information from the progress check is shared with the tutee and the tutor manager.

Selecting and Pairing Tutors With Learners

With availability dictating the pool of potential tutors, teachers cannot always follow their natural preference for older, academically competent tutors; nevertheless, elementary teachers have designed high quality programs using tutors as young as 7, 8, and 9. As a general rule, however, older, more able students are the first choice because they are easier to train, require less supervision, and are better able to manage discipline problems. Academically capable fifth and sixth grade students make ideal tutors, and they are often available because they have little trouble meeting the challenges at their grade level. Often, they are willing to use their classroom study time efficiently or, sometimes, to work on their classroom assignments outside of school time so that they can qualify as tutors.

When teachers select tutors at the secondary level, students currently or formerly enrolled in the target content class are preferred but not necessary. Tenth graders have tutored students in senior health, and eighth graders have tutored in ninth grade social studies or language arts. Given the class notes, study guides, and text, reasonably good students can successfully tutor in a course they have not personally taken (except math).

The more *crucial factors in tutor selection relate to the tutor's personal characteristics*. Program organizers normally seek students who are dependable, responsible, sensitive, and caring, or students who appear likely to develop these traits. Classroom teachers are usually able to identify several students with these traits who have time to participate in tutoring.

CONSIDERATIONS IN IMPLEMENTING A TUTORING PROGRAM: ELEMENTARY

Getting Started

To initiate tutoring in a school, a teacher or program developer first secures the support of the principal, staff, and parents. In beginning a tutoring program, a good rule to follow is to *start small*. The teacher should identify students who need additional practice but who do not present serious behavior management problems. The next step is to assess the students' mastery of curriculum objectives, identifying what they need to learn next.

Designing Lessons and a Measurement System

Tutors are not skilled diagnosticians, curriculum developers, or experts in designing instruction. These are teacher competencies and responsibilities. Lessons can be structured using the same curriculum (e.g., reading and spelling) that is used in the classroom. A typical beginning reading lesson conducted by a tutor would involve several minutes' work on letter sounds, several minutes' instruction on new words, and the remainder of the period devoted to oral reading. The basic structure of the lessons changes little from day to day. Tutors do not have to invent each day's lessons anew; rather, they follow an established lesson format.

The program manager has to develop a procedure for measuring students' performance on each aspect of the lesson. Tutors measure and chart progress daily, and the manager employs these data in making instructional modifications.

Recruiting and Scheduling Tutors

The next step for the program developer is to obtain names of potential tutors from teachers. An orientation meeting is held with these students, and they are requested to obtain parent permission for participating in the program. Tutoring periods agreeable to the tutors and the teachers of tutees are then scheduled.

Designing and Conducting Tutor Training

The content of tutor training varies with the subject area in which they tutor, the kind of performance measures the program employs, and the types of children to be tutored. Nevertheless, training usually addresses these general topics: information about the program and the tutors' responsibilities, measurement procedures, lesson structure and teaching procedures, and personal behavior. To avoid confusion, tutor training should be held during the regularly scheduled tutoring period.

First, trainees are given *information on the purpose of the program and the responsibilities* of being a tutor. Responsibilities pertaining to tutoring itself include a consistent time commitment, punctuality, confidentiality, and positive regard for the learner. The tutor's own classroom responsibilities include maintaining their standard quality of work on their regular assignments and keeping informed about and making up any work they missed while out of the classroom.

Considerable training time is devoted to teaching the tutors *measurement procedures* through a data system. Trainees learn what performance data they will collect (e.g., percent correct and rate of math facts, oral reading, and spelling) and the procedures for collecting these data (e.g., random samples of math facts from specified domains, pre-selected reading passages, and structured spelling lists). Tutors also may have to learn how to use stop watches and pocket calculators to compute summary statistics.

Next the training addresses *lesson structure and teaching procedures*. Depending upon the tutors' academic specialization (e.g., reading or math), trainees learn how to teach specific skills (e.g., sound blending), appropriate use of prompts, error correction procedures, the various components of a lesson, and the amount of time allocated to each component. An outline for training tutors who will teach reading is given in Table 1.

Teachers may demonstrate an entire lesson while trainees observe. Teachers may also model lesson components or small-scale instructional episodes, followed by role-playing opportunities for the trainees, who exchange tutor and student roles. Finally, tutors are introduced to their jobs by allowing them to assume responsibility for parts of lessons, and—as they become comfortable—gradually assume more responsibility.

In the category of interpersonal skills, trainees learn how to display positive verbal and nonverbal *personal behavior,* including active listening, conversing, and praising good effort. They learn not to show impatience, annoyance, or disappointment. They learn that errors are a signal for more teaching, not for punishment and disapproval.

Beginning Tutoring

During the first few solo tutoring sessions, the teacher has to monitor lessons carefully and conduct post-tutoring debriefing sessions. It is wise to stagger the beginning of tutoring with just a few pairs starting on a given day. As tutors grow more accustomed to their roles, monitoring and debriefing sessions can be reduced (but never completely dropped).

TABLE 1
Sample Tutor Training for Reading: Schedule and Skills

Lesson 1 Discriminate and Tally Word Recognition Errors: Omissions	**Lesson 6** Error Correction Procedure
Lesson 2 Discriminate Word Recognition Errors: Additions and Substitutions	**Lesson 7** Praising and Ignoring
Lesson 3 Monitoring Oral Reading: Pauses. Repetitions	**Lesson 8** Teaching Isolated Letter Sounds
Lesson 4 Recording Errors on Data Sheet	**Lesson 9** Comprehension Questions: Asking and Correction Procedures
Lesson 5 Tallying Errors in All Categories	**Lesson 10** Review of All Procedures and Questions and Answers

Maintaining Tutors' Involvement and Interest

Keeping tutors motivated is a challenge to the tutor manager. The most important reinforcer is *personal attention* from the teacher. Time spent with tutors in discussing the tutoring project, as well as other aspects of their school and personal lives, has considerable influence on tutors' interest and continued participation in the program. Another means of maintaining tutors' motivation is by drawing *attention to their accomplishments* with quarterly reports, through informal discussion with their parents, teachers, and principal, school or local newspaper articles, and comments and remarks that remind them of the importance of their contribution to the children they teach.

A third means of maintaining motivation is through *systematic scheduling of reinforcing events* such as tutor luncheons, tutor parties, tutor awards, letters of thanks from principals of tutees, daily material rewards such as candy or stickers, allowing the tutoring room to be a place to meet before school officially opens for students, academic grades or credits for tutoring, and personal letters of recommendation for jobs, camps, or future schooling. This combination of motivational procedures has proven successful in holding the interest of cross-age tutors for as many as three consecutive years of service.

CONSIDERATIONS IN IMPLEMENTING A TUTORING PROGRAM: SECONDARY

General Description of Secondary Tutoring

At the secondary level the tutoring class meets daily throughout a semester. Tutees attend both their content class (e.g., American history) and the tutoring class in which they receive additional instruction and practice.

Tutors and tutees receive training from the teacher at the beginning of each semester and, after tutoring begins, daily for 5–10 minutes. This instruction focuses on social skills and study strategies to improve the study and tutoring skills of the students. To ensure coordination with the classroom teacher and his/her curriculum expectations, tutors meet regularly each week with the classroom teacher. As many as 10–15 tutors may be working with 10–15 tutees at one time in the peer tutoring class.

Both tutors and tutees receive *elective credit* for the tutoring class. Tutees also receive credit for the mainstream class for which they are tutored.

An exemplary student enrolled in a content class is selected by the teacher to be a *notetaker*. The notetaker is given NCR paper on which to record classroom notes. This student delivers a copy of the notes to the tutor program manager. In the tutor room as many as 50 sets of classroom notes may be available each semester. Using these notes, tutors help students complete their own notes and study the class lectures.

Getting Started

To initiate a tutoring program, the program manager obtains a commitment from building and, if appropriate, central administrators. Next, he/she selects staff to teach the classes and identifies the number of periods in which tutoring will be offered. We recommend that tutoring be available to any motivated student who volunteers and that at least half of the tutees come from outside of special education.

The program manager makes a presentation to secure staff approval and support and writes a description of the tutoring class for the course catalogue. Elective or an occupational credit should be arranged for tutors and tutees.

Recruiting Tutors, Tutees, and Notetakers

The most effective recruiters of *tutors* are regular classroom teachers who personally recommend the program to potential tutors. Counselors can also play an important part in the recruitment process because they are likely to know which students would find tutoring appealing. The tutor manager can make presentations in regular classrooms to explain the program. Applications are left with the classroom teacher. Once a program has been established in a building, these presentations can include participation by former tutors and tutees. Before any student is scheduled into the class, the program manager's signature is required. Recruiting tutors is a time-consuming task, requiring 2–3 days of release time each semester.

Recruiting *tutees* follows the same process. Classroom teacher referral and personal contact with the appropriate students is the most effective procedure. Counselors often know students who need assistance in order to pass a class. If parents are aware of the program, they may encourage their child to elect this class. Students themselves may elect this program if they anticipate difficulty in a particular course. The tutor manager should interview tutees to ensure that they are motivated to participate.

After tutees have selected a target class and identified both the teacher and period, the tutor manager consults the classroom teacher to identify a good *notetaker*. The teacher then arranges for this student to take notes on NCR paper (one personal copy, one for the classroom teacher, and one for the tutor). The notetaker delivers a set of the notes and any hand-outs to the tutor room each day. Some classroom teachers, particularly junior high teachers, offer "extra credit" to notetakers. Even without this incentive, obtaining notetakers usually is not difficult.

Scheduling

The more periods per day the program is offered, the easier the scheduling is. Priority registration, especially for tutors who need a particular class for graduation, can be helpful. The tutor manager may need one release day to modify the schedule and balance the classes between tutors and tutees. If fewer tutees are scheduled at the beginning of a semester, space will be available for students who discover they need assistance later in the semester.

Designing and Conducting Tutor Training

At the beginning of the semester, tutors and tutees go through 2–4 weeks of training. The content and skills taught in this phase should be selected to create an atmosphere of acceptance and empathy between the tutors and tutees and to provide instruction in the social skills and study strategies necessary for tutoring. The lessons, developed by the authors in collaboration with Vicki Morrell, Kathy Vranesh, and Vicki Fitzpatrick, are outlined in Table 2.

Devoting the initial 4 weeks of the semester to training can be difficult for some managers as the discrepancy between the two "groups" of students may create pacing and motivational problems. Also, tutees may become panicky about their performance in the content classes. At the junior high school level the discrepancy between tutor and tutee skills is smaller and teachers have been able to maintain the 4-week training model.

A compromise that seems to please most high school teachers is to spend the initial 12–14 days in tutor training. Tutors and tutees are then matched and tutoring begins. The first 5–10 minutes of each class are used for further training. Teaching daily mini-lessons helps focus the students on the tutoring tasks and allows for adjustments of the training, based on students needs. Some tutoring dyads may want to start studying immediately at the beginning of the period, so this 5–10 minutes of training must

TABLE 2
Secondary Tutor Training: Possible Schedule

Lesson 1

Course Introduction
Roles and Responsibilities
Attendance and Grading Policies

Lesson 2

Individual Differences

Lesson 3

Active Listening
Nonverbal Messages

Lesson 4

Task Analysis

Lesson 5

Direct Instruction Model

Lesson 6

Behavior Management

Lesson 7

Goal Setting

Lesson 8

Motivation

Lesson 9

Studying from Notes and Study Guides

Lesson 10

Critical Attributes of a Good Tutor and Tutee Match-Up
Organize Tutor and Tutee Notebooks

"Mini-Lessons" for Daily Instruction

Level of Questioning: Recall, Understanding, Application
Studying from Notes and Study Guides
Paraphrasing
Time Management: Setting Priorities
Personal Presentation and Negotiation Skills
Environmental Analysis of Classrooms
Decision Making and Problem Solving
Test Taking Skills
Memory Strategies
Notetaking
Multipass (Schumacher, Deshler, Alley, Warner, & Denton, 1982)
Visual Imagery

be firmly established as the normal routine.

Training notetakers occurs at the beginning of the semester. In the high school, one 30-minute period will suffice. (In the junior high, an hour's training is necessary.) Training involves describing the use of NCR paper, the location of the tutoring room, how and where to deliver the notes for each class, notetakers' responsibilities for finding substitutes when they are absent, and the importance of their role.

Matching

During the first class, tutors and tutees complete a schedule of their semester classes. Tutees select the class in which they require assistance. (We recommend targeting one content class per tutee, but the tutor manager may allow tutoring in more than one class if a student is able to meet the requirements of the target class with 2 or 3 days of peer tutoring per week.) Tutors identify the subject areas in which they can provide tutoring.

Age and sex differences have not been a problem in matching tutors and tutees. The important characteristics are the tutors' confidence and skill level. More highly skilled and confident tutors are usually placed with the more "difficult" students. Although most students receive one-to-one instruction, some subject areas, such as math or traffic safety, lend themselves to a 1:2 or 1:3 ratio.

Maintaining Tutors' Involvement and Interest

Peer tutoring provides a more caring climate in the school, as students and teachers monitor each other's behavior and invest in each other's success. Interactions between the manager, tutor, and tutee provide abundant opportunities to develop relationships that enhance the tutorial situation. As Goodlad (1984) has reported, secondary students want others to show concern for them as persons; yet, the structure of the secondary school all too often prevents this. Tutoring is a highly personal program, and this may be one of the most reinforcing aspects for all the students involved.

As in the elementary setting, the most important reinforcer is the attention and personal interest of the tutor manager. Tutor managers model interest and concern for each student by greeting them individually as they enter the room and by being available between classes to reinforce the notetakers when they deliver their notes. Tutors and managers draw attention to tutees' accomplishments by posting test and assignment grades on a Student Success Bulletin Board. Tutees write personal notes of thanks to their tutor for the help they have received. Cookies and thank-you notes are sent to the classroom notetakers. Managers write letters to tutors every semester thanking them for their commitment (these letters are also signed by the principal). Tutor managers also write letters of reference for a job or college.

Other reinforcers for tutors include a page in the yearbook, a bulletin board display along with school athletes, awards at the school awards assembly, or a reception for the tutors and tutees that school administrators attend. Both intrinsic and extrinsic reinforcers are used to motivate and maintain the interest of students in the program.

SUMMARY

In addition to the benefits of tutoring to tutees, its consequences to the tutors is an important consideration. Space does not allow discussion of this aspect here. The reader is referred to Coleman (1974), Allen (1976), Cohen et al. (1982), Annis (1983), Gartner, Kohler, and Reissman (1971), and Argyle (1976) for discussion of cognitive and noncognitive benefits to tutors.

Tutoring in some form was probably the first kind of pedagogy among primative peoples, preceding more formal and organized forms of "schooling." Because of its prehistoric origins, tutoring is easily dismissed as "old hat" in today's technologically-oriented world. We believe that this kind of thinking is misguided, reflecting a type of modern, unexamined chauvinism. Sometimes the first ideas are the best ones.

REFERENCES

Allen, V. L. (Ed.) (1976). *Children as teachers: Theory and research on tutoring*. New York: Academic Press.

Annis, L. F. (1983). The processes and effects of peer tutoring. *Human Learning, 2,* 39–47.

Argyle, M. (1976). Social skills theory. In V. Allen (Ed.), *Children as teachers: Theory and research on tutoring*. New York: Academic Press.

Armstrong, S. B., Conlon, M. F., Pierson, P. M., & Stahlbrand, K. (1979). *The cost effectiveness of peer and cross-age tutoring*. Paper presented at the Annual Meeting of the Council for Exceptional Children, Dallas, TX.

Berliner, D. C., Fisher,C. W., Filby, N., & Marlieve, R. (1976). *Proposal for phase III of beginning teacher evaluation study*. San Francisco: Far West Laboratory for Educational Research and Development.

Cohen, P. A., Kulik, J. A., & Kulik, C. C. (1982). Educational outcomes of tutoring. *American Education Research Journal, 19,* 237–248.

Coleman, J. S. (1974). *Youth: Translation to adulthood*. Chicago: University of Chicago Press.

Ellson, D. G., Harris, P., & Barber, L. A. (1968). A field test of programmed and directed tutoring. *Reading Research Quarterly, 3,* 307–367.

Gartner, A., Kohler, M., & Reissman, F. (1971). *Children teach children: Learning by teaching*. New York: Harper & Row.

Goodlad, J. I. (1984). *A place called school*. New York: McGraw-Hill.

Hall, V., Delquadri, J., Greenwood, C. R., & Thurston, L. (1982). The importance of opportunity to respond in children's academic success. In E. Edgar, N. Haring, J. Jenkins, & C. Pious (Eds.), *Mentally handicapped children: Education and training* (pp. 107–140). Baltimore: University Park Press.

Jenkins, J. R., Mayhall, W. F., Peschka, C., & Jenkins, L. M. (1974). Comparing small group and tutorial instruction in resource rooms. *Exceptional Children, 40,* 245–250.

Jenkins, J. R., Mayhall, W. F., Peschka, C., Townsend, V. (1974). Using direct and daily measures to influence learning. *Journal of Learning Disabilities, 7,* 14–17.

Levin, H., Glass, G., & Meister, G. S. (1984). *Cost-effectiveness of four educational interventions*. Stanford, CA: Stanford University Institute for Research on Educational Finance & Governance.

Lippitt, P. (1968, March). Cross-age helpers. *National Educational Association Journal,* pp. 24–26.

Mayhall, W. F., & Jenkins, J. R. (1977). Scheduling daily or less-than-daily instruction: Implications for resource programs. *Journal of Learning Disabilities, 10*(3), 159–163.

Mayhall, W. F., Jenkins, J. R., Chestnut, N., Rose, F., Schroeder, K., & Jordon, B. (1975). Supervision and site of instruction as factors in tutorial programs. *Exceptional Children, 42,* 151–154.

Niedermeyer, F. C. (1970). Effects of training on the instructional behaviors of student tutors. *Journal of Educational Research, 64,* 119, 123.

Rosenshine, B. V., & Berliner, D. C. (1978). Academic engaged time. *British Journal of Teacher Education, 4,* 3–16.

Schumacher, J. B., Deshler, D. D., Alley, G. R., Warner, M. M., & Denton, P. H. (1982). Multipass: A learning strategy for comprehension. *Learning Disability Quarterly, 5,* 295–304.

Stallings, J. A., & Kaskowitz, D. (1974). *Follow-through classroom observation evaluation, 1972–3*. Stanford, CA: Stanford Center for Research & Development in Teaching.

Joseph Jenkins is the director of the Experimental Education Unit, Child Development and Mental Retardation Center, and Professor of Special Education, University of Washington, Seattle. Linda Jenkins works in special education program development in the Lake Washington School District, Kirkland, WA.

Effective instruction has quite naturally gravitated to microcomputers. This article examines the use of microcomputers to teach, reinforce, motivate, improve writing skills, provide reinforcement, and several other uses. The writers offer a considerable number of examples of successful use of microcomputers but also offer words of caution. They fear that educators may settle on practices that have been successful and fail to continue to explore new uses. The authors demonstrate effective ways to employ microcomputers to improve learning and retention. In general, practices that are discussed in this book (amount of engaged time, high rate of responding, and high success ratio) work equally well when used with computers.

Effective Instruction With Microcomputers: Promises, Practices, and Preliminary Findings

Edwin S. Ellis and Edward J. Sabornie

In a recent survey, Mokros and Russell (1986) reported that 88% of the schools surveyed were using microcomputers with learning disabled or behaviorally disordered students. Maddux (1984) reported that 160,000 microcomputers were being used in special education programs. In light of the ever increasing role that microcomputers play in education of mildly handicapped students, the need for clarification of effective instruction with microcomputers is considerable. Though severely lacking in empirically based articles that investigate authenticity, the literature contains many promises related to the advantages and potentials of using microcomputers. The intent of this article is to provide special educators with an overview of the promises of microcomputers and review the extent to which they have been addressed, in relation to effective instruction, by research. On the whole, the studies reflect highly encouraging results, but much research is needed in this area.

PROMISE 1: MICROCOMPUTERS INCREASE MOTIVATION TO LEARN

Perhaps the most common promise of microcomputer applications is associated with its ability to motivate students (e.g., Arms, 1984; Bell, 1983; Furst, 1983; Gray,

1984; Tyler, 1983). Motivational aspects are discussed below from the perspective of primary reinforcers (it is intrinsically motivating to learn when operating the microcomputer) and from the perspective of secondary motivators—using opportunities to interact with the microcomputer as a reward.

Use as a Primary Reinforcer

How motivating is interaction with the computer in an academic setting? Although we found few studies that directly measured motivation, one indicator is whether students are on task when given opportunities to interact with the computer. In a recent investigation that involved surveys, observations, and interviews with teachers and administrators in public schools, Reith (1986) reported a number of interesting findings. First, in classes with computer-based instruction, students spent only 24.1% of their time working at the computer. In fact, students engaged in paper-and-pencil activities more often in computer-use classrooms than in non-computer classes. The extra time created by using the computer as the instructor appeared to be invested in paper-and-pencil activities—an activity found by Reith and Frick (1983) to increase the likelihood of off-task behavior by seven times. Yet in those computer-use classes, students were more likely to be engaged in learning than were their counterparts in non-computer classes. Other educators (e.g., MacArthur, Haynes, & Malouf, 1985; MacArthur, Haynes, Malouf, & Harris, 1986) have reported similar findings of on-task behavior of mildly handicapped students during computer-assisted instruction (CAI). An important issue is to determine whether computers remain motivational as the novelty wears off (Clark, 1983). Limited evidence offered by Romanczyk (1986) and Chiang (1986) indicated that novelty is a key factor in the motivation dimension. Romanczyk reported that when examining the generalization effects of CAI math instruction with learning disabled children, initial positive effects were found to be transitory and appeared to be tied to the novelty effects. During a study investigating the effects of a drill-and-practice program designed to reinforce knowledge of multiplication tables, Chiang observed that the software, *Treasure Hunt,* produced high levels of initial motivation, but students eventually became disillusioned and even resented the features designed to enhance motivation.

Lieber and Semmel (1986) reported similar observations in that students had a high percentage of on-task behavior across special education and mainstreamed settings, but there does seem to be an interaction effect with social variables. For example, Semmel reported that when peers were present, learning handicapped students were more frequently off-task. Studies reported by Romanczyk (1986) suggested that severely emotionally disturbed and autistic students appear to learn effectively with the computer because they do not have to interact with others. Self-stimulatory and acting-out behaviors were observed to virtually disappear when the severely disordered students interacted with the computer.

An issue related to motivation is the perceived need to use entertaining flashing lights, arcade-like sounds, and fancy graphics to maintain the students' motivation while learning. Although these features are used to enhance motivation (Chaffin,

Maxwell, & Thompson, 1982; Malone, 1981), LeBlanc, Hoko, Aangeenbrug, and Etzel (1985) and Christensen and Gerber (1986) noted that many software programs incorporate these features with little or no concern for the appropriateness of the technique. They suggested that such salient stimuli can interfere with learning because of their distracting features.

In a review of the history of CAI as related to its use with mainframe computers, Torgesen (1986a) concluded that programs incorporating effective management routines had consistently more positive effects than those relying heavily on graphics, sound effects, or animation. Following a CAI study, Chiang (1986) concluded that numerous extraneous features and themes (e.g., treasure hunt, meteor shooting) associated with arcade-like games may not be as effective as a simple drill-and-practice program. Christensen and Gerber (1986) also found that when practicing addition through CAI, learning disabled students using a plain CAI performed significantly better than students who trained using the arcade-like game format CAI. Moreover, students using the plain CAI practiced the problems more.

Malouf (1985) provided one of the few studies specifically designed to evaluate the importance of computer games in relation to motivation. The study used sixth, seventh, and eighth grade learning disabled students with varying levels of initial motivation to compare a drill-and-practice computer game with another program that operated identically but contained minimal game features. Results of the study indicated that the program employing game features produced higher continuing motivation than the non-game program with LD students whose motivation was *initially* low. In contrast, no differences in continuing motivation were observed with students who initially had high motivation. The study provided limited evidence that educators' concerns about the distracting features associated with arcade-like games programs may be unfounded, but even tentative conclusions concerning this issue would be premature considering the lack of empirical investigation in this area. Regardless of the interference effects that may accompany some CAI, any form of academic engagement may be welcome for students who are extremely reluctant learners.

Use as a Secondary Reinforcer

Many special education teachers use the microcomputer as a reinforcer to motivate students to complete tasks unrelated to the computer (Reith, 1986). Although few studies have formally addressed the relative salience of the microcomputer as a back-up motivator, this particular application may not be the most desirable for two reasons. *First,* although it admittedly is a motivator for increasing performance at other tasks, it is also a great time thief when used in this manner (Komoshi, 1981). Time playing entertaining arcade-like games is time taken away from more direct forms of instruction. Some instructors use academic drill-and-practice programs, instead of entertaining games, as reinforcers—the argument being that the student is working on academic-related activities. Many teachers, however, simply direct a student to choose from a collection of software drill-and-practice programs those that he or she wishes to use. Little systematic, purposeful planning for review and practice of specific skills takes place in these instances.

The *second* area of concern involves use of extrinsics such as free time for game playing. Several educators have cautioned that nonjudicial use of extrinsic reinforcers can foster external locus of control and dependency—behaviors that run counter to facilitating independence (Adleman & Taylor, 1983; Close, Irvin, Taylor, & Agosta, 1981; Deci, 1975; Ellis, 1986; Ellis, Lenz, & Sabornie, 1987; Licht & Kistner, 1986; Schumaker, Deshler, & Ellis, 1986). Other motivational techniques, however, have been found to be quite effective. These include: (a) providing a high number of success experiences for the students by requiring frequent responses that will assure correct answers (Stevens & Rosenshine, 1981; Anderson, Evertson, & Brophy, 1979; Good & Grouws, 1979); (b) having students chart their prior progress and before each new practice attempt (Adams, Archer, Ellis, & Moorehead, in press); and (c) having students plot a point predicting performance on the next practice attempt (Tollefson, Tracy, Johnson, Buenning, Farmer, & Barke, 1982; Tollefson, Tracy, & Johnson, 1982.) The instructional time and monetary cost in using these procedures is negligible, plus they foster independence of action.

PROMISE 2: MICROCOMPUTERS INCREASE SELF-CONCEPT

Increased self-concept is an often touted advantage of computer-assisted instruction (Furst, 1983; Schiffman, Tobin, & Buchanan, 1982). A search in the available literature does not reveal any studies that have specifically addressed the claim that interactions with the microcomputer using educational software will increase self-concept. Many educators have maintained, however, that one of the most appropriate ways to improve self-concept is to increase the student's level of success and to increase the amount of learning that takes place (Adams et al., in press). A key to effective instruction is the instructor's ability to facilitate students' academic engaged time (Adams et al., in press; Anderson, Evertson, & Brophy, 1979; Good & Grouws, 1979; Stevens & Rosenshine, 1981)—that is, not just to produce on-task behavior but, rather, to manage students' behavior so that they frequently produce a maximum number of academic-related correct responses.

This line of logic can lead one to conclude that the more the students make correct academic responses, the greater is the probability that self-concept will be enhanced. Studies using the microcomputer have demonstrated clearly that *some* programs are able to facilitate academic engaged time with marked effectiveness (e.g., MacArthur, Haynes, Malouf, & Harris, 1986). These studies will be reviewed throughout the remainder of the article.

PROMISE 3: LOGO WORKS WONDERS

A number of writers have noted that LOGO, a simple programming language, has great potential for helping learning disabled and other handicapped students (Abelson & di Sessa, 1982; Gray, 1984; Maddux, 1984; Schiffman, Tobin, & Buchanan, 1982; Weir, 1982). For example, Weir and Watt (1981) indicated that LOGO programming experiences have the potential to improve fine-motor skills, increase short-term memory, help students learn to use feedback more effectively, move from concrete to more abstract levels of thinking, and through successes associated with the experiences, possibly lead to improved attitudes about learning and improved self-confidence. Torgesen (1986b) noted that only ambiguous, anecdotal evidence is offered to support these claims; although it cannot be argued that LOGO experiences do not produce these effects, little empirical data have been provided to substantiate any of the promises made by LOGO enthusiasts.

PROMISE 4: MICROCOMPUTER INSTRUCTION CAN BE SUPERIOR TO TRADITIONAL INSTRUCTIONAL PROCEDURES

A promise that frequently appears in the literature is that microcomputers can be as (or more) effective as traditional teacher-assisted (TA) instructional procedures (Guess, 1981; Hoffman, 1982; Kulik, Kulik, & Cohen, 1980; Magidson, 1978). A number of educators (e.g., Chiang, 1986; Lieber & Semmel, 1985; Romanczyk, 1986) have noted that research has not clearly validated the relative effectiveness of CAI as opposed to TA instruction. A few studies have begun to address this promise, but the claim is too broad to lend itself to precise empirical investigation (Clark, 1983), as instruction consists of multidimensional variables that are difficult to control. Of the few studies designed to compare CAI with TA, findings are ambiguous and do not allow even tentative conclusions concerning the superiority of CAI.

For example, Trifiletti, Frith, and Armstrong (1984) compared a computer-assisted approach with the teacher-guided approach used in a resource room setting for teaching basic math skills to 21 learning disabled students. They reported that the 12 LD students who had received CAI math instruction for 40 minutes a day over a 4-month period learned almost twice as many new math skills as their 9 counterparts in the resource setting room. Although these results are impressive, it is unclear whether they reflect more on the effectiveness of the CAI or the ineffectiveness of the LD resource room teacher in the comparison group (Torgesen, 1986a).

McDermott and Watkins (1983) offer contrasting data. They compared CAI-based math and spelling programs with conventional remedial instruction over a period of one school year. Findings reflected essentially no difference between the 129 LD students in the conventional group and the 38 LD students receiving math CAI and 41 LD students receiving spelling CAI. Further, Fitzgerald, Fick, and Milich (1986), using 9 elementary students characterized by their teachers as having attention deficits, compared CAI designed to teach spelling, a traditional "write-and-check" form of instruction, and a no-practice condition. Students received the instruction over a period of 5 weeks, learning five new words per week. The no-practice condition naturally was found to be inferior, but no differences were found between the CAI and the TA approaches. Fitzgerald et al. concluded that CAI was equal or superior to the traditional method. Even so, learning 15 new words in 5 weeks does not suggest highly efficient instruction in either condition. Other investigators, too, have found no differences between CAI and TA (e.g., Carman & Kosberg, 1982; Kleiman, Humphrey, & Lindsay, 1983).

Some studies have attempted to control for the multidimensional aspects of instructional design by carefully attempting to parallel control group instruction with activities used in the CAI, but results are still equivocal. Hayes, Kapinus, Malouf, and MacArthur (1984) examined the effects of CAI, paired with metacognitive activities (e.g., predicting how many would be correct on the next test) as compared to a TA practice using a paper-and-pencil activity format that closely paralleled spelling, definition, and correct usage of words in sentences. Results revealed no significant differences among the two conditions on either immediate retention or on the amount of time required to practice the new knowledge. Varnhagen and Gerber's (1984) finding that paper-and-pencil activities produced superior performance offers additional evidence in support of TA over CAI. In contrast, Romanczyk (1986) reported that in three studies that matched the conditions on a number of variables (e.g., pacing, difficulty level, degree of interchange, reinforcement) and involved teaching mathematics to neurologically impaired, emotionally disturbed, and LD children, CAI was found to be as effective as teacher-assisted instruction with many of the students.

Torgesen (1986a, 1986b) noted that a relevant dimension appears to be not so much whether the computer or the teacher delivers the instruction but, rather, the extent to which either uses procedures based on mastery learning in which instruction is carefully sequenced and integrated and objectives are well defined and based on established algorithms for making instructional decisions (e.g., determining next instructional procedure based on students' speed and accuracy when performing the skill). Conclusions as such are logically consistent with the effective TA instruction findings (Brophy & Good, 1984; Englemann & Carnine, 1982; Gersten, Woodward, & Darch, 1986; Morsink, Soar, Soar, & Thomas, 1986; Samuels, 1986; Stevens & Rosenshine, 1981), but clarification is needed in how to design programs so that these principles are effectively employed by CAI.

Further, some CAI may be more appropriate for different content and skill areas [e.g., learning math and spelling facts versus developing reading comprehension or problem-solving strategies (Torgesen, 1986b)], and effectiveness may be more related to the level of learning the student is currently performing [e.g., acquiring new skills versus acquiring automaticity of previously learned skills (Carlson & Silverman, 1986; Torgesen, 1986b)], and may be related to the form CAI employed (e.g., tutoring, drill-and-practice, simulations). The following promises address these more specific concerns.

PROMISE 5: MICROCOMPUTERS CAN BE USED AS TUTORS FOR INSTRUCTING NEW SKILLS OR KNOWLEDGE

Although it remains unclear as to whether CAI is as effective or superior in comparison to TA as a general issue, an important area to clarify is how effective CAI is in teaching new skills or knowledge, regardless of how it compares to TA. Carlson and Silverman (1986) noted that current software is either inappropriate or only marginally helpful in the acquisition of new skills or knowledge. Educators should not overgeneralize such statements to believe that CAI is not, or cannot, be effective as a tutor. Existing popular software is more the brunt of that criticism.

Few studies have investigated the role of microcomputers when used as a true tutor of new skills or content, but limited evidence suggests that the microcomputer can be quite effective in teaching knowledge and skills across a variety of domains. The following studies illustrate that, at least to some extent, microcomputers can be effective in providing direct instruction in concepts, processes, and problem solving. Although the primary intent of these studies was not to establish their effectiveness in the various domains, they effectively serve this purpose.

Direct Instruction of New Concepts

Johnson, Carnine, and Gersten (1986) compared two methods of CAI designed to teach vocabulary to mildly handicapped adolescents. The CAI differed in the magnitude of teaching sets offered within a given lesson and the manner in which cumulative review was provided. Both taught the same 50 words and definitions to 24 mildly handicapped students who had been divided randomly into one condition or the other. The program containing the small teaching set presented, in a single set, no more than three new words in conjunction with seven practice words that the student had previously learned. The student had to meet a mastery criterion on each word before the word was removed. The program containing the large teaching set included 25 new words per set; students were able to choose between one of four presentation options: (a) the word was displayed, along with its definition and one sample sentence using the word; (b) a multiple-choice quiz format; (c) an exercise displaying a correct definition, and the student had to spell the correct missing word to complete a sentence; or (d) an arcade-like game in which the student matched words to correct definitions.

To evaluate the effects of the CAI, measures included time to mastery and pre/post test scores on a 50-item multiple-choice test. In addition, transfer measures were taken by an orally administered objective test on the vocabulary words and on a comprehension test that required knowledge of the vocabulary word meanings. Results on the time to mastery measures indicated that the small-set group learned the set of 50 vocabulary words in significantly less time than the large-set group. The small-set group required an average of 7.6 sessions to master the words, whereas the large-set group required a mean of 9.1 sessions. No significant differences were found on the other measures. Results tentatively suggest that information, when presented in small clusters of new information and paired with about twice as much previously learned material, can be an effective way to present new information. More notably, the study illustrates that CAI can be used as an effective tutor in the instruction of concepts.

Direct Instruction of a New Multi-Step Process

A process is a skill that involves application of a number of steps to solve a problem—e.g., reducing fractions, counting coins, writing an enumerative paragraph

(Adams et al., in press). A study by Collins, Carnine, and Gersten (in press) demonstrated that the processes associated with reasoning skills could be successfully taught using a microcomputer as a tutor. The primary intent of the study was to clarify whether "elaborated correction" procedures (detailed corrective feedback, plus modeling steps as necessary to obtain students' correct response) integrated into CAI was more or less effective than "basic corrections" (telling the student that he/she was correct or incorrect and then providing the correct answer if incorrect) when teaching students a new process. The investigation used two versions of a tutoring program designed to teach students to draw conclusions from two statements of evidence and to determine whether a two-statement argument was logical (Englemann, Carnine, & Collins, in press). One of the tutoring programs contained the elaborated form of feedback; the other used the basic corrections form. The Test of Formal Logic (Collins, 1984) was adapted for use as pre, post, and maintenance test measures. Part of the test evaluated acquisition of the logic skills when constructing and analyzing syllogistic arguments similar to those found in the practice exercises. The remainder of the test evaluated the students' ability to generalize the new skills to similar analytic tasks but was presented in prose paragraph form.

Although the finding that the 17 mildly handicapped students who used the elaborated feedback version of the software demonstrated significantly greater skill acquisition and transfer than the 17 students who used the basic correction version is not surprising, the study illustrates a significant point: Even though the effectiveness of much of the commercially available software remains largely an empirical question, software that is effective in tutoring a new skill in applying a process *can* be designed. Moreover, it is possible to design programs employing procedures that provide relatively sophisticated forms of feedback, modeling, and prompting heretofore found only with mainframe computers and live teachers. Which processes lend themselves to CAI and which may be more effectively taught before CAI is introduced, however, remains unclear. The Collins et al. study did not evaluate whether it would have been more effective for the teacher to first provide direct instruction in the logic processes and then allow the computer to follow through with guided practice, as opposed to using only the computer for direct instructional processes.

Evidence from a study by Gleason (1985) suggests that the issue of *when* to use CAI in problem-solving instruction remains in question. In this investigation CAI was used to teach a step-by-step process for solving math story problems. The process focused on choosing the correct operation—multiplication or division. The CAI employed a direct instructional procedure, providing input on a step-by-step basis. Modeling of each step of the process was used, as well as prompting the students' application of the procedure. When a student erred, the CAI provided rule-based instruction. The study compared the direct instruction CAI program with an instructional procedure using software that focused on semantic guiding (*Semantic Calculator*). Rather than providing direct instruction of a step-by-step process for solving the story problem, the semantic guiding procedure guided the student through the story by using questions that prompted answers (e.g., "How many?" "What?") to determine how to solve the problem. When students provided incorrect answers to the guiding questions, they were asked to "go back and try again."

Gleason used a 28-item pre/post test consisting of various word problems requiring all the basic operations. Of the problems, 32% required the student to transfer the problem-solving skill to novel problems unlike those in the practice lessons. When the 13 students who had been randomly assigned to each group were posttested, results indicated no significant differences between the direct instruction CAI and the semantic guide CAI when the number of correct answers and the time required to take the posttest were analyzed. Observations of student performance indicated that they were ignoring computer prompts that told them what to do next; thus, many students were missing opportunities to learn from their errors. Woodward, Carnine, Gersten, Gleason, Johnson, and Collins (1986) speculated that mildly handicapped students may need more direct instruction from the teacher *before* using a computer for practice opportunities. Thus, while some software programs may be effective at teaching a skill at the acquisition level, which processes and procedures lend themselves most effectively to this level of learning remains unclear.

Direct Instruction in Problem Solving

Computers often have been touted as excellent devices for teaching problem solving, but in fact much of the software (e.g., *Lemonade, Snooper Troops, Factory, Oregon Trail*) that claims to promote problem-solving skills (e.g., planning, sequencing, following directions) only remotely address these skills (Russell, 1986) and may be more appropriately classified as entertainment. Many educators have advocated use of simulations to promote problem-solving skills (Doob, 1972; Greenblat & Duke, 1975; Budoff, Thormann, & Gras, 1984), but research comparing simulation instruction with conventional methods has not found the former to be any more effective than the latter. Woodward, Carnine, and Collins (1986) hypothesized that a more effective way to teach problem solving is not to choose between these methods of instruction but, rather, to use both; initially, direct instruction in problem-solving preskills and strategies could be provided, followed by opportunities to practice the new skills while interacting with a simulation. Thus, the simulation activities are used to "enhance rather than replace" problem-solving instruction (p. 14).

Woodward et al. tested this hypothesis using a series of computer simulation activities involving problem solving in health-related areas. Thirty students were randomly divided and assigned to either a conventional or a simulation group. Both groups received the same initial instruction in health-related problem-solving skills. Then the conventional group received application and review activities presented by a resource teacher while the other group worked in a computer lab with the CAI simulation activities. The simulation instruction consisted of interacting with *Health Ways* (Carnine, Lang, & Wong, 1984), a software program consisting of three phases—initial modeling of the problem-solving routines, guided practice using simulation games, and independent practice with individual feedback using simulation games. Measures consisted of tests designed to assess problem-solving ability (diagnosing health problems, prioritizing them as to their effects on a person's longevity, and prescribing appropriate remedies) on items reinforced by the *Health Ways* simulation and items taught in the curriculum but not reinforced by the simulation.

Results indicated significant effects on items reinforced by the simulation, and non-significant effects for items not reinforced. Thus, the simulation appeared to be an effective procedure for reviewing material that already had been taught. When the two groups were compared, the simulation group was significantly superior in problem-solving skills.

One of the most exciting promises of the microcomputer is its ability to provide interactive instruction using simulations, but until recently the relative effectiveness of simulations as an instructional technique has been unimpressive. The Woodward et al. study provides important information about how computer simulations can be effectively used to teach problem solving. Although tentative, the results suggest that use of a structured approach to computer simulations (outcomes are specified and controlled) when preceded by direct instruction in problem-solving strategies may be a highly effective approach.

PROMISE 6: MICROCOMPUTERS CAN BE USED FOR DRILL AND PRACTICE TO ATTAIN AUTOMATICITY OF SKILLS

Drill-and-practice software, one of the most common applications of microcomputer software in special education settings (Reith, 1986; Russell, 1986), has drawn a lot of rhetoric from educators (e.g., Gagne, 1983; Garson, 1983; Hofmeister, 1984; Lepper, 1985; Lesgold, 1983; Russell, 1983; Turkel & Podell, 1984). Some are very critical. For example, LeBlanc et al. (1985) noted that the primary emphasis of current software is on "teaching what already has been taught rather than upon teaching new skills" (p. 28). They noted that most software typically uses trial-and-error procedures that are responsible for the "educational failure of many children who experience learning difficulties" (p. 28). Carlson and Silverman (1986) criticized most CAI software as little more than electronic flashcard machines. When directed at much of the software commonly used, these negative comments are deserving—especially when the CAI does not closely correlate with skills currently under direct instruction by the teacher.

Unfortunately, the criticisms tend to propagate a negative connotation associated with the concept of computer-assisted "drill and practice," (CAP), as opposed to poorly designed software or poor choices as to which software to use with which students. Torgesen (1986b) noted that drill and practice to attain fluency or automaticity of lower order skills (e.g., word decoding or sight word recognition) often is necessary for higher order skill instruction (e.g., metacomprehension strategies) to be appropriate. Several writers (e.g., Lesgold, 1983; Torgesen & Young, 1983; Wilkenson, 1983) have maintained that some forms of CAP, as applied to helping students master basic academic skills, constitute a highly desirable application of the microcomputer. A fundamental question is: How effective are microcomputers for facilitating effective practice?

Representative Studies

Several studies have demonstrated that microcomputers can provide effective practice at increasing mildly handicapped students' word analysis skills. Jones and Torgesen (1985) evaluated *Hint and Hunt* (Beck & Roth, 1984), a program designed to provide practice in analyzing medial vowels and vowel combinations by focusing on accuracy and speed in recognizing vowel sounds in words. Pre and post tests were administered to 20 students who, before the intervention, had an average reading rate of 40 words per minute while correctly reading 70% of the words. The tests required the student to read a word as fast as he or she could after it appeared on the screen. Some of the words from the test were those used during training; others were novel words but contained the same medial vowel and vowel combinations as those addressed by the training.

Results of the drill-and-practice intervention demonstrated that the software can increase decoding fluency. The intervention group demonstrated a 27% increase in speed of responses on generalized words, while the control group increased its speed by only 4%. The increase in speed was accompanied by an increase in accuracy. The intervention group improved its accuracy by about 20%, whereas the control group demonstrated only a 5% increase in accuracy.

Other researchers using other decoding drill-and-practice software have found similar results. For example, Roth and Beck (1984) evaluated the effects of a drill-and-practice program designed to increase decoding by giving the students practice forming many different words from the same sets of beginning and ending word parts. They found that low-achieving fourth graders (i.e., average decoding ability = 1.9 grade equivalent) increased the speed of vocalization of pseudowords by 25%, resulting in a 17% increase in sentence reading speed when provided practice using the CAP software. In contrast, the control group's speed at vocalizing pseudowords increased only slightly, while sentence reading speed increased by only 3%. In addition, Spring and Perry (in press) found similar results when students used CAP software for practicing word analysis skills.

Since decoding skills appear to be an area that can benefit from computerized drill and practice, it would seem logical that sight word recognition also would improve using similar programs. Empirical studies suggest that this is indeed the case. With 9 LD students who had few or no reading skills, Cohen and Torgesen (1985) evaluated the effectiveness of a software program designed to teach sight words. The program used pictures to teach the sight words in groups of 10. Two conditions—typing (to make a response, the student had to type the correct word) versus no-typing (a simple one-button response format)—were employed.

Results of speed and accuracy measures following the intervention suggested that students learned a new word for every 6.7 minutes of study in the no-typing condition, as opposed to 8.7 minutes in the typing condition. The practice also had a slight effect on the students' spelling skills. The authors concluded that the program would be appropriate when used as a supplemental practice activity to teach sight words. Rashotte and Torgesen (1985) demonstrated that fluency of sight word reading in prose also can be improved using CAP. They found that word recognition speed could increase via CAP with a program using a repeated readings format.

Chiang (1986) has provided evidence that drill and practice using the microcomputer also can be effective for teaching multiplication facts. Using 4-minute timings and a software program, *Treasure Hunt*, over a period of 12 days, Chiang demonstrated that students transferred the skills practiced on the computer to paper-and-pencil tasks. As a result of the microcomputer practice, students demonstrated an average gain of 4.7 (girls) and 6.1 (boys) facts per minute on worksheet tasks.

The preceding studies demonstrate that CAI can be applied for effective practice and appear especially appropriate for practicing existing skills to increase automaticity. For the CAI practice to be appropriate, however, teachers should systematically integrate use of the programs with an ongoing instructional plan. Skills practiced with CAI should closely parallel those under TA instruction.

Crossover Instruction

An important question concerning use of CAP is whether new knowledge or skills are being taught or whether existing skills are being practiced. Hasselbring (1986) investigated whether a basic drill-and-practice routine, typically used for practicing existing skills to maintain automaticity, will cross over and have a *tutorial* effect on learning new skills. He investigated the effects of using CAI to teach reproductive math fact recall processes. The subjects were mildly handicapped students with reconstructive math fact skills (students could construct or calculate correct answers by using a process such as counting on fingers) but lacked knowledge of reproductive math facts (immediate recall of correct answers).

In this investigation the students were provided computer-based drill-and-practice activities in the form of arcade-like games for a 20- to 30-day period while working on memorizing answers. Hasselbring used *chronometric analysis,* a process to determine whether students were recalling or reconstructing answers. Results suggested that all students increased their rate of correct responding, but few students moved from reconstructive to reproductive processes. Thus, the drill and practice resulted in a faster answer, but it did not produce a tutoring effect to teach immediate recall of math facts. The drill-and-practice application of the CAI did not produce acquisition of new information (knowledge of math facts). The implications, though tentative, are profound. CAP software, as much of it is commonly designed, does not necessarily teach new skills. Therefore, teachers using these forms of CAI with the intent of teaching new basic facts should carefully monitor the learning process. They might be wise to use a more direct form of instruction during the acquisition phase.

PROMISE 7: MICROCOMPUTERS CAN BE PROGRAMMED TO ACT AS INSTRUCTIONAL ENGINEERS

The term *instructional engineer* refers to the use of both simple and sophisticated instructional techniques and algorithms that have been demonstrated to be highly effective in teaching when used properly (altering the pace of instruction to reflect optimal learning curves for each individual; automatically increasing the requirements for speed of response depending on the student's current level of acquisition of the skill). Although demonstratedly effective, appropriate use of many of the techniques requires intensive training—something that teacher training institutes have not adequately addressed because of overpacked curricula. Thus, many teachers are exposed to only the most rudimentary information about application of principles of learning and teaching (Englert, 1984)—resulting in a form of social invalidity of the more technical procedures. Until problems associated with training and getting teachers to use them are remedied, much of the precise teaching technology remains on the professorial and rhetorical level.

A promise that offers partial resolution to the social validity issue is that persons with high expertise in instructional engineering can design CAI programs that teachers who have relatively little knowledge of precise teaching procedures can use. Many educators (i.e., Fitzgerald, Fick, & Milich, 1986; LeBlanc et al., 1986) have noted promises that the microcomputer can be programmed to make and implement instructional decisions based on data reflecting current performance and specific students' individual needs.

For example, Fitzgerald et al. noted that many hyperactive children appear to learn better when allowed to proceed in a self-paced manner (Whalen et al., 1978) and when feedback is continuous as opposed to intermittent or noncontingent (Douglas & Parry, 1983; Parry & Douglas, 1983). They noted that microcomputers offer the promise of automatic or selected pacing adjustment and feedback features that make them particularly appropriate for these and other populations with unique learning styles. That type of software will allow delivery of engineered instruction in classrooms that heretofore lacked such precision. A number of studies offers evidence to substantiate this promise (e.g., Collins, Carnine, & Gersten, in press; Trifiletti, Frith, & Armstrong, 1984; Fitzgerald et al., 1986). A summary of recent findings related to basic instructional design considerations for CAI and established principles of effective learning is provided below.

Implicit Versus Explicit Instruction

Instructional goals of CAI should be purposeful and explicit (e.g., Carlson & Silverman, 1986; Forman, 1982; Howell & Kaplan, 1980; LeBlanc et al., 1985; Ragosta, 1982; Trifiletti et al., 1984). Although the effectiveness of CAI when the instructional goals are implicit (e.g., *Factory*) remains largely undetermined, much of the CAI with demonstrated effectiveness is based on mastery learning and direct instruction (Collins et al., in press; Woodward et al., 1985).

Frequent, Correct Responses

Eliciting frequent responses from the learner is more important than providing frequent reinforcement for correct answers (LeBlanc et al., 1985). Practice in making correct responses is a key variable to effective learning. To achieve this, programs should be designed to minimize interference effects and make provisions for appropriately spaced review (Salisbury, 1984). Software that limits the size of the set of initial information to be learned appears to be an effective procedure (Johnson, Carnine, & Gersten, 1986). Furthermore, software utilizing isolated practice (practicing a single skill in isolation) is effective during initial stages of learning a new skill, but mixed practice (practicing several different skills) may be more effective in the later stages of learning (Resnick, 1981).

Pacing Instruction

When presenting stimuli based on new information in which a response is required, CAI programs should provide students a brief amount of thinking time until after discrimination has been acquired. In presenting new information, emphasis initially should be on accuracy of responses; later, the program should emphasize both speed and accuracy (e.g., Brophy, 1980; LeBlanc et al., 1985; Torgesen, 1986a, 1986b). Likewise, the pace of the presentation of stimulus materials should be based on learner responding (LeBlanc et al., 1985). For example, several educators (Adams et al., in press; Anderson et al., 1979; Gersten, Carnine, & Williams, 1982) noted that when student responses are in the 80%–90% accuracy range, emphasis should be placed on making accurate responses. When responses are in the 90%–95% accuracy range, emphasis should be placed on speed of accurate responses. Trifiletti et al. (1984) provided an example of this guideline in the following CAI algorithm for teaching math word problems: (a) If less than 60% accuracy on math facts, CAI provided tutorial instruction; (b) if 60%–89% accuracy with a speed of less than 40 digits per minute on math facts, computer-assisted drill-and-practice instruction was provided; (c) if accuracy of ≥90% with speed of 40 digits per minute or more on math facts, word problems were introduced; and (d) the skill was considered mastered when word problem performance was ≥80%.

Torgesen (1986b) noted that careful measurement of student response latency should be built into CAI programs so that decisions can be made to determine whether a skill has been sufficiently overlearned. The importance of this feature was underscored by the research of Taymans, Malouf, and Grogan (1985), who found a strong relationship between latency of response during CAI overlearning activities and retention of the material.

Research investigating the type of response mode (e.g., typing answer versus making a one-button response) has not clearly demonstrated the superiority of one mode over another (Cohen & Torgesen, 1985). The response mode, however, may be closely associated with the nature of the skill being learned (e.g., learning math facts versus spelling words).

Effective Feedback

In research that assessed learning styles of students via computer applications of stimulus-response tasks, LeBlanc et al. (1985) noted that analyzing students' computer-generated errors led to valuable assessment of their task approach behavior. By analyzing pupils' task approach behaviors related to stimuli presented on a computer monitor, they gathered information regarding which discriminative stimulus elements were consistently present when students responded correctly or incorrectly. This information then was used to successfully identify children who had problems in learning complex discrimination tasks and, at the same time, prescribe learning tasks that followed a predetermined sequence and format (i.e., without the stimuli that were closely associated with previous error responses).

LeBlanc et al. concluded that when assessment of learning styles is incorporated into instructional software, CAI can become more reactive to varying learner characteristics. When examining the available educational software for exceptional students who display different types of learning characteristics, however, the latter conclusion appears far easier said than done in CAI software programs.

In terms of general guidelines regarding the manner in which feedback should be engineered, LeBlanc et al. noted that feedback for correct versus incorrect responses should not be more reinforcing than that provided for correct responses. Elaborated forms of corrective feedback (e.g., detailed, corrective feedback paired with modeling and prompts to produce correct responses) are more effective than feedback that merely indicates whether a response is correct or incorrect, or by providing the correct answer following an incorrect response (Collins, Carnine, & Gersten, in press). In addition, following an incorrect response the student should be required to make the correct response (LeBlanc et al., 1985).

Graphics, Sound Effects, and Themes

Too much reinforcer stimulation, as well as repetitious reinforcement, can interfere with learning (LeBlanc et al., 1985; Chiang et al., 1986). The motivation to engage in academic learning of reluctant students, however, appears to increase when the game-like features are included in the program (Malouf, 1985).

To summarize, the studies reviewed underscore the importance of clarifying *intent* when decisions are made to employ CAI. If the intent is to review prerequisite skills or to provide automaticity practice of a skill under current instruction, the skill addressed by the CAI should closely adhere to that where practice is needed. In turn, just because a program addresses a skill of interest does not necessarily mean that the program will effectively instruct in a manner that is needed.

Another issue related to intent concerns criticisms of drill-and-practice applications. Some educators (e.g., Lepper, 1985) have maintained that CAI should focus more on exploratory and discovery aspects of learning and less on passive drill-and-practice applications. The operative word appears to be *intent*. If the intent is to promote curiosity and intrinsic interest in a subject, CAI related to inductive learning might be an effective approach. This remains an empirical question. If the intent, however, is to provide large amounts of effective practice on specific skills, select CAP software is demonstrably effective. Thus, the question is not which is the best application of the technology but, rather, given a specified intent, how effective is the microcomputer in addressing it?

PROMISE 8: USE OF WORD PROCESSORS IMPROVES WRITING ABILITY

Numerous authors have noted many promises associated with using word processors as facilitators of writing ability. Frequently featured are the more motivating aspects of writing when using a word processor (the neat, printed copies of work may positively affect students' evaluations of the work) (MacArthur, Graham, & Skarvold, 1986). Neuman et al. (1985) noted that word processors provide a powerful sense of "authorship" that more conventional techniques cannot offer. Morocco and Neuman (1985) stated the hope that writing on a keyboard will reduce hand cramping. Moreover, revisions are easier; thus, the need for tedious recopying is reduced.

Less optimistically, Degnan (1985) pointed out that because of the memory problems that LD students often experience, many may be precluded from successful application of programs requiring multiple key press or syntax codes for mode crossing; moving between the write, edit, and print modes can be a difficult task for some students to master. Although several educators have mentioned promises associated with using the word processor in the writing process and the teaching of writing (e.g., Bridwell, Nancarrow, & Ross, 1984; Daiute, 1983; Kane, 1983), only a few studies have systematically investigated its impact.

Results, though preliminary, suggest that the value of word processors, in and of itself, may not be as effective or motivating as initially anticipated. For example, MacArthur et al. compared 11 LD students' use of three modes of writing: handwriting, dictation, and word processing. Of the three, dictated stories proved to be the significantly superior mode on a number of variables. For example, dictated stories were longer (median was about 150 words, as compared to a median of about 80 in the other two modes) and had fewer grammatical errors. Notably, no differences were shown between the handwritten stories and those composed on the word processor on a number of variables, including length, quality, structure, vocabulary, mean T-unit length, and mechanical and grammatical errors. On measures of composing rate, dictation again was found superior.

Even though use of the word processor alone may not produce the kind of results initially promised, one should not over-generalize findings to conclude that word processors are not what they have been presumed to be. The medium, paired with specific instruction from the teacher, may yet prove to be a highly valuable instructional tool. But what specific instructional interventions lend themselves effectively to this area is unclear at this time. Some studies have begun to identify some of the problems that mildly handicapped students encounter when using a word processor. Thus, the need for specific instructional skills has begun to be clarified. These are revised briefly here.

Cursor Skills

A naturalistic investigation by McArthur and Shneiderman (1984) provided evidence of specific difficulties that LD students are likely to experience when learning to use the various features of a word processor. They noted that although students had little difficulty moving the cursor, their movements tended to be inefficient. They tended to use the left and right arrows to move the cursor through several lines of text rather than using the up and down arrows. When inserting a single letter, word, or line within a paragraph, students would first use the space bar to make room for the new material, insert it, and then go back and delete the extra space. They were resistant to change, apparently lacking confidence that the words would move by themselves to make room for the new addition, or they would add the space because without it the stimulus was too visually distracting and confusing.

A second problem observed was that the form of the cursor apparently affected deletion of mistakes. Normally, backspace buttons remove the letter immediately preceding the cursor. When the cursor was a block shape that overlapped the next letter, students tended to mistake the letter to be deleted as the one the cursor was on, rather than in front of. Consequently, students frequently deleted the wrong letters. Fewer deleting mistakes were observed when the cursor was shaped like a capital "I." Cursors of this type tend to fall between letters rather than overlapping the letter (MacArthur, Haynes, & Malouf 1985; Neuman et al., 1985).

A third problem related to inefficient deleting procedures. If a mistake was several words behind the cursor, the student tended to delete all the way back to it and retype those words after the mistake was corrected, in lieu of moving the cursor to the error for correction.

Keyboarding Skills

MacArthur, Graham, and Skarvold (1986) found that proficiency in typing was highly correlated with length, quality, and story structure. Thus, this skill appears to be an important variable in the successful application of word processing programs. Also, in a 6-month observation study, Neuman and Morocco (1986) found keyboarding to be a vital skill affecting success in this medium. They observed that teachers tended to use three main approaches to keyboard skill instruction: (a) daily drill and practice with emphasis on hand placement and letter positions; (b) occasional use of computer typing games; and (c) no keyboard practice at all. Of these approaches the first appeared to have the most positive results.

Neuman and Morocco concluded that students should be provided with brief (e.g., 5 minutes) and daily keyboarding instruction on the computer (as opposed to a typewriter or cardboard keyboard). Speed should not be emphasized too early, as students are likely to focus on speed rather than accuracy of response. Further, the teacher should provide careful monitoring of student practice. As the authors noted, if practice is provided routinely, students move from "hunting and pecking" to a much faster "pecking" technique. The authors also pointed out that keyboarding instruction is most effective when provided directly on the monitor. This eliminates the need for continuous switching of eye focal points. Ideally, teachers should select typing practice software that accepts only correct responses and that introduces skills gradually while providing ample reinforcement.

Revisions

An often touted advantage of word processors is that they allow the writer to make quick, easy revisions on a document with a minimal amount of inconvenience. Daiute (1983) explained that this feature allows students to concentrate more on the composition's content, saving the editing process for later. In fact, Neuman et al. (1985) and MacArthur et al. (1986) found that just the opposite tends to occur. Neuman et al. observed that students tended to focus more on the editing process, producing documents that tended to be "technically correct, but shallow in ideas, insight, or the child's own voice" (p. 11).

In an empirical study, MacArthur et al. (1986) verified the observation when they discovered that because of the ease in which revisions can be made, LD students tended to spend more time correcting minor errors during the composing process. They concluded that use of word processors does not necessarily result in greater sophistication of revision strategies, but the word processing may facilitate instruction in revision strategies; students are more willing to make changes when recopying is not necessary.

Composition Skills

Morocco and Neuman (1985) observed that teachers primarily use three basic approaches to writing instruction when students were using a word processor: skill building, guided writing, and strategy instruction. Skill building involved practice with specific subskills to the writing process (e.g., mechanics, conventions). The authors concluded that the skill-building approach limited the students' involvement in the writing process; thus, the motivating features of word processors (e.g., pride, sense of authorship) were not effectively capitalized upon when the microcomputer was used in this manner.

Guided writing involves the teacher as a guide to assist mildly handicapped students in generating and organizing ideas. The authors reported positive findings when teachers used this approach. The word processor's ability to allow insertion or deletion of text made the composing process particularly amenable to teacher prompts or cues (e.g., "What happened next?"). Thus, the focus tended to remain on content.

Strategy instruction taught students processes for planning, organizing, reviewing and revising. Prewriting planning such as brainstorming ideas or generating and outlining subtopics on notecards or tree diagrams is a writing process that many educators have advocated (e.g., Moran, Schumaker, & Vetter, 1981). Some educators have disagreed, stating that this process does not necessarily occur in a linear fashion but, rather, is recursive (Flower & Hayes, 1980, 1981). Neuman et al. observed that when teachers encouraged students to apply the strategies while using a word processor, positive results were observed, including what they described as a "high level of involvement and a strong sense of student ownership of the writing" (p. 17), as well as higher levels of independent work when on the computer than other children. What is unclear is the role the word processor played, as opposed to results that might have been observed if some of the students were writing using the more traditional handwriting methods, but using the writing strategies.

Ellis (in preparation) conducted a study that compared writing strategy instruction under various conditions. The study compared students' ability to defend a position using traditional handwriting versus word processing, and word processing paired with an idea processor (e.g., outlining program) under conditions before and after task-specific strategy instruction in defending a position was provided. Results of the pilot study tentatively suggest no differences between handwriting and word processing conditions before strategy instruction, but the word processor paired with an idea processor produced significantly more positive results.

Following the strategy training, students were able to produce noticeably improved documents under all three conditions. The word processor paired with the idea processor was again the superior technique. The study suggests that generic strategy instruction (e.g., outlining) is better than no strategy instruction, but it is even more effective when paired with a task-specific strategy (e.g., seven explicit steps to defending a position in writing). The microcomputer's ability to handle both word processing and outlining programs simultaneously appeared to be a key variable.

Morocco and Neuman (1985) concluded that the skill building, as opposed to guided and strategy instruction, had the least positive impact on students' involvement in the writing process and on sense of ownership. Although involvement is arguably a key variable to overall success in learning to write, the study did not clarify where the emphasis of writing instruction should be and at what point writing mechanics and conventions should be emphasized. Though still an empirical question, *learning* mechanics may be best handled by direct instruction by the teacher, followed by drill-and-practice programs, whereas the word processor would be used for *applying* mechanics and conventions of print after they had been individually mastered. The word processor also would be used more for developing writing skills in a holistic manner, using guiding and strategic instruction.

In summary, the promise of word processors in relation to improving writing ability is compelling but is yet to be fulfilled. Preliminary studies in this area suggest that using the writing tool does not necessarily improve writing skills, but explorations into effective instruction using this medium have just begun. Although it is unclear whether the problems experienced by mildly handicapped students while learning word processing skills are any different from those of their normal achieving counterparts, specific instruction clearly is needed with this population.

EPILOGUE

Because educators have only just begun to systematically investigate the effectiveness of microcomputers with mildly handicapped students, the findings reported in this article should be considered tentative; they only begin to address and illustrate effective instructional practices in this area. What these studies do show, however, is that the promise, on the whole, eventually may be fulfilled. The emerging research suggests that microcomputers may be used effectively across a wide variety of instructional applications, including instruction and review of content, fact, skills, strategies, and problem solving.

Moreover, promises related to effective instruction across software applications (e.g., simulations, drill-and-practice, word processing) appear to be on their way to becoming fulfilled, although considerable work in each of these areas is needed before the relative roles of the teacher and the microcomputer are clearly indicated. Blackhurst and MacArthur (1985) noted that approximately one-third of the higher education institutions they surveyed reported one or more faculty members engaged in microcomputer research, so the next few years should produce an explosion of information, which should further clarify these issues. In relation to effective instruction and use of microcomputers with mildly handicapped students, the future role of research and the premature locking into practices and beliefs about microcomputer applications are two key areas of concern.

Classroom Computer Use and the Role of Research

If one assumes that computer use in special education is still in its developing stage, future researchers in this domain should be cognizant of practical applications of the microcomputer and the limitations of most educators' experience with the medium. As in most educational research articles, a discussion of the practical educational implications of a particular study's findings is needed. Unfortunately, many of the studies reviewed for this manuscript lacked this basic component. Moreover, future researchers should take great care in experimental design so that research and interpretation problems common in past special education studies (e.g., sampling and other difficulties found in the early efficacy research of special versus regular education for exceptional students) are not repeated. With the exception of many of the studies reviewed in the manuscript, research in classroom computer applications unfortunately appears to be repeating some of the special education never-say-die research difficulties.

Premature Locking into Beliefs and Practices

Despite encouraging results from the studies reviewed in this article, educators concerned with effective instruction when using microcomputers with mildly handicapped students face a major dilemma: Changing basic practices and beliefs is incredibly difficult once they become ingrained in educators' minds. Some less than optimal beliefs and practices associated with using microcomputers with special populations are well on their way to becoming ingrained.

The problem is not unlike that faced by the field of learning disabilities. Because so many educators still practice unsubstantiated remediation procedures that became vogue some 20 years ago, the Council for Learning Disabilities recently issued a belated, but profound, call for a moratorium on assessment and remediation practices based on perceptual-motor theories (Leigh, 1986). Lacking empirally based interventions at its inception, educators provided the best that current knowledge had to offer at that time. These popular services resulted in a bandwagon effect. Now, almost a quarter of a century later, LD professionals are struggling to change ingrained beliefs about aptitude/treatment practices in which the emphasis is on student perceptual deficits and not on effective instruction—an area that a wealth of empirical evidence suggests we should attend to more closely (e.g., Brophy & Good, 1984; Gersten, Woodward, & Darch, 1986; Morsink, Soar, Soar, & Thomas, 1986; Samuels, 1986; Stevens & Rosenshine, 1981). Current beliefs about and practices using microcomputers suggest that many special educators are creating a new bandwagon—only this time they will be riding with microcomputers in their laps!

Current use of microcomputers and the history of learning disabilities have many parallels. Neither was instigated by professionals but, rather, by parents insisting that schools provide a service. Parent organizations have actively raised money and purchased computers for schools, expecting that teachers do something with them; yet few educators had any real idea what to do. Both have been subject to providing services before an empirical basis for the services had been clearly established, and both have been subjected to promoters who have made exaggerated, unsubstantiated claims and promises that far exceeded what the programs were able to produce (Hofmeister, 1982; LeBlanc et al., 1985; Semmel & Lieber, 1986; Semmel, Cosden, Semmel, & Kelemen, 1984; Zientara, 1984).

Further, both the field of learning disabilities and users of educational microcomputers have been subject to simplistic notions regarding what is effective practice. The learning disabilities field has had its share of educators who believe that the key to an individual's success is determining whether the student is a "visual" or "auditory" learner. Likewise, many special educators seem to believe that microcomputers are best used for drill-and-practice, to reward student performance or behavior, or to present games that have no instructional content (LeBlanc et al., 1985).

Since their relative effectiveness appears to be directly related to the extent to which practices draw upon principles of learning and effective instruction (LeBlanc et al., 1985; Ragosta, 1982; Salisbury, 1984; Torgesen, 1986a, 1986b; Trifiletti, Frith, & Armstrong, 1984), both fields share one other commonality: They face the task of changing existing practices and beliefs about what is effective instruction. We hope that the microcomputer field will not take 20 years to come to grips with this task!

REFERENCES

Abelson, A., & di Sessa, A. (1982). *Turtle geometry*. Cambridge: MIT Press.

Adams, A., Archer, A., Ellis, E. S., & Moorehead, M. K. (in press). *Effective instruction of mildly handicapped adolescents*. Reston, VA: Council for Exceptional Children.

Adleman, H. S., & Taylor, L. (1983). *Learning disabilities in perspective*. Glenview, IL: Scott, Foresman.

Anderson, L. M., Evertson, C. M., & Brophy, J. E. (1979). An experimental study of effective teaching in first-grade reading groups. *Elementary School Journal, 79*, 193–222.

Arms, V. M. (1984). A dyslexic can compose on a computer. *Educational Technology, 24*(1).

Beck, I. L., & Roth, S. F. (1984). *Hint and hunt I teacher's manual*. Allen, TX: Developmental Learning Materials.

Bell, T. E. (1983). My computer, my teacher. *Personal Computing, 7*(6).

Blackhurst, A. E., & MacArthur, C. S. (1985). *Microcomputer use in special education personnel preparation programs*. Vienna, VA: Dissemin/Action Products Center.

Bridwell, L. S., Nancarrow, P. R., & Ross, D. (1984). The writing process and the writing machine: Current research on word processors relevant to the teaching of composition. In R. B. Beach & L. S. Bridwell (Eds.), *New directions in composition research*. New York: Guilford Press.

Brophy, J. (1980). *Recent research on teaching*. East Lansing: Michigan State University.

Brophy, J., & Good, T. (1984). Teacher behavior and student achievement. In M. Wittrock (Ed.), *Third handbook of research on teaching* (3rd. ed.). New York: Macmillan.

Budoff, M., Thormann, J., & Gras, A. (1984). *Microcomputers in special education*. Cambridge, MA: Brookline Books.

Carlson, S. A., & Silverman, R. (1986). Microcomputers and computer-assisted instruction in special classrooms: Do we need the teacher? *Learning Disability Quarterly, 9*(2), 105–110.

Carman, G. O., & Kosberg, B. (1982). Educational technology research: Computer technology and the education of emotionally handicapped children. *Educational Technology, 22*(2), 26–30.

Carnine, D., Lang, D., & Wong, L. (1984). *Health ways*. Unpublished computer program, University of Oregon, Eugene.

Chaffin, J. D., Maxwell, B., & Thompson, B. (1982). ARC-ED curriculum: The application of video game formats to educational software. *Exceptional Children 49*(2), 173–178.

Chiang, B. (1986). Initial learning and transfer effects of microcomputer drills on LD students' multiplication skills. *Learning Disability Quarterly, 9*(2), 118–123.

Christensen, C. A., & Gerber, M. M. (1986). *Effects of game format in computerized drill and practice on development of automaticity in single digit addition for learning disabled students* (Tech. Rep. No. 29). Santa Barbara: University of California, Project TEECh.

Clark, R. E. (1983). Reconsidering research on learning from media. *Review of Educational Research, 53*(4), 445–459.

Close, D. W., Irvin, L. K., Taylor, V. E., & Agosta, J. (1981). Community living skills instruction for mildly retarded persons. *Exceptional Education Quarterly, 2*, 75–86.

Cohen, A., & Torgesen, J. K. (1985). *Comparison of two versions of a computer program for increasing sight word vocabulary in learning disabled children*. Unpublished manuscript, Florida State University.

Collins, M. (1984). *Test of formal logic*. Unpublished doctoral dissertation, University of Oregon.

Collins, M., Carnine, D., & Gersten, R. (in press). Elaborated corrected feedback and the acquisition of reasoning skills. A study of computer assisted instruction. *Exceptional Children*.

Daiute, C. A. (1983). The computer as stylus and audience. *College Composition & Communication, 34*, 134–145.

Deci, E. L. (1975). *Intrinsic motivation*. New York: Plenum Press.

Degnan, S. C. (1985). Word processing for special education students: Worth the effort. *Technological Horizons in Education Journal, 12*, 80–82.

Doob, P. (1972). *Prospects for simulation gaming in health planning and consumer health education*. Reston: VA: ERIC ED 070 596.

Douglas, V. I., & Parry, P. (1983). Effects of reward on the delayed reaction time task performance of hyperactive children. *Journal of Abnormal Child Psychology, 11*, 313–326.

Ellis, E. S. (1986). The role of motivation and pedagogy on the generalization of cognitive strategy training. *Journal of Learning Disabilities, 19*, 66–70.

Ellis, E. S. (in preparation). *An examination of the effects of writing strategy instruction using handwriting, word processors, and idea processors with LD adolescents*. Columbia, SC: University of South Carolina Program for Exceptional Children.

Ellis, E. S., Lenz, B. K., & Sabornie, E. J. (1987). Generalization and adaptation of learning strategies to natural environments: Part I. *Remedial and Special Education, 8*(1).

Englemann, S., & Carnine, D. (1982). *Theory of instruction*. New York: Irvington.

Englemann S., Carnine,D., & Collins, M. (1983). *DIAL reasoning skills program* [computer program]. Eugene, OR: Englemann-Becker Corp.

Englert,C. S. (1984). Examining effective direct instruction practices in special education settings. *Remedial & Special Education, 5*, 38–47.

Fitzgerald, G., Fick, L., & Milich, R. (1986). Computer-assisted instruction for students with attentional difficulties. *Journal of Learning Disabilities, 19* (6), 376–379.

Flower, L., & Hayes, J. (1980). The dynamics of composing: Making plans and juggling constraints. In L. Gregg & E. Steinberg (Eds.), *Cognitive processes in writing: An interdisciplinary approach*. Hillsdale, NJ: Lawrence Erlbaum.

Flower, L., & Hayes, J. (1981). Plans that guide the composing process. In C. H. Frederickson and J. Dominic (Eds.), *Writing: The nature, development and teaching of written communication*. Hillsdale, NJ: Lawrence Erlbaum.

Forman, D. (1982). Review of the literature. *Computing Teacher, 9* (5), 37–50.

Furst, M. (1983). Building self-esteem. *Academic Therapy, 19* (1).

Gagne, R. M. (1983). Some issues in the psychology of mathematics instruction. *Journal for Research in Mathematics Instruction, 14,* 7–18.

Garson, J. W. (1983). The case against multiple choice. In D. O. Harper & J. H. Stewart (Eds.), *Run: Computer education.* Monterey, CA: Brooks/Cole.

Gersten, R. M., Carnine, D. W., & Williams, P. B. (1982). Measuring implementation of a structured educational model in an urban school district. *Educational Evaluation and Policy Analysis.* Eugene: University of Oregon.

Gersten, R., Woodward, J. & Darch, C. (1986). Direct instruction: A research-based approach to curriculum design and teaching. *Exceptional Children, 53* (1), 17–31.

Gleason, M. (1985). *A comparison of two CAI approaches in teaching math word problems to handicapped learners.* Unpublished doctoral dissertation, University of Oregon.

Good, T. L., & Grouws, D. A. (1979). The Missouri mathematics effectiveness project. *Journal of Educational Psychology, 71,* 355–362.

Gray, A. (1984, January). LOGO helps remove children's handicaps. *Educational Computer.*

Greenblat, C., & Duke, R. (1975). *Gaming simulation: Rationale, design, and application.* New York: Halsted.

Guess, E. K. (1981). The future of computer education: Invincible innovation of transitory transformation. *Computing Teacher, 9* (1), 39–42.

Hasselbring, T. S. (1986). *A chronometric analysis of the effects of computer-based drill and practice in addition and subtraction.* Paper presented at the Special Education Technology Conference, Washington, DC.

Haynes, J. A., Kapinus, B. A., Malouf, D. B., & MacArthur, C. A. (1984). *Effect of computer assisted instruction on learning disabled readers' metacognition and learning of new words* (Research report #101). College Park, MD: University of Maryland, Institute for the Study of Exceptional Children and Youth.

Hoffman, R. J. (1982). Microcomputers, evaluation, literacy: Will the teacher survive? *Journal of Learning Disabilities, 15* (6), 370–372.

Hofmeister, A. M. (1982). Microcomputers in perspective. *Exceptional Children, 49,* 115–121.

Hofmeister, A. M. (1984). The special educator in the information age. *Peabody Journal of Education, 62* (1), 5–21.

Howell, K., & Kaplan, J. (1980). *Diagnosing basic skills.* Columbus, OH: Merrill.

Johnson, G., Gersten, R., & Carnine, D. (1986). *Effects of instructional design variables on vocabulary acquisition of LD students: A study of computer-assisted instruction.* Manuscript submitted for publication.

Jones, K., & Torgesen, J. K. (1985). *An evaluation of the Hint and Hunt I program with learning disabled children.* Unpublished manuscript, Florida State University.

Kane, J. H. (1983). *Computers for composing* (Tech. Rep. No. 21). New York: Bank Street College of Education.

Kleiman, G., Humphrey, M., & Lindsay, P. H. (1983). Microcomputers and hyperactive children. In D. O. Harper & J. H. Steward (Eds.), *Run: Computer education.* Monterey, CA: Brooks/Cole.

Komoski, K. P. (1981). Instructional materials: Products or processes. *Journal of Special Education Technology, 4* (3), 36.

Kulik, J. A., Kulik, C. L. C., & Cohen, P. A. (1980). Effectiveness of computer-based college teaching: A meta-analysis of findings. *Review of Educational Research, 50,* 525–544.

Larsen, S. C., & Hammill, D. D. (1976). *The test of written spelling.* Austin, TX: PRO-ED.

LeBlanc, J. M., Hoko, J. A., Aangeenbrug, M. H., & Etzel, B. C. (1985). Microcomputers and stimulus control: From the laboratory to the classroom. *Journal of Educational Technology, 7*(1), 23–30.

Leigh, J. (1986). CLD position statements: Measurement and training of perceptual-motor functions. *Learning Disability Quarterly, 9*(3), 247.

Lepper, M. R. (1985). Microcomputers in education: Motivational and social issues. *American Psychologist, 40*(1), 1–18.

Lesgold, A. M. (1983). A rationale for computer-based recording instruction. In A. C. Wilkenson (Ed.), *Classroom computers and cognitive science.* New York: American Press.

Licht, B. C., & Kistner, J. A. (1986). Motivational problems of learning-disabled children: Individual differences and their implications for treatment. In J. K. Torgesen and B. Y. L. Wong (Eds.), *Psychological and educational perspectives on learning disabilities.* New York: Academic Press.

Lieber, J., & Semmel, M. I. (1986). *The effect of group size and configuration on social and performance behaviors of mildly handicapped using microcomputers* (Tech. Rep. No. 22). Santa Barbara: University of California, Project TEECh.

MacArthur, C. A., Graham, S., & Skarvold, J. (1986). *Learning disabled students' composing with three methods: Handwriting, dictation and word processing* (Research report #109). College Park: University of Maryland, Institute for the Study of Exceptional Children and Youth.

MacArthur, C. A., & Shneiderman, B. (1984). Learning disabled students' difficulties in learning to use a word processor: Implications for instruction and software evaluation. *Journal of Learning Disabilities, 19*(4).

MacArthur, C. A., Haynes, J. A., Malouf, D. B., & Harris, K. (1986). *Computer assisted instruction for learning disabled students: Achievement, engagement, and other factors that influence achievement* (Research report #112). College Park: University of Maryland, Institute for the Study of Exceptional Children and Youth.

Maddux, C. D. (1984). Using microcomputers with the learning disabled: Will the potential be realized? *Educational Computer,* pp. 31–32.

Magidson, E. (1978), Trends in computer assisted instruction. *Educational Technology, 18,* 5–8.

Malone, T. W. (1981). Toward a theory of intrinsically motivating instruction. *Cognitive Science, 4,* 333–369.

Malouf, D. B. (1985). *The effects of instructional computer games on continuing student motivation* (Research report #106). College Park: University of Maryland, Institute for the Study of Exceptional Children and Youth.

McDermott, P. A., & Watkins, M. W. (1983). Computerized vs. conventional remedial instruction for learning-disabled pupils. *Journal of Special Education, 17*(1), 81–88.

Mokros, J. R., & Russell, S. J. (1986). Learner-centered software: A survey of microcomputer use with special needs students. *Journal of Learning Disabilities, 19*(3), 185–190.

Moran, M. R., Schumaker, J. B., & Vetter, A. F. (1981). *Teaching a paragraph organization strategy to learning disabled adolescents* (Research report #54). Lawrence: University of Kansas Institute for Research in Learning Disabilities.

Morocco, C. C., & Neuman, S. B. (1985). *Teaching children to write with computers: Comparing approaches* (Tech. Rep. No. 1). Newton, MA: Writing Project, Education Development Center.

Morsink, C. V., Soar, R. S., Soar, R. M., & Thomas, R. (1986). Research on teaching: Opening the door to special education classrooms. *Exceptional Children, 53*(1), 32–40.

Neuman, S. B., Morocco, C. C., Bullock, M., Cushman, H., Neale, A., Packard, D., & Traversi, D. (1985). *A model teaching environment for using word processors with LD children. The Writing Project* (Tech. Rep. No. 2). Newton, MA: Education Development Center.

Neuman, S. B., & Morocco, C. C. (1986). *Two hands is hard for me: Keyboarding and learning disabled children.* Newton, MA: University of Lowell, Education Development Center.

Parry, P., & Douglas, V. I. (1983). Effects of reinforcement on concept identification in hyperactive children. *Journal of Abnormal Child Psychology, 11,* 327–340.

Ragosta, M. (1982). *Computer-assisted instruction and compensatory education: The ETS/LAUSD study—overview of the final report.* Washington, DC: National Institute of Education.

Rashotte, C. A., & Torgesen, J. K. (1985). Repeated reading and reading influency in learning disabled children. *Reading Research Quarterly, 20,* 180–188.

Reith, H. (1986). *An analysis of the instructional and contextual variables that influence the efficacy of computer-based instruction for mildly handicapped secondary school students.* Paper presented at the Special Education Technology Conference, Washington DC.

Reith, H., & Frick, T. (1982). *An analysis of academic learning time (ALT) of mildly handicapped students in special education service delivery systems: Initial report on classroom process variables.* Bloomington, IN: Project ALT Center for Innovation in Teaching the Handicapped.

Resnick, L. B. (1981). The psychology of drill and practice. In L. B. Resnick & W. W. Ford, (Eds.), *The psychology of mathematics for instruction* (pp. 11–37). Hillsdale, NJ: Lawrence Erlbaum.

Romanczyk, R. G. (1986). *Direct computer instruction: Issues of assessment, effectiveness, and generalization.* Paper presented at Special Education Technology Conference, Washington, DC.

Roth, S. F., & Beck, I. L. (1984). *Research and instructional issues related to the enhancement of children's decoding skills through a microcomputer program.* Paper presented at the annual meeting of the American Educational Research Association, New Orleans.

Russell, S. J. (1983, October). LOGO in special education. *Classroom Computer Learning,* pp. 34–39.

Russell, S. J. (1986). But what are they learning? The dilemma of using microcomputers in special education. *Learning Disability Quarterly, 9*(2), 100–104.

Salisbury, D. F. (April, 1984). *Cognitive psychology and its implications for designing drill and practice programs for computers*. Paper presented at Annual Meetings of the American Educational Research Association, New Orleans.

Samuels, S. J. (1986). Why children fail to learn and what to do about it. *Exceptional Children, 53*(1), 7–16.

Schiffman, G., Tobin, D., & Buchanan, B. (1982). Microcomputer instruction for the learning disabled. *Journal of Learning Disabilities, 15*, 557–559.

Schumaker, J. B., Deshler, D. D., & Ellis, E. S. (1986). Intervention issues related to the education of LD adolescents. In J. K. Torgesen & B. Y. K. Wong (Eds.), *Psychological and educational perspectives on learning disabilities*. Orlando, FL: Academic Press.

Semmel, M. I., & Lieber, J. A. (1986). Computer applications in instruction. *Focus on Exceptional Children, 18*(4), 1–12.

Semmel, M. I., Cosden, M. A., Semmel, D. S., & Kelemen, E. (1984). Training special education personnel for effective use of microcomputer technology: Critical needs and directions. *Special Services in the Schools, 1*(1), 63–82.

Spring, C., & Perry, L. (in press). Computer assisted instruction in word decoding for educationally handicapped children. *Journal of Educational Technology Systems*.

Stevens, R., & Rosenshine, B. (1981). Advances in research on teaching. *Exceptional Education Quarterly, 2*, 1–9.

Taymans, J. M., Malouf, D. B., & Grogan, M. M. (1985). *An investigation of the relationship between response latency during over-learning and retention for learning disabled students engaged in computer-assisted instruction* (Research report #105.). College Park: University of Maryland, Institute for the Study of Exceptional Children and Youth.

Tollefson, N., Tracy, D. B., & Johnson, E. P. (1982). *Self-control training of LD adolescents in a resource room setting* (Research report #69). Lawrence: University of Kansas Institute for Research in Learning Disabilities.

Torgesen, J. K. (1986a). Using computers to help learning disabled children practice reading: A research-based perspective. *Learning Disabilities Focus, 1*(2), 72–81.

Torgesen, J. K. (1986b). Computer-assisted instruction with learning disabled children. In J. K. Torgesen & B. Y. L. Wong (Eds.), *Psychological and educational perspectives on learning disabilities*. Orlando, FL: Academic Press.

Torgesen, J. K., & Young, K. (1983). Priorities for the use of microcomputers with learning disabled children. *Journal of Learning Disabilities, 16*, 234–237.

Trifiletti, J. J., Frith, G. H., & Armstrong, S. (1984). Microcomputers versus resource rooms for learning disabled students: A preliminary investigation of the effects on math skills. *Learning Disability Quarterly, 7*, 69–76.

Turkel, S. B., & Podell, D. M. (1984, Summer). Computer-assisted learning for mildly handicapped students. *Teaching Exceptional Children, 16*(4), 258–262.

Tyler, J. G. (1983). Your prescription for CAI success. *Instructional Innovator, 28*(2).

Varnhagen, S., & Gerber, M. M. (1984). Use of microcomputers for spelling assessment: Reasons to be cautious. *Learning Disability Quarterly, 7*, 226–270.

Weir, S. (1982). LOGO: A learning environment for the severely handicapped. *Journal of Special Education Technology, 5*(1).

Whalen, C. K., Collins, B. E., Henker, B., Alkus, S. R., Adams, D., & Stapp, J. (1978). Behavior observations of hyperactive children and methylphenidate (Ritalin) effects in systematically structured classroom environments: Now you see them, now you don't. *Journal of Pediatric Psychology, 3*, 177–187.

Wilkenson, A. C. (1983). Learning to read in real time. In A. C. Wilkenson, (Ed.), *Classroom computers and cognitive science*. New York: Academic Press.

Woodward, J., Carnine, D., & Collins, M. T. (1986). *Closing the performance gap in secondary education*. Unpublished manuscript, University of Oregon, Eugene.

Zientara, A. (1983). Microcomputers in early childhood education? *Young Children, 38*, 61–67.

The authors would like to express our appreciation to Ellen Peters, Abby Adams, Anita Archer, and Ann Knockendoffel for their ideas relating to the format of this article. In addition, we thank Jill Nyland for her library research assistance.

Dr. Ellis and Dr. Sabornie are Assistant Professors in the Department of Educational Psychology, University of South Carolina.

Three

Assessment Strategies

Richard J. Whelan

Some 30 years ago assessment was not a controversial issue. At least the topic did not get the coverage in the professional literature of that time to the extent that it does today. For example, in what was considered to be the primary special education source in 1955 (Frampton & Gall, 1955), only one brief chapter (Corrigan, 1985) in three large volumes was devoted to testing or assessment practices. As might be expected, psychologists (Garrison, 1955) were the key persons for verifying, through tests, a student's eligibility for special education services. And, not surprisingly, a critical point in regard to all tests was the adequacy of their norming sample. Nevertheless, special education in that era formulated questions similar to those of today when selecting assessment procedures:

1. What area requires measurement?
2. What instrument deals with this area?
3. What are the characteristics of the sample used to establish norms for the instrument?
4. Does the child to be tested have experiences comparable to those of the norm group?

This last question is especially important to answer, because lack of experience rather than basic ability may influence test results and lead to a classification error; inattention to norms may produce results that are biased—a violation of today's federal regulations that require unbiased assessment practices (34 CFR, Sec. 300.532).

And to what purposes were test results applied? "The information may be used to adjust the curriculum and teaching procedure so that the exceptional child may use his peculiar abilities to the greatest advantage and overcome his handicap whenever possible" (Corrigan, 1955, p. 58). Obtaining test results that could be used to modify instructional content and practices is clearly a goal that present-day special educators strive to achieve (Hammill, 1987), just as our colleagues of 30 or more years ago tried to do.

The brief excursion into assessment practices of the past serves to point out two important concepts. First, special educators have recognized the relationship of assessment to curriculum and teaching for many years, and the effort to more sharply describe that relationship is ongoing. Second, identification of students for placement in special education and related services was and is a problem area in both the past and the present, but the problem is different now. In 1955 the problem was related to case finding, an issue of underidentification. Today the problem, in simplified terms, is overidentification of students in need of specialized instructional services. Are current assessment procedures used to identify the disability groups specified by the Education for All Handicapped Children Act of 1975 (PL 94–142), or are they also including students who, while they may have school performance problems, are not handicapped?

Assessment to establish eligibility for special education and related services is but one function. Others will be described subsequently. This section of the book contains several chapters that discuss assessment procedures. They are not all-inclusive in the sense that every area to be assessed, and every way to conduct assessment, is covered. Rather, the chapters reflect best practices in the areas addressed.

This introduction focuses on three topics in assessment practices: (a) the purposes of assessment; (b) the legal requirements for assessment practices; and (c) a recent trend in assessment practices. Last, some general comments about assessment procedures and issues are offered.

ASSESSMENT PURPOSES

A basic principle of learning that should be used as a guide for assessment practices is: "Since learners differ in their capacity to make the responses to be acquired, learning will be most efficient if it is planned so that each learner embarks on a program commensurate with his capacity to acquire new responses" (Wallen & Travers, 1963). The key words are *capacity* and *program*. Capacity is, of course, related to individual differences, and program is related to curriculum. Assessment procedures should identify student variables to which a curriculum must respond affirmatively if knowledge and skill gains are to be achieved. In brief, *the central purpose of assessment is to provide data or information that can be used to make instructional and related decisions for a student or a group of students*. More specifically, and with regard to special education, "Assessment is the process of collecting data for the purpose of (1) specifying and verifying problems and (2) making decisions about students" (Salvia & Ysseldyke, 1985, p. 5).

If a part of the central purpose of assessment is to make decisions, the logical question is to ask about the nature of these decisions or sub-purposes. One decision is obviously to make changes in instructional planning or programming, but other decisions have to be made, too. Salvia and Ysseldyke (1978, 1975) have developed a matrix of problems and decisions that best describe the components of assessment practices. The problem areas are related to: (a) academic performance, (b) behavior excesses and deficits, and (c) physical disabilities. Physical disabilities include vision and hearing defects, problems of mobility, and long-term illnesses that affect students' energy levels and capability to sustain academic performance. Academic and social behavior problems usually are associated with students who do not perform up to the teachers' or parents' expectations.

The decision part of the matrix has several types: (a) referral, (b) screening, (c) classification, (d) instructional planning, and (e) determining pupil progress. *Referral* decisions may or may not be made on the basis of an identifiable assessment procedure. A teacher may refer a child based upon a drop in daily achievement scores or a change in behavior such as extensive acting-out or withdrawal from group activities. In a sense, the teacher is using one of the better assessment strategies—the frequent and direct measurement of student performance. In this case, the procedure may be unique to the teacher and is not a school district policy in terms of a required or identifiable assessment procedure.

An identifiable source for referrals is *screening*, a mandated procedure that state and local education agencies must conduct. Local and state plans submitted for PL 94-142 federal funds must contain provisions to locate, identify, and evaluate all students with disabilities as defined by the law and its regulations (see 34 CFR, Sec. 300.5 for definitions of handicapped children; Sec. 300.128 for state plan requirements; and Sec. 300.220 for local plan requirements). To carry out this mandate, school districts engage in child-find activities (e.g., locating handicapped children not in school, and in-school screening of all enrolled students). Vision and hearing screenings usually are included in the process. In addition, a school district might use age-appropriate assessment instruments such as school readiness tests, group tests of intellectual ability, general achievement tests, and a behavior rating scale. Screening is a process applied to all students. Its purpose is to select students who, because of questionable performance in the group screening tests, should have an individual assessment.

For the selected students, additional testing is undertaken to determine eligibility, or *classification* for special education and related services. If eligibility is verified by the assessment results, an individualized education program (IEP) is required, to make instructional planning decisions. An individual assessment may be referred to as a comprehensive evaluation, or a pre-placement evaluation (34 CFR, Sec. 300.531). Because this level of assessment is a special education action, the due process protections guaranteed under PL 94–142 and its regulations take effect. These regulations will be described subsequently, so I will just point out here that the pre-placement assessment requires parent notification and parent consent to complete. Screening that is done for and to *all* students is not a special education action, but because pre-placement assessment is done with an *individual* student, it is a special education action. The primary rationale for the pre-placement assessment is not classification but, rather, to establish eligibility for special education and related services. What is special education? It is "specially designed instruction . . . to meet the unique needs of a handicapped child . . ." (34 CFR, Sec. 300.14). The child is placed (classified) into one of the impairment categories, such as deaf or mentally retarded (34 CFR, Sec. 300.5), because the individual assessment determined that the impairment adversely affects educational performance to the extent that special education is needed.

The point is that *classification or labeling is required for reporting purposes, but it is not required to determine eligibility for special education and related services.* For instance, both state (34 CFR, Sec. 300.124) and local school district plans (34 CFR, Sec. 300.227) require that numbers of students by disability (impairment) category must be reported to the Office of Special Education and Rehabilitative Services (OSERS). But a school district can convey to parents that their child does have an impairment that adversely affects performance in a typical regular education environment, and that specially designed instruction (special education) is needed to meet the child's unique needs. It need not give a label to the child unless the parents demand it. And it need not label the placement settings according to impairment categories under the guise of federal requirements simply because such labeling is not required by federal statute or regulations. It has to use labels only for numerical reporting purposes—and that is an information management issue, not one related to assessment practices or outcomes.

The next decision type is *instructional planning* or the development of a student's IEP. If the assessment data used to establish eligibility are truly comprehensive, they should be applicable to planning instructional services that are described in some detail on the IEP. Once the IEP is developed and approved by parents (because it, too, is a special education action), and school district staff, a placement decision can be made. Again, *the extent of services described in the IEP, rather than the impairment label, prescribes the placement.* For example, to stipulate that a student needs "mentally retarded" services is not enough; that is not a placement. But, if the IEP provides for 30 hours of specially designed instruction per week, placement is likely to be in a self-contained classroom rather than a resource room that has 15 hours of instruction per week for each student.

The last decision for which assessment data are used is to *monitor student progress* in placements that have specially designed instruction. This type of assessment should be functionally related to the curriculum content that the student is expected to achieve and should be used to periodically, if not continuously, measure the student's daily performance in curriculum-related tasks. *This type of measurement for assessment purposes can be used to evaluate instruction.* If the student doesn't progress as expected, is it (a) a problem within the student, or (b) a problem in instructional procedures?

And so the assessment process has come full circle. It started out with a teacher using classroom- or curriculum-based data to make a referral for additional assessments (and possibly help from other colleagues to solve a teaching and learning problem) and ended with the teacher using student performance data in the prescribed curriculum to determine progress or the lack of it. Apparently, then, the most important decisions to be made from student assessment data are twofold. First, what do the data indicate about the needs for instructional and curriculum planning? Once that question is answered and a plan is put into operation, the next decision is to put in place an assessment procedure that will produce data indicative of the plan's success or failure. So we assess to plan and we plan to assess—a continuous process focused upon the educational needs of students.

LEGAL REQUIREMENTS

As indicated previously, the days are gone when one person with one test could transfer a student from regular to special education. It just can't be done today because the federal regulations in support of PL 94–142 preclude such unilateral action. The case law that effectively brought an end to the one person-one test system is more than adequately described in other sources (Calagan, 1985; Martin, 1982; Turnbull, 1986), so the discussion here is devoted to the outcomes produced by litigation. More specifically, those outcomes are embedded in federal regulations (34 CFR, Secs. 300.530–300.543) that guarantee *protection in evaluation procedures*.

Fundamental protections that local school districts and state education agencies must give to parents and students include clearly written requirements for completion of pre-placement evaluations. For example, test materials and procedures must not discriminate among students on the bias of race and culture. If a student's primary language is Spanish, a test of intellectual ability administered in standard English would produce false scores, and this is discriminatory.

Other requirements address the issues of tests and those who give them. Tests must be valid; they must clearly test what they say they will test. A test of arithmetic computation must test that skill. Tests that sample performance in specific areas of instructional needs must be administered in addition to those that yield a single general score such as a numerical value for intelligence. Tests should be selected that probe deeply into areas related to educational performance, (e.g., sound blending skills, place values). In addition, a student's performance on an achievement test, for example, must not be penalized by the examiner's failure to take into account the student's visual impairment or a motor disability. Also, a student must be assessed in all areas related to a suspected disability, including, if appropriate, health, vision, hearing, social skills, emotional status, academic performance levels, math skills, intellectual level, and ability to communicate. Last, only skilled, trained examiners can administer the tests. This means that a multidisciplinary team, including a teacher with knowledge about the student's suspected disability, must conduct the assessment process.

In recommending a placement based upon assessment data, the multidisciplinary team must consider sources of data other than test scores. A former teacher, for instance, may make recommendations and produce a student's daily tasks scores to support them. Further, the group that plans the IEP and recommends a placement must include persons who know the student, who can derive meaning from the assessment information, and who are aware of options that meet the least restrictive environment (LRE) placement rule.

Students who are thought to have a specific learning disability (SLD) have additional assessment requirements. These are even more prescriptive than the ones just described. For example, a regular classroom teacher must be on the evaluation team. At least one person qualified to conduct individual examinations, such as a school psychologist, speech-language pathologist, or remedial reading specialist, has to be on the team. SLD is the only disability area that has such prescriptive evaluation requirements. There must be an observed difference between actual and expected achievement when age and intellectual ability are considered. The actual areas of academic performance are specified in the regulations: basic reading skills, listening comprehension, mathematics reasoning, and so on. So, unless students are observed to have a *severe discrepancy* in one or more of the areas, they are not SLD. And if the severe discrepancy is the result of another disability or ecological disadvantage, SLD is not an appropriate identification. The rather elaborate procedures for evaluating and identifying SLD are a direct result of the dramatic increases in students served under the label, and concerns that many students were misidentified (Bos, Weller, & Vaughn, 1984–1985).

It is, of course, rather a sad indictment when professional and ethical practices have to be mandated by law and regulations. The regulations, however, were the result of numerous, documented abuses in the assessment process. These abuses led to misidentification of students as handicapped, and failure to identify students who were disabled. In both instances, students were denied the opportunity for appropriate educational experiences. But even with the regulations, special education as the central profession involved in the assessment process is still struggling to find accurate, reliable ways to identify students in need of different instructional services than typically available in most regular education classrooms. The regulations help in this effort, but they are not sufficient to guarantee it.

Only dedicated special educators who are committed to the students they serve and to their profession can find functional ways to improve assessment procedures and practices. Or stated another way, "We pass through this world but once. Few tragedies can be more extensive than the stunting of life, few injustices deeper than the denial of an opportunity to strive or even to hope, by a limit imposed from without, but falsely identified as lying within" (Gould, 1981, p. 29). This is the challenge that the profession must confront.

A RECENT TREND IN ASSESSMENT STRATEGIES

What goes around comes around. One of the more identifiable and prominent trends in special education assessment procedures today is curriculum-based assessment (CBA). But CBA is not a new concept (Tucker, 1985) and in fact has been used by effective classroom teacher for years. For instance, Witty and Kopel (1939) made several relevant observations about identifying students with reading problems. Standardized, objective reading tests measure just a small part of students' true reading proficiency. And even though such tests may be useful in estimating grade level, they should not be used to evaluate instruction, and they are not sufficient to identify the cause of poor reading. Moreover, the contents of such tests are fragmented in that words, sentences, and brief paragraphs do not adequately reflect the reading material a student is expected to comprehend. More to the point, they believed that standardized test scores had to be supplemented by assessment of a student's ability to read from the reading curriculum—hence CBA.

Blankenship and Lilly (1981) credit Eaton and Lovitt (1972) with developing the modern-day concept of CBA, although Tucker (1985) believes that Edward Gickling was apparently the first person to use the term in the literature. Eaton and Lovitt (1972) made the point that standard achievement tests provide little, if any, guidance about planning instructional strategies or determining the content of instruction. Instead, they believe that direct and frequent measurement of student responses in, for instance, a basal reader provides functional data to plan and evaluate instruction. They assert that this approach avoids a mismatch between a student's needs and the curriculum that is supposed to be responsive to them. "One of the requisites of a good diagnosis is that it be direct. If the teacher wants information about a child's ability to read in an SRA reader, he should listen to the child read from an SRA reader. . . . The teacher, in other words, should monitor directly the behavior of concern; he should not administer an intelligence, personality, or motor development test that might only be indirectly related to the behavior of concern" (Lovitt, 1977, p. 25).

Tucker (1985) described CBA as "the ultimate in teaching the test, because the materials used to assess progress are always drawn directly from the course of study" (p. 200)—i.e., the curriculum. Assessment on the basis of the curriculum means (a) determining students' instructional needs through (b) frequent and direct observation and recording of their performance on (c) task samples selected from the curriculum (e.g., basal reader) they are expected to master.

Users of CBA report that it has several advantages over other approaches to assessing student performance prior to and concurrent with placement in a teaching and learning environment. Several advantages have been noted by Deno (1985) when the CBA process is used:

1. CBA provides clearly displayed data that can be used to make decisions and communicate information. Data that show a 100% increase in words read accurately communicate more meaningful and relevant instructional planning information than reporting performance at the 2.5 grade level. And, clearly, such data may indicate that a shift to more difficult reading tasks is warranted.
2. CBA is sensitive to short-term changes in student performance. This information, in contrast to yearly achievement test information, allows teachers to make responsive curriculum and instructional modifications.
3. The data base produced by frequent measurement of students' responses to the curriculum represents an improvement over grade-equivalent achievement measures.
4. Using CBA does not preclude comparisons of a student's performance with that of a group of students. For example, in planning to reintegrate a handicapped student into a regular classroom, comparisons of performances on similar tasks can be completed. If there is a reasonable match, mainstreaming may be accomplished successfully.
5. CBA procedures are cost-effective because they do not require purchase of tests or the assignment of another professional's time to administer them. The materials used in CBA (e.g., basal readers, spellers) are readily available in classroom.

Deno (1985) uses the term *curriculum-based measurement* (CBM) instead of CBA. CBM was developed as a system that teachers can use to assess their own instructional effectiveness, as well as their students' progress in content to be learned and performed. In that sense, CBM focuses more on assessing ongoing classroom activities than assessment for placement of students in special education services. But it can be used in the pre-placement evaluation process, too, because the procedures are very similar, if not identical, to the ones used by CBA.

The question surely must arise as to what conditions stimulated a resurgent interest in using the "good old everyday" curriculum as a resource for assessing student problems and for planning instructional programs. One event, of course, was the prescribed procedures for assessment practices as required by PL 94–142. The prescriptions were a direct result of legal challenges to inappropriate applications of intelligence, achievement, and technically flawed tests. Their applications produced observed results that were obviously biased but were still used to place students in special education and related services programs.

Another condition, now recognized by professional special educators, is that norm-referenced and standardized tests of intelligence and achievement (if given correctly) produce valid and reliable results that contribute some information about decisions regarding identification of disabilities and about progress in global academic areas, but the data they produce are not useful for decisions about planning and evaluating a student's instructional program. Instructional program planning is more appropriately conducted by using direct measures of student performance in the curriculum.

A third event is the growing awareness that CBA may be used as an alternative to the referral-pre-placement evaluation sequence. That is, the sequence may become one of referral – CBA – pre-placement evaluation. In this way, CBA can be used (a) to maintain students in LRE environments, (b) to reduce the number of students who are incorrectly placed in special education programs, (c) to divert scarce resources from testing to teaching, and (d) to more effectively serve students with handicaps in appropriate learning environments.

GENERAL COMMENTS

This all-too-brief excursion into the practices and issues associated with special education assessment strategies provides only a foundation for additional study. For example, assessment issues and debates about the merits of CBA versus standardized tests are not confined to the field of special education. These issues represent an ongoing debate in regular education, too (Bracey, 1987; Popham, 1987). This debate in regular education is centered upon the merits of measurement-driven instruction (MDI). In brief, MDI is based upon the notion that if attention has to be drawn to an area, the fastest way to accomplish this is to measure that area. If one wants to improve reading skills in a middle school, the student population is tested and the curriculum is revised after scores are analyzed.

MDI is a product of the competency testing movement in regular education, which is striving to improve the knowledge and skill levels of high school graduates in this country. Once competency standards are established it is but a short conceptual leap to associate them with instructional improvements and curriculum planning. An emphasis is placed upon functional outcomes or competencies so that they became instructional targets in the curriculum. Following curriculum changes, criterion-referenced tests are constructed to reflect what is taught to students. Like CBA, MDI is a response to, among other practices, the extensive reliance upon summative evaluations (i.e., tests follow teaching). Instead, assessment (testing) practices associated with CBA and MDI occur before, during, and after teaching. Both are a part of the instructional process rather than an appendage to it.

MDI, unlike CBA, has been criticized for fragmenting the curriculum. CBA may or may not be focused upon the achievement of specific competencies in the future, but presently it doesn't appear to be inextricably tied to statewide competency testing programs. As noted, however, MDI is associated with statewide programs at the present time, but it could be independently implemented in local districts, too. *Fragmentation* refers to learning pieces of the curriculum in isolation without regard to how the pieces constitute a coherent whole. For example, students may be able to answer discrete questions, but can they combine the answers and use them to complete a project or solve a problem?

Another criticism of MDI is that it reduces curriculum breadth or comprehensiveness. It narrows in on objectives that may or may not be relevant to life-centered needs. If math computation skills are taught too extensively because they are tested by a state, what happens to math concepts or the transfer of such skills to other situations?

Special educators must be aware of the trends in regular education. What are the implications of MDI for handicapped students in mainstream settings? Will CBA, which is obviously a more developed, individualized, clinically responsive approach than MDI, be effective in helping students satisfactorily complete minimum competency tests?

Each of the chapters that follow in this section of the book is, first of all, concerned about individual students. Focus and concern for the individual has been a hallmark of special education and an enduring contribution to regular education practices. All of the chapters emphasize assessment for instructional planning purposes. Further, all of them use assessment data to make decisions about the impact of instruction and its modification if it is not effective in achieving desirable goals. Individually and in sum, these chapters add impressive information to the "why, what, how, and when" of assessment strategies in special education.

REFERENCES

Blankenship, C., & Lilly, S. M. (1981). *Mainstreaming students with learning and behavior problems*. New York: Holt, Rinehart & Winston.

Bos, C. S., Weller, C. A., and Vaughn, S. R. (1984–1985). At the crossroads: Assessment of the learning disabled. *Diagnostique Monograph, 10*(1–4), 98–114.

Bracey, G. W. (1987). Measurement-driven instruction: Catchy phrase, dangerous practice. *Phi Delta Kappan, 68*(9), 683–686.

Calagan, J. E. (1985). Psychoeducational testing: Turn out the lights, the party's over. *Exceptional Children, 52*(3), 288–299.
Corrigan, M. A. (1955). Tests and measurements. In M. E. Frampton & E. D. Gall (Eds.), *Special education for the exceptional* (pp. 152–160). Boston: Porter Sargent Publisher.
Deno, S. L. (1985). Curriculum-based measurement: The emerging alternative. *Exceptional Children, 52*(3), 219–232.
Eaton, M. D., & Lovitt, T. C. (1972). Achievement tests vs. direct and daily measurement. In G. Semb (Ed.), *Behavior analysis and education–1972* (pp. 78–87). Lawrence: University of Kansas, Dept. of Human Development and Family Life.
Frampton, M. E., & Gall, E. D. (Eds.), (1955). *Special education for the exceptional*. Boston: Porter Sargent Publisher.
Garrison, K. C. (1955). The role of psychology in special education. In M. E. Frampton & E. D. Gall (Eds.), *Special education for the exceptional* (pp. 123–130). Boston: Porter Sargent Publisher.
Gould, J. G. (1981). *The mismeasure of man*. New York: W. W. Norton & Co.
Hammill, D. D. (1987). Assessing students in the schools. In D. D. Hammill (Ed.), *Assessing the abilities and instructional needs of students* (pp. 5–37). Austin, Texas: Pro. Ed.
Lovitt, T. C. (1977). *In spite of my resistance, I've learned from children*. Columbus, OH: Charles Merrill.
Martin, R. (1982). Legal issues in assessment in special education. In J. T. Neisworth (Ed.), *Assessment in special education* (pp. 3–9). Rockville, MD: Aspen Systems Corp.
Office of the Federal Register. (1985). *Code of federal regulations, title 34, parts 300–399*. Washington, DC: U.S. Government Printing Office.
Popham, J. W. (1987). The merits of measurement-driven instruction. *Phi Delta Kappan, 68*(9), 679–682.
Salvia, J., & Ysseldyke, J. E. (1978). *Assessment in special and remedial education*. Boston: Houghton Mifflin.
Salvia, J., & Ysseldyke, J. E. (1985). *Assessment in special and remedial education* (3rd ed.). Boston: Houghton Mifflin.
Tucker, J. A. (Ed.). (1985). Curriculum-based assessment [Special issue]. *Exceptional children, 52*(3).
Turnbull, H. R. (1986). *Free appropriate public education: The law and children with disabilities*. Denver: Love Publishing Co.
Wallen, N. E., & Travers, R. M. U. (1963). Analysis and investigation of teaching methods. In N. L. Gage (Ed.), *Handbook of research on teaching* (pp. 448–505). Chicago: Rand McNally.
Witty, P., & Kopel, D. (1939). *Reading and the educative process*. Boston: Ginn & Co.

Even though assessment procedures have always been an important part of the process for providing appropriate instruction to exceptional children and youth, the Education for All Handicapped Children Act of 1975 (PL 94–142) has established national standards that both elevate and strengthen the role of assessment. One person with scores from an assessment instrument or two can no longer decide that a pupil should be placed in a special education program. Instead, the assessment process is much more comprehensive and, as required by PL 94–142, very prescriptive of procedures that can or cannot be used.

Helton has provided a succinct set of guidelines that practitioners can use in conducting assessments. These address (a) assessment goals, (b) federal requirements, (c) ethical practices, and (d) assessment tools. In addition, the author describes the important role of "building-based teams" of competent regular educators in the assessment process, and in reducing errors in determining which pupils are or are not eligible for special education and related services. Last, the author proposes a branching sequence for conducting assessments—a system that clearly identifies process and decision points. All educators concerned with providing a free and appropriate public education for handicapped children and youth will find this selection very useful in completing their day-to-day responsibilities.

Guidelines for Assessment in Special Education

George B. Helton

Assessment in special education is useful when it helps us make decisions that promote appropriate and effective services to students. In particular, assessment should assist us in making two general types of decisions: (1) *who* should be served? (classification decisions); and (2) *how* should eligible students be served? (programming decisions).

Although all of us involved in special education recognize that assessment is crucially involved in our efforts to make appropriate classification and programming decisions, we are often much less sure about how to provide helpful assessment services. We ask questions such as: How should we organize our assessment program? How can we assess all the students who need it and still ensure quality assessment work? What assessment techniques should be used with different types of students?

The specific suggestions in this article may be more easily applied in some school systems than in others. This caution reflects several important points. One is that assessment requires integration of a number of factors including goals of assessment, legal requirements, ethical responsibilities, and available assessment techniques (Helton, Workman, & Matuszek, 1982, pp. 1–2). Partly because of the need to integrate so many factors, assessment is a complex activity, subject to varied emphases and interpretations. It is also an activity that generates much controversy about specific theoretical and applied issues. Hence, each professional involved in assessment and each school system must ultimately make judgments about the varied emphases, interpretations, and viewpoints, rather than depending on others for "packaged" answers. And, of course, a genuine concern for our students and honest teamwork are necessary in any assessment program.

FACTORS TO BE INTEGRATED IN ASSESSMENT

Goals of Assessment

Classification Decisions

Classification decisions, one of the two general types, essentially involve determining whether or not each assessed student has one of the handicapping conditions listed in the regulations implementing Public Law 94–142 (Education of Handicapped Children, 1977). Specific categories of students eligible for special education and related services under these regulations are:

> . . . mentally retarded, hard of hearing, deaf, speech impaired, visually handicapped, seriously emotionally disturbed, orthopedically impaired, other health impaired, deaf-blind, multi-handicapped, or as having specific learning disabilities. (p. 42478)

Although the regulations implementing PL 94–142 also define each of these handicapping conditions, each state department of education may specify more exact criteria for classifying students as handicapped. These criteria must be compatible with the definitions of the handicapping conditions in the regulations implementing PL 94–142. In actual practice, then, classification decisions involve determining whether assessed students meet the criteria used in a particular state for particular handicapping conditions. Since the eligibility criteria for specific handicapping conditions vary from state to state, a student receiving special education services in one state may become ineligible for these services if he or she moves to another state. For instance, a student receiving special education services as a learning disabled student in Georgia might not be classifiable as learning disabled when moving to Tennessee. These situations are confusing and distressing.

Each state also has the right to recognize categories of exceptionality that are not mentioned in the regulations implementing PL 94–142. To illustrate, Tennessee state law recognizes intellectual giftedness as a category of exceptionality. Therefore, special education and support services personnel in Tennessee are required to provide classification and programming services to these students, as well as to students with the handicapping conditions recognized in the regulations implementing PL 94–142.

Programming Decisions

In contrast to classification decisions, programming decisions require us to identify areas in which students classified as exceptional require special education and related services. These areas of need and specific services to address them are incorporated into an individualized education program (IEP), which is basically a service plan, for each eligible student. According to the regulations implementing PL 94–142, an IEP is to be developed by a team including the student's regular classroom teacher, special education personnel, personnel knowledgeable of assessment, and one or both of the student's parents.

Assessment as an aid to classification and programming decisions must be responsive to other legal requirements and to ethical concerns as well. In addition, literally dozens of assessment techniques are available. Some are more appropriate to classification decisions, and others are more appropriate to programming decisions (Coulter, 1980). In light of these considerations, choices about assessment programs and specific assessment practices must be made carefully.

Weatherly and Lipsky (1977) have contended—and I agree—that assessment is easily corrupted, most crucially when its focus is shifted from the needs of students to the needs of school systems and school personnel. Those authors cited examples of such corruption, including "scheduling of assessments in favor of children who had behavior problems, who were not likely to cost the system money, or who met the needs of school personnel seeking to practice their individual specialties" (p. 194). Assessment must serve the needs of school systems and school personnel as well as the needs of students, but it should be concerned *primarily* with the needs of students. Otherwise we may be abiding by the letter of PL 94–142 while neglecting its spirit.

Further, I believe that assessment should place as much emphasis on determining which students are *ineligible* for special education services as it does on determining which students are eligible for these services. This is a controversial stance. On the one hand, numerous court cases have focused on allegations of *misclassification* of ethnic minority students as handicapped (cf., Reschly, 1983), and the regulations implementing PL 94–142 contain a number of requirements for nondiscriminatory assessment and classification of students. On the other hand, students may not receive needed services unless those services are provided by special education programs.

The dilemma involved in providing nondiscriminatory assessment and classification services and, at the same time, providing needed educational and related services to students is perhaps illustrated in a study by Algozzine and Ysseldyke (1981). They found that slightly more than one-half of school staff members in that study judged children as handicapped even though all assessment results for each case presented were within the normal range. Algozzine and Ysseldyke suggested that their findings may indicate concerns about the ability of regular education to adequately serve students referred for assessment, and a corresponding tendency to overdefine who is handicapped.

In contrast, I advocate efforts to make regular education better able to serve a wider variety of students, as well as a continuing emphasis on compensatory education services for economically disadvantaged students. I also advocate that all of us continue to work hard to make special education services more effective for eligible handicapped students. Achieving this goal might lessen the dilemmas involved in special education classification, since classification of students as handicapped can be more easily justified if it is highly likely to lead to effective services.

Finally, I believe that assessment must lead to better programming decisions than it has in the past. Historically, the emphasis in assessment has been on assessment for classification (Helton, Morrow, & Yates, 1977). Though the classification function of assessment cannot be slighted (Helton et al., 1982, xv), the welfare of our students, as well as increasing accountability requirements, demands better assessment for programming (Kaufman, 1983). Our task, then, is to assess students more effectively for both classification and programming—a difficult but unavoidable challenge.

Legal Requirements in Assessment

The regulations implementing PL 94–142 include a number of requirements for assessment practice. These can be grouped in terms of students to receive assessment services, assessment for classification, assessment for programming, and procedural requirements.

Students to Receive Assessment Services

PL 94–142 requires that a free and appropriate education be provided to persons ages 3 through 21 who demonstrate handicapping conditions listed in the regulations implementing the law. School systems, however, are not responsible for providing services to 3 through 5 year-olds and 18 through 21 year-olds if services to persons in those age groups are contrary to state law or court order. The regulations implementing PL 94–142 also require that school systems attempt to identify persons who are or will be eligible for special education services. These "child find" efforts must include persons from birth through age 21 (Helton et al., 1982, p. 47). "Child find" activities and special education services involve assessment for persons in the specified age ranges.

Assessment for Classification

A number of provisions in the regulations implementing PL 94–142 are relevant to assessment for classification:

1. Assessment is to be conducted in all areas related to the suspected disability, including, where appropriate, health, vision, hearing, social and emotional status, general intelligence, academic performance, communicative status, and motor abilities.
2. No single evaluation procedure can be used as the sole basis for making decisions about students.

3. Tests and other methods of evaluating a student must be administered in that student's native language unless this procedure is clearly not feasible.
4. Tests must be administered by qualified personnel who follow the instructions provided by test producers (qualified personnel refers to persons recognized by state departments of education as competent to perform various assessment activities).
5. Test data are not to be interpreted as reflecting poor aptitude or achievement when test scores actually reflect students' sensory, manual, or speech impairments.
6. Tests and other evaluative measures must be validated for the specific purposes for which they are used.
7. Each student receiving special education services must be reassessed at least every 3 years (more frequently if needed or requested by the teacher or parent), and reassessments must conform to the requirements noted above.

Specific wording for each of these requirements may be found in the *Federal Register* (Education of Handicapped Children, 1977, pp. 42496–42497).

These requirements are intended to promote a goal of nondiscriminatory assessment by ensuring that assessment is comprehensive, conducted by qualified personnel, incorporates appropriate tests, and is repeated periodically. While none of us can argue with the goal of "fair" assessment (particularly with ethnic minority, linguistically different, and culturally different students), these requirements are extremely difficult to honor. For one thing, assessment of all areas related to a student's suspected disability can be quite time-consuming. Similarly, reassessing each student receiving special education services at least every 3 years is also time-consuming. Third, some school systems (especially in rural areas) have difficulty locating and employing qualified personnel. In addition, generally qualified personnel may not be able to assess students in their native languages. Even if this is possible with a specific student, it is inappropriate if the norms of the test to be given were developed by giving the test in English (see Helton et al., 1982, pp. 68–69). Finally, there is little agreement on what is required to validate a test for a specific purpose.

Federal courts are now involved in questions of test validation and do not always come to the same conclusions. Consider the *Larry P.* v. *Riles* (1979) case and the *PASE* v. *Hannon* (1980) case. In the former the court held that standardized intelligence tests (such as the Stanford-Binet Intelligence Scale and the Wechsler Intelligence Scale for Children—Revised) had not been sufficiently validated for use in determining whether black students could be classified as mentally retarded. In the latter case the court held that these same tests could be used in making this type of classification decisions. Ultimately, the U.S. Supreme Court will likely be forced to deal with such questions.

At this point, one may be tempted to conclude that the unanswered questions and practical problems are too numerous to allow implementation of beneficial and legally appropriate assessment programs. I do not agree. Instead, I believe that a number of steps can be taken to help us achieve this goal. The following suggestions should be considered in trying to obtain both quality and time efficiency when assessing students who are not currently receiving special education services.

1. Set up screening and programming teams at each of the schools in a school system. These teams can help judge which problematic students are likely to be eligible for special education services and therefore, need comprehensive assessment. Members of the same teams can do further screening, thereby reducing the amount of assessment time that school psychologists and educational diagnosticians must give to each student. School psychologists and educational diagnosticians should meet with the screening and programming teams; and principals, special education teachers, school counselors, school nurses, and school social workers should also be available to meet with the regular teachers who are referring students.
   This group can also brainstorm strategies to try with students who are unlikely to qualify for special education. These strategies should be tried immediately rather than insisting upon comprehensive assessment of each student discussed by the team.
2. Recognize that the idea of screening and programming teams may encounter initial resistance and that objections to creating these teams must be honestly addressed. A "trial period" for these teams in only one or two schools may have to be the starting point. That way, those who object to the concept will experience (or hear about) quicker services to problematic students (since not all students discussed by the teams will be comprehensively assessed and those who are will be served more quickly). Also, team members have a better chance of experiencing the benefits of a support group and the practical advice given by its members.
3. Make sure that the time spent in screening and programming team meetings and related activities (screening, consulting with each other) is spent productively and does not make unreasonable demands on any team member. This effort will require honest negotiations and periodic adjustments (see Fleming & Fleming, 1983).
4. Establish and communicate clear guidelines for assessment, including sequential steps in the process, functions of the screening and programming teams, and specific responsibilities of various members of the school staff. Use both written and verbal communications, addressed to the board of education, the central office staff, the staff of each school, and parents.
5. Encourage honest discussion of how assessment techniques should be chosen for various types of students who are to receive assessment services. Assessment should not be more comprehensive than is needed for appropriate classification and programming decisions; neither should pressure be exerted to cut corners in collecting information needed for appropriate and beneficial classification and programming decisions.
6. Provide time management training for school psychologists, educational diagnosticians, and members of the screening and programming teams (see Maher, 1982).
7. Request additional assessment personnel if the above steps will not or have not provided for an adequate blend of quantity and quality.

Taking these steps will, in itself, be quite time-consuming initially. My experience, however, is that by doing so, time problems will be lessened in the future, and more efficient and beneficial assessment will be provided. A final suggestion is to use consultants from universities, the state department of education, and other school systems as needed in planning these steps and implementing them.

In trying to deal with the time problems associated with the requirement to reassess students currently receiving special education services, I offer two suggestions:

1. Eliminate any local requirement that students who no longer need special education services be reassessed before leaving the program (unless reassessment would be useful in planning for their complete return to regular education). Again, do not provide comprehensive assessment services unless they are truly needed for classification and programming purposes.
2. Explore with the state department of education the possibility of adopting a procedure that is referred to in Tennessee as *modified reassessments*. Under this procedure, a *comprehensive* reassessment is *not* required unless one of the following conditions applies (Tennessee Department of Education, 1982, pp. 4.17–4.18):
   a. The probability of change from the initial evaluation results is high. This is almost always the case with young children.
   b. The initial certification of the child as handicapped marginally met the criteria. This does not apply to the (intellectually) gifted.
   c. Significant or abrupt changes have occurred in the student's environment, which may affect the status of the handicap.
   d. A lack of progress in the student's performance is indicated in his/her annual review of progress in special education.
   e. Current information available is insufficient. Adequate information obtained in the annual review (of progress in special education) should include data such as: individual/group achievement scores, observations, mastery of goals/objectives in the IEP, grades, work samples, and progress reports.
   f. The initial assessment was not consistent with the evaluation components and criteria for certification (as handicapped) in the new state *Rules, Regulations, and Minimum Standards*.

If none of the above conditions apply, a modified reassessment for determining continuing eligibility for special education services may be conducted. These modified reassessments must include (p. 4.18):

1. Personal contact with the student through an observation, interview, and/or testing.
2. Interview with the student's teacher(s).
3. Documentation of the recertification of the student as handicapped and the information on which it is based, written by the appropriate certifying specialist.

State department of education officials in Tennessee hope that allowing modified reassessments will help reduce time requirements for reassessments without sacrificing data needed for appropriate classification decisions. In my opinion, these modified reassessments are appropriate with severely handicapped students but less clearly appropriate with mildly handicapped students. And while it may be tempting to cut corners in determining which students are to receive modified reassessments and in actually performing them, I hope these temptations will be resisted. Again, our task is to provide both appropriate and time efficient assessment, not to corrupt the assessment process in the interest of time efficiency alone.

Many rural school systems, as noted earlier, have problems in locating and employing qualified assessment personnel as required by the regulations implementing PL 94–142. Two possible aids in complying with this requirement are:

1. Join or attempt to establish an educational cooperative—an organization in which two or more school systems combine their resources, enabling them to offer services that none of the member systems could offer alone. For example, two neighboring school systems might jointly hire a school psychologist and agree to share the psychologist's services on a 50/50 basis. (Some states, such as Georgia, fund a statewide network of educational cooperatives; in Georgia these organizations are referred to as Cooperative Educational Service Agencies.)
2. Recruit an interested, capable member of the school system's staff to undergo further training toward state certification as a school psychologist, educational diagnostician, or other needed service provider. Ideally, the school system would assume responsibility for tuition costs and cost-of-living allowances (or salary continuation) if the further training would require the person to move from the community for a time or take a leave of absence from regular duties for an internship. The point here, of course, is that assisting a current staff member to become certified in an area of need may be easier and more productive than trying to recruit an "outsider" who may not want to make a long-range commitment to a rural area.

Most school systems probably have difficulty testing students in their native languages as required by the regulations implementing PL 94–142. This difficulty may be based in part on a lack of qualified personnel who speak languages other than English. Furthermore, testing in languages other than English is not appropriate with some tests. Specifically, it is not recommended with tests that have been normed by administering them in English only. Hence, I offer three suggestions:

1. Administer norm-referenced tests in languages other than English only when those tests provide test norms based on non-English administration. For example, administer a norm-referenced test in Spanish only if that test has norms based on administration of that test in Spanish.
2. When it is necessary to assess the intellectual functioning of a non-English speaking student and tests normed in that student's native language are unavailable, use nonverbal measures of intelligence (Gerken, 1978).
3. Consider the possibility that a non-English speaking student might be more appropriately served in a bilingual education program or through arrangements other than the school system's special education program.

A final difficulty in assessment for classification involves the lack of clarity in what is actually required by federal (and state) regulations in implementing nondiscriminatory assessment practices (as partially illustrated by the conflicting court decisions in the *Larry P.* and *PASE* cases). I offer five suggestions for dealing with this problem:

1. Ensure that all students who are assessed receive prior hearing and vision screening and that any possible problems identified during screening are further evaluated before proceeding with comprehensive assessment. Correct interpretation of assessment data on students is simply not possible unless data on their auditory and visual acuities are available. If health problems other than hearing and vision difficulties are suspected, these should also be investigated before proceeding with comprehensive assessment. City and county health departments are often quite helpful to school systems in providing hearing and vision assessments and assessments of other possible health problems.
2. Using the best possible professional judgment, select assessment techniques appropriate to the decision to be made about a student and to the student's unique characteristics. For example, norm-referenced tests of intelligence, academic achievement, and adaptive behavior provide the kinds of data that are useful in making classification decisions, and criterion-referenced tests of academic achievement and adaptive behavior often provide information helpful to programming decisions. If a norm-referenced test does not provide useful programming information, do not use it as an aid to programming decisions. Similarly, criterion-referenced tests are unlikely to provide information useful for classification decisions and should not be used for that purpose. In choosing tests appropriate to student characteristics, tests that require lengthy verbal responses should not be used with speech-impaired students and tests requiring fine motor skills should not be used with students with motor impairments. Finally, whenever possible try to use tests with adequate reliability, validity, and norms. Since choices of this type require detailed analyses of test appropriateness, readers are urged to consult references such as Helton et al. (1982), Sattler (1982), and Salvia and Ysseldyke (1981) for evaluative comments on a number of specific tests.
3. Take a conservative approach to judgments about students' eligibilities for special education services. Do not classify students as handicapped unless they clearly meet state eligibility criteria. Although a conservative approach to classification decisions will help a school system avoid charges of discriminatory assessment and classification practices, I am not advocating that ineligible students be left to "sink or swim" in their regular classrooms. Instead, investigate other possible sources of assistance to them such as Chapter 1 (formerly Title I) programs or bilingual education programs. In addition, the school screening and programming teams can provide direct and consultative services appropriate to these students' needs.
4. Work hard to make special education services as effective as possible for eligible students. Placement of students in special education programs will less likely be seen as discriminatory if the programs are genuinely helpful.
5. Keep up with changes in state and federal laws and regulations and with court decisions. These changes and decisions determine the legal context for assessment and special education services at any point in time.

Assessment for Programming

Any related service(s) a student needs in order to benefit from special education must be specified in his or her IEP and provided without cost to parents. The regulations implementing PL 94–142 list the following related services to be considered for inclusion in an IEP: audiology, counseling services, early identification of handicapped children, medical services required to classify a student as handicapped, occupational therapy, parent counseling and training, physical therapy, psychological services, recreational services, school health services, speech pathology services, and transportation. Each of these is defined in the regulations (Education of Handicapped Children, 1977, pp. 42479–42480), and the regulations further indicate that other, nonlisted services may have to be provided.

School officials understandably have expressed concern about including related services in IEPs, largely because school systems have to provide them using school personnel or pay outside agencies or practitioners for these services. Of course, related services do not have to be included in IEPs unless they are seen as necessary for students to benefit from special education. The question of whether any of the related services are needed for a specific student often involves a difficult prediction, which in turn requires honest professional judgments. Three suggestions may be helpful:

1. If services are seen as *essential* to progress in special education, include them in IEPs. If services are judged to be helpful but not essential, do not include them. Instead, inform parents that the services are seen as desirable rather than essential, and assist parents in locating such services.
2. Whenever appropriate, use school personnel, including members of each school's screening and programming team, to provide related services. This is more convenient and entails less cost than using mostly outside agencies and practitioners.
3. Consider seeking interagency agreements and state legislation that would help spread the costs of related services to other state agencies (such as community mental health centers and state hospitals for emotionally disturbed and mentally retarded children).

The regulations implementing PL 94–142 require that handicapped students be educated in least restrictive environments. Four suggestions may be of help in dealing with the least restrictive environment requirement:

1. Carefully consider the degrees to which handicapped students will be able to participate in classes and activities with nonhandicapped peers. Make judgments about least restrictive environments on a student-by-student basis rather than in terms of students' handicapping conditions or administrative considerations.
2. Help all members of the school community (board of education, central office staff, principals, teachers, parents) to understand the least restrictive environment requirement.
3. Make consultative services readily available to principals and teachers to help them cope more successfully with perceived problems resulting from placement

of students in least restrictive environments. Members of each school's screening and programming teams might be especially helpful in providing such services.

4. Provide social skills training to handicapped students who require it in order to experience social acceptance from nonhandicapped peers (Gresham, 1982). Such training should occur both prior to students' placements with nonhandicapped peers and following the placements (Strain & Shores, 1983). Again, members of the school's screening and programming team can help, by directly providing social skills training.

Finally, the regulations implementing PL 94–142 require that each student's IEP be reviewed at least annually and modified as needed. Although this is a procedural requirement that is not especially difficult to honor, reviews must be done carefully rather than perfunctorily. Two suggestions illustrate my concerns:

1. Develop and modify IEPs in terms of knowledge of students' characteristics and effective teaching strategies. General teaching strategies that are backed by little research evidence for their effectiveness should not be used in the first place (Kaufman & Kaufman, 1983). In addition, strategies that are not helping a student progress should be modified as soon as possible (Helton et al., 1982). This requires frequent monitoring of student progress.
2. Involve members of the school's screening and programming team in the initial development of IEPs and in their annual (or more frequent) review. This step helps ensure that full knowledge of students' characteristics and progress is brought to decision making and that continuity in services to students is maintained.

Procedural Requirements

A number of procedural requirements contained in the regulations implementing PL 94–142 (Education of Handicapped Children, 1977, pp. 42490–42496) are intended to promote fairness to parents and students in the delivery of assessment and special education services. Among the most significant of these requirements are those that provide for written parental consent to initial assessment and to initial special education placement of students, prior notice to parents before schools take (or fail to take) important actions affecting students' educational programs, parental access to students' records, and due process hearings.

Probably the most important stance in complying with these requirements is that school personnel accept parents as partners in the decision making process and try to treat them as they would wish to be treated if their roles were reversed. Increased and improved collaboration between schools and parents is likely to lead to increased educational progress on the part of handicapped students. If this occurs, the time spent in frequent, honest collaboration is well worth the investment. In this spirit, I offer the following specific suggestions:

1. Try to ensure that parental consent for initial assessment and initial placement of each handicapped student is obtained only after parents clearly understand what is being proposed and voluntarily agree to it.

2. Attempt to use mediation of parent-school disagreements to avoid, if possible, the time, expense, and strain of due process hearings.
3. Respectfully maintain your positions as professionals if you feel that you can honorably defend them in due process hearings.
4. Consider initiating due process hearings or other appropriate actions if you believe, in certain instances, that parents are blocking needed services to their children and if efforts at mediation have failed.

Ethical Considerations in Assessment

While we are often preoccupied with our legal responsibilities to handicapped children, we also face a number of ethical issues in our efforts to provide services to them. Frith (1981) has described a number of instances in which the needs of handicapped students are seen as conflicting with the administrative, financial, and logistical needs of school systems. Conflicts of this nature may necessitate extremely difficult decisions.

As an aid to making such decisions, both a "Code of Ethics" and a set of "Standards for Professional Practice" have been adopted and published by the Council for Exceptional Children (1983a, 1983b). These documents are viewed as binding on the professional activities of CEC members: "Members of the special education profession are responsible for upholding and advancing these principles" (Council for Exceptional Children, 1983a, p. 205). Also, these documents unequivocally stress the need for special educators to abide by laws and regulations governing services to handicapped students. Similarly, support service professionals such as school psychologists are often members of professional organizations having their own ethical codes (e.g., American Psychological Association and National Association of School Psychologists). Hence, school staff members may approach ethical issues from a variety of viewpoints.

Despite the diversity of ethical perspectives that may be present in a school staff, ethical obligations are presented here only from the position of the Council for Exceptional Children documents mentioned. This should be sufficient, in any case, as the CEC, APA, and NASP codes and standards overlap somewhat and have no apparent contradictions. Readers who are interested in the specific content of ethical codes in psychology should consult "Ethical Principles of Psychologists" (American Psychological Association, 1981) and "Principles for Professional Ethics" (National Association of School Psychologists, 1978).

The CEC Code of Ethics includes directives to: (1) promote educational and other quality of life opportunities for handicapped students; (2) exercise objective professional judgment in the delivery of services; (3) uphold and improve laws, regulations, and policies impacting special education services; and (4) avoid condoning or participating in unethical, illegal, or other acts that violate professional standards (Council for Exceptional Children, 1983a, p. 205).

This ethical code has, in turn, been translated into "Standards for Professional Practice" (Council for Exceptional Children, 1983b, pp. 206–209). The Standards include directives to:

1. Use assessment techniques and procedures that are nondiscriminatory.
2. Monitor inappropriate placements of students in special education programs, and correct procedures that lead to inappropriate placements.
3. Intervene when a colleague's behavior is seen as detrimental to handicapped students.
4. Provide accurate information and data to administrators, colleagues, and parents to aid in decision making.
5. Inform parents of their students' educational rights and proposed or actual practices that violate those rights.
6. Use methods and curricula that are effective in meeting the needs of handicapped students.
7. Report to administrators when resources are inadequate for the delivery of services, and promote corrective action.
8. Recognize the competencies of members of other disciplines.

Taken together, these directives support many of the provisions contained in the regulations implementing PL 94–142 and also reinforce some of the suggestions previously offered in this article. Some additional specific suggestions for ethical practice are listed below. These, I believe, are compatible with the APA and NASP ethical codes mentioned above, as well as the CEC "Code of Ethics" and "Standards for Professional Practice."

1. Carefully evaluate your own understandings and skills and engage only in activities in which you are competent. Refer students to other professionals when students require services that other professionals are more competent to provide.
2. Avoid altering or manipulating assessment results in order to qualify students for special education services. Instead, try to promote sufficient flexibility in how data are used in decision making to promote student welfare.
3. Encourage those who have provided assessment services to specific students to participate in meetings where decisions about those students are to be made. Participation prevents misunderstandings of assessment results, allows assessment personnel to ensure that their results are not misused, and enables their expertise in classification and programming to be used in promoting student welfare.
4. Enlist the participation of assessment personnel and others in attempts to resolve conflicts between ethical obligations and financial and administrative considerations. Try to find approaches that better balance legal, ethical, and administrative considerations than approaches previously used.

Available Assessment Techniques

In responding to the PL 94–142 regulations requiring that students be assessed in all areas related to their suspected disabilities, Helton et al. (1982) have described specific assessment techniques in the following assessment domains: health factors (including auditory and visual acuity); general intellectual functioning; modality (or psychoeducational processing) skills; academic functioning; social/emotional functioning; adaptive behavior; and environmental influences on school coping. Salvia and Ysseldyke (1981) also have devoted chapters to assessment techniques appropriate to most of these domains, and in addition have included chapters on the assessment of school readiness and on diagnostic systems.

The point here is that numerous assessment techniques—far too many to discuss in this article—are available for each of these assessment domains. Thus, I provide brief discussions of most of these assessment domains and mention only some representative assessment techniques associated with them. In efforts to choose appropriate assessment techniques, readers are again urged to consult sources such as Helton et al. (1982), Salvia and Ysseldyke (1981), and Sattler (1982).

Health Factors

As previously indicated, I believe that assessment of all referred students' auditory and visual acuities is essential to appropriate assessment practice. Auditory acuity is typically assessed using audiometric techniques. Visual acuity is typically assessed using a Snellen Chart and/or an apparatus such as the Keystone Telebinocular Instrument. The Keystone provides a more comprehensive assessment of visual acuity and is recommended, whenever possible, over less comprehensive procedures such as the Snellen Chart, which measures only far-point vision. If screening for other health factors, the System of Multicultural Pluralistic Assessment (Mercer, 1979) provides several instruments for this purpose. Helton et al. (1982) and Salvia and Ysseldyke (1981) offer descriptions of these instruments.

General Intellectual Functioning

Assessment of general intellectual functioning is required when a student is suspected to be learning disabled or mentally retarded according to the regulations implementing PL 94–142. It also may be required to establish whether a student with a sensory, motor, or other health impairment may additionally be mentally retarded and, hence, multihandicapped. Further, it may be required in determining whether a student is primarily seriously emotionally disturbed or primarily mentally retarded, or possibly both.

Assessment of general intellectual functioning for purposes of classification usually involves administration of one of the following: the Stanford-Binet Intelligence Scale, Form L-M (Terman & Merrill, 1973), the Wechsler Preschool and Primary Scale of Intelligence (Wechsler, 1967), the Wechsler Intelligence Scale for Children—Revised (Wechsler, 1974), or the Wechsler Adult Intelligence Scale—Revised (Wechsler, 1981). Other instruments for assessing intellectual functioning may be particularly appropriate for deaf, blind, and motor-handicapped students (see Gerken, 1979). In addition, a new test of cognitive functioning, the Kaufman Assessment Battery for Children (Kaufman & Kaufman, 1983a, 1983b) is currently attracting great attention.

The Kaufman Assessment Battery for Children is described as appropriate for students 2½ to 12½ years of age and is based on research in cognitive psychology and neuropsychology. Two of its three scales (Simultaneous Processing and Sequential Processing) are designed to assess students' information processing styles, and knowledge of students' performances on these scales is thought to be useful for both classification and programming purposes. A mental processing composite score reflects performance on both of these scales. A third scale, Achievement, is designed to assess the degree to which students have been able to apply their processing skills to the acquisition of various types of learning tasks, including arithmetic and reading tasks (Kaufman & Kaufman, 1983a, 1983b). If the K-ABC proves as useful in classification and programming as its authors suggest, it will represent a valuable addition to the Stanford-Binet Intelligence Scale and the Wechsler scales for preschoolers and children.

Modality Skills

Assessment of modality skills for classification and programming purposes is a complex and controversial topic. Modality skills refer to a student's abilities to interpret sensory information, relate that information to previously acquired information, and respond to that information. The definition of a specific learning disability contained in the regulations implementing PL 94–142 implies that such skills should be assessed in classifying students as learning disabled (Education of Handicapped Children, 1977, pp. 42478–42479). Such a requirement, however, is not specifically contained in the federal regulations, and some states (such as Tennessee) do not require the assessment of modality skills in classifying students as learning disabled.

In addition, debate continues on whether the assessment of modality skills promotes effective programming practices. I am not persuaded that it does, since little research evidence indicates that either attempts to strengthen students' weaknesses in modality skills or attempts to "work around them" in teaching lead to improvements in academic achievement (see Kaufman & Kaufman, 1983c). Techniques typically used to assess modality skills include the Bender Visual-Motor Gestalt Test (Bender, 1938), the Frostig Developmental Test of Visual Perception (Frostig, LeFever, & Whittlesey, 1966), the Goldman-Fristoe-Woodcock Auditory Skills Test Battery (Woodcock, 1976), the Visual-Aural Digit Span Test (Koppitz, 1977) and the Illinois Test of Psycholinguistic Abilities (Kirk, McCarthy, & Kirk, 1968).

Academic Functioning

The regulations implementing PL 94–142 require that assessment of academic functioning be done for classification purposes with students suspected of being learning disabled. In addition, assessment of academic functioning is required with all types of handicapped students for programming purposes. Therefore, this is an extremely important assessment domain. In general, norm-referenced tests of academic functioning are useful for classification, and criterion-referenced tests in this domain are useful for programming.

Examples of the former tests are the Wide Range Achievement Test (Jastak & Jastak, 1978) and the Peabody Individual Achievement Test (Dunn & Markwardt,

1970). Examples of the latter include the Criterion Tests of Basic Skills (Lundell, Evans, & Brown, 1976) and the Brigance Diagnostic Inventory of Basic Skills (Brigance, 1977). Salvia and Ysseldyke (1981) have provided extensive descriptions of diagnostic tests in reading and mathematics, and also tests of oral and written language (including spelling and writing).

Social/Emotional Functioning

Assessment of social/emotional functioning is required by the regulations implementing PL 94–142 for classification of students as seriously emotionally disturbed. Assessing students in this domain may also be necessary to determine if their school problems are primarily the result of a learning disability or emotional disturbance or if they are both emotionally disturbed and experiencing another handicapping condition (multihandicapped). Assessment in this domain may also aid programming decisions for students with a variety of handicaps.

A number of general approaches can be taken for assessing social/emotional functioning. Which of these approaches is most appropriate is the subject of rather heated controversy. Specifically, social/emotional functioning may be assessed through the use of behavior checklists completed by adults who have had extensive contact with a student, self-report instruments (in which a student answers questions about himself/herself), direct behavioral observations of a student, and projective techniques (in which a student responds to ambiguous test materials such as inkblots).

Examples of behavior checklists include the Burks' Behavior Rating Scales (Burks, 1977) and the Walker Problem Behavior Identification Checklist (Walker, 1970). Both of these instruments are norm-referenced and, hence, provide data on the relative severity of a student's behavior problems for classification purposes. Helton et al. (1982) have suggested that data from such instruments be supplemented with direct behavioral observation of a student as a means of both cross-checking data used for classification and collecting additional information for programming. Direct behavioral observation may be conducted using observation systems such as the Ecological Assessment of Child Problem Behavior (Wahler, House, & Stambaugh, 1976). The use of both behavior checklists and direct behavioral observation is recommended by Helton et al. (1982) as an appropriate approach to the assessment of social/emotional functioning and is compatible with their behavioral approach to programming.

Examples of self-report instruments include the Piers-Harris Children's Self-Concept Scale (Piers & Harris, 1969) and the California Psychological Inventory (Gough, 1969). The former attempts to measure a student's self-concept from that student's answers to a number of specific questions, and the latter is seen as a test of general personality and emotional development (Salvia & Ysseldyke, 1981). Although the use of self-report instruments may enrich our understanding of students' personalities, I favor the use of behavior checklists and direct behavioral observation for classification and particularly for programming purposes (see Helton et al., 1982).

The use of projective techniques in social/emotional assessment is quite controversial. Psychodynamically oriented psychologists often consider these techniques essential (see Obrzut & Zucker, 1983), and behaviorally oriented psychologists often view them as having questionable value (see Helton et al., 1982). Projective techniques such as the Rorschach Technique (Rorschach, 1942) and the Thematic Apperception Test (Murray, 1943) should be used only by psychologists well versed in the psychodynamic approach to personality and only after extensive training in their use.

Adaptive Behavior

Assessment of adaptive behavior is required by the regulations implementing PL 94–142 for classification of students as mentally retarded, in which students must demonstrate significantly deficient functioning in both intelligence and adaptive behavior. For classification purposes, norm-referenced measures of adaptive behavior such as the Vineland Social Maturity Scale (Doll, 1965), the Adaptive Behavior Inventory for Children (Mercer & Lewis, 1977), and the AAMD Adaptive Behavior Scale—Public School Version (Lambert, Windmiller, Cole, & Figueroa, 1975) may be appropriate. Each of these measures has strengths and weaknesses (see Helton et al., 1982). Because of this, a new version of the VSMS, the Vineland Adaptive Behavior Scales, has generated much interest. This new instrument is designed for both classification and programming purposes, and it attempts to measure adaptive behavior in both home and school settings (American Guidance Service, 1984). Criterion-referenced measures of adaptive behavior such as the Cain-Levine Social Competency Scale (Cain, Levine, & Elzey, 1977) provide information useful for programming with mentally retarded students. For a detailed discussion of the assessment of adaptive behavior, see Coulter and Morrow (1978).

Environmental Influences on School Coping

Assessment of environmental influences on school coping is required by the regulations implementing PL 94–142 for the classification of students as learning disabled. Specifically, students are not to be classified as learning disabled if their learning problems are primarily the result of environmental, cultural, or economic disadvantage (Education of Handicapped Children, 1977, pp. 42478–42479). Determining whether such factors are present and, if so, whether they are the primary cause of a student's learning problems obviously requires knowledge of that student's life circumstances and judgments about the impact of those circumstances. In making such judgments, I again recommend that Chapter 1 or other nonspecial education services be considered when life circumstances (rather than a learning disability) may be the primary causes of a student's learning problem.

Helton et al. (1982) also proposed that environmental influences be assessed with all referred students for programming purposes. They suggested that a number of environmental influences such as general school climate, nature of the school curriculum, teacher behaviors, peer influences, and home influences be considered when making programming decisions. Their point is that environmental influences that are interfering with school progress should be reduced, if possible, and that positive influences on school performance should be increased, if possible. Readers who are interested in specific techniques for assessing environmental influences should consult sources such as Helton et al. (1982) and Smith, Neisworth, and Greer (1978).

Diagnostic Systems

Diagnostic systems represent the efforts of test authors and publishers to combine measures appropriate to more than one assessment domain into a single package. For example, the Kaufman Assessment Battery for Children (Kaufman & Kaufman, 1983a, 1983b), mentioned earlier, contains measures of both cognitive functioning and achievement.

Similarly, the aforementioned System of Multicultural Pluralistic Assessment (Mercer, 1979) contains measures of health factors (including auditory and visual acuity), intellectual functioning (the Wechsler Intelligence Scale for Children—Revised or WISC-R), and adaptive behavior (the Adaptive Behavior Inventory for Children). Hence, this system provides more comprehensive assessment of students than do single test instruments.

The SOMPA also was designed to promote nondiscriminatory classification of economically disadvantaged and culturally different students. Specifically, this system is intended to help prevent the misclassification of students as mentally retarded, by providing an estimate of a student's intellectual potential. The estimate is referred to as an "estimated learning potential" (ELP) score. The ELP score is based on how well the student performs on the WISC-R compared to the predicted WISC-R performances of other children in the same ethnic group who are judged to have experienced similar sociocultural backgrounds. In essence, the ELP score compares the student to children thought to have had similar life circumstances. This is in contrast to the usual WISC-R IQ scores, which compare a student's performance on the WISC-R to the WISC-R performances of children in general. Mercer (1979) has recommended that ELP scores be used instead of the usual WISC-R IQ scores in determining whether economically disadvantaged and culturally different students should be classified as mentally retarded. Much controversy surrounds the use of ELP scores. Interested readers might want to consult Helton et al. (1982) and Salvia and Ysseldyke (1981) for further discussion.

The Woodcock-Johnson Psychoeducational Battery (Woodcock, 1978) is a third example of a diagnostic system. It is designed to assess cognitive ability, scholastic aptitude, academic achievement, and interests in persons 3 to 80 years of age (Salvia & Ysseldyke, 1981, p. 335). It, like the System of Multicultural Pluralistic Assessment (Mercer, 1979) is complex. Interested readers are referred to Salvia and Ysseldyke (1981) for further information. Those authors made the point that no diagnostic system is likely to provide *all* the information needed on a referred student (p. 343).

SEQUENCING ASSESSMENT AND CHOOSING ASSESSMENT TECHNIQUES

Helton et al. (1982) and Helton and Workman (1982) have advocated the use of an assessment model or system that integrates the needs for assessment to provide adequate information for classification and programming and, at the same time, to be as time efficient as possible. This system, shown schematically in Figure 1, is referred to as a *branching assessment system*.

The Branching Assessment System

The branching assessment system is designed primarily for mildly handicapped students and only for the assessment of students judged by the school's screening and programming team as likely to be eligible for special education services. Students who are unlikely to be eligible for special education services should receive assistance in their regular classrooms. Those who do not benefit from such assistance can, of course, be reconsidered for comprehensive assessment at later dates.

This procedure is designed to save time by not providing comprehensive assessment to all problematic students while, at the same time, allowing students who show compelling need for comprehensive assessment to receive it. The system also promotes time efficiency in that it encourages the use of only those assessment techniques actually needed to provide appropriate information for classification and programming decisions.

In this system, all students to receive comprehensive assessment are first screened for hearing and vision difficulties and for any other suspected health problems. Audiometric testing and testing with the Keystone Telebinocular Instrument are recommended, and screening for other health factors could be done with instruments taken from the System of Multicultural Pluralistic Assessment (Mercer, 1979). Again, any possible problems detected during health screening should receive further evaluation before proceeding with comprehensive assessment.

The next step in the system involves a referral source interview, which is completed by the school's screening and programming team. It should include discussion of the student's cumulative folder and samples of his or her schoolwork. If the team determines that a student needs comprehensive assessment, the team judges whether the student's difficulties suggest an academic behavior problem, a social/emotional behavior problem, or both. Accurate judgments are important for two reasons. First, assessment specialists must choose assessment techniques that are actually relevant to the student's problems. Second, assessment time will be increased if incorrect judgments about the nature of the student's problems lead assessment specialists into the wrong branch of the system. Of course, some students do have both academic and social/emotional problems, and assessment techniques from both branches of the system should be used with these students. Also, in some cases assessment specialists will have to switch from one branch of the system to another if, during assessment, they discover that they are in a wrong branch.

If a student is seen as having primarily an academic behavior problem, the next step in the system is to assess his or her intellectual functioning. The Wechsler scale appropriate for the individual's chronological age (Wechsler, 1976, 1974, or 1981) or the Kaufman Assessment Battery for Children (Kaufman & Kaufman, 1983a, 1983b) if the student is 2½ to 12½ years of age is recommended for this purpose.

If the student's performance on the measure of intellectual functioning is in the mentally retarded range, the assessment specialist next uses a measure of adaptive

FIGURE 1 Branching Assessment System

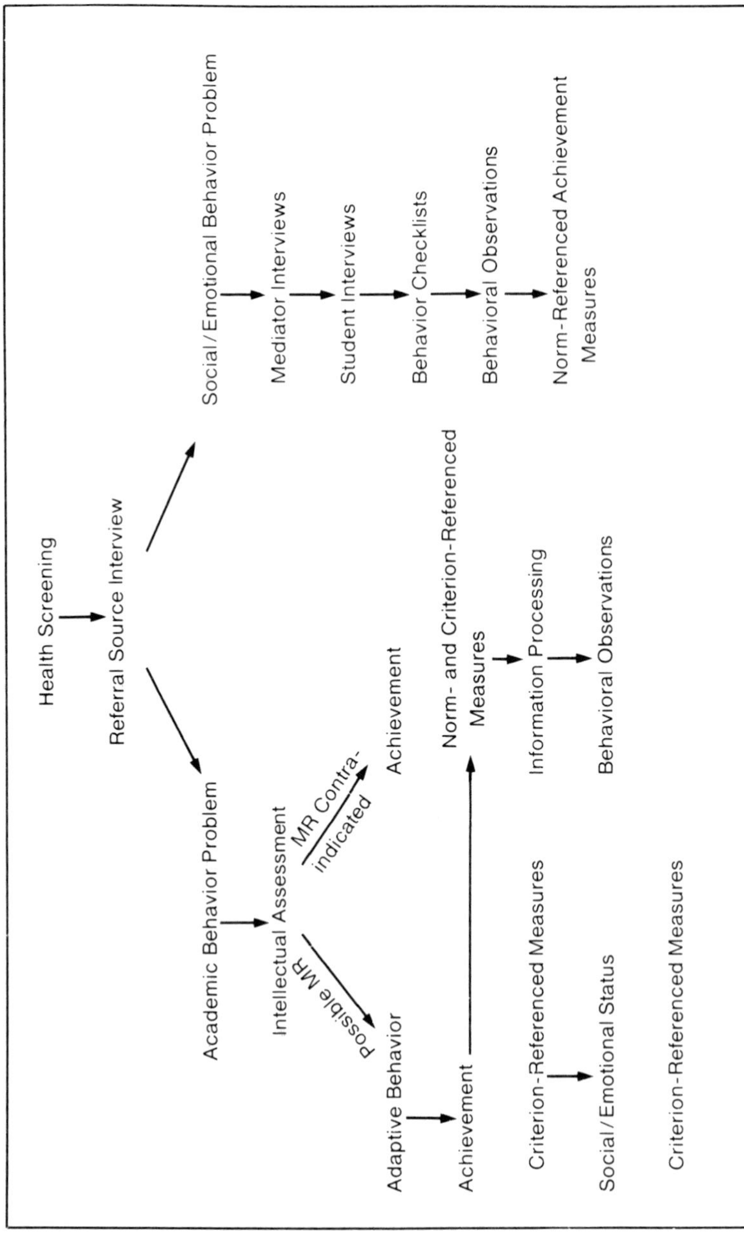

From *Psychoeducational Assessment: Integrating Concepts and Techniques* by G. Helton, E. Workman, and P. Matuszek, New York: Grune & Stratton, 1982. Also from "Considerations in Assessing the Mildly Handicapped" by G. Helton and E. Workman in *The Mildly Handicapped Student* edited by T. Miller and E. Davis, New York: Grune & Stratton, 1982. Used by permission.

behavior to determine if that student can be classified as mentally retarded. (Remember that a student must be deficient in both intellectual functioning and adaptive behavior to be so classified.) I recommend either the Vineland Social Maturity Scale (Doll, 1965) or the Adaptive Behavior Inventory for Children (Mercer & Lewis, 1977) as a measure of adaptive behavior. The Vineland Social Maturity Scale offers the advantage of norms for students of all ages, while the Adaptive Behavior Inventory for Children is normed only for students ages 5 through 11. The Vineland Adaptive Behavior Scales (American Guidance Service, 1984) may become the instruments of choice in this assessment domain.

If the student's adaptive behavior is also significantly below average and if he or she has no sensory, motor, or other impairments, he or she might be classified as mentally retarded. This student is then assessed for programming purposes. Assessment would include the use of criterion-referenced measures of academic achievement, such as the Brigance Diagnostic Inventory of Basic Skills (Brigance, 1977), and criterion-referenced measures of social/emotional status, such as the behavioral observation system contained in the Ecological Assessment of Child Problem Behavior (Wahler, House, & Stambaugh, 1976).

If, on the other hand, the student's measured intellectual functioning is above the mentally retarded range, he or she is next assessed with a norm-referenced measure(s) of academic achievement. This assessment is needed to determine whether the student should be classified as learning disabled. For this classification evidence of a significant discrepancy between expected achievement (based on his or her intellectual functioning) and actual achievement must be shown, as measured through norm-referenced achievement testing (Procedures for Evaluating Specific Learning Disabilities, 1977, p. 65083). Either the Wide Range Achievement Test (Jastak & Jastak, 1978) or the Peabody Individual Achievement Test (Dunn & Markwardt, 1970) could be used for this purpose. Criterion-referenced measures of achievement, such as the Brigance Diagnostic Inventory of Basic Skills (Brigance, 1977), should also be administered to assist with programming decisions.

Figure 1 also indicates that information processing (or modality) skills can be assessed with students suspected of being learning disabled. If this type of assessment is required in a particular state, it should be done using instruments such as those described earlier as appropriate to this assessment domain. Finally, behavioral observations of the learning disabled student are required for classification (Procedures for Evaluating Specific Learning Disabilities, 1977, pp. 65082–65085.). These observations can be accomplished through use of the Ecological Assessment of Child Problem Behavior (Wahler, House, & Stambaugh, 1976) and will be useful for programming as well.

If the screening and programming team sees a student's problems as primarily social/emotional in nature, another branch of the system is entered. Following interviews with mediators (other teachers, parents) and the student, behavior checklists and behavioral observations are used to determine if the student can be classified as seriously emotionally disturbed. I recommend use of the Walker Problem Behavior Indentification Checklist (Walker, 1970) and the Ecological Assessment of Child

Problem Behavior (Wahler, House & Stambaugh, 1976). These measures should be useful in making both classification and programming decisions about the student. Finally, norm-referenced achievement measures such as the Wide Range Achievement Test (Jastak & Jastak, 1978) can be used to estimate achievement levels for programming purposes.

Cautions

The branching assessment system is only one way of sequencing assessment. Readers should judge it or any other system in terms of their own needs. Specific assessment techniques should be chosen carefully.

I have recommended several specific techniques that I and my colleagues have found helpful. Each, however, has its own strengths and weaknesses, and assessment personnel must judge available techniques for themselves.

SUMMARY AND CONCLUSION

This article has presented an assessment system and specific assessment techniques appropriate to classification and programming for mentally retarded, learning disabled, and emotionally disturbed students. Readers concerned with the assessment of students with lower-incidence handicapping conditions should consult sources such as Gerken (1979).

Assessment is a complex activity and one that must be adapted to local needs. Though I believe that appropriate and beneficial assessment is possible, I also believe that it requires our best efforts. These efforts must involve blending our individual talents with those of others in each school and also on a system-wide and community-wide basis. If this occurs, our students will surely benefit.

REFERENCES

Algozzine, B., & Ysseldyke, J. (1981). Special education service for normal children: Better safe than sorry? *Exceptional Children, 48,* 238–243.

American Guidance Service. (1984). *1984 tests and testing services catalog.* Circle Pines, MN: American Guidance Service.

American Psychological Association. (1981). Ethical principles of psychologists. *American Psychologist, 36,* 633–638.

Bender, L. (1938). *A Visual-motor gestalt test and its clinical uses* (Research Monograph No. 3). New York: American Orthopsychiatric Association.

Brigance, A. (1977) *Brigance diagnostic inventory of basic skills.* Woburn, MA: Curriculum Associates, 1977.

Burks, H. (1977). *Burks' behavior rating scales.* Los Angeles: Western Psychological Services.

Cain, L., Levine, S., & Elzey, F. (1977). *Manual for the Cain-Levine Social Competency Scale.* Palo Alto, CA: Consulting Psychologists Press.

Coulter, W. (1980). Adaptive behavior and professional disfavor: Controversies and trends for school psychologists. *School Psychology Review, 9,* 67–74.

Coulter, W., & Morrow, H. (Eds.). (1978). *Adaptive behavior: Concepts and measurements.* New York: Grune & Stratton.

Council for Exceptional Children. (1983a). CEC code of ethics. *Exceptional Children, 50,* 205.

Council for Exceptional Children. (1983b). CEC standards for professional practice. *Exceptional Children, 50,* 206–209. (b)
Doll, E. (1965). *Vineland social maturity scale.* Circle Pines, MN: American Guidance Service.
Dunn, L., & Markwardt, F. (1970). *Peabody individual achievement test—Manual.* Circle Pines, MN: American Guidance Service.
Education of handicapped children (Regulations implementing Education for All Handicapped Children Act of 1975). (1977, August 23). *Federal Register,* pp. 42474–42518.
Fleming, D., & Fleming, E. (1983). Consultation with multidisciplinary teams: A program of development and improvement of team functioning. *Journal of School Psychology, 21,* 367–376.
Frith, G. (1981). "Advocate" vs. "professional employee": A question of priorities for special educators. *Exceptional Children, 47,* 486–492.
Frostig, M., LeFever, W., & Whittlesey, J. (1966). *Frostig developmental test of visual perception.* Palo Alto, CA: Consulting Psychologists Press.
Gerken, K. (1978). Performance of Mexican-American children on intelligence tests. *Exceptional Children, 44,* 438–443.
Gerken, K. (1979). Assessment of high-risk preschoolers and children and adolescents with low-incident handicapping conditions. In G. Phye & D. Reschly (Eds.), *School psychology: Perspectives and issues.* New York: Academic Press.
Gough, H. (1969). *California psychological inventory.* Palo Alto, CA: Consulting Psychologists Press.
Gresham, F. (1982). Misguided mainstreaming: The case for social skills training with handicapped children. *Exceptional Children, 48,* 422–433.
Helton, G., Morrow, H., & Yates, J. (1977). Grouping for instruction: 1965, 1975, 1985. *Reading Teacher, 31,* 28–33.
Helton, G., Workman, E., & Matuszek, P. (1982). *Psychoeducational assessment: Integrating concepts and techniques.* New York: Grune & Stratton.
Helton, G., & Workman, E. (1982). Considerations in assessing the mildly handicapped. In T. Miller & E. Davis (Eds.), *The mildly handicapped student.* New York: Grune & Stratton.
Jastak, J., & Jastak, S. (1978). *Wide range achievement test—Manual of instructions.* Los Angeles: Western Psychological Services.
Kaufman, A. (1983). Intelligence: Old concepts—new perspectives. In G. Hynd (Ed.), *The school psychologist: An introduction.* Syracuse, NY: Syracuse University Press.
Kaufman, A., & Kaufman, N. (1983a). *Kaufman assessment battery for children—Administration and scoring manual.* Circle Pines, MN: American Guidance Service.
Kaufman, A., & Kaufman, N. (1983b). *Kaufman assessment battery for children—Interpretative manual.* Circle Pines, MN: American Guidance Service.
Kaufman, N., & Kaufman, A. (1983c). Remedial intervention in education. In G. Hynd (Ed.), *The school psychologist: An introduction.* Syracuse, NY: Syracuse University Press.
Kirk, S., McCarthy, J., & Kirk, W. (1968). *Illinois test of psycholinguistic abilities.* Urbana, IL: University of Illinois Press.
Koppitz, E. (1977). *The visual aural digit span test.* New York: Grune & Stratton.
Lambert, N., Windmiller, M., Cole, L., & Figueroa, R. (1975). *Manual for the public school version of the AAMD Adaptive Behavior Scale.* Washington, DC: American Association on Mental Deficiency.
Larry P. et al. v. *Wilson Riles et al.* U.S. Dist. Ct., Northern District of California, Case No. C–71–2270 RFP, 1972, 1974, 1979.
Lundell, K., Evans, J., & Brown, W. (1976). *Criterion tests of basic skills.* San Rafael, CA: Academic Therapy Publications.
Maher, C. (1982). Time management training for providers of special services. *Exceptional Children, 48,* 523–528.
Mercer, J. (1979). *Technical manual. System of multicultural pluralistic assessment.* New York: Psychological Corp.
Mercer, J., & Lewis, J. (1977) *SOMPA parent interview manual* New York: Psychological Corp.
Murray, H. (1943). *Thematic apperception test.* Cambridge, MA: Harvard University Press.
National Association of School Psychologists. (1978). *Principles for professional ethics.* Washington, DC: National Association of School Psychologists.
Obrzut, J., & Zucker, S. (1983). Projective personality assessment techniques. In G. Hynd (Ed.), *The school psychologist: An introduction.* Syracuse, NY: Syracuse University Press.
Parents in Action on Special Education (PASE) v. *Joseph P. Hannon.* U.S. Dist. Ct., Northern District of Illinois, Eastern Division, No. 74 (3586), July, 1980.

Piers, E., & Harris, D. (1969). *The Piers-Harris children's self-concept scale*. Nashville: Counselor Recordings and Tests.
Procedures for evaluating specific learning disabilities. (1977, December 29). *Federal Register*, pp. 65082–65085.
Reschly, D. (1983). Legal issues in psychoeducational assessment. In G. Hynd (Ed.), *The school psychologist: An introduction*. Syracuse, NY: Syracuse University Press.
Rorschach, H. (1942). *Psychodiagnostics*. Berne, Switzerland: Verlag Hans Huber.
Salvia, J., & Ysseldyke, J. (1981). *Assessment in remedial and special education* (2nd ed.). Boston: Houghton Mifflin.
Sattler, J. (1982). *Assessment of children's intelligence and special abilities*. Boston: Allyn & Bacon.
Smith, R., Neisworth, J., & Greer, J. (1978). *Evaluating educational environments*. Columbus, OH: Charles E. Merrill.
Strain, P., & Shores, R. (1983). A reply to misguided mainstreaming. *Exceptional Children, 50*, 271–273.
Tennessee Department of Education (1982). *Student evaluation manual*. Nashville: Tennessee Department of Education.
Terman, L., & Merrill, M. (1973). *Stanford-Binet intelligence scale—Manual for the third revision, form L-M, 1972 norms edition*. Boston: Houghton-Mifflin.
Wahler, R., House, A., & Stambaugh, E. (1976). *Ecological assessment of child problem behavior: A clinical package for home, school, and institutional settings*. New York: Pergamon Press.
Walker, H. (1970). *Walker Problem behavior identification checklist*. Los Angeles: Western Psychological Services.
Weatherly, R., & Lipsky, M. (1977). Street-level bureaucrats and institutional innovations: Implementing special education reform. *Harvard Educational Review, 47*, 171–197.
Wechsler, D. (1967). *Manual for the Wechsler Preschool and Primary Scale of Intelligence*. New York: Psychological Corp.
Wechsler, D. (1974). *Manual for the Wechsler intelligence scale for children—Revised*. New York: Psychological Corp.
Wechsler, D. (1981). *Manual for the Wechsler adult intelligence scale—Revised*. New York: Psychological Corp.
Woodcock, R. (1976). *Goldman-Fristoe-Woodcock auditory skills test battery—Technical manual*. Circle Pines, MN: American Guidance Service.
Woodcock, R. (1978). *Woodcock-Johnson psychoeducational battery*. Boston: Teaching Resources.

Dr. Helton is Professor of Educational Psychology and Special Education and Coordinator of the Graduate Program in School Psychology at the University of Tennessee at Chattanooga. He formerly held positions as a school psychologist and as a school administrator.

Second only to prevention, early identification and planned interventions are the most effective strategies to reduce the negative impact of a developmentally disabling condition. The authors have developed and used a comprehensive approach to assessing the developmental needs of young children, and, to their credit, they have organized a system that is instructionally responsive to children's growth needs. Instructional planning, not diagnostic labels, is the primary purpose of assessment. Of importance is the authors' position that assessment and instruction are intertwined; the act of teaching and the child's responses to that act provide assessment data.

A six-step model for assessing the needs of young children is discussed. It is a model that makes sense functionally in that it clearly results in an appropriate instructional program for young children with disabilities. This chapter is especially timely because of the new federal initiatives for handicapped infants and toddlers as specified in PL 99–457, the Education of the Handicapped Amendments of 1986. School districts and other educational agencies that are required to plan and develop programs of instruction and related services for this new mandate should use the guidelines developed in this article.

Assessment of Young Children with Special Needs

Jeanne M. McCarthy, Kathryn A. Lund, and Candace S. Bos

Those concerned with the teaching of young handicapped children are being bombarded by conflicting messages from a variety of professional fields. The growing national priority on early identification, screening, diagnosis, and treatment has emphasized the need for more intensive and specific diagnostic or assessment procedures, at earlier and earlier ages. Investigators in pediatrics, neonatology, psychology, and education are trying to define the variables in each of the developmental areas that will reliably identify the instructional needs of children who need intervention in the early months or years of life. New assessment devices are appearing in large numbers, to augment the sizable number of standardized tests suitable for the early childhood population.

The Arizona Basic Assessment and Curriculum Utilization System (ABACUS) evolved over 12 years of development and field testing. This, basically, is an intervention system representing an early education program for young handicapped children functioning in the developmental age range from 2 to 5½ years. As part of the overall program, the Assessment component follows a philosophy consistent with:

—an emphasis on the needs of the child across all components of the ecological system in which he or she lives.
—an emphasis on instruction as the primary purpose of assessment, and a corresponding deemphasis on etiology (origin) or classification.
—A view of assessment as an ongoing process best done in the teaching-learning situation—thus moving the focus from the psychologist to the teacher and the locus from the specialist's office to the classroom.
—An emphasis on functional levels rather than on quantified statements of performance based on extrapolations from limited samples of behavior.

AN ECOLOGICAL APPROACH TO ASSESSMENT

In the assessment of young exceptional children, the traditional view of assessment, or diagnosis, must be broadened to include the child's total ecological system. Rather than asking, "What is wrong with this child? . . . What are his (her) strengths and weaknesses?" the questions in this approach are, "What does this child need in order to optimize his (her) growth and development? . . . What does he (she) need from each component of his (her) ecosystem to survive and thrive, to become the most socially competent human being possible?" The assessment process must include assessment of the child's service needs and the needs and strengths of significant others in his or her environment. A nutritional assessment may be more important than a cognitive assessment to some children. Assessment of the mother's ability to cope, or her need for respite care, may be more critical than any other type of assessment.

THE PURPOSE OF ASSESSMENT

The purpose of assessment is primarily for instructional purposes and to establish the child's present level of performance in each of the areas considered important for him or her to learn. The assessment process permits the teacher to specify objectives, strategies, and activities keyed to the child's level of performance. In addition, assessment information is useful in making placement decisions and in the evaluation process—both evaluation of program effectiveness and evaluation of child progress. In evaluating child progress, comparing the child with himself or herself, as well as with nonhandicapped peers, has been found useful. With these purposes in mind, both criterion-referenced assessment instruments and norm-referenced instruments may have to be utilized.

THE TEACHER'S ROLE IN THE ASSESSMENT PROCESS

In the ABACUS model, assessment is viewed as an ongoing process. The teacher is involved in all facets of the process—as the generator of data on criterion-referenced instruments, as an adjunct to the psychologist responsible for the norm-referenced intelligence testing, and as a sophisticated consumer of norm-referenced data. Further, observation of the child in the process of learning may yield information critical to the assessment process.

In addition to the teacher's involvement in standardized testing, his or her role in the use of criterion-referenced tests becomes even more critical because of the nature of these tests. The teacher, with his or her detailed knowledge of what the child can do, is the most logical person to utilize criterion-referenced instruments. The teacher is in the best position to judge when to test the child, to select the time at which he or she is functioning best, and to determine appropriate entry points on the assessment device. In the ABACUS as long as two or three weeks may be necessary to complete the process, with short daily sessions of 5 to 10 minutes interspersed in the daily program. This would be impossible for anyone not in daily contact with the child.

Because the assessment of young handicapped children is an art, not a science, it must be done with extreme care, not on a one-shot basis in surroundings that are strange to the child. Also, testing children in familiar surroundings, usually a corner of the classroom, has been found most fruitful. In some cases, the teacher might have to interpret verbal or signed responses that may not be totally intelligible. In all cases, the teacher is the major translator of data from tests administered by the support staff into each child's instructional program. The total assessment process in the ABACUS encompasses clinical observations, clinical teaching, and norm-referenced and criterion-referenced testing. The classroom teaching staff plays an important role in all three phases, complementing and enhancing the contribution of support staff traditionally assigned these functions.

ASSUMPTIONS BASIC TO THE ASSESSMENT OF YOUNG HANDICAPPED CHILDREN

Implicit in the approach to assessment of young children in the ABACUS model are the following basic assumptions:

1. The word "assessment," rather than "diagnosis," is used in relation to instruction because it places emphasis on the current level of developmental functioning. "Diagnosis" is best left to the medical model, since a medical diagnosis leads to definitive statements about etiology, clinical symptomatology, treatment, and prognosis, whereas "assessment" leads to an appropriate educational program.

   Educational and psychological testing provide little or no information about etiology, some about clinical symptomatology, little or none about treatment, and none about prognosis. Rather than "diagnosing" a problem, we should be describing a preschool child's current level of functioning in such a way that the assessment leads to appropriate instructional programming.
2. The testing situation elicits only a limited sample, at best, of the child's behavior. In many cases, the behavior is better described than quantified or labeled.
3. Intelligence develops out of continuous interaction between the child and his or her environment. This dynamic commitment to the educability of intelligence must be uppermost in the mind of anyone involved in assessing young children. Intelligence is not static. It may fluctuate in response to environmental stimulation. Assessing the environment may be an important adjunct to assessing the child.

4. Given the instability of the IQ in young children and their response to environmental stimulation, the traditional labels should be used with extreme caution, if at all. Labeling a 3-year-old as educable mentally retarded or learning disabled appears to be unwarranted because of the permanence implied in these labels.

   A term such as "developmentally delayed" is preferable to describe the child's level of functioning at the moment and does not convey the permanence inherent in most other labels. Labeling before the age of 6 or 7, for most of the "soft" categories of handicapping conditions, should be avoided if possible. In any case, the label should be as far removed as possible from the child. Maturation, time, and spontaneous recovery of function may make liars of the most competent assessors.
5. The idea that every child is learning something every waking moment is important to the educator of preschool children. Children are processing all environmental stimuli with or without our being aware of it.
6. The younger the child, the less reliable will be the predictions across all dimensions measured. The purpose of early intervention is to change the outcome for each child, thus reducing the predictive reliability of assessment instruments.
7. The more complex the multiplicity of handicaps, the more difficult, sensitive, and demanding will be the assessment process.
8. If three or four years in the home environment have not helped a child develop at a rate commensurate with peers, recommending a change in his or her environment makes good sense. Nursery school, a Head Start program, or a special preschool program are among the viable options, matching the intensity of service to the severity of the delay.
9. The functioning of a child at home, on the bus, on the playground, with peers, is more relevant than his or her performance in the specialist's office and has to be considered in the assessment process.
10. Screening procedures for young children should not be implemented until a service plan has been carefully thought out. Unless service is to follow, identifying and labeling children may prove to be a disservice. The kinds of service and the numbers of children for whom service is available will dictate details of the screening procedures.
11. The task of assessment is to pinpoint where children *are,* what they *can* do, what they *are* doing. Little emphasis should be placed on what they cannot do. This is especially true for severely and profoundly involved children. After describing what the child *can* do, the development of an instructional program is relatively simple, since the program is to be built upon what he or she can do, using sequenced steps to teach new skills.

PREVALENCE OF HANDICAPPING CONDITIONS AMONG PRESCHOOL CHILDREN

When planning a total assessment process for preschool handicapped children, the numbers of children to be served at each step of the process should be estimated. A review of the literature on the prevalence of handicapping conditions among children under five years of age reveals a dearth of reliable data useful to the person responsible for program development. Because of variability in criteria in the reported studies, prevalence figures range from 3% to 17% of the total preschool population in need of special education programming in the preschool years. The lower figures have been found in studies of physically handicapped children, excluding the categories of speech impaired, emotionally handicapped, educable mentally retarded, and learning disabled.

The U.S. Office of Education, Special Education Programs, limited the percentage of the total population to be counted for reimbursement (under Public Law 94–142) to 12% of the school-aged population. The actual percentage of children being served is 8–9%, with some variability between states. Given these figures, we can probably estimate that 5–10% of the preschool population of an average school district would be in need of intervention because of a handicapping condition. Sociocultural variations, as well as socioeconomic factors, require these estimates to be increased or decreased accordingly.

Using the "guesstimates," a school district of 10,000–15,000 children, with 1,000 3-year-olds and 1,000 4-year-olds, could reasonably expect between 100 and 200 children to be eligible for a preschool program, across all categories of the handicapped. Some sensory impaired children may already have been placed in a state program for the deaf, blind, or multiply handicapped. Some of the mildly involved children may be viewed as "immature" and not identified as handicapped. If the community is characterized by closely knit, extended families, the preschoolers in need of special services may not surface until they reach kindergarten age. If the community is economically deprived, the prevalence of handicapping conditions may be higher.

As a general rule of thumb, we may start with a 10% prevalence estimate and cut it in half for a new program, planning at the 5% level until the program becomes established. In a poverty level community the figure could be safely estimated at 15–20% for purposes of planning to meet the needs of the handicapped. Larger numbers of children initially identified during the first steps of the screening process will be gradually reduced to a lower figure.

A TOTAL ASSESSMENT PROCESS FOR PRESCHOOL HANDICAPPED CHILDREN

Assessment as used in the ABACUS calls for six steps, which are briefly outlined in this article.

Step 1: Screening

Screening is defined as *a process to determine if a problem exists*. Some of the important questions to be asked before instituting a screening program are as follows:

- What age group will be served?
- What kinds of handicapping conditions will be served?
- What will you do with the children once you find them?

- What philosophy underlies your intervention approach?
- Which curriculum is most appropriate for the children you will find?
- What instructional methodology is most appropriate?
- What will be the organizational structure of the program?
- Where will it be?
- How many persons will be needed for the screening process, and who will be utilized (volunteers, paraprofessionals)?
- To which clinics, agencies, or professionals will the parents be referred for further diagnosis of the child?
- How many children will be identified as having special needs in screening?
- How much will the screening program cost? How about the cost of diagnosis? Assessment?
- Who will pay for it?

In the ABACUS, the screening is divided into two levels with two instruments—the *PreABACUS Screening Scale I* (PASS I) and the *PreABACUS Screening Scale II* (PASS II). The face sheets of these instruments are shown here as Figures 1 and 2.

PASS I is a checklist for behavioral observations. Little professional time is required to use or score this checklist, so the cost per child is relatively low. PASS I has been developed for ages 2, 3, 4 (as indicated by Figure 1), and 5. Each checklist consists of 10 items in the five developmental areas of the ABACUS to be rated by the parent or care-giver—Body Management, Self-Care, Communication, Pre-Academics, and Socialization.

Children functioning in the lower quartile for their chronological age in any of the developmental areas would be singled out for further consideration. A rough estimate of the numbers being singled out at this stage of the screening process depends upon the characteristics of the total population, with higher prevalence figures for low socioeconomic groups. In normal populations 15% of the population might appear to need further study at this point.

These children would be candidates for the more intensive screening of the PASS II, which contains 60 selected items from the full ABACUS that are considered to be marker variables in each developmental area. PASS II would be administered to the smaller subset of the total population—only to those children who appear to have problems on the PASS I or to those referred by parents or other professionals.

Children who show significant delays on the items of PASS II would then receive careful consideration and possible referral for further diagnosis or assessment. At this stage of the screening process, vision and hearing screening might be wise. A general physical examination may also be considered. Although extreme variability is found among populations of children, probably 10–12% may indicate the need for further evaluation.

Step 2: Diagnosis

Diagnosis, within the ABACUS, refers to the process of determining the nature and extent of the problem. This step in the assessment process is applied to a small

FIGURE 1 PreABACUS Screening Scale Level I (PASS I)—Face Sheet

Age
4

PASS I—Scoring Booklet
PreABACUS Screening Scale Level I

NAME ______________________ DATE ______________________

BIRTHDATE ______________________ OBSERVER/RATER ______________________

RELATIONSHIP TO CHILD ______________________

Instructions

Check child's performance in each skill on the following pages. After checking the child's skills within an area, total the number of *"Can Do"* responses. Write this number in the box marked "Total 'Can Do' Responses." Transfer each of those numbers to the corresponding box below.

Screening Summary

Developmental Area	**Number of *"Can Do"* Responses**		
	0-4	**5-8**	**9-10**
Body Management			
Self-Care			
Communication			
PreAcademics			
Socialization			

Do you consider this child to be a: ☐ Slow Learner ☐ Average Learner ☐ Rapid Learner

Comments:

---

subset of the population determined to have some sort of problem. Diagnosis may be done by representatives of the medical or health-related professions. The most common types of diagnostic assessment of young handicapped children are done by pediatricians, neurologists, audiologists, otologists, ophthalmologists, orthopedists, speech and language pathologists, physical or occupational therapists, and the like. With the assistance of these specialists, medical or physiological correlates of the

FIGURE 2 PreABACUS Screening Scale Level II (PASS II)—Face Sheet

PASS II — Scoring Booklet
PreABACUS Screening Scale Level II

Name ____________________

Teacher ____________________ Birthdate ____________

School ____________________ Age ____________

	Curriculum Area				
	BM	SC	C	PA	S
Date Administered					
Examiner					

Developmental Area	1	2	3	4	5	6	7	8	9	
I. BODY MANAGEMENT (BM)										**COMMENTS:**
A. Gross Motor	*	*	*	*	*	*	*	*		
B. Fine Motor	*	*	*	*	*	*	*			
II. SELF-CARE (SC)										
A. Dressing	*	*								
B. Toileting	*	*	*							
C. Grooming	*									
D. Eating	*	*	*							
E. Mechanical Know-How	*									
F. Safety	*									
III. COMMUNICATION (C)										
A. Prerequisites	*	*	*	*	*					**RECOMMENDATIONS:**
B. Comprehension and Production	*	*	*	*	*	*	*	*	*	
IV. PREACADEMICS (PA)										
A. Thinking	*	*	*	*	*	*	*			
B. Reading	*	*	*							
C. Mathematics	*	*	*							
D. Writing	*	*	*	*						
V. SOCIALIZATION (S)										
A. Awareness of Self and Others	*	*								
B. Awareness of Feelings	*									
C. Social Information	*									
D. Play Behavior	*									
E. Interactive Behavior	*	*	*							

After administering the items in this booklet, translate the correct responses (+) from the Score column to this sheet by drawing a horizontal line through the corresponding asterisk above.

problem may be identified, and programs may be designed to ameliorate them.

Closely related to this type of diagnostic assessment are the psychological assessments done primarily for purposes of eligibility for a special education program. In many states the school psychologist is largely responsible for declaring eligibility for programs for mentally retarded, learning disabled, or emotionally handicapped children. In cooperation with other members of the transdisciplinary team, a child may be declared eligible for the special program. In addition, the school psychologist at this step in the assessment process is to determine the psychological correlates of the disability that are relevant to total assessment of the child.

An estimated 5%–10% of the total population will be declared eligible for special programs because of a handicapping condition. But two questions require answers:

1. Does a significant developmental delay exist in one or more of the functional life skills, (body management, self-help, communication (including cognition), preacademics, or socialization)?
2. Is a significant discrepancy apparent within the psychological processes that underlie learning (attending, discrimination, visualization, auditorization, concept formation, receptive or expressive language, etc.)?

"Significant delay" for the preschool child may be defined in terms of standard deviations, stanines, or percentiles. On quantifiable measures, a child with a significant delay functions more than 1.5 standard deviations below the mean of his or her age group, or within the lowest 10% of the population, or in the first or second stanines of norm-referenced measures. Each of these criteria encompasses approximately 8%–11% of the population. The clinical judgment of team members can sharpen the criteria as they relate to a specific child.

On the Wechsler Preschool and Primary Scale of Intelligence, for example, 1.5 standard deviations below the mean would yield an IQ of 77, with subtest scores of 5 and 6. Although an IQ of 77 would not currently fall within the mentally retarded range, it could indicate a significant discrepancy within the psychological processes that underlie learning and might indicate a learning disability. This would be corroborated if the full-scale score were to reflect some sub-scale scores of 2, 3, or 4 and others of 6, 7, or 8, or higher. In situations where services can be delivered to "developmentally delayed" children, an IQ of 77 could indicate a significant delay.

On measures that cannot be quantified, including many criterion-referenced measures, clinical judgment has to dictate the significance of the delay. Neither criterion-referenced measures nor screening devices should be used to reach eligibility decisions. The clinical judgment of the team may have to be relied upon.

Valid and reliable formal test data on very young children are difficult and often impossible to gather. Thus, the answers to the questions may have to come from structured observations of the child's performance and from informal testing, coupled with formal testing. The family's and the preschool teacher's perceptions and observations have to be heavily emphasized, since the role of the child's support system in ameliorating the impact of biological insult has been documented in longitudinal research.

Step 3: Assessment

For instructional purposes, assessment is a process for determining the present level of performance and the prioritized goals and objectives in all areas of the curriculum. The total ABACUS assessment device is used at this point—after the child has been accepted into the program and individual programs have begun on the basis of PASS II and other available data.

The ABACUS consists of 214 items, in the five developmental areas mentioned previously:

1. *Body Management*. This incorporates gross motor skills involving large muscle development (such as sitting, walking, running, climbing, balancing, and throwing) and fine motor skills (grasping objects, stacking blocks, putting pegs in a pegboard, stringing beads, fitting pieces into puzzles, cutting, and the like).
2. *Self-Care*. The skills involved here are those that allow the child to function independently and to take care of personal needs (dressing, toileting, grooming, eating, mechanical know-how, and safety).
3. *Communication*. Communication allows for the exchange of ideas or thoughts. The skills involved are divided, in the ABACUS, into prerequisite skills (attending, imitating vocalizations, etc.), comprehension (understanding gestures, words, and concepts), and production (expressing ideas either verbally or through the use of total communication).
4. *Pre-Academics*. Cognitive skills and knowledge labeled as readiness skills for school can be classified by thinking (e.g., matching objects and pictures, labeling the shape and color of objects), reading (print awareness, book handling, and reading basic words), mathematics (identifying numbers and numeral concepts 1 to 5), and writing (scribbling, making pre-writing strokes, copying first name, etc.).
5. *Socialization*. Skills that increase a child's ability to get along with other children and adults and to function and learn in school comprise socialization.

These five developmental areas form the basis for not only the assessment, but the ABACUS curriculum and all components of the system. Figure 3 gives a sample page from the Pre-Academics assessment section.

During assessment of the child's communication skills using the ABACUS, speech and language pathologists assigned to the program might be called upon to assess language skills beyond those assessed on the ABACUS. A communication sample is taken. It has three major components: content, form, and use. This three-dimensional model of language is basic to describing the development of language and for understanding language delays.

Step 4: Ecological Assessment/Family Assessment

Ecological assessment is defined as a process to determine the physical, environmental, nutritional, and social correlates of the child's problem. It includes maternal perceptions, mother-child interactions, family strengths and needs, environmental

FIGURE 3 Sample Page from ABACUS Assessment

ITEM	(MATERIALS) PROCEDURES	CUE	NO.	SCORE PRE	SCORE POST	CRITERIA
19. Labels shapes	(4 basic two-dimensional shapes: circle, square, triangle; all shapes 2"-3" in size and same color) Put all shapes on table. Cue.	"What shape is this?" a. circle. b. square. c. triangle. d. rectangle.	a. b. c. d. 19.			Labels all 4 shapes.
*20. Finds like pictures	(Set of picture strips) Present strips in the following order: a. fruit, b. vehicles, c. balls. For each strip, point to the first picture. Cue. a. b. c. 	"Point to the one like this." a. banana. b. car. c. ball.	a. b. c. 20.			Does 2 of 3 correctly.
21. Tells if pictures are same/different	(Set of 5 cards; each card has 2 simple line drawings) Present cards one at a time in the following order: a. 2 identical houses. b. sock, hat. c. bird, dog. d. 2 identical trees e. ball, block.	"Are these two the same? Are they alike?" a. houses. (same) b. sock, hat. c. bird, dog. d. trees. (same) e. ball, block.	a. b. c. d. e. 21.			Does 4 of 5 correctly.
B. Reading *1. Turns pages of a book	(Book with colorful pictures and easy-to-turn pages) Give child the book. Cue.	"Look at the book. Turn the pages."	1.			Turns 1 to 3 pages at a time.
*2. Points to named picture	(Pictures of 5 objects: doll, spoon, ball, car, shoe) Put all 5 pictures on table. Cue.	"Point to the ______ " a. doll. b. spoon. c. ball. d. car. e. shoe.	a. b. c. d. e. 2.			Points to 4 of 5 pictures.

variables, parental attitudes, nutrition, social support systems, and the like. The importance of parental input at this stage is obvious. And data supplied by the nurse or social worker might also be useful, with consideration given to specifics such as nutritional status, adequacy of diet, sleeping arrangements at home, and so on.

Questions to be asked are not, "What is wrong with this child?" but, rather: "What does this child need to optimize his or her growth and development? What does the child need from each component of his or her ecosystem in order to survive and thrive?"

In the area of nonorganically defined high-risk infants, toddlers, and preschool youngsters, major efforts have succeeded in producing efficient early detection procedures and effective methods of measuring the effects of early intervention (Garber & Heber, 1981; Gordon & Guinagh, 1974; Gutelius et al., 1972; Raimey & Haskins, 1981). Data have been collected on home environments, family support networks, mothers' attitudes and teaching styles, and a host of other psychosocial variables that play a part in programs of early intervention and prevention of functional mental retardation.

Assessment instruments appropriate to ecological aspects of the child's environment have begun to appear in large numbers. One of the first was the Vineland Adaptive Behavior Scales (Sparrow, Balla, & Cicchetti, 1984), an interview checklist covering socialization, self-help, interpersonal relationships, and other areas. Another scale of interest is Caldwell's (1981) Home Observation for Measurement of the Environment (HOME). A home screening questionnaire developed by the John F. Kennedy Child Development Center in Denver (Frankenburg, 1981) provides for gaining similar information on variables in the home that have been found to influence development. These are only examples of many possible choices available to measure family strengths and needs.

Step 5: Formulation of an Instructional Hypothesis

All the data collected in the previous steps (screening data, medical and health-related correlates, psychological correlates, ecological correlates, and educational data) are utilized in formulating a hypothesis upon which instructional decisions are to be based. This hypothesis could be stated succinctly. An example might be:

> Although José was diagnosed as hydrocephalic at birth, and placed in a home for dying infants at nine days of age, the shunts seem to be working, and the present adoptive home appears to offer adequate support for his emotional needs. The delays present at 4 years of age appear to be residuals of the traumatic first two or three years of life. Current progress has been documented, with gradual closing of the gaps expected as school and home work to ameliorate the delays, and as José and his mother become more secure in their relationships. Based on this hypothesis, current levels of functioning will be identified, and the objectives based on what he needs to do next.

This type of statement puts the pieces of an extremely complex assessment process into an organized form that will lead to an instructional program.

Step 6: Development of the Individualized Education Plan/ Individual Family Service Plan

This final step in the process is based upon all five preceding steps in the total assessment. The decision on eligibility and most appropriate placement now has to be made. If a continuum of services is available, the choice must be based upon the best option to meet the child's individual needs as identified in the assessment process. If a child's prioritized needs can be met in an integrated setting, placement in this less restrictive environment may be indicated. If the prioritized needs indicate that a more intensive individualized program is required, placement in a self-contained class may be called for. In every case, the severity of the child's needs must be matched by the intensity of the service.

The IEP/IFSP serves as the bridge between assessment and instruction and leads directly into the curriculum. The format developed for the ABACUS incorporates the essential requirements of the federal regulations. Each item in the ABACUS IEP/IFSP form has a corresponding program in the ABACUS curriculum.

The six steps in the assessment process—screening, diagnosis, assessment for instruction, ecological/family assessment, formulation of an instructional hypothesis, and development of the IEP/IFSP—should lead smoothly into a curriculum that will help correct developmental delays in the areas of body management, self-care, communication, pre-academics, and socialization. This is the objective of the ABACUS program—to intercede in the lives of children who may be at-risk for later failure, and to direct them in the path of a better life through a systematic, coordinated program of intervention.

REFERENCES

Caldwell, B. (1965). *Daily program II—A manual for teachers*. Washington, DC: Office of Economic Opportunity.

Frankenburg, W. (1981). *Home screening questionnaire*. Denver: John F. Kennedy Development Center/Ladoca.

Garber, I. J., & Heber, R. (1981). The efficacy of early intervention with family rehabilitation. In M. Begab, H. C. Haywood, & H. L. Garber (Eds.), *Psychosocial influences in retarded performance*. Baltimore: University Park Press.

Gordan, I. J., & Guinagh, B. J. (1974). *A home learning center approach to early stimulation* (Final report to the National Institute of Mental Health). Gainesville, FL: University of Florida Institute for Development of Human Resources.

Gutelius, M. F., Kirsch, A. D., MacDonald, S., Brooks, M. R., McErlearn, T., & Newcomb, C. (1972). Promising results from a cognitive stimulation program in infancy. *Clinical Pediatrics, 11*, 585–593.

Raimey, C. T., & Haskins, R. (1981). The causes and treatment of school failure: Insights from the Carolina Abecedarian Project. In M. Begab, H. Garber, & H. C. Haywood (Eds.), *Causes and prevention of retarded development in psychosocially disadvantaged children*. Baltimore: University Park Press.

Sparrow, S., Balla, D., & Cicchetti, D. (1984). *Vineland adaptive behavior scales*. Circle Pines, MN: American Guidance Service.

Jeanne McCarthy and Candace Bos are with the Division of Special Education and Rehabilitation, University of Arizona. Kathryn Lund is with the Flagstaff (Arizona) Public Schools.

Transition from the world of school to the world of work within a community has now been recognized as a problem in need of solutions. After a person with a disability completes the last individualized education program at age 17 or 21, the need for supportive services does not magically disappear. But what can school programs do about transition problems? Cobb and Larkin provide a realistic solution via their paradigm of assessment and placement for effective vocational programming. Their approach has several advantages in comparison to traditional assessment procedures. First, it uses direct measures of behaviors rather than scores describing interests or traits. Second, direct measures of behaviors are used for program planning. Third, assessment is viewed as a continuous process instead of a one-time administration of a battery of tests.

The authors have added a unique ecological component to their approach to assessment. They do not limit vocational planning to the school or work setting. Instead, the planning includes interaction analyses—e.g., student-curriculum, student-teacher, student-peer, student-home/community, and student-work facility. Finally, the authors call for a new view of the role assigned to a vocational assessment specialist. The revised role would require abilities to function as a team member with both regular and special educators and would move the specialist from a laboratory site to settings in which programs are operational. This model has much to commend it to school districts and has direct implications for training personnel to function in a new vocational assessment role.

Assessment and Placement Of Handicapped Pupils Into Secondary Vocational Education Programs

R. Brian Cobb and Dave Larkin

As educational alternatives develop and evolve, so too must assessment strategies. Prior to the 20th century, assessment was primarily a matter of monitoring competence in the "three Rs." During the early 1900s, as the Industrial Revolution reshaped the way we worked, vocational education curricula (primarily agriculture, industrial arts, and home economics) appeared as a means to provide a well-trained labor force. During this same time, compulsory education and child labor laws required our schools to educate an ever increasing range of pupils, foreshadowing the need for a general education curriculum track. It is not surprising, then, that the early 1900s marked the beginning of the standardized testing movement. School counselors and administrators needed a means to place students into the various curriculum alternatives.

Progressing through the first half of the 1900s, curriculum options expanded even more. New divisions such as health, distributive, business, and technical education appeared in vocational education, and our increasingly sophisticated assessment techniques opened the door for placement among special education alternatives. The 1950s and early 1960s saw a rapid expansion in school placement alternatives in mental retardation, followed closely by the learning disabilities category in the 1970s and, more recently, that of emotional disturbance/behavioral disorders.

The expanding curriculum alternatives and the inclusion of children with a greater range of abilities and needs has made educators increasingly aware of complex interactions among curriculum, instructional delivery, and child characteristics. One small, yet troublesome, portion of that interaction—the assessment and placement of handicapped students who are likely candidates to receive secondary vocational education in a mainstreamed environment—is the subject of this article. The discussion here relates only to *high school* vocational assessment, and it is not intended to be critical of all of current vocational evaluation, both within and outside of schools. We recognize that the quality of vocational evaluation ranges to extremes. Our aim is to be constructive, not perjorative, and we trust the reader will apply that intent to the following discussion and paradigm.

BACKGROUND AND CURRENT PROBLEMS

Assessment of handicapped students in our public schools has occurred in systematic, albeit varied forms for several decades now. With the mandates in the PL 94–142 legislation associated with non-biased testing, least restrictive placements, and multidisciplinary staffing teams, the propriety and utility of many of our school assessment practices have come under intense scrutiny (for recent examples of critiques from several different perspectives, see Messick, 1984, Ysseldyke & Mirkin, 1982; Snow, 1984; Leinhardt, Bickel, & Pallay, 1982; Lilly, 1983). At a minimum, traditional practices in assessment for screening, placement, and program planning in special education seem to have become confounded by technical, methodological, and functional service delivery issues.

Although the empirical research base is not nearly as extensively developed, these same kinds of problems seem to hold for vocational/special education assessment as well. We have recognized for years the value of the vocational assessment process for handicapped students, including those with mildly handicapping conditions. These processes are commonly perceived to yield extrinsic benefits for a particular student in terms of team planning and placement decisions, and intrinsic rewards in the student's growth in confidence and maturity vis-à-vis the world of work. Recently, school guidance personnel and psychologists have recognized the potential that vocational assessment can play in their work in the schools (see, for example, Hohenshil, 1984; Shepard, Dielman, & Ellenwood, 1984; entries in Hohenshil, Anderson, & Salwan, 1982; Batsche, 1982; Peterson & Housley, 1982). These school personnel, however, have also expressed chagrin over many aspects characterizing much of traditional vocational assessment (Zytowski, 1982; Thurlow & Ysseldyke, 1982).

It seems evident, then, that vocational assessment of handicapped students will continue to demand the attention of professional vocational and special educators. This assessment area received a tremendous impetus in the 1960s with parallel development of the fields of vocational evaluation in rehabilitation and the civil rights focus on individual needs in education. In the 1970s vocational assessment again received attention as a result of the symbiotic relationship established in the PL 94–482 and PL 94–142 laws. Mainstreamed enrollments in regular vocational education have increased (Phelps, 1982), and programs and services have expanded, although at uneven rates (Wright, Cooperstein, Renneker, & Padilla, 1982). The new vocational education legislation (The Carl D. Perkins Vocational Education Act of 1984-H.R. 4164) has strengthened both the fiscal and the programmatic attention that handicapped students must receive in vocational education. Indeed, vocational assessment appears specifically in legislative language for the first time.

Historically, vocational assessment has been perceived by virtually all special education professionals as a fundamentally important supportive service for handicapped adolescents. Model processes have evolved in many states (e.g., Maryland State Department of Education, 1980; Arizona Department of Education, 1982; Peterson & Hill, 1982; California State Department of Education, 1983), and it is not unusual for school districts to require all handicapped students who enroll in a vocational education course to undergo comprehensive, formal vocational evaluation. A common theme underlying all models of vocational assessment is that results from that process should be used in developing the IEP (Phelps & McCarty, 1984), although local policy requiring the use of vocational assessment results in IEP processes is much less frequent.

This burgeoning evolution of vocational assessment models and processes notwithstanding, difficulties remain in the development of a consistent vocational assessment process that fulfills an equally useful function for parents, educators, support personnel, and students alike. Although considerable overlap exists, these areas will be discussed in terms of: (a) problems with the relationship between vocational assessment and vocational evaluation, and (b) definition of the process and environmental constructs assessed.

The Relationship between Vocational Assessment and Vocational Evaluation

Those describing the vocational assessment process have yet to achieve a consensus about what is meant by *vocational evaluation* and *vocational assessment* and how the two differ, if at all. These distinctions are more than just semantic, as evidenced by the extreme variability in the perceived relationship between the two. Consider the following examples.

Sitlington and Wimmer (1978), in an often cited article on vocational assessment, began:

> The terms *vocational assessment* and *vocational evaluation* have been used to mean anything from a 1-week deluge of aptitude and interest tests to a 3- to 4-week period of data collecting using a wide variety of assessment procedures. (p. 74)

The clear implication here is one of synonymy; the authors did nothing in the remainder of their manuscript to dispel that notion. Other writers have concurred. Several authors, however, have attempted to differentiate between the two. Unfortunately, no two seem to differentiate the relationship consistently.

Peterson (1982), who chaired a National Association of Vocational Education Special Needs Personnel (NAVESNP) task force on vocational assessment and produced a draft position paper in that effort, views vocational assessment as a comprehensive and systematic process, of which *vocational evaluation is but a subcomponent*. Just the reverse status is assigned by Kiernan and Petzy (1982), who stated:

> The terms *vocational assessment* and *vocational evaluation* are often used interchangeably. In this chapter, a distinction is drawn between assessment—as a process in which a characteristic factor is appraised in order to assign it a rating, description, or score—and evaluation—as a process in which data or information derived from an assessment is analyzed in order to determine its value in light of specific decisions that must be made. (p. 118)

Thus, these authors are telling us that vocational assessment is synonymous with test administration and vocational evaluation is the larger act of putting those assessment (test) results to use. This interpretation is not only at odds with Peterson's (1982) but is also counter to how most assessment specialists in special education perceive testing vis-a-vis assessment.

We believe that an effort to distinguish between the two terms as they relate to child assessment is counter-productive. What is needed in child assessment is a distinction between the many purposes for which vocational assessments are conducted rather than a distinction between the terms *assessment* and *evaluation*. We propose to eliminate the term *vocational evaluation* as it pertains to the entire range of assessment activities associated with screening, placement, and program planning and monitoring for an individual child. If local or state education personnel want to *evaluate* (assess merit or worth) local service delivery at the programmatic level, the term *vocational evaluation* may have some utility. For purposes of this article, however, we believe one should *assess individuals* (and their match with curriculum and instructional delivery) and *evaluate programs*.

Definition of Vocational Assessment and Environmental Constructs Assessed

Related to the problem of distinguishing between vocational assessment and vocational evaluation is that of defining the process. Again, the literature is equivocal stemming from confusion about the variety of purposes for which vocational assessment might be conducted, as well as confusion about what constructs are being assessed. Although conceptually separating these two issues from each other is impossible, we will treat them separately to make our position clearer.

Definition of Vocational Assessment

It would seem that whether it is vocational *assessment* or vocational *evaluation*, the definition of that process would be relatively consistent. Not so. Definitional disparities appear to gravitate toward an emphasis on predicting an individual/employment "fit" at one extreme, to a more exploratory, learning-centered, and school-based approach at the other extreme. An example of the former is provided by Botterbusch (1978):

> Vocational assessment is the process of assessing a person to determine the specific nature of his or her aptitudes, skills, characteristics, and work-related behaviors. (p. 2)

Knowledge derived through this assessment process is then matched with what is known about the knowledge, skills, and abilities requisite in a particular occupation. The ultimate purpose is to generate an occupational profile of a handicapped individual and match that with occupational information from specific jobs, most often through the *Dictionary of Occupational Titles* or some similar manual.

Contrast the above definition with the following definitions of vocational assessment:

> . . . a comprehensive process conducted over a period of time, involving a multi-disciplinary team . . . with the purpose of identifying individual characteristics, education, training, and placement needs, which provides educators the basis for planning an individual's program. (Dahl, Appleby, & Lipe, 1978, p. 103)

or

> . . . a holistic approach which considers an individual's total career development . . . [whose purpose] is to collect and provide objective career information for parents, educators, the student, and others to use in planning appropriate educational experiences to enhance the student's employability. (Peterson & Hill, 1982, p. 1)

We believe these latter definitions convey a much more utilitarian process at the public school level. As has been pointed out repeatedly (Zytowski, 1982; Phelps & Wentling, 1977; Dunn, 1976), our instrumentation is simply not advanced enough to make accurate predictive decisions about handicapped adolescents' occupational traits or abilities. As a result, some profoundly mistaken assumptions about the employment potential of a handicapped student may be made at the local level.

Environmental Constructs Assessed

No doubt the confusion about the definition of the terms is associated, in large measure, to the lack of clarity about *what* is being assessed. This construct validity problem is compounded by the nature of vocational education and the origin of vocational assessment within the realm of vocational rehabilitation.

Formal vocational assessment, as it has evolved in the public schools and has typically been described in the literature, has been directly adapted from the vocational rehabilitation evaluation process. This process is grounded in predictive attempts to assess disabled adults for a "fit" with workplace requirements, either through competency-based assessment procedures, occupational trait analysis, or a behavioral consistency approach (Dunn, 1976). This model can be considered "diagnostic-prescriptive" in that the assessment attempts to diagnose individual vocational interests/aptitudes and results in a prescription of how those client characteristics can be matched with suitable workplace requirements. (Much more detailed discussions of this process are available in Schneck, 1981; Dunn, Korn, & Andrew, 1976.)

On the surface, then, transfer to the special/vocational education environment would appear to be appropriate, since special education service delivery has taken primarily a diagnostic-prescriptive model approach. Unfortunately, though, the "prescriptive" component of this rehabilitation assessment model does not adapt well to the didactic purposes that underlie educational functions. Hence, vocational assessment processes in our schools have evolved attempting to make predictions about employment suitability, but not very often about curricular ecology. Thus, our instructional planning personnel are confronted with vocational assessment systems and instrumentation that yield information essentially unrelated to, or only tangentially related to, curriculum.

Increasingly in recent years, this anomaly in service delivery has received critical attention in the literature (Cobb, 1981, 1983; Halpern, Lehmann, Irvin, & Heiry, 1982; Gugerty & Crowley, 1982; Menchetti, Rusch, & Owens, 1982; Miller, Sachs, & Stadt, 1982; Petzy, 1983; Rosenberg & Tesolowski, 1982; Stodden & Ianacone, 1981; Zytowski, 1982). The Halpern et al. (1982) book has described this dualistic approach to conceptualizing vocational assessment in terms of traditional versus contemporary approaches. Traditional assessment:

> . . . has been based upon the assumption that measures of existing aptitudes, interests, and traits can be used to predict subsequent learning, performance, and adjustment.

Contemporary assessment, on the other hand:

> . . . refers to those practices that clearly link the purposes and outcomes of assessment with the goals and techniques of instruction and other forms of service intervention. . . . (p. 1)

The authors then elaborated upon the differences between the two approaches:

> Rather than rely on traits or aptitudes to infer performance, the contemporary approach emphasizes the importance of direct assessment of actual competencies, [and] requires the outcomes of measurement to have direct implications for program planning. (p. 4)

We believe the contemporary notion of vocational assessment for handicapped adolescents represents the most viable and responsive assessment alternative, given the didactic purpose of vocational education. Linking assessment procedures directly to instruction is inherently more opportunity-expanding, and, we believe, may lead in general to less restrictive placements in vocational education. Most assessment models for use with mildly handicapped students, however, are bereft of systematic components that assess the match between a student's skills and deficits on the one hand and classroom curriculum, ecology, instructional delivery, and availability of supportive services on the other. What is clearly needed in our conceptualization of vocational assessment at the school level is the addition of a systematic process that includes this component as well.

A PARADIGM OF VOCATIONAL ASSESSMENT

A logical paradigm for vocational assessment that relates the activities and instrumentation to instructional delivery has been repeatedly utilized in the regular special education assessment literature (e.g., Salvia & Ysseldyke, 1981; Hawkins, 1979) and has more recently been characterized by Halpern et al. (1982) as falling within the contemporary assessment domain discussed earlier. What makes our paradigm different in its utility for model development is that it relates activities to *instructionally relevant purposes* rather than to processes and instrumentation that have characterized much of the model literature to date. We believe that if educational professionals perceive a clear chronological sense of *why* assessment occurs and *how* those notions relate to ongoing school-based activity for an individual student, the utility of the entire process will be greatly enhanced.

In this paradigm the vocational assessment process is assigned five chronological purposes: screening, placement, program planning, monitoring of individual progress, and individual program evaluation. Figure 1 depicts the chronology of these five purposes. Each of these purposes is discussed here, with examples of instrumentation and processes relative to the vocational assessment of handicapped learners in mainstreamed settings. For similar and highly compatible resources and example documents, the reader could refer to Albright, Fabac, and Evans (1978) and Albright (1979).

A fundamental underlying assumption of this model, it should be pointed out, is a *team* approach to vocational assessment. We do not adhere to the more traditional assessment processes characterized by a vocational evaluator conducting an in-lab assessment, collecting information from outside sources, and synthesizing those data into an assessment report. We believe vocational, special, and regular educators can and should *conduct* some of the assessment activities (with proper training), not only pass judgment on the information derived from them. Thus, our assessment specialist must recognize the need for and propriety of having some assessments conducted in completely normalized settings by regular education professionals.

Each of the purposes discussed here fits well within the IEP process model as well. By indexing each of these purposes to the multiple processes in IEP development and implementation, we anticipate increasing the use of vocational assessment results in IEP development and making the IEP a more dynamic component of ongoing instruction.

FIGURE 1 ***Purposes of Assessment and Their Relationship to Ongoing Instructional Delivery***

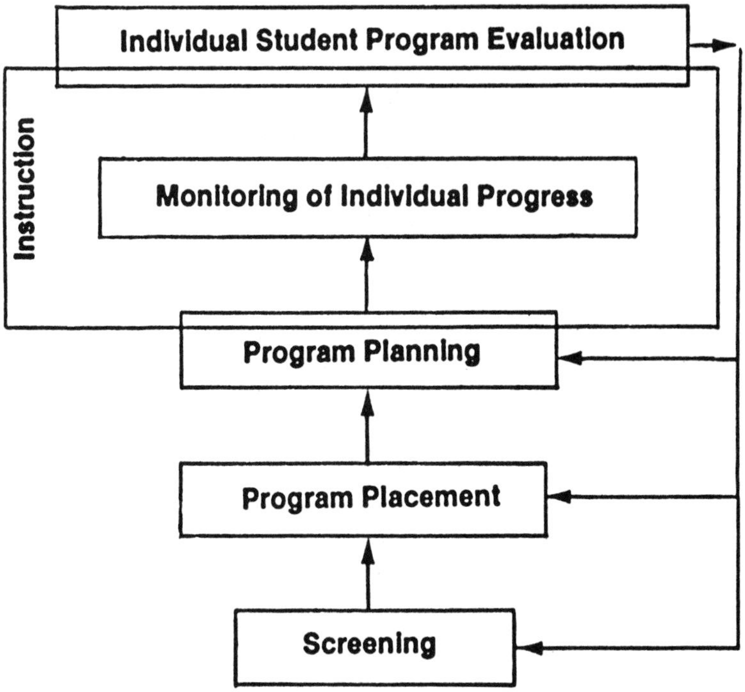

Screening

Vocational assessment for the purpose of screening is the first component in our paradigm. It can be conceptualized in terms of the fundamental question a staffing team may want to answer: "Is vocational education an appropriate curriculum option for this particular handicapped student, or should he/she be in some other curriculum such as college preparatory or general track?" This question assumes that a viable set of curriculum alternatives exists and that the choice between them can be based upon direct assessment information rather than local district policy.

How do we determine whether vocational education is appropriate for a particular student? The traditional assessment approach would suggest a set of standardized procedures to determine aptitudes and interests, then try to match them with existing vocational curricula through a primarily predictive process. To screen a student for vocational education, however, we suggest the following less formal (standardized) activities.

First, we suggest using parent input as to their aspirations for the child. Bellamy and Wilcox (1982) recently introduced the notion of *opportunity costs* in the selection of curriculum alternatives for secondary-aged handicapped students. By the time a student reaches high school, he or she has only a few school years left in which to prepare for the complex demands of participatory citizenship. Many students still need remedial education in academics, domestic living, and recreating, as well as employment preparation. Parents are likely to provide important validation of a curriculum selection such as vocational education.

Parent input by itself, however, is not enough. Equally important, students at the secondary level are capable of self-selection, and vocational assessment personnel must determine whether a student is committed to that choice. We recommend a review of the student's previous scholastic record in industrial arts or prevocational coursework, as well as interviews with his/her teachers in those subjects.

Assuming the student and/or parent(s) favors placement in vocational education, assessment personnel must then determine whether program alternatives exist and are accessible. Questions the vocational assessor should address include:

- To what extent does the school district and/or regional vocational center policy promote accessibility of programs to handicapped students exhibiting skill deficits similar to those possessed by this student?
- To what extent is the individual ready for vocational education?
- How well-trained and receptive are teachers in the regional vocational center toward teaching handicapped students?
- How well does the related services system function so that success is likely? Related services should be broadly defined to include not only in-school support but also transportation, sending school guidance/counseling, etc.

Placement

Once a student has been screened and a decision has been made that vocational education is the appropriate curriculum option, the next decision that must be made is: "*Which program* within vocational education?" Currently, vocational education is made up of nine different divisions, although all may not be available at every vocational school.

School-Related Options

These are: (a) agriculture, (b) trades and industrial, (c) business and office occupations, (d) distributive, (e) technical, (f) home economics, (g) health occupations, (h) industrial arts, and (i) cooperative education.

Within each division a variety of program alternatives may be available. For example, a student may be interested in agriculture education; yet the diversity of occupational preparation alternatives within that option might range from ornamental horticulture to agribusiness technology. Likewise, with health occupations, selections may vary from a program to train nurses' aides to one preparing laboratory technicians. Consistent with the notions of free appropriate public education and least restrictive environment, assessment for placement assumes the existence of bona fide choices for students with handicapping conditions. If local district policy presupposes the placement of all students with a particular handicapping condition in food services, for example, assessment for placement becomes superfluous.

What mechanisms and information sources can assist in assessment for placement? Again, parents can provide important information in deciding program selection. And the student, through interviews and informal interest inventories and tours of different programs, can clearly focus the selection process.

As in assessment for screening, a number of programmatic variables must be considered along with student and parent interests. For example, assessing the match between student academic skills and entry-level program competencies would be important. Similarly, some sense of a likelihood for achieving exit-level competencies must be taken into account, since mainstreamed placements should require that students achieve the same competency *levels*, if not the same range of competencies, as nonhandicapped students.

Another critical variable may well be the characteristics of instructional delivery. A vocational assessor's brief observation of vocational teacher teaching styles may assist greatly in making placement decisions. Likewise, the use of teaching strategies such as peer teaching and peer tutoring, multiple media in lecture, and logical, well-sequenced presentations may be important variables in selecting a placement.

An additional concern may be the physical requirements associated with multiple locations of instruction. A building trades program is likely to require that a majority of instructional time take place at a building site. Given that on-site instruction may be much less structured than in-class instruction, a student requiring close supervision might not best be placed in that curriculum.

A placement consideration that may be extremely important is the existence of a cooperative work education (CWE) experience culminating the program selection or concurrent with it. A recent 4-year follow-up study of mildly to moderately handicapped graduates of vocational programs in Vermont suggested that part-time employment prior to leaving school greatly enhanced the employment prospects of those individuals (Hasazi & Gordon, 1982). A CWE experience features paid work placement in the community in an occupation for which training has occurred during a student's vocational education program. Typically, CWE experiences occur in the final semester of a student's program and involve a half-day of work and a half-day of instruction.

Evans and Herr (1978) have also characterized the advantages of CWE programs as follows:

> Cooperative work education stimulates desirable attitudes toward work. Work atmosphere is extremely difficult to reproduce outside of a real work situation, and the importance of promptness and regular attendance at work are much more demonstrable on the job than in school. Moreover, because of the difficulty of marketing goods and services produced within school laboratories, it is also extremely difficult in laboratory-based programs to develop realistic attitudes towards speed, quality, and efficiency. (p. 238)

Those authors continued by documenting extremely high employment rates of CWE completers—often as high as 80% in many school districts. Thus, the value of a CWE component in programs for mildly to moderately handicapped students is particularly compelling.

Equally important to a CWE placement in a business outside of the school may be an in-school entrepreneurial experience. Stern (1984) recently found that participants in school-based work enterprises viewed these activities, when compared to out-of-school jobs, as providing "more opportunity to work in teams, to learn skills they think will be valuable in future jobs, and to experience work that is more intrinsically motivating" (p. 422). Given that work attitudes and overall career maturity are frequently cited by employers as important qualities in prospective employees, high-quality school-based enterprises that are attached to a vocational program (such as the school store in a distributive education program) may be an important placement consideration for a handicapped youngster.

Job Availability

Finally, local job availability may be a prime consideration (assessment technique) for determining program selection. We place *little* emphasis upon predicating program selection decisions upon community employment opportunities existing at the time of placement in a training program. In many communities the jobs most available are those requiring little or no prior training, such as many of those in the fast-food industry. Mildly handicapped students are no more in need of *job-specific training* for these positions than are nonhandicapped students. Students should be placed in vocational education programs for jobs that legitimately require or make use of job-specific training. It is no more appropriate to let job availability in these businesses overly affect program selection decisions (such as food service programs) for mildly handicapped students than for nonhandicapped students.

Local vocational education programming has a history of responsiveness to local employer needs. Although that responsiveness has been much more evident at the post-secondary level than at the secondary level, these natural controls for determining the entire range of local vocational education programs are as satisfactory for mildly handicapped students as for nonhandicapped students. The risk of imperfections in the existing system of natural controls is preferable to the stereotypical response of over-enrolling handicapped students in training programs for "least preferred" employment.

Program Planning

Assessment for the purpose of program planning represents one of the most traditional notions of why special educators should assess their students. Yet, in the vocational assessment literature its treatment is markedly absent or underdeveloped. Overall, vocational assessment specialists are attempting to answer the question: "What support service(s) must be provided for this student to ensure success in this placement?" As with regular special education service delivery, development of the vocationally-related component to the IEP evolves in this process as well. Halpern et al. (1982) discussed this assessment component:

> The development of specific goals and objectives is the major activity within program planning. If this is done in a "behavioral" fashion, specifying expected performance of the student, the articulation of performance criteria will also emerge from the planning process, along with the stipulation of "targeted" services that directly address the stated objectives. (p. 16)

Thus, the specification of annual goals and short-term behavioral objectives directly relating student deficits to placement curriculum results from this process, in addition to a specification of the necessary supportive services.

How is this accomplished? To best explain our notion of assessment for program planning, we will first fit this process into an ecological perspective. Figure 2 depicts this ecological perspective and suggests that a host of variables (and interactions between them) should be examined in the identification of goals, objectives, and supportive services. Two underlying considerations are particularly important:

- No handicapping condition exists in a student until he or she comes in contact with one or more program variables, and through an assessment of that contact, the need for support arises. Students are not handicapped until a deficit occurs in the manner in which they interact with some aspect of the school environment—what Gearheart and Weishahn (1984) called a "handicapping situation." That is why most mildly to moderately handicapped students "lose" their handicapping condition upon leaving the public schools.

FIGURE 2 The Ecological Perspective for Program Planning

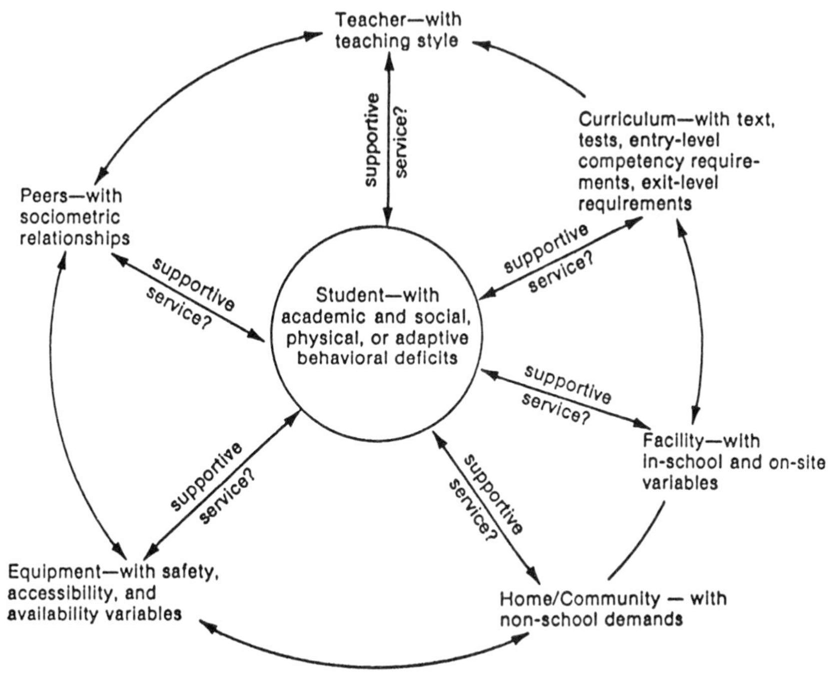

- Assessment of the contact between student and program variables can best occur through direct observation of that interaction. Granted, most IEPs are developed in the spring well in advance of the student's actual program placement, and much of this advanced program planning is guided by needed administrative efficiency. Nonetheless, we suggest that vocational assessors be guided in their program planning activities, to the maximum extent feasible, by direct observation of the student interacting in the classroom environment.

Student-Curriculum Interaction

To assess the interaction between a student and his/her placement curriculum, we suggest employing a 10-step strategy adapted from Zigmond, Vallecorsa, and Silverman (1983).

1. *Decide what to assess.* Many mildly handicapped students in mainstreamed vocational programs have to be assessed in basic academics. In addition, things such as general laboratory safety, performance in gross and fine motor operations, adaptive behavior, and knowledge of specific entry-level competencies unique to the curriculum may require attention as well.
2. *Select or develop a skill hierarchy for each skill to be assessed.* This step is most germane if the results of step 1 suggest a need to assess in either mathematics or in the performance of some sequenced task (e.g., finishing a piece of cabinetry or assembling a carburetor). Many commercially-developed vocational curricula, such as the Vocational-Technical Consortium of the States (V-TECS) guides, contain well-developed skill sequences in a large number of vocational offerings to assist assessors in developing performance-based skill hierarchies.
3. *Decide where to begin.* Testing down rather than up, for speed and efficiency, is generally recommended. This would hold for mildly to moderately handicapped vocational education students, many of whom read and compute at better than fourth or fifth grade levels, and who many times possess significant technical knowledge in content areas. The point here is not to waste a lot of time testing students for skills they already have but, rather, let prior records (such as those in existing files and available from guidance personnel) and informal "quick" assessments dictate the likely upper limits of the area to be tested.
4. *Select or develop the survey instrument.* We recommend curriculum-referenced techniques, such as cloze procedures, for assessing a student's competence with the class text. If the course is competency-based (as are many vocational education curricula), competency checklists can provide excellent referents for instrument development to assess performance-related areas. Similarly, the V-TECS task analyses can provide valuable assistance, provided they are congruent with classroom-based task requirements. In general, criterion-referenced, informally-developed instruments are recommended (Albright, 1978b; Albright & Hux, 1984).
5. *Get ready to test.* This is an especially important consideration for performance testing. With many students, observing the process of assessment in environ-

ments with naturally-occurring contingencies may be just as valuable in supportive service planning as is evaluation of results of the test itself.

6. *Administer the survey.* Again the student's performance and his/her process of completing the instrument are the primary considerations—*not* the score obtained.
7. *Note errors and performance style.* In many cases, noting the students' interaction with the laboratory environment as well as performance with the test will assist in interpretation of results and the most effective targeting of supportive services. It is also extremely important to consider the antecedents to the testing situation. Often, knowledge about a student's home life or classroom activity immediately prior to testing will temper the interpretation of results.
8. *Analyze findings and summarize outcomes.* Again, the goal is not to develop a score but, rather, to interpret findings in such a way as to develop hypotheses about supportive service needs. And as Halpern et al. (1982) suggest, reasonable performance levels for goals and objectives can begin to evolve through analysis and summary of outcomes, provided the focus is upon patterns of errors and single persistent errors (Zigmond et al., 1983).
9. *Hypothesize reasons for errors and determine areas to probe.* As Zigmond et al. (1983) have suggested, one must be certain that errors were not a result of disinterest or variables unrelated to the skills being tested, such as a poor night's sleep or anxiety over an upcoming test. If these kinds of exogenous variables appear to have influenced error patterns, results of the assessment should be discarded and arrangements made to redesign the testing environment. If, however, it is assured that the assessment reflects "motivated performance," the authors suggest four other possible hypotheses for errors: (a) the task was too complex; (b) the response mode was inappropriate; (c) the response level was too difficult, or (d) the student required cues/prompts. As was stated before, antecedents to testing should also be considered in developing hypotheses for errors.
10. *Complete record keeping forms and generate teaching objectives.* In all likelihood, annual goal statements will have been already identified prior to this 10-step process. Albright (1978b) recommended development of annual goals and targeting areas for potential supportive services in the spring annual reviews, and developing specific short-term objectives and the intensity of the supportive services in the fall, shortly after classes begin. Assessment of student-curriculum interaction, if developed in this manner, engenders a high likelihood of resulting in an IEP that is a dynamic, useful management tool.

This 10-step strategy can be extremely valuable in developing specific objectives, reasonable criteria, and effective supportive services. We would also recommend, however, that vocational assessment specialists systematically examine the interaction of the curriculum, the facility/equipment, and the instructor's teaching style, specifically as they relate to entry-level skills required of program participants. Peterson and Housley (1982) have developed a relatively simple system for assessing these interactions, and documenting them on a "Training Analysis Form" for every vocational program available to special needs students. By referencing the results of specific assessments to information contained on that program's Training Analysis Form, targeted supportive services are likely to be more effective.

Student-Teacher Interaction

The interaction between handicapped students and regular classroom teachers has long been recognized as an important variable in the likely success of a mainstreamed placement and clearly should be assessed in program planning activities. Peterson and Housley's (1982) Training Analysis Form, for example, has a section devoted to assessing teaching style. Also, knowledge of teacher attitudes, skills, and flexibility toward teaching handicapped students will have been taken into account in previous placement decisions. In program planning, we are particularly concerned with the teacher's ability to manage classroom behavior, to encourage positive student-student interaction (through the use of cooperative learning arrangements, buddy systems, or peer tutoring arrangements), and to individualize instruction for handicapped students in difficult units within the curriculum.

Student-Student Interaction

Johnson and Johnson (1978) provided an expanded definition of least restrictive placement that has important implications for program planning for some mainstreamed handicapped students:

> Mainstreaming is defined as providing an appropriate educational opportunity for all handicapped students in the least restrictive alternative, based on individualized educational programming and aimed at providing handicapped students with access to and constructive interaction with nonhandicapped peers. (p. 152)

For many handicapped students in vocational education classes, student-student interaction presents no problem; for others, it may. For students at risk, the vocational assessor will want to pay close attention to these interactions and plan support accordingly.

Student-Facility/Equipment Interaction

Consideration of this interaction is primarily relegated to planning programs for orthopedically, hearing, and vision impaired students. Voluminous guides of equipment modifications exist (e.g., Gugerty, Roshal, Tradewell, & Anthony, 1981), and Erekson (1981) has developed a systematic approach for assessing facility/equipment accessibility.

Student-Home/Community Interaction

Handicapped students, like all others, bring with them to school a complex mix of home/community interactions that can profoundly affect the efficacy of supportive service delivery in school. Vocational assessment specialists must be sensitive to these antecedent variables and determine as best they can their influence on a student's performance and how supportive services must be shaped around them.

Monitoring Individual Progress

Assessment for the purpose of monitoring individual progress has typically been ignored or addressed only perfunctorily in the vocational assessment literature (with a notable exception of Albright, 1978a). This is probably because it is difficult to monitor individual progress of handicapped students in a classroom setting when one's notion of vocational assessment is circumscribed by short-term administration of a battery of standardized instruments and commercial work samples. We suggest that vocational assessment specialists must include progress monitoring within their assessment domain, through training regular teachers, aides, or student mentors to collect data, or doing it themselves.

We recommend curriculum-based, direct, frequent, and informal measures to monitor progress. Ysseldyke, Thurlow, Graden, Wesson, Algozzine, and Deno (1983), reporting on 5 years of research on assessment for instructional decision-making, found that frequent 1- to 3-minute informal measures could reliably and validly monitor the quality of supportive service interventions. Earlier, Ysseldyke and Mirkin (1982) extolled the virtues of direct and frequent measurement:

> Those who propose direct and continuous measurement . . . assume that no matter how carefully assessment might have been done initially, at the present time educational program planners are unable to predict which interventions will consistently have certain effects . . . When direct and continuous measurement information is available to the teacher there is a higher probability the teacher will make better decisions, which in turn will lead to increased student achievement. (p. 399)

Van Etten and Van Etten (1976) have developed a relatively simple yet insightful model to measure student progress and have tested it empirically for its efficiency. It involves four elements. *Continuous measures* involve recording progress daily or every other day. *Noncontinuous measures* are those that are administered at regular intervals, such as every 6 weeks, at semester's end, or at the end of an instructional unit. *Direct measures* involve performance-based measurement in the same response mode as those used in the initial teaching of the skills. *Indirect assessment* means testing a student with related items that may not necessarily have been taught or may have been taught in a different response mode.

These distinctions have important implications for vocational assessment specialists in that handicapped students in vocational education programs frequently are taught performance-based skills (e.g., correctly taking blood pressure or installing new brake shoes), yet are required to demonstrate competence through written measures. Vocational assessors must sensitize regular vocational teachers to the difficulties of students who are placed in jeopardy by indirect measurement of competence, and they must cooperatively seek more direct measures. In any event, to the extent that we can generalize from the academic literature, vocational assessment specialists should include frequent and direct monitoring of student progress as part of their assessment domain for the students they serve.

Individual Program Evaluation

Assessment for individual program evaluation seeks to answer two interacting questions: "How well has the support service structure served this student?" and "Is a curriculum change warranted?" If a curriculum placement has not succeeded, the vocational assessment specialist must sort out whether the support service structure was inadequate or the placement simply was not right for the student. As with monitoring individual progress, evaluation should be based upon curriculum-referenced and direct measurement techniques.

Typically, this program evaluation occurs at semester's or year's end and, depending upon the outcome, will recycle the process. Figure 3 depicts a chronological sequence of how this assessment paradigm functions for a child throughout 3 years of vocational education. Some districts begin their vocational education programs in the ninth grade, which would extend the cycle one more year.

CONCLUSION

The foregoing discussion suggests some rather striking changes in vocational assessment for handicapped students in the public schools. We see these changes being characterized by two fundamental shifts in assessment service delivery, particularly as it relates to placement and training in vocational education.

Vocational Evaluation Laboratories

First, school districts that are operating, or considering operating, formal vocational evaluation laboratories should closely examine the expected outcomes (benefits) associated with those laboratories, and how well those benefits match teacher and student assessment needs. Vocational evaluation centers typically have high start-up costs, require substantial staff to operate them, and utilize a fair amount of building space. Thus, to make them pay off, school districts must be certain that the benefits associated with operating these evaluation centers exceed the benefits that might accrue with some alternative allocation of operating budget, building space, and personnel.

Research examining costs and benefits of different vocational assessment models is virtually nonexistent. One study nearing completion (Neubert, 1984) does suggest that vocational assessment centers may function best in a screening/placement capacity, offering exploratory experiences to assist students in developing or refining areas of vocational interest (although Kiss, 1984, found no differences in career maturity for students who were recipients of a formal vocational assessment versus those who were not). Neubert also found little evidence of the results of a formal vocational assessment process being used to assist vocational or special educators in student pro-

FIGURE 3 Chronological Sequence of Assessment Paradigm

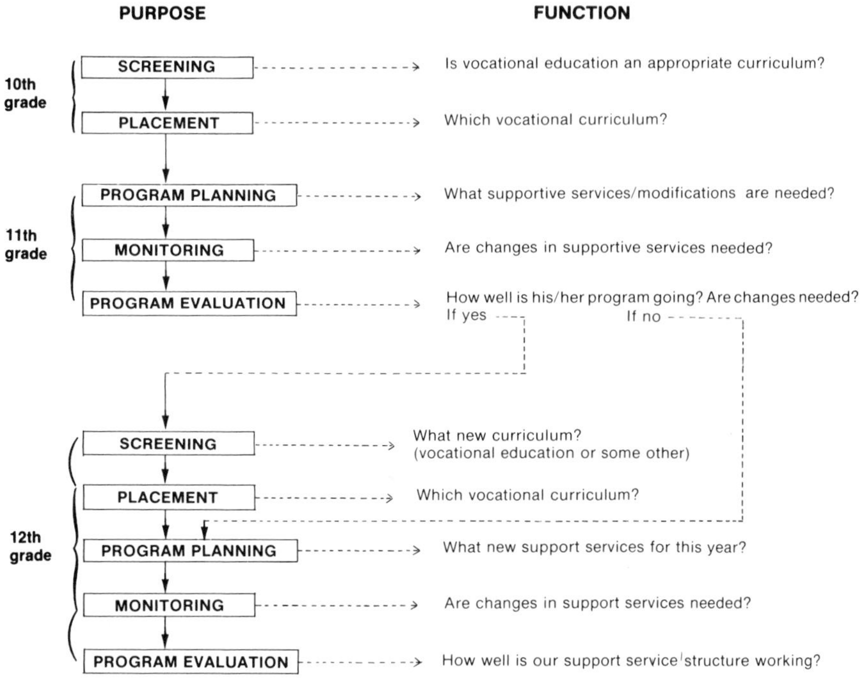

gram planning, monitoring, or evaluation. Similarly, articulation of assessment results into the present levels of performance sections of IEPs was virtually nonexistent.

We believe that in many school districts the vocational assessment needs of students and teachers alike may best be served by eliminating most commercial laboratory processes and involving assessment staff more directly in classroom environments, their curricula, and development of classroom-based performance samples directly related to those curricula. We believe most interviewing, document analyses, and interest testing can occur in vocational guidance offices. Similarly, direct observation of student behavior should clearly occur in normalized environments where handicapped students interact with the regular curriculum (or work setting) and its natural contingencies rather than with commercial work samples or in simulated work settings. We question the increasingly heavy reliance that vocational assessment specialists seem to be placing upon commercial assessment systems. Instead, we favor more informal, direct, and curriculum-based processes that reinforce interaction between assessors and teachers/support personnel rather than discourage it.

This recommendation for movement away from highly specialized vocational assessment laboratory activities has one important exception—the relatively new and promising area of rehabilitation engineering technology (see, for example, Hobson,

1984). We do not suggest that the public schools should begin to adopt these extremely expensive units. They are currently far too costly for the schools to absorb and presently serve only a small segment of the handicapped population—severely orthopedically impaired, blind, and deaf students. Nonetheless, rehabilitation engineering does focus upon interactions between an individual and his/her natural work or home environment. This technology will likely spread into the schools and find utility in instructional or curricular modification for students with severe learning handicaps as well.

Our recommendation for reduced reliance upon vocational assessment laboratory processes is predicated upon the assumption that in its absence, more informal, classroom-based processes would replace it. We recognize, however, that in many cases alternative considerations might come into play that would render this assumption invalid. For example, in some districts elimination of a vocational assessment laboratory might result in elimination of staff associated with it. We obviously would not recommend that. Likewise, some districts use an extensive situational/work sample approach almost as an intervention to *stimulate* (as opposed to determine) vocational interests in handicapped students. While we would recommend short (1–2 week) mini-courses in actual vocational classrooms instead, we do recognize the importance of "hands-on" assessment activities to generate interest among students.

Vocational Assessment Specialists

The second major shift we envision is in the role and competencies of the vocational assessment specialist. We see the technical competencies necessary for the vocational assessment specialist to be things such as: (a) ability to function as part of a team whose responsibility is to synthesize information from diverse sources—regular, vocational, special, and rehabilitation personnel—to make the most informed choices about students; (b) ability to consult with and train regular vocational education or special/vocational education teachers to monitor progress of handicapped students; (c) ability to interview students, parents, and other teachers to ascertain enduring vocational interests of individual handicapped students; (d) familiarity with all vocational curriculum options and their teacher's teaching styles and skills, as well as familiarity with community-based employment training alternatives; (e) ability to identify and direct modifications to curriculum, instructional delivery, and laboratory and equipment to accommodate mainstreamed students; and (f) ability to analyze the school/community supportive services system and orchestrate its utility for students served by the schools who will be in need of some form of transition services when they exit from it.

Clearly, these competencies describe an individual who spends a majority of his/her time outside the confines of a vocational assessment laboratory. They suggest a proactive, interventionist orientation, rather than a reactive, medical-model orientation. And they clearly suggest downplaying the predictive attempts of vocational aptitude testing in lieu of more short-term, intensive intervention planning. We envision, for example, our vocational assessment specialist's day beginning with traditional activities such as student interviewing, reviewing cumulative files, scheduling or organizing job shadowing or mini-tours of vocational courses, or informal interest testing. These traditional activities would then shift to visits to classrooms, home-based or telephone interviews with parents, community visits for job analyses and development, and monitoring of students who have been placed in the community. In short, this individual's skills fit the description of any highly trained supportive service personnel. The difference is that this person fits his/her activities into a vocational assessment paradigm, and that each activity fulfills a purpose within it.

This article has examined the vocational assessment process as it relates primarily to mainstreamed, in-school vocational education. Some of these paradigmatic components would change significantly or even disappear under other service delivery alternatives. For example, if a school district places all ninth grade children labeled educable mentally retarded in a prevocational program, the need for assessment for purposes of screening and placement is eliminated and assessment for program planning is sharply reduced. Similarly, many handicapped students who are likely candidates for mainstreamed vocational education programs could also fit into other nonrestrictive placements, such as community-based employment training programs.

The intensity with which a vocational assessor engages in different assessment purposes varies throughout a student's vocational education program. For example, at the beginning of a student's 2-year program, the assessor would want to make certain that screening and placement purposes were well met. Program planning and monitoring would receive attention continually throughout the student's program, and program review probably would not occur until the end of the first year. If the program is successful, assessment for screening and placement the following year is not necessary, since most vocational curriculum sequences are fairly well-defined after initial selection. As a student nears the end of a program, however, assessment for screening and placement (for CWE or transitional planning) again becomes of much more concern.

REFERENCES

Albright, L. (1978a). Monitoring the student's individualized vocational plan. In L. Albright, J. Fabac, & R. Evans (Eds.), *A system for the identification, assessment, and evaluation of the special needs learner in vocational education*. Urbana-Champaign: University of Illinois, Bureau of Educational Research.

Albright, L. (1978b). Strategies for assessing the student's present level(s) of performance. In L. Albright, J. Fabac., & R. Evans (Eds.), *A system for the identification, assessment, and evaluation of special needs learners in vocational education*. Urbana-Champaign: University of Illinois, Bureau of Educational Research.

Albright, L. (1979). *Administering programs for handicapped students* (Professional Development Series, No. 3). Arlington, VA: American Vocational Association.

Albright, L., Fabac, J., & Evans, R. (1978). *A system for the identification, assessment, and evaluation of the special needs learner in vocational education*. Urbana-Champaign: University of Illinois, Bureau of Educational Research.

Albright, L., & Hux, T. (1984, February). Program aids in IEP development. *School Shop*, 22–23.

Arizona Department of Education. (1982). *Arizona model for vocational assessment: A procedural manual*. Phoenix: Author.

Batsche, C. (1982). *Handbook for vocational school psychology.* Des Moines: Iowa Department of Public Instruction.

Bellamy, G. T., & Wilcox, B. (1982). Secondary education for severely handicapped students: Guidelines for quality services. In K. P. Lynch, W. E. Kiernan, & J. A. Stark (Eds.), *Prevocational and vocational education for special needs youth: A blueprint for the 1980s*. Baltimore: Paul H. Brookes.

Botterbusch, K. F. (1978). *A guide to job site evaluation*. Menomonie: University of Wisconsin-Stout, Stout Vocational Rehabilitation Institute.

California State Department of Education. (1983). *Career/vocational assessment of California secondary students with exceptional needs*. Sacramento: Office of Special Education.

Cobb, R. B. (1981). Vocational assessment of the special needs learner: The utility of commercial work sampling systems. *Journal of Vocational Special Needs Education, 3*(3), 30–32.

Cobb, R. B. (1983). A curriculum-based approach to vocational assessment. *Teaching Exceptional Children, 15*(9), 216–219.

Dahl, T., Appleby, J., & Lipe, D. (1978). *Mainstreaming guidebook for vocational educators teaching the handicapped.* Salt Lake City, UT: Olympus Publishing.

Dunn, D. J. (1976, October). What occupations or jobs will the individual be successful at in the future? In D. J. Dunn, T. A. Korn, & J. Andrew (Eds.), *Critical issues in vocational evaluation*. Menomonie: University of Wisconsin-Stout, Stout Vocational Rehabilitation Institute.

Dunn, D., Korn, T., & Andrew, J. (Eds.). (1976). *Critical issues in vocational evaluation*. Menomonie: University of Wisconsin-Stout, Stout Vocational Rehabilitation Institute.

Erekson, T. L. (1981, January). *Accessibility to laboratories and equipment for the physically handicapped: A handbook for vocational education personnel*. DeKalb: Northern Illinois University, College of Education.

Evans, R. N., & Herr, E. L. (1978). *Foundations of vocational education* (2nd ed.). Columbus, OH: Charles E. Merrill.

Gearheart, B. R., & Weishahn, M. W. (1984). *The exceptional student in the regular classroom* (3rd ed.). St. Louis: Mosby.

Gugerty, J. J., & Crowley, C. B. (1982). Informal vocational assessment for special needs students. *Journal of Vocational Special Needs Education, 4*(2), 16–18.

Gugerty, J. J., Roshal, A. F., Tradewell, M. D. J., & Anthony, L. (1981, January). *Tools, equipment and machinery adapted for the vocational education and employment of handicapped people*. Madison: University of Wisconsin, Stout Vocational Studies Center.

Halpern, A. S., Lehmann, J. P., Irvin, L. K., & Heiry, T. J. (1982). *Contemporary assessment for mentally retarded adolescents and adults*. Baltimore: University Park Press.

Hasazi, S. B., & Gordon, L. R. (1982). Follow-up study of graduates-leavers of diversified education programs in Vermont. Montpelier: Vermont State Department of Education.

Hawkins, R. P. (1979). The functions of assessment: Implications for selection and development of devices for assessing repertoires in clinical, educational, and other settings. *Journal of Applied Behavior Analysis, 12*(4), 501–516.

Hobson, J. (1984). Rehabilitation engineering—a developing speciality. *Prosthetics & Orthotics International, 1*, 56–60.

Hohenshil, T. H. (1984). School psychologists facilitating career development programs in secondary education. *Career Development for Exceptional Individuals, 7*(2), 51–58.

Hohenshil, T. H., Anderson, W. T., & Salwan, J. W. (Eds.). (1982). *Secondary school psychological services: Focus on vocational assessment procedures for handicapped students*. Blacksburg: Virginia Polytechnic Institute and University, College of Education.

Johnson, D. W., & Johnson, R. T. (1978). Mainstreaming: Will handicapped students be liked, rejected, or ignored? *Instructor, 87*, 152–154.

Kiernan, W. E., & Petzy, V. (1982). A systems approach to career and vocational education programs for special needs students grades 7–12. In K. P. Lynch, W. E. Kiernan, & J. A. Stark (Eds.), *Prevocational and vocational education for special needs youth: A blueprint for the 1980s*. Baltimore: Paul H. Brookes.

Leinhardt, G., Bickel, W., & Pallay, A. (1982). Unlabeled but still entitled: Toward more effective remediation. *Teachers College Record, 84*(2), 391–422.

Lilly, M. S. (1983, August). *Divestiture in special education: An alternative model for resource and support services*. Urbana-Champaign: University of Illinois, College of Education.

Maryland State Department of Education. (1980). *Vocational student assessment*. Baltimore: Division of Vocation-Technical Education.

Menchetti, B. M., Rusch, F. R., & Owens, D. M. (1982). Assessing the vocational training needs of mentally retarded adults. In J. L. Matson, & S. E. Breuning (Eds.), *Assessing the mentally retarded*. New York: Grune & Stratton.

Messick, S. (1984). Assessment in context: Appraising student performance in relation to instructional quality. *Educational Researcher, 13*(3), 3–8.

Miller, S. R., Sachs, J. J., & Stadt, R. (1982). Assessment of secondary exceptional students' vocational interests and aptitudes: Need, status, and recommendations. *ICEC Quarterly, 31*(4), 13–19.

Neubert, D. (1984). *A study of vocational evaluation recommendations used in the educational planning and placement process for handicapped students* (preliminary data analysis). Unpublished doctoral dissertation. University of Maryland, Department of Industrial, Technological, and Occupational Education, College Park.

Peterson, M. (1982, December). *Vocational assessment of the visually impaired*. Paper presented at the annual meeting of the American Vocational Association, Anaheim, CA.

Peterson, M., & Hill, P. (1982). *Vocational assessment of students with special needs: An implementation manual*. Commerce: East Texas State University, Occupational Curriculum Laboratory.

Peterson, M., & Housley, W. (1982). Entry skills needed for special needs students in vocational programs. *Vocational Guidance Quarterly*, 149–153.

Petzy, V. (1983). Vocational assessment for special needs students in the middle/junior high school. *Career Development for Exceptional Individuals, 6*(1), 15–24.

Phelps, L. A. (1982, May). Testimony delivered before the joint hearing of the Subcommittee on Elementary, Secondary, and Vocational Education and the Subcommittee on Select Education of the Committee on Education and Labor. Washington, DC: U.S. Government Printing Office.

Phelps, L. A., & McCarty, T. (1984). Student assessment practices. *Career Development for Exceptional Individuals, 7*(1), 30–37.

Phelps, L. A., & Wentling, T. L. (1977). A proposed system for the identification, assessment, and evaluation of special needs learners. *Journal of Industrial Education, 14*(3), 19–35.

Rosenberg, H., & Tesolowski, D. G. (1982). Assessment of critical vocational behaviors. *Career Development for Exceptional Individuals, 5*(1), 25–37.

Salvia, J., & Ysseldyke, J. E. (1981). *Assessment in special and remedial education* (2nd ed.). Boston: Houghton Mifflin.

Schneck, G. R. (1981, June). Program improvement in vocational assessment for the handicapped. In R. A. Stodden (Ed.), *Vocational assessment* (Policy Paper series, Document 6). Urbana-Champaign: University of Illinois, Leadership Training Institute/Vocational and Special Education.

Shepard, J. W., Dielman, M. B., & Ellenwood, A. E. (1984). School psychologists and vocational education programs. Participation in career development for the handicapped. *Journal for Vocational Special Needs Education, 6*(2), 13–14; 22.

Sitlington, P. L., & Wimmer, D. (1978). Vocational assessment techniques for the handicapped adolescent. *Career Development for Exceptional Individuals, 1*(2), 74–87.

Snow, R. E. (1984). Placing children in special education. Some comments. *Educational Researcher, 13*(3), 12–14.

Stern, D. (1984). School-based enterprise and the quality of work experience: A study of high school students. *Youth & Society, 15*(4), 401–427.

Stodden, R. A., & Ianacone, R. N. (1981). Career/vocational assessment of the special needs individual: A conceptual model. *Exceptional Children, 47*(8), 600–608.

Thurlow, M. L., & Ysseldyke, J. E. (1982). Instructional planning: Information collected by school psychologists vs. information considered useful by teachers. *Journal of School Psychology, 20*(1), 3–10.

Van Etten, C., & Van Etten, G. (1976). The measurement of pupil progress and selecting instructional materials. *Journal of Learning Disabilities, 9*(8), 469–480.

Wright, A. R., Cooperstein, R. A., Renneker, E. G., & Padilla, C. (1982, December). *Local implementation of P.L. 94–142; Final report of a longitudinal study* (SRI Project 7124). Menlo Park, CA: SRI International Social Sciences Center.

Ysseldyke, J. E., & Mirkin, P. E. (1982). The use of assessment information to plan instructional interventions: A review of research. In C. R. Reynolds & T. B. Gutkin (Eds.). *The handbook of school psychology*. New York: John Wiley & Sons.

Ysseldyke, J. E., Thurlow, M., Graden, J., Wesson, C., Algozzine, B., & Deno, S. (1983). Generalizations from five years of research on assessment and decision making: The University of Minnesota Institute. *Exceptional Education Quarterly, 4*(1), 75–93.

Zigmond, N., Vallecorsa, A., & Silverman, R. (1983). *Assessment for instructional planning in special education*. Englewood Cliffs, NJ: Prentice-Hall.

Zytowski, D. (1982). Assessment in the counseling process for the 1980's. *Measurement & Evaluation in Guidance, 15*(1), 15–20.

We wish to thank the following individuals for their insightful and incisive comments on drafts of this manuscript: Len Albright, Barbara and John Banks, Susan Brody-Hasazi, Pat Decoteau, Nishma Duffy, Pam Leconte, Deb Neubert, Mike Peterson, Al Phelps, and Pat Sitlington.

Brian Cobb is an Assistant Professor in the Department of Special Education, University of Maryland. Dave Larkin is an Assistant Professor in the Department of Professional Education, Bemidji State University.

Assessment procedures are often associated with academic areas, and as important as that domain is for appropriate instructional planning, it is just one area of student functioning that requires examination. Another important area is adaptive behavior. Taylor defines adaptive behavior as the "ability to . . . deal effectively with personal and social demands." Assessment procedures and instruments usually include the performance areas of (a) communication skills, (b) daily living skills, (c) social skills, and (d) motor skills. Students need to acquire skills in those performance areas so they can function with success in home, school, and community settings. For example, a student who exhibits deficient interpersonal relationship styles (e.g., hitting others) will undoubtedly have difficulty coping with the classroom expectations.

As Taylor points out, adaptive behavior instruments can be used for different purposes. Data from them may be used to establish eligibility for special education services. Hence, they serve to help in making classification decisions, or they can be used to develop goals and objectives in the IEP. Taylor has provided a brief, yet effective, review of several of the most commonly used adaptive behavior scales. Strengths and problems associated with each scale are clearly presented. The information in this selection will be useful to school personnel who conduct assessments of students and to teacher educators who prepare others to complete reliable and valid assessments of adaptive behaviors.

Measuring Adaptive Behavior: Issues and Instruments

Ronald L. Taylor

In the broadest sense, adaptive behavior refers to an individual's ability to cope or deal effectively with personal and social demands. Although many formal definitions of adaptive behavior have been set forth, the definition proposed by the American Association on Mental Deficiency (AAMD) is perhaps the most widely accepted: ". . . the effectiveness with which the individual meets the standards of personal independence and social responsibility" (Grossman, 1983, p. 1). In a review of the various definitions and interpretations of adaptive behavior, Witt and Martens (1984) noted that most considered adaptive behavior as being age- and culture-specific and included areas such as independent functioning, social responsibility, and cognitive development.

Regardless of the formal definition used, one caveat regarding adaptive behavior is necessary: It is a difficult construct to operationalize and, subsequently, to measure.

For example, some conceptions of adaptive behavior include academic and more cognitively oriented skills, whereas others intentionally omit these types of behavior. Also, as previously noted, adaptive behavior is age-specific and, to a certain extent, culture-specific. Adaptive behavior for a 3-year-old child might include skills such as eating and toileting; for an adult it might include behaviors related to social and economic responsibility.

The AAMD provides general categories of adaptive behavior skills for preschoolers, children and early adolescents, and late adolescents and adults (Grossman, 1983). *Preschool* skills include sensorimotor, communication, and self-help skills. *Childhood and early adolescent* skills are aimed primarily at practical application of academic skills and appropriate interpersonal functioning. *Late adolescent and adult* skills focus largely on community, vocational, and economic responsibilities.

The culture-specific nature of adaptive behavior relates not as much to the *general* skills expected of individuals but, rather, to the *specific nature* of the expected skills. For example, Reschly (1984) noted that "crossing traffic properly with a traffic light" is an important and reasonable behavior to expect from school-age children and could fall into the general category of using judgment to cope effectively with the environment. If, however, a child is from a rural area that has no traffic lights, the *nature* of that skill is culture-specific.

Difficulties in identifying universal, specific skills make the measurement or assessment of these skills problematic at best. Before the instruments used to measure adaptive behavior can be analyzed, however, the history and purported uses of adaptive behavior assessment should be discussed, to shed additional light on this somewhat confusing area.

THE HISTORY OF ADAPTIVE BEHAVIOR ASSESSMENT

Adaptive behavior is not a new concept in special education, although it only recently has gained its present level of attention—partly as a result of litigation and legislation related to the identification of mentally retarded students. In the 1970s several noteworthy court cases (e.g., *Guadalupe v. Tempe, Arizona School District*, 1972) brought attention to the inadequate and inappropriate assessment methods used to identify mildly retarded students. In part, sole use of IQ in determining eligibility for special education was criticized because of the alleged bias of IQ scores against minority children. The result was a disproportionate number of ethnic minority children in classes for mildly retarded students.

In the early 1970s Mercer, a leading proponent of the adaptive behavior movement, characterized this phenomenon by referring to many of these students as "six-hour retarded children" (Mercer, 1973). This characterization implied that although they had difficulty during the 6 hours spent in the school environment, these children were able to meet demands required in other environments. Phrased another way, these students were *not deficient in adaptive behavior skills*.

The increased public awareness led, in part, to development of Public Law 94–142 (which includes a nondiscriminatory evaluation clause) and revised definitions of mental retardation. Specifically, the changes indicated a need for multiple assessment measures, including adaptive behavior testing, in determining the classification of mentally retarded students.

Recent definitions of mental retardation by the AAMD have specifically used the term *adaptive behavior deficit* to describe the criteria necessary for that classification (Grossman, 1977, 1983). Even so, the *concept*, if not the *term* adaptive behavior, has been considered in classification systems for a number of years. In fact, as early as 1941, Doll referred to "social incompetence" as one of the criteria necessary to identify an individual as retarded (in Reschly, 1984).

PURPOSES OF ADAPTIVE BEHAVIOR ASSESSMENT

Until recently, the vast majority of adaptive behavior measures were informal checklists or sequential lists of behavior that were inadequate for the assessment of such an important and conceptually difficult area (Taylor, 1988). In the past 10 years, however, more time, research, and effort have been expended in developing new adaptive behavior instruments. The more commonly used and widely accepted of these are *norm-referenced tests*. Norm-referenced tests are those that compare an individual's score to the performance of a standardization sample or *normative group;* a student's test performance is interpreted on the basis of its comparison to the performance of students on whom the test was normed.

Comparing the child's test performance to the norm is not necessarily the same as comparing the performance to "normal." Rather, the child's performance is being compared to the performance of individuals in the standardization sample. This sample might be a random group of nonhandicapped children across the United States for one test, and on another test it might be a trainable mentally retarded sample. The test's purpose partially determines the nature of the standardization sample. Clearly, the nature of the comparison group must be kept in mind when interpreting the results of adaptive behavior instruments.

In general, adaptive behavior instruments are used for two purposes. The first relates to identification of individuals who vary significantly from "normal" expectations in areas such as independent functioning and socialization. The applicable tests, sometimes referred to as *descriptive* (Cone & Hawkins, 1977), are used to help make classification decisions as well as to identify overall problem areas and general strengths and weaknesses. Most descriptive adaptive behavior instruments are standardized on nonhandicapped individuals.

Other adaptive behavior instruments yield much more specific information related to identification of educational/instructional objectives. These types of tests, referred to by Cone and Hawkins as *prescriptive*, often are developed for and standardized on more severely handicapped children. Compared to descriptive tests, prescriptive tests typically include more specific and sequential items related to a fewer number of areas. Some instruments include both descriptive and prescriptive components.

Both types of instruments are important in the overall measurement of adaptive behavior, and individuals interested in assessing this area clearly should have a specific purpose in mind so that the appropriate type of instrument can be chosen. Unfortunately, many of the norm-referenced tests that are available have generally poor technical characteristics, including problems with reliability and validity. *Reliability* problems frequently surface as a function of the type of format used to gather the test information. Most adaptive behavior instruments rely on an interview with an informant (e.g., teacher, parent) to provide the test data. Often, the information obtained differs depending on the informant. For example, some evidence suggests that parents rate the same child higher than a teacher does (e.g., Mealor & Richmond, 1980). Problems in *validity* occur for many reasons, not the least of which is the previously mentioned problem in defining and operationalizing the adaptive behavior construct.

DESCRIPTION AND CRITIQUE OF ADAPTIVE BEHAVIOR INSTRUMENTS

The instruments discussed here represent only a fraction of the many available adaptive behavior scales, but they are some of the newer, more frequently used scales, and they exemplify the various purposes of adaptive behavior assessments as well as the various formats of the tests themselves. Readers are encouraged to investigate the test manuals or relevant textbooks (e.g., Taylor, 1984) for more in-depth descriptions of these and other tests.

Adaptive Behavior Inventory for Children (ABIC)

The Adaptive Behavior Inventory for Children (Mercer, 1979) is a descriptive instrument that is a part of the battery of tests called the System Of Multicultural Pluralistic Assessment (SOMPA). One of the primary uses of the ABIC is to assist in the declassification of minority children labeled as mentally retarded. As such, it contains items that focus only on behaviors *outside* of the school environment. This test is the only adaptive behavior measure that has this feature. Information is obtained via a structured interview with a parent (usually the mother). The test is designed for use with 5- to 11-year-old children and yields standard scores (mean = 50, standard deviation = 15).

Overall, the ABIC includes 242 items divided into six scales: family, community, peer relations, nonacademic school roles, earner/consumer, and self-maintenance. An example of a test item is: "Does (name of child) take telephone and other messages correctly and give them to the right person?"—to which the mother must respond "sometimes," "regularly," or "never." The test also includes a veracity scale used to determine whether the informant is artificially inflating the child's score.

Most of the research on the SOMPA centers on its use within the SOMPA model and its resulting effect on the declassification of minority special education students. For example, Reschly (1981) and Talley (1979) found that use of the ABIC greatly reduced the number of children in classes for mildly retarded students. Other research on the ABIC has focused on issues of validity—what type of skills the test is actually measuring. In general, there is a lack of supportive validity data to indicate what the test is measuring. Low correlations have been reported using achievement (Kazimour & Reschly, 1981) and intelligence test results (e.g., Taylor, Ziegler, & Partenio, 1985) as criterion measures.

AAMD Adaptive Behavior Scale—School Edition (ABS-SE)

The AAMD Adaptive Behavior Scale—School Edition (Lambert, Windmiller, Tharinger, & Cole, 1981) is the most recent in a series of revisions of the original AAMD scale. The same general areas (called domains) and items have been included in the various revisions, but the standardization sample and the various scoring and interpretative procedures have been changed. For example, the ABS-SE was standardized on a school-based population (as opposed to an institutional group in the original test) and includes a scoring procedure that allows the separate comparison of an individual's performance to a regular education, an educable mentally retarded population, and a trainable mentally retarded population. The various purposes of the ABS-SE, as well as the procedural steps to follow, are shown in Figure 1.

This scale was designed for use with individuals age 3–16. The information about the child usually is provided on the test form by someone who is very familiar with his or her behavioral repertoire (e.g., teacher, parent). Part One of the instrument focuses on adaptive behavior such as self-help skills and personal independence; Part Two includes items related to maladaptive behavior.

Part One includes the following domains: Independent Functioning, Physical Development, Economic Activity, Language Development, Numbers and Time, Prevocational Activity, Self-Direction, Responsibility, and Socialization. In general, these domains contain items that require the informant to rate the child's behavior within a dependence-independence continuum. For example, the item concerned with *use of table utensils* (in the Independent Functioning domain) requires that the child be rated on a 6-point scale from "feeds self with fingers or must be fed" (rating of 0) to "uses knife and fork correctly and neatly" (rating of 6).

The domains in Part Two are Aggressiveness, Antisocial vs. Social Behavior, Rebelliousness, Trustworthiness, Withdrawal vs. Involvement, Mannerisms, Appropriateness of Interpersonal Manners, Acceptability of Vocal Habits, Acceptability of Habits, Activity Level, Symptomatic Behavior, and Use of Medications. For each of these domains, several items are included in the form of behavioral descriptions (e.g., "uses threatening gestures"). The informant must indicate whether the examinee exhibits each behavior occasionally, frequently, or not at all.

Percentile ranks are available for all 23 domains. In addition, various domains have been collapsed into five factors: Personal Self-Sufficiency, Community Self-Sufficiency, Personal-Social Responsibility, Social Adjustment, and Personal Adjustment. Scores from these five factors can be compared to the various groups (EMR, etc.) mentioned earlier.

The original ABS has been studied extensively. Most of this research has focused on technical characteristics of the instrument. Part Two has been scrutinized in particular. For example, the reliability has been questioned (Isett & Spreat, 1979) and the

FIGURE 1 Purposes of and Procedural Steps in the ABS-SE

The ABS-SE Assessment Process

Preparation: Gain experience with ABS-SE components. Training by someone familiar with the process is recommended.*

Administration: Complete the Assessment Booklet by one of two methods:
First-person Assessment: A teacher or well-trained aide completes the scale by rating the student on each item.
Third-party Assessment: A teacher, psychologist, social worker or other trained person reads the scale items to someone unfamiliar with the scale, but who knows the student well, and records the reponses.

Scoring: Totals are obtained as each item, subdomain, and domain is completed in the Assessment Booklet.*

For Screening or Instructional Planning: The teacher or aide completes the Instructional Planning Profile, converts raw domain scores from the Assessment Booklet to percentile scores, and plots a profile.

Results indicate whether further evaluation is needed and what areas of adaptive behavior require remediation.*

For Diagnosis and Placement: The psychologist or other trained personnel completes the Diagnostic Profile using the Assessment Booklet to obtain scaled scores and a Comparison Score and plots a profile of factor scores.

Results indicate how a student's scores compare to scores of students in a similar age group.**

For Progress Evaluation: The teacher readministers the scale and compares results with those from a prior administration. Comparison indicates the extent of student progress and achievement of IEP goals and objectives.*

For IEP Evaluation: The teacher or psychologist readministers the scale and the IEP committee compares results with those from a prior administration. Comparison indicates the extent of student progress and appropriateness of educational placement.**

*For further information, refer to the Administration and Instructional Planning Manual.

**For further information, refer to the Diagnostic and Technical Manual.

Adapted from Adaptive Behavior Scale—School Edition *by N. Lambert, M. Windmiller, D. Tharinger, & M. Rosen (Washington, DC: American Association on Mental Deficiency, 1981). Used by permission.*

norms criticized (McDevitt, McDevitt, & Rosen, 1977). In addition, the fact that the severity of the maladaptive behavior is not taken into account can lead to misleading interpretations (Taylor, Warren, & Slocumb, 1979). Little research data have been reported regarding the School Edition. The differences between the two tests would preclude any direct generalization of the previously noted research. Similarities of the tests, however, indicate that research is warranted with the School Edition.

Balthazar Scales of Adaptive Behavior (BSAB)

A good example of an instrument designed primarily for *prescriptive* reasons is the Balthazar Scales of Adaptive Behavior (Balthazar, 1976). Specifically, it was intended to be used for developing programs for severely and profoundly retarded individuals. Unlike most other scales, the BSAB uses a direct observational approach (rather than an interview) for obtaining the information.

The first section of the BSAB, the Scales of Functional Independence, measures the areas of eating, dressing, and toileting. The second section, the Scales of Social Adaptation, includes items measuring self-directed behavior, interpersonal behavior, verbal communication, play activities, and response to instructions. The items measuring these areas are broken down sequentially into much smaller steps than necessary for adaptive behavior instruments designed for more descriptive purposes. Thus, the items are frequently used as instructional objectives.

Research on the BSAB is generally lacking—probably because the normative use of the instrument is limited. Overall, the standardization sample was quite restricted, and the technical characteristics have not been explored adequately. In general, the test is used informally—almost as a checklist of possible instructional objectives.

The Children's Adaptive Behavior Scale (CABS)

The Children's Adaptive Behavior Scale (Richmond & Kicklighter, 1980) is a unique instrument in that it tests the child directly rather than relying on interviews or observation. According to its authors, this feature was incorporated because of the lack of agreement when multiple raters (e.g., teachers and parents) provide information about a child's typical behavior. The scale was designed to be brief and to provide information that would be helpful to teachers in developing educational programs for 5- to 10-year-old children. As such, the items are heavily weighted toward school-type tasks.

Five separate areas or domains of adaptive behavior are measured: Language Development, Independent Functioning, Family Role Performance, Economic-Vocational Activity, and Socialization. A total score combines these five areas. Age-equivalents are available for each domain, as well as for the total score. Examples of the types of items include, "Name three kinds of animals that have four legs" (Language Development domain) and, "What would you do if you got lost in (nearest city or town)?" These items represent the more academic nature of the test as compared to other adaptive behavior instruments. They also indicate that it measures what the child *would do* as opposed to what he/she *typically does*.

Undoubtedly, the CABS will have a relatively high correlation with cognitive and academic measures. This is in contrast to the ABIC, for example, which has low correlations with those measures. The problems with the CABS relate to whether the items are different enough from other types of tests to warrant its addition in a psychometric battery and, if so, how the results can be used. Both of these issues relate to the validity of the test and would best be answered through empirical studies and continued use.

Comprehensive Test of Adaptive Behavior (CTAB)

The Comprehensive Test of Adaptive Behavior (Adams, 1984) uses a combination of direct observation and completion from memory to provide information. Unlike many other adaptive behavior tests, the CTAB has clearly identified criteria to indicate whether the subject has passed or failed an item. As a result, the information gathered is more reliable than that from many other scales. Figure 2 shows an example of the items and the criteria for passing.

There are over 500 items measuring the general areas of Self-Help Skills, House-Living Skills, Independent-Living Skills, Social Skills, Sensory and Motor Skills, and Language Concepts and Academic Skills. The CTAB was standardized using both retarded and nonretarded individuals so that various comparisons can be made.

Overall, the CTAB was appropriately named; it is a comprehensive instrument. As such, it has the possibility of being used for prescriptive purposes. Its use as a descriptive instrument is somewhat limited because of its length, however. For persons interested in a relatively fast, normative, descriptive instrument, the Normative Adaptive Behavior Checklist, designed to be used in conjunction with the CTAB, is available. This instrument contains 120 items that are answered in a yes-no format.

The Scales of Independent Behavior (SIB)

The Scales of Independent Behavior (Bruininks, Woodcock, Weatherman, & Hill, 1984) is a relatively new instrument that can be used by itself or as a part of the Woodcock-Johnson Psychoeducational Battery. By using the scales as a component of the total Battery, one can get a profile of an individual in the areas of cognitive ability, achievement, and interests, as well as adaptive behavior. The format of the SIB is highly structured (similar to the ABIC). The interviewer asks a series of questions such as, "Does ____ eat with a fork by spearing the food when appropriate?" The respondent must indicate whether the individual can do that task without help or supervision "never or rarely," "about ¼ of the time," "about ¾ of the time," or "almost always."

Overall, the SIB is easy to administer and score, although the number of tables used to transform the raw score to derived scores is burdensome. It is designed for use with infants through adults and provides a variety of scores, including percentile ranks and standard scores.

FIGURE 2 Examples of Items and Criteria from the CTAB

48-② Stores refrigerated food

Criterion: Student puts food needing refrigeration into airtight containers and places containers in refrigerator.

Test: After a meal and with containers available, say "______, put the (name of the food) away."

48-③ Prepares frozen juice

Criterion: Student gets juice from freezer, opens can, and makes juice by mixing according to directions.

Test: Place student in front of freezer (frozen juice inside) with can opener and pitcher available. Say "______, there is some (name of the juice) in the freezer. Make some for me."

48-④ Freezes food

Criterion: Student puts food needing freezing into the freezer.

Test: Place student in front of a variety of food (some of which needs freezing, for example, ice cream). Say "______, put the food away."

49-① Operates stove burners

Criterion: Student turns appropriate burner on and adjusts to proper temperature. Student turns burner off when finished.

Test: Place student in front of stove burners. Point to one of the burners and say "______, turn this burner on to ?______ (the temperature reading will vary depending on the stove available)."

49-② Makes instant hot beverages

Criterion: Student makes instant hot beverages (for example, instant coffee or tea).

Test: Place student in front of stove, pan (kettle), cup, and beverage (for example, instant coffee). Say "______, make a cup of (name of beverage)."

Adapted from *The Comprehensive Test of Adaptive Behavior* by G. Adams (Columbus, OH: Charles E. Merrill, 1984). Used by permission.

The SIB can be given in its entirety or can be administered using one of several options. For example, a short form consisting of 32 items is available for screening purposes. The full battery contains 226 items broken down into the following areas: Gross Motor, Fine Motor, Social Interaction, Language Comprehension, Language Expression, Eating and Meal Preparation, Toileting, Dressing, Personal Self-Care, Domestic Skills, Time and Punctuality, Money and Value, Work Skills, and Home-Community Orientation. In addition, certain of the areas are combined to form Motor Skills, Social Interaction and Communication Skills, Personal Independence Skills, and Community Independence Skills *clusters* that can be administered and scored separately. A Problem Behavior Scale, such as that in Figure 3, allows for the evaluation of maladaptive behavior.

In general, the SIB should be used for descriptive purposes, primarily for mildly/moderately retarded individuals. The items are neither sequential enough to use as a prescriptive instrument nor "low enough" to use with severely/profoundly retarded individuals. As with many new adaptive behavior tests, there is not enough research to date to explore its uses and limitations adequately.

Vineland Adaptive Behavior Scales (VABS)

Although the Vineland Adaptive Behavior Scales (Sparrow, Balla, & Cicchetti, 1984) has a name similar to its predecessor, the Vineland Social Maturity Scale (VSMS), the two instruments are relatively dissimilar. Authors of the VABS acknowledge that Doll (author of the VSMS) made a significant contribution to the overall area of adaptive behavior, and they have used many of his concepts in designing the new instrument; however, Sparrow et al. have expanded this conception and developed a more comprehensive measure.

The test, designed for use with individuals aged 3 to 18 years, has three separate editions that can be used separately or in combination. The Interview Edition-Survey Form is most like the original Vineland and consists of 261 items. This edition provides an overall measure of adaptive behavior and can be helpful in identifying strengths and weaknesses. The Interview Edition-Expanded Form is composed of 541 items. This edition offers a prescriptive component to the VABS model because the items are more sequential and appropriate for use in developing Individual Education Plans. The Classroom Edition has a unique feature in that it allows the assessment of adaptive behavior within the classroom environment and is completed entirely by teachers. The two Interview Editions, in contrast, are administered in a semi-structured format with the parents or primary caregivers as the respondents. For example, the interviewer encourages the parent/caregiver to respond to the item, "Imitates sounds of adults immediately after hearing them." The interviewer then rates the response on a 0 (no, never) to a 2 (yes, usually) scale. A "don't know" (DK) and a "no opportunity" (NO) category are also available.

All three editions include five domains broken down into 12 subdomains. These are: Communication (Receptive, Expressive, Written), Daily Living Skills (Personal, Domestic, Community), Socialization (Interpersonal Relationships, Play and Leisure

FIGURE 3 Problem Behavior Areas Measured by the SIB

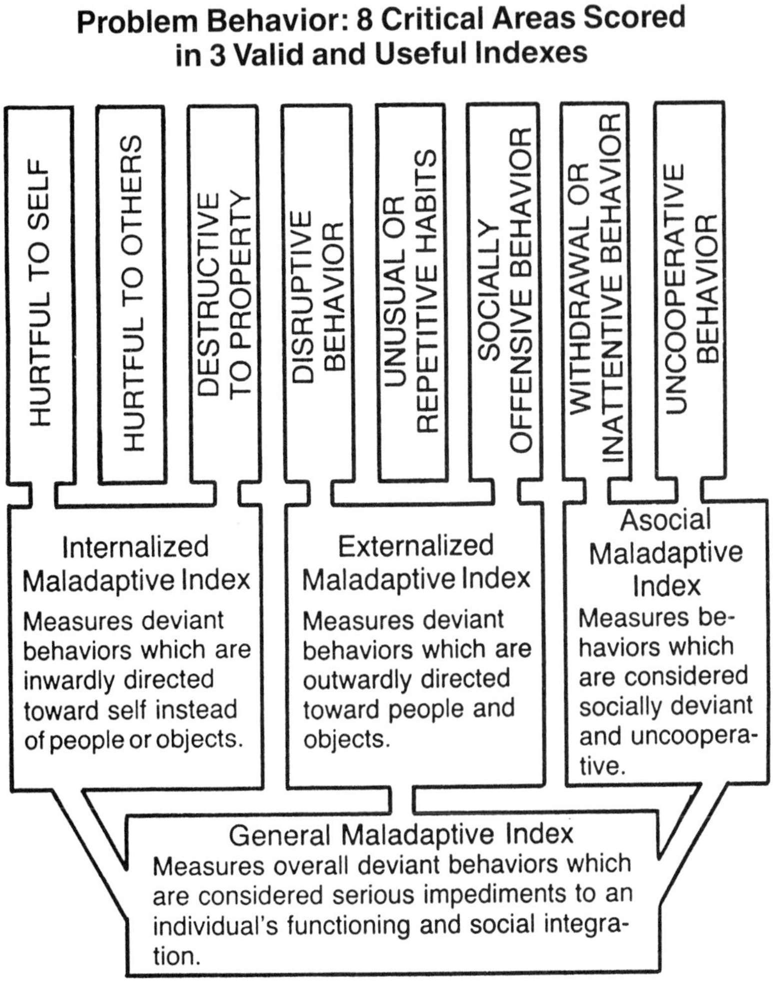

Adapted from R. Bruininks, R. Woodcock, R. Weatherman, & B. Hill, The Scales of Independent Behavior (Allen, TX: DLM Teaching Resources, 1984). Used by permission.

Time, Coping Skills), Motor Skills (Gross, Fine), and the Adaptive Behavior Composite (a combination of the other four domains). In addition, the two Interview Editions include an optional Maladaptive Behavior Domain focusing on undesirable behaviors that interfere with individual adaptive functioning.

A variety of scores are available from all three editions of the VABS: standard scores, national percentile ranks, stanines, and age equivalents. One particularly nice feature is a summary report for parents, presented in nontechnical language. This is shown in Figure 4.

FIGURE 4 Parent Report from the VABS

			Above Average	Average	Below Average
COMMUNICATION	**Receptive**	What your child understands			
	Expressive	What your child says			
	Written	What your child reads and writes			
DAILY LIVING SKILLS	**Personal**	How your child eats, dresses, and practices personal hygiene			
	Domestic	What household tasks your child performs			
	Community	How your child uses time, money, the telephone, and job skills			
SOCIALIZATION	**Interpersonal Relationships**	How your child interacts with others			
	Play and Leisure Time	How your child plays and uses leisure time			
	Coping Skills	How your child demonstrates responsibility and sensitivity to others			
MOTOR SKILLS	**Gross**	How your child uses arms and legs for movement and coordination			
	Fine	How your child uses hands and fingers to manipulate objects			

Adapted from Vineland Adaptive Behavior Scales *by S. Sparrow, D. Balla, & D. Cicchetti. Reprinted by permission of American Guidance Service, Inc., Publishers' Bldg., Circle Pines, MN 55014. Copyrighted 1984. Rights reserved.*

Overall, the VABS promises to be one of the better adaptive behavior instruments published in the last 10 years. Its standardization was well-constructed, and its theoretical base is sound. The instrument can be used for both descriptive and prescriptive purposes so that an overall adaptive behavior package is available within the same instrument. In addition, a large portion of the standardization sample was also used in the norming of the Kaufman Assessment Battery for Children, so that measures of cognitive skills, achievement, and adaptive behavior are possible using the same comparison group.

SUMMARY

Most adaptive behavior instruments include items in the areas of independent functioning, self-help skills, sensory and motor skills, and social skills. Adaptive behavior scales are used for a variety of purposes. In some situations they are used to aid in decisions about special education classifications. In other situations they are used to help develop educational objectives for students receiving special education (particularly lower-ability students). Adaptive behavior instruments have been traditionally used with mentally retarded students or those suspected of being mentally retarded, although many have relevance for other types of students.

The measurement of adaptive behavior is age-related and, to a certain extent, culture-related. For example, adaptive behavior would be defined differently for a 3- to 7-year-old than for a 13-year-old child. Similarly, opportunities for exhibiting certain behaviors considered to be "adaptive" might be related to the geographic/socioeconomic/cultural background of an individual.

In general, the technical characteristics of many adaptive behavior instruments are limited. In particular, the reliability of adaptive behavior instruments has been questioned, partially because of the interview format that is so commonly used. The validity of many of these tests has also been questioned, primarily because of the difficulty in defining the adaptive behavior construct.

These differing opinions regarding the definition and conceptualization of adaptive behavior have resulted in tests that are very different in terms of format as well as their purported use. Table 1 summarizes the instruments discussed in this article.

TABLE 1
Summary Profile of the Adaptive Behavior Scales

Name	Age Range	Type	Source of Information
Adaptive Behavior Inventory for Children	5-11 years	Descriptive	Structured Interview
AAMD Adaptive Behavior Scale-School Edition	3-16 years	Descriptive/Prescriptive	Semi-structured interview
Balthazar Scales of Adaptive Behavior	5-57 years	Prescriptive	Observation
Children's Adaptive Behavior Scale	5-10 years	Descriptive	Direct administration to child
Comprehensive Test of Adaptive Behavior	preschool - adult	Descriptive—Prescriptive (with NABC)	Completion from memory; observation
The Scales of Independent Behavior	infant - 40+ years	Descriptive	Structured interview
Vineland Adaptive Behavior Scale, Birth - 18 years	birth - 18 years	Descriptive/Prescriptive	Semi-structured interview

REFERENCES

Adams, G. (1984). *The comprehensive test of adaptive behavior.* San Antonio, TX: Psychological Corp..

Balthazar, E. (1976). *Balthazar scales of adaptive behavior.* Palo Alto, CA: Consulting Psychologists Press.

Bruininks, R., Woodcock, R., Weatherman, R., & Hill, B. (1984). *Scales of independent behavior.* Allen, TX: DLM Teaching Resources.

Cone, J., & Hawkins, R. (1977). Behavioral assessment: New directions in clinical psychology. New York: Brunner/Mazel.

Grossman, H. (1977). *Manual on terminology and classification in mental retardation.* Washington, DC: American Association on Mental Deficiency.

Grossman, H. (1983). *Classification in mental retardation.* Washington, DC: American Association on Mental Deficiency.

Guadalupe v. Tempe, Arizona School District, Civ. No. 71–435 (D. Ariz. 1972).

Isett, R., & Spreat, S. (1979). Test-retest and interrater reliabilities of the AAMD Adaptive Behavior Scale. *American Journal of Mental Deficiency, 84,* 93–95.

Kazimour, K., & Reschly, D. (1981). Investigation of the norms and concurrent validity for the Adaptive Behavior Inventory for Children. *American Journal of Mental Deficiency, 85,* 512–520.

Lambert, N., Windmiller, M., Tharinger, D., & Cole, L. (1981). *AAMD adaptive behavior scale—School edition.* Washington, DC: American Association on Mental Deficiency.

McDevitt, S., McDevitt, S., & Rosen, M. (1977). Adaptive behavior scale—Part two: A cautionary note and suggestions for revisions. *American Journal of Mental Deficiency, 82,* 210–212.

Mealor, D., & Richmond, B. (1980). Adaptive behavior: Teachers and parents disagree. *Exceptional Children, 46,* 386–389.

Mercer, J. (1973). *Labeling the mentally retarded: Clinical and social system perspectives on mental retardation.* Berkeley: University of California Press.

Mercer, J. (1979). *System of multicultural pluralistic assessment.* New York: Psychological Corp.

Reschly, D. (1981). Evaluation of the effects of SOMPA measures on classification of students as mildly mentally retarded. *American Journal of Mental Deficiency, 86,* 16–20.

Reschly, D. (1984). Best practices in conceptualizing adaptive behavior. In J. Grimes & A. Thomas (Eds.), *Best practices in school psychology.* Stratford, CT: NASP Publications.

Richmond, B., & Kicklighter, R. (1980). *The children's adaptive behavior scale.* Atlanta: Humanics, Ltd.

Sparrow, S., Balla, D., & Cicchetti, D. (1984). *Vineland adaptive behavior scales.* Circle Pines, MN: American Guidance Service.

Talley, R. (1979). Evaluating the effects of implementing the System of Multicultural Pluralistic Assessment: A qualitative perspective. *School Psychology Digest, 8,* 71–78.

Taylor, R. (1988). Assessment policies and procedures. In L. Sternberg (Ed.), *Educating students with severe or profound handicaps* (2nd ed.). Rockville, MD: Aspen.

Taylor, R. (1984). Assessment of exceptional students: Educational and psychological procedures. Englewood Cliffs, NJ: Prentice-Hall.

Taylor, R., Warren, S., & Slocumb, P. (1979). Categorizing behavior in terms of severity: Considerations for part two of the Adaptive Behavior Scale. *American Journal of Mental Deficiency, 83,* 411–414.

Taylor, R., Ziegler, E., & Partenio, I. (1985). An empirical investigation of the Adaptive Behavior Inventory for Children. *Psychological Reports, 57,* 640–642.

Witt, J., & Martens, B. (1984). Adaptive behavior: Tests and assessment issues. *School Psychology Review, 13,* 478–484.

The author extends a special thanks to Yvette Taylor for her careful technical editing of this manuscript.

Ronald Taylor is affiliated with the Department of Exceptional Student Education, Florida Atlantic University.

Among the three recognized "r's," the biggest "R" probably refers to reading. If students can read with comprehension, they have clearly learned an important survival and self-growth skill. Yet reading is only one form of communication through language. Another important and often overlooked or neglected form is written language. Why, one may ask, is it important that students with disabilities learn to write? As Moran points out, if writing instruction is focused upon conventions such as proper placement of periods and commas, the importance of written expression in the overall cognitive development of students may be ignored. If writing is taught as a thinking process, however, the opportunities for students to grow cognitively and affectively are very much enhanced.

In this article, Moran clearly describes the options for language assessment. Options must be carefully associated with the expected outcomes of instruction in written expression. For example, if a priority goal is to write a one-page classroom assignment with correct grammar and spelling, assessment of transcription skills may be all that is required. This chapter provides functional information for classroom teachers who integrate written language into the general curriculum. It is a must, too, for teacher educators to include in their methods courses for preservice special education teachers.

Options for Written Language Assessment

Mary Ross Moran

"Since writing is a learned set of skills, not an innate ability, comprehensive assessment of writing skills must be understood in terms of the educational goals of a society and the chief expression of those goals—the schools" (Faigley, Cherry, Jolliffe, & Skinner, 1985, p. 99).

"Writing is more likely to be assessed than to be taught" (Applebee, 1984, p. 184).

"Time and again, the methods that have been employed to measure writing have been criticized as either unreliable or invalid" (Charney, 1984, p. 65).

Concerns about writing assessment are summarized in the above quotations. Why do educators want students to learn to write? Should schools teach learners merely to imitate, in answers to essay questions, the ideas and organization previously presented by lectures or textbooks? Is writing to be conceptualized as communicative and interpersonal in purpose? Should writing also be taught as a noncommunicative means of self-expression, discovery of meaning, application of inductive and deductive reasoning to the development of a personal set of values?

Do adopted assessment practices reflect the instructional program, or has measurement lagged behind teaching progress? Do schools indeed assess more than they teach writing? Might available assessment instruments and practices dictate which writing skills are taught? What are prevailing assessment procedures for writing? How do reported reliabilities and validities differ across options?

Only the last two of these questions are addressed in this article. The other questions raise policy issues and implications for empirical research extending well beyond the scope of this discussion. Any consideration of writing assessment, however, must acknowledge the context in which assessment occurs. Administrators and instructors, including special educators, select assessment practices in accord with desired educational or social outcomes of writing instruction.

If, for example, the goal of writing proficiency for handicapped learners is merely to meet the demands of classroom assignments and to be able to take notes and written tests in mainstream classes, it is enough to measure skills in textbook organization of referential material with attention to surface conventions of grammar, punctuation, and spelling. If, on the other hand, writing instruction for handicapped learners is to encompass all six language functions described by Jakobson (1960)—referential, persuasive, emotive, metalingual, poetic, and interpersonal—assessment practices must be broadened to cover more types of writing for varied audiences and purposes.

TERMINOLOGY

For purposes of this discussion, terms are defined as follows.

Writing encompasses both composition and transcription, both process and product.

Composition refers to the substantive activities of selecting appropriate relationships among form, audience, and purpose, generating original text, and organizing text into a variety of styles in accord with conventions of literary forms.

Transcription skills are those superimposed upon composition when language is in written form; that is, writing requires transcribing language into another medium requiring a literary, rather than a colloquial, language register. Conventions include end punctuation and capitalization to mark sentences, commas and other internal marks for clarity, spelling, handwriting, segmenting with subheadings, and paragraphing.

Indirect measures are those that do not require composing skills—no decisions about audience or purpose, no original text; tests measure knowledge of transcribing rules.

Direct measures apply evaluation criteria to writing samples to examine both composition and transcription skills across varied tasks.

Process is the act of writing while it is in progress, typically including recursive stages of preplanning, drafting, revising, and editing.

Product is the completed version of a writing task as submitted to meet an assignment or conveyed to a reader as a final form of a communication.

Holistic evaluation is based on an impressionistic reaction to a product on first reading without attempting to account for the relative contributions of individual components; raters rank products in accord with anchor papers and assign a single score for overall merit.

Analytic evaluation involves examination of selected components of the writing task to isolate skills for instruction; instruments may include checklists, numerical scores, or qualitative judgments based on sets of decision criteria.

ASSESSMENT SELECTIONS

Researchers, administrators of writing programs, and individual instructors have developed assessment procedures for written language. A review of mainstream composition literature discloses a number of options, along with expert opinion on their respective merits. The search for reliable procedures—those yielding consistent results—and valid measures—those that comprehensively assess the real tasks in which writers engage—is ongoing.

Current choices permit relative emphasis upon (a) *composition* or *transcription* proficiencies, (b) *indirect* or *direct* measurement, (c) *process* or *product* direct evaluation, and (d) *holistic* or *analytic* product examination. Members of these pairs are not polar opposites; rather, they are extreme points on a continuum with some degree of overlap at the center. Though the pairs are useful to organize information, they are not parallel concepts; some pairs are subsumed under others. *Process* and *product* are types of *direct* measurement; *holistic* and *analytic* are subtypes of *product* evaluation.

Each procedure has advantages and disadvantages for different purposes. Choices are made on the basis of cost-benefit ratio according to the way results are to be used.

For *administrative* purposes—determining which students are assigned to remedial or honors English sections, for example, or estimating district students' writing status in comparison to national peers—*indirect* methods limited to *transcription* skills or *direct* evaluation of *products* using *holistic* procedures have been considered appropriate. When assessment is conducted for *instructional* planning, however, emphasis on *composition* through *direct* measurement, and use of *analytic* procedures have been recommended.

For special educators, the three purposes of writing assessment are:

—to establish whether a performance problem contributes to eligibility for special services.
—to gain diagnostic information to plan appropriate instruction.
—to monitor progress through and outcomes of instruction.

Indirect norm-referenced measures limited to *transcription* skills offer relative data useful for documenting an academic performance problem in general English proficiency. Special educators who wish to teach *composition* as well as *transcription* skills, however, employ *direct* measurement of multiple writing samples to derive short-term objectives. The following discussion offers options to be considered before selecting writing assessment procedures to be incorporated into the process of developing individualized education programs.

COMPOSITION EVALUATION

Composing is the act of creating novel connected discourse, either oral or written. The task imposes substantive demands on formulation and arrangement of language.

Composition acknowledges three discourse variables—writer, text, and audience. Closely associated with this communicative triangle is the notion of classes of discourse, typically identified as *expressive, narrative, descriptive, expository,* and *argumentative* prose, along with types of poetry and drama (D'Angelo, 1984). Discourse aims (Jakobson's six as listed earlier) overlap with, but offer concepts broader than, discourse classes. Composing further subsumes recursive activities called *prewriting, drafting, revising,* and *editing* (Flower & Hayes, 1981).

The communicative interaction of writer, text, and audience is based on classical rhetorical theory. Composing demands decisions about appropriate relationships among the three. Voice or tone, relative formality or informality, and selection of informative, emotive, or logical content depend upon a writer's perception of the intended audience and the desired effect on that audience. Bases for decisions are multiple—familiarity with the topic, how well a writer knows the readers, which genre or medium is conventionally used for specific purposes, and the importance of the task to personal goals (Selzer, 1984).

The assessment question is the extent to which writers have integrated their purposes with the needs or interests of their audiences by selections of content and form. For example, a mismatch occurs when a writer chooses slang vocabulary for logical and ethical arguments in an essay designed to persuade school administrators to delete a dress code.

Though the five discourse types listed above are frequently mentioned, numbers of other taxonomies have been suggested (D'Angelo, 1984). Discourse modes have been criticized as inadequate conceptual frameworks for writing or as secondary to the aim of the writing task (Lloyd-Jones, 1977). Nevertheless, the notion that identifiable combinations of purpose and audience give rise to specific requirements of content and form has persisted in writing assessment. Evaluators attempt to determine the extent of compliance with those constraints. For instance, a writer embarking on a narrative is expected to establish characters, setting, and chronological sequence of events; a writer developing an argument must provide a conclusion drawn from premises and support. Furthermore, writing for the referential purpose of explaining a procedure requires less emotive and poetic vocabulary but more rigid sequence than does an imaginative work.

Cognitive processes involved in composing have been described in working hypotheses resting on four key points: (a) writing is a set of distinctive thinking processes; (b) these processes have a hierarchical, embedded organization; (c) writing is guided by the writer's developing goals; (d) writers create and alter goals throughout the composing process (Flower & Hayes, 1981, p. 366). "Composing theory has moved beyond the old linear 'stage models' of composition (prewriting, writing, revising) to a recognition that composing activities are more recursive than linear, more flexible than constrained" (Selzer, 1984).

When Flower and Hayes conceptualized stages as recurring throughout the composing process (p. 367), they also identified a need for a novel type of assessment procedure to investigate the nature of rhetorical and stylistic decisions. Insight into stages is dependent upon *process* assessment. The assessment question is whether writers appropriately incorporate into their composing strategies, in accordance with the communicative triangle and constraints of discourse type and purpose, elements of planning, drafting, revision, and editing. For example, an argumentative term paper on nuclear disarmament demands more planning, organization, and revision than does a weekly one-page formatted laboratory report for biology class.

TRANSCRIPTION EVALUATION

As distinct from substantive elements of the writing task, components discussed under this category are variously addressed in the literature as *mechanics, conventions,* or *surface features*. The concept of *transcribing* is used here because the student writer's task is analogous to transcribing music into another key; oral and written language codes differ, and a developing writer must learn to transcribe from a known, relatively informal code to a sometimes more formal one with different cues.

To give an obvious example, oral features of falling or rising intonation are marked in writing by a period or a question mark—an adjustment that may not be difficult to master; but speaking permits *phrases* to be so marked whereas most school writing allows only independent *clauses* to be marked as sentences. More complex relationships between oral and written codes, described by Elbow (1985), include many similarities but enough differences to demand greater clarity in "final drafts . . . that could survive outside the context of local author and local audience" (p. 291).

Six features might be subsumed under *transcription*—literary language register, spelling, punctuation, capitalization, handwriting, and spatial conventions such as paragraph indentations, margins, headings, and footnotes. With the exception of personal notes or letters, written English in schools is to be in literary register—as opposed to the colloquial version appropriate for most spoken language. Spelling, punctuation, and capitalization can obscure messages of writers who are unfamiliar with these conventions (Shaughnessy, 1977). Handwriting is less critical in an age of word processing, but some studies have shown that it affects judgments of writing quality (Charney, 1984). Conventional spatial features clearly are related to overall coherence of text (Bamberg, 1983).

Evaluation of transcribing skills has been characterized as unrelated to language competence, as "a test of social conformity, of how well a person recognizes the language forms most commonly used by those in authority . . . but that does not make it a test of skills in discourse" (Lloyd-Jones, 1977, p. 34). Nevertheless, transcribing skills that have not reached an automatic level cannot be ignored in writing assessment because, "For children and inexperienced writers, this extra burden may overwhelm the limited capacity of short-term memory. If the writer must devote conscious attention to demands such as spelling and grammar, the task of translating can interfere with the more global process of planning what one wants to say" (Flower & Hayes, 1981, p. 373).

INDIRECT MEASURES

Indirect procedures require students to make judgments about correctness of contrived items, to correct another writer's errors, or to spell or punctuate dictated material. Occasionally an item requires rewording a sentence or paragraph, but testees do not engage in formulation of original connected text. Instead, tasks follow a multiple-choice format, a cloze procedure, or, infrequently, sentence-combining activities. The focus of measurement is *knowledge* about writing conventions, rather than *application* of those principles to real or simulated writing purposes.

Indirect measures carry the advantages of ready availability, quick administration, and objective scoring requiring limited professional time. Indirect methods far outperform direct procedures in terms of interrater agreement (Charney, 1984). Indirect tests typically are norm-referenced, offering advantages of known reliability and standard error of measurement, and they establish testees' status relative to national age and grade peers. This information can be useful when the assessment question is the extent of conformity with conventions.

One disadvantage of indirect measures has been associated with the cost-benefit ratio. Because they are quick to score, objective tests are said to save examiner time, offsetting the limited data they provide (Stiggins, 1982). As White (1984) pointed out, however, expenses associated with developing a standardized indirect measure are considerable; costs to consumers are not reflected in professional scoring time, but expenses of field testing and norming are passed on to schools in the purchase price of indirect instruments.

A more critical disadvantage is inadequate validity because of failure to tap *composition* components of the writing task. Because indirect items are selected to permit scoring ease or to provide variability across groups of testees rather than to cover essential skills, indirect measures are extremely limited in coverage (Cooper & Odell, 1977). They typically measure only *transcription* skills of literary usage, punctuation, capitalization, and spelling.

The very qualities that make indirect measures reliable therefore result in inadequate validity. In particular, *content* validity is questionable because tasks are so far removed from the desired outcome of writing instruction—the ability to generate written text. Results depend on inferences about a complex set of skills that are never demonstrated. Indirect tests "are insensitive to a student's ability to write cogent, coherent and fluent prose" (Charney, 1984, p. 67).

Criterion-related validity has been estimated by a number of studies correlating objective usage scores with evaluation of direct writing samples. Six studies over subjects ranging from third grade through college reported correlations as high as .75

(Stiggins, 1982). Writing samples for these studies, however, were evaluated holistically; because some evidence indicates that holistic scores may be unduly influenced by surface features such as grammatical usage, punctuation, capitalization, spelling, and even handwriting (Charney, 1984), criterion-related validity studies may be contaminated by limitations of the direct measures.

Studies of *predictive* validity of specific indirect measures typically compare test scores to grades assigned for language arts or English classes. Again, studies have produced correlations in satisfactory ranges (Cooper & Odell, 1977). Class grades, however, are based on reading and interpretation of literature, and many activities other than writing. Indeed, writing of paragraph length or more occupies a minor role in English classes (Applebee, 1984). Therefore, critics have argued that indirect measures correlate with *general language* proficiency rather than with *writing* skill (Lloyd-Jones, 1977).

Examples of individually administered indirect measures illustrate some of the validity problems. For instance, the Written Language Cluster of Part Two of the Woodcock-Johnson Psychoeducational Battery (Woodcock & Johnson, 1977) includes spelling to dictation and proofreading of sentences to locate spelling, punctuation, or usage errors and provide an oral correction. This battery is used as a survey of academic achievement of students referred to special services (McLaughlin & Lewis, 1986).

Beyond the central issue of testing knowledge rather than application, several questions arise about whether the test measures what could be called a *written language cluster*. Testees are asked to spell to dictation a series of single words (not a real-life writing task) that have not first been tested to establish that the words are in testees' oral or reading vocabularies. Sentences presented for proofreading not only have been written by someone else (not a real editing situation) but also are read silently so an examiner cannot judge whether testees have read accurately, and thus cannot determine possible contamination attributable to reading disability.

Other examples of indirect individual tests identified by publishers as measures of written language skills are the Spelling, Word Usage, and Style subtests of the Test of Written Language (TOWL) (Hammill & Larsen, 1983). Again, spelling words are dictated without first being presented for vocabulary knowledge or sight reading, and sentences to be completed for Word Usage and those rewritten for Style are read silently. Although examiners are instructed to decode words for testees on request, students may not ask for help when needed. These subtests thus share with the Woodcock-Johnson subtests the problem of unknown contribution of reading skills to the outcomes. The TOWL however, includes an examination of a single narrative direct product—though far from comprehensive—along with indirect measures.

The Brigance set of criterion-referenced Writing measures, like the Woodcock-Johnson norm-referenced instrument, is limited to indirect items. In the instrument designed for older subjects, the Diagnostic Inventory of Essential Skills (Brigance, 1981), transcription skills of letter formation, handwriting quality, capitalization, punctuation, and eight subtests of spelling are covered. A contrived task involves composing sentences using required words; other items require filling in blanks on standard forms. Generating a letter, which is analyzed for formal elements, constitutes the single composing task. Most of the same items occur in two other Brigance volumes. Inferences about *composing* cannot be drawn from these subtests, though they have some utility as measures of *transcribing* proficiency.

In summary, indirect measures offer advantages as screening instruments to estimate general knowledge of formal, literary language and written conventions. These tests, however, are inadequate for purposes of planning writing instruction as they cannot predict how an individual writer will apply knowledge when presented with a task requiring *composition* skills (Cooper & Odell, 1977).

DIRECT MEASURES

Direct procedures require testees to engage in production of original, connected discourse. Examiners may observe writers in action, videotape them, or ask them to verbalize the *process* to create a protocol. When the task is completed, direct *products* in the form of written language samples can be evaluated.

Typically an examiner presents testees with a brief writing prompt, such as a question or a statement that invites writers to express feelings, recount an event, describe an object, person or place, explain a procedure, express and support an opinion, or any combination thereof. Well stated prompts identify the form of the writing to be produced, the specific audience to be addressed, and the purpose of the communication. Writers respond by preparing original written discourse of at least paragraph length, in accordance with directions accompanying the prompts.

Direct measures offer advantages of original connected text available for examination, a simulated communicative purpose for the exercise, and at least potential application of a broad variety of composition and transcription skills (Cooper & Odell, 1977). Writers are required to interpret the prompt, to plan, generate, draft, revise, and edit original text in accord with the demands of a specific communicative task (Flower & Hayes, 1981). Testees have considerably more control over the material than over indirect items.

Direct measures generally are conceded to provide much higher content or face validity than do indirect tests. Since testees are engaging in the criterion, real-life task, evaluation is applied to the very skills that most experts would call *writing* (Cooper & Odell, 1977). The major disadvantage of direct measures is that they are time-consuming. The cost in professional staff commitment is high (Stiggins, 1982).

Acceptable intrarater and interrater reliabilities, as well as content validity, depend upon controlling variables associated with elicitation, process protocols, and scoring. But most experts have argued that *only* direct procedures can be said to measure *writing* as defined to include both *composition* and *transcription*. Therefore, the many precautions that must be taken to ensure reliable and valid outcomes are considered to be balanced by the utility of the data provided by direct measurement.

Process Evaluation

Scardamalia and Bereiter (1986) have argued that the distinction between process and product is somewhat artificial because "the more realistically learners are aware of what product characteristics they should be striving for and of how successful they are in achieving them, the more likely it is that the attendant cognitive processes will develop" (p. 798). These two types of assessment become better integrated as research on process continues to uncover writers' strategies (Gorrell, 1983).

The rationale for process analysis is that developing writers can benefit from bringing to consciousness the strategies used in composing. Process is a set of problem-solving sequences through recursive stages of planning, drafting, revising, and editing. Bases for choices become accessible by verbalizing and studying decision points.

Several researchers (Flower & Hayes, 1981; Perl, 1979; Sommers, 1980) have compared inexperienced writers with experts to study similarities and differences in strategies. Research has shown that some writers plan and revise extensively for most purposes, while others engage in relatively planless single-draft writing for many tasks (Selzer, 1984). "While nothing approaching a comprehensive theory of development of composing processes has yet been suggested, researchers have identified certain cognitive strategies that seem to be requisite of mature writing ability. Moreover, the work of some researchers has suggested that writers' increasing awareness of these strategies may signal their having achieved greater control of composing processes" (Faigley, Cherry, Jolliffe, & Skinner, 1985, p. 165).

Two methods, which may be combined in various ways, have been associated with assessing writing process—(a) thinking-aloud protocols, and (b) interviews, both following and during the task. Thinking-aloud protocols, the most widely reported procedure, have been described by Emig (1971), Flower and Hayes (1981), and Perl (1979). Examiners ask writers to verbalize musings during the composing act. Writers' talk is tape-recorded; then transcripts are prepared and subjected to analysis. Protocols offer the advantage of immediate access to what is going through writers' minds rather than relying on recall. A disadvantage is the intrusiveness of the procedure, which distracts writers from the task by requiring them to verbalize.

Interviews usually follow completion of a written product. Researchers observe writers composing, then question them about their practices. This approach has the advantage of introducing no intrusive procedures during the task, but it is potentially hampered by failures of recall or inferences drawn by writers about processes of which they were not conscious during composition.

Instead of asking writers to wait until the process has been completed, Faigley et al. (1985) have developed a *process log* to present questions at various points prior to and between drafting, revision, and editing stages. Intermittent interviews reduce the likelihood of losing data through memory lapse. If, however, writers engage in processes not covered by the specific questions and the accompanying scales, examiners are not likely to learn about them.

Interview methods sometimes make use of videotapes that record writing in progress for later playback Examiners ask open-ended questions with the tape serving as a prompt. Though Rose (1984) reported that his use of this procedure improved recall, he also concluded that reports of strategies were less accurate than thinking-aloud procedures about the order of activities and the time spent on each.

Research methodologies to document writers' strategies are not yet sufficiently operationalized to provide immediate assessment information to instructors, nor have reliability and validity studies received attention. Nevertheless, procedures are described in the literature for those who would like to investigate process and are willing to translate research methods into classroom assessment tools. To date, methods of assessing process strategies have been limited to single-subject procedures rather than systems applicable to groups (Faigley et al., 1985). Therefore, process methods can be expected to serve instructional, rather than administrative, purposes.

Product Evaluation

Direct *product* evaluation involves examining samples collected in natural settings, such as classroom assignments, or samples elicited specifically for assessment. Because classroom writing samples may be contaminated by inappropriate assignments, inadequate or misunderstood directions, and other unfavorable conditions (Applebee, 1984), elicited samples are more widely used.

Score stability within raters, across raters, and over time has been satisfactorily established for some types of scoring systems applied to *direct products* (White, 1984). But a list of variables affects the statistical consistency of ratings. "The list includes: the number of separate readings of each writing sample, the number of writing samples evaluated per student, the writing topic, the size of the writing scale, the consistency with which the readers are trained, the conditions under which the papers are read and so on" (Charney, 1984, p. 70).

Though content validity is superior to that of indirect measures, some types of direct-product evaluation nevertheless have been criticized on the basis of validity. Bias has been ascribed to the nature of writing prompts, including the extent to which they tap prior topic knowledge (Langer, 1984). Different discourse modes (Lloyd-Jones, 1977), varying cognitive demands (Flower & Hayes, 1981), and specific audiences to whom writing is addressed (Applebee, 1984) alter writing quality to such an extent that experts judge content validity on a case-by-case basis. "Thus it is possible to disagree on the validity of any given test, depending upon its design" (Charney, 1984, p. 71).

When the decision has been made to employ direct product measurement, evaluators may choose *holistic* or *analytic* scoring procedures. Holistic scoring has achieved prominence over the past 20 years or so as a means of permitting direct measurement of writing in programs involving large numbers of students. Analytic evaluation has evolved more recently to supplement holistic impressions of quality with detailed information for instructional planning.

Holistic Rating

Through the period of development of holistic rating, several practices have become standard. White (1984) summarized prevailing procedures. Trained raters read papers at the same time and place to reduce distractions and to standardize conditions. Scoring criteria are stated, defining points on a rating scale. Anchor papers are provided as concrete examples of points on the scale. Table leaders check intrarater consistency for five to seven readers and may retrain raters who demonstrate scoring drift. Two readers from two tables score each essay independently for interrater agreement.

Charney (1984) also listed conditions prerequisite to reliable and valid assessments. Precautions include employing qualified readers from similar backgrounds and training readers to conform to agreed criteria.

Noting that few studies of consistency across various types of writing have been reported, Mishler and Hogan (1982) estimated interscorer reliabilities from published studies at .85 and intrascorer reliabilities at .90. The consensus seems to be that the procedure demonstrates acceptable reliabilities if standard practices and precautions are followed rigorously (Stiggins, 1982).

White (1984) argued that content validity of holistic ratings is higher than that of either *indirect* or direct *analytic* methods. According to him, writing is "an artistic and human whole, not merely . . . a collection of scraps and parts" (p. 409). By this reasoning, holistic scoring is valid because it provides an overall human response to a human activity that resists reductionism.

Charney (1984), however, questioned the validity of holistic rating on two grounds. First, whether criteria are set up in advance by experts or are derived by a homogeneous group of readers, the standards of what constitutes the "best" papers are disputable as subject to bias (p. 73). Second, the extent to which readers use standards set in advance has been called into question by studies showing that separable traits correlate with holistic ratings. "It is disconcerting to find holistic scores, which are supposed to be a *qualitative* measure, so directly predictable by such mundane quantitative measures as the length of the sample, the number of errors and the number of unusual vocabulary items" (p. 75).

In addition to advantages of satisfactory reliabilities, and face validity superior to other types of assessment, holistic scoring is generally considered to be cost-efficient for scoring writing in quantity. Though two readers are involved (three in cases of disagreement), each spends an average of only 30 seconds to 1 minute (Mishler & Hogan, 1982) or 2 to 3 minutes (Cooper & Odell, 1977) on each paper.

Disadvantages center on the inability of holistic evaluation to provide any information for instructional planning. Holistic scoring merely assigns values to writing samples and yields judgments of quality relative to other papers in the same group. "It gives no meaningful diagnostic information beyond the comparative ranking it represents. . . . All we have is a single score, where we might wish to have a profile" (White, 1984, p. 406).

An example of a specialized type of holistic scoring developed for the National Assessment of Educational Progress has been described by Lloyd-Jones (1977). Primary Trait Scoring relies upon elicited samples in response to writing prompts that specify the form, audience, and purpose of the writing. Traits associated with those specifics are identified in advance and applied to the written product to determine the extent of compliance. Development of differing criteria for varied writing assignments sets this procedure apart from holistic systems that attempt to use the same criteria for several writing assignments. Descriptions of a variety of other holistic scoring procedures were presented by Myers (1980), along with examples of scored papers.

Analytic Scoring

Analytic methods yield a series of scores, checklist marks, or descriptions for presumably separable subskills derivable from writing samples. Because this is the most recent type of measurement to develop, there is some inconsistency in terminology. Cooper (1977) used *analytic scale* to describe what he called a type of *holistic* scoring that considers separate features of the sample without requiring readers "to stop and count or tally incidents of the feature" (p. 4). In contrast, Mishler and Hogan (1982) clearly distinguished *holistic* from *analytic* scoring, which they described as a system "in which papers are rated on any number of different facets" (p. 12). A resolution to the conflict is to consider systems that result in a single score as *holistic* and those incorporating separable components that do not sum up to one score as *analytic*.

Analytic scoring often has been equated with counting or, in even narrower interpretations, with counts of *errors* only, without acknowledgement of strengths (Ney, 1986). But the concept appears to be expanding to include qualitative judgments as well as quantitative measures, strengths as well as weaknesses.

Analytic scoring involves selecting, from the many possible ways of categorizing writing subskills, some characteristics that will be measured. For example, a developer of an analytic system might consult Cooper and Odell (1977), Myers (1985), or Purves (1984) for lists of components that could be included. Under superordinate categories such as *content, organization, vocabulary,* and *syntax,* for instance, subskills might be judged according to criteria.

In contrast to holistic rating, which compares products with those of peers in the same group, analytic scoring uses only *intrastudent* comparisons across subskills. By studying a profile, examiners determine proficiencies and limitations not apparent in an impressionistic reading of papers.

Advantages of analysis have been variously described. A complex task is rendered manageable so that teachable components can be isolated (Gorrell, 1983). Identified subskills then can be taught with some concentration of effort so instructors and students do not have to try to deal with all aspects of a complex task simultaneously (Simmons, 1984). Writers' tendency to become overloaded if too many skills are attempted at once (Ammon & Keech, 1985) is avoided. Forcing evaluators to go beyond surface conventions reduces that potential source of invalidity and may lead to discovery of composition strengths obscured by transcription errors (Moran, 1987a).

Disadvantages of analytic scoring have been summarized by White (1984), who argued that although "analytic scoring should provide the diagnostic information that holistic scoring fails to provide," it has thus far failed to do so (p. 407). Experts have not agreed that subskills of the complex writing task are in any way separable, so artificial designation of discrete components may involve overlap and interdependence of skills. Intrarater and interrater reliabilities are difficult to establish for multiple characteristics. Because scoring is complicated and involves a number of passes through several papers, the procedure is time-consuming and, therefore, costly in professional hours. Mishler and Hogan (1982) estimated 15 minutes per paper for analytic scoring, but considerable training may be required to reach that level of efficiency.

Examples of analytic evaluations include Shaughnessy's (1977) procedures for inexperienced writers. Three systems that have been applied to writing by samples of handicapped learners illustrate varying approaches.

The Diagnostic Evaluation of Writing Skills (DEWS) (Weiner, 1980) has been applied to one direct product per writer elicited in timed writing sessions that include a segment set aside for revision. "The 41 criteria for assessment are divided into six categories to include most of the common writing errors" (p. 54).

Graphic features subsume handwriting and spacing; 18 *Orthographic* and *Phonologic* items focus on spelling; *Syntactic* subskills include six covering standard literary usage and four concerned with variety and productivity at the sentence level. The *Semantic* category includes composition items that tap vocabulary, coherence, sequencing, transitions, and focus. *Self-monitoring* is credited if the writer engages in revision and editing. Scoring consists of "simple tabulation of the number of errors" (p. 55). The measure was described by its developer as "providing a permanent record of the student's deficiencies, which subsequently become the basis for remedial teaching" (p. 59).

Poteet's (1980) Inventory of Written Expression and Spelling features a Checklist of Written Expression, which the developer recommends applying to multiple samples. Elicitation procedures are not specified. Transcription items are grouped under "Penmanship" and "Spelling." Literary register and conventions (capitalization, punctuation, and syntax) appear under "Grammar." An "Ideation" section combines composition skills of comprehensibility, level of abstraction, tone, word choice, and sentence variety with tallies of total words produced and numbers of complete, run-on, and fragmented sentences. The checklist is marked to indicate whether the subskill under consideration is too advanced or adequate for the writer's age and grade level or whether it should be introduced. The developer described the system as yielding "results which suggest instructional strategies" (p. 98).

The Analytic Profile of Composing and Transcribing Skills (Moran, 1987b) is applied to multiple samples representing at least three relationships among writer, text, and purpose. Samples are elicited under controlled conditions. Following an oral reading of papers for impressionistic reactions by the writer and at least one peer, a scoring guide presents decision criteria under four major categories, three covering *composition* and one devoted to *transcription*.

Under "Complexity," the system measures percentage of complex T-units (one independent clause plus embedded or attached dependent clauses) (Hunt, 1970), mean words, morphemes and free modifiers per T-unit, and varieties of clause construction. The "Continuity" section identifies five types of relationships among writer, text, and audience and provides weighted scores for degrees of compliance with constraints of each type. "Connections" cover some semantic and syntactic ties associated with unifying written discourse. "Conventions" include basic T-unit construction, sentence boundaries, spelling, and formal language register. Each section yields numerical data, some in percentages and others in arbitrary weighted figures.

The described analytic systems were not designed to be normed; therefore, profiles of normally developing, randomly selected writers are unknown. These measures can be called criterion-referenced because the components identified and subjected to analysis are drawn from a general domain described by writing experts in the professional literature, and results are referenced only to *intra*student rather than *inter*student comparisons. Validity decisions depend upon which list of subskills might be considered representative of *writing* by the specific experts selected to review a given analytic system.

These criterion-referenced measures are appropriately used, if applied to multiple samples written for different purposes, to describe writing characteristics of individuals for instructional planning. Criterion levels, which determine whether a given component is subject to intervention, are set by users of these systems.

Alternatively, an analytic system can be developed by school district personnel directly from the writing curriculum to which their own students are exposed. Because curriculum-based assessment takes into account the methods and materials employed in direct writing instruction, content validity is satisfied. A major advantage is that analytic systems based on district instructional objectives are specific enough to call attention to writing components that might be overlooked by more global methods of evaluation.

CONCLUSION

Consideration of similarities and differences among the options available for writing assessment leads to a conclusion that no method is inherently superior to another. Relative usefulness or relevance varies as a function of the purpose of assessment.

Therefore, indirect methods, yielding screening data on general proficiency in recognizing standard English, can contribute to evidence for or against a performance problem in language arts, though they may not distinguish *reading* from *writing* problems. Direct methods, capable of describing application of a variety of skills to a complex task, are preferable for developing preintervention and progress data for instruction, despite time-consuming precautions necessary to safeguard reliability and validity.

In turn, purpose is related to the goals of writing instruction. Assessment procedures must reflect the expectations, writing assignments, and focus of classroom lessons. Writing instruction in the mainstream has undergone shifts away from transcription skills toward increasing attention to writing as a thinking process (Faigley et al., 1985). For educators planning instruction for handicapped learners, assessment decisions will be formed by the extent to which writing programs attempt to incorporate the higher cognitive and linguistic functions of composition.

REFERENCES

Ammon, P., & Keech, C. (1985). Longitudinal research on writing assessment. In K. Greenberg & V. Slaughter (Eds.), *Notes from the National Testing Network in Writing* (pp. 13–22). New York: City University of New York.

Applebee, A. (1984). *Contexts for learning to write*. Norwood, NJ: Ablex.

Bamberg, B. (1983). What makes a text coherent? *College Composition & Communication, 34*, 417–429.

Brigance, A. (1981). *Diagnostic inventory of essential skills*. North Billerica, MA: Curriculum Associates.

Charney, D. (1984). The validity of using holistic scoring to evaluate writing: A critical overview. *Research in the Teaching of English, 18*, 65–81.

Cooper, C. (1977). Holistic evaluation of writing. In C. Cooper & L. Odell (Eds.), *Evaluating writing: Describing, measuring, judging* (pp. 3–32). Urbana, IL: National Council of Teachers of English.

Cooper, C., & Odell, L. (Eds.) (1977). *Evaluating writing: Describing, measuring, judging*. Urbana, IL: National Council of Teachers of English.

D'Angelo, F. (1984). Nineteenth-century forms/models of discourse. *College Composition & Communication, 35*, 31–42.

Elbow, P. (1985). The shifting relationships between speech and writing. *College Composition & Communication, 36*, 283–303.

Emig, J. (1971). *The composing processes of twelfth graders* (Research Report No. 13). Urbana, IL: National Council of Teachers of English.

Faigley, L., Cherry, R., Jolliffe, D., & Skinner, A. (1985). *Assessing writers' knowledge and processes of composing*. Norwood, NJ: Ablex.

Flower, L., & Hayes, J. (1981). A cognitive process theory of writing. *College Composition & Communication, 32*, 365–387.

Gorrell, R. (1983). How to make Mulligan stew: Process and product again. *College Composition & Communication, 34*, 272–277.

Hammill, D., & Larsen, S. (1983). *Test of written language*. Austin, TX: Pro-Ed.

Hunt, K. (1970). Syntactic maturity in school children and adults. *Monographs of the Society for Research in Child Development, 35*(Serial No. 134), 1–44.

Jakobson, R. (1960). Linguistics and poetics. In T. Sebeok (Ed.), *Style in language* (pp. 350–376). New York: John Wiley.

Langer, J. (1984). The effects of available information on responses to school writing tasks. *Research in the Teaching of English, 18*, 27–44.

Lloyd-Jones, R. (1977). Primary trait scoring. In C. Cooper & L. Odell (Eds.), *Evaluating writing* (pp. 33–68). Urbana, IL: National Council of Teachers of English.

McLoughlin, J., & Lewis, R. (1986). *Assessing special students*. Columbus, OH: Charles E. Merrill.

Mishler, C., & Hogan, T. (1982). Holistic scoring of essays. *Diagnostique, 8*, 4–16.

Moran, M. (1987a). Individualized objectives for writing instruction. *Topics in Language Disorders, 7*, 42–54.

Moran, M. (1987b). *Analytic profile of composing and transcribing skills*. Kansas City, MO: Mss. Press.

Myers, M. (1980). *A procedure for writing assessment and holistic scoring*. Urbana, IL: National Council of Teachers of English.

Myers, M. (1985). *The teacher researcher: How to study writing in the classroom*. Urbana, IL: National Council of Teachers of English.

Ney, J. (1986). Error analysis, theories of language, and the teaching of writing. *Written Communication, 3*, 15–30.

Perl, S. (1979). The composing processes of unskilled college writers. *Research in the Teaching of English, 13*, 317–336.

Poteet, J. (1980). Informal assessment of written expression. *Learning Disability Quarterly, 3*, 88–98.

Purves, A. (1984). In search of an internationally valid scheme for scoring compositions. *College Composition & Communication, 35*, 426–438.

Rose, M. (1984). *Writer's block: The cognitive dimension*. Carbondale, IL: Southern Illinois University Press.

Scardamalia, M., & Bereiter, C. (1986). Research on written composition. In Wittrock, M. (Ed.), *Handbook of research on teaching* (pp. 778–803). New York: Macmillan.

Selzer, J. (1984). Exploring options in composing. *College Composition & Communication, 35*, 276–284.

Shaughnessy, M. (1977). *Errors and expectations*. New York: Oxford University Press.

Simmons, J. (1984). The one-to-one method of teaching composition. *College Composition & Communication, 35*, 222–229.

Sommers, N. (1980). Revision strategies of student writers and experienced adult writers. *College Composition & Communication, 31,* 378–388.
Stiggins, R. (1982). A comparison of direct and indirect writing assessment methods. *Research in the Teaching of English, 16,* 101-114.
Weiner, E. (1980). The diagnostic evaluation of writing skills (DEWS). *Learning Disability Quarterly, 3,* 54–59.
White, E. (1984). Holisticism. *College Composition & Communication, 35,* 400–409.
Woodcock, R., & Johnson, M. (1977). *Woodcock-Johnson psychoeducational battery.* Allen, TX: DLM.

Dr. Moran is Associate Professor in the Department of Special Education, University of Kansas Medical Center, Kansas City.

Clearly, curriculum-based assessment (CBA), a concept old in time but new in revised interest among special educators, has attained a prominent position in priority lists for research and applications in classrooms. It is difficult to argue against the notion that assessment practices should be based upon the curriculum that is taught to students. Given that an instructional goal is known and measurable, a student's progress, or lack of it, in relation to the goal can be assessed. But the question of how CBA should be implemented is not as easy to answer as it is to say "yes" to the question of whether it should be used.

Deno and Fuchs have offered an answer in their problem-solving approach known as curriculum-based measurement (CBM). The approach provides for the direct measurement of a student's responses to an assignment. For example, a minute reading sample from an appropriate instructional level can be used two or three times weekly to chart correct and incorrect words. If the instruction is having a desired impact, several results should occur. First, oral reading rate should increase. Second, number of words read correctly should increase. And third, number of words read incorrectly should decrease and stabilize at a very low level. A teacher and student chart of progress based upon the reading samples provides immediate feedback of progress in attaining an instructional target or goal. The measurement principles used in CBM have been around for many years and have been used extensively in modifying deviant social behaviors in classroom settings. Their application to instructional problem solving, however, is relatively recent. Deno and Fuchs have provided regular and special education professionals with a highly functional approach to CBA.

Developing Curriculum-Based Measurement Systems For Data-Based Special Education Problem Solving

Stanley L. Deno and Lynn S. Fuchs

Special education is characterized most often as a service delivery system (Deno, 1970). Indeed, The Education for All Handicapped Children Act (Public Law 94–142) is written to guarantee provision of educational services to all students classified as handicapped. Although viewing special education as a service delivery system may be useful, this conceptualization tends to cast special education in the mold of a welfare program, designed to serve an educationally needy segment of the population through special funding. An alternative—perhaps more constructive—conceptualization is to view special education as a component of the general education system, designed to solve individual students' problems.

The advantage of recasting special education as a problem-solving mechanism is that programmatic goals can be specified more precisely, and the steps or procedures for solving the problems for which special education was created can be identified more clearly. Consider the generic steps followed in problem-solving activities:

1. Identify the problem to be solved.
2. Identify alternative solutions to the problem.
3. Implement and test the alternative solutions.
4. Revise unsuccessful solutions.
5. Terminate the problem-solving process.

How do we apply these steps to describe special education practice? The answer to this question is apparent when we recast the problem-solving steps as the following series of decisions special educators formulate in building effective educational programs:

1. What are the problems that gave impetus to referral to special education and suggest the need for modifying the student's program?
2. What alternative individual education plans can be created that might solve these problems?
3. Have we implemented the Individualized Education Program (IEP) designed to solve problems that led to referral, and does the problem solution appear to be effective?
4. Have we revised an unsuccessful attempt at problem solution, and does that revised problem solution appear to be more successful?
5. Does evidence exist that the problems that led to referral have been solved and the student may be exited from special education?

When special education is viewed in terms of these questions, which correspond to the generic problem-solving process, the essence of special education becomes *constructive problem solving,* whatever the overlay of regulations and policies created through federal and state laws. The focus of special education shifts from simply serving handicapped students through special resources to solving pupils' problems in order to produce optimal progress in least restrictive environments.

Problem solving in this regard can be approached as an entirely intuitive and subjective process, but it also is possible to approach problem solving systematically and objectively. Although intuitive approaches to problem solving may be valuable, in special education we increasingly have been required to objectify the basis for our decisions. The process that produces the greatest objectification in human endeavor is, of course, *measurement*. Now, more than ever, we are required to provide data not only to justify the allocation of resources but also to demonstrate the effectiveness of problem-solving efforts we undertake.

The requirement for data collection is not new in special education. For years we have used all manner and means of formal educational and psychological tests and informal observations to identify those to serve and, to a lesser extent, to evaluate the effectiveness of what we do. The problems with our traditional approach to measurement and data collection are many and have been chronicled elsewhere (see, for example, Galagan, 1985). They will not be repeated here. Rather, the focus of this article is an alternative approach to data-basing our special education problem-solving decisions: curriculum-based measurement.

Here, curriculum-based measurement first is defined and its decision-making purposes reviewed. Then, several advantages of this approach are discussed. Next, a framework for developing curriculum-based measurement systems is presented and applied to demonstrate how curriculum-based assessment methodology can be specified. Finally, a case study illustrating how a practitioner actually might employ the framework and design a curriculum-based measurement system for one specific student is presented.

CURRICULUM-BASED MEASUREMENT

Definition

The term *curriculum-based measurement* (CBM) has been applied to a variety of approaches for describing student progress (Deno, Marston, & Tindal, 1986). As Tucker (1985) pointed out, however, the essential characteristic of all approaches to CBM is that "the measure of success in education is the student's progress in the curriculum of the local school" (p. 199). What makes CBM distinct from traditional psychoeducational measurement, then, is that the stimulus material that provides the occasion for student responses is the actual curriculum of the local school rather than a set of independent items or problems created by commercial test developers.

Purposes

CBM systems have begun to be applied widely for a variety of special education problem-solving purposes (see Tucker, 1985). First, CBM has been validated (Marston, Deno, & Mirkin, 1984) and used (Germann & Tindal, 1985) to create a data base from which screening and referral decisions are made. Quick, standardized samples of student performance on curricular materials can be used as a meaningful, efficient, objective tool for identifying pupils who are (a) academically discrepant from classroom peers (Shinn & Marston, 1985) and (b) in need of in-depth assessment (Marston et al., 1984).

Second, CBM may provide the richest, most valid data source for developing effective programs. Systematic observations of performance in the curriculum provide the basis for formulating initial hypotheses about strategies for improving student growth (Howell, 1986). Additionally, ongoing assessment of students' curricular progress, in response to alternative instructional programs, has been demonstrated to effect much higher achievement levels than traditional approaches to program development (Fuchs, Deno & Mirkin, 1984; Fuchs & Fuchs, 1986b).

Finally, CBM has been employed innovatively and effectively to (a) summatively assess the effectiveness of individual education programs in relation to specific exit criteria, and (b) evaluate the efficacy of special education programs in general along important dimensions such as time in program, type of handicap, and level of service (see Germann & Tindal, 1985). Consequently, CBM provides a suitable and uniform data base for processing through the entire five-step problem-solving process constituting special education practice.

Advantages

The many advantages of using the local school curriculum as the stimulus material for measuring student performance have been reviewed elsewhere (see Deno, 1985). Three fundamental strengths are addressed here. Foremost, perhaps, is that CBM improves the match between testing and teaching. As demonstrated by Jenkins and Pany (1978) and Armbruster, Stevens, and Rosenshine (1977), the potential discrepancy between what is taught and what is tested can be considerable and can result in significant biasing of student achievement decisions. The correspondence between the test and the curriculum, known as *curricular validity,* has been shown to be an important element of effective instruction (see Fuchs & Fuchs, 1986a).

A second important advantage of CBM relates to the fact that the primary goal for most special education students is successful functioning within the mainstream curriculum. This means that special education student success must be defined in terms of competence in the mainstream curriculum. Relatedly, useful measurement indexes mainstream curricular growth, and CBM successfully addresses this requirement. It enables direct appraisal of the extent to which a student is performing successfully in the mainstream curriculum and whether sufficient improvement has accrued for the student's reintegration with mainstream peers.

Another key consideration in the selection of a measurement approach is the degree to which it communicates clearly among those who use the measurement data. Although psychoeducational testing represents the historical and predominant measurement strategy, it would be an overstatement to claim that all who communicate regarding student progress understand the derived scores from traditional tests. Finally, a related, important strength of CBM is that its direct measurement of progress within the curriculum used by mainstream teachers enables clear and direct communication between regular and special educators. This enhancement of communication applies to parents as well, because their children's performance in special education can be compared to the performance of mainstream children within the same curriculum. Mainstream curriculum, then, becomes the common standard against which all student performance is tracked for decision-making purposes.

DEVELOPING CURRICULUM-BASED MEASURES: A FRAMEWORK

CBM has been shown to provide an effective data base for special education problem solving, and compelling arguments can be made for why student performance in the curriculum of the local school ought to be the basis for measuring student achievement. Nevertheless, adopting a CBM approach raises formidable technical issues.

The technical issues related to adopting CBM are summarized by the question: *How do we reliably measure student performance in the curriculum so that the data are valid for making special education problem-solving decisions?* A framework for answering this question is presented in Tables 1 and 2. Table 1 is a matrix combining a set of measurement issues with factors that constrain the answers to those questions. Table 2 lists the questions that must be addressed when the issues in the matrix intersect with the related constraints to form matrix cells. Explication of this matrix proceeds in the following way. First, the constraints, issues, and currently available answers to the matrix questions are addressed for the "What" and "How" to measure components of the matrix. Then, for the "How to Use Data" portion of the matrix, the measurement issues and constraints with currently available answers to the matrix questions are specified.

Constraints: "What" and "How" to Measure

Technical Adequacy

Whereas some technical adequacy issues important in developing a CBM system are unique to the concerns of CBM, several issues are similar to the concerns of traditional, norm-referenced assessment. The relevant technical adequacy issues of traditional psychometric testing are the validity and reliability of the curriculum-based stu-

TABLE 1
Decision-Making Matrix

	Technical	Effectiveness	Logistical
What to Measure	T-1	E-1	L-1
How to Measure	T-2	E-2	L-2
How to Use Data	T-3	E-3	L-3

Numbers are given to label cells. Corresponding questions are presented in Table 2.

TABLE 2
Questions Posed in the Decision-Making Matrix

Technical

T-1. *What to measure:* What behaviors clearly index growth and are responsive to the effects of instruction?

T-2. *How to measure:* What measurement procedures generate reliable and valid data that are sensitive to short- and long-term growth?

T-3. *How to use data:* How should the data be summarized, analyzed, and interpreted to ensure reliable and valid decision making?

Effectiveness

E-1. *What to measure:* Does measuring different behaviors relate to different achievement outcomes?

E-2. *How to measure:* Do different measurement procedures result in different rates of student improvement?

E-3. *How to use data:* What data-based decision rules result in more successful programs?

Logistical

L-1. *What to measure:* What behaviors are readily accessible for repeated measurement?

L-2. *How to measure:* What measurement procedures are most efficient and least intrusive?

L-3. *How to use data:* What data utilization procedures are most efficient and cost-effective?

---

dent achievement measure. *Validity* refers to the extent to which measurement data relate to the measurement purposes or improve decision making. Three relevant types of validity are criterion, content, and construct validity.

For a measure to demonstrate strong *criterion validity,* scores should correlate highly with other data that are deemed important. For a reading achievement measure, for example, to have criterion validity, it should correlate with technically adequate standardized tests of reading, teacher placement in the curriculum, or placement in special reading programs. If we explore "reading aloud from text" as a potential behavioral indicator of reading proficiency, low scores on textual material should be associated with poor performance on global, norm-referenced reading tests, and high scores should be associated with good performance on the global, norm-referenced tests.

Content validity is dependent upon the adequacy with which a specified domain of content is sampled. For example, measuring "reading aloud from text" would possess content validity if teachers agree that their goal is to teach students to read text aloud proficiently.

Finally, *construct validity* represents the extent to which measures correlate in expected ways with other measures or are affected in predictable ways by experimental treatments. Once a domain of behaviors is specified, along with the ways in which those behaviors relate to one another, experimental evidence is sought to confirm or disconfirm that those behaviors actually relate to one another as hypothesized.

A second technical adequacy issue that applies to CBM is *reliability* including test-retest reliability, alternate-form reliability, and interscorer agreement. *Test-retest reliability* is illustrated in the following example. John makes the most errors of anyone in his reading group when reading words from a third-grade word list on Monday; on Wednesday, when all read the same list again, we can expect his performance to be similar. Test-retest reliability is the extent to which a set of students' relative scores are alike on two testings.

A second form of reliability, *alternate-form reliability,* is highly relevant for CBM when monitoring progress requires repeated testing with a different test form at each measurement session. Alternate-form reliability is the extent to which the relative scores of a group of students are similar on alternate test forms. A third type of reliability, *interscorer agreement,* refers to the extent to which a group of students' performances are scored alike by independent examiners. All forms of reliability indicate the extent to which scores on a test are free from error and represent a student's "true score."

In addition to these traditional technical concerns, CBM, wherein student performance is monitored over time, requires consideration of a number of other technical issues. One of these is the reliability of the trend or slope of the data, which is indicative of changing student achievement across days in school. Other technical concerns include: (a) the amount of intra-individual variability from day to day or week to week, (b) the degree to which the measurement data are linked directly to the goal specified on the IEP, and (c) the reliability or consistency of teachers' interpretations of data.

Instructional Effectiveness

The ultimate purpose of a CBM system is to solve problems. Therefore, in addition to technical concerns, selection among measurement and evaluation components should reflect the effects those elements have on teacher decision making and student achievement. Instructional effectiveness concerns have, in fact, been shown to be relevant. A meta-analysis of the effects of CBM on student achievement indicated that procedural differences in CBM produce differential student growth (Fuchs & Fuchs, in press-b). Instructional effectiveness, consequently, is included in the decision-making matrix.

Logistical Feasibility

A major teacher concern is that CBM may be too time consuming (Wesson, King, & Deno, 1984). In research conducted in a rural special education cooperative (Fuchs, Wesson, Tindal, Mirkin, & Deno, 1981), elementary resource teachers initially spent an average of 2¼ minutes preparing for, administering, scoring, and graphing one curriculum-based measure for one student. Multiplied across a full caseload of students, this figure represents a large portion of teacher time. In designing a feasible measurement system, then, one must make logistical changes to reduce teacher and student time in measurement. Consequently, logistical feasibility also is incorporated within the decision-making matrix of a constraint on determining CBM procedures.

Measurement Issues: "What" and "How" to Measure

What to Measure

In developing an adequate set of CBM procedures, the first issue to address is selection of a behavior to be measured. In reading, for example, students can be observed reading isolated words aloud or silently, reading text aloud or silently, answering questions based on text reading, decoding nonsense words, completing cloze passages, and completing worksheets. In spelling, students can be measured writing from dictation, editing word lists, recognizing correct alternatives, writing paragraphs, and doing various "spelling" worksheets. Before curriculum-based data can be collected, the specific behaviors that are vital, global indicators of student academic growth must be identified.

How to Measure

Decisions constituting "How to Measure" vary by academic domain. Figures 1 and 2 illustrate the decision flows for reading and spelling, and for written expression, respectively. The following discussion briefly describes each decision referenced in Figures 1 and 2.

Selection of a *basic measurement strategy* for monitoring student progress is an essential decision in designing a measurement system. Two strategies are performance measurement and progress measurement (Deno & Mirkin, 1977). *Performance measurement* provides information on how a student's behavior changes on a task of constant difficulty. In performance measurement, increases in fluent performance on equivalent forms of the task should represent growth or achievement. For example, a teacher might decide to measure a student's performance on reading aloud

FIGURE 1 Decision Flow for Academic Domains of Reading and Spelling

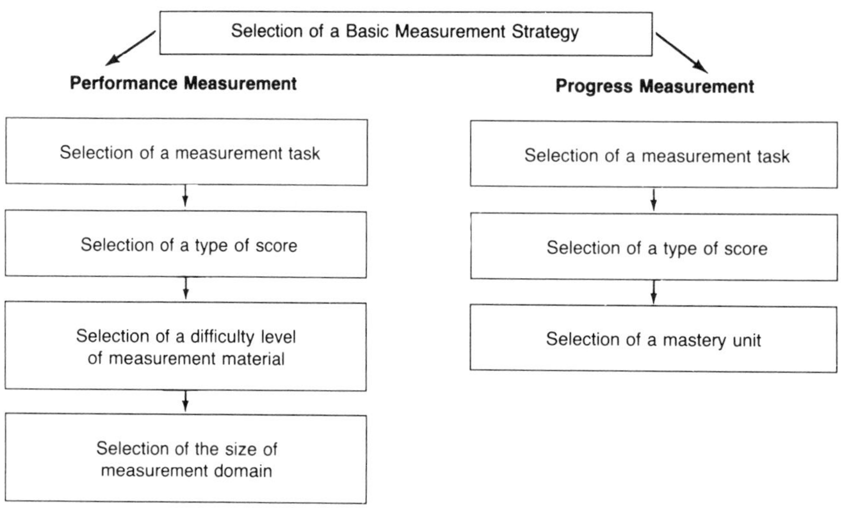

FIGURE 2 Decision Flow for Academic Domain of Written Expression

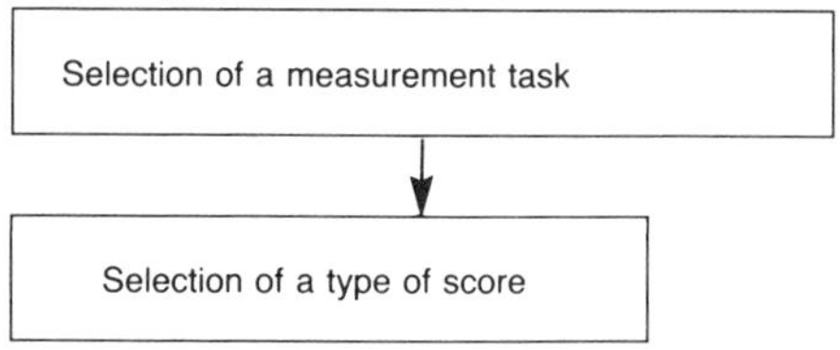

from a fourth-grade reader. Each day the teacher would select randomly a passage to measure student performance and ask the student to read aloud for 1 minute. With this strategy the student's graph might display the number of words correct and the number of errors per day during 1 minute of reading from the fourth-grade text.

As illustrated in the work of Deno and Mirkin (1977), *progress measurement,* a second strategy, involves monitoring student mastery through a curriculum over a period of time. In progress measurement, a sequence of objectives is specified and a criterion of mastery is established for each objective. Mastery of objectives then is assessed frequently to monitor student progress. For instance, a teacher might establish a series of phonics skills as the sequence of objectives to be mastered. Then the teacher might determine that a performance standard of reading 50 words per minute correctly with no more than two errors is the criterion of mastery to be met before a student can progress to the next objective. The student's graph, therefore, would display objectives mastered per time unit, and improved progress would be indicated by an increased rate of mastery through the objectives.

Performance and progress measurement are different in two essential ways:

1. In performance measurement, the measurement task is sampled constantly from the same pool of material; in progress measurement, the measurement task changes each time the student masters a segment of the curriculum;
2. In performance measurement, the goal is to describe changes in performance on one specific level of material; in progress measurement, the object is to describe the rate of progress through a series of tasks. Table 3 summarizes this concept.

Within each measurement strategy one must select a score (correct rate, percentage correct, or incorrect rate) to employ in analyzing the measurement sample. Depending on the level of student behavior, one might want to score small units of behaviors, such as letter sequences spelled correctly, or large units of behavior, such as words or even sentences spelled correctly. Depending on teacher time available to score, one might want to analyze types of phonetic errors or just number of errors.

Within performance measurement two additional decisions remain. First, one must determine *at what difficulty level management will occur* (e.g., at instructional level, at age/grade-appropriate material). This difficulty level remains constant as the

TABLE 3
Differences Between Progress and Performance Measurement

Type of Measure	Difficulty Level of Measurement Material	Goal
Performance	remains constant	to improve performance on same level of material
Progress	increases through a skills sequence	to improve rate of progress through increasingly more difficult material

student's proficiency changes. One also must select the *size of the measurement domain*. That is, given a difficulty level of material, one must determine the size of the material pool from which frequent measurement tasks will be sampled (from several grade levels of material, within one grade level of material, within one unit of material, etc.).

Within progress measurement, one additional decision remains. A *unit of mastery* (pages, stories, units, books in reading; words, lists, units, books in spelling) must be determined. Often this is problematic because curricula are not designed so that mastery units are equivalent—a requirement for a technically adequate measurement system.

Once the basic measurement is established, *measurement frequency* must be determined. Will measurement occur daily, twice per week, weekly, monthly? Further, one must establish student *mastery criteria*. Within progress measurement one must determine mastery criteria for each step or objective within the hierarchy of skills. Within performance measurement one must determine criteria that specify when acceptable performance has been met on the long-range goal or outcome behavior.

Three remaining decisions relevant to "How to Measure" involve (a) *procedures for generating test samples,* (b) *procedures for administering test,* and (c) *determining duration of test samples*—whether each measurement sample will involve a constant time (e.g., a duration of 30 seconds, 1 minute, 3 minutes) or fixed number of stimuli (e.g., 20 words, 30 words). These parameters specify the mechanics of measurement. The mechanics must be outlined and held constant if the measurement data are to be interpreted meaningfully. Generation of test samples refers to how the many equivalent measurement samples will be created. Administration of test samples relates to the standard procedures (directions, setting, schedule) employed in administering the measures. Duration of test samples addresses the length of time to administer a test.

Current Answers: "What" and "How" to Measure

Because CBM is a generic concept, various CBM systems have been developed and integrated into teaching systems (cf., Deno, Marston, & Tindal, 1986). Each of these systems has answered somewhat differently the questions of what and how to measure. In providing an example of how these questions might be answered, results of research and development of CBM through the Institute for Research on Learning Disabilities at the University of Minnesota, focusing on the areas of reading, spelling, and written expression, are used. That research is described elsewhere (cf., Deno, 1985; Deno, Marston, & Mirkin, 1982; Deno, Mirkin, & Chiang, 1982). Guidelines for answering what should be measured and how measurement should occur, derived from that research, are summarized below.

Reading

What to measure: Reading aloud from text passages randomly selected from one level of the school's basal reading series (elementary) or a subject matter text (secondary).

How to Measure and Score Reading Performance

1. Select one of the reading passages that corresponds to the appropriate level for the student's long-range goal.*
2. For each passage there are two forms—an unnumbered copy for the student and a numbered copy for the teacher. Put the student copy in front of and facing the student.
3. Put the teacher copy in front of and facing yourself.
4. Say to the student: "When I say 'start,' begin reading aloud at the top of this page. Try to read each word. If you wait for a word too long, I'll tell you the word. You can skip words that you don't know. At the end of one minute, I'll say 'stop.'" (Give student 3 seconds before supplying words.)
5. Turn on the stopwatch as you say "start."
6. Follow along on your copy, circling with a pencil incorrectly read words (omissions, substitutions, mispronunciations, insertions).
7. At 1 minute, say "stop" and turn off the stopwatch.
8. Place a slash after the last word read.
9. Count the number of words correct and the number of errors. (The teacher copy lists the number of words per line.)
10. Record both correct and incorrect scores on an equal-interval graph labeled "Number of Words Read Aloud from Text Passages."
11. Repeat steps 1–10 at least twice weekly.

Spelling

What to Measure: Writing words or letter sequences (White & Haring, 1980) dictated from a constant level of the school's spelling curriculum or basal reading series.

How to Measure and Score Spelling Performance

1. Find the spelling list that corresponds to the appropriate level for the student.*
2. Give the student a pencil and a response form with his/her name written on it.
3. Say to the student, "I am going to read some words to you. I want you to write the words on the sheet I just gave you. Write the words in the first column, and then go to the top of the second column. I'll give you 10 seconds to spell each word. When I say the next word, try to write it even if you haven't finished the last one."
4. Say, "Let's begin," as you start the stopwatch.
5. Begin, dictating each word in order. In the case of homonyms, a short sentence incorporating appropriate use of the word should be presented following pronunciation of the word.

---

* *Ask regular classroom teachers what the expected curricular level of average students of the same age and grade as the target student will be at the time of the next annual review. For additional information on placement criteria, see Mirkin, Deno, et al. (1981).*

6. Present each word upon the student's completion of the previous word. After 10 seconds present the next word even if the student has not completed the previous word.
7. Dictate words for 2 minutes. If the student is near completion of a word and the time is up, allow him/her to finish that word. Do not present any new words in the last 3 seconds of the test.
8. Count the number of correctly spelled words or correct letter sequences.
9. Record correct scores on an equal-interval graph labeled "Number of Words Correct/Incorrect" or "Number of Letter Sequences Correct/Incorrect."
10. Repeat steps 1–9 at least twice weekly.

Written Expression

What to Measure: Writing words or letters in stories in response to a story starter or topic sentence.

How to Measure and Score Written Expression Performance

1. Give the child a pencil and a response form. (Story starters may be individually or group administered.)
2. Give the student the following instructions. "Today I want you to write a story. I am going to read a sentence to you first, and then I want you to write a short story about what happens. You will have 1 minute to think about the story you want to write and then have 3 minutes to write it. When I say 'begin', start writing."
3. Time the student as he/she writes for 3 minutes.
4. When 3 minutes have elapsed, tell the student to stop writing.
5. Count the total number of words or letters written in the composition, including words spelled incorrectly. Count all personal nouns and names. Do not count numbers.
6. Record the total number of words or letters written by the student on an equal-interval chart labeled "Number of Words or Letters Written."
7. Repeat steps 1–6 at least twice weekly.

As is evident in this description of the Minnesota CBM procedures, the measurement procedures are standardized, even as the stimulus items for the test are generated from the local school curriculum. These standardized measurement procedures produce reliable data that also have demonstrated validity for making special education programming decisions (cf., Germann & Tindal, 1985; Marston & Magnusson, 1985).

Measurement Issues: "How to Use Data"

Evidence suggests that teachers who collect student performance data do not necessarily use those data to make instructional decisions (Baldwin, 1976; White, 1977), and that systematic procedures for interpreting student performance data appear to be an important dimension of an effective CBM. In a meta-analysis, Fuchs and Fuchs (1986b) found that the effectiveness of CBM was enhanced when teachers used a systematic data utilization strategy. For that reason, careful attention should be given to how CBM data will be recorded, graphed, and interpreted. The decision-making matrix presented in Table 1 is used as a framework for considering data utilization strategies with CBM.

Charting Student Progress

A feature common to virtually all approaches to CBM is that student progress over days is displayed visually. The number of charting options is great (Deno & Mirkin, 1977). The procedures described here focus on those selected for use with the CBM systems developed at the University of Minnesota.

A first decision that has to be made is whether to chart mastery of successive levels of the curriculum (progress measurement) or to chart change in proficiency on a level of constant difficulty (performance measurement). For progress measurement, cumulative units of curriculum per time unit are graphed. For performance measurement, changing levels of performance on samples from the same material pool per time unit are graphed. Few alternative procedures are available within each measurement format. Further, little evidence supports the superiority of any one graphing procedure. Given the lack of research data, the technical, effectiveness, and logistical constraints influencing the decision of what and how to graph progress are grouped below and discussed by basic measurement strategy.

A critical problem in *progress measurement* is the lack of equal intervals to represent curriculum units along the vertical axis. Therefore, an essential rationale for employing a particular graphing convention within progress measurement is how it resolves this problem.

Deno and Mirkin (1977) advocated a graphing procedure wherein mastery units along the vertical axis are plotted so that the units are spaced in accordance with the mastery time demonstrated by average students. The feasibility of this approach has been demonstrated by Peterson, Heistad, Peterson, and Reynolds (1985). The graph is organized so that for the average student the level of progress is one-to-one; for each time unit the average student is expected to master the number of pages or stories designated for that period. Average rate of progress through the curriculum, then, is depicted by a diagonal line from the lower left corner to the upper right corner of the graph.

A problem inherent in the progress measurement graph is that curricula are not designed so that the mastery units sequentially plotted at these equal intervals actually represent equivalent segments of the curriculum. For example, if a story is more difficult than the one it follows, the second story represents a larger unit of mastery even though the two stories were plotted as equal units.

Although no available research addresses the relative effectiveness or logistical feasibility of alternative mastery units, selection of a mastery unit can be based on technical considerations. Selection of a very small mastery unit should increase the probability that units on the vertical axis will represent equal intervals. Pages are much more likely to be equivalent mastery units than are stories, clusters of stories, or entire books.

An additional advantage in selecting a very small mastery unit is that it virtually ensures that the data will be sensitive to student change. With pages as the mastery unit, students easily can register growth. In contradistinction, if books are the unit of mastery, the measurement format might be insensitive to student improvement because the pupil would have to gain much proficiency before mastering an entire book and registering any growth. Therefore, both of these technical considerations—approximating equivalent mastery units and ensuring sensitivity to student growth—support the use of a relatively small mastery unit within a measurement and evaluation system.

With respect to additional graphing conventions within progress measurement, logistical and instructional considerations support students graphing their own data. Once students are competent graphers, this procedure should reduce teacher time and therefore improve the feasibility of frequent measurement. Additionally, Frumess (1973) demonstrated that students who scored and graphed their daily reading performance achieved significantly better than students who only scored their performance.

Within *performance measurement,* the relative merits of equal-interval and semi-logarithmic paper have been explored. In two crossover studies, Brandstetter and Merz (1978) compared the reinforcement value of semi-log graphs and linear graphs with the reinforcement value of raw scores. In the first study, reading gains made while charting on linear graphs were significantly greater than gains made while recording raw scores. In the second study, the difference between charting on semi-log graphs and recording raw scores was not significant. Because the children in both studies were neither randomly assigned nor similar to each other, however, valid comparisons cannot be made between the effectiveness of the two types of graphs.

Marston (in press) compared the prediction capabilities of both types of charts. After calculating the performance slope for each of 82 elementary students who were measured weekly over 7 weeks, predictions of student scores for weeks 8, 9, and 10 were determined. Actual student performance for weeks 8, 9, and 10 then was compared to the predictions made with equal-interval and semi-logarithmic charts. For the academic areas of reading, spelling, and written expression, predictions were significantly better on the equal-interval graphs. Therefore, given that teachers may prefer equal-interval graphs and find them easier to interpret and share with students, currently available research on graphing, albeit scant, seems to indicate the use of equal-interval graphs.

Data Interpretation

Once student performance data have been collected and graphed, the educator must summarize and interpret these data to determine whether the instructional program appears effective or whether that program should be changed. Two approaches to data summarization and interpretation are goal-oriented and program-oriented analyses.

In *goal-oriented data analysis,* the objective is to ensure that a student's performance reaches a prespecified goal by a certain date. This goal may represent any reasonable performance level selected by the teacher. Or, in a more systematic fashion and in consonance with the principles of normalization (Wolfensberger, 1972), this goal may be a performance level (a) commensurate with a student's mainstream peers, or (b) representing a reduced discrepancy between the student's current performance and his or her age/grade appropriate level.* This goal, designated the "static aim" (Liberty, 1972, 1975), is marked on the graph with an X at the intersection of the desired performance level and the anticipated attainment date. Then a line of desired progress, the "dynamic aim," connects the student's baseline median score with the static aim on the graph.

Throughout the delivery of instruction, data summarization consists primarily of determining median performance within intervention periods. Data interpretation consists of application of some form of the following rule: If on N consecutive days (2, 3, or more), student performance data fall below the dynamic aimline, the program is judged ineffective and should be changed. Two possible consequences are: (a) A new aimline is drawn on the graph, parallel to the old aimline but originating from the intersection of the middle day on which performance was inadequate and the median performance level of those inadequate data points, or (b) the student's program is changed. A change in the program is designated on the graph with a vertical line running through the data on which the program change was introduced.

In *program-oriented data analysis,* the student performance level and attainment date may be specified but are not essential to data utilization. Instead, the directive is to test changes in a student's program frequently and systematically, to move the student's performance toward the highest possible rate of improvement. One assumes that only by implementing an unending series of program changes and by comparing the effects of those program changes on a student's performance can an effective individual program emerge (Deno, & Mirkin, 1977). Therefore, program changes are introduced regularly and are treated as experimental hypotheses to be tested by observing their effect on a student's performance.

Data Summarization

In goal-oriented analyses, drawing trend lines through actual student progress is the primary method of summarizing student performance. By contrast, data summarization in a program-oriented analysis is more comprehensive. Data interpretation is directed toward judging the effectiveness of a program or experimental treatment by comparing student performance across different interventions.

The four indices of performance are: (a) the *median,* a measure of central tendency representing the score that falls at the 50th percentile; (b) the *trend,* a line of

* *Ask regular classroom teachers what the expected curricular level of average students of the same age and grade as the target student will be at the time of the next annual review. For additional information on placement criteria, see Mirkin, Deno, et al. (1981).*

best fit through the data points, which indicates how fast and in what direction student performance is changing; (c) the *shift* up or down on the first day of intervention (i.e., the size and direction of the difference between the last data point of the previous intervention and the first data point of the current program); and (d) the *variability* or "bounce" (Pennypacker, Koenig, & Lindsley, 1972) of the data points around the trend line. These indices are compared across phases of a program to determine whether a program change has improved student performance. Changes in median, trend, step up/down, or variability among phases are inspected and interpreted to formulate decisions about the effectiveness of programs.

Constraints and Current Answers: "How to Use Data"

Technical Considerations

In exploring the technical strengths of goal- and program-oriented data summarization and interpretation, two relevant considerations are (a) accuracy of judgments and (b) interjudge agreement. With respect to the *accuracy of judgments,* goal-oriented analysis appears to be stronger (Tindal, Wesson, Mirkin, Deno, & Fuchs, 1982). Ten teachers in a rural special education cooperative were assigned randomly and then trained to use either a goal-oriented or program-oriented procedure to analyze their students' graphs. Midway through the study each teacher crossed over to the other data analysis condition. Results indicated that, by the end of the study, teachers summarized data more accurately with the goal-oriented analysis rules (47% vs. 12% correct summarizations), and the timing of changes in students' programs was more accurate with the goal-based rules (70% vs. 33% correctly timed changes).

With respect to *interjudge reliability,* program-oriented analysis may be stronger. In the same study (Tindal et al., 1982), teachers' judgments with the program-oriented analysis rules were more reliable for both when program changes should be introduced (76% vs. 62% agreements) and when program changes were producing student growth (88% vs. 74% agreements).

The technical superiority of one data summarization/utilization method over the other, therefore, has not been established clearly. Program-oriented analysis appears to be more reliable and goal-oriented analysis more accurate. Certainly, differences in the results were larger and more dramatic for the reliability contrasts; goal-oriented accuracy was an average 3 times greater. On the basis of these results, one might conclude tentatively that each data utilization method has some technical strength. Perhaps the goal-oriented method renders more correct, and therefore technically superior, decisions.

Effectiveness Considerations

Scant evidence exists for the superiority of either data utilization procedure in producing greater student gains. Available studies have contrasted the relative effectiveness of monitoring short-term objectives using weekly aimlines with monitoring long-term objectives using program-oriented methods (Mirkin, Fuchs, Tindal, Christenson, & Deno, 1981; Tindal, Fuchs, Christenson, Mirkin, & Deno, 1981). Results indicated that teachers believed they were more effective in the short-term objective conditions, even though there actually were no student performance differences.

Perhaps the only piece of evidence directly contrasting goal- and program-oriented methods supports the instructional effectiveness of a goal-oriented analysis because of its effect on teacher behavior. Tindal et al. (1982) demonstrated that teachers more accurately judged effective interventions when they applied goal-oriented analysis procedures (100% vs. 80% accurate judgments).

Logistical Considerations

Goal-oriented analysis also appears stronger for two logistical reasons. First, data summarization is less time consuming; it entails the computation of one rather than four statistics. Second, over two training sessions in the study described above (Tindal et al., 1982), teachers were more accurate in the goal-oriented analysis group (79% vs. 68% correct decisions). Therefore, goal-oriented analysis methods appear to be more feasible because they are less time consuming during both training and day-to-day implementation.

Nevertheless, evidence suggests that teachers may prefer a combination of the two data utilization methods. Fuchs, Wesson, Tindal, Mirkin, and Deno (1982) found that teachers preferred the goal-oriented approach for (a) monitoring progress toward IEP goals, (b) the ease of its use, (c) its efficiency, (d) a guide concerning when to change a student's instructional program, (e) the ease with which it could be described to parents and other teachers, (f) its more adequate representation of student performance, and (g) its overall usefulness. The program-oriented approach was preferred by most teachers only as a guide for what to change in a student's instructional program.

When asked to name the data utilization system of their choice, one-half of the surveyed teachers indicated that they preferred to use a combination of the two approaches. Therefore, despite the teachers' overwhelming preference for goal-oriented evaluation, many chose a combination of the two. This finding may be attributed to the fact that goal-oriented evaluation addresses the question of *when,* not what, to change in a student's program and that teachers preferred program-oriented evaluation for determining *what* to change in an educational plan. For handicapped children, the question of what to change may be especially problematic. This may have led some teachers to conclude that a combination of the two strategies is optimal.

A strong experimental contrast of the two data utilization strategies, one with dramatic and persuasive results, currently is not available. Nevertheless, evidence suggests that a goal-oriented analysis may be more technically adequate, more feasible, more efficient, and more instructionally useful. Given these results, along with teachers' preference for a combination of the two data utilization approaches, a combined data utilization method that borrows more heavily from the goal-oriented approach is recommended.

In this approach (Mirkin, Deno, et al., 1981), teachers draw the dynamic aimline on the graph. Then a trendline based on 7 to 10 student performance data points is graphed and compared to the slope of the dynamic aimline. If the student performance slope is less steep than the aimline, a program change is introduced. Logistically, this data utilization rule is facilitated by the availability of computer software packages whereby teachers can enter student performance data and access a student graph with aimline and a decision concerning whether a program change is indicated.

In a significant experimental study comparing the effectiveness of teachers using CBM procedures to those not using CBM procedures, this combination strategy was employed (Fuchs, Deno, & Mirkin, 1984), with significant achievement benefits accruing to students taught with CBM. Therefore, tentative support for the value of this combined CBM data-utilization approach is provided.

USING CBM TO DATA-BASE A STUDENT'S PROGRAM: A CASE STUDY

CBM Decision Sequence

As presented above, the process of formulating a CBM system entails a 10-step sequence. Each of these decisions is reviewed here, illustrating how a special education teacher, Mrs. R., applied the decision-making matrix to design a CBM strategy for one specific student, Michael, for the purpose of formatively developing an effective instructional program.

1. *What to Measure: Selection of a Behavior*

Consistent with the recommended CBM procedures, Mrs. R. decided that she would measure Michael's reading aloud from text. Reading aloud from text increases developmentally and demonstrates both construct and criterion validity (see Deno, Mirkin & Chiang, 1982). Measuring reading aloud in context provides rich information for making sound program improvement decisions and is easy to measure relative to other reading behaviors (see Mirkin, Fuchs, & Deno, 1982).

2. *How to Measure: Selection of a Basic Strategy*

Mrs. R. decided that her basic measurement strategy would be performance measurement. She decided to select one level of difficulty for the reading selections on which she would measure Michael's progress with a goal of improving Michael's performance on that material. Because neither progress nor performance measurement had a clear advantage, Mrs. R. chose performance measurement because of personal preference.

3. *How to Measure: Selection of a Score, a Difficulty Level, and a Measurement Domain*

Mrs. R. chose to record the number of correctly and incorrectly read words as the scores she would monitor. She selected level 2 of the SRA Series as the material from which she would draw selections for measuring Michael's reading aloud in context because it represented a mid-range difficulty for Michael. (He initially read 55 words per minute correct with no more than 11 errors.) She decided to monitor correct and error scores because the correct scores represent technically adequate data and the error scores would provide supplemental information for generating instructional hypotheses (see Mirkin et al., 1982).

Having decided on correct and error scores, as well as Level 2 of the SRA series, Mrs. R was ready now to determine what the size of the measurement domain would be. She decided on a mid-sized domain, all of Level 2, because it was likely to render data with relatively low variability and with an acceptable slope; further, it probably would remain an appropriate difficulty level for Michael over the entire school year (see Fuchs, Tindal, & Deno, 1984).

4. *How to Measure: Selection of a Measurement Frequency and a Sample Duration*

Given the associated technical, logistical, and effectiveness constraints (see Mirkin et al., 1982), Mrs. R. selected a schedule of at least twice weekly and a sample duration of 1 minute.

5. *How to Measure: Selection of a Criterion of Mastery or Goal*

Mrs. R. decided on a mastery criterion of 80 words correct with no more than 8 errors (a 90% accuracy criterion). This criterion of mastery or goal represented to Mrs. R a reasonable but ambitious amount of improvement for Michael. Additionally, it fell close to the recommended rates (see Fuchs, Fuchs, & Deno, 1982; Mirkin et al., 1982).

6. *How to Measure: Selection of a Procedure for Generating Test Samples*

Mrs. R. used a random selection procedure for generating test samples, wherein she (a) selected passages from the level representing the annual goal and wrote on equal-size slips of paper the number of each of the pages in stories that did not have excessive dialogue, indentations, or unusual pronouns; (b) put the slips of paper into a drawbag and shook it; (c) randomly picked a slip of paper; and (d) had the student begin reading on the page number shown on the slip of paper (see Mirkin, Deno, et al., 1981).

7. *How to Measure: Selection of Administration and Scoring Procedures*

Once the practitioner has defined a measurement system, only a few alternatives exist for administering and scoring tests. The two primary considerations in choosing among alternatives are: (a) *technical*—maintaining consistent procedures across testing occasions, and (b) *logistical*—designing efficient administration and scoring procedures. Mrs. R. used the CBM procedures described for reading that were presented above (see Mirkin, Deno, et al., 1981, for rationale).

8. *Specification of a Goal and Objective Form*

Having specified "What to Measure" and "How to Measure," Mrs. R. was ready to complete the following Goal and Objective Form.

Goal In ______19 weeks______, when presented with stories for 1 minute from
(# school weeks until year's end)
Level 2-SRA Series, ____Michael____, will read aloud ______80______ with no
(Level #, series) (student's name) (words per minute correct)
more than __6__ errors.
(#)

Objective Each successive week, when presented with a random selection for 1 minute from Level 2-SRA Series, the student will read aloud at an average increase
(same level # and series as above)
of 2.6 words per week and no increase in errors.
(#)

9. *Specification of a Measurement System Form*

To summarize further the decisions Mrs. R. made, she next completed the Measurement System Form.

Behavior: reading aloud in context
Frequency: at least twice weekly
Duration of Test: 1 minute
Difficulty Level: Level 2—SRA Series
Size of Domain: all of Level 2
Test Administration Procedure: see description
Scoring Procedure: see description

10. *How to Use Data*

Having specified what and how she would measure, Mrs. R. had to determine how she would use the data she collected. The first decision she made was to graph the data on equal-interval paper. Figure 3 displays Michael's graph with "Words Read Per Minute" on the vertical axis and "Months" (and school days within them) on the horizontal axis. The first three data points on this figure indicate Michael's baseline performance (A) on the Level 2 material. The vertical lines following these baseline data indicate the introduction of new dimensions into Michael's reading program. These program dimensions are labeled A, B, and C at the top of the vertical lines. The large X on the right side of the graph indicates the mastery criterion or goal that Mrs. R. set for Michael. The diagonal line from the baseline median to the X is Michael's dynamic aimline, depicting the rate of progress Michael would have to exhibit to meet his goal as anticipated.

With this graph established, Mrs. R. could plot data points and easily see, on any given day, how Michael's performance compared to his dynamic aim, or the level at which he had to perform to reach the long-term goal. Then Mrs. R. adopted the combined data utilization rule described previously: If a trendline drawn through the last 7 to 10 data points was greater than or equal to the slope of the dynamic aimline, she

FIGURE 3 Example of Correct Words and Errors Per Minute by Michael Across Time and Using Three Instructional Strategies

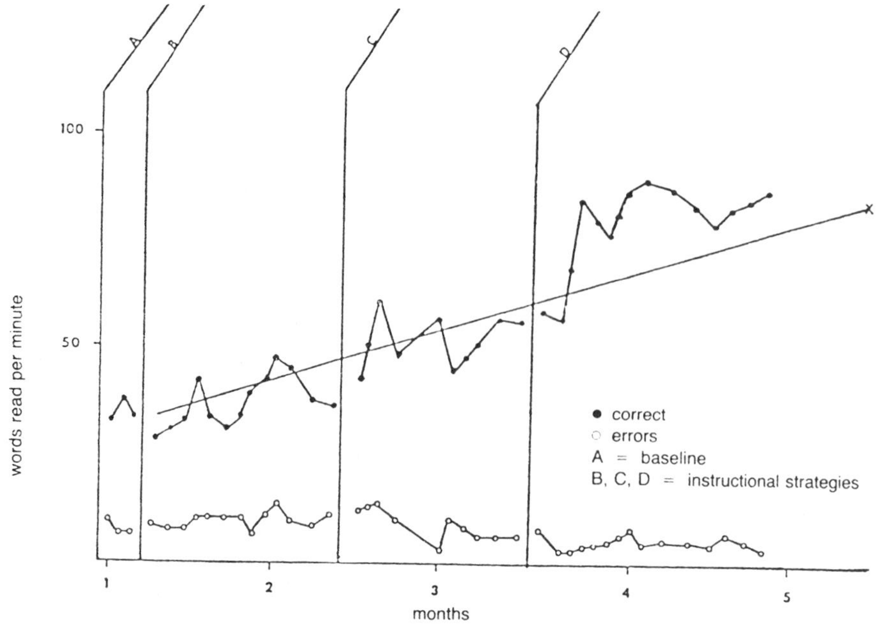

maintained the student's program; if the trendline was less than the aimline slope, she introduced a change into Michael's program. With the introduction of the third program change, Michael's performance improved dramatically over his previous performance.

Using the decision framework and procedures described here to formulate a CBM system, Mrs. R. established a close connection between the instruction she provided Michael and the way she measured and evaluated his progress. With this measurement and evaluation system, Michael's educational program and progress toward goals was evaluated formatively. In response to measurement data, Michael's program was modified throughout the school year to improve his reading achievement.

SUMMARY AND CONCLUSIONS

CBM is a data-based strategy by which special education problems can be solved and by which decisions about referral, program development, and summative evaluation can be formulated. With CBM, assessment demonstrates strong curricular validity, addresses the overall special education goal for competence within mainstream curricula, and is easily understood. Nevertheless, designing a comprehensive, reliable, and valid CBM system that simultaneously is instructionally effective and logistically feasible can be difficult. A decision-making framework, employing technical, instructional, and logistical considerations for determining what to measure, how to measure, and how to use data, can systematize the process of specifying CBM systems and result in more adequate measurement, along with improved special education problem solving.

The procedures selected and described here may incorporate answers based on the most currently available empirical investigation, but further unresolved issues represent fertile territory for additional research to illustrate many sound CBM procedures. In addition to facilitating the design of measurement systems, the decision-making matrix represents a useful framework for conceptualizing useful research questions in the area of curriculum-based measurement.

REFERENCES

Armbruster, B. B., Stevens, R. G., & Rosenshine, B. (1977). *Analyzing content coverage and emphasis: A study of three curricula and two tests.* (Technical Report N26). Urbana: University of Illinois, Center for the Study of Reading.

Baldwin, V. (1976). Curriculum concerns. In M. A. Thomas (Ed.), *Hey, don't forget about me.* Reston, VA: Council for Exceptional Children.

Brandstetter, G., & Merz, C. (1978). Charting scores in precision teaching for skill acquisition, *Exceptional Children, 45*(1), 42–48.

Deno, E. N. (1970). Special education as developmental capital. *Exceptional Children, 37*(3), 229–237.

Deno, S. (1985). Curriculum-based measurement: The emerging alternative, *52*(3), 219–231.

Deno, S., Marston, D., & Mirkin, P. (1982). Valid measurement procedures for continuous evaluation of written expression. *Exceptional Children, 48*(4), 368–371.

Deno, S., Marston, D., & Tindal, G. (1986). Direct and frequent curriculum-based measurement: An alternative for educational decision making. *Special Services in the Schools, 2*, 5–27.

Deno, S. L., & Mirkin, P. K. (1977). *Data based program modification: A manual.* Arlington, VA: Council for Exceptional Children.

Deno, S., Mirkin, P., & Chiang, B. (1982). Identifying valid measures of reading. *Exceptional Children, 49*(1), 36–45.

Frumess, S. (1973). *A comparison of management groups involving the use of the standard behavior chart.* Unpublished doctoral dissertation, University of Texas.

Fuchs, L., Deno, S., & Mirkin, P. (1984). The effects of frequent curriculum-based measurement and evaluation on pedagogy, student achievement and student awareness of learning. *American Educational Research Journal, 21*(2), 449–460.

Fuchs, L. S., & Fuchs, D. (1986a). Curriculum-based assessment of progress toward long- and short-term goals. *Journal of Special Education, 20*, 69–82.

Fuchs, L. S., & Fuchs, D. (1986b.). Effects of systematic formative evaluation: A meta-analysis. *Exceptional Children, 53*, 199–208.

Fuchs, L. S., Fuchs, D., & Deno, S. L. (1982). Reliability and validity of curriculum-based informal reading inventories. *Reading Research Quarterly, 18*, 6–26.

Fuchs, L. S., Tindal, G., & Deno, S. L. (1984). Methodological issues in curriculum-based assessment. *Diagnostique, 9*, 191–207.

Fuchs, L., Wesson, C., Tindal, G., Mirkin, P., & Deno, S. (1981). *Teacher efficiency in continuous evaluation of IEP goals (Research Report No. 53). Minneapolis: University of Minnesota, Institute for Research on Learning Disabilities.*

Fuchs, L., Wesson, C., Tindal, G., Mirkin, P., & Deno, S. (1982). *Instructional changes, student performance, and teacher preferences: The effects of specific measurement and evaluation procedures* (Research Report No. 64). Minneapolis: University of Minnesota, Institute for Research on Learning Disabilities.

Galagan, J. (1985). Psychoeducational testing: Turn out the lights, the party's over. *Exceptional Children, 52*(3), 288–298.

Germann, G., & Tindal, G. (1985). An application of curriculum-based assessment: The use of direct and repeated measurement. *Exceptional Children, 52*(3), 288–298.

Howell, K. (1986). Direct assessment of academic performance. In L. S. Fuchs & D. Fuchs (Eds.), Linking assessment to instructional intervention. *School Psychology Review, 15*, 324–335.

Jenkins, J., & Pany, D. (1978). Standardized achievement tests: How useful for special education? *Exceptional Children, 44*, 448–453.

Liberty, K. A. (1972). *Data decision rules* (Working Paper No. 20). Eugene: University of Oregon, Regional Resources Center.

Liberty, K. A. (1975). *Decide for progress: Dynamic aims and data decisions*. Seattle: University of Washington, Experimental Education Unit, Child Development and Mental Retardation Center.

Marston, D. (in press). Measuring academic progress of students with learning difficulties: A comparison of the semi-logarithmic chart and equal interval graph paper. *Exceptional Children*.

Marston, D., Deno, S., & Mirkin, P. (1984). Curriculum-based measurement: An alternative to traditional screening, referral and identification. *Journal of Special Education, 18*(2), 109–117.

Marston, D., & Magnusson, D. (1985). Implementing curriculum-based measurement in special and regular education settings. *Exceptional Children, 52*(3), 266–276.

Mirkin, P., Deno, S., Fuchs, L., Wesson, C., Tindal, G., Marston, D., & Kuehnle, K. (1981). *Procedures to develop and monitor procedures toward progress on IEP goals*. Minneapolis: University of Minnesota, Institute for Research on Learning Disabilities.

Mirkin, P., Fuchs, L., & Deno, S. (1982). *Considerations for designing a continuous evaluation system: An integrative review* (Monograph No. 20). Minneapolis: University of Minnesota, Institute for Research on Learning Disabilities.

Mirkin, P., Fuchs, L., Tindal, G., Christenson, S., & Deno, S. (1981). *The effect of IEP monitoring strategies on teacher behavior* (Research Report No. 62). Minneapolis: University of Minnesota, Institute for Research on Learning Disabilities.

Pennypacker, H. S., Koenig, C. H., & Lindsley, O. R. (1972). *Handbook of the standard behavior chart* (prelim.). Kansas City, KS: Precision Media.

Peterson, J., Heistad, D., Peterson, D., & Reynolds, M. (1985). Montevideo individualized prescriptive instructional management systems. *Exceptional Children, 52*(3), 239–243.

Shinn, M., & Marston, D. (1985). Differentiating mildly handicapped, low achieving and regular education students: A curriculum-based approach. *Remedial & Special Education, 6*(2), 31–38.

Tindal, G., Fuchs, L., Christenson, S., Mirkin, P., & Deno, S. (1981). *The relationship between student achievement and teacher assessment of short- or long-term goals*. (Research Report No. 61). Minneapolis: University of Minnesota, Institute for Research on Learning Disabilities.

Tindal, G., Wesson, C., Mirkin, P., Deno, S., & Fuchs, L. (1982). *Comparison of goal-oriented and program-oriented data utilization procedures* (Research Report in preparation). Minneapolis: University of Minnesota, Institute for Research on Learning Disabilities.

Tucker, J. (1985). Curriculum-based assessment: An introduction. *Exceptional Children, 52*(3), 199–204.

Wesson, C., King, R. P., & Deno, S. (1984). Direct and frequent measurement of student performance: If it's good for us, why don't we do it? *Learning Disability Quarterly, 7*(1), 45–48.

White, O. R. (1977). Behaviorism in special education: An area for debate. In R. D. Kneedler & S. G. Tarver (Eds.), *Changing perspectives in special education*. Columbus, OH: Charles E. Merrill.

White, O. R., & Haring, N. G. (1980). *Exceptional teaching (2nd ed.)*. Columbus, OH: Charles E. Merrill.

Wolfensberger, W. (1972). *The principle of normalization in human services*. Toronto: National Institute on Mental Retardation.

Dr. Deno is a Professor in the Department of Educational Psychology, Special Education Programs, University of Minnesota. Dr. Fuchs is Assistant Professor, Department of Special Education, Peabody College of Vanderbilt University.

High levels of academic responding are directly related to achievement gains. This is a statement that probably will stand without challenge, a truism. Yet, how many educators are aware that the interactions among (a) subject matter, (b) materials and instruction, and (c) students produce differential rates of responding? Greenwood and Carta describe a system to Code for Instructional Structure and Student Academic Response (CISSAR). This code enables a teacher or assessment specialist to analyze the ecology of the classroom—the interdependent interaction between a child and conditions for learning. Applying the code results in data across student behaviors and tasks, which are used to determine which combinations of subjects and instructional approaches result in high levels of academic responding. This is important information to know because some combinations, such as passive attention during lectures, are not conducive to achievement gains.

At first inspection the modified CISSAR described in this chapter may seem unduly complicated for classroom use. Such is not the case, because with practice and cross-checks by colleagues, it can be used successfully and accurately. As will be noted upon reading the article, the ecobehavioral approach offers a major advancement when compared to child deficit and environmental deficit approaches to problem-solving interventions. An ecobehavioral approach uses precise measurement procedures of applied behavior analysis within the context of student-environment interactions. It is a major contribution to the special education profession.

An Ecobehavioral Interaction Analysis of Instruction Within Special Education

Charles R. Greenwood and Judith J. Carta

A fundamental principle in special education is that the performance outcomes of instruction must be assessed in order to evaluate the success of educational programs. But little general agreement exists on exactly how this assessment should be conducted (e.g., Deno, 1985). We have identified three general approaches to the assessment of instruction and instructional outcomes: (a) the deficit approach, (b) the environmental-adequacy approach, and (c) the environment-behavior interaction approach (Greenwood, Schulte, Kohler, Dinwiddie, & Carta, 1986).

The deficit approach is based upon the premise that the student is deficient in terms of organismic, cognitive, or behavioral variables, or any combination thereof. Assessment and treatment based upon this approach focus on identifying the deficit areas and providing the necessary instruction or prosthetic intervention to ameliorate them. This approach has given rise to the many categories of handicaps and disabilities in the field of special education and the wealth of intervention and instructional methods focusing on these particular problems.

The environmental-adequacy approach is based upon the assumption that the environment in which the student is operating lacks the features necessary to support the student's performance (e.g., Bijou, 1981; Engelmann, Granzin, & Severson, 1979). Assessment and treatment based upon this approach are directed at identifying ineffective aspects of the home, school, and community environments and correcting them. This approach has given us the various service delivery settings (e.g., residential, resource room, mainstream) and special education professionals (e.g., resource room teachers, itinerant teachers) trained to provide specific educational services (e.g., Peterson, Zabel, Smith, & White, 1983). This approach has also heavily influenced our initiatives for least restrictive placements, optimal classroom and school physical structures, and the removal of barriers.

A third, and rapidly growing, approach is that of ecobehavioral interaction (e.g., Greenwood, Dinwiddie, et al., 1984; Rogers-Warren, 1984). This approach rests on the premise that students' interactions with environmental (or ecological) factors either optimize or limit their performance. The assumption is that assessment focusing exclusively on student performance or on the instructional program is inadequate and seldom leads to optimal learning outcomes.

The ecobehavioral approach is a recent development within the field of applied behavior analysis. It combines ecological psychologists' concerns with "broader" aspects of the environment (e.g., Barker, 1968) with strategies for observational assessment and the designs of applied behavior analysis (Baer, Wolf, & Risley, 1968). As Bijou and Baer (1978) noted:

> The interaction between the child and the environment is continuous, reciprocal, and interdependent. We cannot analyze a child without reference to an environment, nor is it possible to analyze an environment without reference to a child. The two form an inseparable unit consisting of an interrelated set of variables, or an interactional field (p. 29).

The ecobehavioral approach is an attempt to operationalize this interactional field. It requires that student performance be observed and assessed concurrently with specific instructional variables within the classroom environment. For example, in an ecobehavioral approach to assessment, student performance would be measured in relationship to teacher behavior.

This approach to assessment rejects the notion that instruction should be uniform for all students. What goes on in one special classroom and what one student receives may not be identical in terms of goals, objectives, and curriculum to what is received by a student in the same class, the one next door, in the next building, or in the next state. Students' academic gains within a classroom setting depend heavily on the nature of instruction during individual lessons and what students do during these lessons. Student performance therefore must be evaluated in terms of the multitude of factors that define instruction and how those factors change from moment to moment and day to day.

> The ecobehavioral approach to program evaluation "is a means of assessing program variables through systematic observation and measuring the moment-to-moment effects of an array of variables upon student behavior. The temporal interactions between immediate program variables as ecological factors and student behaviors are the units of analysis for predicting or otherwise investigating program outcomes (e.g., developmental gain or long-term achievement)" (Carta & Greenwood, 1985, p. 92).

Using the ecobehavioral approach to assessment, student behaviors during a lesson, for example, will be evaluated in relationship to the actual activities and materials presented, size and location of the instructional group, and the teacher behavior that accompanies them. As a result, student behaviors can be quantified within very specific contexts of instruction. One can examine the extent to which instruction actually occurs, how it changes over time, and the extent to which the observed student response is congruent with the goals of instruction (Greenwood et al., 1981; Ysseldyke & Algozzine, 1982).

Ultimately, the ecobehavioral approach to assessment can provide teachers with information about their classrooms and their teaching that can be most helpful in arranging more effective instruction. It can provide answers to the following questions:

- What are the best ways to arrange the classroom environment (e.g., use of activities, materials, instructional groups) to optimize particular forms of performance?
- How can modifications in instructional practices influence student behavior?
- What are the promoters of these behaviors?

WHY ASSESS ECOLOGICAL VARIABLES?

The ecology of a special education environment is composed of both physical and social structures. These include the physical arrangements of classrooms, homes, and community and related service settings. It is widely recognized that physical structures mediate the performance of persons within them. Similarly, social structures—the interactions with caregivers, teachers, and peers—provide the contexts for behavior in ways that either facilitate or hinder performance. Ecological factors define the "standing patterns of behavior" that can operate. Without information concerning the physical and social structure of environments, an analysis of student performance cannot be completed.

WHY ASSESS STUDENT BEHAVIOR VARIABLES?

Students' behavior within special education has been a traditional measure of the effects of special education. Research has demonstrated clearly that specific student behaviors, such as attention to task and task orientation (defined as looking, writing, and speaking during instruction) are correlates of academic achievement (e.g., Rosenshine & Stevens, 1986). Recent research has refined these findings and determined that student achievement is highly related to the actual time spent in behaviors relative to specific instructional topics. Obviously, what students do during lessons has a profound effect on learning outcomes regardless of how they are measured (e.g., as curriculum-based measures, criterion-referenced measures, or standardized achievement measures).

ECOBEHAVIORAL FINDINGS FROM RESEARCH ON TEACHING

In our work we have developed several ecobehavioral observation systems including the Code for Instructional Structure (CISSAR) (Stanley & Greenwood, 1981; Greenwood & Delquadri, in press), the CISSAR-Special Education version (Rotholz, Whorton, McGrale, Norris, & Greenwood, 1985), the CISSAR-Mainstream version (Carta et al., 1987), and the Ecobehavioral System for Complex Assessment of Preschool Environments (ESCAPE) (Carta, Greenwood, & Atwater, 1985; Carta, Greenwood, & Robinson, 1987). These systems have been used in both descriptive and experimental studies of instruction.

We have reported that specific academic responses (i.e., reading aloud, talk academic, writing) were better correlates of achievement than passive attention defined as "looking at the teacher" (e.g., Greenwood et al., 1981; Stanley & Greenwood, 1983). Specific ecological arrangements were associated with low levels of academic responding. We defined these arrangements, which included relatively frequent use of audiovisual media and teacher-student discussion, as "decelerator variables" (Greenwood et al., 1985). Arrangements that increased academic responding, called "accelerator arrangements," included the frequent use of readers and paper-and-pencil tasks. Interestingly, we found that teachers in the suburbs more frequently incorporated accelerator variables and that inner-city teachers more frequently used decelerator arrangements of variables.

Finally, we have conducted a number of experimental studies that have determined that classroom interventions affect changes both in ecological arrangements and in student behaviors (Greenwood, Delquadri, & Hall, 1984; Greenwood, Dinwiddie, et al., 1984). For example, the use of Classwide Peer Tutoring (Delquadri, Greenwood, Whorton, Carta, & Hall, 1986) brought increases in the use of accelerator variables, decreases in the use of decelerator variables, and associated increases in academic responses such as writing and academic talk. When these ecobehavioral changes occurred in classrooms, students in these classes demonstrated gains in curriculum-based measures (weekly spelling, math, and vocabulary test scores, and correct oral reading rate checks).

Collectively, these descriptive, correlational, and experimental studies have demonstrated the importance of examining ecobehavioral interactions within special education programs. The information obtained can lead to modifications in instructional procedures that quickly enhance student academic responding during daily lessons. In contrast, assessment based on the former approaches does not reveal either the efforts to teach (deficit approach) or the immediate effects on student behavior (environmental adequacy approach) and therefore are less useful to the teacher and program designer. The benefit of the ecobehavioral interaction approach is the advantage gained by information on the *interaction* of events rather than single events.

A PRACTICAL ECOBEHAVIORAL OBSERVATIONAL MEASURE

An observation system for use by special education personnel employing two categories of ecology (activities and tasks/materials) and one category of student behavior (student academic responding) is presented here. This system is a down-sized version of the CISSAR system previously discussed. It contains a few of the most important categories and codes to make it both functional and easy to implement by the teacher or a support staff member.

Purpose

The purpose of this system is to provide a means of examining the percentage of time in which a student uses various tasks and materials during a specific instructional activity (e.g., reading) and to determine how the student responded in relationship to each particular task. Data from this system can be used to assess, plan, and monitor the effects of changes in the use of instructional materials and related teaching procedures.

Ecological Variables (Activities, Tasks/Materials)

Two categories of ecological variables are included: Activities and Tasks/Materials. Activities are defined as the subject or content of instruction. In this system we have included: daily living skills (Dl), handwriting (H), language (L), mathematics (M), motor skills (Ms), prevocational and vocational skills (Pv), reading (R), spelling (S), self-care (Sf), science (Sc), and social studies (Ss). These basic skills activities are defined in the Appendix. Only codes for basic skills activities are provided. Thus, we have excluded codes for arts/crafts, music, and free time.

Tasks/Materials are defined as the stimuli or setting events currently available to guide students' responding. In some cases these stimuli are materials (e.g., readers or worksheets). At other times they emanate from teachers (e.g., lecture, student-teacher discussion, or instructions to clean up and end the session). The eight tasks included in the system are: fetch/put away (Fp), lecture (Ll), other media (Om), paper/pencil (Pp), readers (Rr), teacher-student discussion (Tsd), workbook (Wb), and worksheet (Ws). The definitions for these variables are included in the Appendix.

Student Academic Responding

Seven academic responses are included in this system: answer question (ANQ), ask question (ASK), task participation (TP), read aloud (RA), read silent (RS), talk academic (TA), and write (W). Two additional codes are included: attention (AT) and other behavior (OB). Attention is considered a passive response and is recorded only when the prior seven academic responses are not observed. Other behavior refers to task management behaviors such as raising hand, moving to academic stations, looking for materials, and the like, and also includes inappropriate behaviors such as inappropriate locale and inappropriate play. The definitions for all of these behaviors are provided in the Appendix.

Method of Recording

Observations focus on an individual student. *The student is the unit of ecobehavioral study.* Thus, a sufficient amount of observation sampling of the activities and tasks of one student and his or her behavior is necessary. This means at least 15 minutes of continuous data for one student. As a result, the system is data-intensive for the individual student. We do not recommend sampling many students for shorter periods of time (5 to 10 minutes) with this system.

Students to be observed should be selected as either (a) representative of students in the class generally (i.e., at random or as average achieving), or (b) of special interest because of behavior problems or low academic achievement. In some cases teachers may wish to conduct observations of a high, average, and low achieving student to estimate the ecobehavioral effects for students of differing skill levels.

Before conducting observations three requirements must be satisfied. First, the observer must be familiar and practiced with the data recording sheet. Second, the observer must know the procedure necessary for cuing 10-second time intervals. Third, the observer must be trained in the ecobehavioral definitions and be reliable in identifying these events in the classroom.

An illustration of the data recording sheet is provided in Figure 1. The first line provides for recording the student's and the teacher's names, followed in line two with identification of the *activity* of instruction; the activity code is check-marked or circled. If the activity changes during the observation, a new sheet is initiated and a new activity marked. The third line is used to record the total observation time, which is the ending time (ET) minus the start time (ST) or [(ET – ST) = total time observed].

Events are recorded in the Activity/Task/Behavior Matrix, which is defined by eight task codes listed down the left side of the matrix and nine student behaviors listed across the top of the matrix. At both the right side and at the bottom of the matrix, space is provided for summing the total numbers of events recorded.

FIGURE 1 Activity/Task/Behavior Matrix

Student Name: ____________ Teacher Name ________

Activity: Dl H L M Ms Pv R Sc Ss Sf S (CHECK ONE)

START TIME: _____ END TIME: ______ TIME OBSERVED: _____ (ET - ST)

EVENT TALLY

TASKS	STUDENT BEHAVIORS									TOTALS	
	W	TP	RA	RS	TA	ANQ	ASK	AT	OTHER	AR COMP	TOTAL
Rr											
Wb											
Ws											
Pp											
Ll											
Om											
Tsd											
Fp											
COMBINED											

PERCENT SCORES SUMMARY

TASKS	STUDENT BEHAVIORS										
	W	TP	RA	RS	TA	ANQ	ASK	AT	OTHER	AR COMP	TASK COMP
Rr											
Wb											
Ws											
Pp											
Ll											
Om											
Tsd											
Fp											
COMBINED											

Note: AR COMP = Academic Response Composite Score. It is the sum of tallies for the behaviors W through ASK.

Observations are made every 10 seconds using momentary time sampling. Observations can be paced using the second sweep hand of a watch, a digital stopwatch, or a Walkman-type tape player with an audiocassette on which 10-second observe prompts have been recorded.

At the onset of the interval (e.g., when the sweep hand crosses a 10-second point), the observer looks at the target student and notes both the task and the student's behavior. This momentary observation is completed in approximately the first 3 to 4 seconds of the interval. The observer then looks at the recording sheet, locates the correct task and behavior cell, and marks a tally in the cell. Thus, if the student were observed using a paper/pencil task and concurrently engaged in writing behavior, a tally would be made in the cell defined by Pp and W. If the student were receiving a lecture (Ll) and looking at the teacher (AT), a tally would be marked in the cell defined by Ll and AT.

Using this system, the observer records ecobehavioral events, those tasks and student behaviors occurring simultaneously. When the tally is marked, that observation sample is completed. The observer then should look away from the student, resting until onset of the next 10-second interval. At the onset of the next interval, the observe-tally-rest cycle is repeated.

When the student is not engaged in an academic response or an attention response, the Other behavior code is tallied. Only the specific student behaviors defined in the Appendix as academic responses or attention are tallied in this system. All other responses are recorded as Other behavior. This enables the recording of just those events and behaviors we wish to promote.

Learning to Use the System

Certainly there is a price to be paid to obtain the information available in this system. That price is memorizing the 15 task/behavior definitions, becoming fluent with the Activity/Task/Behavior Matrix, and the actual time required for data collection. Before learning the system, a partner is needed both for collecting the data and supporting your efforts. A partner can be a fellow teacher, an aide, or any other professional (e.g., school psychologist, resource teacher) who is interested in the system. To memorize the definitions, a set of flash cards should be prepared with the code (e.g., Rs or RS) on one side and the code name (e.g., Readers or Read Silent) and the definition (from Appendix) on the other side. The names and definitions will have to be mastered before trying to use the Matrix. We recommend studying them individually and testing them with a partner.

The second step involves practice observations using the Matrix and the timing device selected. We recommend the tape player option because it leaves the observer free to look at only the student or the tally sheet. It provides an auditory prompt to observe every 10 seconds. We suggest that a person who is learning the system should conduct at least five practice observations with the partner, noting any problems, either with definitions or perhaps missing the pace (failing to complete a tally before onset of the next interval). An agreement check, comparing the consistency with which the partners apply the task and behavior definitions, also is recommended.

To complete an agreement check the timing devices must be synchronized. The procedure to do this depends on the type of device being used. If using a tape player, for example, a dual jack should be obtained so that both headphones are powered by a single player. Also, partners should make certain that they both begin and stop the observations at the same time.

Agreement is analyzed by comparing the tallies made by each observer in each task/behavior cell in the matrix. If the accounts agree exactly or disagree by no more than ± 2 tallies, agreement is scored for this cell. If the counts in a cell disagree by more than 2 tallies, a minus is scored for the cell. After checking the 72 cells (8 tasks × 9 behaviors = 72 cells), divide the total number of agreements by 72 and multiply by 100. This figure is the percentage of agreement for the observation. If it is 85% or higher, adequate use of definitions has been demonstrated. If below this level, the definitions in the Appendix should be reviewed.

Method of Analysis

A completed observation is presented in the upper panel of the Matrix in Figure 2. In this observation the student, Chris L., in Ms. Davis' class, was observed during reading (R). The observation lasted from 9:00 to 9:20 (20 minutes). A number of task/student behavior events have been recorded. For example, four intervals were tallied as Wb (workbook) and W (writing behavior). Three intervals were tallied as Wb (workbook) and RA (reading aloud), and three intervals were tallied as Wb (workbook) and Other behavior. Of the 10 student behaviors concurrently observed with Wb (workbook), 7 were academic responses (writing and reading aloud), and 3 were other behaviors.

In contrast, 26 behavior tallies were made in association with Rr (readers). Six were RA (read aloud), 10 were RS (read silent), 2 were ANQ (answer question), 3 were AT (attention), and 5 were Other behaviors. In this case, 18 (6 RA + 10 RS + 2 ANQ) of the tallies were academic responses.

The combined set of tallies for behaviors over the entire observation displays the baseline levels of student behavior across all task situations. These ranged from 0 (TP—task participation) to 22 (W—writing) across the academic responses. AT—attention received 24, Other received 37, and the academic response composite was 51. The total number of intervals recorded was 112.

The combined tallies for tasks over the entire observation are displayed down the far right in the Total column. These ranged from 7 for Tsd (teacher-student discussion) to 26 total tallies for Rr.

These raw data from the observation are analyzed by converting them to percentages. Completed percentages are shown in the lower panel of Figure 2—the Percent Scores Summary. To convert the *behavior tallies* to percent requires that each cell count be divided by the total count for each task row (see the upper panel for these values). For example, 6 Rr/RA events divided by 26 total Rr events times 100 produces 23%. The percentages are computed from the tallies and recorded in the correct cell in the Percent Scores Summary.

FIGURE 2 Completed Activity/Task/Behavior Matrix

Student Name: CHRIS L. Teacher Name MS. DAVIS

Activity: DI H L M Ms Pv R Sc Ss Sf S (check one)

START TIME: 9:00 END TIME: 9:20 TIME OBSERVED: 20 (ET - ST)

EVENT TALLY

TASKS	W	TP	RA	RS	TA	ANQ	ASK	AT	OTHER	AR COMP	TOTAL
	STUDENT BEHAVIORS									TOTALS	
Rr			卌 /	卌 卌		//		///	卌	18	26
Wb	////		///						///	7	10
Ws	卌 卌			卌					卌	15	20
Pp	卌 ///								//	8	10
Ll					/		/	卌 /	卌	2	13
Om							/	卌 卌	卌	1	16
Tsd								卌	//	0	7
Fp									卌 卌	0	10
COMBINED	22	0	9	15	1	2	2	24	37	51	112

PERCENT SCORES SUMMARY

TASKS	W	TP	RA	RS	TA	ANQ	ASK	AT	OTHER	AR COMP	TASK COMP
	STUDENT BEHAVIORS										
Rr			23	38		8		12	19	69	23
Wb	40			30				0	30	70	9
Ws	50			25				0	25	75	18
Pp	80							0	20	80	9
Ll					8		8	46	38	15	12
Om							6	63	31	6	14
Tsd								71	29		6
Fp									100		9
COMBINED	20	0	8	13	1	2	2	21	33	46	100

To convert the *task tallies* to percentages requires that the task totals be divided by the grand total, or 112. Thus, the percentage for Rr is computed by dividing 26 by $112 \times 100 = 23\%$. The most efficient method of converting tallies to frequencies is to use a microcomputer. A program can be created for this purpose using a spread sheet program such as SuperCalc III or Lotus 1–2–3.

Interpretation

With all the percent scores computed, several interesting comparisons can be made. *First,* the relative use of tasks during the observation period is evident in the far right column marked TASK COMP (task composite) score. In rank order, the use of tasks was 23% Rr (readers), 18% Ws (worksheets), 14% Om (electronic media), 12% Ll (lecture), 9% Wb (workbook), 9% Pp (paper/pencil), 9% Fp (fetch/put away), and 6% Tsd (teacher-student discussion).

Second, the baseline percentage of student behaviors over the entire observation (see the Combined row at the bottom) can be seen. The academic responses from highest to lowest were 20% W (write), 13% RS (read silent), 8% RA (read aloud), 2% each for ANQ (answer question) and ASK (ask question), 1% for TA (talk academic), and 0% for TP (task participation). The academic response composite was 46%. Passive attention (AT) was 21%. Other behavior accounted for 33%.

Third, the effects of tasks on behaviors can be seen by comparing the profiles of student behaviors (the rows). For example, the first four tasks (rows)—Rr (readers), Wb (workbook), Ws (worksheet), and Pp (paper/pencil)—produced academic response composite scores (AR COMP) ranging from 69% in Rr to 80% in Pp. The last four rows—Ll (lecture), Om (media), Tsd (teacher-student discussion), and Fp (fetch/put away)—were associated with academic response levels ranging from 0% to 15%.

When we compare tasks on the percentages of specific academic responses, we see that Rr (readers) produced both RA (read aloud) and RS (read silent) responses. We also see that Wb (workbook), Ws (worksheet), and Pp (paper/pencil) produced high levels of writing (W) in conjunction with RS—read silent. Pp (paper/pencil) produced the highest levels of writing behavior (W) at 80%.

The highest levels of passive attention were associated with Ll (lecture), Om (media), and Tsd (teacher-student discussion), at 46%, 63%, and 71%, respectively. During Fp (fetch/put away) academic responses and attention were at zero levels as other behaviors accounted for 100% of the tallies.

Fourth, the magnitude of these specific task effects on student behavior can be compared to the combined levels. For example, the baseline level over the entire session for W (write) was 20%, the combined level. Wb, Ws, and Pp, at 40%, 50%, and 80%, were producing these behaviors at 2–4 times greater levels. Similarly, Ll, Om, Tsd, and Fp all produced zero levels of writing behavior and were significantly lower than the 20% base level.

A similar analysis of RS (read silent) indicates that compared to a baseline level of 16%, during Rr (readers) and Wb (workbook) tasks, RS (read silent) occurred at nearly twice this level (37% and 30%). This same comparison to baseline levels demonstrates that the accelerators of passive attention (AT), compared to a base level of 21%, were Ll, Om, and Tsd, at 46%, 63%, and 71%.

These four comparisons—(a) the percentages of tasks used during an observation, (b) the base levels (combined) of student behavior, (c) the specific behavioral profiles produced by different tasks, and (d) the task/behavior levels relative to the base (combined) level—provide an instructive method for evaluating eco-behavioral effects during instruction. This information can be used in several ways to improve instructional methods.

Applications

Tasks that are clear accelerators of active academic responses—those producing more than double the base level—can be identified using this system. Many teachers are unaware that different tasks can have differential effects on student performance. Furthermore, many teachers do not have clear goals regarding the specific types of student behaviors they would like during lessons. As noted earlier, our work has demonstrated that high levels of academic responding are directly related to achievement gains. Based on the data produced by this system, two general approaches to improving instruction are available to teachers:

1. Increase the time devoted to tasks that naturally promote academic responding (accelerators).
2. Modify the student response requirements of decelerator tasks so that they produce more active academic responding.

The first strategy—increasing the time spent in accelerator tasks—can be implemented by simply providing more time with particular tasks. This strategy, however, eventually will be limited by aspects of the lesson that require explanation, review, or sustained periods of attention to instructions. These situations, in which students are required to sit and listen, are potential decelerators. For example, audiovisual media as typically used by teachers are not promoters of academic responding, but this is usually because teachers require students only to look at the screen during these lessons.

By using the second strategy and introducing frequent opportunities for student responses during this audiovisual lesson, by requiring students to write each item or to read each item in unison, the number of writing and reading responses can be substantially increased (e.g., Heward, 1978).

Similarly, teacher-student discussion is typically not a promoter of academic responses. Yet, by building in increased response opportunities such as questions, student prompts to respond, and unison responding, the levels of academic talk or asking and answering questions, which typically are less than 1% of a lesson, can be increased to over 10%–20% of a lesson. Teachers can use the current observation system to monitor the success of these instructional changes.

Additional Applications

The system has several other special education applications. For special education personnel who supervise teacher trainees, the system can be *a basis for objective evaluation and feedback*. Otis-Wilborn (1986) reported the use of the CISSAR system in this capacity. She noted that with feedback based upon observations, trainees were able to modify their instructional procedures to increase levels of active student responding. She also noted that in the absence of an objective system, feedback to trainees was little more than personal advice.

Ecobehavioral approaches also can be used as *an objective means for assessing the match or fit between a student and a potential placement setting*. Hoier, McConnell, and Pallay (1987) used an observation system to select the best match between (a) the patterns of behavior of single-target students, and (b) representative students in several placement settings. Walker and Rankin (1983) provided data on (a) the behaviors of students in relationship to (b) the behavioral expectancies of the teacher in potential placement settings. Although both of these systems provide objective bases for optimizing matches between settings and students, neither has provided information on the subsequent success of these placements. Moreover, these systems have not yet been used to improve placement through systematic monitoring and revision of instructional procedures after placement. The CISSAR observation system could provide this additional information.

Last, this system can serve as *a research tool for personnel interested in evaluating interventions that include specific tasks and their effects on students' academic behavior.* Too often in the past, observational systems have focused on just the inappropriate behaviors of students when in fact the goal of special education is to increase academic performance and appropriate social behavior. Our system provides an efficient, direct measure of the levels of these behaviors.

SUMMARY AND CONCLUSION

The ecobehavioral approach, a recent development within applied behavior analysis, is addressing both ecological and behavioral concerns. This approach is based on the use of observational methods of assessment and behavioral research design. Results from descriptive and experimental studies of instruction completed at the Juniper Gardens Children's Project, in which ecobehavioral observational assessments have been used, were reported. These results (a) support the importance of assessing specific active academic responses rather than global measures of attention, (b) reveal that certain instructional arrangements are accelerators of academic responding, and (c) indicate that gains in curriculum-based assessments occur when these accelerators are used frequently in classrooms. We have described an ecobehavioral observation system for analyzing activity/task/student behavior interactions appropriate for use by classroom teachers and other special education personnel.

The advantages of an ecobehavioral interaction approach to the assessment of special education, relative to the costs of using these systems, is the leverage they provide in terms of validity, utility, and precision over many other existing methods. As Deno, Mirkin, and Chiang (1982) noted: "To be useful in evaluating the ongoing instructional program, the data produced must be immediately sensitive to the effects of relatively small adjustments made in (a) instructional methods and materials, (b) motivational techniques, and (c) administrative arrangements (e.g., adjustments in groupings, setting for instruction, teacher versus peer tutor, and allocated time)" (p. 37). Clearly, ecobehavioral assessment meets all three of these important criteria.

REFERENCES

Baer, D. M., Wolf, M. M., & Risley, T. R. (1968). Some current dimensions of applied behavior analysis. *Journal of Applied Behavior Analysis, 1,* 91–97.

Barker, R. G. (1968). *Ecological psychology.* Stanford, CA: Stanford University Press.

Bijou, S. W. (1981). The prevention of retarded development in disadvantaged children. In M. J. Begab, H. C. Haywood, & H. L. Garber (Eds.), *Psychosocial influences in retarded performance: Issues and theories in development* (Vol. 1)(pp. 29–46). Baltimore: University Park Press.

Bijou, S. W., & Baer, D. M. (1978). *Behavior analysis of child development.* Englewood Cliffs, NJ: Prentice-Hall.

Carta, J. J., & Greenwood, C. R. (1985). Ecobehavioral assessment: A methodology for expanding the evaluation of early intervention programs. *Topics in Early Childhood Special Education, 5,* 88–104.

Carta, J. J., Greenwood, C. R., & Atwater, J. (1985). *Ecobehavioral system for complex assessments of preschool environments (ESCAPE).* Kansas City, KS: University of Kansas, Bureau of Child Research, Juniper Gardens Children's Project.

Carta, J. J., Greenwood, C. R., Schulte, D., Arreaga-Mayer, C., Hughes, V., & Terry, B. (1987). *Code for instructional structural and student academic response: Mainstream version.* Kansas City, KS: University of Kansas, Bureau of Child Research, Juniper Gardens Children's Project.

Carta, J. J., Greenwood, C. R., & Robinson, S. (1987). Application of an ecobehavioral approach to the evaluation of early intervention programs. In R. J. Prinz (Ed.), *Advances in behavioral assessment of children and families* (Vol. 3) (pp. 123–156). Greenwich, CT: JAI Press.

Delquadri, J., Greenwood, C. R., Whorton, D., Carta, J. J., & Hall, R. V. (1986). Classwide peer tutoring. *Exceptional Children, 52,* 535–542.

Deno, S. L. (1985). Curriculum-based measurement: The emerging alternative. *Exceptional Children, 52,* 219–232.

Deno, S. L., Mirkin, P. K., & Chiang, B. (1982). Identifying valid measures of reading. *Exceptional Children, 49,* 36–45.

Engelmann, S., Granzin, A., & Severson, H. (1979). Diagnosing instruction. *Journal of Special Education, 13,* 355–363.

Greenwood, C. R., & Delquadri, J. (in press). Code for instructional structure and student academic response (CISSAR). In M. Hersen & A. S. Bellack (Eds.), *Dictionary of behavioral assessment.* New York: Pergamon.

Greenwood, C. R., Delquadri, J., & Hall, R. V. (1984). Opportunity to respond and student academic performance. In W. L. Heward, T. E. Heron, J. Trap-Porter, & D. S. Hill (Eds.), *Focus on behavior analysis in education* (pp. 58–88). Columbus, OH: Charles Merrill.

Greenwood, C. R., Delquadri, J., Stanley, S., Sasso, G., Whorton, D., & Schulte, D. (1981, Summer). Allocating opportunity to learn as a basis for academic remediation: A developing model for teaching. *Monograph in Behavioral Disorders,* pp. 22–23.

Greenwood, C. R., Delquadri, J., Stanley, S., Terry, B., & Hall, R. V. (1985). Assessment of ecobehavioral interaction in school settings. *Behavioral Assessment, 7,* 331–347.

Greenwood, C. R., Dinwiddie, G., Terry, B., Wade, L., Stanley, S., Thibadeau, S., & Delquadri, J. (1984). Teacher- versus peer-mediated instruction: An ecobehavioral analysis of achievement outcomes. *Journal of Applied Behavior Analysis, 17,* 521–538.

Greenwood, C. R., Schulte, D., Kohler, F., Dinwiddie, G., & Carta, J. (1986). Assessment and analysis of ecobehavioral interaction in school settings. In R. J. Prinz (Ed.), *Advances in behavioral assessment of children and families* (Vol. 2)(pp. 69–98). Greenwich, CT: JAI Press.

Heward, W. L. (1978). Visual response system. *Exceptional Children, 44*, 466–468.

Hoier, T. S., McConnell, S., & Pallay, A. G. (1987). Observational assessment for planning and evaluating educational transitions: An initial analysis of template matching. *Behavioral Assessment, 9*, 6–20.

Otis-Wilborn, A. (1986, May). Using eco-behavioral data in training student teachers in instructional management. In C. R. Greenwood (Chair), *Applied uses of eco-behavioral data*. Symposium presented at the 12th Annual Convention of the Association for Behavior Analysis, Milwaukee, WI.

Peterson, R. L., Zabel, R. H., Smith, C. R., & White, M. A. (1983). Cascade of services model and emotionally disabled students. *Exceptional Children, 49*, 404–410.

Rogers-Warren, A. K. (1984). Ecobehavioral analysis. *Education & Treatment of Children, 7*, 283–304.

Rosenshine, B., & Stevens, R. (1986). Teaching functions. In M. C. Wittrock (Ed.), *Handbook of research on teaching* (3rd ed.)(pp. 376–391). New York: Macmillan.

Rotholz, D., Whorton, D., McGrale, J., Norris, M., & Greenwood, C. R. (1985). *Code for instructional structure and student academic response: Special education version (CISSAR-SPED)*. Kansas City, KS: University of Kansas, Bureau of Child Research, Juniper Gardens Children's Project.

Stanley, S. O., & Greenwood, C. R. (1981). *CISSAR: Code for instructional structure and student academic response: Observer's manual*. Kansas City, KS: University of Kansas, Bureau of Child Research, Juniper Gardens Children's Project.

Stanley, S. O., & Greenwood, C. R. (1983). How much "opportunity to respond" does the minority disadvantaged student receive in school? *Exceptional Children, 49*, 370–373.

Walker, H. M., & Rankin, R. (1983). Assessing the behavioral expectations and demands of less restrictive settings. *School Psychology Review, 12*, 274–284.

Ysseldyke, J. E., & Algozzine, B. (1982). Where to begin in diagnosing reading problems. *Topics in Learning & Learning Disabilities, 2*, 60–69.

APPENDIX

CISSAR-Classroom Teacher: Categories, Codes, and Definitions

Ecological Categories

Activity: The activity is the subject area or topic of instruction.

Dl — *Daily living and community skills*
Daily living and community activities are those devoted to independent living in the home and community. Examples are budgeting, laundry, cooking, and use of public transportation.

H — *Handwriting*
Handwriting is the activity devoted to learning to print or to write in cursive letters.

L — *Language*
Language is the activity devoted to either speech or language learning. Language learning can range from the study of word meaning (vocabulary) to English poetry.

M — *Mathematics*
Mathematics is the activity devoted to quantitative reasoning, calculation, and computation.

Ms — *Motor skills*
Motor skills are activities devoted to developing both fine and gross motor skills. These activities are similar to physical education but with adaptations for certain handicaps. Examples include peg board, stencils, bead stringing (fine motor); scooter boards, balance beams (gross motor).

Pv — *Pre-vocational/vocational*
Pre-vocational/vocational activities are those devoted to learning work and job skills.

R — *Reading*
Reading is the activity devoted to decoding and comprehending written words.

Sc — *Science*
Science is the activity devoted to topics such as insects, health, personal hygiene, weather, biology, and related topics.

Ss — *Social Studies*
Social studies is the activity devoted to topics related to mental health, behavior, cultures, ways of life, history, roles, and the like.

Sf *Self-care*
Self-care activities are those devoted to personal hygiene, grooming, and other body care. Examples include dressing, toileting, toothbrushing, and bathing.

S *Spelling*
Spelling is the activity devoted to learning to spell and to write spelling words from memory.

Tasks/Materials

Tasks and materials are the stimuli set by the teacher to occasion students' academic responding. These may be curricula materials or either immediate or standing instructions by the teacher, as defined below:

Fp *Fetch/put away*
Fp is coded when the student is instructed to: (a) change tasks or (b) stop a current task and change to a new one. For example: "All right, students, it is time to clean up for recess" or "Go to reading groups."

Ll *Listen to lecture*
Ll is coded when the task is to listen to the teacher lecture or make a presentation (e.g., a chalkboard lesson or reading a story).

Om *Other media*
Om is coded when the task is based on *electronic* media (e.g., overhead projector, tape recorder, computer, telephone) or other *manipulative* materials (e.g., abacus, counting rods, clocks, word cards).

Pp *Paper/pencil*
Pp is coded when the task consists of paper-and-pencil materials, including pens and other writing instruments. Paper may be lined or unlined.

Rr *Readers*
Rr is coded when the task is based on a reading primer or reading textbook (e.g., a basal reader or library book or other textbook).

Tsd *Teacher-student discussion*
Tsd is coded when task involves listening and talking with the teacher. For example, Ll may change to Tsd when a teacher asks a question and it is answered by the student. Tsd also is coded when the teacher talks with the student individually.

Wb *Workbook*
Wb is coded when the task involves paperbacked, bound materials that require both reading and writing by the student. These may be programmed reading workbooks or exercise books that accompany the main curriculum in reading, math, spelling, or language.

Ws *Worksheet*
Ws is coded when the task is a single printed sheet or a set of printed sheets on which students are expected to read and write responses. These may be from spirit duplicating masters and prepared by the teacher.

Student Behavior Categories

Active academic responses are specific, active responses made in relation to specific academic tasks.

ANQ *Answer question*
ANQ is coded when the student writes, gestures, or orally provides an answer in response to a teacher's, aides's, or peer's academic question. The answer may be correct or incorrect.

ASK *ASK question*
ASK is coded when the student verbally asks the teacher, aide, or peer tutor a question related to the activity or task.

TP *Task participation*
TP is coded when the student is observed to be using an academic game or participating in a social game, either individually or with peers. The response may be verbal, motor, or social. The student may be manipulating flash cards, coloring, using scissors, playing with a toy, spinning a wheel, moving a pawn on a board, etc.

RA *Read aloud*
RA is recorded when the student is looking at printed material and speaking aloud what is written. This may be words or numbers.

RS *Read silent*
RS is recorded when the student is looking directly at printed material and eye movements suggest that student is scanning the material. Materials may be books, flash cards, words on the chalkboard, etc. Students may be reading words or numbers.

TA *Talk academic*
TA is recorded when the student is verbalizing about the activity or task (i.e., the subject matter). Spelling words aloud, presenting words to be spelled by a peer, and correcting a peer are examples.

W *Write*
W is recorded when the student is observed marking tasks with a pencil, pen, crayon, or other writing tool. This involves holding the instrument between the thumb and forefinger and moving it in a manner likely to produce letters, words, or drawings.

Task Management: Prerequisite or Enabling Response

AT *Attention*
AT is recorded in the absence of above active responses and consists of looking at the teacher, aide, or peer tutor.

Other

OB *Other Behaviors*
Other is recorded in the absence of any of the above behaviors. This may include *task management behaviors* such as moving to a new location in the class, raising one's hand, looking for materials, and appropriate nonacademic play. Other also includes *inappropriate behaviors* such as disruptive, inappropriate talk, self-stimulation, inappropriate play, looking around, self-abuse, and inappropriate locale.

Dr. Greenwood is Research Director, Juniper Gardens Children's Project; Associate Scientist, Bureau of Child Research; and Associate Professor, Department of Special Education, and Human Development and Family Life, University of Kansas. Dr. Carta is a Project Director with the Juniper Gardens Children's Project and Research Associate, Bureau of Child Research, University of Kansas.

Index of Contributors